D1495849

Making, Breaking Codes:
An Introduction to Cryptology

Paul Garrett
University of Minnesota, Minneapolis

PRENTICE HALL, Upper Saddle River, NJ 07458

Library of Congress Cataloging-in-Publication Data

Garrett, Paul B.
Making, breaking codes: an introduction to cryptology / Paul Garrett.
    p. cm.
Includes bibliographical references and index.
ISBN 0-13-030369-0
1.Coding theory. I. Title.

QA268 .G37 2001
652.8dc21   00-042742

Acquisitions editor: George Lobell
Assistant Vice President of Production and Manufacturing: David W.
Executive Managing Editor: Kathleen Schiaparelli
Senior Managing Editor: Linda Mihatov Behrens
Production Editor: Betsy A. Williams
Manufacturing Buyer: Alan Fischer
Manufacturing Manager: Trudy Pisciotti
Marketing Manager: Angela Battle
Marketing Assistant: Vince Jansen
Director of Marketing: John Tweeddale
Editorial Assistant: Gale Epps
Art Director: Jayne Conte
Cover Designer: Bruce Kenselaar
Front and Back Cover Photos: Christopher Simon Sykes/The Interior Archive.
  Title: Blenheim/Great Houses of England and Wales. *The lock and the key
  for the great door at Blenheim Palace.*

e United States of America
  3 2

69-0

ational (UK) Limited, London
ralia Pty. Limited, Sydney
  Inc., Toronto
mericana, (S.A.) Mexico
  rivate Limited, New Delhi
    Pte. Ltd.
  o Brasil, Ltda., Rio de Janeiro

Making, Breaking Codes:
An Introduction to Cryptology

Paul Garrett
University of Minnesota, Minneapolis

PRENTICE HALL, Upper Saddle River, NJ 07458

Library of Congress Cataloging-in-Publication Data

Garrett, Paul B.
Making, breaking codes: an introduction to cryptology / Paul Garrett.
    p. cm.
Includes bibliographical references and index.
ISBN 0-13-030369-0
1.Coding theory. I. Title.

QA268 .G37 2001
652.8dc21   00-042742

Acquisitions editor: George Lobell
Assistant Vice President of Production and Manufacturing: David W. Riccardi
Executive Managing Editor: Kathleen Schiaparelli
Senior Managing Editor: Linda Mihatov Behrens
Production Editor: Betsy A. Williams
Manufacturing Buyer: Alan Fischer
Manufacturing Manager: Trudy Pisciotti
Marketing Manager: Angela Battle
Marketing Assistant: Vince Jansen
Director of Marketing: John Tweeddale
Editorial Assistant: Gale Epps
Art Director: Jayne Conte
Cover Designer: Bruce Kenselaar
Front and Back Cover Photos: Christopher Simon Sykes/The Interior Archive.
    Title: Blenheim/Great Houses of England and Wales. *The lock and the key*
    for the great door at Blenheim Palace.

 ©2001 by Prentice-Hall, Inc. Upper Saddle River, NJ 07458

Printed in the United States of America
10 9 8 7 6 5 4 3 2

ISBN 0-13-030369-0

Prentice-Hall International (UK) Limited, London
Prentice-Hall of Australia Pty. Limited, Sydney
Prentice-Hall Canada, Inc., Toronto
Prentice-Hall Hispanoamericana, (S.A.) Mexico
Prentice-Hall of India Private Limited, New Delhi
Pearson Education Asia Pte. Ltd.
Editora Prentice-Hall do Brasil, Ltda., Rio de Janeiro

Contents

Preface

This book is an introduction to modern ideas in cryptology and how to employ these ideas. It includes the relevant material on number theory, probability, and abstract algebra, in addition to descriptions of ideas about algorithms and complexity theory. Three somewhat different terms appear in the discussion of secure communications and related matters: *cryptography, cryptanalysis*, and *cryptology*. The first, cryptography, refers to writing using various methods to keep the message secret, as well as more modern applications of these methods. By contrast, cryptanalysis is the science of attacking ciphers, finding weaknesses, or possibly proving that there are none. Cryptology covers both, and is the most inclusive term.

In an introduction to cryptography, cryptanalysis, and cryptology that is more than just recreational, several things should be accomplished:

- Provide some historical perspective. Specifically, we should see why the classical cipher systems *fail* by contemporary standards.

- Survey uses of cryptography. (It is not just for keeping secrets.)

- Introduce mathematics relevant to classical and modern cryptosystems.

- Give examples of types of hostile cryptanalytic attacks.

- Explain that *key management* and *implementation details* are fundamental.

Prerequisites here are minimal: the reader need only have the mathematical sophistication associated with having taken calculus and a bit of linear algebra.

We will first selectively review *classical cryptology*. This refers to the time prior to the 1940s. Some mechanical and primitive electronic devices were automated decryption/encryption and hostile cryptanalytic attacks, especially during 1935–1945, but these devices were slow, limited in their programmability, and not very portable. Part of the limitation was that they were fundamentally mechanical or electromechanical, rather than being 'software.'

By contemporary standards, the classical ciphers (prior to Enigma) definitively fail. This doesn't mean what one might think, though. It is much more than just the fact that contemporary computers are much better than the tube-based machines of the 1940s. Rather, it is now demanded that 'strong' ciphers be resistant to types of attacks which might have seemed irrelevant in the past.

One interesting idea that pervades both the classical and modern cryptanalysis and underlying mathematics is that of *stochastic algorithm* or *probabilistic algorithm*, by contrast to the more traditional and usual *deterministic* algorithms used in elementary mathematics. The point is that for many purposes there are algorithms that run *much faster* but with less than 100% chance of success, or, on the other hand, *usually* run fast, but not always. And this appears to be a fact of life, rather than just an artifact of our ignorance.

It must be noted that the advent of widely available high-speed computing machinery has drastically altered the landscape of cryptology. Simultaneously:

- Encryption and (authorized) decryption can be automated, massive computation to perform encryption/decryption is enormously easier, and more elaborate systems become feasible.

- Storage, transfer, and manipulation of data on computer networks has sharply increased the *need* for effective encryption and related techniques.

- Cryptanalytic attacks have become commensurately easier. So issues which might have previously been viewed as of interest mostly to little kids (?) or spies (?) are now of quite general interest.

This is a subject in *applied mathematics*, since most of the mathematics we do will be motivated by application. The necessary mathematics will include some number theory, linear algebra, abstract algebra, probability theory, complexity theory, and other things. We can't pretend to be doing justice to these subjects, but will only provide an introduction with some concrete motivation. At the same time, we do not assume prior experience with any of these subjects.

There is also not enough space in a single book to pretend to give any sort of complete coverage of either historical developments or current developments in cryptology itself. What *is* possible is giving some representative and important examples and indicating other directions.

We will not be able to simulate full-scale real-life examples of contemporary issues, especially of cryptanalysis, because we do not have access to the right kind of computing machinery, and the actual simulations would take many hours or days in any case, with enormous memory usage. Ordinary computers can do encryptions and (authorized) decryptions very fast, but real-life *attacks* on today's cipher systems take days or months of computer time.

So at first we'll discuss some representative 'classical' cryptosystems, and the mathematics on which they are based, or which can be used to understand or break them. This is a good warm-up. Then, a little later, we'll describe a *real symmetric* encryption system in current use: DES ('Data Encryption Standard'). DES is considerably more complicated than the classical ciphers, and for good reason: much more is required of it. And, partly because of its success, it is not possible to say how to attack it successfully. A little more specifically: the fact that DES reveals very little mathematical structure is all in its favor, since this is what makes it less vulnerable to attack. DES has been the U.S. standard (for symmetric ciphers) since the mid-1970s, and has been used extensively outside the U.S. as well. Extensive analysis over 20 years has not found any fatal weakness in DES, but by now computers are so much faster than in 1976 that a brute-force attack is feasible. In fact, in mid-1998 the Electronic Frontier Foundation (EFF) spent $100,000 to construct a *DES-cracker* from off-the-shelf parts, which is able to obtain a DES key in about 2 days. Still, triple encryption by DES, reasonably enough called *triple DES*, seems to be secure for the foreseeable future. Nevertheless, the National Institute of Standards has called for submission of candidates for a new symmetric cipher with 128-bit block size. This contest is still going on now (mid-2000), and the winner will be known as the *Advanced Encryption Standard* (AES).

There is much more mathematical content in the discussion of the *asymmetric ciphers* (also called *public-key* ciphers). We will mostly discuss two sorts: the RSA system (Rivest, Shamir, Adleman), and the ElGamal system and its generalizations. RSA is simpler and more popular, but ElGamal lends itself better to generalizations such as *elliptic curve ciphers*. The security of RSA hinges on the apparent difficulty of factoring very large integers into primes. The security of the ElGamal system depends upon the difficulty of computing 'logarithms in finite fields.' (What this means exactly will be explained later.) And practical operation of either system depends upon generating a good supply of very large primes, which is an interesting problem in itself. As a further sample of asymmetric cipher, we briefly mention the NTRU cipher, which is newer and mathematically more sophisticated. In contrast to the symmetric systems, the more mathematical nature of the asymmetric systems does seem to make them naturally more vulnerable. There are important and subtle auxiliary mathematical issues in this part.

More specifically, after reviewing classical issues, we'll give an introduction to the application of *number theory* to contemporary cryptology, especially *public-key* ciphers such as RSA and ElGamal. This will introduce

- public-key (asymmetric) ciphers

- pseudo-random-number generators (pRNGs)

- protocols

The necessary mathematics will include

- results from number theory and abstract algebra

- primality testing, factorization, and related algorithms

- informal ideas from complexity theory

We won't do much with complexity theory except to keep rough track of the difficulty with which various computations can be performed, separating 'hard' from 'easy.'

The primality testing and factoring issues are fundamental for almost everything here. Many of the actual algorithms can be described in elementary terms, although the explanations for *why* they work at all usually require more preparation. But even without the explanation it is possible to *experiment* with these algorithms to get a feeling for their performance and accuracy.

A central underlying issue is *the structure of* integers-modulo-n, denoted $\mathbf{Z}/n$ (explained later), and generalizations of this. Especially we want to understand the differences in the nature of $\mathbf{Z}/n$ between n *composite* and n *prime*.

Randomization plays a very important role in some of the most efficient algorithms. For those of us accustomed to *certainty* in mathematics, this may be disconcerting, but it seems to be a necessary price to pay in many situations. The immediate goal is to motivate consideration of probabilistic primality tests such as Solovay–Strassen and Miller–Rabin, and *prove that they work*.

There is much more material here than could fit into a one-semester course, but in good conscience I couldn't have left anything out. A year-long course probably could go straight through and cover nearly everything.

I have used this material several times in a course that does *not* presume that students know any number theory, abstract algebra, probability, or cryptography. The mathematical topics are interwoven with cryptological applications in a style that is intended to provide adequate motivation for applications-minded people and interesting sidelights for theoretically-minded people. I've tried to make the different chapters maximally independent of each other to allow readers to skip topics that don't appear interesting to them without impairing the intelligibility of subsequent writing. In some cases this required that I repeat some small discussions of technical points because I could not be sure that the reader would have seen the earlier discussion. From a pedagogical viewpoint a modest amount of repetition is probably a good thing anyway.

A one-semester course in number theory could use this text, with the cryptographic and computational parts skipped but left as optional reading. There is more abstract algebra included than here in some traditional number theory courses. When I've taught traditional undergraduate number theory courses I always faced the choice between pretending to do number theory *without* abstract algebra, *requiring* abstract algebra as prerequisite, or developing some abstract algebra as motivated by number theory. The latter (somewhat non-traditional) choice has been my choice, but there are few texts that hit that mark. Some parts of the present text are an outgrowth of notes I've written for undergraduate courses in which I coordinated number theory and abstract algebra, using number theory as a tangible entry point to algebra and as a beneficiary of basic results from it. Thus, a one-semester course in number theory could skip over the first six chapters on classical ciphers and probability, and also skip the chapter on the Hill ciphers. The chapter on public-key ciphers *could* be skipped, but this *is* one of the chief applications of mathematics to communication.

A short introductory course in cryptography could use this text, with much of the more serious mathematical sections omitted. To make this feasible, I've tried to write about the mathematical aspects in a manner that is intelligible from both relatively elementary and relatively high-level viewpoints. In some cases this means that I've given both an elementary proof of a special case and a more elegant higher-level proof of a more general case. Since this is probably good educational strategy anyway, I don't feel bad about spending the time and space. At the same time, a common limitation of more serious cryptography texts is that the relevant mathematics is given short shrift. A related common limitation is that the reader is assumed to have already reached a high level of mathematical sophistication. By contrast, here I've attempted to *require* as little as possibly, while still providing appropriate resources for the cryptography student who wants to see how the underlying mathematics works. Thus, a short introductory course in cryptography could simply proceed straight through the text and stop when time ran out. In some sense this is the most natural use of this material.

A course in computational number theory could focus on the algorithms, and soft-pedal the cryptography and the more theoretical mathematical parts. In the classes I've taught from this material I have *not* assumed that students are able to or want to do computer work of any sort, but of course the material begs for CPU time! My descriptions of the algorithms are intended to be fairly clear, but I've not written out pseudo-code or specific language implementations of the algorithms. One reason for this is that I want students to think about what the algorithms are doing, at least a little, rather than just to execute them. Another reason for not writing out algorithms in a proprietary language is that I am disinclined to implicitly endorse a language and all it entails. And, while I strongly favor students' learning how to write programs, I don't encourage them to study *software packages*. Still, friendly-interface software packages do provide an easy entry to computing.

In courses for students who have already seen some probability or number theory the corresponding chapters and sections can be skipped. In structuring the text I have incorporated necessary material into the text itself rather than relegating it to appendices. This allows a knowledgeable reader to skip over material while not requiring that eveyone else flip back and forth to appendices. Such integration of the material better shows the logical dependencies, too.

I thank the reviewers of the manuscript for their constructive criticism and for their positive responses to some of my non-standard stylistic choices: Professors Irvin Roy Hentzel, Iowa State University; Yangbo Ye, University of Iowa, Iowa City; Joachim Rosenthal, U. of Notre Dame; Daniel Lieman, U. of Missouri, Columbia; Jonathan Hall, Michigan State University. My students in the last few years deserve thanks for tolerating half-baked versions of this text, making helpful suggestions, and finding many errors, hopefully making the reviewers' job less gruesome than it might have been otherwise.

Paul Garrett
University of Minnesota, Minneapolis
garrett@math.umn.edu
paul.garrett@acm.org
http://www.math.umn.edu/~garrett/

Introduction

Uses of cryptography. The traditional and easiest-to-understand goal of cryptography is *keeping secrets*. Unavoidably this idea makes reference to an *adversary*. Usually the secret-keeping has meant *encrypting* a message so that even if the adversary should eavesdrop, or capture the messenger, or obtain a copy, the adversary still would have relatively great difficulty in understanding the content of the message. At the same time, the intended and *authorized* receiver of the message should be able to figure out, with relative ease, what the message says.

A more recent use is *authentication* of a message, whether or not the message is secret. That is, the receiver of a message (encrypted or not) wants to be sure that the claimed sender is the true sender, and that the message has not been altered. It is important to be able to ensure that documents have not been altered. This issue is also known as maintaining *data integrity*. In cases where it is presumed that there is no adversary other than noise in the environment, a relatively simple *checksum* may suffice, but in more hostile environments, the device must be more complicated in order to thwart or detect cheating.

We might want a cryptographic equivalent of a *signature* when a literal, physical signature in ink on paper is not available. In communication among networked computers, these non-physical signatures are called *digital signatures*.

A less obvious use of cryptography is the issue of *non-repudiation*, although this is an aspect of *signatures*: it must be impossible for the signer of a digital signature to later deny the signing. There arises a distinction about *cheating*: do we try to make cheating *impossible*, or merely *detectable*? The latter should be easier, though perhaps unacceptable in some scenarios.

Oblivious transfer. The goal is that Alice should communicate a secret to Bob so that afterward Alice does not know whether or not Bob received the secret (but Bob knows whether or not he received it). Or, as a variant, it might be that Alice offers to sell Bob one of several secrets so that Alice will not know which secret Bob actually bought. Here we should think of political situations, where it might be embarrassing for Bob to admit his ignorance of certain secrets. In such a context the easy solution of using a *trusted referee* is infeasible.

Zero-knowledge proofs are protocols in which Alice proves to Bob that she knows a secret, without divulging the secret. Generally, a *minimum-disclosure proof* minimizes the information Alice imparts while proving that she knows the secret. *Cheating* should be difficult: if Alice does not really know the secret, then the probability that she is able to falsely convince Bob should be negligible; and, Bob cannot acquire more information from Alice's proof than he had without it. In particular, Bob should *not* be able to (falsely) demonstrate to anyone else that *he* knows the secret. (The fact that minimum-disclosure proofs are possible may remind the reader of mathematics and other technical courses in which students become convinced mostly that the lecturer does indeed know how to prove the theorems, without disclosing any further information to the audience.)

Terminology. A **cryptosystem** or **cipher** is a procedure to render messages unintelligible except to the authorized recipient. The **encryption** process, performed by the sender, is intended to render the message unintelligible to any eavesdropper or interceptor of the encrypted message. The **decryption** process is conducted by the legitimate intended receiver, recovering the original message (the **plaintext**) from the obscured version (the **ciphertext**). Paraphrasing: it is intended to be significantly harder for anyone eavesdropping or intercepting the ciphertext to recover the plaintext than for the intended recipient to decrypt it. In symmetric cryptosystems, at least, this is accomplished by having the sender and receiver **share a secret**, called the **key**. Not knowing the key should be sufficient to prevent an eavesdropper from decrypting the ciphertext.

One might imagine that secrecy of the whole encryption/decryption process would be the best approach. However, it seems that it is unreasonable to depend on this. Rather, the standard viewpoint nowadays is that the encryption and decryption should be viewed as potentially public knowledge, with the only secret being the *key*. This viewpoint, sometimes called **Kerckhoff's principle**, has several arguments in its favor. The most compelling such argument is simply that it is *possible* to design cryptosystems that meet this requirement, so any system that does *not* is unacceptable.

An argument in favor of acting in accord with Kerckhoff's principle is that *standardization* of algorithms makes large-scale communication easier. We will assume throughout that the mechanics of the cryptosystem in use is *publicly known*. This does *not* mean that it does not matter what cipher is used: quite the contrary. But the only **secret** will be the **key**. Since the *secret* resides entirely in the *key*, **key distribution** and **key management** are fundamental issues.

Although 'code' and 'cipher' are synonyms in colloquial English, we will use them in different ways here. For our purposes, a **code** is a method for concealing the content of messages by exchanging words or phrases in English for different ones, according to some dictionary. This transformation usually depends to some degree on the *meaning* and *grammar* of the message: nouns and verbs are recognized and converted to other nouns and verbs, for example. By contrast, a **cipher** treats messages as streams of **characters** without reference to any possible meaning. (A *character* is a letter, number, space, or punctuation mark.) A similar word, **encode**, refers to a transformation not for purposes of concealment, but for subsequent manipulation. For example, very often letters a–z are *encoded* as numbers 0–25 before being manipulated in an *encryption* process.

By a **classical cipher** we mean (approximately) a cipher used or developed prior to the advent of electronic computing machinery. The Enigma machines and some others used in the Second World War represent the zenith of pre-electronic cryptography. Since that time the issues have changed somewhat, and the standards for performance have risen. So by chance it happens that 'classical cipher' also may mean 'not very good cipher' (by current standards).

A **symmetric cipher** is one in which knowledge of the encryption key is equivalent to knowledge of the decryption key, or in extreme cases the same key is used for both encryption and decryption. That is, the sender and receiver really do share the *same* secret. All the classic ciphers were of this form. In fact, until about 1975 no other sorts were known. But in 1975–1978 Merkle and Hellman conceived of the first examples of **asymmetric ciphers**, in which knowledge of the encryption key gives little information about the decryption key, and vice versa. These asymmetric ciphers also provide the most mathematical interest, since their success is contingent upon the intractability of various natural mathematical problems. By contrast, the symmetric ciphers are considerably less mysterious. (It has recently become known that 10 years before Merkle and Hellman, people in the British secret service conceived the idea of public-key ciphers.)

An **attack** on a cryptosystem is an attempt to decrypt encrypted messages without knowledge of the key. There are four basic sorts of attacks:

- **Ciphertext only**: In this case, the cryptanalyst possesses a fragment of the encrypted message but has no knowledge of the plaintext or of the key. There are two levels of attack: to decrypt a *particular* message, or to obtain the key, thereby being able to decrypt *all* subsequent messages.

- **Known plaintext**: In this case, the cryptanalyst possesses all or part of a plaintext and corresponding ciphertext. The goal would be to deduce the key. Most 'classical' ciphers are vulnerable to such an attack.

- **Chosen plaintext:** Here the cryptanalyst is able to *choose* some number of plaintexts and to see the corresponding encryptions. The goal is to obtain the key. 'Classical' ciphers are very vulnerable to such attacks.

- **Encryption key**: This is relevant to asymmetric systems where (by design) knowledge of the encryption key does not easily yield the decryption key. The goal is to *preprocess* to obtain the decryption key prior to interception of any ciphertext.

This classification of attacks is not as clear as the words indicate. Often an attacker does not know the *whole* plaintext, but for circumstantial reasons can be fairly sure that some specific words or phrases will occur in the plaintext. A word which is known to occur *somewhere* in a plaintext is a **crib**. Adroit use of *cribs* played a central role in cryptanalysis as late as the Second World War, but since then the issues are somewhat different.

The first three sorts of attacks are relevant to symmetric cryptosystems. Of the three, clearly the ciphertext-only attack is most difficult for the cryptanalyst, while the chosen-plaintext attack is the easiest. It is clear that any reasonable cryptosystem should be reasonably resistant to ciphertext-only attacks. The presumption is that eavesdropping or interception of messages is a fact of life. In general, it might be harder to arrange a known-plaintext or chosen-plaintext attack, although there are clichéd descriptions of such scenarios. Rather than argue the plausibility or not of such attacks, the point seems to be that there are cryptosystems strong enough to resist even chosen-plaintext attacks. As a consequence, resistance to such attacks becomes the standard. Thus, while already some of the classical cryptosystems are too vulnerable to ciphertext-only attacks, and therefore are unacceptable, in fact by current standards they should be even more strongly rejected since they are completely vulnerable to chosen-plaintext attacks. We shall consider the more difficult ciphertext-only attack on some 'classical' cryptosystems, both because that was what they were intended to withstand, and also to illustrate some points of interest. We will also point out vulnerability to known-plaintext and chosen-plaintext attacks. Again, however, the reader should understand that the current standard is that *a cryptosystem should be able to withstand chosen-plaintext attacks.*

The word **heuristic** will be used often. A *heuristic* approach to a problem is by no means guaranteed to work or to be correct, but suggests a course of action or suggests what is true. In the best circumstances, this hint can be *checked.*

In intuitive terms, an **algorithm** is a computational or decision-making procedure that can be completely automated (for example, programmed on a computer). A **probabilistic algorithm** is one which may not always work, or may not give a result guaranteed to be correct.

The standard measures of information are *bit*, *byte*, etc. A **bit** is the smallest unit of information, being either a 0 or a 1 (true or false, on or off). Some sources claim that 'bit' is an abbreviation for 'binary digit,' and this may be true. A **byte** is an ordered collection of 8 bits, but usually one of the bits is used as a *parity-check* (meaning to verify that no single-bit error has occured), so only 2^7 rather than 2^8 bits of information are conveyed by one byte. Playing around with Greek prefixes, a **kilobyte** is 1,000 bytes, a **megabyte** is 1,000,000 bytes, a **gigabyte** is 1,000,000,000 bytes, a **terabyte** is 1,000,000,000,000 bytes, and so on.

In countries where the Latin alphabet ('A' through 'Z' but without diacritical marks) is used, usually a *character* is encoded as an integer 0–255, that is, as a *byte*. Most of these are non-printing or control characters. There are other systems as well, but in the United States the so-called **ASCII system** (American Standard Code for Information Interchange) is very often used: characters 0–9 are numbered 48–57, uppercase A–Z are 65–90, and lowercase a–z are 97–122. The other integers are allocated to punctuation marks and control characters.

Unicode is a relatively new idea for encoding larger alphabets (or ideograph systems, such as Chinese), by using *two* bytes per character. This will (in the future) give $2^{16} = 65,536$ available encodings of characters (and ideographs) rather than the measly 256 available with a single byte.

1

Simple Ciphers

This section introduces three relatively simple ciphers, the shift cipher, the one-time pad, and the affine cipher. The shift cipher and the affine cipher are hopelessly bad, while the one-time pad is perfectly secure, *if* used properly. That 'if' is a *big* 'if', however.

With these three ciphers we will begin our general pattern of *description* of ciphers, followed by discussion of their *weaknesses*. Relevant mathematical ideas are introduced along the way, as necessary either for the function of the cipher or for the attacks on the ciphers.

One reason to discuss weak ciphers is to understand the weaknesses, both to avoid such weaknesses in the future, and to know how to exploit them if necessary. Certainly if we only looked at impregnable ciphers we'd have no idea what the failure of a cipher would look like, nor a successful attack. So, as silly as the shift cipher is, for example, it is worthwhile looking at its silliness in some detail, as a lesson.

1.1 The Shift Cipher

The simplest kind of encryption is the **shift cipher**. This evidently dates back at least to Julius Caesar, since this cipher is sometimes called the *Caesar cipher*, although there were earlier (and better) ciphers of other sorts (Polybios, for example). Although this is actually a *bad* encryption system, it is instructive to see *why* it is bad.

First we describe Caesar's apparent special case of this cipher, and then the general encryption scheme. In this discussion, the message (**plaintext**) will be written in all lower-case letters, while the encrypted version (**ciphertext**) will be written in all upper-case. Also, we will use the English alphabet, with 26 letters, in the usual order. All messages will be in English.

In Caesar's case, to *encrypt*, each letter in a message would be moved forward by 3, so that 'a' became 'D', 'b' became 'E', 'c' became 'F', and so on. At the end of the alphabet, the shifting would *wrap around*, meaning that 'x' would move off the end of the alphabet, but then start back at the beginning, to become 'A'. And 'y' would become 'B', and 'z' would become 'C'.

To *decrypt* in Caesar's system, the letters in the alphabet would be shifted *backward* by 3, using the wrap-around as necessary: 'A' goes to 'x', 'B' to 'y', 'C' to 'z', 'D' to 'a', 'E' to 'b', and so on.

Thus, in Caesar's system, the message

> all of gaul is divided into three parts

would become

> DOO RI JDXO LV GLYLGHG LQWR WKUHH SDUWV

Facing a population where most people could neither read nor write in the first place, this may have been effective for keeping secrets even when messages might be intercepted. However, once a (literate) adversary became aware of the system, the only obstacle in decrypting intercepted messages was the time it took to do the actual letter-shifting. Since the letter-shifting had to be done by the intended recipient anyway, once the secret of the encryption method was known it became just as easy for an adversary to decrypt the message as for the intended recipient. This is not good.

We can enhance the method by adding a additional *secret* to it, in order to cause an adversary to have to work harder than the intended recipient to decrypt the message. Namely, the sender and receiver of messages agree in advance upon a **key**, which in the present circumstance would be a number from 1 to 25 telling *how far to shift* the letters in the alphabet, rather than just shifting forward and backward by 3 all the time (as does the original Caesar cipher). This key would be a **shared secret** between the sender and receiver of the messages, agreed upon at some earlier point. This encryption system is a **shift cipher**.

Thus, a naive adversary who had intercepted a message encrypted by a shift cipher (with a secret amount of shifting) would be missing some information and would not know where to begin. By contrast, the intended receiver could immediately start letter-shifting and thereby produce the plaintext.

The naive but determined adversary might start trying every possible shifting, and wait to see which message seemed to make sense. This is a **brute force attack**. For example, suppose that the message

RCC FW XRLC ZJ UZMZUVU ZEKF KYIVV GRIKJ

is intercepted by the adversary. The adversary successively tries shifting backwards, by 1, then by 2, then by 3, then by 4, and so on, waiting until a message comes out that makes sense:

(shift back by 01:) qbb ev wqkb yi tylytut ydje jxhuu fqhji
(shift back by 02:) paa du vpja xh sxkxsts xcid iwgtt epgih
(shift back by 03:) ozz ct uoiz wg rwjwrsr wbhc hvfss dofhg
(shift back by 04:) nyy bs tnhy vf qvivqrq vagb guerr cnegf
(shift back by 05:) mxx ar smgx ue puhupqp uzfa ftdqq bmdfe
(shift back by 06:) lww zq rlfw td otgtopo tyez escpp alced
(shift back by 07:) kvv yp qkev sc nsfsnon sxdy drboo zkbdc
(shift back by 08:) juu xo pjdu rb mrermnm rwcx cqann yjacb
(shift back by 09:) itt wn oict qa lqdqlml qvbw bpzmm xizba
(shift back by 10:) hss vm nhbs pz kpcpklk puav aoyll whyaz
(shift back by 11:) grr ul mgar oy jobojkj otzu znxkk vgxzy
(shift back by 12:) fqq tk lfzq nx inaniji nsyt ymwjj ufwyx
(shift back by 13:) epp sj keyp mw hmzmhih mrxs xlvii tevxw
(shift back by 14:) doo ri jdxo lv glylghg lqwr wkuhh sduwv
(shift back by 15:) cnn qh icwn ku fkxkfgf kpvq vjtgg rctvu
(shift back by 16:) bmm pg hbvm jt ejwjefe joup uisff qbsut
(shift back by 17:) all of gaul is divided into three parts
(shift back by 18:) zkk ne fztk hr chuhcdc hmsn sgqdd ozqsr
(shift back by 19:) yjj md eysj gq bgtgbcb glrm rfpcc nyprq
(shift back by 20:) xii lc dxri fp afsfaba fkql qeobb mxoqp
(shift back by 21:) whh kb cwqh eo zerezaz ejpk pdnaa lwnpo
(shift back by 22:) vgg ja bvpg dn ydqdyzy dioj ocmzz kvmon
(shift back by 23:) uff iz auof cm xcpcxyx chni nblyy julnm
(shift back by 24:) tee hy ztne bl wbobwxw bgmh makxx itkml
(shift back by 25:) sdd gx ysmd ak vanavwv aflg lzjww hsjlk

All possible unshiftings are shown here so that they can be compared. In particular, only one attempted decryption makes any sense at all (in English). (And, while immersed in the purely mechanical process of letter-shifting, the adversary might indeed overlook the fact that shifting backward by 17 seems to yield a sensible message.) Note that this naive adversary has done 20 times the work that the legal recipient would, since the legal recipient would have *known* that the shift was by 17. If the message was very long, the 20-times-greater task of the adversary might have been prohibitive.

A somewhat less naive adversary might realize that unshifting the whole message is silly if an initial fragment of it is already gibberish. That is, the whole message need not be unshifted in order to tell whether it will make any sense. Indeed, by looking at just the first 3 letters in the 25 attempted decryptions listed, few could possibly be part of an English word. And even when the first 3 letters *might* be part of an English word, by continuing to attempted decryption to the next 2 letters we have only one plausible candidate, which is the true decryption.

In terms of speeding up the brute-force attack, this means that the adversary need only decrypt at most 5 characters for each guess at the key, in order to decide whether that guess at the key is correct or not. Since there are only 25 possibilities, very little work has to be done in order to find the key for a shift cipher.

This all means that a shift cipher is very easy to *break* by a *ciphertext-only* attack: any message in coherent English of more than about 3 characters can be decrypted by trying the 25 different unshifting possibilities on the first few letters of the message. Thus, trying 5 characters each time, there will be at most 24×5 wasted character decryptions before the true key is found. For a 10-line message of 80 characters each, this means that an adversary would only do 15% more work than the intended recipient. This is bad.

Even worse, consider what happens in the case of a *known-plaintext attack*: if the attacker knows a single character and its encryption, then the key (an integer 1-25) is known immediately by seeing how far the encrypted character is shifted over from the plaintext character. (A *chosen-plaintext* attack is no easier in this case, but how much easier could it get?)

As bad as this encryption system may be for keeping secrets against active hostile opponents, it has some uses. Such encryption can be viewed as a very thin but opaque wrapper on plaintext messages, in the sense that it precludes *accidental reading* of the message. That is, while it is essentially worthless for keeping secrets against *active adversaries*, it can be completely effective in keeping secrets with *cooperating agents*. After all, while from a mechanical viewpoint a shift cipher is easy to break, few people can naturally read shift-encrypted messages without considerable effort. Thus, the answer to a puzzle can be shift-enciphered so that it won't accidentally be read prematurely, and jokes of dubious taste can be shift-enciphered (with attached warnings in plaintext) so that no one will be offended by inadvertently reading them.

Terminology: The shift cipher is **symmetric**, in the sense that knowing the *encryption* key gives the *decryption* key, and vice versa. It is **monoalphabetic** in the sense that it will always encrypt a letter the same way (for the same key).

Exercises

1.1.01 Shift-encrypt 'this is the message' with key 13.

1.1.02 Shift-encrypt 'this is the message' with key 7.

1.1.03 Shift-encrypt 'this is the message' with key 19.

1.1.04 Shift-encrypt 'this is the message' with key 8.

1.1.05 Shift-encrypt 'this is the message' with key 12.

1.1.06 Decrypt the Caesar-encrypted message 'WKLV VKRXOG EH TXLWH HDVB'.

1.1.07 Decrypt the Caesar-encrypted message 'WDNH PH RXW WR WKH EDOO JDPH'.

1.1.08 Decrypt the Caesar-encrypted message 'UIFTF BSF UJNFT UIBU NBLF VT UJSFE'.

1.1.09 Decrypt the shift-encrypted message 'VO DOHA H ILHBAPMBS TVYUPUN'.

1.1.10 Decrypt the shift-encrypted message 'YRQ QEFP BUXJMIB FP IBPP BXPV'.

1.1.11 Decrypt the shift-encrypted message 'JYRIB YRJ GIVKKP KVVKY'.

1.1.12 Decrypt the shift-encrypted message 'WX KDBRWNBB URTN BQXF KDBR-WNBB'.

1.1.13 Decrypt the shift-encrypted message 'KTBG BG LITBG YTEEL BG MAX IETBG'.

1.1.14 Why is it silly to shift by amounts larger than 25?

1.1.15 Why is shifting forward by t the same as shifting backwards by $26 - t$?

1.1.16 (*) Discuss the effectiveness of padding a legitimate message with nonsense characters, possibly with a preselected statistical bias, prior to encryption with (for example) a shift cipher. Would this adversely affect the legal recipient's decryption?

1.2 Reduction/Division Algorithm

For a nonzero integer m, there is the process of **reduction modulo** m which is none other than the division-with-remainder by m from elementary arithemetic, with the quotient discarded. That is, the **reduction modulo** m **of** N is the remainder when N is divided by m. This procedure is also called the **division algorithm**, for that reason.

More precisely, the reduction modulo m of N is the unique integer r (the **remainder**) in the range

$$0 \leq r < |m|$$

so that N can be written as

$$N = q \cdot m + r$$

with an integer q (the **quotient**). Then we write

$$N \% m = r$$

(Very often the word 'modulo' is abbreviated as 'mod'.) The non-negative integer

m is the **modulus**. For example,

$$
\begin{aligned}
10 \mathbin{\%} 7 &= 3 &&(\text{because } 10 = 1 \cdot 7 + 3) \\
10 \mathbin{\%} 5 &= 0 &&(\text{because } 10 = 2 \cdot 5 + 0) \\
12 \mathbin{\%} 2 &= 0 &&(\text{because } 12 = 6 \cdot 2 + 0) \\
15 \mathbin{\%} 7 &= 1 &&(\text{because } 15 = 2 \cdot 7 + 1) \\
100 \mathbin{\%} 7 &= 2 &&(\text{because } 100 = 14 \cdot 7 + 2) \\
1000 \mathbin{\%} 2 &= 0 &&(\text{because } 1000 = 500 \cdot 2 + 0) \\
1001 \mathbin{\%} 2 &= 1 &&(\text{because } 1001 = 500 \cdot 2 + 1)
\end{aligned}
$$

In some sources, and sometimes for brevity, this terminology is abused by replacing the phrase 'N reduced mod m' by 'N mod m'. This is not so terrible, but there is also a related but significantly different meaning that 'N mod m' has, as we will see later. Usually the context will make clear what the phrase 'N mod m' means, but watch out. We will use a notation which is fairly compatible with most computer languages that include such an operation: write

$$ x \mathbin{\%} m $$

for

$$ x \text{ reduced modulo } m $$

Reductions mod m can be computed by hand by the familiar *long division* algorithm. For m and N both *positive*, even a simple hand calculator can be used to easily compute reductions. For example: divide N by m, obtaining a decimal. Remove (by subtracting) the integer part of the decimal, and multiply back by m to obtain the reduction mod m of N. Another way, which is more stable when the modulus m is large, is to divide N by m, remove the *fractional* part of the decimal, multiply back by m, and subtract this from N. While it might seem that there's no difference between these two computations, calculators implicitly retain only a certain number of decimal places of precision, and this makes a difference, so the second version behaves better when the numbers get large enough so that this becomes an issue.

The process of reduction mod m can also be applied to negative integers. For example,

$$
\begin{aligned}
-10 \mathbin{\%} 7 &= 4 &&\text{since } -10 &&= (-2) \cdot 7 + 4 \\
-10 \mathbin{\%} 5 &= 0 &&\text{since } -10 &&= (-2) \cdot 5 + 0 \\
-15 \mathbin{\%} 7 &= 6 &&\text{since } -15 &&= (-3) \cdot 7 + 6
\end{aligned}
$$

But neither the hand algorithm nor the calculator algorithm mentioned above give the correct output directly: for one thing, it is not true that the reduction mod m of $-N$ is the negative of the reduction mod m of N. And all our reductions mod m are supposed to be non-negative, besides. For example,

$$ 10 = 1 \cdot 7 + 3 $$

shows that the reduction of 10 mod 7 is 3, but if we simply negate both sides of this equation we get

$$ -10 = (-1) \cdot 7 + (-3) $$

That '−3' does not fit our requirements. The trick is to add another multiple of 7 to that '−3', while subtracting it from the $(-1) \cdot 7$, getting

$$-10 = (-1 - 1) \cdot 7 + (-3 + 7)$$

or finally

$$-10 = (-2) \cdot 7 + 4$$

And there is one last 'gotcha': in case the remainder is 0, as in

$$14 = 2 \cdot 7 + 0$$

when we negate to get

$$-14 = (-2) \cdot 7 + 0$$

nothing further needs to be done, since that 0 is already in the right range. (If we *did* add another 7 to it, we'd be in the wrong range.) Thus, in summary, let r be the reduction of N mod m. Then the reduction of $-N$ mod m is $m - r$ if $r \neq 0$, and is 0 if $r = 0$.

The modulus can be negative, as well: however, it happens that always the reduction of N modulo m is just the reduction of N mod $|m|$, so this introduces nothing new.

Note that by our definition the reduction mod m of any integer is always non-negative. This *does not match* the usage in some computer languages, where the reduction of a negative integer $-N$ is the negative of the reduction of N. This difference has to be remembered when writing code.

A **multiplicative inverse mod** m of an integer N is another integer t so that $N \cdot t \% m = 1$. It is important to realize that this new notion of 'inverse' is entitled to this label because it shares the abstract property that multiplication by it (and then reduction) *returns to 1*. However, knowing that 2-inverse is 0.5 as a rational or real number gives no clue as to what 2-inverse-mod-5 might be. Thus, while inverse-mod-m has a very strong abstract connection to a more ordinary sense of 'inverse', it would be misleading to think that there was a direct tangible relation.

For example, since $2 \cdot 3 = 6$, which reduces mod 5 to 1, we can say that 3 is a multiplicative inverse mod 5 to 2. This is *not* to say that '$3 = \frac{1}{2}$' or '$3 = 0.5$' or any such thing. As another example, 143 is a multiplicative inverse to 7 modulo 100, since $7 \times 143 = 1001$, which reduces mod 100 to 1. On the other hand, we can anticipate that, for example, 2 has no multiplicative inverse modulo 10, because any multiple $2 \times t$ is an *even* number, but all expressions $q \times 10 + 1$ are *odd*.

At this point it is not clear which integers might or might not have multiplicative inverses, and it is even less clear how we might efficiently *find* such inverses. We will leave this as a small mystery for the moment, but resolve it decisively a little later.

Last, let's prove *existence* and *uniqueness* of the quotient and remainder in the assertion of the Reduction/Division Algorithm:

Proposition. Given a nonzero integer m and arbitrary integer N, there are unique integers q and r so that $0 \leq r < |m|$ and

$$N = q \cdot m + r$$

Proof: For fixed N and m, let X be the collection of all integers of the form $N - x \cdot |m|$. Let r be the least non-negative integer in X, and let q be the corresponding integer, so that $N - q|m| = r$.

First, we claim that $0 \leq r < |m|$. If $r \geq |m|$, then $r - |m| \geq 0$. Since $r - |m|$ is writeable as $N - (q+1)|m|$, it is in the collection X. But $r - |m| < r$, contradicting the fact that r is the smallest non-negative integer in X. Thus, it could not have been that $r \geq |m|$, and we conclude that $r < |m|$, as desired. Then from the expression $N = q|m| + r$, if $m > 0$ we have $N = qm + r$, and if $m < 0$ we replace q by $-q$ again to obtain $N = qm + r$, as desired.

Next, we prove uniqueness of the q and r. Suppose that

$$qm + r = q'm + r'$$

were two expressions as in the proposition, with $0 \leq r < m$ and $0 \leq r' < m$. By symmetry, we can suppose that $r \leq r'$ (if not, reverse the roles of r and r' in the discussion). Then

$$(q' - q) \cdot m = r' - r$$

and $r' - r \geq 0$. If $r' - r \neq 0$, then necessarily $q' - q \neq 0$, but if so then

$$r' - r = |r' - r| = |q' - q| \cdot |m| \geq 1 \cdot |m|$$

(Again, $r' - r = |r' - r|$, since $r' - r \geq 0$.) But

$$r' - r \leq r' < |m|$$

Putting these together, we get the impossible

$$|m| \leq r' - r < |m|$$

This contradicts the supposition that $r \neq r'$. Therefore, $r = r'$. Then, from $(q' - q)m = r' - r = 0$ (and $m \neq 0$) we get $q' = q$, as well. This proves the uniqueness.

We need to be sure that X contains *some* non-negative integers, or our reference to the least non-negative element of X would be fallacious. This is not mysterious. On one hand, if $N > 0$, then $N - 0 \cdot |m|$ is certainly positive. On the other hand, if $N < 0$, then for sufficiently large negative x the quantity $N - x \cdot |m|$ is positive. ♣

Remark: The assertion that any (non-empty) collection of positive integers has a least element is the **Well-Ordering Principle** for the positive integers.

Proposition. Let n and N be two integers, with $N = kn$ for some integer k. Then for any integer x

$$(x \% N) \% n = x \% n$$

Proof: Let $x = Q \cdot N + R$ with $0 \leq R < |N|$. This R is the reduction of x mod N. Further, let $R = q \cdot n + r$ with $0 \leq r < |n|$. This r is the reduction of R mod n. Then

$$x = QN + R = Q(kn) + qn + r = (Qk + q) \cdot n + r$$

So r is also the reduction of x modulo n.   ♣

Exercises

1.2.01 Find the reduction mod 99 of 1000.

1.2.02 Find the reduction mod 81 of 1001.

1.2.03 Find the reduction mod 81 of 10.

1.2.04 Find the reduction mod 73 of 1000.

1.2.05 Find the reduction mod 89 of 1000.

1.2.06 Find the reduction mod 88 of -10.

1.2.07 Find the reduction mod 67 of -23.

1.2.08 Find the reduction mod 123 of -1.

1.2.09 Find the reduction mod 88 of -1000.

1.2.10 Find the reduction mod 123 of -1.

1.2.11 Find the reduction mod 59 of -10.

1.2.12 Find the reduction mod 279 of -1000.

1.2.13 Find the reduction mod 399 of -997.

1.2.14 Prove that the reduction mod 10 of a positive integer N is simply the ones'-place digit of N in decimal notation.

1.2.15 Prove that the reduction mod 100 of a positive integer N is the two-digit number made up of the tens'- and ones'-place digits of N.

1.2.16 Let m be any nonzero integer. Prove that the reduction mod $-m$ of N is the same as the reduction mod m of N.

1.2.17 Prove in general that if r is the reduction of N mod m, and if $r \neq 0$, then $m - r$ is the reduction of $-N$ mod m.

1.2.18 By brute force, find a multiplicative inverse to 13 mod 100.

1.2.19 By brute force, find a multiplicative inverse to 87 mod 100.

1.2.20 By brute force, find a multiplicative inverse to 29 mod 100.

1.2.21 By brute force, find a multiplicative inverse to 31 mod 100.

1.2.22 By brute force, check that among 1, 2, ..., 25 the integers with multiplicative inverses modulo 26 are the *odd* integers in that range, excluding 13. Is there any shortcut here, by cleverness alone, without invoking any fancier mathematics?

1.2.23 (*) (This is a little hard to do without using anything more than what we have already!) Let m be a positive integer. Prove that for all integers x, y

$$((x \% m) + (y \% m)) \% m = (x + y) \% m$$

and

$$((x \% m) \times (y \% m)) \% m = (x \times y) \% m$$

1.3 The One-Time Pad

The **one-time-pad** (OTP) is *perfectly secure*, when used properly. Further, we can even *prove* that it is perfectly secure, not merely *believe* it. It is very simple in concept. It is the *only* known cipher in the world that can keep messages secret no matter how long an adversary attacks, and no matter what machinery the adversary has. For this reason, some of the most sensitive communications in the world use OTP: nuclear weapon launch codes, etc. OTP is sometimes called *Vernam cipher* after Gilbert Vernam, who advocated use of such ciphers around 1917. We'll explain what it is very shortly.

Of course there is a *gotcha*: notice that we said 'used properly'. If keys are reused, or if inferior keys are used, then an OTP can very easily fail. For example, if a key is reused, then the OTP effectively becomes a Vigenere cipher, which we'll later show how to successfully attack.

The apparatus and vocabulary of reduction modulo m, and the notion of *function* generally, make discussion of encryption and decryption easier. For example, if we now encode a as 0, b as 1, up through z as 25 (as we will frequently do), then the shift cipher's encryption was given by a very simple type of *function E_k* (depending on the key k, telling how much to shift) from the set $\{0, 1, \ldots, 25\}$ to itself, given by the formula

$$E_k(x) = (x + k) \% 26$$

Likewise, the decryption for the shift cipher with key k can be thought of as a function D_k in the other direction:

$$D_k(x) = (x - k) \% 26$$

But even with 'only' a ciphertext-only attack, the shift cipher is weak because the keyspace is so tiny (just 25).

Going to another extreme, we could arrange to have *keys which are as big as the message* itself. This certainly helps, by creating a huge keyspace. An even more essential idea of the OTP is that, in addition, keys are *used only once*. Because of this one-time use of a key, the OTP achieves a better effect than just having a large keyspace: from the ciphertext of a properly OTP-encrypted message *nothing* can be learned, no matter how much time or energy an attacker spends. It's not just an issue of having an intractably huge keyspace.

The OTP works as follows. Suppose that we anticipate sending a single very important message of n characters, which we want to encrypt using a one-time pad. For this, we choose a *key* consisting of a string of *random n characters* $k = (k_1, \ldots, k_n)$. For the present discussion we view a character as being an integer in the range 0–25 (encoding 'a' as '0', 'b' as '1', and so on). The message will be $x = (x_1, x_2, \ldots, x_n)$, with the same encoding of letters by integers. Using the idea of encryption as a function, we can view encryption with key k as a *function E_k* from the set of lists of n characters to itself. Using the idea of reduction modulo 26, we can write a *formula* for such a function: for brevity, write

$$x \ \% \ 26$$

for

$$x \text{ reduced modulo } 26$$

Now we can write our one-time pad encryption function:

$$E_k(x) = ((x_1 + k_1) \ \% \ 26, (x_2 + k_2) \ \% \ 26, \ldots, (x_n + k_n) \ \% \ 26)$$

That is, each character in the plaintext x is shifted by an amount determined by the corresponding character in the key. Then the decryption function D_k with key k is simply shifting backward by the corresponding amounts:

$$D_k(x) = ((x_1 - k_1) \ \% \ 26, (x_2 - k_2) \ \% \ 26, \ \ldots, (x_n - k_n) \ \% \ 26)$$

For example, with plaintext of length 10, the sender and receiver might agree in advance to use a key consisting of a fairly random-looking sequence of ten numbers in the range 0–25, such as $k = (8, 13, 24, 19, 9, 1, 0, 7, 20, 3)$. Then the plaintext 'impossible' would be first encoded by integers as

$$x = (8, 12, 15, 14, 18, 18, 8, 1, 11, 4)$$

Then

$$E_k(x) = ((8+8) \ \% \ 26, (12+13) \ \% \ 26, (15+24) \ \% \ 26, (14+19) \ \% \ 26, (18+9) \ \% \ 26,$$

$$(18+1) \ \% \ 26, (8+0) \ \% \ 26, (1+7) \ \% \ 26, (11+20) \ \% \ 26, (4+3) \ \% \ 26)$$

$$= (16, 25, 13, 7, 1, 19, 8, 8, 5, 7) = QZNHBTIIFH$$

(We converted it back to letters just for effect.)

An incidental virtue of a OTP is that it is **polyalphabetic**, meaning that the same letter may be encrypted different ways depending upon where it occurs in the plaintext. This is generally an advantage over **monoalphabetic** systems (such as the shift cipher) where the same plaintext letter is encrypted as the same ciphertext letter every time.

We can sketch the proof of the perfect security of an OTP very briefly as follows. First we should say what **perfect security** should mean: it should be that an attacker who intercepts the ciphertext has no more information about the plaintext than if they didn't even have the ciphertext. Yes, this sounds funny, but if you think about it you may agree that this is what *perfect* security would have to mean. Why does an OTP achieve this? The *rough* idea is that

$$\text{random } n \text{ bits} + \text{meaningful } n \text{ bits} = \text{random } n \text{ bits}$$

In isolation, this simplifies to

$$\text{random 0-or-1} + \text{meaningful 0-or-1} = \text{random 0-or-1}$$

It is important that there is as much random stuff as there is message, or it won't completely mask the meaning.

Yet there are weaknesses here. First, there is the temptation to use a key which is (the encoding into integers in the range 0–25 of) some word or phrase which is memorable to the sender and receiver, such as someone's name, the name of a pet, a book title, etc. An attacker familiar with the sender and receiver would surely try such keys. Even if there were no personal details of sender and receiver available to the attacker, a clever attacker might try as keys (encodings of) 10-letter phrases in English. It would still be a daunting task to run through a list of such keys, but the number of 10-letter phrases in English is still much much smaller than 10^{10}. Running through such a short list hunting for keys is called a **dictionary attack**.

Note that a dictionary attack can succeed only if *both* the message and the (bad!) key are non-gibberish. In any case, if the message itself *is* gibberish, especially if it consists of non-printing characters in ASCII, it would be difficult for an adversary to tell the correct decryption from among equally gibberish-seeming incorrect decryptions.

There is the temptation to *reuse* the key to a one-time pad, which would be a fatal mistake, since reuse would make possible Friedman's index-of-coincidence attack as if the cipher were a Vigenere cipher. But if the keys are *not* reused, then *creation* and *distribution* of huge keys (without *their* being stolen) is as difficult a problem as sending the messages themselves. This is the first example of the fundamental problem(s) of **key distribution** and/or **key management**. Any practical discussion of encryption must address these.

In the context of a true one-time pad, meaning that the key *will not be reused*, the idea of a known-plaintext attack makes no sense, since obtaining the key will serve no further purpose than acquiring the plaintext anyway. Likewise, a chosen-plaintext attack makes no sense.

Another potential problem is that with very long plaintexts it may be a little complicated to arrange 'random' keys of such length. If the key for a long message is *not* very random, there are several ciphertext-only attacks possible, as we will see when looking at other classical ciphers.

Terminology: The one-time pad is **symmetric**: knowing the encryption key is equivalent to knowing the decryption key, and vice versa. It is **polyalphabetic**: a letter is not generally encrypted the same throughout a message.

Exercises

1.3.01 Encrypt 'nevermore' by a one-time-pad with key 'excelsior'.

1.3.02 Encrypt 'nevermore' by a one-time-pad with key 'idiosyncratic'.

1.3.03 Encrypt 'nevermore' by a one-time-pad with key 'tangentially'.

1.3.04 Encrypt 'nevermore' by a one-time-pad with key 'inconsequential'.

1.3.05 Encrypt 'dog has fleas' by a one-time-pad with key 'antedeluvian'.

1.3.06 Encrypt 'idealism' by a one-time-pad with key 'hypeoversubstance'.

1.3.07 (*) Estimate how much easier it would be to find an 8-character OTP key knowing that it is an English word, rather than an arbitrary string of 8 characters (among a–z encoded as 0–25).

1.4 The Affine Cipher

So far, the shift cipher has too small a keyspace, which makes it vulnerable to a brute-force ciphertext-only attack. (And it is completely transparent to known-plaintext or chosen-plaintext attacks with just a single known or chosen character.) On the other hand, while a one-time pad is perfectly secure, the keys are not so easy to produce, are not reusable, and distribution of keys is a huge problem. So let's go back to the shift cipher, and try to improve it a little.

Using the idea of encoding letters as numbers, and the idea of reduction modulo 26, we can enlarge the shift cipher keyspace a bit by considering more complicated **affine cipher** encryption functions of the form

$$E_{a,b}(x) = (a \cdot x + b) \% 26$$

for integers a, b in the range 0–25. This generalizes the shift cipher, which is just the case $a = 1$. For example,

$$E_{3,11}(\text{hello how are you}) = \text{GXSSB GBZ LKX FBT}$$

(We continue to write plaintext in lowercase and ciphertext in uppercase.) Thus, in this scenario the key is a pair (a, b) of integers in the range 0–25. This is still a *monoalphabetic cipher*, but the keyspace is bigger. (This cipher, like all classical ciphers, is *symmetric*, meaning that knowledge of encryption and decryption keys is essentially the same thing.)

Of course, we want the ciphertext to be decryptable in only one way. In terms of the language of functions, this means that we want $E_{a,b}$ to have an inverse function, or, to be technical, at least a *left* inverse. Therefore, we want the encryption function $E_{a,b}$ to be **bijective**. In fact, it turns out that the decryption function is of the same form as the encryption function:

Proposition. For a possessing a multiplicative inverse a^{-1} mod 26, the affine encryption function $E_{a,b}$ has an inverse

$$D_{a,b} = E_{a,b}^{-1} = E_{a^{-1}, -a^{-1} \cdot b}$$

Proof: We have

$$E_{a,b} = E_{1,b} \circ E_{a,0}$$

and we know that the simpler shift $E_{1,b}$ does have the inverse $E_{1,-b}$ so $E_{a,b}$ will surely be invertible if $E_{a,0}$ is invertible. And, finally, if a has a multiplicative inverse a^{-1} mod 26, then the inverse of $E_{a,0}$ is given quite explicitly as

$$E_{a,0}^{-1}(x) = a^{-1} \cdot x \,\%\, 26 = E_{a^{-1},0}(x)$$

In this case, using the general principle that $(f \circ g)^{-1} = g^{-1} \circ f^{-1}$ for suitable invertible functions, we conclude that

$$E_{a,b}^{-1} = (E_{1,b} \circ E_{a,0})^{-1} = E_{a,0}^{-1} \circ E_{1,b}^{-1} = E_{a^{-1},0} \circ E_{1,-b} = E_{a^{-1}, -a^{-1} \cdot b}$$

as we wanted to show.   ♣

If we grant ourselves the verifiable fact that there are 12 invertible integers mod 26 among 1, 2, ..., 25 (the odd integers other than 13), then we have $12 \times 26 - 1 = 311$ keys (a, b) now, rather than the mere 25 for the shift cipher. (There are 12 choices for the 'a', and for each such choice there are 26 choices for 'b', excluding $b = 0$ only in the case $a = 1$.) At least in a relative sense this enlargement of the keyspace is an improvement over the shift cipher.

Thus, at least on the scale we're operating, we might decide that a **brute-force** *ciphertext-only* attack (trying the 311 possible keys and seeing which yields a recognizable output) is daunting, even if we take the shortcut of using only the first 5 or so characters in each key trial.

Before worrying about improving our technique to launch a more effective ciphertext-only attack, let's note that a *known-plaintext* or *chosen-plaintext* is also harder than in the case of the shift cipher.

Let's do the chosen-plaintext attack first, since it's the easiest: two chosen plaintext characters will suffice to disclose the key very directly. Given a key (a, b) to be disclosed, we will choose two different plaintext characters x, y (from among 0–25) so that knowledge of $E_{a,b}(x)$ and $E_{a,b}(y)$ determines the key (a, b). Take $x = 0$ (corresponding to 'a'). Then

$$E_{a,b}(0) = (a \cdot 0 + b) \,\%\, 26 = b \,\%\, 26 = b$$

since we certainly may suppose that b was reduced in the first place. That is, the b part of the key is immediately disclosed with one chosen character of plaintext. Next,

$$E_{a,b}(1) = (a \cdot 1 + b) \% 26 = (a + b) \% 26$$

Since we already know b, this gives a (by subtracting and reducing mod 26).

The *known-plaintext* attack is slightly more complicated than the chosen-plaintext attack. For example, suppose that we are given $E_{a,b}(x)$ and $E_{a,b}(y)$ for two different x, y among 0–25, although now we have no control over which x, y are given. Then

$$E_{a,b}(x) - E_{a,b}(y) = (a \cdot (x - y)) \% 26$$

since the b's cancel, and since we can reduce before or after doing arithmetic. Now, if we were lucky enough that $x - y$ had a multiplicative inverse $(x - y)^{-1} \bmod 26$, then

$$a = (x - y)^{-1}(E_{a,b}(x) - E_{a,b}(y)) \% 26$$

Granting that, b is easy to find by subtraction:

$$b = (E_{a,b}(x) - a \cdot x) \% 26$$

Thus, if we are a little *lucky*, a known-plaintext attack with two plaintext characters will succeed, providing we can find inverses modulo 26.

Further delaying discussion of a better ciphertext-only attack, let's contemplate the usefulness of *repeated applications* of an affine cipher, with the same key or not. Quite generally, when an encryption scheme S is applied one time, it is called a **single-round** S. If an encryption scheme S is applied 3 times, then this is called **3-round** S, and so on. The motivation for repeated application of an encryption scheme is the intuitive notion that if a single application 'mixes up' the message, then repeated applications will 'mix it up' even more. And, with good contemporary cryptosystems this really is the case.

However, multiple rounds of many classical ciphers don't provide any extra security at all. Already this is clear for the shift cipher: the net effect of repeated shiftings by various amounts is simply one shifting. Much less obviously, in the case of the affine cipher, the formula

$$E_{a,b} \circ E_{c,d} = E_{ac,ad+b}$$

implies that application of an affine cipher with key (c, d), followed by application of an affine cipher with key (a, b) has the same effect as a single encryption with key $(ac, ad + b)$. Continuing in this manner, it follows that *any number* of affine cipher encryptions have the net effect of a single such encryption.

The fact that multiple-round affine ciphers (even with varying keys) give nothing new might be construed as demonstrating that these ciphers don't really 'mix up' the set 0–25 very much.

A little later we'll use basic statistical properties of English to give a simple ciphertext-only attack on affine ciphers.

An even more devastating ciphertext-only attack on affine ciphers can be made from a variant of the Friedman index-of-coincidence attack (that we'll use on Vigenere ciphers later). Assuming that the message is in coherent English (for example) and is more than a few letters long, this would *completely automate* hostile decryption. When an attack can be fully automated, it is even more clear that the modest increase in the keyspace is pointless.

Exercises

1.4.01 Encrypt 'meet me at midnight' with an affine cipher keyed as $E_{3,7}(x) = 3 \cdot x + 7 \% 26$.

1.4.02 Encrypt 'meet me at midnight' with an affine cipher keyed as $E_{11,1}(x) = 11 \cdot x + 1 \% 26$.

1.4.03 Encrypt 'meet me at midnight' with an affine cipher keyed as $E_{9,3}(x) = 9 \cdot x + 3 \% 26$.

1.4.04 Encrypt 'meet me at midnight' with an affine cipher keyed as $E_{11,19}(x) = 11 \cdot x + 19 \% 26$.

1.4.05 Encrypt 'meet me at midnight' with an affine cipher keyed as $E_{19,8}(x) = 19 \cdot x + 8 \% 26$.

1.4.06 Determine the decryption key for an affine cipher with encryption $E_{3,7}(x) = 3 \cdot x + 7 \% 26$.

1.4.07 Determine the decryption key for an affine cipher with encryption $E_{11,5}(x) = 11 \cdot x + 5 \% 26$.

1.4.08 Determine the decryption key for an affine cipher with encryption $E_{7,3}(x) = 7 \cdot x + 3 \% 26$.

1.4.09 Determine the decryption key for an affine cipher with encryption $E_{13,16}(x) = 13 \cdot x + 16 \% 26$.

1.4.10 Fix a positive integer m, and let $E_{a,b}$ be the function from $\{0, 1, \ldots, m-1\}$ to itself given by $E_{a,b}(x) = ax + b \% m$. Prove that $E_{a,b} = E_{1,b} \circ E_{a,0}$.

1.4.11 More generally, in the situation of the previous exercise, prove that $E_{a,b} \circ E_{c,d} = E_{ac,ad+b}$.

1.4.12 Known-plaintext attack: suppose that $E_{a,b}(3) = 5$ and $E_{a,b}(4) = 7$. Find a and b.

1.4.13 Known-plaintext attack: suppose that $E_{a,b}(3) = 19$ and $E_{a,b}(4) = 2$. Find a and b.

1.4.14 Known-plaintext attack: suppose that $E_{a,b}(3) = 5$ and $E_{a,b}(6) = 7$. Find a and b.

1.4.15 Known-plaintext attack: suppose that $E_{a,b}(11) = 8$ and $E_{a,b}(4) = 11$. Find a and b.

1.4.16 Known-plaintext attack: suppose that $E_{a,b}(8) = 16$ and $E_{a,b}(19) = 21$. Find a and b.

1.4.17 Known-plaintext attack: suppose that $E_{a,b}(8) = 11$ and $E_{a,b}(11) = 1$. Find a and b.

1.4.18 Known-plaintext attack: suppose that $E_{a,b}(9) = 16$ and $E_{a,b}(20) = 11$. Find a and b.

1.4.19 Known-plaintext attack: suppose that $E_{a,b}(3) = 5$ and $E_{a,b}(5) = 7$. What are the possibilities for a and b?

1.4.20 Show that a two-round affine cipher can actually have no net effect in some cases: show that for any character x (in 0–25) we have $E_{25,25}(E_{25,25}(x)) = x$.

1.4.21 Show that a three-round affine cipher can possibly have no net effect: show that for any x in 0–25 we have $E_{3,2}(E_{3,2}(E_{3,2}(x))) = x$.

2
Probability

The goal of this chapter is to develop a few simple ideas about probability in order to give names to some features of English and other natural languages. One question already helps to illustrate what we're trying to understand: when we see a string of letters (and numbers and punctuation), how do we go about answering the question **'Is it English?'** To say that it's English if an English-speaking person can recognize it as English is too evasive: we haven't told *how* we recognize it as English in a way that anyone else could reproduce, or that could be described in machine instructions. We won't pretend to give a very good answer to that question here, but we *can* talk about some low-level features of English that can be recognized and used in a systematic mechanical fashion.

The most important and basic feature is the frequency of occurrence of single letters. This already is a significant-enough aspect of English to make attacks on weak ciphers possible, and to understand why probabilistic attacks work.

We introduce a bit of probability, first looking at some basic counting principles which underlie the probability as we use it here. All these things will be used and reused frequently in the rest of this book.

2.1 Counting

Here are some simple but important examples of **counting** in preparation for many other things. Of course, by 'counting' we mean *structured* counting.

First example: Suppose we have n different things, for example, the integers from 1 to n inclusive. *How many different* **orderings** *or* **ordered listings**

$$i_1, i_2, i_3, \ldots, i_{n-1}, i_n$$

of these numbers are there? The answer is obtained by noting that there are n choices for the first thing i_1, then $n-1$ remaining choices for the second thing i_2 (since we can't reuse whatever i_1 was), $n-2$ remaining choices for i_3 (since we can't reuse i_1 or i_2, whatever they were!), and so on down to 2 remaining choices for i_{n-1} and then just one choice for i_n. *Thus, there are*

$$n \cdot (n-1) \cdot (n-2) \cdot \ldots \cdot 2 \cdot 1$$

possible **orderings** *of n distinct things.* Since this kind of product arises often, there is a notation for it and a name for it: n-**factorial**, denoted $n!$, is the product

$$n! = n \cdot (n-1) \cdot (n-2) \cdot \ldots \cdot 2 \cdot 1$$

Second example: How many subsets of k elements are there in a set of n things? There are n possibilities for the first choice, $n-1$ remaining choices for the second (since the first item is removed), $n-2$ for the third (since the first and second items are no longer available), and so on down to $n-(k-1)$ choices for the kth. This number is $n!/(n-k)!$, but is *not* what we want, since it includes a count of all different *orders* of choices, but subset are not ordered. That is,

$$\frac{n!}{(n-k)!} = k! \times \text{the actual number}$$

since we saw in the previous example that there are $k!$ possible orderings of k distinct things. Thus, there are

$$\frac{n!}{k!\,(n-k)!} = \binom{n}{k}$$

choices of subsets of k elements in a set with n elements.

The number $n!/k!(n-k)!$ also occurs often enough to warrant a name and notation: it is called a **binomial coefficient**, is written

$$\frac{n!}{k!\,(n-k)!} = \binom{n}{k}$$

and is read 'n choose k'.

Third counting example: How many *disjoint pairs* of 3-element and 5-element subsets are there in a set with 10 elements? We just saw that there are $\binom{10}{3}$ choices for the *first* subset with 3 elements. Then the remaining part of the original set has just $10 - 3 = 7$ elements, so there are $\binom{7}{5}$ choices for the *second* subset of 5 elements. Therefore, there are

$$\binom{10}{3}\binom{7}{5} = \frac{10!}{7!\,3!}\frac{7!}{5!2!}$$

$$= \frac{10!}{3!\,5!\,2!}$$

pairs of disjoint subsets of 3 and 5 elements inside a set with 10 elements.

Fourth counting example: How many *disjoint pairs* of subsets, each with k elements, are there in a set with n elements, where $2k \leq n$? We saw that there are $\binom{n}{k}$ choices for the *first* subset with k elements. Then the remaining part of the original set has just $n - k$ elements, so there are $\binom{n-k}{k}$ choices for the *second* subset of k elements. But our counting so far accidentally takes into account a *first* subset and a *second* one, which is not what the question is. By now we know that there are $2! = 2$ choices of ordering of two things (subsets, for example). Therefore, there are

$$\frac{1}{2}\binom{n}{k}\binom{n-k}{k} = \frac{1}{2}\frac{n!}{(n-k)!k!}\frac{(n-k)!}{k!(n-2k)!}$$

$$= \frac{n!}{2\,k!\,k!(n-2k)!}$$

pairs of disjoint subsets of k elements each inside a set with n elements.

Generalizing the previous: For integers n, ℓ, k with $n \geq k\ell$, we could ask *how many families of ℓ disjoint subsets of k elements each are there inside a set of n elements?* There are

$$\binom{n}{k}$$

choices for the first subset,

$$\binom{n-k}{k}$$

for the second,

$$\binom{n-2k}{k}$$

for the third, up to

$$\binom{n-(\ell-1)k}{k}$$

for the ℓth subset. But since *ordering* of these subsets is accidentally counted here, we have to divide by $\ell!$ to have the actual number of families. There is some cancellation among the factorials, so that the actual number is

$$\frac{n!}{\ell!\,(k!)^\ell\,(n-\ell k)!}$$

Exercises

2.1.01 How many different ways are there to *order* the set $\{1,2,3\}$?

2.1.02 How many different ways are there to *order* the set $\{1,2,3,4\}$?

2.1.03 How many different ways are there to *order* the set $\{1,2,3,4,5\}$?

2.1.04 How many different ways are there to *order* the set $\{a,b,c,d,e\}$?

2.1.05 How many choices of 3 things from the list $1,2,3,\ldots,6,7$?

2.1.06 How many choices of 3 things from the list $1,2,3,\ldots,9$?

2.1.07 How many subsets of $\{1,2,3,4,5,6,7\}$ with exactly 4 elements?

2.1.08 How many subsets of choices of $\{1,2,3,\ldots,10\}$ with exactly 5 elements?

2.1.09 How many subsets of choices of $\{1,2,3,\ldots,12\}$ with exactly 4 elements?

2.1.10 How many different choices are there of an *unordered* pair of *distinct* numbers from the set $\{1,2,\ldots,10\}$? How many choices of *ordered* pair?

2.1.11 How many subsets of all sizes are there of a set S with n elements? (*Hint:* Go down the list of all elements in the set: for each one you have 2 choices, to *include* it or to *exclude* it. Altogether how many choices?)

2.1.12 How many pairs of disjoint subsets each with 3 elements are there inside the set $\{1,2,3,4,5,6,7,8\}$?

2.2   Basic Ideas

Elementary ideas of *probability* are part of our culture, although in some cases are misrepresented. For that matter, some very reasonable conclusions of elementary probability are counter-intuitive, and require a bit of reflection before one's intuition can refine itself to match.

In fact, the uneasy relation between the mathematized form of 'probability' and the real-world version is bad enough that probability theory was not considered a fully legitimate part of mathematics until 1930 or later. What *randomness* or *random choice* means in the real world is unclear, yet we are accustomed to feeling that these words do have content. We may speculate that the decimal digits of π are 'random', and while we cannot directly *see* the pattern, of course the pattern is that they describe π.

Nevertheless, at the very least our abstract version of 'probability' and 'randomness' provides a vocabulary and a *heuristic* for addressing a variety of real-world issues. At the end of this section we do a general computation important for applications to **birthday attacks**.

First, there is the conversion from the colloquial notion of the 'chance' of something occurring to the notion of its 'probability'. While usually the 'chance' of something happening is given as a percentage, a **probability** is given as a number between 0 and 1, inclusive. The simple conversion rule is the following: if in colloquial English the 'chance' of something happening is $x\%$, then its probability is $x/100$. (This change introduces no new content.)

The first example involves coin-tossing. A 'fair coin' is presumed to have 'equal chances' of landing heads-up or tails-up. Further, each toss of the coin is presumed to have an outcome *independent* of other tosses before and after. That is, there is no mechanism by which the outcome of one toss affects another. Then, out of (for example) 10 coin tosses we expect about half to be heads and about half to be tails. We expect that it would very seldom happen that 10 out of 10 tosses would all be 'heads'. So far, in this vague language, there is no obvious problem.

Yet experimentation will show that out of repeated batches of 10 coin flips, only about $1/4$ of the time will there be *exactly* 5 heads and 5 tails. (Only once in about $2^{10} = 1024$ times will one get *all* heads.) In fact, about $2/5$ of the time there will be *either* 6 heads and 4 tails, or *vice versa*. That is, a 6-4 or 4-6 distribution of outcomes is more likely than the 'expected' 5-5.

But this is not a paradox, since our intuition surely tells us not that there will be *exactly* half heads and half tails, but only *approximately* half and half. And we can retell the story in a better way as follows.

In a **trial** of n coin flips, each flip has two possible outcomes, so there are

$$\underbrace{2 \times \ldots \times 2}_{n} = 2^n$$

possible sequences of n outcomes. The assumptions that the coin is 'fair' and that the separate coin tosses do not 'influence' each other are interpreted as saying that *each one of the 2^n possible sequences of coin-toss outcomes is equally likely.* Therefore, the probability of any *single* sequence of n outcomes is $1/2^n$. Further, for any subset S of the set A of all 2^n possible sequences of outcomes, we assume that

probability of a sequence of n tosses giving an outcome in S

$$= \frac{\text{number of elements in } S}{\text{number of elements in } A} = \frac{\text{number of elements in } S}{2^n}$$

Then the probability that *exactly* k heads will occur out of n tosses (with $0 \le k \le n$) is computed as

probability of k heads out of n tosses

$$= \frac{\text{the number of sequences of } n \text{ flips with exactly } k \text{ heads}}{\text{the total number of sequences of } n \text{ flips}}$$

$$= \frac{\text{the number of sequences of } n \text{ flips with exactly } k \text{ heads}}{2^n}$$

To count the number of sequences of n heads-or-tails with exactly k heads, we may think of this problem as that of *counting the number of subsets with k elements from a set with n elements*. That is, the 'whole set' is the set of all n flips, and 'the subset' is the set of flips that come up 'heads'. This number is the binomial coefficient

$$n\text{-choose-}k \;=\; \frac{n!}{k!\,(n-k)!} \;=\; \binom{n}{k}$$

Thus, for example, the probability that exactly 5 heads come up in 10 tosses is

$$\frac{\binom{10}{5}}{2^{10}} = \frac{\left(\frac{10\cdot 9\cdot 8\cdot 7\cdot 6}{5\cdot 4\cdot 3\cdot 2\cdot 1}\right)}{1024} = \frac{252}{1024} \approx \frac{1}{4}$$

as commented just above. And the probability that 6 heads and 4 tails *or* 4 heads and 6 tails occur is

$$\frac{\text{number of sequences of 10 flips with exactly 6 or exactly 4 heads}}{2^{10}}$$

$$= \frac{\binom{10}{4} + \binom{10}{6}}{1024} = \frac{2\cdot(10\cdot 9\cdot 8\cdot 7\,/\,4\cdot 3\cdot 2)}{1024} = \frac{420}{1024} \approx \frac{2}{5}$$

Not too surprisingly, the probability of getting *exactly* half heads and half tails out of $2n$ flips goes *down* as the number of flips goes up, and in fact goes to 0 as the number of flips goes to infinity:

$$\frac{\binom{2}{1}}{2^2} \approx 0.5$$

$$\frac{\binom{4}{2}}{2^4} \approx 0.375$$

$$\frac{\binom{6}{3}}{2^6} \approx 0.3125$$

$$\frac{\binom{8}{4}}{2^8} \approx 0.2734$$

$$\frac{\binom{10}{5}}{2^{10}} \approx 0.2461$$

$$\frac{\binom{12}{6}}{2^{12}} \approx 0.1813$$

$$\frac{\binom{14}{7}}{2^{14}} \approx 0.1683$$

But of course it might not be *exactly* half heads and half tails, but *close*. What should this mean? One approach which was used in the past, but is not to be taken too literally, is the idea of **limiting frequency**, described as follows. Let $h(n)$ be the number of times that a head came up in n trials. Then as n grows larger and larger, the ratio $h(n)/n$ should get 'closer and closer' to $1/2$. Or, more precisely, in the language of limits,

$$\lim_{n\to\infty} \frac{h(n)}{n} = \frac{1}{2}$$

We would say that the **limiting frequency** of heads is $\frac{1}{2}$. For *any* infinite sequence of flips, this limit should be $1/2$.

There are many objections to this as a fundamental definition, but we should be aware of interpretations in this direction.

A slightly more complicated scenario involves picking colored balls out of an urn. Suppose, for example, that there are N balls in the urn, r red ones and $b = N - r$ blue ones, and that they are indistinguishable by texture, weight, or size. Then a blindfolded person choosing a single ball from the urn is 'equally likely' to choose any one of the ten. Thus, we would say that the probability is r/N that a red ball will be chosen and b/N that a blue ball will be chosen. For convenience, let's call the cycle of drawing a ball, identifying the color of the ball (with blindfold momentarily off), and replacing the ball a **trial**. We will suppose that one trial has no effect on the next one, so that they are **independent**. Let $r(n)$ be the number of red balls drawn in a sequence of n trials. Then, in parallel with the discussion just above, we would presume that for any infinite sequence of trials

$$\lim_{n\to\infty} \frac{r(n)}{n} = \frac{r}{N}$$

Running this in the opposite direction: if there are N balls in an urn, some red and some blue, if $r(n)$ denotes the number of red balls chosen in n trials, and if (for any infinite sequence of trials)

$$\lim_{n\to\infty} \frac{r(n)}{n} = f$$

then we would deduce that

$$\text{number of red balls in the urn } = f \cdot N$$

That is, we would deduce that the *probability* of drawing a red ball in a *single* trial is f, since the *limiting frequency* of drawing red balls is f.

Further, we might consider an urn with N balls of *various* colors (but otherwise indistinguishable). For any particular color c, if there are n_c balls of that color in the urn, then we would postulate that the *probability* of drawing a ball of color c out of the urn (in a single trial) would be n_c/N. Letting $n(c)$ be the number of balls of color c drawn in a sequence of n trials, we would likewise postulate that the **limiting frequency** $\lim \frac{n(c)}{n}$ has value

$$\lim_{n\to\infty} \frac{n(c)}{n} = \frac{n_c}{N}$$

Contrariwise, if the limiting frequency of drawing a ball of color c is f, then we presume that the number of balls of that color in the urn is $f \cdot N$, and we say that the *probability* of drawing a ball of color c is f.

It bears repeating that the 'frequency' version of probability has serious drawbacks, and is not really the 'industrial strength' version of the idea. But it gives us something to hang our hat on. We'll gradually move away from this viewpoint.

Suppose that some experiment X has possible different outcomes $x_1, \ldots, x_n$. The collection of possible outcomes is the **sample space**. Each episode in which the experiment X is carried out is called a **trial**. Each possible x_i is an **event**. We suppose that each possible outcome x_i has a **probability** $p_i \geq 0$, and

$$p_1 + p_2 + \cdots + p_n = 1$$

A standard notation for this is

$$P(X = x_i) = P(x_i) = p_i$$

which is read as *the probability of x_i is p_i*, or *the probability that $X = x_i$ is p_i*.

A more general idea of **event** (sometimes called **compound event**) is any subset A of the sample space, that is, of the set $\Omega = \{x_1, \ldots, x_n\}$ of all possible atomic events. The **probability of** A is

$$P(A) = \sum_{x_i \in A} P(x_i)$$

where (to repeat) the sum is over the 'points' x_i that lie in A. The event A **occurs** if any one of the $x_i \in A$ occurs. Thus, for $A = \{x_{i_1}, \ldots, x_{i_k}\}$,

$$P(A) = P(x_{i_1} \text{ or } x_{i_2} \text{ or } \ldots \text{ or } x_{i_k})$$

As extreme cases,
$$P(\Omega) = 1$$

and
$$P(\phi) = 0$$

Generally, for an event A, the event **not-**A is the set-theoretic *complement* $A^c = \Omega - A$ of A inside Ω. Then

$$P(\text{not } A) = P(A^c) = P(\Omega - A) = 1 - P(A)$$

For two events A and B, the event $A - \textbf{or} - B$ is simply $A \cup B$, and

$$P(A \text{ or } B) = P(A \cup B)$$

For two events A and B, the event $A - \textbf{and} - B$ is $A \cap B$, and

$$P(A \text{ and } B) = P(A \cap B)$$

Two events A and B (subsets of $\{x_1, \ldots, x_n\}$) are **mutually disjoint** or **mutually exclusive** if $A \cap B = \phi$. If two events are disjoint, then we have

$$P(A \text{ or } B) = P(A \cup B) = P(A) + P(B)$$

We can assign these probabilities p_i *by intuition*, by limiting frequency, or by other means. In fact, they might be measured experimentally, or assigned in some heuristic manner. Let's repeat the limiting-frequency story one more time in this situation. We imagine that the same experiment X is conducted over and over, and that subsequent trials are unaffected by the earlier ones, that is, they are **independent trials**. For n such independent trials let $n(x_i)$ be the number of times that the event x_i occurs. Suppose that for any infinite sequence of trials the limit

$$p_i = \lim_{n \to \infty} \frac{n(x_i)}{n}$$

exists. Then this **limiting frequency** p_i should be the **probability of** the event x_i.

For example, the experiment X might be the drawing of a ball from an urn in which there are 3 red balls, 3 blue balls, and 4 white balls (otherwise indistinguishable). We would intuit that the probability of drawing any particular individual ball is 1/10. (These 'atomic' events are indeed mutually exclusive, because we only draw one ball at a time.) Thus, the 'smallest' events $x_1, x_2, \ldots, x_{10}$ are the possible drawings of each one of the 10 balls. Since they have equal chances of being drawn, the probabilities $p_i = P(x_i)$ are all the same (and add up to 1):

$$p_1 = p_2 = p_3 = \ldots = p_{10}$$

Then the ('compound') event A of 'drawing a red ball' is the subset with three elements consisting of 'draw first red ball,' 'draw second red ball,' and 'draw third red ball.' Thus,

$$P(A) = \frac{1}{10} + \frac{1}{10} + \frac{1}{10} = \frac{3}{10}$$

Let B be the event 'draw a white ball.' Then, since A and B are disjoint events, the probability of drawing *either* a red ball *or* a white ball is the sum:

$$P(A \cup B) = P(A) + P(B) = \frac{3}{10} + \frac{4}{10} = \frac{7}{10}$$

Extending this further, we might have two different experiments, X and Y, with possible outcomes $x_1, \ldots, x_m$ and $y_1, \ldots, y_n$, respectively. Then we say that X and Y are **independent** if for all indices $1 \le i \le m$ and $1 \le j \le n$

$$P(X = x_i \ \& \ Y = y_j) = P(X = x_i) \cdot P(Y = y_j)$$

As an example of a basic computation, we have the following result. The conclusion of this proposition will be used often in subsequent probabilistic discussions.

Proposition. Let X be an experiment with possible different outcomes $x_1, \ldots, x_n$ with respective probabilities $P(x_1) = p_1, \ldots, P(x_n) = p_n$. Let A be a subset of the sample space $\{x_1, \ldots, x_n\}$ with probability $P(A) = p$. Let $k \le N$ be integers with $N > 0$ and $k \ge 0$. The probability is

$$\binom{N}{k} \cdot p^k \, (1-p)^{N-k}$$

that A occurs in exactly k of N trials.

Proof: When $N = 1$, the probability that A occurs is p, and the binomial coefficient $\binom{1}{1}$ is 1. The probability that A does not occur is $1 - p$, and $\binom{1}{0} = 1$ also.

The main part of the argument is an induction on N. Since the different trials are independent, we have

$$P(A \text{ occurs in } k \text{ of } N)$$

$$= P(A \text{ occurs in } k \text{ of the first } N - 1 \text{ }) \cdot P(A \text{ does not occur in the } N\text{th})$$

$$+ P(A \text{ occurs in } k - 1 \text{ of the first } N - 1 \text{ }) \cdot P(A \text{ occurs in the } N\text{th})$$

$$= \binom{N-1}{k} p^k (1-p)^{N-1-k} \times (1-p)$$

$$+ \binom{N-1}{k-1} p^{k-1} (1-p)^{N-1-(k-1)} \times p$$

We want to prove that this is equal to

$$\binom{N}{k} p^k (1-p)^{N-k}$$

We can see already that the powers of p and of $1-p$ will match, so it's just a matter of proving that

$$\binom{N-1}{k} + \binom{N-1}{k-1} = \binom{N}{k}$$

Writing the binomial coefficients out, the left-hand side of the latter alleged equality is

$$\frac{(N-1)!}{k!(N-1-k)!} + \frac{(N-1)!}{(k-1)!(N-1-(k-1))!}$$

$$= \frac{(N-1)! \cdot (N-1-(k-1))}{k!(N-1-k)! \cdot (N-1-(k-1))} + \frac{(N-1)! \cdot k}{k \cdot (k-1)!(N-1-(k-1))!}$$

where we are putting both terms over a common denominator in order to really add them. Since in general $t \cdot (t-1)! = t!$, this is equal to

$$\frac{(N-1)! \cdot [(N-1-(k-1)) + k]}{k! \, (N-k)!} = \frac{(N-1)! \cdot N}{k! \, (N-k)!} = \frac{N!}{k! \, (N-k)!} = \binom{N}{k}$$

This completes the induction and the proof. ♣

Let Ω be a set of possible outcomes, and let A be a ('compound') event with $P(A) > 0$. Let B be another ('compound') event. Then the **conditional probability**

$$P(B \text{ given that } A \text{ occurs})$$

is denoted $P(B|A)$ and is computed as

$$P(B|A) = \frac{P(A \cap B)}{P(A)}$$

In effect, the phrase 'given that A occurs' means that we replace the 'universe' Ω of possible outcomes by the smaller 'universe' A of possibilities, and 'renormalize' all the probabilities accordingly.

The formula $P(B|A) = P(A \cap B)/P(A)$ allows us to compute the conditional probability in terms of the other two probabilities. In 'real-life' situations, it may be that we know $P(B|A)$ directly, for some other reasons. If we also know $P(A)$, then this gives us the formula for

$$P(A \text{and } B) = P(A \cap B)$$

namely

$$P(A \cap B) = P(B|A) \cdot P(A)$$

This will be used in the following example.

We'll do another another important basic computation which explains why **birthday attacks** work. Let

$$\Omega = \{1, 2, \ldots, N\}$$

be the sample space of all possible 'atomic' events. Assign equal probabilities

$$P(i) = 1/N$$

for all $i = 1, \ldots, N$. The experiment X is random choice of an element of Ω (without actually removing it from the set). The question is: *what is the probability that after n trials at least 2 of the outcomes will be the same?*

Proposition. In this situation, the probability that after n trials at least 2 outcomes will be the same is *at least*

$$1 - e^{-\frac{1}{2}(n-1)n/N}$$

Therefore, for

$$n > \sqrt{2 \ln 2} \ \sqrt{N}$$

the probability is at least $1/2$ that two outcomes will be the same.

Proof: It is wisest to compute the probability that *no two* outcomes are the same, and subtract this result from 1 to obtain the desired result. We consider the n trials in order and compute the probability of no two identical outcomes for n trials in terms of the result for $n - 1$ trials.

After one trial, there is only one outcome, so the probability is 1 that no two are the same.

After two trials, there is only $1/N$ chance that the second trial had an outcome equal to the outcome of the first one (whichever that first outcome was), so the probability is $1 - \frac{1}{N}$ that the outcomes of two trials will be all different.

After 3 trials, *given* that the first two outcomes are different, the *conditional probability* is $2/N$ that the third trial would give an outcome equal to *one* of the first two. Thus, given that the first two outcomes are different, the conditional probability that the third will differ from both is $1 - \frac{2}{N}$. Since the probability that the first two were different was $1 - \frac{1}{N}$, the formula above gives

$$P(\text{first 3 different}) = (1 - \frac{1}{N})(1 - \frac{2}{N})$$

After 4 trials, *given* that the first two outcomes are different, the *conditional probability* is $3/N$ that the third trial would give an outcome equal to *one* of the first two. Thus, given that the first two outcomes are different, the conditional probability that the third will differ from all of the first 3 is $1 - \frac{3}{N}$. Using the previous step, and the formula above,

$$P(\text{first 4 different}) = (1 - \frac{1}{N})(1 - \frac{2}{N})(1 - \frac{3}{N})$$

Continuing, we get

$$P(n \text{ trials all different}) = (1 - \frac{1}{N})(1 - \frac{2}{N})(1 - \frac{3}{N})\ldots(1 - \frac{n-1}{N})$$

The logarithm of the probability that they're all different is

$$\ln(1 - \frac{1}{N}) + \ln(1 - \frac{2}{N}) + \cdots + \ln(1 - \frac{n-1}{N})$$

We certainly assume that $n < N$, or the whole thing is silly. Then we invoke the first-order Taylor expansion for the function $\ln(1 - x)$ for $|x| < 1$:

$$\ln(1 - x) = -(x + \frac{x^2}{2} + \frac{x^3}{3} + \frac{x^4}{4} + \cdots)$$

In particular, it is certainly true that for $0 < x < 1$

$$\ln(1 - x) \leq -x$$

Thus,

$$\ln(1 - \frac{1}{N}) + \ln(1 - \frac{2}{N}) + \cdots + \ln(1 - \frac{n-1}{N}) \leq -(\frac{1}{N} + \frac{2}{N} + \cdots + \frac{n-1}{N})$$

We may (or not?) recall the formula

$$1 + 2 + 3 + 4 + \cdots + (k - 1) + k = \frac{1}{2}k(k + 1)$$

If we use this, then we have the **estimate**

$$\ln\left(P(n \text{ trials all different})\right) \leq \frac{-\frac{1}{2}(n - 1)n}{N}$$

Exponentiating (and subtracting from 1) gives the assertion of the proposition, since the exponential function is an increasing function.

As n gets larger and larger, the expression $(n-1)n$ is for 'practical' purposes less and less distinguishable from n^2. Thus, we have an *approximate* formula

$$\ln\left(P(n \text{ trials all different})\right) \leq -\frac{n^2}{2N}$$

The probability that some two will be the same is therefore bigger than or equal $1/2$ when the probability that no two are the same is *less* than $1/2$. Thus, for given N we *solve* to find the smallest n so that

$$-\frac{n^2}{2N} < \ln\frac{1}{2}$$

From this we get the assertion of the proposition.   ♣

Exercises

2.2.01 What is the probability of exactly 3 heads out of 10 flips of a fair coin?

2.2.02 What is the probability of exactly 5 heads out of 10 flips of a fair coin?

2.2.03 What is the probability that there will be *strictly more* heads than tails out of 6 flips of a fair coin?

2.2.04 What is the probability that there will be *strictly more* heads than tails out of 8 flips of a fair coin?

2.2.05 What is the probability that there will be *strictly more* heads than tails out of 9 flips of a fair coin?

2.2.06 If there are 3 red balls and 7 blue balls in an urn, what is the probability that in two trials two red balls will be drawn?

2.2.07 If there are 5 red balls and 6 blue balls in an urn, what is the probability that in two trials two red balls will be drawn?

2.2.08 If there are 3 red balls and 7 blue balls in an urn, what is the probability that in 10 trials at least 4 red balls will be drawn?

2.2.09 Prove that

$$1 + 2 + 3 + 4 + \cdots + (n-1) + n = \frac{1}{2}n(n+1)$$

2.2.10 What is the probability that a roll of two fair dice will give either a '7' or an '8'? What is the probability of a '2'?

2.2.11 What is the probability that there will be at most N heads out of $3N$ flips of a fair coin?

2.2.12 The *Birthday Paradox*: Show that the probability is greater than $1/2$ that, out of a given group of 23 people, at least two will have the same birthday.

2.2.13 (*) In the derivation of the formula for the minimum number of trials necessary to have probability greater than $1/2$ that at least two outcomes are the same, did we give up anything of significance by using the simple estimate

$$\ln(1 - x) < -x$$

valid for $0 < x < 1$?

2.2.14 (**) Suppose that two real numbers are chosen "at random" between 0 and 1. What is the probability that their sum is greater than 1? What is the probability that their product is greater than $1/2$?

2.3 Statistics of English

What features do English sentences have that random streams of characters do not? How can this be described in purely mechanical terms? Specifically, how can we tell whether an alleged decryption is really a decryption, or is just gibberish?

In some circumstances, when trying to decrypt a message, we are done when what we have looks like English. And directions for further partial decryption are indicated by trying to imagine a sensible message into which known fragments would fit.

In such contexts, there is a strong presumption that the message *will not be gibberish*, so that a correct decryption will be immediately and easily recognizable. Especially in classical pre-computer cryptanalysis, study of the *content* of a 'partial plaintext' was a fundamental device. If the message were pure gibberish anyway, then the contents of a correct decryption would be indistinguishable from the contents of an incorrect decryption, and the process would be both futile and pointless.

Even in the context of a presumably coherent and 'meaningful' plaintext, there is the issue of *automation* of the process of distinguishing a plausible message from an implausible one. This amounts to giving a sufficiently precise description of features that English sentences have that random strings of characters do not. For the moment we will not attempt to describe the *meaning* that English sentences have, but only their *form*. Even that we only address in a very low-level statistical way.

So we will pick out some characteristics of English plaintext for two uses: First, these would be features that we would want to *obscure* in order to frustrate an adversary attempting to break *our* cryptosystem. Second, these would be features to *employ* in attempting to break an adversary's cryptosystem. In this section we will simply delineate some of these features, postponing both exploitation and masking of them to a later section.

The main device we'll use is the heuristic device of **frequency** of letters or words in 'typical samples' of English text. This starts from very crude observations such as that the letter 'e' seems to occur much more often than the letter 'z'. Pursuing this, if we pretend that English texts are sequences of characters selected according to some probabilities, then the '*probability*' f_e of a character being an 'e' should be approximately the ratio

$$\frac{\text{number of 'e's in that body of text}}{\text{total number of characters in large body of text}}$$

Similarly, the '*probability*' f_{the} that a *word* in an English text is 'the' is the ratio

$$\frac{\text{number of 'the's in large body of text}}{\text{total number of words in that body of text}}$$

Thus, to pretend to 'compute' the probability that a character will be 'e', we count the number of 'e's in a large body of text and divide by the total number of characters. To 'compute' the probability that a word will be 'the', we count the number of 'the's in a large body of text and divide by the total number of words.

While this idea is *compatible* with the notion of **limiting frequency** in probability (introduced earlier), it is really just a heuristic, since the 'selection' of characters and words in English is not a 'random' process. Nevertheless, especially in pre-computer cryptanalysis this heuristic proved very useful. Specifically, it *does* become clear that some letters occur much more often than others, as do certain combinations of letters and short words. Thus, even from the viewpoint of this very simple probabilistic heuristic, English is very distinguishable from a 'random' sequence of letters. This fact is essential in ciphertext-only attacks on classical cryptosystems.

Some of the distinguishing features of English are as follows.

First are **small words**. In English, there are few very short words. Thus, if word boundaries are detectable in an encrypted text, quite sharp inferences can be made. The only single-letter words are *a* and *I*, out of 26 possibilities. Not counting abbreviations, in a 500-kilobyte sample of filtered email, only 35 two-letter words occur, out of $26 \times 26 = 676$ possibilities. And, in that sample, only 196 3-letter words appear, out of $26 \times 26 \times 26 = 17,576$ possibilities for combination of 3 letters.

Next are **common words**. In the 500-kilobyte sample used, more than 5000 distinct words appear. The 9 most common words already account for 21% of all words, the 20 most common account for 30%, the 104 most common give 50%, the most common 247 give 60%. A listing of common words and their frequency (as percentage) is given at the end of this section.

Blanks: In ordinary English, counting characters 'A' through 'Z' *and blanks* (but ignoring uppercase and lowercase) shows that blanks are by far the most common characters: about 17–18% of characters are blanks, while the next most numerous characters such as 'e', 't', 'o', 'a', and 'i' each occur less than 9% of the time. Thus, if blanks are treated as characters and encrypted, their high frequency may give away information. On the other hand, if they are *not* encrypted, then *other* information is given away more directly: a cryptanalyst can make use of knowledge about frequencies of small words and statistics about letter frequencies at word boundaries. For these reasons, in 'classical' cryptosystems the blanks often are removed from messages.

Character frequency. Counting characters 'A' through 'Z' but ignoring uppercase/lowercase distinctions in a megabyte of old email (after removing the headers), we find approximate frequencies (as percentages)

e	11.67	t	9.53	o	8.22	i	7.81	a	7.73	n	6.71	s	6.55
r	5.97	h	4.52	l	4.3	d	3.24	u	3.21	c	3.06	m	2.8
p	2.34	y	2.22	f	2.14	g	2.00	w	1.69	b	1.58	v	1.03
k	0.79	x	0.30	j	0.23	q	0.12	z	0.09				

That is, 11.67% of all characters are 'e', 9.53% of all characters are 't', and so on, down to 0.09% of all characters being 'z'. In particular, the letter 'e' occurs more than 100 times as often as does 'z', and the other letters occur with frequencies in between these. Thus, there is a quite marked *statistical bias*, meaning that the 26 characters do not occur with equal frequency. Far from it.

Presenting this sort of information can be misleading, since even 500,000 characters of filtered email is not a very random sample of English. And, more important, one would need to know something about the likelihood of deviation from these frequencies. Such deviations would be very likely in small samples. And some people have in fact gone to the trouble of writing novels without using the specific letter 'e'.

And, without having done considerable testing, it is not at all clear how well the plausibility that a stream of characters is English is established by knowing that the frequencies of individual letters do or do not resemble these numbers. And, on the other hand, it is not clear at all that a stream of characters whose frequencies are *different* than these *can't* be English. A more serious and legitimate statistical study would take into account **sample size** and other variables.

Digrams are *adjacent pairs* of characters. The $26 \times 26 = 676$ different digrams which do or do not occur in a character stream tell much more about that stream of characters than do the single-character frequencies. Indeed, while every letter of the alphabet really does occur in many English words, the same is not true for digrams. We can also discuss digrams that include *blanks*, digrams that can occur at word boundaries, etc.

In the same sample of 500 kilobytes of email (with headers removed), *with spaces left in*, only 611 of the possible 676 digrams occur at all. (If blanks are removed, then 659 of the possible 676 digrams occur.) The top 44 digrams already give more than 50% of the total, the top 102 give 75%, the top 175 give 90%, and the top 279 give 98%. With blanks eliminated before counting, the frequencies are spread out a bit: the top 54 give 50%, the top 126 give 75%, the top 222 give 90%, and the top 359 give 98%. Tables of the most common digrams are given at the end of this section.

Trigrams are *adjacent triples* of characters. Out of $26 \times 26 \times 26 = 17,576$ possible trigrams, relatively few occur often. From the same megabyte of filtered email, looking only at the trigrams that occur *within English words*, the top 241 already give 50% of all trigrams occurring. This is quite extreme: fewer than 1/70 of all trigrams account for 50% of all occurrences! The top 652 give 75%, the top 1271 give 90%, and the top 2520 account for 98% of all trigrams that occur. If blanks are removed, then the frequencies are spread out, as with digrams: the top 430 give 50%, the top 1162 give 75%, the top 2314 give 90%, and the top 4408 give

98%. Tables of the most common trigrams are given at the end of this section.

There are several points here. First, even just looking at frequencies of occurrence of single characters, a stream of English text is not at all random: some letters persistently occur much more often than others. Further, some *adjacent pairs of characters* (digrams) occur much more often than others. Similarly for *adjacent triples of characters* (trigrams). This low-level statistical bias can be put to use in cryptanalysis, on one hand, and must be masked in order to have a secure cryptosystem, on the other hand.

As a simple special statistical feature, *blanks* occur about twice as frequently as any other character. Since messages are still fairly readable even after blanks have been removed, on many occasions blanks *are* removed before encryption. This removes some information which otherwise could be used by the cryptanalyst. For example, the statistics on digrams and trigrams show that the statistical bias is considerably sharper when word boundaries are clear, by contrast to the situation when word boundaries have been obliterated.

There still remains the issue of making systematic (and efficient) use of this information. Some simple illustrations will be given later.

The 100 most common words in the sample, with percentages of the total:

the 4.65	*to* 3.02	*of* 2.61	*i* 2.2	*a* 1.95
and 1.82	*is* 1.68	*that* 1.62	*in* 1.57	*it* 1.22
for 1.17	*you* 1.06	*be* 0.99	*not* 0.84	*on* 0.76
have 0.71	*this* 0.69	*as* 0.57	*at* 0.56	*would* 0.55
are 0.55	*but* 0.54	*if* 0.53	*my* 0.53	*with* 0.5
your 0.48	*so* 0.48	*or* 0.46	*some* 0.43	*will* 0.41
do 0.39	*about* 0.39	*me* 0.38	*from* 0.35	*by* 0.33
no 0.33	*more* 0.33	*what* 0.32	*an* 0.32	*there* 0.32
one 0.32	*all* 0.32	*was* 0.30	*we* 0.30	*just* 0.27
which 0.27	*can* 0.26	*very* 0.25	*series* 0.25	*am* 0.24
things 0.24	*people* 0.24	*get* 0.23	*hi* 0.23	*time* 0.22
think 0.22	*course* 0.22	*etc* 0.22	*also* 0.21	*any* 0.21
other 0.20	*than* 0.2	*know* 0.19	*could* 0.19	*they* 0.19
too 0.19	*only* 0.18	*up* 0.18	*good* 0.18	*out* 0.18
has 0.17	*such* 0.17	*had* 0.16	*should* 0.16	*now* 0.16
dont 0.16	*like* 0.15	*its* 0.15	*want* 0.15	*well* 0.15
here 0.14	*might* 0.14	*who* 0.14	*may* 0.14	*then* 0.14
make 0.14	*thanks* 0.14	*much* 0.13	*thing* 0.13	*did* 0.13
how 0.12	*really* 0.12	*he* 0.12	*students* 0.12	*maybe* 0.12
yours 0.12	*see* 0.12	*been* 0.12	*were* 0.12	*rather* 0.11
when 0.11	*paper* 0.11	*even* 0.11	*our* 0.11	*still* 0.11
case 0.11	*since* 0.11	*while* 0.11	*use* 0.1	*ill* 0.10
email 0.10	*stuff* 0.10	*seems* 0.10	*them* 0.10	*book* 0.10
work 0.10	*please* 0.10	*online* 0.10	*into* 0.10	*does* 0.10
two 0.10	*university* 0.09	*little* 0.09	*page* 0.09	*number* 0.09

Note that some words that have reached this 'high-frequency' list, such as 'university', 'number', and 'students', would very likely have a different frequency if the text sample were not taken from the correspondence of a university professor. This bias occurs *after* the more obvious technical words and such things are filtered out. On one hand, we might want to have statistics that are more universal than this. On the other hand, any particular information about an adversary is potentially useful.

The top 77 digrams occurring *within words* in the sample, with percentages:

th 3.18	*in* 2.59	*he* 2.17	*er* 1.95	*re* 1.85	*on* 1.63	*an* 1.59
at 1.54	*ou* 1.43	*or* 1.26	*es* 1.26	*ha* 1.24	*to* 1.22	*te* 1.21
is 1.18	*ti* 1.17	*it* 1.16	*en* 1.13	*nt* 1.09	*ng* 1.08	*al* 1.07
se 1.05	*st* 1.01	*nd* 0.98	*le* 0.91	*ar* 0.90	*me* 0.90	*hi* 0.86
ve 0.85	*of* 0.84	*ed* 0.78	*co* 0.74	*as* 0.73	*ll* 0.72	*ne* 0.70
om 0.70	*ri* 0.68	*ic* 0.67	*ro* 0.67	*ea* 0.66	*et* 0.64	*ur* 0.64
io 0.64	*ra* 0.62	*li* 0.62	*no* 0.62	*so* 0.62	*be* 0.61	*de* 0.59
ma 0.59	*si* 0.58	*ly* 0.54	*ut* 0.53	*ot* 0.53	*pr* 0.53	*fo* 0.53
yo 0.52	*il* 0.50	*ca* 0.50	*pe* 0.50	*ch* 0.49	*ho* 0.49	*ul* 0.47
ce 0.47	*ta* 0.45	*di* 0.45	*rs* 0.45	*el* 0.44	*ge* 0.44	*us* 0.44
ec 0.42	*ss* 0.42	*ac* 0.41	*ct* 0.41	*em* 0.41	*wh* 0.40	*oo* 0.40

The most 77 frequent digrams *including blanks*:

*e_* 3.15	*_t* 2.55	*th* 2.11	*s_* 1.97	*t_* 1.93	*_a* 1.81	*in* 1.72
_i 1.69	*he* 1.44	*er* 1.29	*d_* 1.24	*re* 1.23	*_s* 1.18	*n_* 1.15
on 1.08	*an* 1.05	*_o* 1.04	*y_* 1.03	*at* 1.03	*r_* 0.99	*ou* 0.95
*o_* 0.92	*_w* 0.92	*or* 0.84	*es* 0.83	*ha* 0.83	*to* 0.81	*te* 0.80
is 0.79	*ti* 0.78	*it* 0.77	*en* 0.75	*nt* 0.72	*ng* 0.72	*_c* 0.71
al 0.71	*se* 0.70	*_m* 0.69	*_b* 0.67	*st* 0.67	*_p* 0.65	*nd* 0.65
_f 0.62	*le* 0.60	*ar* 0.60	*me* 0.60	*f_* 0.59	*l_* 0.59	*g_* 0.58
hi 0.57	*ve* 0.57	*_h* 0.56	*of* 0.55	*ed* 0.52	*_d* 0.51	*co* 0.49
as 0.48	*ll* 0.48	*ne* 0.47	*om* 0.46	*i_* 0.45	*ri* 0.45	*a_* 0.45
_n 0.44	*ic* 0.44	*ro* 0.44	*ea* 0.44	*et* 0.42	*ur* 0.42	*io* 0.42
_r 0.42	*_e* 0.41	*ra* 0.41	*li* 0.41	*no* 0.41	*so* 0.41	*be* 0.41

The top 77 digrams occurring *after blanks are removed*:

th 2.63	*in* 2.08	*he* 1.75	*er* 1.67	*re* 1.52	*on* 1.33	*es* 1.32
an 1.29	*at* 1.28	*ti* 1.26	*nt* 1.16	*ou* 1.16	*to* 1.13	*st* 1.12
ha 1.05	*or* 1.05	*et* 1.03	*en* 1.01	*te* 1.01	*is* 0.98	*it* 0.97
ea 0.93	*se* 0.90	*al* 0.89	*ng* 0.89	*nd* 0.81	*ed* 0.76	*hi* 0.75
le 0.75	*ar* 0.74	*si* 0.73	*me* 0.73	*so* 0.71	*of* 0.70	*ve* 0.68
ri 0.64	*as* 0.64	*om* 0.64	*ra* 0.61	*no* 0.61	*ne* 0.60	*co* 0.60
ro 0.59	*ll* 0.59	*ta* 0.58	*ic* 0.57	*ot* 0.57	*tt* 0.57	*li* 0.57
yo 0.52	*ur* 0.51	*ec* 0.51	*io* 0.51	*de* 0.51	*di* 0.51	*ma* 0.51
ei 0.49	*be* 0.49	*sa* 0.47	*ss* 0.47	*el* 0.46	*em* 0.46	*rs* 0.45
fo 0.44	*ut* 0.44	*ly* 0.44	*rt* 0.43	*ca* 0.42	*pr* 0.42	*na* 0.42
ts 0.41	*ho* 0.41	*il* 0.41	*pe* 0.40	*ch* 0.40	*ul* 0.38	*ee* 0.38

The 77 most common trigrams *within English words*, with percentages:

the 2.44	*ing* 1.26	*and* 0.82	*hat* 0.78	*tha* 0.77	*ion* 0.75	*you* 0.67
ent 0.66	*for* 0.63	*tio* 0.63	*thi* 0.60	*her* 0.51	*ati* 0.47	*our* 0.47
ere 0.45	*all* 0.43	*ter* 0.43	*ver* 0.40	*not* 0.40	*hin* 0.40	*ome* 0.36
oul 0.36	*uld* 0.36	*int* 0.34	*rea* 0.34	*pro* 0.34	*res* 0.33	*ate* 0.33
hav 0.30	*ave* 0.30	*ill* 0.30	*his* 0.30	*com* 0.30	*ons* 0.30	*are* 0.28
ple 0.28	*ers* 0.28	*con* 0.27	*ess* 0.27	*out* 0.27	*one* 0.26	*ith* 0.25
som 0.25	*ive* 0.25	*tin* 0.25	*nce* 0.24	*ble* 0.24	*ted* 0.24	*han* 0.23
ine 0.23	*per* 0.23	*ect* 0.23	*nte* 0.23	*wit* 0.22	*men* 0.22	*but* 0.22
wou 0.21	*ica* 0.21	*eve* 0.21	*cal* 0.21	*pre* 0.21	*cou* 0.21	*lin* 0.21
est 0.20	*eri* 0.20	*mor* 0.20	*ser* 0.20	*ore* 0.19	*any* 0.19	*abl* 0.19
tic 0.19	*urs* 0.19	*ant* 0.19	*sti* 0.18	*ear* 0.18	*hou* 0.18	*ies* 0.18

The 77 most common trigrams *including blanks*:

_th 1.67	*the* 1.22	*he_* 0.80	*ing* 0.63	*_to* 0.62	*to_* 0.55	*ng_* 0.52
_an 0.50	*_in* 0.49	*_of* 0.49	*at_* 0.45	*is_* 0.44	*of_* 0.44	*e_t* 0.43
*on_* 0.43	*er_* 0.42	*nd_* 0.42	*and* 0.41	*ed_* 0.40	*es_* 0.39	*hat* 0.39
tha 0.38	*ion* 0.37	*re_* 0.37	*_i_* 0.36	*_co* 0.35	*or_* 0.33	*t_t* 0.33
you 0.33	*e_a* 0.33	*ent* 0.33	*in_* 0.33	*_is* 0.32	*e_i* 0.32	*for* 0.31
_yo 0.31	*tio* 0.31	*_a_* 0.31	*thi* 0.30	*_be* 0.30	*ly_* 0.30	*s_a* 0.29
_re 0.29	*_no* 0.28	*nt_* 0.27	*t_i* 0.27	*_fo* 0.27	*_it* 0.27	*s_t* 0.26
_ha 0.26	*e_s* 0.26	*le_* 0.26	*_on* 0.25	*it_* 0.25	*her* 0.25	*ll_* 0.25
*me_* 0.25	*_so* 0.24	*n_t* 0.24	*_wh* 0.23	*ati* 0.23	*our* 0.23	*ve_* 0.23
_se 0.22	*s_i* 0.22	*ut_* 0.22	*ere* 0.22	*all* 0.21	*al_* 0.21	*ter* 0.21
*st_* 0.21	*d_t* 0.21	*_pr* 0.21	*se_* 0.20	*ver* 0.20	*not* 0.20	*_wi* 0.20

The 77 most common trigrams *after blanks have been removed*:

the 1.49	*ing* 0.77	*tha* 0.52	*and* 0.50	*hat* 0.47	*ion* 0.45	*ent* 0.43
you 0.41	*thi* 0.38	*for* 0.38	*ati* 0.38	*tio* 0.38	*her* 0.35	*ere* 0.35
eth 0.34	*int* 0.32	*our* 0.28	*tth* 0.27	*all* 0.27	*rea* 0.26	*ter* 0.26
nth 0.26	*ome* 0.25	*hin* 0.25	*ver* 0.25	*not* 0.24	*res* 0.23	*est* 0.22
oul 0.22	*ont* 0.22	*ate* 0.21	*uld* 0.21	*ers* 0.21	*tin* 0.21	*oth* 0.20
pro 0.20	*sth* 0.20	*ons* 0.20	*his* 0.19	*ith* 0.19	*ave* 0.19	*eri* 0.19
sin 0.19	*ess* 0.18	*are* 0.18	*hav* 0.18	*ist* 0.18	*ill* 0.18	*out* 0.18
com 0.18	*rth* 0.18	*ese* 0.17	*ore* 0.17	*ple* 0.17	*con* 0.17	*one* 0.16
att 0.16	*iti* 0.16	*ert* 0.16	*ica* 0.16	*ein* 0.16	*eto* 0.16	*som* 0.16
han 0.15	*oft* 0.15	*nte* 0.15	*ine* 0.15	*sto* 0.15	*ted* 0.15	*ive* 0.15
ear 0.15	*fth* 0.15	*nce* 0.15	*ret* 0.14	*ngt* 0.14	*ble* 0.14	*lin* 0.14

Exercises

2.3.01 Suppose that the probability that a given letter in English is 'e' really is 0.1167. What is the probability that in a 'random text' of 10 characters there will be *no* 'e'? In 100 characters?

2.3.02 Suppose that the probability that a given English word is 'the' really is 0.0465. What is the probability that in a "random text" of 10 words there will be *no* 'the'? In 100 words?

2.3.03 Suppose that there is a language which uses just two characters, '1' and '0'. Suppose that the '1' occurs with probability 2/3 and the '0' occurs with probability 1/3 in that language, in general. What is the probability that a stream of N 1's and 0's in that language could have $N/2$ or fewer 1's? Address this for $N = 3, 6, 9, 12$.

2.4 Attack on the Affine Cipher

With some information about *frequencies* of characters, words, digrams, etc., it is possible to give a more graceful ciphertext-only attack on an affine cipher than the brute-force attack of trying all the possible keys.

For example, suppose we are given the ciphertext

$$\text{JFFGJFDMGFSJHYQHTAGHQGAFDCCFP}$$

Our goal is to find the key (a, b) so that (with notation as earlier in discussion of the affine cipher)

$$E_{a,b}(\text{plaintext}) = JFFGJFDMGFSJHYQHTAGHQGAFDCCFP$$

Since the spaces have been removed, we cannot make direct use of small-word frequencies. Nevertheless, looking at single-letter percentages, we have

F	20.68
G	13.79
H	10.34
J	10.34
Q	6.89
A	6.89
C	6.89
D	6.89
P	3.44
S	3.44
T	3.44
Y	3.44
M	3.44

This would cause us to think that the encryption of the letter 'e' is 'F', since 'e' is by far the most common letter in English and 'F' is by far the most common letter in the ciphertext. Then, just hoping for luck, the second-most common letter in English is 't', and (by a good margin) the second-most common letter in this ciphertext is 'G', so we might guess that 't' is encrypted as 'G'. To assess the quality of this guess, we must determine the key (a, b) so that

$$E_{a,b}(e) = F \qquad E_{a,b}(t) = G$$

Numerically, since 'e' is encoded as 4, 'F' is 5, 't' is 19, and 'G' is 6. Thus, in terms of the numbers,

$$(a \cdot 4 + b) \% 26 = 5$$
$$(a \cdot 19 + b) \% 26 = 6$$

As mentioned in the discussion of the *chosen-plaintext* on the affine cipher, this gives (by subtracting)

$$a \cdot (19 - 4) \% 26 = 6 - 5 = 1$$

That is,

$$15 \cdot a \% 26 = 1$$

We find (by brute force or otherwise) that the multiplicative inverse of 15 mod 26 is 7, so $a = 7$ is our guess. Then going back to the equation

$$(a \cdot 4 + b) \% 26 = 5$$

with the tentative $a = 7$ we get

$$(7 \cdot 4 + b) \% 26 = 5$$

This gives $2 + b = 5$, so (we guess) $b = 3$.

That is, based on *frequencies*, we guess that the key is $(7, 3)$. If so, by our general formula for the inverse

$$E_{a,b}^{-1} = E_{a^{-1}, -a^{-1}b}$$

where the a^{-1} denotes inverse modulo 26. We have already noted that $15 \cdot 7 \% 26 = 1$, so 15 is the multiplicative inverse of 7. We compute

$$-7^{-1} \cdot 3 \% 26 = -15 \cdot 3 \% 26$$
$$= -45 \% 26 = 7$$

Thus, the inverse of $E_{7,3}$ is $E_{15,7}$. Applying $E_{15,7}$ to the ciphertext should *decrypt* and recover the plaintext:

$$E_{15,7}(JFFGJFDMGFSJHYQHTAGHQGAFDCCFP)$$

$$= meetmeaftermidnightinthealley$$

which is readily broken up into *meet me after midnight in the alley*. We were lucky that our first guess was correct.

Note that in this ciphertext-only attack we used frequency analysis to bring us closer to what amounted to a known-plaintext attack. If we had been less lucky, we would have had to guess again, and go through the determination of the alleged key, then decrypt to see if what came out looked reasonable.

Exercises

2.4.01 Decrypt the affine cipher with ciphertext 'VCLLCP BKLC LJKX XCHCP'

2.4.02 Decrypt the affine cipher with ciphertext 'LBBKL BJMKB OLTQW TXIKT WKIBJ AABN'

2.4.03 (*) Decrypt 'DBUHU SPANO SMPUS STMIU SBAKN OSMPU SS'

3

Permutations

Now we briefly look at some other classical ciphers inadequate for serious use, but which illustrate ideas used as components in modern ciphers. These are **substitution** and **transposition** ciphers. Substitution ciphers are also known as **cryptograms**, and transposition ciphers are also called **anagrams**.

The mechanism underlying these two types of cipher is that of moving things around, either moving letters within an alphabet in cryptograms, or moving the location of letters within a message in anagrams. In a mathematical context, moving elements of a set around is a **permutation** of that set. Permutations can be analyzed and have an intelligible internal structure. We look at some examples of card shuffling and other naturally occurring mixing. A few surprises emerge.

A challenging pastime only indirectly related to cryptography is the construction of **palindromes**, phrases which read the same forward and backward. A simple one is 'A man, a plan, a canal, Panama'. There is Napoleon's 'Able was I ere I saw Elba'. A much longer one due to Peter Hilton at Bletchley Park, 1943, is 'Doc, note, I dissent, a fast never prevents a fatness. I diet on cod'.

3.1 Cryptograms: Substitutions

Cryptograms, or **monoalphabetic substitution ciphers**, are the sort of ciphers that are presented in the daily newspapers as puzzles. One would infer from the fact that millions of people solve the puzzle every day that cryptograms are not secure. This is correct, and gives another illustration of the fact that a huge keyspace by itself gives no assurance of security. Shift ciphers and affine ciphers are just very special (by being more structured) examples of monoalphabetic substitution ciphers. So when we see that cryptograms are breakable, this certainly means that the special cases are breakable as well.

Again, the name **monoalphabetic substitution cipher** refers to the fact that each letter of the alphabet is encrypted the same way every time it occurs in the plaintext ('monoalphabetic cipher'), and that the encrypted form of a character of the plaintext occurs in the same location as the the plaintext character ('substitution cipher').

In case you are unfamiliar with cryptograms, here's what they are. The *key* is an arbitrary mixing-up of the alphabet. Of course, we need a method to describe and remember such mixing-arounds. Basically, we can give a **look-up table** for encryption:

$$a \quad b \quad c \quad d \quad e \quad f \quad g \quad h \quad \ldots \quad x \quad y \quad z$$
$$C \quad E \quad A \quad T \quad X \quad H \quad B \quad R \quad \ldots \quad D \quad S \quad U$$

The top row gives characters of plaintext, and the character underneath each character is what it encrypts to. For example, in this case a encrypts to C, b encrypts to E, c to A, etc. To remember the key, agree upon a secret phrase in English, such as

$$ASTITCHINTIMESAVESNINE$$

Then remove the duplicate letters (as well as spaces and punctuation)

$$ASTICHNMEV$$

and then stick the unused letters of the alphabet on the end:

$$ASTICHNMEVBDFGJKLOPQRUWXYZ$$

Then this can be used to make the table for encoding:

$$a \quad b \quad c \quad d \quad e \quad f \quad g \quad h \quad i \quad j \quad k \quad l \quad m \quad n \quad o \quad p \quad q \quad r \quad s \quad t \quad u \quad v \quad w \quad x \quad y \quad z$$
$$A \quad S \quad T \quad I \quad C \quad H \quad N \quad M \quad E \quad V \quad B \quad D \quad F \quad G \quad J \quad K \quad L \quad O \quad P \quad Q \quad R \quad U \quad W \quad X \quad Y \quad Z$$

Of course, for fast decryption it would be sensible to make a separate table, since it's not convenient to search the lower row.

As an example, with this key we'd encrypt the plaintext

'The history of the National Security Agency is shrouded in secrecy.
Even its budget is classified.'

to ciphertext

'QMC MEPQJOY JH QMC GAQEJGAD PCTROEQY ANCGTY EP
PMOJRICI EG PCTOCTY CUCG EQP SRINCQ EP TDAPPEHECI'.

The simplest effective attack on a monoalphabetic cipher is use of frequencies
in natural languages: single letters, bigrams/trigrams, small words, end/beginning
of words, etc. We'll only consider English here. We'll use some empirical facts about
single-letter frequencies, as well as knowledge about common English words. Again,
the most common single letters English are e and t, with all others considerably
less frequent.

Thus, to attack a cryptogram, first do an accounting of the most common
letters in the ciphertext. For example, in

QCIV XY KEO JLYYW JBRO XN KEO JKGOOK. TOK SO KX KEO AELGAE
XY KBSO. KEO NBJE CGO MLSDBYT CYR KEO AXKKXY BJ EBTE. XLG
JKCKO NCBG BJ KEO HOJK JKCKO NCBG.

we find, ranked by order of frequency of appearance,

K - 15, O - 13, E - 9, B - 7, J - 7, C - 6, X - 6, Y - 6, G - 5, L - 3, N - 3, A - 2,
S - 2, T - 2, R - 2, with D, H, I, M, Q, V, W occurring much less often.

Thus, we would imagine that 'K' is either 'e' or 't', and perhaps 'O' is the other of
the two. Trying first $K = e$ and $O = t$, we have (in part)

QCIV XY eEt JLYYW JBRt XN eEt JeGtte. Tte St eX eEt AELGAE XY ...

The 'Tte' in the second sentence immediately raises a problem: it seems unlikely
that 'T' can be anything that would make this a word that could begin a sentence.
So try $K = t$ and $O = e$ instead:

QCIV XY tEe JLYYW JBRe XN tEe JtGeet. Tet Se tX tEe AELGAE XY tBSe.
tEe NBJE CGe MLSDBYT CYR tEe AXttXY BJ EBTE. XLG JtCte NCBG BJ
tEe HeJt JtCte NCBG

The 'tEe' suggests $E = h$, the 'tX' suggests $X = o$, and then 'XY' suggests $Y = n$.
This gives

QCIV on the JLnnW JBRe oN the JtGeet. Tet Se to the AhLGAh on tBSe. the
NBJh CGe MLSDBnT CnR the Aotton BJ hBTh. oLG JtCte NCBG BJ the HeJt
JtCte NCBG.

The 'Tet Se to the' suggests 'get me to the', so $T = g$ and $S = m$. And 'JtGeet'
could be 'street', so $J = s$, $G = r$:

QCIV on the sLnnW sBRe oN the street. get me to the AhLrAh on tBme. the
NBsh Cre MLmDBng CnR the Aotton Bs hBgh. oLr stCte NCBr Bs the Hest
stCte NCBr.

The ending on 'MLmDBng', and also 'Bs hBgh', suggest $B = i$. Also the 'oLr'
suggests $L = u$. Rewrite:

QCIV on the sunnW siRe oN the street. get me to the AhurAh on time. the Nish
Cre MumDing CnR the Aotton is high. our stCte NCir is the Hest stCte NCir.

Then 'sunnW siRe oN' suggests $W = y$, $R = d$, and $N = f$:

QCIV on the sunny side of the street. get me to the AhurAh on time. the fish Cre
MumDing Cnd the Aotton is high. our stCte fCir is the Hest stCte fCir.

The 'Cre MumDing' suggests $C = a$, and 'the Hest' suggests H is b. Also, the word 'AhurAh' suggests $A = c$. And 'Aotton' suggests $A = c$. There are not many possible plaintext letters left. The 'MumDing' cannot use $M = b$, because 'b' is already used, etc. After some fooling around, we might decide on $M = j$, $D = p$. We're almost done:

QaIV on the sunny side of the street. get me to the church on time. the fish are jumping and the cotton is high. our state fair is the best state fair.

The point is that with a little boost from looking at single-letter frequencies, and some trial-and-error, cryptograms (monoalphabetic substitution ciphers) can be broken.

Breaking such a cipher is especially easy if *word boundaries* are preserved, since this allows use of knowledge about small words in English. The popular newspaper cryptograms mostly *do* preserve word boundaries, since otherwise breaking such a cipher is considerably harder. Still, especially for messages large enough so that statistical features of English can be used with confidence, breaking monoalphabetic ciphers is quite feasible.

By the way, notice that the keyspace is huge: there are 26 choices for what a encrypts to, 25 remaining choices for what b encrypts to, 24 choices for what c encrypts to, etc. Thus, there are

$$26 \cdot 25 \cdot 24 \cdot \ldots 5 \cdot 4 \cdot 3 \cdot 2 \cdot 1 = 403, 291, 461, 126, 605, 635, 584, 000, 000$$

different keys. If solving a cryptogram really meant considering this many possibilities, no one could do it with mere pencil and paper. So quite clearly thinking in terms of keyspace size can be misleading: too small a keyspace is bad, but a huge keyspace does not by itself assure security!

Exercises

3.1.01 Decrypt the cryptogram 'PBIYGR GRQQRO KORNSRIEBRP CGJIR JKQRI IRCOGX PSKKBER QJ VREOXMQ PSLPQCIQBCG RIYGBPA PRIQRIERP, CGQAJSYA FRRMBIY UJOV LORCFP BI HCFRP CI RIJOHJSP VBKKRORIER.' The breaks are genuine breaks between English words.

3.1.02 Decrypt the cryptogram 'UHNDJST NO P MTFPQNVTFY HTW NSTP RJM THDJSNHI FPMITM PFKAPETQO PHS NSTJIMPKAND OYOQTGO EY UONHI QWJ EYQTO KTM DAPMPDQTM'. The breaks are genuine breaks between English words.

3.1.03 Decrypt the cryptogram 'EPKH RTD RTDKPDH BUQR MPKVDJ RTD PCRIK KE MPIHIRIVD PKKRQ RK CGG DGDHDJRQ IQ HKQR KERDJ CLKVD KJD OUCPRDP'. The breaks are genuine breaks between English words.

3.1.04 Decrypt the cryptogram 'KOS UVXW YFD YMY CFK VUUFQ KOS HNMRA EIFQC LFT KF ZNBG FPSI MK, QOMRO VUUFQJ BNRO QIMKMCD QMKOFNK NJMCD KOS BFJK RFBBFC ROVIVRKSI NCKMU ZNJK CFQ.'

3.2 Anagrams: Transpositions

Simple transposition ciphers or **anagrams** are ciphers in which the individual characters are unchanged but their locations are changed. That is, the ciphertext is created by shuffling around the plaintext suitably. The mixing-around process itself is known as a **transposition** or **anagramming**. Also, a meaningful rearrangement of an already meaningful phrase is called an **anagram** of the original. Of course the fact that many people solve anagrams on a regular basis as puzzles is an indication that these ciphers are insecure.

For example, a cipher which simply *reverses* the characters of a text looks like this: the plaintext

> Education ought not be merely vocational training

is encrypted as

> GNINIART LANOITACOV YLEREM EB TON THGUO NOITACUDE

Decryption is achieved by the same reversal process. Certainly a naive person wouldn't be able to read this. But the *secret* is just a single simple thing, and once it's discovered the cipher is broken. A phrase which is *meaningful* both forward and backward is a **palindrome**.

But if we are given a large jumble of letters, such as

> MOPOOMSEHCWEELNEA (from 'please come home now')

with no information whatseover about what kind of transposition was used to obtain it from English, there may be a great number of ways to rearrange it to make sensible English. This is true *regardless of message length*, in contrast to some other cipher types. The problem (in terms of cryptanalytic attack) of multiple decryptions is already visible with certain small words: 'ant' and 'tan' are anagrams, 'keep' and 'peek', 'live' and 'evil' and 'vile', and so on.

The pastime of rearranging meaningful phrases in a natural language into other completely different but yet meaningful phrases in the same or another natural language is **anagramming**. The fact that this is possible means that very often when a *single* message is encrypted with a transposition cipher that acts on a block at least as large as the whole message, a ciphertext-only attack will give many different possible decryptions. The possibility of this seems to increase, rather than decrease, with the size of the message. Yet if a specific transposition encryption scheme is used more than once, the *multiple anagramming* method below provides a decisive ciphertext-only attack. This is somewhat parallel to the nature of one-time pads, which are vulnerable if used more than once.

A **block transposition cipher** would operate on the characters of a fixed-size *block*, mixing the characters of each block among themselves, and in a manner that is the same for all blocks. Decryption would reverse the mixing. For example, we might have a transposition cipher which operates on blocks of length n, reversing the characters in each such block. When a message is broken into n-characer pieces, any leftover block at the end might be padded with random characters to make it have length n, and then treated as the other blocks. An extreme case of this is when $n = 2$, so that the $2k$th and $(2k + 1)$th characters in the message are interchanged. This last cipher has the effect of turning plaintext

The rain in spain falls mainly in the plain

into ciphertext

HT EARNII NPSIA NAFLL SAMNIYLI NHT ELPIAXN

Of course, this looks like gibberish, but it is easy to decrypt, even by sight, when the mechanism is known.

By the way, how can we conveniently specify a mixing-around of plaintext, in order to change keys when the old transposition is discovered? It's not obvious how to do this nicely, and the awkwardness of this question illustrates again the problem of specifying a family of encryption processes in a simple way depending upon a key. But let's ignore the issue of describing transpositions gracefully in terms of keys, and just see how to implement and *attack* transposition ciphers.

Remark: As remarked above, it turns out that simple transposition ciphers acting on blocks less than half the size of the message are quite breakable when used to encrypt a natural language such as English. Or, equivalently, the same vulnerability exists if the same cipher is used to encrypt more than one message. Nevertheless, transposition is an essential *ingredient* in many secure modern ciphers.

The basic *ciphertext-only attack* on these simple transposition ciphers is an attempt to *maximize common-bigram adjacencies*. This means to figure out re-arrangements so that the number of impossible or unlikely bigrams is minimized, and the number of common bigrams is maximized. This is sometimes called **the contact method**. Note that a transposition cipher does *not* affect the single-letter frequencies, since an 'e' remains an 'e', and so on, so single-letter frequencies give no helpful information about a cipher already known to be a simple transposition cipher. Indeed, if the single-letter frequencies of a ciphertext are essentially identical to those of English, then we should infer that it *is* a simple transposition cipher. This method works fairly well on short anagrams, and is after all a low-level (and therefore automate-able) version of the by-hand approach which picks out common word fragments or small words and then tries to allocate the remainder in some reasonable fashion.

As a very simple example, given a ciphertext *KTICH*, the contact method might proceed as follows. The most common bigram of all is 'th', and 'ck' is another. Thus, instead of 5 separate pieces 'K', 'T', 'I', 'C', 'H' we try looking at a smaller number of pieces, just the 3 pieces 'TH', 'CK', and 'I'. Thus, instead of $5! = 120$ possible rearrangements, we have cut down the search space to $3! = 6$

rearrangements. Further, since we only have one vowel, which must be in the middle, there are only two possibilities for decryption, 'ckith' and 'thick'. The latter is it, and we're done. If, instead, we take a different path and (incorrectly) suppose that the fairly common 'CH' will appear, and simultaneously *exclude* the unlikely 'KT' and 'TK', then either the 'I' or the 'CH' must occur between the 'T' and 'K', but clearly we need a vowel, namely the 'I'. Likewise, the 'CH' can't be adjacent to the 'K', and 'TCH' and 'CHT' are not at all common in English. But by now this excludes all the (likely) possibilities that use 'CH', so we would infer (fairly mechanically) by the *contact method* that 'CH' does not occur.

Remark: Note that this is indeed a probabilistic approach. If the most likely possibilities eventually fail, one must backtrack and try less likely approaches, much as with cryptograms.

As a slightly larger example, consider ciphertext 'SEGHCAN'. There would be $7! = 5040$ possible rearrangements. We would want to mechanically eliminate as many as possible before 'eyeballing' a list to identify recognizable words. Let's try to cut the search space down by *excluding* bigrams which are unlikely to appear: 'hc', 'hs', 'gn', 'ae', 'sg', 'gc', 'cg', 'hg' are all unlikely. Here a 'gs' is also unlikely, due to the paucity of vowels. Further, in this situation, a decryption *ending* in 'a', 'c', 'g', 'h', 'n', or 'e' is unlikely. And we might restrict our attention to decryptions containing either 'sh' or 'ch'. A purely mechanical (if tedious) process shows that there are only 22 (rather than 5040) remaining possibilities. Listing these so that we can look at them, we have *egachns, echngas, gechans, gechnas, geachns, genchas, gachens, gachnes, ganches, chegans, chengas, chagens, changes, chnegas, chngeas, chnages, agechns, achnges, ngechas, ngaches, nchegas, nchages.* The plausible decryption 'changes' is visible.

However, with large anagrams (with block size as large as the text) there will be many plausible decryptions, and this method fails. For example, ciphertext 'RHETDA' (with $6! = 720$ possible rearrangements) can be rearranged to 'thread' and also 'dearth' and 'at herd' and 'red hat' and so on. How can we tell which is correct? We can't. It is true that further context might help, but it might well be that much of the additional information to establish the context is also encrypted in this manner, so the ambiguities won't go away. Thus, in sharp contrast to many other classical ciphers, there is a serious problem of decrypting transposition ciphers where the encryption block size is as large as the message.

But, if the attacker has two or more simple transposition ciphertexts *with the same key*, or (equivalently) if the block size is less than half the size of the message, there is also the **multiple anagram attack**. The principle of this attack is that although a single anagram may allow many different sensible rearrangements, evidently it is extremely unlikely that two anagrams would be rendered sensible *simultaneously* by more than one rearrangement.

For example, suppose the two ciphertexts 'ESROL' and 'VIERD' are received, known to be encrypted with the same key by a simple transposition cipher. 'ESROL' has at least two plausible decryptions, 'loser' and 'sorel', while 'VIERD' has at least two as well, 'drive' and 'diver'. However, the only *simultaneous* rearrangement that turns *both* into something sensible is by moving the 1st letter to the 4th position, 2nd to the 3rd, 3rd to 5th, 4th to 2nd, and 5th to 1st, giving 'loser' and 'drive' as decryptions.

Remark: From the viewpoint of the contact method, cutting down the search space is the goal. There would be $5! = 120$ different rearrangements of 5 things if we didn't manage to be a little clever. But we can decide to *ignore* any rearrangements in which

'ESROL' decrypts so as to include 'sr', 'lr', or 'oe'

'VIERD' decrypts so as to include 'vr', 'vd', or 'dv'

since those are very uncommon bigrams. It is a bit tedious to check, but this leaves only 24 possibilities of simultaneous rearrangement. We could further exclude occurrences of 'eo' in any decryption of 'ESROL', but this is the same condition as prohibiting 'vr' in decrypting 'VIERD', so nothing is gained. But excluding the case that the decryption of 'VIERD' ends in 'v' or 'i' cuts the search space down to 15, and prohibiting the decryption of 'ESROL' to end in 'o' cuts the number of possibilities down to 10. (These numbers can be obtained mechanically, since they require no high-level understanding of English!) The remaining list of 10 possibilities is small enough for a human to look at:

oserl rived

oresl revid

olser rdive

loser drive

esorl vired

eslor vidre

ersol veird

erosl verid

serol iverd

resol evird

The only case in which the two attempted decryptions make sense in English is in the fourth case, giving 'loser' and 'drive'.

Remark: Note that, as with all other classical ciphers, a chosen-plaintext attack can be made to reveal the key immediately. That is, from a modern viewpoint simple transposition ciphers are very far from meeting the basic standards for ciphers. Still, it is also important to understand that plaintext-only attacks can succeed.

Remark: The distinction between what is mechanical and what requires some exercise of human judgment is important in cryptanalysis. Machines are able to perform extremely repetitive tasks with a low error rate, but humans are not. Therefore, maximizing the mechanical pre-sorting or pre-filtering (before a human being is required to look at possible decryptions) is a primary goal. While development of more sophisticated models of language is certainly both interesting and potentially useful, it appears that approaches which succeed with simple models of language are more robust.

Exercises

3.2.01 Decrypt 'IIVLC', which was encrypted with a simple transposition cipher.

3.2.02 Decrypt 'HETEM', which was encrypted with a simple transposition cipher.

3.2.03 Decrypt 'ALBST', which was encrypted with a simple transposition cipher.

3.2.04 Decrypt 'RIGYM', which was encrypted with a simple transposition cipher.

3.2.05 Decrypt 'EPSILTP', which was encrypted with a simple transposition cipher.

3.2.06 Decrypt 'TSAALPEN', which was encrypted with a simple transposition cipher.

3.2.07 Decrypt 'EAGGAR' and 'DAIREP', which were encrypted with the same simple transposition cipher (anagram).

3.2.08 Decrypt 'YLAINLF' and 'ELYICCB', which were encrypted with the same simple transposition cipher (anagram).

3.2.09 Decrypt 'QHEIASUMS' and 'LYGCAHIRO', which were encrypted with the same simple transposition cipher (anagram).

3.3 Permutations

Intuitively, to apply a **permutation** to a bunch of things means just to move them around. More precisely, a **permutation** f **of a set** X is defined to be a *bijective* function f from X to itself.

The crudest question we can ask about permutations of X is *how many are there?* If X has n (distinct) elements $x_1, x_2, \ldots, x_n$ and $f : X \to X$ is a permutation of X, then there are n choices for what $f(x_1)$ can be, $n - 1$ remaining choices for what $f(x_{n-1})$ can be (since it can't be whatever $f(x_n)$ was), and so on. Thus, there are $n!$ permutations of a set with n elements.

Another significant question is *how many times can a given permutation be applied before everything returns to its original position?* This is not only relevant in *card shuffling*, but also in thinking about random-number generation and other things.

To study permutations themselves it doesn't matter much exactly what the elements of the set are, so long as we can tell them apart, so let's just look at the set

$$\{1, 2, 3, \ldots, n - 1, n\}$$

as a good prototype of a set with n (distinct) elements. The standard notation is to write S_n for the **group of permutations** of n things. This S_n is also called the **symmetric group** on n things.

Despite the name 'symmetric group,' these groups are not directly related to 'groups of symmetries' of familiar geometric objects. At the same time, it certainly can happen that a group of symmetries turns out to be a symmetric group. And if we are willing to say that a set with n things in it is a 'geometric object,' then the symmetric group is a group of symmetries. The point is that the terminology

*is intended to suggest something, but the reference is a little delicate, so be careful
what inferences you make from terminology alone.*

A standard way to write permutations f of $\{1, 2, \ldots, n\}$ in order to describe
in detail what f does is to effectively *graph* f but in the form of a list: write

$$f = \begin{pmatrix} 1 & 2 & 3 & \ldots & n \\ f(1) & f(2) & f(3) & \ldots & f(n) \end{pmatrix}$$

Thus, altering the notation just slightly, the permutation

$$g = \begin{pmatrix} 1 & 2 & 3 & \ldots & n \\ i_1 & i_2 & i_3 & \ldots & i_n \end{pmatrix}$$

is the one so that $g(\ell) = i_\ell$.

Always we have the **trivial permutation**

$$e = \begin{pmatrix} 1 & 2 & 3 & \ldots & n \\ 1 & 2 & 3 & \ldots & n \end{pmatrix}$$

which does not 'move' any element of the set. That is, for all i, $e(i) = i$.

Of course, one permutation may be applied after another. If g, h are two
permutations, write

$$g \circ h$$

for the permutation that we get by first applying h, and then applying g. This is the
composition or **product** of the two permutations. It is important to appreciate
that, *in general,*

$$g \circ h \neq h \circ g$$

We'll see examples of this below. But in any case this notation is indeed compatible
with the notation for (and the idea of) *composition of functions*. Thus, for $1 \leq i \leq
n$, *by definition,*

$$(g \circ h)(i) = g(h(i))$$

It is a consequence of the definition of permutations as (bijective) *functions*
from a set to itself that *composition of permutations is associative:* for all permutations g, h, k of a set,

$$(g \circ h) \circ k = g \circ (h \circ k)$$

Indeed, for any element i of the set, the definition of composition of permutations
gives

$$\begin{aligned}
((g \circ h) \circ k)(x) &= (g \circ h)(k(x)) & \text{(definition of } (g \circ h) \circ k, \text{ applied to } x) \\
&= g(h(k(x))) & \text{(definition of } g \circ h, \text{ applied to } k(x)) \\
&= g((h \circ k)(x)) & \text{(definition of } h \circ k, \text{ applied to } x) \\
&= (g \circ (h \circ k))(x) & \text{(definition of } g \circ (h \circ k), \text{ applied to } x)
\end{aligned}$$

(This even works for infinite sets.)

And for any permutation g there is the **inverse** permutation g^{-1} which has the effect of reversing the permutation performed by g. That is,

$$g \circ g^{-1} = g^{-1} \circ g = e$$

Often the little circle indicating composition is suppressed, and we just write

$$g \circ h = gh$$

as if it were ordinary multiplication. The hazard is that we cannot presume that $gh = hg$, so a little care is required.

The graph-list notation for permutations is reasonably effective in computing the *product* of two permutations: to compute, for example,

$$\begin{pmatrix} 1 & 2 & 3 \\ 2 & 3 & 1 \end{pmatrix} \circ \begin{pmatrix} 1 & 2 & 3 \\ 3 & 2 & 1 \end{pmatrix}$$

we see what this composite does to each of $1, 2, 3$. The permutation on the right is applied first. It sends 1 to 3, which is sent to 1 by the second permutation (the one on the left). Similarly, 2 is sent to 2 (by the permutation on the right), which is sent to 3 (by the permutation on the left). Similarly, 3 is sent to 1 (by the permutation on the right), which is sent to 2 (by the permutation on the left). Listing-graphing this information, we have

$$\begin{pmatrix} 1 & 2 & 3 \\ 2 & 3 & 1 \end{pmatrix} \circ \begin{pmatrix} 1 & 2 & 3 \\ 3 & 2 & 1 \end{pmatrix} = \begin{pmatrix} 1 & 2 & 3 \\ 1 & 3 & 2 \end{pmatrix}$$

If we multiply (compose) in the opposite order, we get something different:

$$\begin{pmatrix} 1 & 2 & 3 \\ 3 & 2 & 1 \end{pmatrix} \circ \begin{pmatrix} 1 & 2 & 3 \\ 2 & 3 & 1 \end{pmatrix} = \begin{pmatrix} 1 & 2 & 3 \\ 2 & 1 & 3 \end{pmatrix}$$

This is the simplest example of the **non-commutativity** of the 'multiplication' of permutations, that is, that $gh \neq hg$ in general.

It is certainly true that permutations, especially of big sets, can be very complicated things which are hard to visualize. Still, they can be broken up into simple pieces, as we'll see just below.

First, the simplest permutations are the **cycles** of various lengths. A k-**cycle** is a permutation f so that (for some numbers $i_1, \dots, i_k$)

$$f(i_1) = i_2, \quad f(i_2) = i_3, \quad f(i_3) = i_4, \quad \dots, \quad f(i_{k-1}) = i_k, \quad f(i_k) = i_1$$

and so that $f(j) = j$ for any number j not in the list $i_1, \dots, i_k$. Note that i_k is sent back to i_1. Thus, as the name suggests, f *cycles* the $i_1, \dots, i_k$ among themselves. A more abbreviated notation is used for this: write

$$(i_1 \quad i_2 \quad \dots \quad i_{k-1} \quad i_k)$$

for this k-cycle.

For example, comparing with the more general notation,

$$\begin{pmatrix} 1 & 2 & 3 \\ 2 & 1 & 3 \end{pmatrix} = (1\ 2)$$

$$\begin{pmatrix} 1 & 2 & 3 \\ 3 & 2 & 1 \end{pmatrix} = (1\ 3)$$

$$\begin{pmatrix} 1 & 2 & 3 \\ 2 & 3 & 1 \end{pmatrix} = (1\ 2\ 3)$$

These are, in order, two 2-cycles and a 3-cycle.

Unlike the more general notation, there is some *ambiguity* in the cycle notation: for example,

$$(1\ 2\ 3) = (2\ 3\ 1) = (3\ 1\ 2)$$

Generally, there are k different ways to write a k-cycle in this cycle notation. In a similar vein, it is pretty clear that

- If g is a k-cycle, then $g^k = e$.

This means that applying g to the set k times has the net effect of *moving nothing*. How do cycles interact with each other? Well, generally not very well, but if $g = (i_1 \ldots i_k)$ and $h = (j_1 \ldots j_\ell)$ are a k-cycle and an ℓ-cycle with *disjoint* lists $\{i_1, \ldots, i_k\}$ and $\{j_1, \ldots, j_\ell\}$ then g and h do interact nicely: *they commute with each other*, meaning that

$$gh = hg$$

in this special scenario. Such cycles are called (reasonably enough) **disjoint cycles**. Pursuing this idea, we have

- Any permutation can be written as a product of disjoint cycles, and in essentially just one way.

The 'essentially' means that multiplying the same cycles in a different order is not to be considered different, since after all they *commute*. This is called a **decomposition into disjoint cycles**.

Knowing the decomposition into disjoint cycles of a permutation g is the closest we can come to understanding the nature of g. Happily, this decomposition can be determined in a systematic way (effectively giving an explicit proof of this assertion). For example, consider

$$g = \begin{pmatrix} 1 & 2 & 3 & 4 & 5 & 6 & 7 \\ 4 & 3 & 2 & 5 & 7 & 6 & 1 \end{pmatrix}$$

We just trace the 'path' of elements under repeated applications of g. To start, let's see what happens to 1 under repeated applications of g: first 1 goes to 4, which then goes to 5, which then goes to 7, which then goes to 1. Since we have returned to 1, we have *completed the cycle*: we see that one cycle occurring inside g is

$$(1\ 4\ 5\ 7)$$

Next, look at a number, for example 2, which didn't already occur in this cycle. First 2 goes to 3, which then goes to 2, which already completes another cycle. Thus, there is also the 2-cycle

$$(2 \ 3)$$

inside g. The only number which hasn't yet appeared in either of these cycles is 6, which is not moved by g. Thus, we have obtained the *decomposition into disjoint cycles*:

$$\begin{pmatrix} 1 & 2 & 3 & 4 & 5 & 6 & 7 \\ 4 & 3 & 2 & 5 & 7 & 6 & 1 \end{pmatrix} = (1 \ 4 \ 5 \ 7)(2 \ 3) = (2 \ 3)(1 \ 4 \ 5 \ 7)$$

In the last example, 6 was sent to itself by g: $g(6) = 6$. That is, 6 is a **fixed point** of g. In our cycle-decomposition notation we just didn't refer to 6 at all, implying that 6 didn't move. But we could also explicitly refer to elements that don't move by writing **1-cycles**. In this case the 1-cycle (6) mentions 6, but only says that it doesn't move it. So if we wanted to be explicit about what happened to 6 in that last example, we could write

$$\begin{pmatrix} 1 & 2 & 3 & 4 & 5 & 6 & 7 \\ 4 & 3 & 2 & 5 & 7 & 6 & 1 \end{pmatrix} = (1 \ 4 \ 5 \ 7)(2 \ 3) = (2 \ 3) \ (1 \ 4 \ 5 \ 7) \ (6)$$

The decomposition into disjoint cycles also can be used to tell how many times a permutation must be repeated in order to have no net effect: *the least common multiple of the lengths of the disjoint cycles appearing in its decomposition.*

The **order** of a permutation is the number of times it must be applied in order to have *no net effect*. (Yes, there is possibility of confusion with other uses of the word 'order'.) Thus,

- The order of a k-cycle is k. The order of a product of disjoint cycles is the least common multiple of the lengths.

We might imagine that permutations with larger orders 'mix better' than permutations with smaller orders, since more repetitions are necessary before the mixing effect is 'cancelled'. In this context, it may be amusing to realize that if a card shuffle is done perfectly, then after *some* number of repetitions the cards will be returned to their original order! The number is eight with a 52-card deck, but it's not easy to do perfect shuffles anyway.

As an example, let's examine all the elements of S_7, determining their structure as products of disjoint cycles, counting the number of each kind, and noting their order.

First, let's count the 7-cycles $(i_1 \ldots i_7)$: there are 7 choices for i_1, 6 for i_2, and so on, but there are 7 different ways to *write* each 7-cycle, so there are $7!/7$ distinct 7-cycles altogether.

Next, 6-cycles $(i_1 \ldots i_6)$: there are 7 choices for i_1, 6 for i_2, and so on down to 2 choices for i_6, but there are 6 different ways to *write* each 6-cycle, so there are $7!/6$ distinct 6-cycles altogether.

Next, 5-cycles $(i_1 \ldots i_5)$: there are 7 choices for i_1, 6 for i_2, and so on down to 3 choices for i_5, but there are 5 different ways to *write* each 5-cycle, so there are $7!/2!5$ distinct 5-cycles altogether.

For variety, let's count the number of permutations writeable as a product of disjoint 5-cycle and 2-cycle. We just counted that there are 7!/2!5 distinct 5-cycles. But each choice of 5-cycle leaves just one choice for 2-cycle disjoint from it, so there are again 7!/2!5 distinct products of disjoint 5-cycle and 2-cycle. And we note that the *order* of a product of disjoint 5 and 2-cycle is lcm(2, 5) = 10.

There are 7!/3!4 distinct 4-cycles, by reasoning similar to previous examples.

There are $7!/3!4 \cdot 3!/2$ choices of disjoint 4-cycle and 2-cycle. The order of the product of such is $lcm(2, 4) = 4$.

There are $7!/3!4 \cdot 3!/3$ choices of disjoint 4-cycle and 3-cycle. The order of the product of such is $lcm(3, 4) = 12$.

There are 7!/4!3 distinct 3-cycles, by reasoning similar to previous examples.

There are $7!/4!3 \cdot 4!/2!2$ choices of disjoint 3-cycle and 2-cycle. The order of the product of such is $lcm(2, 3) = 6$.

The number of disjoint 3-cycle, 2-cycle, and 2-cycle is slightly subtler, since *the two 2-cycles are indistinguishable*. Thus, there are

$$\frac{7!}{4!3} \frac{4!}{2!2} \frac{2!}{0!2} \cdot \frac{1}{2!}$$

where the last division by 2! is to take into account the 2! different orderings of the two 2-cycles, which make only a *notational* difference, *not* a difference in the permutation itself. The order of such a permutation is $lcm(2, 2, 3) = 6$.

The number of disjoint pairs of 3-cycle and 3-cycle is similar: the two 3-cycles are not actually ordered although our 'choosing' of them gives the appearance that they are ordered. There are

$$\frac{7!}{4!3} \frac{4!}{1!3} \cdot \frac{1}{2!}$$

such pairs, where the last division by 2! is to take into account the 2! different orderings of the two 3-cycles, which make only a *notational* difference, *not* a difference in the permutation itself. The order of such a permutation is $lcm(3, 3, 1) = 3$.

There are 7!/5!2 distinct 2-cycles, each of order 2.

There are $7!/5!2 \cdot 5!/3!2 \cdot 1/2!$ pairs of disjoint 2-cycles, where the last division by 2! is to take into account the possible orderings of the two 2-cycles, which affect the notation but not the permutation itself.

Finally, there are

$$\frac{7!}{5!2} \frac{5!}{3!2} \frac{3!}{1!2} \cdot \frac{1}{3!}$$

triples of disjoint 2-cycles, where the last division by 3! is to account for the possible orderings of the 3 2-cycles, which affect the notation but not the permutation itself. The order of such a permutation is just $lcm(2, 2, 2) = 2$.

As a by-product of this discussion, we see that the largest order of any permutation of 7 things is 12, which is obtained by taking the product of disjoint 3 and 4-cycles.

As a more extreme example of the counting issues involved, let's count the disjoint products of three 2-cycles and three 5-cycles in S_{24}. As above, this is

$$\frac{24!}{22!2} \frac{22!}{20!2} \frac{20!}{18!2} \frac{1}{3!} \cdot \frac{18!}{13!5} \frac{13!}{8!5} \frac{8!}{3!5} \frac{1}{3!}$$

where both of the divisions by 3! come from discounting the possible orderings of the 2-cycles, and the possible orderings of the 5-cycles. Note that since 2-cycles are distinguishable from 5-cycles, there is no further accounting necessary for the ordering of the 2-cycles *relative to the 5-cycles*, etc.

Exercises

3.3.01 Express the following permutation as a product of disjoint cycles, and determine the order:

$$\begin{pmatrix} 1 & 2 & 3 & 4 & 5 \\ 2 & 5 & 4 & 3 & 1 \end{pmatrix}$$

3.3.02 Express the following permutation as a product of disjoint cycles, and determine the order:

$$\begin{pmatrix} 1 & 2 & 3 & 4 & 5 & 6 & 7 \\ 2 & 5 & 4 & 7 & 1 & 3 & 6 \end{pmatrix}$$

3.3.03 Express the following permutation as a product of disjoint cycles, and determine the order:

$$\begin{pmatrix} 1 & 2 & 3 & 4 & 5 & 6 & 7 \\ 2 & 3 & 4 & 7 & 1 & 5 & 6 \end{pmatrix}$$

3.3.04 Express the following permutation as a product of disjoint cycles, and determine the order:

$$\begin{pmatrix} 1 & 2 & 3 & 4 & 5 & 6 & 7 \\ 6 & 5 & 4 & 2 & 7 & 1 & 3 \end{pmatrix}$$

3.3.05 Compute the product

$$\begin{pmatrix} 1 & 2 & 3 & 4 & 5 & 6 & 7 \\ 7 & 5 & 1 & 6 & 4 & 3 & 2 \end{pmatrix} \times \begin{pmatrix} 1 & 2 & 3 & 4 & 5 & 6 & 7 \\ 2 & 3 & 5 & 7 & 1 & 4 & 6 \end{pmatrix}$$

3.3.06 Compute the product

$$\begin{pmatrix} 1 & 2 & 3 & 4 & 5 & 6 & 7 \\ 2 & 5 & 4 & 7 & 1 & 3 & 6 \end{pmatrix} \times \begin{pmatrix} 1 & 2 & 3 & 4 & 5 & 6 & 7 \\ 2 & 3 & 4 & 7 & 1 & 5 & 6 \end{pmatrix}$$

3.3.07 Compute the product

$$\begin{pmatrix} 1 & 2 & 3 & 4 & 5 & 6 & 7 \\ 6 & 5 & 1 & 7 & 4 & 3 & 2 \end{pmatrix} \times \begin{pmatrix} 1 & 2 & 3 & 4 & 5 & 6 & 7 \\ 2 & 3 & 4 & 7 & 1 & 5 & 6 \end{pmatrix}$$

3.3.08 How many distinct 3-cycles are there in the symmetric group S_5 of permutations of 5 things?

3.3.09 How many distinct 4-cycles are there in the symmetric group S_5 of permutations of 4 things?

3.3.10 Count the number of elements of S_4 of each possible order, by identifying them as products of disjoint cycles of various orders.

3.3.11 Count the number of elements of S_5 of all possible orders, by identifying them as products of disjoint cycles of various orders.

3.3.12 What is the largest *order* of any element of S_5? Of S_{14}?

3.4 Shuffles

Shuffles by cutting a deck of cards, and riffle shuffles of decks of cards, viewed as permutations of the set of cards in the deck, are amenable to analysis. Some of the conclusions may be surprising. A mixing procedure identical to a riffle shuffle is used in interleaving *convolutional* codes.

The simplest type of **cut** applied to a deck of n cards consists of choosing a random spot to break the deck in two, and then interchanging the two parts. For example, with a deck of just 6 cards, $0, 1, 2, 3, 4, 5$, the deck might be broken into pieces $0, 1$ and $2, 3, 4, 5$. Then the two pieces are put back together as $2, 3, 4, 5, 0, 1$. With a deck of n cards, the cut has the effect

$$0, 1, 2, 3, \ldots, n-2, n-1 \;\rightarrow\; i+1, i+2, \ldots, n-2, n-1, 0, 1, 2, 3, \ldots, i$$

That is, in terms of reduction of integers modulo n, as a function

$$f_i : \mathbf{Z}/n \rightarrow \mathbf{Z}/n$$

this shuffle is
$$f_i(x) = (x + i) \ \% \ n$$

That is, a cut on a deck of n cards simply amounts to adding modulo n. In particular,
$$f_j(f_i(x)) = f_{i+j}(x)$$

That is, the effect of two cuts is identical to that of a single cut. In particular, in that regard cuts are not very thorough mixers, since you can cut a deck all day long and have no more effect than just doing a single cut.

A good **riffle shuffle** of a deck of $2n$ cards consists of breaking the deck into two equal pieces

$$1, 2, 3, \ldots, n \quad n+1, n+2, \ldots, 2n-1, 2n$$

and then interleaving the cards from one half with the cards with the other as

$$n+1, 1, n+2, 2, n+3, 3, \ldots, 2n-1, n-1, 2n, n \text{ (good riffle)}$$

Note that the top and bottom cards do *not* stay in their original positions. There is a *bad* riffle shuffle, which may be useful in various card tricks, in which the top and bottom cards stay in the same position: the interleaving in the bad case is

$$1, n+1, 2, n+2, 3, n+3, 3, \ldots, n-1, 2n-1, n, 2n \text{ (bad riffle)}$$

This bad riffle shuffle is the same thing as a good riffle shuffle on the deck of cards obtained by removing the top and bottom cards from the deck. Also, note that there is really just one riffle shuffle, (or maybe two) unlike the cuts, where there is a parameter.

Proposition. The good riffle shuffle on a deck of $2n$ cards $1, 2, \ldots, 2n-1$ is the function

$$f(x) = (2 \cdot x) \text{ \% } (2n+1)$$

which is multiplication by 2 followed by reduction modulo $2n+1$.

Proof: On one hand, if $1 \le x \le n$, then by its definition the riffle shuffle sends x to the $2x$th spot in the deck, because of the interleaving. On the other hand, if $n < x \le 2n$, write $x = n+i$. Then by definition of the shuffle x is sent to the $(2i-1)$th spot in the deck. We can re-express this as

$$f(n+i) = 2i - 1 = 2(n+i) - (2n+1) = 2(n+i) \text{ \% } 2n+1$$

since $2n+1 < 2(n+i) < 2(2n+1)$. This proves that the riffle shuffle is just multiplication by 2 modulo $2n+1$, as claimed.   ♣

Corollary. Let e be the order of 2 modulo $2n+1$. That is, e is the smallest positive integer such that $2^e = 1 \bmod 2n+1$. The good riffle shuffle on a deck of $2n$ cards first returns all cards to their original position after e shuffles.

Proof: The xth card is put into position $2^t x \bmod 2n+1$ by t applications of the riffle shuffle. The equations

$$2^t x = x \bmod 2n+1$$

for $x = 1, 2, 3, \ldots, 2n$ include as a special case $x = 1$, which is

$$2^t = 1 \bmod 2n+1$$

The smallest positive solution is $t = e$, and then $2^e x = x \bmod 2n+1$ for all x.   ♣

Exercises

3.4.01 Show that when a good riffle shuffle on a deck of 50 cards is executed just 8 times in a row, then all cards return to their original positions.

3.4.02 Show that if a good riffle shuffle on a deck of 52 cards is executed repeatedly, no card returns to its original position until the riffle shuffle has been executed 52 times.

3.4.03 Determine the cycle decomposition of a good riffle shuffle on a deck of 10 cards.

3.4.04 Determine the cycle decomposition of a good riffle shuffle on a deck of 12 cards.

3.4.05 Determine the cycle decomposition of a good riffle shuffle on a deck of 14 cards.

3.4.06 Determine the cycle decomposition of a good riffle shuffle on a deck of 16 cards.

3.4.07 Determine the cycle decomposition of a good riffle shuffle on a deck of 18 cards.

3.4.08 Determine the cycle decomposition of a good riffle shuffle on a deck of 20 cards.

3.4.09 On a deck of 12 cards, alternate a good riffle shuffle with an overhand shuffle that breaks the deck into two equal parts. How many times must this be repeated before the cards return to their original positions?

3.4.10 What is the disjoint cycle decomposition of the riffle shuffle followed by overhand shuffle in the previous example?

3.5 Block Interleavers

These 'interleaver' permutations are used in classical transposition ciphers, as well as in concatenated error-correcting codes. Rather like the riffle shuffles, there is an attractive analysis of these permutations. Fix positive integers m, n. We will define a permutation, called the m-by-n **classic block interleaver**, on $N = m \cdot n$ things. (In fact, this is a *left-to-right, top-to-bottom* interleaver, for reasons that will be apparent shortly.)

The physical description of the m-by-n block interleaver is quite straightforward: write the numbers $0, 1, 2, \ldots, N-1$ *by row*, from left to right, top to bottom into an m-by-n rectangular array:

$$
\begin{array}{ccccc}
0 & 1 & 2 & \ldots & n-1 \\
n & n+1 & n+2 & \ldots & 2n-1 \\
& & \ldots & & \\
mn-n & mn-n+1 & mn-n+2 & \ldots & mn-1
\end{array}
$$

Then read the numbers out by *by columns*, from left to right, top to bottom:

$$0, n, 2n, \ldots, mn - n, 1, n + 1, 2n + 1, \ldots, mn - n + 1, \ldots, mn - 1$$

This has the bad feature that 0 and $mn - 1$ are left in the same positions. This disadvantage is offset by some other positive features and simplicity.

From the physical description of the interleaver, we can get a formula for the effect of the m-by-n block interleaver: given x, let $x = qn + r$ with $0 \leq r < n$. Then

$$qn + r = x \to q + rm$$

Indeed, notice that the row into which x gets put is the integer part of x/n, while the column is $x \% n$. Then reading out of the array reverses the roles of column and row, and replaces n by m.

For example, the 3-by-4 block interleaver is computed by creating the array

$$\begin{array}{cccc} 0 & 1 & 2 & 3 \\ 4 & 5 & 6 & 7 \\ 8 & 9 & 10 & 11 \end{array}$$

which is read out, by columns, to 0, 4, 8, 1, 5, 9, 2, 6, 10, 3, 7, 11. We can compute the cycle decomposition of this:

$$(13954)\ (267108)\ (0)\ (11)$$

By contrast, the 3-by-6 block interleaver is a 16-cycle (ignoring the fixed points 0 and 15 which give 1-cycles)

$$1, 3, 9, 10, 13, 5, 15, 11, 16, 14, 8, 7, 4, 12, 2, 6$$

Proposition.   Ignoring the two obvious fixed points 0 and $mn - 1$, the m-by-n block interleaver acts on the set

$$\{1, 2, 3, \ldots, mn - 2\}$$

by multiplication by m followed by reduction mod $mn-1$, $x \to (mx)\ \%\ (mn-1)$.

Proof: Let $x = qn + r$, with $0 \leq r < n$. Then

$$m \cdot x = m(qn + r) = mn \cdot q + mr = (mn - 1)q + q + mr = q + mr \bmod mn - 1$$

This is the asserted formula.   ♣

Exercises

3.5.01 Find the cycle decomposition of the 2-by-6 block interleaver.

3.5.02 Find the cycle decomposition of the 3-by-5 (left-to-right, top-to-bottom) block interleaver.

3.5.03 Find the cycle decomposition of the 3-by-4 (left-to-right, top-to-bottom) block interleaver.

3.5.04 Find the cycle decomposition of the 3-by-7 (left-to-right, top-to-bottom) block interleaver.

3.5.05 Show that a 2-by-n left-to-right, **bottom-to-top** block interleaver has the same effect as a *good* riffle shuffle. Show that a 2-by-n left-to-right, **top-to-bottom** block interleaver has the same effect as a *bad* riffle shuffle.

4

A Serious Cipher

4.1 The Vigenere Cipher

While the affine cipher is slightly better than the pathetic shift cipher in resisting ciphertext-only attacks, it still has too small a keyspace, so that relatively small pieces of ciphertext are sufficient to break an affine cipher (that is, to find the key), using frequency analysis. Yet the idea of the one-time pad does not quite hit the mark, either, since key distribution is hard.

The **Vigenere cipher** has a relatively large keyspace, and the encryption and decryption use ideas similar to what we've already seen, arranged slightly differently. It is *symmetric*: that is, knowing the encryption key is essentially the same as knowing the decryption key. It is *polyalphabetic*: a given character from the ciphertext occurring in different locations will not *usually* be encrypted the same way.

However, the Vigenere cipher is **periodic**, meaning that if two identical characters occur a distance apart which is a multiple of the key length, then they will be encrypted identically. This *periodicity* property is the exploitable weakness.

For a Vigenere cipher, a *key* is a sequence $k = (k_1, \ldots, k_m)$ of characters, where m is arbitrary. Thus, in principle, there are infinitely many keys. A plaintext $x = (x_1, \ldots, x_N)$ will be broken up into pieces of length m. If the message doesn't happen to have length which is a multiple of m, then random characters are added at the end to pad it out. Again writing x % 26 for the reduction modulo 26 of an integer x, the encryption function E_k is

$$E_k(x_1, \ldots, x_N) = ((x_1 + k_1) \% 26, (x_2 + k_2) \% 26, \ldots, (x_m + k_m) \% 26,$$

$$(x_{m+1} + k_1) \% 26, (x_{m+2} + k_2) \% 26, \ldots, (x_{2m} + k_m) \% 26,$$

$$(x_{2m+1} + k_1) \% 26, (x_{2m+2} + k_2) \% 26, \ldots, (x_{3m} + k_m) \% 26,$$

$$\cdots$$

$$(x_{N-m+1} + k_1) \% 26, (x_{N-m+2} + k_2) \% 26, \ldots, (x_N + k_m) \% 26)$$

That is, the first character of the key is added to the first, $(m + 1)$th, $(2m + 1)$th, $(3m + 1)$th, characters of the plaintext (and reduced mod 26), the second character of the key is added to the second, $m + 2$th, $2m + 2$th, $3m + 2$th, characters of the plaintext (and reduced mod 26), and so on.

Note that if m is very large by comparison with the planned message size we're basically back to the one-time pad.

The decryption function D_k is the same as the encryption function, but with subtraction instead of addition:

$$D_k(x_1, \ldots, x_N) = ((x_1 - k_1) \% 26, (x_2 - k_2) \% 26, \ldots, (x_m - k_m) \% 26,$$

$$(x_{m+1} - k_1) \% 26, (x_{m+2} - k_2) \% 26, \ldots, (x_{2m} - k_m) \% 26,$$

$$(x_{2m+1} - k_1) \% 26, (x_{2m+2} - k_2) \% 26, \ldots, (x_{3m} - k_m) \% 26,$$

$$\cdots$$

$$(x_{N-m+1} - k_1) \% 26, (x_{N-m+2} - k_2) \% 26, \ldots, (x_N - k_m) \% 26)$$

Here it bears repeating that for any integers s, t

$$(s - t) \% 26 = (s + (26 - t)) \% 26$$

(and other similar identities), so that subtraction (and reduction mod 26) is really a special case of addition (and reduction mod 26).

If we relabel the elements of the text stream, we can give a nice formula for the character-wise encryption and decryption: instead of having the indices start at 1, we'll have them start at 0. So the key is $k = (k_0, k_1, \ldots, k_{m-1})$. Then

$$E_k(x_0, x_1, \ldots) = (y_0, y_1, \ldots)$$

where for any index i

$$y_i = (x_i + k_{i \% m}) \% 26$$

Yes, the *index* gets reduced modulo the keylength. Here we see the *periodicity* of the cipher.

For example, with key $k = gopher = (6, 14, 15, 7, 4, 17)$, and with plaintext

> meet me in the alley after midnight, bring money and dont tell

becomes

SSTAQ VOBIO IRRZT FEWZS GTMUT WVOXS XWCNQ FTSNH

RUJCC AXVRZ

(with all non-alphabetic characters removed, and regrouped by blocks of five characters).

Here is the first situation in which a **multiple-round** encryption serves any purpose at all. If a plaintext is encrypted by the Vigenere cipher with a key of length m, and the resulting ciphertext is again encrypted by the Vigenere cipher with a key of length n, the net effect is the same as encryption by the Vigenere cipher with a key of length which is the **least common multiple** of m and n. On one hand, if m and n are relatively prime, then this *lcm* is mn, and this is a much larger keysize. On the other hand, one might have used a longer key to begin with.

Let's verify that a 2-round Vigenere cipher is a 1-round Vigenere with a key whose length is the least common multiple of the key lengths. Indeed, using notation in which the indices start at 0, with two keys

$$k^{(1)} = (k_0^{(1)}, k_1^{(1)}, k_2^{(1)}, \ldots, k_m^{(1)})$$

$$k^{(2)} = (k_0^{(2)}, k_1^{(2)}, k_2^{(2)}, \ldots, k_n^{(2)})$$

of lengths m and n, then by the formula above

$$E_{k^{(2)}} \left(E_{k^{(1)}} (x_0, x_1, x_2, x_3, \ldots) \right) = (y_0, y_1, y_2, \ldots)$$

with (for all indices i)

$$y_i = (x_i + k_{i \% n}^{(2)} + k_{i \% m}^{(1)}) \% 26$$

Let $N = lcm(m, n)$. Define a key $k = (k_0, \ldots, k_{N-1})$ of length N by

$$k_i = (k_{i \% n}^{(2)} + k_{i \% m}^{(1)}) \% 26$$

Then check that single-round E_k gives the same effect as the two-round encryption: that is, we must check that for any non-negative integer index i

$$k_{i \% N} \equiv (k_{i \% n}^{(2)} + k_{i \% m}^{(1)}) \bmod 26$$

What's the issue? It is to verify that

$$(i \% N) \% m = i \% m$$

and

$$(i \% N) \% n = i \% n$$

for all integers i. But we did already verify this if $m|N$ and $n|N$. Ah, well, the *least* common multiple of m and n is the smallest value of N that makes this work.

A *chosen-plaintext* attack is nearly transparent: using plaintext consisting of a string of N 'a's (that is, 0's) gives ciphertext consisting of the key itself repeated as many times as it takes to cover N characters. Since it is not known how long the key is, several attempts might be necessary before the string of 'a's is long enough so that the ciphertext starts repeating itself. But apart from these annoyances, the Vigenere cipher yields easily to a chosen-plaintext attack. For example, with the key 'gopher', a chosen plaintext 'aaaaaaaaaaaaaaaaaaaa' (consisting of 20 'a's) becomes

GOPHERGOPHERGOPHERGO

A *known-plaintext* attack is not much more difficult than the chosen-plaintext attack. If a string $x = (x_1, x_2, \ldots)$ of characters is encrypted with key k as $y = (y_1, y_2, \ldots)$, then, at least if the message length is considerably longer than the key length, we find the key $k = (k_1, \ldots, k_m)$ by

$$k_1 = (y_1 - x_1) \% 26$$

$$k_2 = (y_2 - x_2) \% 26$$

$$\ldots$$

$$k_m = (y_m - x_m) \% 26$$

That is, if we take as new key

$$k' = (-x_1 \% 26, \ldots, -x_N \% 26)$$

then *encryption* of the ciphertext y by k' yields a number of copies of the key as output. As in the chosen-plaintext attack, in principle there remains some ambiguity about the key length.

A *ciphertext-only attack* needs considerable further preparation.

Exercises

4.1.01 Encrypt 'meet me in the alley after midnight' with the Vigenere cipher with key 'gandolf'.

4.1.02 Encrypt 'meet me in the alley after midnight' with the Vigenere cipher with key 'pandora'.

4.1.03 Encrypt 'meet me in the alley after midnight' with the Vigenere cipher with key 'platitude'.

4.1.04 Encrypt 'meet me in the alley after midnight' with the Vigenere cipher with key 'horrific'.

4.1.05 Observe that for m and n relatively prime and both > 2 the number of length mn keys is "lots" bigger than the number of length m keys times the number of length n keys.

4.1.06 Why is there no point to multiple-round Vigenere encryption all with keys of the same length?

4.1.07 Why is it better to Vigenere encrypt with a 'random' key of length mn than to two-round Vigenere encrypt with two keys of lengths m and n (supposing m and n relatively prime)?

4.1.08 What is the longest effective key length achievable with a 3-round Vigenere cipher with each individual key length ≤ 12?

4.1.09 The ciphertext 'OCXJIW, JCBR JC XDQCO KFBKGDFQ GK REC XJICV, ZBDLPB WLS DM EMJC CPLK TMOI, XLA BLLQ RBJI YKWLLB' was obtained by using a Vigenere cipher with a key of length 2. Decrypt it by brute force, treating it as two shift ciphers taken every-other-character.

4.2 LCMs and GCDs

It is *not* always the case that we can divide one integer by another and obtain an *integer* quotient. For example, 7 divided by 3 gives a quotient of $2\frac{1}{3}$, while by contrast 12 divided by 3 is 4. This motivates a simple definition: for two integers d, n, the integer d **divides** n (or is a **divisor** of n) if n/d is an integer. This is equivalent to there being another integer k so that $n = kd$. As equivalent terminology, we may also (equivalently) say that n is a **multiple** of d if d divides n. The notation is

$$d|n$$

for 'd divides n.'

Let m, n be integers, not both zero. The **greatest common divisor** $\gcd(m, n)$ of m, n is the largest positive integer d so that d divides m and d divides n. The **least common multiple** $\operatorname{lcm}(m, n)$ of m and n is the smallest positive integer N so that N is a multiple of m and N is a multiple of n.

The use of the words 'greatest' and 'least' is meant to suggest properties that these things have, but some of the ramifications are not clear. An important property we'd want to prove, but can't without more work (later), is:

> **Theorem.** The greatest common divisor $\gcd(m, n)$ of m, n has the property that for *every* divisor e of both m and n we have $e|\gcd(m, n)$. The least common multiple $\operatorname{lcm}(m, n)$ of m, n has the property that for *every* multiple N of both m and n we have $\operatorname{lcm}(m, n)|N$.

Prime numbers p are integers which have no divisors d with $1 < d < p$. For example, the beginning of the list of primes is 2, 3, 5, 7, 11, 13, 17, 19, 23, 29, 31,

37, ... For several reasons, 1 is not called a prime. A theorem we'll prove later is that *every positive integer can be factored into primes, and in only one way.* This fact is more or less familiar to us in the case of small integers, anyway:

$$
\begin{aligned}
12 &= 2^2 \cdot 3 \\
35 &= 5 \cdot 7 \\
1001 &= 7 \cdot 11 \cdot 13 \\
47268 &= 2^2 \cdot 3^2 \cdot 13 \cdot 101
\end{aligned}
$$

For small integers we can do these factorizations intuitively. A little later we'll be more systematic, but it turns out that factorization into primes is one of the abidingly difficult mathematical problems in the world.

If we *already have* the prime factorizations of two numbers m, n, then we can easily find the greatest common divisor and least common multiple by looking at prime factors they have in common. This is a very suboptimal approach, but it matches our intuition about factorization into primes. For example, to find the greatest common divisor of 12 and 15, first factor $12 = 2^2 \cdot 3$ and $15 = 3 \cdot 5$. The greatest common factor is visibly just 3.

Generally, for each prime number p, the power of p dividing the *gcd* of m and n is the *minimum* of the powers of p dividing m and dividing n. Since this is true for each prime, we know the prime factorization of the greatest common divisor. In a bigger example,

$$gcd(2^3\ 3^5\ 5^2\ 11,\ 3^2\ 5^3\ 7^2\ 11^2) = 3^2\ 5^2\ 11$$

since 2^0 is the smaller of the two powers of 2 occurring, 3^2 is the smaller of the two powers of 3 occurring, 5^2 is the smaller of the two powers of 5 occurring, 7^0 is the smaller of the two powers of 7 occurring, and 11^1 is the smaller of the two powers of 11 occurring.

Similarly, the least common multiple is obtained by taking the *larger* of the two powers of each prime occurring in the factorizations of m, n.

It is very important to realize, as we will see later, that there is a much better approach to computing greatest common divisors or least common multiples.

Exercises

4.2.01 Find the greatest common divisor and least common multiple of 12 and 15.

4.2.02 Find the greatest common divisor and least common multiple of 15 and 18.

4.2.03 Find the greatest common divisor and least common multiple of 15 and 21.

4.2.04 Find the greatest common divisor and least common multiple of 18 and 24.

4.2.05 Find the greatest common divisor and least common multiple of 19 and 23.

4.2.06 Find the greatest common divisor and least common multiple of 31 and 47.

4.2.07 Find the least common multiple of 24 and 36.

4.2.08 Find the greatest common divisor of 231 and 343.

4.2.09 Find the greatest common divisor of 5609 and 5767.

4.2.10 Find the greatest common divisor of 51051 and 55913.

4.3 Kasiski Attack

In any ciphertext-only attack on the Vigenere cipher, determination of the key length is a fundamental issue. (Though, still, even if the key length m is known, and we try to treat the ciphertext as an aggregate of m interwoven shift ciphers, hostile decryption is still much harder than with a single shift, since it might be very hard to tell when the decryption is correct for batches of characters that are not adjacent to each other!)

One ingenious attack on the Vigenere cipher is the **Kasiski attack** or **Kasiski test**, whose goal is exactly the determination of key length (Friedrich Kasiski, 1863). This attack is by no means guaranteed to succeed. Also, at best it acquires limited information (just the key length). In fact, these peculiar features of the Kasiski attack are characteristic of more serious cryptanalytic scenarios, so in this regard the Kasiski attack is representative.

The idea is that if two trigrams in the plaintext occur at a distance apart which is a multiple of the key length, then they will encrypt to the same trigram in the *ciphertext*. Thus, if two identical trigrams in the *ciphertext* arise because of such reason, they will be separated by a distance which is a multiple of the key length. Thus, we *look for trigrams which occur more than once in the ciphertext, and speculate that their distances apart may be multiples of the keylength.*

What is true about this 'method' is that *if* there are two trigrams in the plaintext whose distance apart is a multiple of the key length, then this multiple *will* occur in the list of distances-apart of identical trigrams in the ciphertext. But there are at least two problems. First, if the ciphertext is too small, then the chances are small that the same trigram will occur twice or more at a distance apart which happens to be a multiple of the key. Second, if the ciphertext is too large, the chances are greater that identical trigrams appear in the *ciphertext* for other reasons (not because they are the encryptions of identical trigrams occuring keylength multiples apart).

Our implementation of this is the following. For each trigram in the ciphertext that occurs more than once, we compute the **greatest common divisor** of the collection of all the distances apart of all its occurences. If this greatest common divisor is greater than 1, then we list the trigram and the associated greatest common divisor. Then we would *guess* that the key length is a divisor of at least one of these greatest common divisors. Let's see what the Kasiski attack yields in various scenarios:

For example, consider the plaintext

friendinthecomputerbusinesssentmeth
isiwonderwhatthenetworkserviceschec
kingmodementeredpasswordsforcrackab
ilityorfromthewallstreetjournalemai

lsnoopingisokintheeyesofthelawarece
ntusdistrictcourtdecisioninpennsylv

Using a Vigenere cipher with a key *ab* of length 2, this gives ciphertext

FSIFNEIOTIEDONPVTFRCUTIOETSTEOTNEUH
JSJWPNEESWIAUTIEOEUWPRLSFRWIDETCIED
KJNHMPDFMFNUESEEPBSTWPRESGOSCSADKBB
JLJTZOSFSONTIEXAMLTTSEFTKOVROAMENAJ
LTNPOQIOGJSPKJNUHFEZETOGTIEMAXASEDE
OTVSEITTSIDTDOVRUDFCJSJOOIOPFNOSZLW

Among trigrams which occur more than once, we find *greatest common divisors* of distances apart as follows:

TIE	:	4
EOT	:	146
OVR	:	58
TTS	:	58
UTI	:	27
IED	:	58
WPR	:	36
JSJ	:	160
KJN	:	82

It is certainly true that 2 (the key length) does divide *most* of these greatest common divisors. But one of the *gcd*'s is 27. Using a Vigenere cipher with a key *abc* of length 3, this gives ciphertext

FSKEOFIOVHFEONRUUGRCWSJPETUSFPTNGTI
KSJYOOFESYHBVTIGNFVWPTKTGRWKCFUCIGC
LKNHOOEGMFPTFTEERATUWPTDTHOSERBEKBD
IMKTZQRGTONVHFYAMNSUTEFVJPWROCLFOAJ
NSOQOQKNHKSPMIOVHFGYFUOGVHFNAXCRFEE
OVUTFITVRJETDQUSVDFEITKOOKNQGNOUYMX

Among trigrams which occur more than once, we find *greatest common divisors* of distances apart as follows:

IOV	:	147
KNH	:	75
VHF	:	3
FPT	:	51
OVH	:	147
WPT	:	36

It is true that 3 (the key length) does divide these greatest common divisors. Using a Vigenere cipher with a key *abcd* of length 4, this gives ciphertext

FSKHNEKQTIGFONRXTFTEUTKQETUVEOVPEUJ
LSJYRNEGUWICWTIGQEUYRRLUHRWKFETEKED

MLNHORDFOHNUGUEERDSTYRREUIOSEUADMDB
JNLTZQUFSQPTIGZAMNVTSGHTKQXROCOENCL
LTPROQKQGJURKJPWHFGBETQITIGOAXCUEDG
QTVUGITVUIDVFOVTWDFELSJQQIORHNOUBLW

Among trigrams which occur more than once, we find *greatest common divisors* of distances apart as follows:

$$
\begin{array}{rcl}
TIG & : & 4 \\
LSJ & : & 160 \\
TKQ & : & 107 \\
YRR & : & 36 \\
TVU & : & 5
\end{array}
$$

Here, the key length (namely 4) divides only 3 out of 5 of the *gcd*'s. This is disturbingly ambiguous. But using a Vigenere cipher with a different key *abcx* of length 4, this gives ciphertext

FSKBNEKKTIGZONRRTFTYUTKKETUPEOVJEUJ
FSJYLNEGOWICQTIGKEUYLRLUBRWKZETEEED
MFNHOLDFOBNUGOEERXSTYLREUCOSEOADMXB
JNFTZQOFSQJTIGTAMNPTSGBTKQRROCIENCF
LTPLOQKKGJULKJPQHFGVETQCTIGIAXCOEDG
KTVUAITVOIDVZOVTQDFEFSJQKIORBNOUVLW

Among trigrams which occur more than once, we find *greatest common divisors* of distances apart as follows:

$$
\begin{array}{rcl}
TIG & : & 4 \\
YLR & : & 36 \\
FSJ & : & 160
\end{array}
$$

Here, the key length (namely 4) divides all of the *gcd*'s. So it appears that the 'bad' *gcd*'s in the previous paragraph were a result of 'bad luck'. Using a Vigenere cipher with a key *abcde* of length 5, this gives ciphertext

FSKHRDJPWLEDQPTUUGUFUTKQISTUHRTNGWL
ITKZSNEGUAHBVWLEOGWAOSMVIRWKFISDJHG
KJPJQOEGPINUGUIDQCVWWPTGWFPTFVADMDF
IMKWCOSHUSMUJHAAMNVXRFGWNOVTQELFODM
LTPRSPJPJMSPMLRTIGHCETQIXHFNDAASGFI
NUWVHITVUMCUERYRUFHGITKRRIORHRNTAOZ

Among trigrams which occur more than once, we find *greatest common divisors* of distances apart as follows:

$$
\begin{array}{rcl}
UGU & : & 65 \\
WLE & : & 40 \\
JPJ & : & 75 \\
ITK & : & 160 \\
INU & : & 95
\end{array}
$$

Here, the key length (namely 5) divides all of the *gcd*'s. Using a Vigenere cipher with a key *abcdef* of length 6 give *gcd*'s

$$
\begin{array}{rcl}
VMS & : & 107 \\
VXW & : & 53 \\
WPT & : & 36 \\
VKI & : & 12
\end{array}
$$

Here, the key length 6 divides only two of the *gcd*'s. But using a different key *abcdex* of length 6 gives *gcd*'s

$$
\begin{array}{rcl}
WPT & : & 36 \\
VKI & : & 12
\end{array}
$$

which are both divisible by the key length 6. A Vigenere cipher with key *abcdefg* of length 7 gives *gcd*'s

$$
\begin{array}{rcl}
NUJ & : & 147 \\
UJH & : & 147 \\
ONU & : & 147 \\
MKW & : & 11 \\
PHW & : & 139
\end{array}
$$

The first 3 are divisible by the key length 7, but the latter two are not. A different key *abcdefx* of length 7 gives

$$
\begin{array}{rcl}
NUJ & : & 147 \\
FNU & : & 147 \\
UJH & : & 147 \\
PHW & : & 139
\end{array}
$$

(with the 139 not divisible by the key length 7), and a third key *abcdxxx* gives

$$
\begin{array}{rcl}
OSF & : & 31 \\
NUJ & : & 147 \\
FNU & : & 147 \\
UJH & : & 147 \\
PVV & : & 191
\end{array}
$$

Still the 31 and 191 are not divisible by 7. With key *abcdefgh* of length 8, we get

$$
\begin{array}{rcl}
TIG & : & 40 \\
XMK & : & 48 \\
LWN & : & 160 \\
ORH & : & 127
\end{array}
$$

The key length 8 does divide 3 of the 4. With key *abcdefghi* of length 9, we get

$$VMS \quad : \quad 107$$
$$BHF \quad : \quad 108$$
$$YAZ \quad : \quad 53$$
$$JWU \quad : \quad 75$$
$$WPT \quad : \quad 36$$
$$VKI \quad : \quad 9$$

The key length 9 divides 3 of the 6. With key *abcdefghij* of length 10, we get

$$QIX \quad : \quad 139$$
$$BQE \quad : \quad 40$$
$$NYP \quad : \quad 160$$

The key length 10 divides 3 of the 6. With key *abcdefghijk* of length 11, we get

$$GOS \quad : \quad 50$$
$$CIO \quad : \quad 87$$

This shows that *no* trigrams occur a multiple of 11 apart in the plaintext. So *any* encryption of that particular plaintext with a key of length 11 will give meaningless results to the Kasiski attack. Bad luck. With key *abcdefghijklm* of length 13, we get

$$FHF \quad : \quad 39$$
$$WMW \quad : \quad 35$$
$$BQO \quad : \quad 156$$
$$WIW \quad : \quad 65$$

The keylength 13 divides *all*.

Exercises

4.3.01 Suppose (falsely, but for simplicity) that all 26 characters occur with equal probability in a character stream of length N. For a positive integer m, what is the probability (as a function of m and of N) that no two identical characters occur any multiple of m apart?

4.3.02 Suppose (falsely, but for simplicity) that all 26^3 trigrams occur with equal probability in a character stream of length N. For positive integer m, what is the probability (as function of m and N) that *no* two identical trigrams occur *any* multiple of m apart?

4.3.03 Referring to both the previous exercises: if we concede that in fact some letters and trigrams are much more likely to occur than others, does this *increase* or *decrease* the probability that *no* two identical ones occur at a multiple of m apart?

4.3.04 Would it be reasonable to apply the Kasiski attack using not trigrams but just single characters?

4.3.05 Why would it be silly to apply the Kasiski attack to the encryption of a plaintext consisting of a stream of 'random' characters?

4.3.06 (*) Are multiple-round Vigenere ciphers with several small keys (but large *lcm*) more vulnerable to Kasiski than single-round Vigenere with a single "random" key of length the *lcm* of all the single keys?

4.3.07 (*) Here is a variant of the Kasiski attack: in the ciphertext, look for characters which are the *least common* in ordinary English, and compute the greatest common divisor of the distances apart of occurrences of identical ones. We'd then guess that the key length should divide many of these *gcd*'s. Is this reasonable?

4.3.08 (*) If we apply the Kasiski attack to a plaintext, what does the outcome mean? How can the Kasiski attack tell that a text is encrypted?

4.3.09 (*) Why does the Kasiski attack work at all?

4.3.10 (*) Quantify the impact that size of the ciphertext has upon the effectiveness of the Kasiski attack.

4.4 Expected Values

Let $\Omega = \{\omega_1, \ldots, \omega_n\}$ be a sample space, with 'atomic' event ω_i having probability p_i. A real-valued function X defined on the set Ω is called a **random variable**. (In fact, it is fine to allow random variables be have somewhat more general values, like complex numbers or vectors, but for our purposes real-valued random variables are enough.)

Yes, due to tradition at least, instead of the 'f' otherwise often used for functions, an 'X' is used, perhaps to be more consonant with the usual use of x for a (non-random?) 'variable'. Further, there is a tradition that makes the *values* of X be labelled 'x_i' (in conflict with the calculus tradition). Also, there is some conflict with use of the letter 'E' for 'encryption'. Context will make clear what is meant.

For a possible *value* x of X, we extend the notation by writing

$$P(X = x) = P(\{\omega \in \Omega : X(\omega) = x\})$$

That is, the probability that $X = x$ is defined to be the probability of the subset of Ω on which X has the value x. The **expected value** of such a random variable is defined to be

$$E(X) = p_1 \cdot X(\omega_1) + p_2 \cdot X(\omega_2) + \cdots + p_n \cdot X(\omega_n)$$

Of course, the idea is that after a 'large' number of independent trials with outcomes $\omega_{i_1}, \omega_{i_2}, \ldots, \omega_{i_N}$ the *average* value

$$\frac{1}{N}\left(X(\omega_{i_1}) + X(\omega_{i_2}) + \cdots + X(\omega_{i_N}) \right)$$

will be 'close to' $E(X)$. But this viewpoint has the same limitations as the analogous idea that probability is a sort of limiting frequency.

The simplest models for the intuitive content of this idea have their origins in gambling. For example, suppose Alice and Bob ('A' and 'B') have a fair coin (meaning heads and tails both have probability 0.5) and the wager is that if the coin shows 'heads' Alice pays Bob a dollar, and if it shows 'tails' Bob pays Alice a dollar. Our intuition tells us that this is fair, and the expected-value computation corroborates this, as follows. The sample space is $\Omega = \{\omega_0, \omega_1\}$ (index '0' for heads and '1' for tails), with each point having probability 0.5. Let X be the random variable which tells Alice's gain (or loss):

$$X(\omega_0) = -1, \qquad X(\omega_1) = +1$$

Then the expected value of X, Alice's *expected* gain, is

$$E(X) = 0.5 \cdot (-1) + 0.5 \cdot (+1) = 0$$

In general, a **fair wager** is one so that everyone's expected gain is 0. (What's the point of it then? Probably that *perceptions* of probabilities can differ.)

It is important to notice that an expected value is more sophisticated than the most naive idea of 'average'. For example, suppose we choose an integer at random in the range 1–10 and square it. With equal probabilities assigned, the expected value of the square is

$$\frac{1}{10}1^2 + \cdots + \frac{1}{10}10^2 = \frac{1}{10}385 = 38.5$$

It is *not* true that we can take the average of 1–10 first (namely, 5.5) and square it (getting 30.25) to obtain the expected value.

Proposition. Let X and Y be two random variables on a sample space $\Omega = \{\omega_1, \ldots, \omega_n\}$, with probabilities $P(\omega_i) = p_i$. The **sum** random variable $X + Y$ is defined in the natural way as

$$(X + Y)(\omega_i) = X(\omega_i) + Y(\omega_i)$$

Then

$$E(X + Y) = E(X) + E(Y)$$

Proof: This is a direct computation from the definition:

$$E(X + Y) = \sum_i p_i \left(X(\omega_i) + Y(\omega_i) \right)$$

$$= \sum_i p_i X(\omega_i) + \sum_i p_i Y(\omega_i)) = E(X) + E(Y)$$

which proves what we want.   ♣

Proposition. Let X be a random variable on a sample space $\{\omega_1, \ldots, \omega_n\}$, with probabilities $P(\omega_i) = p_i$. Let c be a constant. The random variable cX is defined in the natural way as $cX(\omega_i) = c \cdot X(\omega_i)$. Then $E(cX) = c \cdot E(X)$.

Proof: This is a direct computation from the definition:

$$E(cX) = \sum_i p_i\, cX(\omega_i) = c \sum_i p_i\, X(\omega_i) = c \cdot E(X)$$

as asserted.   ♣

Let Ω be a sample space. Let X and Y be random variables on Ω. The **product random variable** XY is defined on the sample space Ω in the reasonable way:

$$(XY)(\omega) = X(\omega)\, Y(\omega)$$

These two random variables are **independent random variables** if for every pair x, y of possible *values* of X, Y, we have

$$P(X = x \text{ and } Y = y) = P(X = x) \cdot P(Y = y)$$

(This definition of independence is really just a paraphrase of the earlier definition of independence of *events.*)

The following assertion is not generally true without the hypothesis of independence.

Proposition.   For two *independent* random variables X, Y on a sample space Ω, the expected value of the product is the product of the expected values:

$$E(XY) = E(X) \cdot E(Y)$$

Proof: The definition of the expected value of the product is

$$E(XY) = \sum_{\omega \in \Omega} P(\omega) XY(\omega)$$

By the definition of XY, this is

$$\sum_{\omega \in \Omega} P(\omega) X(\omega)\, Y(\omega)$$

To prove the proposition gracefully it is wise to use the notation introduced above: let x range over possible *values* of X and let y range over possible values of Y. Then we can rewrite the expected value by grouping according to values of X and Y: it is

$$\sum_{x,y} \sum_{\omega} P(\omega) X(\omega)\, Y(\omega)$$

where for fixed (x, y) the inner sum is over ω so that

$$X(\omega) = x \quad \text{and} \quad Y(\omega) = y$$

Then use the new notation to rewrite this as

$$= \sum_{x,y} P(X = x \text{ and } Y = y)\, x\, y$$

The assumption of independence is exactly that

$$P(X = x \text{and } Y = y) = P(X = x) \cdot P(Y = y)$$

so the expression becomes

$$\sum_{x,y} P(X = x)\, P(Y = y)\, x\, y$$

which we can now separate as a product

$$= \sum_{x} P(X = x)\, x \; \cdot \; \sum_{y} P(Y = y)\, y = E(X) \cdot E(Y)$$

giving the desired result.   ♣

An important case of independent random variables arises when several independent trials are conducted (with the same 'experiment'). Let Ω be a sample space. Consider N independent trials. Consider the product

$$\Omega^N = \underbrace{\Omega \times \ldots \times \Omega}_{N}$$

consisting of ordered N-tuples of elements from Ω. Let X_i be a random variable on Ω^N whose value only depends upon the *outcome of the ith trial*. Then for $i \neq j$ the two random variables X_i and X_j are independent.

Exercises

4.4.01 If there are 3 red balls in an urn and 7 black balls, what is the *expected* number of red balls to be drawn in 20 trials (replacing whatever ball is drawn in each trial)?

4.4.02 If there are 5 red balls in an urn and 9 black balls, what is the *expected* number of red balls to be drawn in 10 trials (replacing whatever ball is drawn in each trial)?

4.4.03 If there are 2 red balls in an urn and 13 black balls, what is the *expected* number of red balls to be drawn in 30 trials (replacing whatever ball is drawn in each trial)?

4.4.04 What is the expected number of heads (before any tail comes up) as a result of tossing a fair coin?

4.4.05 What is the expected number of heads (before any tail comes up) as a result of tossing a coin that gives heads $1/3$ of the time?

4.4.06 What is the expected number of heads (before any tail comes up) as a result of tossing a coin that gives heads $3/4$ of the time?

4.4.07 What is the expected number of heads (before any tail comes up) as a result of tossing a coin that gives heads 3/5 of the time?

4.4.08 What is the expected number of coin flips before a head comes up (with a fair coin)?

4.4.09 What is the expected number of coin flips before two consecutive heads come up?

4.4.10 What is the expected distance between two 'e's in a random character stream where 'e's occur 11% of the time?

4.4.11 What is the expected distance between two 'ee's in a random character stream where 'e's occur 11% of the time?

4.4.12 Let X be the random variable defined as "the number of heads in 10 flips of a fair coin". The sample space is all 2^{10} different possible sequences of outcomes of 10 flips. The expected value of X itself is 5. What is the expected value of the random variable $(X-5)^2$?

4.4.13 What is the expected number of coin flips before n consecutive heads come up?

4.4.14 (*) Choose two real numbers "at random" from the interval $[0,1]$. What is the expected value of their product?

4.5   Friedman Attack

This section introduces methods which made a broad class of classical ciphers obsolete, because they became completely vulnerable to ciphertext-only attacks. Until late in the 19th century it was widely believed that **polyalphabetic (periodic) substitution ciphers** (such as Vigenere) were secure. But the **Index of Coincidence** [William Friedman, 1925] was a decisive attack on *periodic substitution ciphers*. In particular, it completely breaks Vigenere: it can guess key length more effectively than the Kasiski attack, and can make good guesses at the key for a given key length. Further, it is quite amenable to automation. In fact, during the Second World War both mechanical and electronic devices implemented this method, which played an important role.

The class of ciphers to be attacked is the **periodic substitution ciphers**. Again, both the *shift* and *affine* ciphers are examples of *monoalphabetic* substitution ciphers, although in those two cases the substitution is of a special sort. The Vigenere cipher is a *polyalphabetic* substitution cipher.

The methods of this section are effective in determining the *key length* of *any* periodic substitution cipher. Then the particular vulnerabilities of the Vigenere will be exploited, giving a complete ciphertext only attack on it.

So far, in a ciphertext-only attack on the Vigenere cipher, even if we have used the Kasiski attack to make a good guess as to the key length, the remaining decryption is relatively difficult by comparison to the shift cipher or affine cipher. If the key length is m, there are (in principle) 26^m possible keys.

Of course, if we believe that the key was *not* a random stream of m characters, but rather was a phrase having meaning in English (for example) then the effective number may be much smaller. Further, even without knowing the key length, all too often the person who chose the key used the name of their dog, favorite football team, or most-feared math professor. Then the effective **key space** is relatively tiny. Instead of a list of 26^m or more keys to try, we might develop a much smaller list of most-likely candidates. This is a **dictionary attack**.

But we want a ciphertext-only attack that does not depend upon **bad keys**. Even with a good guess that the key length is some particular number m, we still have 26^m keys to consider. While it is true that the plaintext characters

$$x_i, \ x_{i+m}, \ x_{i+2m}, \ x_{i+3m}, \ \ldots$$

all are shifted by the same amount (for any fixed index i), this plaintext fragment will not likely be *recognizable*. That is, we *cannot* successfully treat a Vigenere cipher with key of length m merely as m different shift ciphers. (If we *could*, things would be easy, since shift ciphers are very easy to break even in ciphertext-only attacks.) Again, this is because we rely upon the plaintext being coherent in order to tell when we've got it: if an alleged decryption gives a character stream that is not obviously English, we reject it. This criterion is not applicable if we're looking at mere slivers of the plaintext.

For example, from the plaintext

> friendinthecomputerbusinesssentmethisiwonderwhatthenetworkserviceschec
> kingmodementeredpasswordsforcrackabilityorfromthewallstreetjournalemai
> lsnoopingisokintheeyesofthelawarecentusdistrictcourtdecisioninpennsylv

take out just every eight character and see if it is still visibly English:

> ftteentrennsobfateokeatidil

No. Nevertheless, the *single-letter frequencies* should be the same in such a 'slice' of English as they would be for ordinary English (at least if the slice is large enough). (The digrams and trigrams would certainly get disrupted.)

Just as the Kasiski method magically *isolated* a particular bit of information, Friedman's **index of coincidence** which we will introduce also addresses just a little bit of the problem at a time, thereby allowing us to *decrypt* a little bit at a time. Kasiski's method could be viewed as a coarse version of Friedman's.

Given two streams of characters, of the same length,

$$y = (y_0, y_1, \ldots, y_N)$$

$$z = (z_0, z_1, \ldots, z_N)$$

the **index of coincidence** is

$$I(y, z) = \frac{1}{N} \sum_{i=0}^{N} \delta(y_i, z_i)$$

where

$$\delta(y_i, z_i) = \begin{cases} 1 & (y_i = z_i) \\ 0 & (y_i \neq z_i) \end{cases}$$

Thus, if the two streams were identical, the index would be 1.

If one (or both) of the two streams were completely random, the index of coincidence would be expected to be about $\frac{1}{26} = 0.038$, as may seem intuitively reasonable. After all, if all the letters are random, then the probability is $1/26$ that the two characters at the ith place will match. So the index would be expected to be about

$$\text{index} = \frac{\frac{1}{26} + \cdots + \frac{1}{26}}{N} = \frac{N \cdot \frac{1}{26}}{N} = \frac{1}{26}$$

If both streams have the frequency distributions of typical English, then we can compute that the expected value of the index of coincidence is approximately 0.067 (or higher). Just below we'll see where these numbers come from.

Proposition. Let E be any *substitution* cipher. For two plaintext character streams y and z, the index of coincidence $I(y,z)$ is *not changed* if they are both encrypted with the same key k: for any key k,

$$I(E_k(y), E_k(z)) = I(y, z)$$

Proof: This is easy: if $y_i = z_i$ in the plaintext streams, then $E_k(y_i) = E_k(z_i)$, since the encryption does not depend upon anything beyond the key k and the point i at which we are in the plaintext stream. ♣

There is a *probabilistic version* of the index of coincidence that has certain virtues, as well. Note that if we have ℓ different texts of length N, and if we want to compute the index of coincidence between each two of them, then we must compare $\ell(\ell-1)/2$ pairs of texts. If we compute the index of coincidence as indicated above, then this means examining $N \cdot \ell(\ell-1)/2$ pairs of characters for equality. If N should be large this might be burdensome. Rather, we can compute the **expected value** of the index, based on the *single-letter frequencies* in the two texts, viewed as *probabilities*, as follows.

Assign probabilities p_i to the characters i in the range $0 - -25$. Fix a positive integer N. We consider the sample space Ω_N of all character streams $y = (y_0, \ldots, y_{N-1})$ of length N with probability of occurrence

$$P(y) = p_{y_0} p_{y_1} \cdots p_{y_{N-1}}$$

That is, we imagine that these streams are 'generated' by a 'source' which produces character i with probability p_i, and so that the production of the ith character is independent of the previous ones. Let p_i' be another (possibly different) assignment of probabilities, and Ω_N' the corresponding sample space of character streams of length N with probabilities

$$P(y) = p_{y_0}' p_{y_1}' \cdots p_{y_{N-1}}'$$

Proposition. Define a random variable X on $\Omega_N \times \Omega'_N$ by

$$X(y, z) = I(y, z) = \text{index of coincidence of } y, z$$

Then the *expected value* EX of X is computed by the formula

$$EX = \sum_{i=0}^{25} p_i \cdot p'_i$$

Proof: The random variable X can be expressed as

$$X(y, z) = \sum_{j=0}^{N-1} X_j(y, z)$$

where the random variable X_j is defined to be

$$X_j(y, z) = \delta(y_j, z_j)$$

where δ is defined by

$$\begin{cases} 1 & (y_j = z_j) \\ 0 & (y_j \neq z_j) \end{cases}$$

Since the selections of the characters at different spots in the stream are independent, these random variables are independent. Thus, as observed earlier, the expected value is computed as

$$EX = \sum_{j=0}^{N-1} EX_j$$

And each of the random variables X_j is really just the expected value of δ on $\Omega_1 \times \Omega'_1$. We compute this.

Two characters y_1 and z_1 will both be 0 (and hence equal) with probability $p_0 p'_0$. They will both be 1 (and hence equal) with probability $p_1 p'_1$. Generally, they will both be i (and hence equal) with probability $p_i p'_i$. These different events, that is, both being equal to different characters i, are certainly *independent*, so the probability that $y_1 = z_1$ is the sum

$$P(y_1 = z_1) = \sum_{i=0}^{25} p_i p'_i$$

This finishes the proof.   ♣

The previous result also suggests *defining* an **averaged** index of coincidence of two *specific* streams $y = (y_0, \ldots, y_{N-1})$ and $z = (z_0, \ldots, z_{N-1})$ by putting

$$p_i^y = \frac{\text{number of characters } i \text{ in } y}{N}$$

$$p_i^z = \frac{\text{number of characters } i \text{ in } z}{N}$$

and

$$I_{\text{avg}}(y, z) = \sum_{i=0}^{25} p_i^y p_i^z$$

In particular, this version of the index has a different sense for a *single* stream, revealing something about the family of frequencies p_i:

$$I_{\text{avg}}(y) = \sum_{i=0}^{25} (p_i^y)^2$$

This probabilistic version of the index of coincidence can be interpreted as being the 'typical' index for streams with the same frequencies as y and z. (Indeed, we showed that it *is* the expected value taken over the sample space of all streams of that length with the same frequencies.)

Proposition. The *average* index of coincidence $I_{\text{avg}}(y, z)$ of two streams y, z with frequencies $\{p_i^y\}$ and $\{p_i^z\}$ (respectively) is unchanged if both streams are encrypted by a *transposition cipher* using the same key.

Proof: The numbers of occurrences of the various characters in a block of characters are unchanged by reordering them, which is all that a transposition cipher does. The frequencies p_i^y and p_i^z are unchanged by this.   ♣

Thus, if we are willing to use this expected value of the index of coincidence, we can encapsulate the relevant information about a character stream in just the list of 26 probabilities (frequencies), after making just *one* pass through each stream.

If the stream y is in English, or is encrypted from English by a *simple* substitution cipher, then we know approximate frequencies p_i for characters: 'e' occurs with probability about 0.11, etc. Using the formula above, and the list of probabilities, a little computation gives

$$I_{\text{avg}}(y) \approx \sum_{i=0}^{25} p_i^2 \approx 0.064$$

In particular, this should still be true for a 'random fragment' of an English plaintext.

On the other hand, for a character stream y produced by a truly random source, with all characters occurring with probability $p_i = 1/26$, the *expected* index of coincidence is about

$$I_{\text{avg}}(y) \approx \sum_{i=0}^{25} p_i^2 = 26 \cdot \left(\frac{1}{26}\right)^2 = \frac{1}{26} \approx 0.0385$$

Conversely, if y is a character stream with $I_{\text{avg}}(y)$ *not* close to the number 0.067 just computed, then we would doubt that y was an English text or a random fragment thereof. In practice, a stream v of Vigenere-encrypted English has

$$I_{\text{avg}}(v) \approx 0.047$$

or so. This is slightly above the truly random value, but well below the English plaintext value.

The expressions

$$I_{\text{avg}}(y) = \sum_{i=0}^{25} (p_i^y)^2$$

and

$$I_{\text{avg}}(y, z) = \sum_{i=0}^{25} p_i^y \, p_i^z$$

have *geometric* interpretations as well, which give some clarification of their behavior. Specifically, to each character stream $y = (y_0, \ldots, y_{N-1})$ we associate the 26-dimensional **vector** of frequencies

$$p^y = (p_0^y, \, p_1^y, \, \ldots, \, p_{25}^y)$$

where as usual

$$p_i^y = \frac{\text{number of characters } i \text{ in } y}{N}$$

Then

$$I_{\text{avg}}(y) = \sum_{i=0}^{25} (p_i^y)^2$$

is the **norm** of this vector. For another character stream z (not necessarily of the same length as y), with associated frequency vector p^z, the averaged index

$$I_{\text{avg}}(y, z) = \sum_{i=0}^{25} p_i^y p_i^z$$

is the usual **inner product** of the two frequency vectors.

Proposition. Always

$$0 \le I_{\text{avg}}(y, z) \le \sqrt{I_{\text{avg}}(y)} \, \sqrt{I_{\text{avg}}(z)}$$

If both $I_{\text{avg}}(y)$ and $I_{\text{avg}}(z)$ are close to the magic number 0.064, the averaged index $I_{\text{avg}}(y, z)$ will be close to 0.064 if the angle between the frequency vectors p^y and p^z is small, and will decrease from 0.064 as that angle increases.

Proof: The asserted inequality is just the Cauchy-Schwarz-Bunyakowsky inequality for the frequency vectors. For that matter, we have the formula for the cosine of the angle θ between p^y and p^z:

$$\cos \theta = \frac{I_{\text{avg}}(y, z)}{\sqrt{I_{\text{avg}}(y)} \, \sqrt{I_{\text{avg}}(z)}}$$

And the frequencies are non-negative in any case, so $I_{\text{avg}}(y, z) \ge 0$.   ♣

Now we return to the attack which determines key length for periodic substitution ciphers. Suppose that the ciphertext is $y = (y_0, y_1, y_2, \ldots)$ encrypted by a periodic substitution cipher, and that we wish to test whether or not the *period* is m. For any stream $y = (y_0, y_1, \ldots)$ and positive integer ℓ let

$$y^{(+\ell)} = (y_\ell, y_{\ell+1}, y_{\ell+2}, \ldots)$$

That is, $y^{(+\ell)}$ is the stream y shifted forward by ℓ. If the period length *were* m (or a *divisor* of ℓ), then the stream y and the *shifted* stream $y^{+\ell m}$ would be encrypted by the same periodic substitution cipher (with the same key). Therefore, *if the* period divided ℓ, we would have

$$I(y, y^{(+\ell)}) \approx 0.067$$

By contrast, if the period length did *not* divide m, we would expect

$$I(y, y^{(+\ell)}) \approx 0.047 \text{ (or less)}$$

Note that we do not want to look at shift 0 because the index would be a meaningless '1'. For that matter, since English is not really random, insofar as characters near each other are not actually very independent (see the digram statistics earlier), even if we suspect a Vigenere key of small length such as 3, it would be unwise to use $\ell = 3$, since the index of coincidence would be low. Thus, we should try shifting by amounts $\ell \geq 3$ at least and compute the index of coincidence, but look for the *high* values at *multiples* of the period.

For example, with a filtered 980-character piece of unencrypted old email, computing the index of coincidence for various shifts, *multiplied by 100* for legibility:

Shift	Index of coincidence $\times$ 100
3	5.93
4	6.96
5	7.48
6	6.46
7	6.16
8	8.12
9	6.9
11	7.84
12	7.64
13	5.99
14	6.1
15	5.8
16	6.95
17	6.64
18	6.86
19	5.2
20	6.14
21	6.56

The point of this is to see the fluctuations in the index. With larger samples there is less fluctuation.

By contrast, using a Vigenere cipher on the same plaintext, with key *prognosti-cate* (length 13), computing the same indices of the ciphertext against itself shifted, we get

Shift	Index × 100
1	4.69
2	4.8
3	3.48
4	4.09
5	2.56
6	2.97
7	4.62
8	4.32
9	4.73
10	4.12
11	4.23
12	4.13
13	5.99
14	3.2
15	4.24
16	4.46
17	3.94
18	3.43
19	3.22
20	3.22
21	4.58
22	4.07
23	3.03
24	4.28
25	3.97
26	6.6
27	3.04
28	3.88
29	3.57
30	4.52
31	3.47
32	5.06
33	3.69
34	2.85
35	4.23
36	3.81
37	3.92
38	3.71
39	6.69
40	3.82

Looking down the list of numbers, the only ones above 5.0 are obtained at 13 (value 5.99), 26 (value 6.6), 32 (value 5.06), and 39 (value 6.69). The pattern is clear: the

'32' is anomalous, and the others are multiples of 13. So we would conclude that the keylength is a multiple of 13 (as it really is). Thus, screening out any shifts with index at or below 4.7 seems a safe way to proceed.

The same text, Vigenere encrypted with keyword '*xyzqwe*', gives indices

Shift	Index × 100
6	6.46
12	7.64
18	6.86
24	4.91
30	7.26
36	8.26
42	6.82
48	7.72

The keyword is short enough for the text size (1000 characters) so that this attack unequivocally gives the key length 6.

The same plaintext, Vigenere encrypted with keyword '*praxisperfect*,' gives (looking at shifts under 50)

Shift	Index × 100
3	5.32
6	5.03
13	5.99
26	6.6
27	5.03
32	4.85
39	6.69
49	4.72

The multiples of 13 stand out, so we conclude that the keylength is 13.

In the same scenario with a longer keyword, '*praxisperfectoyster*,' we get (looking at shifts under 50)

Shift	Index × 100
7	5.65
19	5.2
33	4.75
38	6.47
48	5.79

The multiples of 19 are the obvious choices.

In the same scenario with an even longer keyword

asdfgqwertzxcvbyuiopqwertkjhyuixwqpty

(length 37), looking at shifts up through 80, we have

Shift	Index × 100
15	4.97
16	5.08
20	5.31
22	4.9
26	5.03
37	5.51
48	4.72
59	4.99
63	4.79
74	7.94
78	4.76

Here, there are only about 26 characters encoded with the same shift, yet the 37 and especially the 74 stand out. The key length is 37.

Next, we see how Friedman's index can be used to determine the key $k = (k_0, k_1, \ldots, k_{m-1})$ for a Vigenere cipher, assuming that we have already determined a very likely candidate m for the key length, as above.

We take 'slices' of the ciphertext:

$$
\begin{aligned}
y^{(0)} &= (y_0, y_m, y_{2m}, \ldots) \\
y^{(1)} &= (y_1, y_{1+m}, y_{1+2m}, \ldots) \\
y^{(2)} &= (y_2, y_{2+m}, y_{2+2m}, \ldots) \\
y^{(3)} &= (y_2, y_{3+m}, y_{3+2m}, \ldots) \\
y^{(4)} &= (y_3, y_{4+m}, y_{4+2m}, \ldots) \\
y^{(m-1)} &= (y_{m-1}, y_{(m-1)+m}, y_{(m-1)+2m}, \ldots)
\end{aligned}
$$

If the key length really is m (or a *divisor of m*), then for each index j the slice $y^{(j)}$ is encoded from the corresponding substream of the plaintext by a shift cipher with key k_j. Recall that the shift cipher has the property that

$$E_s \circ E_t = E_{s+t}$$

for any two integers s, t. Therefore, for any two indices i, j, the two character streams $y^{(i)}$ and $E_{k_i-k_j} y^{(j)}$ are the encryptions by shift cipher E_{k_i} of an English text (or a random slice thereof).

In particular, the *difference* $k_i - k_j$ should be the number t among 0–25 for which the index

$$I(E_t(y^{(i)}), \, y^{(j)})$$

is close to the magic number 0.064, while this index should be 0.047 or lower for all other values of t. However, since the adjacent characters in reality *do* have some relation to each other, we should instead compute something like

$$I(E_t(y^{(i)}), \, y^{(j)(+3m)})$$

using the notation above, meaning to shift the slice $y^{(j)}$ forward by 3 times the (presumed) keylength.

Or, we might consider using the *averaged* version $I_{\text{avg}}(y, z)$ of the index.

For example, using the same 980 characters as above, encrypting with Vigenere and keyword '*abcxq*', presuming that the keylength is 5, computing

$$I(E_t(y^{(0)}),\ y^{(1)(+15)})$$

for t ranging from 0 to 25 (and omitting mention of any indices below 5.5) we find

Shift	*Index* $\times$ 100
1	7.77
2	6.21
12	6.21
21	6.21
23	5.69

This gives 1 as the leading candidate for the *relative* shift $k_1 - k_0$ between the 0th and 1st slices, as is indeed the case. In the same scenario but computing

$$I(E_t(y^{(0)}),\ y^{(2)(+15)})$$

to guess at $k_2 - k_0$, we get

Shift	*Index* $\times$ 100
2	6.72
8	6.72
17	6.21

which is rather equivocal about $k_2 - k_0$. But to get information on $k_2 - k_0$ from another side, we can also guess at $k_2 - k_1$ by computing

$$I(E_t(y^{(1)}),\ y^{(2)(+15)})$$

which gives

Shift	*Index* $\times$ 100
1	8.8
8	5.69
17	6.73

This gives 1 as the best guess for $k_2 - k_1$, although the other two values are also plausible.

Therefore, in this example, $k_1 - k_0$ is almost surely 1, while $k_2 - k_0$ is among 2, 8, 17, and $k_2 - k_1$ is most likely 1, though it is plausibly 8 or 17. Looking at these simultaneously, since certainly

$$(k_2 - k_0) - (k_1 - k_0) = k_2 - k_1$$

we can conclude that the 8's and 17's are impossible. Thus, by exclusion, we reach the (correct) conclusion that the first three characters k_0, k_1, k_1 of the key fall into the pattern $i, i+1, i+2$.

Continuing in this example, computing

$$I(E_t(y^{(0)}), y^{(3)(+15)})$$

gives

Shift	Index $\times$ 100
19	6.2
23	6.72

which is ambiguous, suggesting that $k_3 - k_0$ is either 19 or 23. Computing

$$I(E_t(y^{(1)}), y^{(3)(+15)})$$

gives

Shift	Index $\times$ 100
8	6.72
11	7.24
22	6.72

This in itself is also ambiguous, suggesting that $k_3 - k_1$ is either 8, 11, or 22. But we have already concluded (at least tentatively) that the difference $k_1 - k_0$ is 1, so since

$$(k_3 - k_0) + (k_1 - k_0) = k_3 - k_0$$

The only way these fit together is that $k_3 - k_0 = 23$, which is indeed the correct conclusion. For corroboration, we compute

$$I(E_t(y^{(2)}), y^{(3)(+15)})$$

finding

Shift	Index $\times$ 100
2	5.69
6	7.25
11	5.69
16	5.69
21	5.18
24	6.21

which is not such great corroboration (since the '21' is correct!), but the 5.18 is high enough to be plausible. The other higher numbers are incompatible with the earlier numbers.

And let's do the last batch of differences, to approach k_4 in this example. Computing for

$$I(E_t(y^{(0)}), y^{(4)(+15)})$$

we get

Shift	Index $\times$ 100
9	5.68
16	5.16
17	7.23
18	5.68
20	5.68
22	6.19

which makes a relative shift of 17 look best for $k_4 - k_0$, but we secretly know that this relative shift is 16, the least appealing of the numbers that reached our threshhold. But because the threshhold really must be rather low, the conclusion we should reach here is that it isn't clear. Computing

$$I(E_t(y^{(1)}),\ y^{(4)(+15)})$$

gives

Shift	Index $\times$ 100
0	5.68
5	6.2
15	7.75
21	5.17
22	5.17
24	6.2

Since $k_1 - k_0 = 1$, for compatibility all possibilities are excluded except $k_4 - k_0 = 16$ and $k_4 - k_1 = 15$ (as is correct). Looking for corroboration, we compute

$$I(E_t(y^{(2)}),\ y^{(4)(+15)})$$

hoping to have 14 suggested as $k_4 - k_2$:

Shift	Index $\times$ 100
8	5.17
11	5.17
14	6.21
15	6.21
20	5.17
21	6.21

This is ambiguous, but leaves $k_4 - k_2 = 14$ plausible at least. Last, we try

$$I(E_t(y^{(3)}),\ y^{(4)(+15)})$$

hoping to have 19 suggested as $k_4 - k_3$ in order to be compatible:

Shift	Index $\times$ 100
1	5.18
5	5.18
9	5.18
15	5.18
19	7.25
23	6.21

Remark: The ambiguities occurring above are entirely expectable, considering the sample size of 980 characters, as about 196 characters are encrypted by each simple shift cipher in the 'slices'. The fact that for (presumed) keylength 5 we have altogether 10 lists of indices is a help.

Now we are almost done with this ciphertext-only attack on Vigenere. By using Friedman's index we have established that the key is of the form

$$k = (k_0, \, k_0 + 1, \, k_0 + 2, \, k_0 + 23, \, k_0 + 16)$$

Thus, the remaining complexity is essentially that of a simple shift cipher done on the whole plaintext, since there is only the single unknown parameter k_0. Determination of k_0 can be done by *brute force*, by simply looking at the 26 different possible decryptions with a key of this form. Further, this final brute force attack can be *automated* to a certain degree, by computing the index of coincidence of

$$D_k(\text{ciphertext})$$

against some character stream of plaintext English with keys of this very restricted sort, and seeing which value of k_0 gives the highest index. In the present example, computing the index against a character stream of 'generic English', with k_0 ranging from 0 to 25, with the key of the special form above, gives

$Shift$	$Index \times 100$
0	7.64
4	4.85
7	5.06
12	5.06
25	5.57

This shows that (with this special form of key) the frequencies of the ciphertext *decrypted* via D_k most closely resemble those of ordinary English when the k_0 is taken to be 0. This is correct. If the numbers had been more ambiguous, we would have had to do trial decryptions to see which message made sense.

Exercises

4.5.01 Consider an alphabet with just two characters, '0' and '1', and a language in which these characters occur with respective probabilities 2/3 and 1/3. Say that a stream of '0's and '1's is *random* if the '0's and '1's both occur with probability 1/2. Define an index of coincidence $I(y, z)$ for character streams y, z of '0's and '1's (of the same length).

4.5.02 In the context of the previous problem, what is the expected value E_{rand} of the index of two random character streams? What is the expected value E_{lang} of the index of two character streams from that language?

4.5.03 In the context of the previous problem, what is the probability that the index of two *random* streams of length 5 is as large as E_{lang}? What if the length is 10?

4.5.04 In the context of the previous problem, what is the probability that the index of two streams of length 5 *from the language* is as small as E_{rand}? If the length is 10?

4.5.05 Explain why the *average* indices $I_{\text{avg}}(y, y^{+t})$ are *not* useful in guessing the period length of a periodic substitution cipher.

4.5.06 Explain why the *average* indices $I_{\text{avg}}(y^{(i)}, y^{(j)})$ *are* useful in guessing the relative shifts $k_i - k_j$ in a ciphertext-only attack on a Vigenere cipher.

5

More Probability

This little chapter is not directly used in the sequel, but it does give more perspective on probabilistic arguments and phenomena. In particular, we introduce *variance* as another fundamental quantity attached to a random variable (in addition to *expected value*, discussed earlier). This allows us to formulate a simple case of the Law of Large Numbers, which gives substance to the idea that outcomes really do approach the expected as more and more trials are performed. The quantitative limitations in such an assertion can be important, and we study them here.

The proof we give for our special case of the Law of Large Numbers uses an inequality due to Chebycheff, which itself asserts a sharper and more quantitative version of the Law of Large Numbers. Roughly, Chebycheff's inequality tells how fast the result of larger and larger samples will approach the expected value of the associated random variable. For example, this inequality tells how close to n we might expect the number of heads from $2n$ flips of a fair coin to be. Certainly it is unreasonable to expect it to be *exactly* n, but we have an intuitive expectation that it be *close*.

5.1 Generating Functions

Let X be the random variable on the probability space Ω consisting of all ordered n-tuples of 0's and 1's, and whose value on each n-tuple is the number of 1's in that n-tuple. Suppose that 1's occur with probability p and 0's occur with probability q (with $p + q = 1$, of course), and that the 0's and 1's at different positions in the sequence are independent. **What is the expected value of X?**

There is an easier approach than what we'll do here, which in some ways is even more intuitive, but this question gives a relatively simple opportunity to illustrate the use of generating-function computational methods.

First, we can *group* the possibilities according to the total number of 1's that occur: there are $\binom{n}{k}$ ways that k 1's can occur among n positions. By the assumed independence, the probability of any particular pattern of k 1's and $n - k$ 0's is $p^k q^{n-k}$. Thus, the probability of getting exactly k 1's is

$$P(X = k) = \binom{n}{k} p^k q^{n-k}$$

Thus, the expected value is

$$EX = \sum_{k} P(X = k) \cdot k = \sum_{k=0}^{n} \binom{n}{k} p^k q^{n-k} \cdot k$$

Here's the trick. Replace p by a variable x in this expression, obtaining

$$\sum_{k=0}^{n} \binom{n}{k} x^k q^{n-k} \cdot k$$

From calculus, we know that

$$\frac{\partial}{\partial x} x^k = k \cdot x^{k-1}$$

Multiplying this by x so that the exponent is still k gives

$$x \frac{\partial}{\partial x} x^k = k \cdot x^k$$

Thus, in the sum, the $x^k \cdot k$ part can be expressed as being obtained by a differentiation:

$$\ldots = \sum_{k=0}^{n} \binom{n}{k} x \frac{\partial}{\partial x} x^k q^{n-k}$$

Of course the sum of derivatives is the derivative of the sum, so this is

$$x \frac{\partial}{\partial x} \sum_{k=0}^{n} \binom{n}{k} x^k q^{n-k}$$

Ah! Now the sum is recognizable as being the binomial expansion of $(x + q)^n$. Great! So the whole thing is

$$x\frac{\partial}{\partial x}(x + q)^n = xn(x + q)^{n-1}$$

Substituting back p for x gives

$$EX = pn(p + q)^{n-1} = pn \cdot 1^{n-1} = pn$$

Remark: Yes, this answer is also possibly fairly intuitive, so it is not surprising. Also, X is the sum of the random variables X_i where X_i tells how many 1's occur at the ith position in the sequence. The expected value of each X_i is very easy to compute:

$$EX_i = p \cdot 1 + q \cdot 0 = p$$

and the expected value of a sum is the sum of expected values, so we can more simply compute

$$EX = E(X_1 + \cdots + x_n) = EX_1 + \cdots + EX_n = \underbrace{p + \cdots + p}_{n} = pn$$

This approach is simpler *for this particular example*. But the generating-function method illustrated is very important to appreciate!

Exercises

5.1.01 Using the fact that

$$x^n + \binom{n}{1}x^{n-1}y + \binom{n}{2}x^{n-2}y^2 + \cdots + \binom{n}{n-1}xy^{n-1} + y^n = (x + y)^n$$

evaluate the sum

$$1 \cdot \binom{n}{1} + 2 \cdot \binom{n}{2} + 3 \cdot \binom{n}{3} + \cdots + (n-1) \cdot \binom{n}{n-1} + n$$

5.1.02 Evaluate the sum

$$1^2 \cdot \binom{n}{1} + 2^2 \cdot \binom{n}{2} + 3^2 \cdot \binom{n}{3} + \cdots + (n-1)^2 \cdot \binom{n}{n-1} + n^2$$

5.1.03 Evaluate the sum

$$1^2 \cdot \binom{n}{1} + 2^2 \cdot \binom{n}{2} + 3^2 \cdot \binom{n}{3} + \cdots + (n-1)^2 \cdot \binom{n}{n-1} + n^2$$

5.1.04 Using the fact that for $|x| < 1$ $1 + x + x^2 + x^3 + \cdots = \frac{1}{1-x}$, sum the series $x + 2x^2 + 3x^3 + 4x^4 + \cdots$.

5.1.05 Sum the series $x + 2^2 x^2 + 3^2 x^3 + 4^2 x^4 + \cdots$.

5.1.06 Sum the series $x + 2^3 x^2 + 3^3 x^3 + 4^3 x^4 + \cdots$.

5.1.07 Consider a coin which has probability p of heads. Let X be the random variable which tells how long we wait before 2 heads in a row come up. What is the expected value of X?

5.2 Variance, Standard Deviation

Let X be the random variable on the probability space Ω consisting of all ordered n-tuples of 0's and 1's, and whose value on each n-tuple is the number of 1's in that n-tuple. Suppose that 1's occur with probability p and 0's occur with probability q (with $p + q = 1$, of course), and that the 0's and 1's at different positions in the sequence are independent. We just saw that the expected value of X is the intuitively reasonable number pn. **What is the variance of X?**

Recall that for a random variable X with expected value (also called *mean*) μ, the variance σ is defined by

$$\text{variance}(X) = \sigma^2(X) = E(\,(X - \mu)^2\,)$$

(Yes, there is indeed an exponent 2 on that σ.) That is, σ^2 is the expected value of the random variable $(X - \mu)^2$. The quantity σ itself is the **standard deviation**.

For computing, this can be simplified a little by using basic properties of expected values, keeping in mind that μ is just a number:

$$\sigma^2 = E(\,(X-\mu)^2\,) = E(X^2 - 2\mu X + \mu^2) = E(X^2) - 2\mu\,E(X) + \mu^2$$

$$= E(X^2) - 2\mu \cdot \mu + \mu^2 = E(X^2) - \mu^2$$

This is true for any random variable X, since we didn't use any properties of the specific example we're actually interested in.

So to compute the variance of the X here the thing we need to compute is $E(X^2)$:

$$E(X^2) = \sum_{k=0}^{n} P(X = k) \cdot k^2$$

As usual, there are $\binom{n}{k}$ ways to have exactly k 1's, and each way occurs with probability $p^k q^{n-k}$. Thus,

$$E(X^2) = \sum_{k=0}^{n} \binom{n}{k} p^k q^{n-k} \cdot k^2$$

This is very similar to the expression that occurred above in computing the expected value, but now we have k^2 instead of k. But of course we might *repeat* the trick we used above, and see what happens: since

$$x \frac{\partial}{\partial x} x^k = k x^k$$

then by repeating it we have

$$x \frac{\partial}{\partial x} \cdot x \frac{\partial}{\partial x} x^k = k^2 x^k$$

Thus, in the expression for $E(X^2)$, replace p by x, and compute

$$\sum_{k=0}^{n} \binom{n}{k} x^k q^{n-k} \cdot k^2 = \sum_{k=0}^{n} \binom{n}{k} x \frac{\partial}{\partial x} \cdot x \frac{\partial}{\partial x} x^k q^{n-k}$$

$$= x \frac{\partial}{\partial x} \cdot x \frac{\partial}{\partial x} \sum_{k=0}^{n} \binom{n}{k} x^k q^{n-k} = x \frac{\partial}{\partial x} \cdot x \frac{\partial}{\partial x} (x+q)^n$$

since after getting the k^2 out from inside the sum we can recognize the binomial expansion. Taking derivatives gives

$$x \frac{\partial}{\partial x} \cdot x \frac{\partial}{\partial x} (x+q)^n = x \frac{\partial}{\partial x} (x \cdot n(x+q)^{n-1}) = x(1 \cdot n(x+q)^{n-1} + x \cdot n(n-1)(x+q)^{n-2})$$

Substituting back p for x, and using $p + q = 1$, gives

$$E(X^2) = p(1 \cdot n(p+q)^{n-1} + p \cdot n(n-1)(p+q)^{n-2}) = p(n + p \cdot n(n-1))$$

So then

$$\sigma^2 = E(X^2) - \mu^2 = p(n + p \cdot n(n-1)) - (pn)^2 = pn + p^2 n^2 - p^2 n - p^2 n^2 = p(1-p)n$$

That is, the **standard deviation** σ is

$$\sigma = \sqrt{p(1-p)n} = \sqrt{\text{variance}}$$

Exercises

5.2.01 Compute the variance of the random variable which tells the sum of the result of the roll of one fair die.

5.2.02 Compute the variance of the random variable which tells the sum of the result of the roll of two fair dice.

5.2.03 Compute the variance of the random variable which tells the sum of the result of the roll of three fair dice.

5.2.04 (*) Compute the variance of the random variable which tells the sum of the result of the roll of n fair dice.

5.2.05 Consider a coin which has probability p of heads. Let X be the random variable which tells how long before 2 heads in a row come up. What is the variance of X?

5.3 Chebycheff's Inequality

The *idea* of what the 'variance' $\sigma^2(X)$ of a random variable X means is that it tells roughly how much the random variable tends to deviate from its expected value. Chebycheff's inequality gives this some substance, and is a precursor to a weak version of a **Law of Large Numbers**.

> **Theorem.** Let X be a random variable with expected value μ and variance σ^2. Let $t > 1$. Then $P(|X - \mu| \geq t \cdot \sigma) \leq \frac{1}{t^2}$.

Proof: Using just the definition of σ^2,

$$\sigma^2 = E(|X - \mu|^2) = \sum_x P(X = x) \cdot (x - \mu)^2 \geq \sum_{x|x-\mu|\geq t\sigma} P(X = x) \cdot (x - \mu)^2$$

since summing non-negative quantities over a possibly smaller index set cannot increase the value of the sum. Then this is

$$\sum_{x:|x-\mu|\geq t\sigma} P(X = x) \cdot (x - \mu)^2 \geq \sum_{x:|x-\mu|\geq t\sigma} P(X = x) \cdot (t\sigma)^2$$

since on the set of real numbers x where $|x - \mu| \geq t\sigma$ replacing the expression $(x - \mu)^2$ by $(t\sigma)^2$ certainly does not increase the sum. And then this is

$$\sum_{x:|x-\mu|\geq t\sigma} P(X = x) \cdot (t\sigma)^2 = (t\sigma)^2 \sum_{x:|x-\mu|\geq t\sigma} P(X = x)$$

since now the constant $t\sigma$ does not depend on the index x, and this gives

$$\sigma^2 = (t\sigma)^2 P(|X - \mu| \geq t\sigma)$$

Rearranging and cancelling the σ^2 gives $\frac{1}{t^2} \geq P(|X - \mu| \geq t\sigma)$ as claimed.   ♣

Exercises

5.3.01 Gracefully estimate the probability that in 100 flips of a fair coin the number of heads will be at least 40 and no more than 60.

5.3.02 Gracefully estimate the probability that in 1000 flips of a fair coin the number of heads will be at least 900 and no more than 1100.

5.3.03 Gracefully estimate the probability that in 10,000 flips of a fair coin the number of heads will be at least 9000 and no more than 11,000.

5.3.04 With a coin that has probability only 1/10 of coming up heads, show that the probability is less than 1/9 that in 100 flips the number of heads will be more than 20.

5.3.05 With a coin that has probability only 1/10 of coming up heads, show that the probability is less than 1/900 that in 10,000 flips the number of heads will be less than 2000.

5.4 Law of Large Numbers

By using Chebycheff's inequality we can prove a special case of what is called the **(Weak) Law of Large Numbers**, at least in the special case of repeated trials with a probability space $\{H, T\}$, where $P(H) = p$, $P(T) = 1 - p$.

It is too naive to expect to get the expected value as the value of a random variable, since the expected value is only an average. But we certainly imagine that most of the values we get are *close* to the expected value, in a quantifiable way, which turns out to depend upon the variance. There are many ways of formulating such results, and it is important also to realize that such results hold for a much wider variety of random variables than we mention here, but we have chosen a simple instance to avoid some needlessly technical details.

> **Theorem.** Let X be the random variable which tells how many H's occur out of n trials in a probability space $\Omega = \{H, T\}$, with $P(H) = p$. Let ε be a small positive number. Then
>
> $$\lim_{n \to \infty} P(|X - p \cdot n| > \varepsilon \cdot n) = 0$$
>
> where we know that the expected value of X is $p \cdot n$.

Proof: We will obtain this result by making a reasonable choice of the parameter in the assertion of Chebycheff's inequality. Let μ be the expected value of X and let σ be the standard deviation of X. We know from computations above that $\mu = p \cdot n$ and $\sigma = \sqrt{p(1-p)} \cdot \sqrt{n}$. Then Chebycheff's inequality asserts in general that $P(|X - \mu| > t\sigma) < \frac{1}{t^2}$, which here gives

$$P(|X - p \cdot n| > t \cdot \sqrt{p(1-p)} \cdot \sqrt{n}) < \frac{1}{t^2}$$

Now take

$$t = \frac{\varepsilon}{\sqrt{p(1-p)}} \cdot \sqrt{n}$$

to obtain

$$P(|X - p \cdot n| > \varepsilon \cdot n) < \frac{\sqrt{p(1-p)}}{n}$$

The right-hand side certainly goes to 0 as n goes to infinity, so we're done.   ♣

Exercises

5.4.01 How many times must one flip a fair coin so that the probability is at least 9/10 that

$$\frac{1}{2} \leq \frac{\text{number of heads}}{\text{number of tails}} \leq 2 \ ?$$

5.4.02 How many times must one roll a pair of fair dice so that the probability is at least 3/4 that a 7 comes up?

5.4.03 How many times must one roll a pair of fair dice so that the probability is at least 9/10 that a 12 comes up?

5.4.04 How many times must one roll a pair of fair dice so that the probability is at least 9/10 that a 7 comes up?

6

Modern Symmetric Ciphers

6.1 Design Goals

Having seen some examples of ciphers, and how they fail, we can formulate a little more clearly the design goals for a *successful* cipher. First let's review the examples we've seen so far.

A **simple substitution cipher** or **simple permutation cipher** has a key which is a **permutation** f of the alphabet $\{a, b, c, \ldots, z\}$ (or whatever alphabet is being used), and has encryption step

$$E_f(x_0, x_1, x_2, \ldots) = (f(x_0),\ f(x_1),\ f(x_2),\ \ldots)$$

This is also called a **monoalphabetic** substitution cipher to emphasize that the same change is made to a character no matter where it occurs in the plaintext.

Recall that a permutation f of the set $\{a, b, c, \ldots, z\}$ is simply a *bijective* function

$$f : \{a, b, c, d, \ldots, y, z\} \to \{a, b, c, d, \ldots, y, z\}$$

Thus, we view f as 'mixing up' the alphabet. The *same* substitution f is used at every step. The decryption step uses the inverse function f^{-1} in place of f:

$$D_f = E_{f^{-1}}$$

so that

$$D_f(x_0, x_1, x_2, \ldots) = (f^{-1}(x_0),\ f^{-1}(x_1),\ f^{-1}(x_2),\ \ldots)$$

Both the *shift* and *affine* ciphers are examples of simple substitution ciphers. 'Cryptograms' are the most general version of this. In the case of shift and affine ciphers the permutation is of a very restricted sort, described in terms of arithmetic modulo 26, and so on.

By using single-letter frequencies and other low-level information about the structure of English (or whatever natural language is being used), ciphertext-only attacks on monoalphabetic substitution ciphers succeed. So these are hopelessly bad.

Increasing in complexity, a **polyalphabetic substitution cipher** uses possibly different substitutions at different steps, according to some prescription. One general class of prescription gives rise to a **periodic polyalphabetic substitution cipher**: here the key is an m-tuple $(f_0, f_1, \ldots, f_{m-1})$ of substitutions f_i (where m is also part of the key), and the encryption is

$$E_f(x_0, x_1, x_2, \ldots) = (f_0(x_0),\ f_1(x_1), \ldots, f_{i \% m}(x_i), \ldots)$$

That is,

$$f_{i \% m}$$

(with the *index* reduced modulo m) is used to encrypt the ith character of the plaintext. The decryption is

$$E_f(x_0, x_1, x_2, \ldots) = (f_0^{-1}(x_0),\ f_1^{-1}(x_1), \ldots, f_{i \% m}^{-1}(x_i), \ldots)$$

So the encryption of the ith character of plaintext only depends upon what that character is, and on what i is *modulo m*. The **period** is the length m at which the encryption of the individual characters repeats itself. The Vigenere cipher is of this sort, being the periodic polyalphabetic version of the shift cipher.

We saw that *periodic* polyalphabetic substitution ciphers (such as Vigenere) fail, essentially because an attacker can isolate the *subsequences* of ciphertext characters that are all encrypted by the same *monoalphabetic* cipher.

By contrast, using a different mechanism, a **(simple) transposition cipher** does not alter the individual *characters*, but rather changes their *positions* in the message. Many of the more picturesque classical examples of ciphers that involved viewing messages through grilles, or writing messages on paper tapes wound around conical cylinders, are of this sort. The general abstract description is as follows. Choose a positive integer *block size* m, and let f be a bijective function from $\{0, 1, \ldots, n-1\}$ to itself (a *permutation* of the latter set). The m and f are the key. Then to encode a plaintext

$$x = (x_0, x_1, \ldots)$$

break it into pieces of length exactly m:

$$(x_0, \ldots, x_{m-1})$$

$$(x_m, \ldots, x_{2m-1})$$

$$(x_{2m}, \ldots, x_{3m-1})$$

$$\ldots$$

and encrypt each **block** $(x_{km}, \ldots, x_{km+m-1})$ as follows. For simplicity of notation, for a fixed block $(x_{km}, \ldots, x_{km+m-1})$ write

$$z = (z_0, \ldots, z_{m-1}) = (x_{km}, \ldots, x_{km+m-1})$$

Then

$$E_{m,f}(z) = (z_{f(0)}, z_{f(1)}, z_{f(2)}, \ldots, z_{f(m-1)})$$

Yes, this is described by *permuting the indices*. This has the effect of moving around the characters within the block, without altering them individually (apart from their location). The popular puzzles called **anagrams** are encryptions by transposition ciphers. As with cryptograms, the fact that small anagrams are solved by many people as recreation is a negative indicator about their security.

As with substitution ciphers, a complication in implementing transposition ciphers is in the *description* of the permutation that moves plaintext characters around, and in the description of how this should change depending upon the key. The charming picturesque classical tricks do not scale up very well, since most often once the key mechanism is discovered there's no replacement in sight: the key material consists of a single monolithic secret for which there is no feasible replacement mechanism.

And we saw that *double anagramming* is an effective attack on simple transposition ciphers.

The *key* to either a substitution or transposition cipher is a *permutation*. For substitution ciphers the *alphabet* itself is permuted, so that each character of the message is changed, while for transposition ciphers the *positions* of characters within the message are permuted, while the each character itself is unchanged.

A cipher such as a transposition cipher which acts on *blocks* of plaintext is (reasonably enough) called a **block cipher**, in contrast to **stream ciphers** which by definition more-or-less act on each plaintext character as it comes along. Thus, substitution ciphers can reasonably be called **stream ciphers** (of the simplest sort), because the encryption of each character does not depend upon the *plaintext* characters before or after it. *Periodicity* in a substitution cipher, such as exhibited by the Vigenere cipher, proves to be a fatal weakness.

However, the supposed distinction between block and stream ciphers is not clear-cut, and from a slightly abstract viewpoint hardly exists. After all, any block cipher can be thought of as a periodic stream cipher, with period equal to the block size.

It must be noted that while many classical ciphers were *either* substitution *or* transposition ciphers, contemporary ciphers are in effect combinations of the two. And the attempted distinction between block and stream ciphers is likewise a bit futile, since in reality many ciphers treat the plaintext as a sequence or stream of blocks, while the encryption of each block can depend upon its position in the stream of blocks.

In the context of stream ciphers, perhaps thinking of the plaintext stream as broken into blocks, the encryption of a block may or may not depend upon previous parts of the *plaintext*. If the encryption of each block is *independent* of the previous *plaintext*, the cipher is **synchronous** (apparently also called **key auto-key** in the military). If the encryption of a block *does* depend on the previous plaintext, then the cipher is **asynchronous**.

In the late 1940s Claude Shannon laid out some good design criteria for (symmetric) ciphers. First, he repeated Kerckhoff's principle that the only secret should be the key, not the larger mechanism of the cipher. Second, Shannon emphasized that a good cipher will incorporate both *confusion* and *diffusion*. Not only does this sound catchy, it also pinpoints the weaknesses in the classical ciphers. By **confusion** we mean that a cipher should hide *local* patterns in language from an attacker. By *diffusion* we mean that the cipher should mix around different parts of the plaintext, so that nothing is left in its original position. A rough paraphrase of these requirements is that both *small-scale* and *large-scale* structure should be destroyed.

For example, a monoalphabetic substitution cipher (cryptogram) fails both criteria. Local features such as doubled letters (like 'ee') will still appear as double letters. And single-letter frequencies will still be revealing.

A polyalphabetic substitution cipher such as Vigenere is more effective at *confusion* (concealing local features of language) because it does not encrypt the same character the same way every time. But Vigenere fails at *diffusion*, because it does not move anything. In particular, this (together with the periodic-ness of the substitution) allows Friedman's attack.

The cute classical transposition ciphers excel at *diffusion* by design, because exactly what they do is move things around. And if this could be done in an ideal way, it would certainly obliterate small-scale features of language too, thus achieving *confusion*. But, as commented above, it is not so easy to describe how the mixing should change depending upon the key.

But by now it is clear that a good cipher should combine both substitution and transposition to achieve Shannon's goals of *confusion* and *diffusion*. Most contemporary (symmetric) ciphers repeat cycles of one or the other: a substitution, then a transposition, then a substitution, then a transposition, and so on. And a substantial part of the specifics should depend upon the key.

Further, when we encode characters as *numbers* (whether modulo 26 or as strings of 0's and 1's), then we open up many more possibilities for substitutions and transpositions.

Exercises

6.1.01 (*) Is there any good argument *against* Kerckhoff's and Shannon's principle that only the key should be secret, not the larger mechanism of a cipher?

6.1.02 (*) Why is resistance to known and adaptive plaintext attacks really necessary, rather than mere resistance to ciphertext-only attacks?

6.1.03 (*) Since one-time pads are potentially perfectly secure, why aren't they used as the default general-purpose cipher?

6.2 Data Encryption Standard

The **Data Encryption Standard**, DES, is more than 20 years old, and due to its too-small keyspace is now essentially obsolete. After years of general speculation about the cost and speed of a DES-cracking machine, the Electronic Frontier Foundation spent $100,000 in 1998 and built one that could get a key in about two days. Nevertheless, DES did survive for more than 20 years without any discovery of hidden or unsuspected weaknesses. And it seems that **triple DES** (triple encryption with DES) is still secure. Also, DES is reasonably easy to implement in either hardware or software. Altogether, DES has fared better than many later symmetric ciphers in terms of resistance to new ideas of cryptanalytic attacks. For that matter, DES is built into so many pieces of software that it will be in use for many years to come whether or not we declare it 'obsolete'. Even if it is 'obsolete' by a high standard, in some situations it may provide sufficient security even in the face of increased computing speed.

As you would expect, DES is more complicated than classical ciphers. Part of the reason for taking the trouble to describe DES here is to make clear that it's not easy to understand. In particular, rather than trying to focus on the details, it is probably better to simply see how many details there *are*.

DES uses a 64-bit key, of which 8 bits are error-check bits, so really it has a 56-bit key. (Every eigth bit is parity-check.) The **Advanced Encryption Standard** (AES), currently under competition, will have 128-bit, 192-bit, and 256-bit keys. DES (a *block cipher*), encrypts blocks of 64 bits of plaintext at a time. The AES will encrypt blocks of 128 bits.

There has always been political turmoil surrounding DES. A team at IBM designed its predecessor **Lucifer** in early 1970, and NSA finalized its design. NSA reduced the key size and modified some of the so-called *S-boxes*. After 20 years of looking for a built-in weakness without finding any, many people have concluded that perhaps NSA did not build in a weakness. The key size was considered suspiciously small all along, but that was not a secret.

All that we'll do here is look at a *description* of DES. The subtler design specifications need a lot of computer time for verification. Apart from brute-force attacks, two 'modern' cryptanalytic attacks have been invented: **differential cryptanalysis** and **linear cryptanalysis**. Very roughly, differential cryptanalysis makes a systematic study of how small changes in plaintext affect the ciphertext. Linear cryptanalysis tries to 'approximate' the effect of encryption by a *linear* function. In either case, any detectable pattern allows the attacker some sort of increased efficiency in hunting for the key. A trick which reduces the **workload** by a factor of 10^3 helps a little, while an idea which reduces the workload by a factor of 10^9 might be decisive.

A DES encryption consists of 16 **rounds**, meaning repetitions of a simpler process. Each round is **Feistel network**, which we'll describe in detail shortly. People have shown that using various smaller numbers of rounds results in ciphers ('12-round DES', for example) that are significantly more vulnerable than full DES.

The basic idea of a **Feistel network** is simple, and gives a function which is *guaranteed to be invertible* and *to be its own inverse*. Fix a positive integer n, which would be 32 in the case of DES. Given a string of $2n$ bits, group them in two parts, the *left* and *right* halves, L and R. We can view L and R as **vectors** of length n with entries *reduced mod 2*. Let f be *any* function whatsoever that accepts as inputs n bits and produces an output of n bits. Then the corresponding Feistel network F_f takes two $2n$-bit pieces L and R as inputs, and produces $2n$ bits of output by

$$F_f(L, R) = (L \oplus f(R), R)$$

where the $\oplus$ as used here means vector (component-wise) addition and then reduction modulo 2. (This is the same as bit-wise XOR, if you know what that means.) For some reason it is traditional to write this addition as $\oplus$, although we'll only follow that tradition for this little chapter.

For example, with $n = 5$ this vector addition mod 2 is

$$(1, 1, 1, 0, 0) \oplus (1, 0, 1, 1, 1) = (1 + 1, 1 + 0, 1 + 1, 0 + 1, 0 + 1) \% 2$$

$$= (2, 1, 2, 1, 1) \% 2 = (0, 1, 0, 1, 1)$$

The key property of a Feistel network is that if you do it twice with the same f, then you come back to the same thing:

$$F_f(F_f(L, R)) = F_f(L \oplus f(R), R) = (L \oplus f(R) \oplus f(R), R) = (L, R)$$

since for any vector v

$$v \oplus v = (0, 0, 0, \dots)$$

when we're working modulo 2. After all, both $0 + 0 = 0$ and $1 + 1 = 0$.

So, however wacky the function f is, we don't have to worry about invertibility or about *finding* the inverse. This is good, since we can put all our energy into making choices which create lots of **confusion and diffusion**. We'd want to repeat this process with some simple mixing in-between, using some sort of tricky functions f depending on a key. This is what DES does.

Each **round** of DES is an enhanced version of the Feistel network we just described, with a specific choice of the function f, depending on the key.

At the very outset, the 64-bit key has every eighth bit removed, and is rearranged according to the following formula, called the **key permutation**:

57	49	41	33	25	17	9	1	58	50	42	34	26	18
10	2	59	51	43	35	27	19	11	3	60	52	44	36
63	55	47	39	31	23	15	7	62	54	46	38	30	22
14	6	61	53	45	37	29	21	13	5	28	20	12	4

This should be read in order, starting at the top left, reading left-to-right, down the page. Note that there is some pattern to the numbers: in each row they decrease by 8 each time, and then wrap around if they reach 0. The meaning of the notation is that the 57th bit of the key goes to the first bit of the rearrangement (since 57 is the first number listed), the 49th bit of the key goes to the second bit of the rearrangement (since 49 is the second number listed), the 41st bit of the key goes to the third bit of the rearrangement (since 41 is the third number listed), and so on. The pattern is simple.

An important part of the game is that each round uses a different 48-bit **subkey** of the 56-bit key. (We dropped every eighth bit from the original 64-bit key.) The description of the details of how to use the key is called **key scheduling**. First, for each round of DES, the key is broken into two 28-bit halves, each of which is shifted left (with wrap-around) by either 1 or 2 bits, depending upon which round we're in. The prescription for the number of bits to shift is

1	2	3	4	5	6	7	8	9	10	11	12	13	14	15	16
1	1	2	2	2	2	2	2	1	2	2	2	2	2	2	1

(Don't ask me why!) Then the *shifted* batch of 56 bits is mapped to 48 bits by what is called a **compression permutation**, meaning that it's not invertible. The formula is the same for each round's **compression permutation**:

14	17	11	24	1	5	3	28	15	6	21	10
23	19	12	4	26	8	16	7	27	20	13	2
41	52	31	37	47	55	30	40	51	45	33	48
44	49	39	56	34	53	46	42	50	36	29	32

That is, the 14th bit goes to the first position (because 14 is the first number), the 17th bit goes to the second position (because 17 is the second number listed), etc. *This* finally is really mysterious-looking. So the result of the initial key permutation, together with the varying shifts by 1 or 2 bits, followed by the compression permutation, is what produces the 48-bit **subkey** for each of the 16 rounds. We'll tell how to *use* it shortly.

As indicated above, each round of DES manipulates halves of the text, in a manner that depends on the key (and on which round we're in). Let L_i be the left half in the ith round, and let R_i be the right half in the ith round. Then the formula to get from one round to the next is of the form

$$(L_i, R_i) = (R_{i-1}, L_{i-1} \oplus f(R_{i-1}))$$

where f also depends on the ith subkey. Note that in addition to the Feistel trick we *interchange* halves of the text, so that both halves will get obscured. We must describe the function f and how it depends on the ith subkey.

For each round, first the right half R_{i-1} has applied to it a fixed (rather simple) **expansion permutation** or **E-box**, which accepts 32-bit inputs and creates a 48-bit output, given by the formula (using the same system as above)

32	1	2	3	4	5	4	5	6	7	8	9	8	9	10	11
12	13	12	13	14	15	16	17	16	17	18	19	20	21	20	21
22	23	24	25	24	25	26	27	28	29	28	29	30	31	32	1

Note that the pattern is *not* very complicated. But by allowing one bit of the text to affect more than one bit of the expanded version, we get an **avalanche effect**, meaning that changes in relatively few bits of the original plaintext should cause many bits of the ciphertext to change: as we go through the 16 rounds of DES, changing a single bit should cause more and more bits to change. Hence the name.

At each round, the 48-bit output from the E-box is XOR'd (added mod 2) to the 48-bit subkey (which depends on what round we're in).

The most serious part of DES, and also the most mysterious, from which it gets its security, is the application of the **substitution boxes**, or **S-boxes** to the 48-bit XOR'd subkey with the 48-bit output from the E-box. There are 8 S-boxes, each of which takes a 6-bit input and produces a 4-bit output. The 48 bits are broken into 8 pieces of 6 bits each and fed to the 8 S-boxes. (The first 6 bits are acted upon by the first S-box, the second by the second, etc.) The outputs are stuck back together again to give a 32-bit total output. Each of the 8 S-boxes can be described by a table with 4 rows and 6 columns. Each entry in the table is a 4-bit number, meaning in the range 0–15, which (written in binary) will be the output of the S-box. The 6-bit input to the S-box specifies the row and column as follows. Let the 6 bits be $b_1, b_2, \ldots, b_5, b_6$. Then

$$\text{row} = 2 \cdot b_1 + b_6$$

$$\text{column} = 8 \cdot b_2 + 4 \cdot b_3 + 2 \cdot b_4 + b_5$$

where the indexing of rows and columns starts at the upper left and begins with 0, not with 1. For example, the 6 bits 111010 would specify row 10 (in binary, from the first and sixth bits), and column 1101 (in binary, from the middle 4 bits). That is, we'd look in the 2nd row and 13th column, starting with 0 in both cases.

The S-boxes are, from first to eighth:

14	4	13	1	2	15	11	8	3	10	6	12	5	9	0	7
0	15	7	4	14	2	13	1	10	6	12	11	9	5	3	8
4	1	14	8	13	6	2	11	15	12	9	7	3	10	5	0
15	12	8	2	4	9	1	7	5	11	3	14	10	0	6	13

```
15  1  8 14  6 11  3  4  9  7  2 13 12  0  5 10
 3 13  4  7 15  2  8 14 12  0  1 10  6  9 11  5
 0 14  7 11 10  4 13  1  5  8 12  6  9  3  2 15
13  8 10  1  3 15  4  2 11  6  7 12  0  5 14  9
```

```
10  0  9 14  6  3 15  5  1 13 12  7 11  4  2  8
13  7  0  9  3  4  6 10  2  8  5 14 12 11 15  1
13  6  4  9  8 15  3  0 11  1  2 12  5 10 14  7
 1 10 13  0  6  9  8  7  4 15 14  3 11  5  2 12
```

```
 7 13 14  3  0  6  9 10  1  2  8  5 11 12  4 15
13  8 11  5  6 15  0  3  4  7  2 12  1 10 14  9
10  6  9  0 12 11  7 13 15  1  3 14  5  2  8  4
 3 15  0  6 10  1 13  8  9  4  5 11 12  7  2 14
```

```
 2 12  4  1  7 10 11  6  8  5  3 15 13  0 14  9
14 11  2 12  4  7 13  1  5  0 15 10  3  9  8  6
 4  2  1 11 10 13  7  8 15  9 12  5  6  3  0 14
11  8 12  7  1 14  2 13  6 15  0  9 10  4  5  3
```

```
12  1 10 15  9  2  6  8  0 13  3  4 14  7  5 11
10 15  4  2  7 12  9  5  6  1 13 14  0 11  3  8
 9 14 15  5  2  8 12  3  7  0  4 10  1 13 11  6
 4  3  2 12  9  5 15 10 11 14  1  7  6  0  8 13
```

```
 4 11  2 14 15  0  8 13  3 12  9  7  5 10  6  1
13  0 11  7  4  9  1 10 14  3  5 12  2 15  8  6
 1  4 11 13 12  3  7 14 10 15  6  8  0  5  9  2
 6 11 13  8  1  4 10  7  9  5  0 15 14  2  3 12
```

```
13  2  8  4  6 15 11  1 10  9  3 14  5  0 12  7
 1 15 13  8 10  3  7  4 12  5  6 11  0 14  9  2
 7 11  4  1  9 12 14  2  0  6 10 13 15  3  5  8
 2  1 14  7  4 10  8 13 15 12  9  0  3  5  6 11
```

In each round the 32-bit output of the S-boxes is first fed into the **P-box**, which performs a genuine permutation according to the formula

$$
\begin{array}{cccccccccccccccc}
16 & 7 & 20 & 21 & 29 & 12 & 28 & 17 & 1 & 15 & 23 & 26 & 5 & 18 & 31 & 10 \\
2 & 8 & 24 & 14 & 32 & 27 & 3 & 9 & 19 & 13 & 30 & 6 & 22 & 11 & 4 & 25
\end{array}
$$

(using the same interpretation of the notation as above).

After all 16 rounds, **not exchanging left and right halves after the last (16th) round**, there is also the **final permutation** which is applied to the text. This has formula (interpreted as all the others above except the S-box descriptions)

$$
\begin{array}{cccccccccccccccc}
40 & 8 & 48 & 16 & 56 & 24 & 64 & 32 & 39 & 7 & 47 & 15 & 55 & 23 & 63 & 31 \\
38 & 6 & 46 & 14 & 54 & 22 & 62 & 30 & 37 & 5 & 45 & 13 & 53 & 21 & 61 & 29 \\
36 & 4 & 44 & 12 & 52 & 20 & 60 & 28 & 35 & 3 & 43 & 11 & 51 & 19 & 59 & 27 \\
34 & 2 & 42 & 10 & 50 & 18 & 58 & 26 & 33 & 1 & 41 & 9 & 49 & 17 & 57 & 25
\end{array}
$$

The pattern in columns is evident. The output from this is the ciphertext.

Happily, because of the Feistel network property, and by the relatively simple choice of the initial and final permutation, exactly the same process (with the same key) **decrypts**.

Apparently the S-boxes were optimized to resist *differential cryptanalysis*. This came to light in the public domain in 1990 with the work of Bihan and Shamir. Any similar sort of cipher with *fixed S-boxes* evidently has a certain weakness that can be exploited by adaptive plaintext attacks.

A sort of attack that was evidently not directly anticipated was *linear cryptanalysis*, which appeared in public in about 1993 in work of Mitsuru Matsui. Nevertheless, DES resists this reasonably well.

In the end, it seems that no attack is significantly better than an adroit brute-force key search. This is a success.

Remark: The description above only deals with encryption of a single block. When larger quantities of information are encrypted, it would be *a mistake* to encrypt each block of data individually. If that were done with large amounts of data, an adversary could mount a **code-book attack**, meaning that a dictionary of the encrypted blocks could be built up. From frequencies, cribs, and known ciphertext, inferences could be made about the plaintext, without having any idea of the key. To avoid this attack, encryption should be done with some form of **block chaining**, meaning that each block affects the encryption of the next, as well, thwarting a code-book attack.

Remark: For the same reason, it is unwise to use the same DES key for many sessions (messages), since a code-book could be built up. In fact, current usage is to use a 'new' key, called a **session key**, for each message. But then there is the obvious *key management* problem: how are all these session keys arranged? It is here that *public-key* methods are important in current usage: these methods such as Diffie–Hellman key exchange (discussed later) allow session keys to be set up securely and at low cost. It may be hard to imagine how this is accomplished, and indeed the fact that it is possible is the 'miraculous' aspect of public-key cryptography.

Exercises

6.2.01 (*) Since the S-boxes in DES have no variable controls, they are called *static*. What are the possible advantages and disadvantages of using static S-boxes in a cipher analogous to DES?

6.2.02 (*) What is the point of using so-called *expansion permutations* rather than 'ordinary' permutations?

6.2.03 (*) Program a nice graphical demonstration of the manner in which changes in single bits in input to DES propagate with successive rounds, eventually to affect many other bits in the output.

6.3 Advanced Encryption Standard

The **AES** is the **Advanced Encryption Standard**, which as of early 2000 is still in competition. This future standard is not yet specified completely, but in any case it will replace the DES (Data Encryption Standard) in future usage, although of course DES (and other old symmetric ciphers) are built into so much old software that analysis of DES will remain relevant for some time.

The first round of the competition is over, and the AES round-2 finalists are

- MARS from IBM

- RC6 from RSA Laboratories

- Rijndael from Joan Daemen and Vincent Rijmen

- Serpent from Ross Anderson, Eli Biham, and Lars Knudsen

- Twofish from Bruce Schneier, John Kelsey, Doug Whiting, David Wagner, Chris Hall, and Niels Ferguson

Part of the specification for the new standard *is* clear: whatever else the AES turns out to be, the following are required. The AES should have a larger block size, 128 bits instead of the 64-bit blocks of DES. The AES should allow 128-bit, 192-bit, and 256-bit keys. It is also supposed to be faster than triple-DES (and hopefully faster than DES, too). The National Institute of Standards (NIST) also requires that any patent rights to a candidate cipher be given up if it is chosen as the new standard.

An interesting idea that is raised in some of the candidates is that of **dynamic S-boxes**, in contrast to DES, in which the S-boxes are *static* (unchanging). That is, the key material changes the parameters in the S-boxes to some degree. This has potential advantages, but also potential disadvantages. On one hand, if the S-boxes are dynamic, then attackers cannot analyze them in advance. On the other hand, the cipher designer cannot as easily systematically test dynamic S-boxes to make sure that they have desirable characteristics.

The issue of static versus dynamic S-boxes raises another issue, that of the analyzability of S-boxes. It appears that the primary evidence for the goodness of the S-boxes in DES is simply that they've withstood decades of experimental analysis. On the other hand, it might be better to have S-boxes with *provable* properties, rather than only experimentally and statistically verifiable ones. But it is not clear whether or how this could be achieved.

Supposedly the new standard will be chosen from among the round-2 finalists sometime in mid-2000.

(Note: in late 2000 Rijndael was chosen as AES.)

Exercises

6.3.01 Give at least two different reasons why the AES should allow a range of key sizes.

6.3.02 Explain why security considerations would encourage a larger block size in AES than in DES.

6.3.03 Why do we need a *standard* cipher like AES, as opposed to a variety of ciphers available from different sources?

7

The Integers

7.1 Divisibility

We all have a pretty good intuition for the ordinary integers $\mathbf{Z}$ and the operations of addition, subtraction, multiplication, and division (*when possible*, since not every quotient x/y of integers is an integer itself). Here we establish some terminology especially regarding **divisibility**. The most naive **primality test** is included.

Noting that it is *not* always the case that we can divide one integer by another and obtain an *integer* answer, we give a definition: for two integers d, n, the integer d **divides** n (or is a **divisor** of n) if n/d is an integer. This is equivalent to there being another integer k so that $n = kd$. As equivalent terminology, we may also (equivalently) say that n is a **multiple** of d if d divides n.

It turns out that it is better always to use the criterion that d divides n if and only if there is an integer k so that n = k · d (rather than use the quotient n/d).

A divisor d of n is **proper** if it is not $\pm n$ nor ± 1. A multiple N of n is **proper** if it is neither $\pm n$. The notation

$$d|n$$

is read as 'd divides n'. Notice that *any* integer d divides 0, since $d \cdot 0 = 0$. On the other hand, the *only* integer 0 divides is itself.

A positive integer is **prime** if it has no proper divisors. That is, it has no divisors but itself, its negative, and ± 1. Usually we only pay attention to *positive* primes.

The following is the simplest but far from most efficient test for primality. It does have the virtue that if a number is not prime, then this process finds the smallest divisor $d > 1$ of the number.

Proposition. A positive integer n is prime if and only if it is not divisible by any of the integers d with $1 < d \leq \sqrt{n}$.

Proof: First, if $d|n$ and $2 < d \leq \sqrt{n}$, then the integer n/d satisfies

$$\sqrt{n} \leq \frac{n}{d} \leq \frac{n}{2}$$

(where we are looking at inequalities among *real* numbers!). Therefore, neither of the two factors d or n/d is ± 1 nor $\pm n$. So n is not prime.

On the other hand, suppose that n has a proper factorization $n = d \cdot e$, where e is the larger of the two factors. Then

$$d = \frac{n}{e} \leq \frac{n}{d}$$

gives $d^2 \leq n$, so $d \leq \sqrt{n}$. ♣

Two integers m, n are **relatively prime** or **coprime** if the only integers that divide both m and n are ± 1. Also we may say that m is **prime to** n if they are relatively prime. For a positive integer n, the number of positive integers less than or equal n and relatively prime to n is denoted by $\varphi(n)$. This is called the **Euler phi-function**. (The trial-and-error approach to computing $\varphi(n)$ is suboptimal. We'll get a better method later.)

Proposition.

- If $a|b$ and $b|c$, then $a|c$.

- If $d|x$ and $d|y$, then for any integers a, b we have $d|(ax + by)$.

Proof: If $a|b$, then there is an integer k so that $ak = b$. If $b|c$, then there is an integer ℓ so that $b\ell = c$. Then, replacing b by ak in the latter equation, we have

$$c = b\ell = (ak) \cdot \ell = a \cdot (k\ell)$$

so $a|c$.

If $d|x$, then there is an integer m so that $dm = x$. If $d|y$, then there is an integer n so that $dn = y$. Then

$$ax + by = a(md) + b(nd) = (am + bn) \cdot d$$

Thus, $ax + by$ is a multiple of d.   ♣

Proposition.   Let n and N be two integers, with $n|N$. Then for any integer x

$$(x \% N) \% n = x \% n$$

Proof: Write $N = kn$ for some integer k, and let $x = Q \cdot N + R$ with $0 \leq R < |N|$. This R is the reduction of x mod N. Further, let $R = q \cdot n + r$ with $0 \leq r < |n|$. This r is the reduction of R mod n. Then

$$x = QN + R = Q(kn) + qn + r = (Qk + q) \cdot n + r$$

So r is also the reduction of x modulo n.   ♣

An integer d is a **common divisor** of a family of integers $n_1, \ldots, n_m$ if d divides each one of the integers n_i. An integer N is a **common multiple** of a family of integers $n_1, \ldots, n_m$ if N is a multiple of each of the integers n_i.

Theorem.   Let m, n be integers, not both zero. Among all *common* divisors of m, n there is a unique one, call it d, so that for *every* other common divisor e of m, n we have $e|d$, and also $d > 0$. This divisor d is the *greatest common divisor* or **gcd** of m, n. The greatest common divisor of two integers m, n (not both zero) is the *least positive integer* of the form $xm + yn$ with $x, y \in \mathbf{Z}$.

Remark: The greatest common divisor of m, n is denoted $\gcd(m, n)$. Two integers are **relatively prime** or **coprime** if their greatest common divisor is 1. Also we may say that m is **prime to** n if they are relatively prime. The theorem gives a curious but important characterization of the *gcd*.

Proof: Let $D = x_0 m + y_0 n$ be the least positive integer expressible in the form $xm + yn$. First, we show that any divisor d of both m and n surely divides D. Write $m = m'd$ and $n = n'd$ with $m', n' \in \mathbf{Z}$. Then

$$D = x_0 m + y_0 n = x_0(m'd) + y_0(n'd) = (x_0 m' + y_0 n') \cdot d$$

which certainly presents D as a multiple of d.

On the other hand, apply the Division Algorithm to write $m = qD + r$ with $0 \leq r < D$. Then

$$0 \leq r = m - qD = m - q(x_0 m + y_0 n) = (1 - qx_0) \cdot m + (-y_0) \cdot n$$

That is, this r is also expressible as $x'm + y'n$ for integers x', y'. Since $r < D$, and since D is the smallest positive integer so expressible, it must be that $r = 0$. Therefore, $D|m$. Similarly, $D|n$.   ♣

A companion or 'dual' notion concerning *multiples* instead of *divisors* is:

Corollary.   Let m, n be integers, not both zero. Among all *common* multiples of m, n there is a unique one, call it N, so that for *every* other common multiple M of m, n we have $N|M$, and also $N > 0$. This multiple N is the *least common multiple* or **lcm** of m, n.

Remark: As we noted much earlier, if we *already have* the prime factorizations of two numbers m, n, then we can easily find the greatest common divisor and least common multiple: for each prime number p, the power of p dividing the *gcd* is the *minimum* of the powers of p dividing m and dividing n. Since this is true for each prime, we know the prime factorization of the greatest common divisor. For example,

$$gcd(2^3 \cdot 3^7 \cdot 5^2 \cdot 11^3, 2^1 \cdot 3^2 \cdot 5^3 \cdot 7^2 \cdot 11^2) = 2^1 \cdot 3^2 \cdot 5^2 \cdot 11^2$$

since 2^1 is the smaller of the two powers of 2 occurring, 3^2 is the smaller of the two powers of 3 occurring, 5^2 is the smaller of the two powers of 5 occurring, 7^0 is the smaller of the two powers of 7 occurring, and 11^2 is the smaller of the two powers of 11 occurring. The least common multiple is obtained by taking the *larger* of the two powers of each prime occurring in the factorizations of m, n.

However, we will soon see that this approach to computing greatest common divisors or least common multiples (by way of prime factorizations) is needlessly inefficient.

Exercises

7.1.01 Find all the divisors of 60. Why are you sure that you have them all?

7.1.02 Find all the divisors of 80. Why are you sure that you have them all?

7.1.03 Find all the divisors of 90. Why are you sure that you have them all?

7.1.04 Find all the divisors of 96. Why are you sure that you have them all?

7.1.05 For all the numbers under 100, either verify that they are prime, or factor them into primes.

7.1.06 Show directly from the definition of divisibility that if $d|m$, then $d|(-m)$.

7.1.07 Prove directly, from the very definition of divisibility, that if $d|x$ and $d|y$, then $d|(x - y)$ and $d|(x + y)$.

7.1.08 Observe that 1331 and 14641 cannot be prime, without computation.

7.1.09 Observe that 10510100501 cannot be prime, without computation.

7.1.10 Find the smallest divisor $d > 1$ of 10001.

7.1.11 Find the smallest divisor $d > 1$ of 12344321.

7.1.12 Find the least common multiple of 2, 4, 8, 16, 32, 64, 128.

7.1.13 Show that for any integer n if $d|n$ and $d|(n+2)$, then $d|2$.

7.1.14 Show that for any integer n the two integers n and $n+1$ are invariably relatively prime.

7.1.15 Show that for any integer n exactly one of $n, n+2, n+4$ is divisible by 3. In particular, except for $3, 5, 7$, there are no triples of primes occuring in the pattern $n, n+2, n+4$.

7.1.16 Show that for any integer n, the integers n and $n^2 + 1$ are relatively prime.

7.1.17 (*) Show that for any integer n the greatest common divisor of $16n^2 + 8n + 1$ and $16n^2 - 8n + 1$ is 1.

7.1.18 Prove that for any two integers m, n, the least common multiple $lcm(m, n)$ exists, and is given by the formula $lcm(m, n) = m \cdot n/gcd(m, n)$. (*Caution:* Do not accidentally assume that it exists to prove the formula.)

7.1.19 (*) Let m and n be relatively prime positive integers. Show that $\varphi(mn) = \varphi(m) \cdot \varphi(n)$, where $\varphi(N)$ is Euler's φ-function, counting the number of positive integers less than N and relatively prime to N.

7.1.20 (**) How likely is it that two *randomly chosen positive integers* will be relatively prime?

7.2 Unique Factorization

We now can prove the *unique factorization of integers into primes*. This very possibly may already seem 'intuitively true', since our experience with small integers bears witness to the truth of the assertion. And it is true, after all. But it is worth paying attention to *how* such a thing can be proven, especially since we will later want to *try* to prove unique factorization for fancier kinds of 'numbers', for which our intuition is not adequate. Since it is *not* true in general that 'all kinds' of numbers can be factored uniquely into primes, we must be alert.

While we're here, we also give a formula for Euler's *phi-function* $\varphi(n)$, whose definition is

$$\varphi(n) = \text{number of integers } i \text{ in the range } 0 \le i \le n \text{ relatively prime to } n$$

While this definition can be used directly to determine values of $\varphi(n)$ for small integers n, such a *brute force* approach is painfully inefficient, and the formula we'll give will be considerably better.

We also look at the most naive algorithm to obtain the **factorization** of an integer into primes. To obtain the list of all primes less than a given bound, we mention **Eratosthenes' sieve**, which is reasonably efficient for what it does.

Also, we can take this occasion to review some algebraic identities which occasionally provide shortcuts in the otherwise potentially laborious task of ascertaining whether a given number is prime, and/or factoring it into primes.

Theorem. *(Unique Factorization)* Every integer n can be written in an *essentially unique* way as $\pm$ a product of primes:

$$n = \pm\, p_1^{e_1}\, p_2^{e_2} \ldots p_m^{e_m}$$

with positive integer exponents and distinct primes $p_1, \ldots, p_n$.

Remark: The 'essentially unique' means that, of course, writing the product in a different order does not count as truly 'different'. The use of the word 'distinct' is typical of mathematics usage: it means 'no two of them are the same.' (This is a sharpening of the more colloquial use of 'different'.) The $\pm$ in the theorem is necessary, since n might be negative but prime numbers themselves are positive. And of course the factorizations of ± 1 includes no primes.

Corollary. Let N be a positive integer factored into primes as

$$n = p_1^{e_1}\, p_2^{e_2}\, \ldots\, p_n^{e_n}$$

where $p_1, \ldots, p_n$ are distinct primes, and the exponents e_i are all non-negative integers. Then the Euler phi-function of N has the value

$$\varphi(N) = (p_1 - 1)p_1^{e_1 - 1}\, (p_2 - 1)p_2^{e_2 - 1}\, \ldots\, (p_n - 1)p_n^{e_n - 1}$$

The proof of the theorem starts from the following key lemma, which may *feel* obvious, but is not.

Lemma. Let p be a prime number, and suppose that a and b are integers, with $p|(ab)$. Then either $p|a$ or $p|b$, or both.

Proof: *(of Lemma)* If $p|a$, we are done. So suppose that p does not divide a. Then the *greatest* common divisor $gcd(p, a)$ can't be p. But this greatest common divisor is also a divisor of p, and is positive. Since p is *prime*, the only positive divisor of p other than p itself is just 1. Therefore, $gcd(p, a) = 1$. We saw that there exist integers x, y so that $xp + ya = 1$.

Since $p|(ab)$, we can write $ab = hp$ for some integer h.

$$b = b \cdot 1 = b \cdot (xp + ya) = bxp + yba = (bx + yh) \cdot p$$

This shows that b is a multiple of p.   ♣

Corollary. *(of Lemma)* If a prime p divides a product $a_1 a_2 \ldots a_n$, then necessarily p divides at least one of the factors a_i.

Proof: *(of Corollary)* This is by induction on n. The Lemma is the assertion for $n = 2$. Suppose $p|(a_1 \ldots a_n)$. Then write the latter product as

$$a_1 \ldots a_n = (a_1 \ldots a_{n-1}) \cdot a_n$$

By the lemma, either p divides a_n or p divides $a_1 a_2 \ldots a_{n-1}$. If $p|a_n$, we are done. If not, then $p|(a_1 \ldots a_{n-1})$. By induction, this implies that p divides one of the factors $a_1, a_2, \ldots, a_{n-1}$. Altogether, we conclude that in any case p divides one of the factors $a_1, \ldots, a_n$.   ♣

Proof: *(of Theorem)* First we prove that for every integer there *exists* a factorization, and then that it is *unique*. It certainly suffices to treat only factorizations of *positive* integers, since factorizations for $-n$ and n are obviously related.

For *existence*, let $n > 1$ be the least integer *not* to have a factorization into primes. Then n cannot be prime itself, or just '$n = n$' is a factorization into primes. Therefore n has a proper factorization $n = xy$ with $x, y > 0$. Since the factorization is *proper*, both x and y are strictly smaller than n. Thus, x and y both can be factored into primes. Putting together the two factorizations gives the factorization of n. This contradicts the assumption that there exist any integers lacking prime factorizations.

Now prove *uniqueness*. Suppose we have

$$q_1^{e_1} \ldots q_m^{e_m} = N = p_1^{f_1} \ldots p_n^{f_n}$$

where (without loss of generality)

$$q_1 < q_2 < \ldots < q_m$$

are primes, and also

$$p_1 < p_2 < \ldots < p_n$$

are all primes. And the exponents e_i and f_i are positive integers. We must show that $m = n$, $q_i = p_i$ for all i, and $e_i = f_i$ for all i.

Since q_1 divides the left-hand side of the equality, it must divide the right-hand side. Therefore, by the corollary to the lemma just above, q_1 must divide one of the factors on the right-hand side. So q_1 must divide some p_i. Since p_i is prime, it must be that $q_1 = p_i$.

We claim that $i = 1$. Indeed, if $i > 1$, then $p_1 < p_i$. And p_1 divides the left-hand side, so divides one of the q_j, so is equal to some q_j. But then we string these inequalities together:

$$p_1 = q_j \geq q_1 = p_i > p_1$$

which is impossible. Therefore, $q_1 = p_1$.

Further, by dividing through by e_1 factors $q_1 = p_1$, we see that the corresponding exponents e_1 and f_1 must also be equal.

The rest of the argument about uniqueness is by induction on N. First, 1 has a unique factorization (of sorts), namely the product '1'. In any case, since 2 is prime, *it* has the factorization $2 = 2$. This begins the induction in earnest. Suppose that all integers $N' < N$ have unique factorizations into primes (and prove that N likewise has a unique factorization).

From the equation

$$q_1^{e_1} \ldots q_m^{e_m} = N = p_1^{f_1} \ldots p_n^{f_n}$$

by cancelling off $q_1^{e_1} = p_1^{f_1}$ we obtain

$$q_2^{e_2} \ldots q_m^{e_m} = \frac{N}{q_1^{e_1}} = p_2^{f_2} \ldots p_n^{f_n}$$

We had supposed that all the exponents e_i were positive, so $N/q_1^{e_1} < N$. Thus, by induction, $N/q_1^{e_1}$ has unique factorization, and we conclude that all the remaining factors must match up. This finishes the proof of unique factorization. ♣

Now we prove the corollary, giving the formula for Euler's phi-function:

$$\varphi(N) = (p_1 - 1)p_1^{e_1-1} (p_2 - 1)p_2^{e_2-1} \ldots (p_n - 1)p_n^{e_n-1}$$

where $n = p_1^{e_1} \ldots p_n^{e_n}$ is the factorization into *distinct* prime factors p_i, and all exponents are positive integers. The argument is by *counting*: we'll count the number of numbers x in the range from 0 through $N - 1$ which *do* have a common factor with N, and subtract. And, by unique factorization, if x has a common factor with N then it has a common *prime* factor with N. There are exactly N/p_i numbers divisible by p_i, so we would be tempted to say that the number of numbers in that range with *no* common factor with N would be

$$N - \frac{N}{p_1} - \frac{N}{p_2} - \ldots - \frac{N}{p_n}$$

However, this is not correct in general: we have accounted for numbers divisible by two *different* p_i's *twice*, so we should add back in all the expressions $N/p_i p_j$ with $i \neq j$. But then we've added back in too many things, and we have to *subtract* all the expressions $M/p_i p_j p_k$ with i, j, k distinct. And so on:

$$\varphi(N) = N - \sum_i \frac{N}{p_i} + \sum_{i \neq j} \frac{N}{p_i p_j} - \sum_{i,j,k \text{distinct}} \frac{N}{p_i p_j p_k} + \ldots$$

$$= N \cdot \left(1 - \frac{1}{p_1}\right) \left(1 - \frac{1}{p_2}\right) \ldots \left(1 - \frac{1}{p_n}\right)$$

$$= p_1^{e_1} \left(1 - \frac{1}{p_1}\right) \cdot p_2^{e_2} \left(1 - \frac{1}{p_2}\right) \ldots p_n^{e_n} \left(1 - \frac{1}{p_n}\right)$$

$$= (p_1 - 1)p_1^{e_1-1} (p_2 - 1)p_2^{e_2-1} \ldots (p_n - 1)p_n^{e_n-1}$$

This is the desired formula.

Remark: The style of discussion at the end of the last proof is a very important principle in counting, sometimes called the **inclusion-exclusion principle**.

The most obvious (but not most efficient) means to *obtain* the **prime factorization** is an extension of the *naive primality test* mentioned just above. It is as follows. Attempt division by integers $d = 2, 3, 4, 5, 6, 7, \ldots \le \sqrt{N}$ until either the smallest divisor $d_1 > 1$ of N is found, or it is determined that N has no proper divisors $\le \sqrt{N}$. In the latter case, N is prime. In the former case, attempt division by integers $d = d_1, d_1 + 1, d_1 + 2, \ldots \le \sqrt{N/d_1}$ until either the smallest divisor $d_2 > 1$ of N/d_1 is found, or it is determined that N/d_1 has no proper divisors $\le \sqrt{N/d_1}$. In the latter case, N/d_1 is prime. In the former case, attempt division by integers $d = d_2, d_2 + 1, d_2 + 2, \ldots \le \sqrt{N/d_1 d_2}$ until either the smallest divisor $d_3 > 1$ of $N/d_1 d_2$ is found, or it is determined that $N/d_1 d_2$ has no proper divisors $\le \sqrt{N/d_1 d_2}$. In the latter case $N/d_1 d_2$ is prime. In the former case...

This *recursive* procedure ends when some $N/d_1 d_2 \ldots d_m$ is prime. At the same time, if N has no divisor d in the range $1 < d < \sqrt{N}$, then N is prime.

Remark: It is possible to make the procedure slightly more economical in an obvious way: in attempting division by d as indicated, there is no reason to use non-primes, since if $d = ab$ with $a, b > 1$, then we would already have detected divisibility by both a and b earlier and divided out by them. On the other hand, the larger the numbers being tested the less advantage there is in avoiding trial division by non-primes.

Some sort of compromise approach is reasonable: for example, there is no reason to attempt division by *even* numbers other than 2, nor by numbers bigger than 5 other than 5 (nor numbers divisible by 10). The point is that for integers represented as decimals, divisibility by 2 or 5 (or 10) is very easy to identify.

Addressing a slightly different question, we might wish to find all primes less than a given bound N. A reasonable procedure for this is **Eratosthenes' Sieve**, described as follows. List all the integers from 2 through N.

- Starting with $2 + 2$, mark every 2nd integer on the list. (This marks all even numbers bigger than 2.)

- The next integer (after 2) on the list which hasn't been marked is 3. Starting with $3 + 3$, mark every 3rd integer (counting those *already* marked). (This marks all multiples of 3 bigger than 3 itself.)

- The next integer (after 3) on the list which hasn't been marked is 5. Starting with $5 + 5$, mark every 5th integer (counting those *already* marked). (This marks all multiples of 5 bigger than 5 itself.)

- ...

- Take the *next* integer n on the list which has not yet been crossed off. This n **is prime**. Starting with $n + n$, cross off every nth integer (counting those *already* marked). (This marks all multiples of n bigger than n itself.)

- ...

- Stop when you've marked all multiples of the largest prime less than $\sqrt{N}$.

For example, looking at the list of integers from 2 through 31 and executing this procedure, we first have the list

$$\begin{array}{ccccccccccc}
2 & 3 & 4 & 5 & 6 & 7 & 8 & 9 & 10 & 11 \\
12 & 13 & 14 & 15 & 16 & 17 & 18 & 19 & 20 & 21 \\
22 & 23 & 24 & 25 & 26 & 27 & 28 & 29 & 30 & 31
\end{array}$$

Marking multiples of 2 after 2 itself gives

$$\begin{array}{ccccccccccc}
2 & 3 & 4* & 5 & 6* & 7 & 8* & 9 & 10* & 11 \\
12* & 13 & 14* & 15 & 16* & 17 & 18* & 19 & 20* & 21 \\
22* & 23 & 24* & 25 & 26* & 27 & 28* & 29 & 30* & 31
\end{array}$$

Marking multiples of 3 after 3 itself gives

$$\begin{array}{ccccccccccc}
2 & 3 & 4* & 5 & 6* & 7 & 8* & 9* & 10* & 11 \\
12* & 13 & 14* & 15* & 16* & 17 & 18* & 19 & 20* & 21* \\
22* & 23 & 24* & 25 & 26* & 27* & 28* & 29 & 30* & 31
\end{array}$$

Marking multiples of 5 after 5 itself gives

$$\begin{array}{ccccccccccc}
2 & 3 & 4* & 5* & 6* & 7 & 8* & 9* & 10* & 11 \\
12* & 13 & 14* & 15* & 16* & 17 & 18* & 19 & 20* & 21* \\
22* & 23 & 24* & 25* & 26* & 27* & 28* & 29 & 30* & 31
\end{array}$$

By this point, the next unmarked integer is 7, which is larger than $\sqrt{31}$, so all the integers in the list unmarked by this point are *prime*.

There are **standard identities** which are useful in anticipating factorization of special polynomials and special forms of numbers:

$$\begin{aligned}
x^2 - y^2 &= (x - y)(x + y) \\
x^3 - y^3 &= (x - y)(x^2 + xy + y^2) \\
x^3 + y^3 &= (x + y)(x^2 - xy + y^2) \\
x^4 - y^4 &= (x - y)(x^3 + x^2y + xy^2 + y^3) \\
x^5 - y^5 &= (x - y)(x^4 + x^3y + x^2y^2 + xy^3 + y^4) \\
x^5 + y^5 &= (x + y)(x^4 - x^3y + x^2y^2 - xy^3 + y^4)
\end{aligned}$$

and so on. Note that for *odd* exponents there are *two* identities, while for *even* exponents there is just *one*.

Thus, for example, we might be curious whether there are infinitely many primes of the form $n^3 - 1$ for integers n. To address this, use

$$n^3 - 1 = (n - 1) \cdot (n^2 + n + 1)$$

Therefore, *if* both factors $n - 1$ and $n^2 + n + 1$ fall strictly between 1 and $n^3 - 1$, then this is a proper factorization of $n^3 - 1$, so $n^3 - 1$ could not be prime. In fact, it suffices to show that *one* of the factors is both > 1 and $< n^3 - 1$. Note that for $n = 2$ the expression $n^3 - 1$ has value 7, which *is* prime, so we'd better not try to prove that this expression is *never* prime.

For $n > 2$ certainly $n - 1 > 2 - 1 = 1$. This is one comparison. On the other hand, also for $n > 2$,

$$n - 1 < 2 \cdot 2 \cdot n - 1 < n \cdot n \cdot n - 1$$

Thus, $0 < n - 1 < n^3 - 1$ if $n > 2$. This shows that $n^3 - 1$ is *never* prime for $n > 2$.

One special algebraic form for numbers, which was historically of recreational interest, but is now also of practical interest, is $2^n - 1$. If such a number *is* prime, then it is called a **Mersenne prime**. It is not known whether or not there are infinitely many Mersenne primes.

Another special form is $2^m + 1$. If such a number *is* prime, it is called a **Fermat prime**. It is not known whether there are infinitely many primes of this form. Fermat evidently thought that every expression $2^{2^n} + 1$ might be prime, but this was disproved by Euler about 100 years later.

Exercises

7.2.01 Factor the integers $1028, 2057$ into primes.

7.2.02 Find a proper factor of $111, 111, 111, 111, 111$ without using a calculator.

7.2.03 Find a proper factor of $110, 111, 101, 111, 011$ without using a calculator.

7.2.04 Find a proper factor of $101, 010, 101, 010, 101$ without using a calculator.

7.2.05 Prove/observe that the one's-place digit of a decimal number *cannot* be sufficient information (by itself) to determine whether the number is divisible by 3, or by 7.

7.2.06 Explain why $n^2 - 1$ cannot be prime for *any* $n > 2$.

7.2.07 Explain why $3^n - 1$ cannot possibly be a prime number if $n > 1$.

7.2.08 Explain why $2^m + 1$ cannot possibly be a prime number unless m is a power of 2.

7.2.09 While we mostly know that $x^2 - y^2$ has a factorization, that $x^3 - y^3$ has a factorization, that $x^3 + y^3$ has, and so on, there is a factorization that seldom appears in 'high school': $x^4 + 4y^4$ has a factorization into two quadratic pieces, each with 3 terms! Find this factorization. *Hint:* $x^4 + 4y^4 = (x^4 + 4x^2y^2 + 4y^4) - 4x^2y^2$.

7.2.10 Can $n^4 + 4$ be a prime if the integer n is bigger than 1?

7.2.11 Factor $x^6 - y^6$ in two different ways.

7.2.12 (*) (*Euclid's proof of the infinitude of primes*) Suppose there were only finitely many primes $p_1, p_2, \ldots, p_n$. Consider the number $N = p_1 \ldots p_n + 1$. Show that none of the p_i can divide N. Conclude that there must be some other prime than those on this list, contradiction.

7.3 Euclidean Algorithm

The **Euclidean algorithm** is a very important, efficient, and non-obvious systematic procedure to find the *greatest common divisor* d of two integers m, n.

It also provides a good algorithm for finding integers x, y so that

$$xm + yn = d$$

(Recall that this odd sort of expression comes up in the proof that greatest common divisors exist.) Further, the Euclidean algorithm provides the most efficient procedure to find *multiplicative inverses modulo m*. As we'll see just below, each step in the Euclidean algorithm is an instance of the division algorithm.

One important aspect of the Euclidean algorithm is that it *avoids* factorization of integers into primes, and at the same time is a reasonably *fast* algorithm to accomplish its purpose. This is true at the level of hand calculations *and* for machine calculations, too.

The use of the Euclidean algorithm to *express* the greatest common divisor of x, y in the form $ax + by = gcd(x, y)$ (and the related application of finding the multiplicative inverse of x mod y) can be implemented in a form which requires less 'memory'. At the end of the section, we'll explain this.

We'll describe the Euclidean algorithm by examples.

To perform the Euclidean algorithm for the two integers $513, 614$:

$$
\begin{aligned}
614 - 1 \cdot 513 &= 101 && \text{(reduction of 614 mod 513)} \\
513 - 5 \cdot 101 &= 8 && \text{(reduction of 513 mod 101)} \\
101 - 12 \cdot 8 &= 5 && \text{(reduction of 101 mod 8)} \\
8 - 1 \cdot 5 &= 3 && \text{(reduction of 8 mod 5)} \\
5 - 1 \cdot 3 &= 2 && \text{(reduction of 5 mod 3)} \\
3 - 1 \cdot 2 &= 1 && \text{(reduction of 3 mod 2)}
\end{aligned}
$$

Notice that the first step is reduction of the larger of the given numbers modulo the smaller of the two. The second step is reduction of the smaller of the two modulo the remainder from the first step. At each step, the 'modulus' of the previous step becomes the 'dividend' for the next step, and the 'remainder' from the previous step becomes the 'modulus' for the next step.

In this example, since we obtained a 1 as a remainder, we know that the greatest common divisor of 614 and 513 is just 1. That is, 614 and 513 are *relatively prime*. By the time we got close to the end, it could have been clear that we were going to get 1 as the gcd, but we carried out the procedure to the bitter end.

Notice that we did not need to find prime factorizations in order to use the Euclidean algorithm to find the greatest common divisor. Since it turns out to be a time-consuming task to factor numbers into primes, this fact is worth something.

As another example, let's find the *gcd* of 1024 and 888:

$$
\begin{aligned}
1024 - 1 \cdot 888 &= 136 && \text{(reduction of 1024 mod 888)} \\
888 - 6 \cdot 136 &= 72 && \text{(reduction of 888 mod 136)} \\
136 - 1 \cdot 72 &= 64 && \text{(reduction of 136 mod 72)} \\
72 - 1 \cdot 64 &= 8 && \text{(reduction of 72 mod 64)} \\
64 - 8 \cdot 8 &= 0 && \text{(reduction of 64 mod 8)}
\end{aligned}
$$

In this case, since we got a remainder 0, we must look at the remainder on the *previous* line: 8. The conclusion is that 8 is the greatest common divisor of 1024 and 888.

At this point it is worthwhile to give a simple estimate of the number of steps the Euclidean algorithm might take in the *worst-case scenario*. In particular, the estimate we give shows that this method for finding *gcd*'s is *much* faster than factoring the numbers into primes and then comparing the factors explicitly. The advantage increases as the sizes of the numbers increase.

Proposition. The number of steps required by the Euclidean algorithm to compute the *gcd* of two integers $x > y$ is less than or equal to $2 \cdot \log_2 y$.

Proof: We look at a few consecutive steps in the execution of the algorithm. This would look something like

$$\begin{aligned} \ldots &= y' \\ x' - q'y' &= r' \\ y' - q''r' &= r'' \end{aligned}$$

where $0 \leq r' < y'$ and $0 \leq r'' < r'$. Our specific claim is that $r'' < y'/2$. That is, we claim that in each *two* steps of the algorithm the remainder decreases at least by a factor of $1/2$. (Keep in mind that all symbols denote non-negative integers.)

If already $r' \leq y'/2$, then, since $r'' < r'$ we certainly have what we want. On the other hand, if $r' > y'/2$ (but still $r'' < r'$), then evidently q'' must be 1, and

$$r'' = y' - q''r' = y' - r' < r' - y'/2 = y'/2$$

as desired.

Likewise, already in the *first two* steps $x - qy = r$ and $y - q'r = r'$ of the algorithm the r' satisfies $r' < \frac{1}{2}y$. Thus, after $2n$ steps, the size of the remainder is less than

$$\frac{1}{2} \cdot (\frac{1}{2})^{n-1} \cdot |y| = (\frac{1}{2})^n \cdot |y|$$

(The first factor of $1/2$ is from the first two steps, and after that each *two* steps give another factor of $1/2$.) Since the algorithm stops when the remainder is ≤ 1, we are done as soon as n is large enough so that

$$(\frac{1}{2})^n \cdot |y| \leq 1$$

Rearranging, this is

$$2^n \geq |y|$$

or

$$n \geq \log_2 |y|$$

That is, n is (at *worst*) the *smallest* integer so that this inequality is true. The actual number of steps is $2n$, so

$$\text{number of steps needed } \leq 2\log_2 |x| \leq 2\log_2 |y|$$

This proves the proposition.   ♣

So far we've only seen how to find $gcd(x, y)$. For small numbers we might feel that it's not terribly hard to do this just by factoring x, y into primes and comparing factorizations, as mentioned above. However, the problem of finding integers a, b so that

$$gcd(x, y) = ax + by$$

is much more of a hassle even for relatively small integers x, y.

The Euclidean algorithm provides means to find these a, b with just a bit more trouble, requiring that we have kept track of all the numbers occurring in the Euclidean algorithm, and that we *run it backward*, as follows.

In the case of 614 and 513:

$$
\begin{aligned}
1 \;=\; & 3 - 1 \cdot 2 \\
& \text{(last line of algorithm)} \\
=\; & 3 - 1 \cdot (5 - 1 \cdot 3) \\
& \text{(replacing 2 by expression from previous line)} \\
=\; & -1 \cdot 5 + 2 \cdot 3 \\
& \text{(rearranging as sum of 5s and 3s)} \\
=\; & -1 \cdot 5 + 2 \cdot (8 - 1 \cdot 5) \\
& \text{(replacing 3 by expression from previous line)} \\
=\; & 2 \cdot 8 - 3 \cdot 5 \\
& \text{(rearranging as sum of 8s and 5s)} \\
=\; & 2 \cdot 8 - 3 \cdot (101 - 12 \cdot 8) \\
& \text{(replacing 5 by expression from previous line)} \\
=\; & -3 \cdot 101 + 38 \cdot 8 \\
& \text{(rearranging as sum of 101s and 8s)} \\
=\; & -3 \cdot 101 + 38 \cdot (513 - 5 \cdot 101) \\
& \text{(replacing 8 by expression from previous line)} \\
=\; & 38 \cdot 513 - 193 \cdot 101 \\
& \text{(rearranging as sum of 513s and 101s)} \\
=\; & 38 \cdot 513 - 193 \cdot (614 - 513) \\
& \text{(replacing 101 by expression from previous line)} \\
=\; & 231 \cdot 513 - 193 \cdot 614 \\
& \text{(rearranging as sum of 614s and 513s)}
\end{aligned}
$$

That is, we have achieved our goal: we now know that $1 = 231 \cdot 513 - 193 \cdot 614$.

In order to successfully execute this algorithm, it is important to keep track of which numbers are mere *coefficients*, and which are the numbers to be *replaced* by more complicated expressions coming from the earlier part of the algorithm. Thus, there is considerable reason to write it out as done just here, with the *coefficients first*, with the numbers to be substituted-for *second*.

Exercises

7.3.01 Find gcd(102313, 103927) without factoring.

7.3.02 Find gcd(82933, 145393) without factoring.

7.3.03 Find gcd(216793, 256027) without factoring.

7.3.04 Find $\gcd(1112, 1544)$ and express it in the form $1112x + 1544y$ for integers x, y.

7.3.05 Find $\gcd(117, 173)$ and express it in the form $117x + 173y$ for integers x, y.

7.3.06 Find $\gcd(10201, 32561)$, and express it in the form $10201x + 32561y$.

7.3.07 Find $\gcd(12345, 54321)$ and express it in the form $12345x + 54321y$.

7.3.08 For an integer n, show that the greatest common divisor of the two integers $n^3 + n^2 + n + 1$ and $n^2 + n + 1$ is unavoidably just 1.

7.3.09 For an integer n, show that the greatest common divisor of the two integers $n^3 + n^2 + n + 1$ and $n^8 + n^7 + n^6 + n^5 + n^4 + n^3 + n^2 + n + 1$ is unavoidably just 1.

7.4 Multiplicative Inverses

Now we apply the Euclidean algorithm to find **multiplicative inverses** mod m. First, though, we can prove that they exist in certain circumstances.

Recall that y is a multiplicative inverse of x modulo m if

$$x \cdot y \,\% \, m = 1$$

For example, 3 is a multiplicative inverse of 2 modulo 5, since

$$2 \cdot 3 \,\% \, 5 = 6 \,\% \, 5 = 1$$

But also 8 is a multiplicative inverse of 2 modulo 5, because also

$$2 \cdot 8 \,\% \, 5 = 16 \,\% \, 5 = 1$$

That is, there appear to be several different multiplicative inverses of 2 modulo 5. We'll now resolve this ambiguity, as well as the question of existence.

Proposition.   Let m be an integer not $0, \pm 1$, and let x be an integer *relatively prime* to m. Then x has a multiplicative inverse modulo m. In particular, in any expression $ax + bm = 1$, the integer a is a multiplicative inverse for x modulo m. On the other hand, if x does have a multiplicative inverse mod m, then x and m are relatively prime.

Proof: In proving the existence of greatest common divisors, we showed that always the *gcd* of two integers x, m is the smallest positive integer of the form $ax + bm$ (for integers a and b). In particular, if x, m are relatively prime, then their *gcd* is 1, so there are integers a, b so that $ax + bm = 1$. That is, we have $ax = -bm + 1$. Thus, we have expressed ax in the form $qm + r$ with $0 \le r < |m|$, since m is not $0, \pm 1$. That is, ax reduced modulo m is 1, as desired.

On the other hand, suppose that y is a multiplicative inverse of x modulo m. That is, $xy \,\% \, m = 1$. That is, for some integer q,

$$xy = q \cdot m + 1$$

Let d be a divisor of both x and m, and let $x = dx'$ and $m = dm'$. Then, rearranging,

$$1 = xy - qm = dx'y - qdm' = d \cdot (x'y - qm')$$

That is, d divides 1. This implies that $d = \pm 1$. Therefore, the only possible common divisors of x and m are ± 1, so they're relatively prime, as asserted. ♣

Corollary. Let m be an integer other than $0, \pm 1$. Let x be an integer. Then the Euclidean algorithm finds the *gcd* of x and m. If this *gcd* is 1, then the expression $ax + bm = 1$ obtained by 'reversing' the Euclidean algorithm yields the multiplicative inverse a of x modulo m.

Now we return to address the issue of characterizing all the possible inverses of x modulo m, if there are any.

Proposition. If y is a multiplicative inverse of x modulo m, and if m divides $y - y'$ for some other integer y', then y' is also a multiplicative inverse of x modulo m. Conversely, if y and y' are multiplicative inverses to x modulo m, then $y - y'$ is divisible by m.

Proof: Suppose that $y - y' = km$ for some integer m, and also let q be the integer so that $xy = qm + 1$, in the definition of the assertion $xy \% m = 1$. Then

$$xy' = x(y - km) = xy - xkm = (qm + 1) - xkm = 1 + m(q - xk)$$

That is, $xy' \% m = 1$.

On the other hand, suppose that $xy \% m = 1$ and $xy' \% m = 1$. Let k, k' be integers so that $xy = mk + 1$ and $xy' = k'm + 1$. Then

$$x(y - y') = (k - k')m$$

We will show that m divides $y - y'$ by a trick that will reappear later: since x and m are relatively prime, there are integers a, b so that $ax + by = 1$. Then

$$y - y' = 1 \cdot (y - y') = (ax + bm)(y - y') = a(x(y - y')) + bm(y - y')$$

$$= a((k - k')m) + bm(y - y')$$

by replacing the $x(y - y')$ by $(k - k')m$, invoking the equality above. That is

$$y - y' = m \cdot (a(k - k') + b(y - y'))$$

so $y - y'$ is indeed a multiple of m. ♣

Exercises

7.4.01 By trial and error, find a multiplicative inverse to 3 mod 7.

7.4.02 By trial and error, find a multiplicative inverse to 5 mod 11.

7.4.03 By trial and error, find a multiplicative inverse to 7 mod 11.

7.4.04 By trial and error, find a multiplicative inverse to 5 mod 13.

7.4.05 By trial and error, find a multiplicative inverse to 9 mod 11.

7.4.06 Find a multiplicative inverse to n mod $2n - 1$.

7.4.07 Find a multiplicative inverse to n mod $2n + 1$.

7.4.08 Find a multiplicative inverse to n mod $3n + 1$.

7.4.09 Find a multiplicative inverse to n mod $n^2 + 1$.

7.4.10 Find a multiplicative inverse to n mod $n^2 - 1$.

7.5 Computing Inverses

When we want to run the Euclidean algorithm 'backward' to find those numbers a, b to express the *gcd* of x, y as $ax + by$, we can be a little cleverer than indicated above. First, we need to recall how two-by-two **matrices** are multiplied. A two-by-two matrix is just a block of numbers

$$\begin{pmatrix} a & b \\ c & d \end{pmatrix}$$

The product of two such things is defined to be

$$\begin{pmatrix} a & b \\ c & d \end{pmatrix} \begin{pmatrix} A & B \\ C & D \end{pmatrix} \begin{pmatrix} aA + bC & aB + bD \\ cA + dC & cB + dD \end{pmatrix}$$

If you are unacquainted with the seemingly peculiar pattern here, we can break it down a little. In general, to compute the entry in the product in the ith row and jth column, we only need the entries from the ith row of the first factor, and from the jth column of the second factor. Thus,

$$\begin{pmatrix} a & b \\ * & * \end{pmatrix} \begin{pmatrix} A & * \\ C & * \end{pmatrix} \begin{pmatrix} aA + bC & * \\ * & * \end{pmatrix}$$

where the $*$'s denote entries that we don't know or don't care. The other three entries are computed, respectively, as

$$\begin{pmatrix} a & b \\ * & * \end{pmatrix} \begin{pmatrix} * & B \\ * & D \end{pmatrix} = \begin{pmatrix} * & aB + bD \\ * & * \end{pmatrix}$$

$$\begin{pmatrix} * & * \\ c & d \end{pmatrix} \begin{pmatrix} A & * \\ C & * \end{pmatrix} = \begin{pmatrix} * & * \\ cA + dC & * \end{pmatrix}$$

$$\begin{pmatrix} * & * \\ c & d \end{pmatrix} \begin{pmatrix} * & B \\ * & D \end{pmatrix} = \begin{pmatrix} * & * \\ * & cB + dD \end{pmatrix}$$

We can use matrices of other shapes and sizes, too. For now, we care especially about two-by-one matrices, of the form

$$\begin{pmatrix} x \\ y \end{pmatrix}$$

We can multiply such things on the left by two-by-two matrices, by an analogous formula

$$\begin{pmatrix} a & b \\ c & d \end{pmatrix} \begin{pmatrix} x \\ y \end{pmatrix} = \begin{pmatrix} ax + by \\ cx + dy \end{pmatrix}$$

This multiplication can be used to express the operations that occur in the Euclidean algorithm. Suppose we want to apply the Euclidean algorithm to two positive integers x, y. Let q_1 and r_1 be the integers so that

$$x - q_1 \cdot y = r_1$$

(with $0 \leq r_1 < y$). Then the next step will be to do the same with the pair y, r_1 in place of x, y. This can be expressed as

$$\begin{pmatrix} y \\ r_1 \end{pmatrix} = \begin{pmatrix} 0 & 1 \\ 1 & -q_1 \end{pmatrix} \begin{pmatrix} x \\ y \end{pmatrix}$$

Continuing in this vein, at each step of the Euclidean algorithm, we have a pair of integers x_i, y_i (with $x_0 = x$ and $y_0 = y$), and

$$\begin{pmatrix} x_{n+1} \\ y_{n+1} \end{pmatrix} = \begin{pmatrix} 0 & 1 \\ 1 & -q_{n+1} \end{pmatrix} \begin{pmatrix} x_n \\ y_n \end{pmatrix}$$

where q_{n+1} is the integer so that

$$0 \leq x_n - q_{n+1} \cdot y_n < |y_n|$$

For all indices i, let

$$M_i = \begin{pmatrix} 0 & 1 \\ 1 & -q_i \end{pmatrix}$$

Then the Euclidean algorithm continues until

$$M_n \, M_{n-1} \, M_{n-2} \, \ldots \, M_3 \, M_2 \, M_1 \begin{pmatrix} x \\ y \end{pmatrix} = \begin{pmatrix} \gcd(x, y) \\ 0 \end{pmatrix}$$

Note that if this big product of matrices has the value

$$M_n \, M_{n-1} \, M_{n-2} \, \ldots \, M_3 \, M_2 \, M_1 = \begin{pmatrix} a & b \\ c & d \end{pmatrix}$$

then we have

$$ax + by = \gcd(x, y)$$

Therefore, to have a more economical version of the Euclidean algorithm we simply want a more economical means to obtain the product $M_n \ldots M_1$.

Let the ith accumulated product of the M'_js be denoted by

$$\begin{pmatrix} a_i & b_i \\ c_i & d_i \end{pmatrix} = M_i \, M_{i-1} \, M_{i-2} \, \ldots \, M_2 \, M_1$$

Then of course (granting the *associativity* of matrix multiplication!)

$$\begin{pmatrix} a_i & b_i \\ c_i & d_i \end{pmatrix} = M_i \begin{pmatrix} a_{i-1} & b_{i-1} \\ c_{i-1} & d_{i-1} \end{pmatrix}$$

Also, to get started, we have

$$\begin{pmatrix} a_0 & b_0 \\ c_0 & d_0 \end{pmatrix} = \begin{pmatrix} 1 & 0 \\ 0 & 1 \end{pmatrix}$$

Therefore, to minimize the 'memory' used in execution of the Euclidean algorithm on a pair x, y, we need only keep track of *six* things:

$$(x_i, y_i, a_i, b_i, c_i, d_i)$$

where $x_0 = x$, $y_0 = y$, $a_0 = 1$, $b_0 = 0$, $c_0 = 0$, and $d_0 = 1$. To get from the ith to the $(i+1)$th list-of-six, we find q_{i+1} so that

$$0 \le x_i - q_{i+1} \cdot y_i < |y_i|$$

and then

$$(x_{i+1}, y_{i+1}, a_{i+1}, b_{i+1}, c_{i+1}, d_{i+1}) = (y_i, \, x_i - q_{i+1}y_i, \, c_i, \, d_i, \, a_i - q_{i+1}c_i, \, b_i - q_{i+1}d_i)$$

The procedure ends at step n when $y_n = 0$. At that point, we have

$$a_n \, x + b_n \, y = \gcd(x, y)$$

Remark: We still didn't prove that the Euclidean algorithm really does what we've claimed!

Exercises

7.5.01 Find a multiplicative inverse of 21 mod 25.

7.5.02 Find a multiplicative inverse to 11 mod 26.

7.5.03 Find a multiplicative inverse to 12 mod 29.

7.5.04 Find a multiplicative inverse of 210 mod 251.

7.5.05 Find a multiplicative inverse to 19 mod 24.

7.5.06 Find a multiplicative inverse of 2101 mod 2513.

7.5.07 Find a multiplicative inverse of 1234 mod 4321.

7.5.08 Find a multiplicative inverse of 21017 mod 25139.

7.6 Equivalence Relations

The idea of thinking of *integers modulo m* as necessarily having something to do with *reduction modulo m* is dangerously seductive, but is a trap, if for no other reason than this: a somewhat richer vocabulary of concepts is necessary in order to discuss more sophisticated ciphers (and other things).

The idea of **equivalence relation** (defined below) is an important extension and generalization of the traditional idea of *equality* and occurs throughout mathematics. The associated idea of **equivalence class** (also defined just below) is equally important.

The goal here is to make precise both the idea and the notation in writing something like '$x \sim y$' to mean that x and y have some specified common feature. We can set up a general framework for this without worrying about the specifics of what the features might be.

Recall the 'formal' definition of a *function* f from a set S to a set T: while we *think of* f as being some sort of rule which to an input $s \in S$ 'computes' or 'associates' an output $f(s) \in T$, this way of talking is inadequate, for many reasons.

Rather, the formal (possibly non-intuitive) definition of function f from a set S to a set T is that it is a subset G of the cartesian product $S \times T$ with the property

- For each $s \in S$ there is exactly one $t \in T$ so that $(s, t) \in G$.

Then connect this to the usual notation by

$$f(s) = t \quad \text{if} \quad (s, t) \in G$$

(Again, this G would be the *graph* of f if S and T were simply the real line, for example.)

In this somewhat formal context, first there is the primitive general notion of **relation** R on a set S: a *relation* R on a set S is simply a subset of $S \times S$. Write $x R y$ if the ordered pair (x, y) lies in the subset R of $S \times S$.

This definition of 'relation' compared to the formal definition of 'function' makes it clear that every function is a relation. But most relations do not meet the condition to be functions. This definition of 'relation' is not very interesting except as set-up for further development.

An **equivalence relation** R on a set S is a special kind of relation, satisfying

- **Reflexivity**: $x R x$ for all $x \in S$

- **Symmetry**: If $x R y$ then $y R x$

- **Transitivity**: If $x R y$ and $y R z$ then $x R z$

The fundamental example of an equivalence relation is ordinary equality of numbers. Or equality of sets. Or any other version of 'equality' to which we are accustomed. It should also be noted that a very popular notation for an equivalence relation is

$$x \sim y$$

(that is, with a tilde rather than an 'R'). Sometimes this is simply read as x *tilde* y, but also sometimes as x **is equivalent to** y with only *implicit* reference to the equivalence relation.

A simple example of an equivalence relation on the set $\mathbf{R}^2$ can be defined by

$$(x, y) \sim (x', y') \quad \text{if and only if} \quad x = x'$$

That is, in terms of analytic geometry, two points are *equivalent* if and only if they lie on the same vertical line. Verification of the three required properties in this case is easy, and should be carried out by the reader.

Let $\sim$ be an equivalence relation on a set S. For $x \in S$, the $\sim$-**equivalence class** $\bar{x}$ containing x is the subset

$$\bar{x} = \{x' \in S : x' \sim x\}$$

The **set of equivalence classes** of $\sim$ on S is denoted by

$$S/\sim$$

(as if we were taking a quotient of some sort). Every element $z \in S$ is certainly contained in an equivalence class, namely the equivalence class of all $s \in S$ so that $s \sim z$.

Note that in general an equality $\bar{x} = \bar{y}$ of equivalence classes $\bar{x}, \bar{y}$ is no indication whatsoever that $x = y$. While it *is* always true that $x = y$ implies $\bar{x} = \bar{y}$, in general there are many *other* elements in $\bar{x}$ than just x itself.

Proposition. Let $\sim$ be an equivalence relation on a set S. If two equivalence classes $\bar{x}, \bar{y}$ have any common element z, then $\bar{x} = \bar{y}$.

Proof: If $z \in \bar{x} \cap \bar{y}$, then $z \sim x$ and $z \sim y$. Then for any $x' \in \bar{x}$, we have

$$x' \sim x \sim z \sim y$$

so $x' \sim y$ by transitivity of $\sim$. Thus, every element $x' \in \bar{x}$ actually lies in $\bar{y}$. That is, $\bar{x} \subset \bar{y}$. A symmetrical argument, reversing the roles of x and y, shows that $\bar{y} \subset \bar{x}$. Therefore, $\bar{x} = \bar{y}$.   ♣

It is important to realize that while we tend to refer to an equivalence class in the notational style $\bar{x}$ for some x in the class, there is no requirement to do so. Thus, it is legitimate to say 'an equivalence class A for the equivalence relation $\sim$ on the set S'.

But of course, given an equivalence class A inside S, it may be convenient to *find* x in the set S so that $\bar{x} = A$. Such an x is a **representative** for the equivalence class. Any element of the subset A is a representative, so in general we certainly should *not* imagine that there is a *unique* representative for an equivalence class.

Proposition.   Let $\sim$ be an equivalence relation on a set S. Then the equivalence classes of $\sim$ on S are mutually disjoint sets, and their union is all of S.

Proof: The fact that the union of the equivalence classes is the whole thing is not so amazing: given $x \in S$, x certainly lies inside the equivalence class

$$\{y \in S : y \sim x\}$$

Now let A and B be two equivalence classes. Suppose that $A \cap B \neq \phi$, and show that then $A = B$ (as sets). Since the intersection is non-empty, there is some element $y \in A \cap B$. Then, by the definition of 'equivalence class', for all $a \in A$ we have $a \sim y$, and likewise for all $b \in B$ we have $b \sim y$. By transitivity, $a \sim b$. This is true for all $a \in A$ and $b \in B$, so (since A and B are equivalence classes) we have $A = B$. ♣

A set $\mathcal{S}$ of non-empty subsets of a set S whose union is the whole set S, and which are mutually disjoint, is called a **partition** of S. The previous proposition can be run in the other direction, as well:

Proposition.   Let S be a set, and let X be a set of subsets of S so that X is a partition of S. Define a *relation* $\sim$ on S by $x \sim y$ if and only if there is $T \in X$ so that $x \in T$ and $y \in T$. That is, $x \sim y$ if and only if they both lie in the same element T of X. Then $\sim$ is an *equivalence relation*, and its equivalence classes are the elements of X.

Proof: Since the union of the sets in X is the whole set S, each element $x \in S$ is contained in *some* $T \in X$. (Note that T is a sub*set* of the set S.) Thus, we have the reflexivity property $x \sim x$. If $x \sim y$, then there is $T \in X$ containing both x and y, and certainly $y \sim x$, so we have symmetry.

Finally, the mutual disjointness of the sets in X assures that each $y \in S$ lies in just one of the sets from X. For $y \in S$, let T be the *unique* set from X which contains y. If $x \sim y$ and $y \sim z$, then it must be that $x \in T$ and $z \in T$, since y lies in no other subset from X. Then x and z both lie in T, so $x \sim z$, and we have transitivity. Verification that the equivalence classes are the elements of X is left as an exercise. ♣

Exercises

7.6.01 Show that the subset $\{(1,1), (2,2), (3,3), (1,2), (2,1)\}$ of $\{1,2,3\} \times \{1,2,3\}$ is an equivalence relation on the set $\{1,2,3\}$.

7.6.02 Show that the relation $x\,R\,y$ on real numbers, defined by $x\,R\,y$ if and only if $x \leq y$, is *not* an equivalence relation.

7.6.03 Let X be a set of non-empty subsets of a set S, whose union is all of S and which are mutually disjoint. (So X is a **partition**.) Let $\sim$ be the equivalence relation defined by this partition. Prove that the equivalence classes are the elements of X.

7.6.04 How many equivalence relations are there on the set $\{1,2,3,4\}$?

7.7 The Integers mod m

Now it will be possible (among other things) to prove that we can reduce mod m (or not) whenever we wish in the course of an arithmetic computation whose answer will be reduced modulo m. This plausible-sounding (and true) fact is very clumsy to prove in 'raw' form.

If two integers x, y differ by a multiple of a nonzero integer m, we say that x is **congruent to** y **modulo** m, written

$$x \equiv y \bmod m$$

Any relation such as the latter is called a **congruence** modulo m, and m is the **modulus**. Equivalently, $x \equiv y \bmod m$ if and only if $m|(x - y)$.

For example, $3 \equiv 18 \bmod 5$ because $5|(18 - 3)$. This is 'just' a different way of writing a divisibility assertion. But this notation (due to Gauss, almost 200 years ago) is meant to cause us to think of *congruence* as a variant of *equality*, with comparable features. That congruences really do have properties similar to equality requires some proof, even though the proofs are not so hard. In giving the statements of these properties the corresponding terminology is also introduced.

Proposition. For a fixed integer m, congruence modulo m is an *equivalence relation*. That is, as defined earlier,

- *Reflexivity:* Always $x \equiv x \bmod m$ for any x.

- *Symmetry:* If $x \equiv y \bmod m$, then $y \equiv x \bmod m$.

- *Transitivity:* If $x \equiv y \bmod m$ and $y \equiv z \bmod m$, then $x \equiv z \bmod m$.

Proof: Since $x - x = 0$ and always $m|0$, we have reflexivity. If $m|(x - y)$, then $m|(y - x)$, since $y - x = -(x - y)$. Thus, we have symmetry. Suppose that $m|(x - y)$ and $m|(y - z)$. Then there are integers k, ℓ so that $mk = x - y$ and $m\ell = y - z$. Then

$$x - z = (x - y) + (y - z) = mk + m\ell = m \cdot (k + \ell)$$

This proves the transitivity.   ♣

The **integers mod** m is the collection of *equivalence classes* of integers with respect to the equivalence relation *congruence modulo* m. It is denoted $\mathbf{Z}/m$ (or sometimes $\mathbf{Z}_m$). Given an integer x and a modulus m, the equivalence class

$$\{y \in \mathbf{Z} : y \equiv x \bmod m\}$$

of x modulo m is often denoted $\overline{x}$, and is also called the **congruence class** or **residue class** of x mod m. On other occasions, the bar notation is not used at all, so that x-mod-m may be written simply as 'x' with only the *context* to make clear that this means x-mod-m and not the integer x.

Thus, for example, modulo 12 we have

$$\bar{0} = \overline{12} = \overline{-12} = \overline{2400}$$

$$\bar{7} = \bar{7} = \overline{-5} = \overline{2407}$$

$$\bar{1} = \overline{13} = \overline{-11} = \overline{2401}$$

or, equivalently,

$$0 \bmod 12 = 12 \bmod 12 = -12 \bmod 12 = 2400 \bmod 12$$

$$7 \bmod 12 = 7 \bmod 12 = -5 \bmod 12 = 2407 \bmod 12$$

$$1 \bmod 12 = 13 \bmod 12 = -11 \bmod 12 = 2401 \bmod 12$$

Remark: There is one traditionally popular collection of representatives for the equivalence classes modulo m, namely

$$\{\bar{0}, \bar{1}, \bar{2}, \ldots \overline{m-2}, \overline{m-1}\}$$

In fact, some flawed sources *define* integers-mod-m as being this set of things, but this is too naive an understanding of what kind of thing integers-mod-m really is. We should distinguish the set of integers *reduced* mod m (which really *is* $\{0, 1, 2, \ldots, m-1\}$!) from the set of integers *modulo* m, which is the set of equivalence classes of integers modulo m. The latter is a more abstract object.

So while it is certainly true that (for example)

$$\mathbf{Z}/3 = \{\bar{0}, \bar{1}, \bar{2}\}$$

it is also true that

$$\mathbf{Z}/3 = \{\overline{10}, \overline{31}, \overline{-1}\}$$

and that there are many other ways of describing it as well.

Again: $\mathbf{Z}/n$ is *not* the set of integers $\{0, 1, 2, 3, \ldots, m-1\}$. Rather, $\mathbf{Z}/n$ is the set of *equivalence classes* modulo m. The set $\{0, 1, 2, 3, \ldots, m-1\}$ is the set of integers *reduced modulo* m (for which there is no special symbol). Still, we do have:

Proposition. Fix two integers x, x'. Let $x = qm + r$ and $x' = q'm + r'$ with integers q, q', r, r' and $0 \le r < |m|$ and $0 \le r' < |m'|$. Then $x \equiv x' \bmod m$ if and only if $r \equiv r' \bmod m$.

Proof: If $x \equiv x' \bmod m$, then there is an integer k so that $x' = x + km$. Then

$$r' = x' - q'm = (x + km) - q'm = x + m \cdot (k - q') = qm + r + m \cdot (k - q')$$

$$= r + m \cdot (q + k - q')$$

This proves that $r \equiv r' \bmod m$. The opposite direction of argument is similar. ♣

Beyond being just an equivalence relation, congruences behave nicely with respect to the basic arithmetic operations of addition, subtraction, and multiplication:

Proposition. For fixed modulus m, if $x \equiv x'$, then for all y

$$x + y \equiv x' + y \bmod m$$

$$xy \equiv x'y \bmod m$$

In fact, if $y \equiv y'$, then

$$x + y \equiv x' + y' \bmod m$$

$$x \cdot y \equiv x' \cdot y' \bmod m$$

Proof: It suffices to prove only the more general assertions. Since $x' \equiv x \bmod m$, $m|(x' - x)$, so there is an integer k so that $mk = x' - x$. That is, we have $x' = x + mk$. Similarly, we have $y' = y + \ell m$ for integer ℓ. Then

$$x' + y' = (x + mk) + (y + m\ell) = x + y + m \cdot (k + \ell)$$

Thus, $x' + y' \equiv x + y \bmod m$. And

$$x' \cdot y' = (x + mk) \cdot (y + m\ell) = x \cdot y + xm\ell + mky + mk \cdot m\ell = x \cdot y + m \cdot (k + \ell + mk\ell)$$

Thus, $x'y' \equiv xy \bmod m$.   ♣

As a corollary of this last proposition, congruences immediately *inherit* some properties from ordinary arithmetic, simply because $x = y$ implies $x \equiv y \bmod m$:

- *Distributivity:* $x(y + z) \equiv xy + xz \bmod m$
- *Associativity of addition:* $(x + y) + z \equiv x + (y + z) \bmod m$
- *Associativity of multiplication:* $(xy)z \equiv x(yz) \bmod m$
- *Property of* 1: $1 \cdot x \equiv x \cdot 1 \equiv x \bmod m$
- *Property of* 0: $0 + x \equiv x + 0 \equiv x \bmod m$

We should feel reassured by these observations that we can do arithmetic 'mod m' without anything messing up. As a matter of notation, we write

$$\mathbf{Z}/m$$

for **the integers mod** m, viewing two integers x, y as 'the same' if $x \equiv y \bmod m$. Thus, there are only m 'things' in $\mathbf{Z}/m$, since there are only m congruence classes (equivalence classes) modulo m. Very often, one thinks of $0, 1, 2, \ldots, m - 2, m - 1$ as being the 'things' in $\mathbf{Z}/m$, but this is not quite good enough for *all* purposes.

There are some more practical observations which also deserve emphasis, although at the same time they should not be surprising:

- $m \equiv 0 \bmod m$, and generally $km \equiv 0 \bmod m$ for any integer k
- $x + (-x) \equiv 0 \bmod m$
- $x \pm m \equiv x \bmod m$, and generally $x + km \equiv x \bmod m$ for any integer k

Note that in all this discussion we only look at one modulus m at a time.

Corollary.   For a fixed modulus m in each residue class there is exactly one integer which is *reduced mod m*. Therefore, $x \equiv y \bmod m$ if and only if x and y have the same *reduction mod m*. That is, $x \equiv y \bmod m$ if and only if x and y have the same remainder when divided by m.

Proof: Fix an integer x. Invoking the division algorithm, there is a *unique* $0 \le r < |m|$ and an integer q so that $x = qm + r$. Then $x - r = qm$ is divisible by m, so x and r are in the same residue class. Since r is reduced, this proves that there is at least one reduced representative for each residue class.

On the other hand, (reproving the uniqueness part of the reduction algorithm!), suppose that $x \equiv r'$ for r' in the range $0 \le r' < |m|$. If $0 \le r < r'$, then

$$0 < r' - r = (r' - x) - (r - x)$$

is multiple of m. Yet also $0 < r' - r \le r' < |m|$. But a multiple of m cannot be > 0 and $< |m|$, so it cannot be that $0 \le r < r'$. Or, supposing that $0 \le r' < r$, by a symmetrical argument we would again reach a contradiction. Thus, $r = r'$. This proves the uniqueness.   ♣

Corollary.   Fix a modulus m, and integers x and y. For brevity write

$$x \% m$$

for x reduced modulo m. Then

$$(x + y) \% m = ((x \% m) + (y \% m)) \% m$$

$$(x \cdot y) \% m = ((x \% m) \cdot (y \% m)) \% m$$

Proof: The residue class of $x' = (x \% m)$ is the same as the residue class of x itself. Therefore, modulo m, we have

$$((x \% m) + (y \% m)) \% m \equiv (x \% m) + (y \% m) \equiv x + y$$

since we proved that $x' \equiv x$ and $y' \equiv y$ gives $x' + y' \equiv x + y$. Further, similarly, $x + y \equiv (x + y) \% m$. Thus, by transitivity,

$$((x \% m) + (y \% m)) \% m \equiv (x + y) \% m$$

The same argument works for multiplication.   ♣

One would correctly get the impression that all properties of congruences follow from properties of ordinary equality together with properties of elementary arithmetic.

We return again to *multiplicative inverses modulo m*. That is, to find a multiplicative inverse mod m for a, we want to solve for x in the equation

$$ax \equiv 1 \bmod m$$

where the integer a is given. Unless $a = \pm 1$ the solution $x = \frac{1}{a}$ of the equation $ax = 1$ is *not* an integer. But that's not what's going on here. Rather, recall that if $gcd(a, m) = 1$, then there are integers x, y so that

$$ax + ym = gcd(a, m) = 1$$

Then $ax - 1 = ym$ is a multiple of m, so with this value of x

$$ax \equiv 1 \bmod m$$

Unless $a = \pm 1$, this x can't possibly be $\frac{1}{a}$, if only because $\frac{1}{a}$ is not an integer. We are doing something new.

Recall that we *did* prove that a has a multiplicative inverse if and only if $gcd(a, m) = 1$, in which case the Euclidean algorithm is an effective means to actually *find* the inverse.

In light of the last observation, we have a separate notation for the integers-mod-m which are relatively prime to m and hence have inverses:

$$\mathbf{Z}/m^{\times}$$

The superscript is not an 'x', but is a 'times', making a reference to multiplication and multiplicative inverses, but mod m.

Proposition. The product xy of two integers x and y both prime to m is again prime to m.

Proof: One way to think about this would be in terms of *prime factorizations*, but let's do without that. Rather, let's use the fact that the *gcd* of two integers a, b can be expressed as

$$gcd(a, b) = sa + tb$$

for some integers s, t. Thus, there are integers a, b, c, d so that

$$1 = ax + bm \qquad 1 = cy + dm$$

Then

$$1 = 1 \cdot 1 = (ax + bm)(cy + dm) = (ac)(xy) + (bcy + axd + bdm)m$$

Thus, 1 is expressible in the form $A(xy) + Bm$, so (by the sharp form of this principle!) necessarily xy and m are relatively prime.   ♣

So in the batch of things denoted $\mathbf{Z}/m^{\times}$ we can multiply and take inverses (so, effectively, divide).

Exercises

7.7.01 Find an integer x so that

$$(x \% 1009) \% 1013 \neq x \% 1013$$

7.7.02 Take two positive integers n and N with n *not* dividing N. Find an integer x so that

$$(x \% N) \% n \neq x \% n$$

7.7.03 How many elements does the set $\mathbf{Z}/n$ have?

7.7.04 How many elements does the set $\mathbf{Z}/30^{\times}$ have?

7.7.05 How many elements does the set $\mathbf{Z}/24^{\times}$ have?

7.7.06 Reduce $100,000,000,001$ modulo 10.

7.7.07 Compute and *reduce modulo* the indicated *modulus:* 110×124 modulo 3, and $12 + 1,234,567,890 \bmod 10$.

7.7.08 In the decimal expansion of 2^{99}, compute the ones-place digit.

7.7.09 Compute $2^{1000} \% 11$. (*Hint:* Don't use numbers much larger than 11.)

7.7.10 Compute $3^{1000} \% 11$. (*Hint:* Don't use numbers much larger than 11.)

7.7.11 In the decimal expansion of 3^{999}, compute the ones-place digit.

7.7.12 Find the multiplicative inverse of 3 modulo 100.

7.7.13 Find the multiplicative inverse of 1001 modulo 1234.

7.7.14 Find three distinct residue classes x modulo 105 so that $x^2 \equiv 1 \bmod 105$.

7.7.15 Find three distinct residue classes x modulo 143 so that $x^2 \equiv 1 \bmod 143$.

7.7.16 Show that $x^2 - y^2 = 102$ has no solution in integers. (*Hint:* When squares are involved, always first try looking mod 4, and realize (check!) that the only squares mod 4 are $0, 1$.)

7.7.17 Show that $x^3 + y^3 = 3$ has no solution in integers. (*Hint:* Look at this mod 7: see what the cubes are mod 7.)

7.7.18 Show that $x^3 + y^3 + z^3 = 4$ has no solution in integers. (*Hint:* Mod 9?)

7.7.19 Show that $x^2 + 3y^2 + 6z^3 - 9w^5 = 2$ has no solution in integers.

7.7.20 Casting out nines: Show that for an integer $n = a_k \ldots a_1 a_{\leq}$ with decimal digits $a_k, \ldots, a_1, a_{\leq}$, that

$$n \equiv a_k + \cdots a_1 + a_0 \bmod 9$$

7.7.21 By casting out nines, show that

$$123456789123456789 + 234567891234567891$$
$$\neq 358025680358025680$$

7.7.22 By casting out nines, show that

$$123456789123456789 \times 234567891234567891$$
$$\neq 28958998683279996179682996625361999$$

Certainly in *this* case it's not possible to check *directly* by hand, and probably most calculators would overflow.

7.8 Primitive Roots, Discrete Logs

In this section we simply *explain* what a *primitive root* is supposed to be, and state what is true. The *existence* of primitive roots will be proven later. That proof requires a lot of preparation! Along with this, we can define *discrete logarithms*.

Let n be a positive integer. An integer g is a **primitive root modulo** n if for every x relatively prime to n there is an integer ℓ so that

$$g^\ell = x \bmod n$$

For fixed g and for given x, an integer ℓ with this property is a **discrete logarithm** of x base g modulo m. To avoid confusion with more ordinary logarithms, sometimes the discrete log of x base g modulo m is called the **index** of x base g modulo m.

For 'most' integers n there is *no* primitive root modulo n. As an example, modulo the prime 7, 3 is a primitive root because (all modulo 7)

$$
\begin{array}{rcrcl}
3^1 & = & 3 & & \\
3^2 & = & 9 & = & 2 \\
3^3 & = & 27 & = & 6 \\
3^4 & = & 81 & = & 4 \\
3^5 & = & 243 & = & 5 \\
3^6 & = & 729 & = & 1
\end{array}
$$

That is, just by taking successive powers, we see that everything nonzero mod 7 is a power of 3 (mod 7, of course). This would be called a *brute-force* verification.

By contrast, the candidates mod 8 are 1, 3, 5, 7, but all of these fail to be primitive roots. By just computing, we see that, of course, all powers of 1 (mod 8) are just 1, powers of 3 mod 8 are either 3 or 1, powers of 5 mod 8 are either 5 or 1, and powers of 7 mod 8 are either 7 or 1. There is no primitive root modulo 8.

Yes, there is more structure here than we have the vocabulary to explain for the moment! A little bit of an explanation, at least a precise statement about when there is or isn't a primitive root modulo m, is

Theorem. *(Proof later.)* The only integers n for which there is a primitive root modulo n are those of the forms

- $n = p^e$ with an odd prime p, and $e \geq 1$
- $n = 2p^e$ with an odd prime p, and $e \geq 1$
- $n = 2, 4$

In particular, there *do* exist primitive roots modulo *primes*.

Further, since $\mathbf{Z}/n$ is a finite set, we would anticipate that a list h, h^2, h^3, h^4, ... (powers of a fixed element h of $\mathbf{Z}/n$), although infinite itself, cannot contain infinitely many *different* things modulo n. In particular, whether or not h is a primitive root modulo n, we might imagine that for some *positive* integer t we have

$$h^t = 1 \bmod n$$

The smallest positive integer t so that this holds is the **exponent** or **order** of h (mod n). Later, after we show that primitive roots exist in certain situations, we'll also prove:

Proposition. Let p be an odd prime, and e a positive integer. Let g be a primitive root mod p^e. Then

$$g^{p-1} = 1 \bmod p$$

and more generally

$$g^{(p-1)p^{e-1}} = 1 \bmod p^e$$

And these are the smallest positive exponents with these properties. That is, the *order* of a primitive root modulo a prime p is $p - 1$, and the order of a primitive root modulo p^e is $(p-1)p^{e-1}$. *(Proof later.)*

Remark: It's necessary to introduce these things far in advance of all the proofs, because we need these things in our applications, and because some aspects of the proofs are difficult. Several later topics are related to issues about primitive roots, orders, exponents, and discrete logarithms: Fermat's little theorem, Euler's theorem, cyclotomic polynomials, and others.

Exercises

7.8.01 Verify that 2 is a primitive root mod 5.

7.8.02 Verify that 2 is a primitive root mod 11.

7.8.03 Verify that 2 is a primitive root mod 25.

7.8.04 Verify that 2 is a primitive root mod 10.

7.8.05 Find the ('discrete') logarithm of 3 base 2 mod 5.

7.8.06 Find the ('discrete') logarithm of 2 base 3 mod 7.

7.8.07 Find the ('discrete') logarithm of 2 base 3 mod 5.

7.8.08 Find the ('discrete') logarithm of 2 base 3 mod 23.

7.8.09 Find the ('discrete') logarithm of 3 base 2 mod 25.

7.8.10 Find the ('discrete') logarithm of 2 base 3 mod 101.

7.8.11 Find the ('discrete') logarithm of 3 base 2 mod 125.

7.8.12 Choose two different primitive roots r and s modulo 17, and let $\log_r$ and $\log_s$ denote discrete logarithms base r and base s modulo 17, respectively. Verify numerically that

$$\log_r 2 = \log_r s \cdot \log_s 2$$

7.8.13 *Prove* that for any two different primitive roots r and s modulo m, letting $\log_r$ and $\log_s$ denote discrete logarithms base r and base s modulo m, respectively, we have the identity

$$\log_r x = \log_r s \cdot \log_s x$$

for any x which is nonzero modulo m.

8

The Hill Cipher

8.1   Hill Cipher Operation
8.2   Hill Cipher Attacks

The Hill cipher is another example of a cipher that is a failure by modern standards, but which illustrates some interesting points nevertheless. It was one of the first *block ciphers*, meaning that it manipulated chunks of the message larger than single characters.

8.1 Hill Cipher Operation

Having seen the weaknesses of substitution ciphers (especially periodic ones) such as the Vigenere cipher, one might seek a somewhat different or at least more complicated mechanism for encryption.

The **Hill cipher** (Lester Hill, 1929) may be thought of as a *block* cipher, although the distinction between block and stream ciphers is always merely a matter of degree. It seems that the increased mathematical-ness of the mechanism of this cipher made a deep impression at the time, and substantially influenced the greater role that mathematics has played in cryptology since that time. This cipher was apparently used for encryption of radio call signs in the Second World War. Encryption and decryption were done by mechanical (not electronic) devices designed for this purpose.

Fix a block size N (this can be part of the key), and choose an *invertible* N-by-N matrix K with entries in $\mathbf{Z}/26$. This K is the *key*. Rewrite a block

$$y = (y_1, y_2, \ldots, y_N)$$

of N characters as an N-by-1 matrix (column vector)

$$y = \begin{pmatrix} y_1 \\ y_2 \\ y_3 \\ \ldots \\ y_N \end{pmatrix}$$

Such a block is encrypted by *matrix multiplication*:

$$E_K(y) = K \cdot y$$

That is, the ℓth character $E_K(y)_\ell$ in $E_K(y)$ is

$$E_K(y_\ell) = \sum_{j=1}^{N} K_{\ell j}\, y_j$$

where $K_{\ell j}$ is the (ℓ, j)th entry of K. Here we are using integers-mod-26 as convenient *encodings* for characters.

The decryption step D_K uses the (multiplicative) *inverse matrix* K^{-1} of K, which we have assumed exists. In effect, decryption for key K is the same as encryption with key K^{-1}:

$$D_K(E_K(y)) = K^{-1}\,(K\,y) = (K^{-1}\,K)\,y = 1_N\,y = y$$

by *associativity* of matrix multiplication.

Note that it is *not* the process of finding the multiplicative inverse that is supposed to be difficult, thereby discouraging unauthorized decryption. As tedious as inversion of large matrices may be, this difficulty is not the primary 'secret' here.

The keyspace here is potentially *infinite*, as with the Vigenere cipher, since in principle there is no limitation on the size N of the plaintext blocks (and of the matrix). The Vigenere cipher has 26^N keys for block size N. While not every N-by-N matrix with coefficients in $\mathbf{Z}/26$ is invertible, more than $\frac{1}{4}$ *are* invertible (as we will understand later). Thus, for block size N, the Hill cipher has more than $\frac{1}{4} \cdot 26^{N^2}$ keys. This cipher, being a 'pure' block cipher, is certainly periodic of period equal to the size of the matrix used.

Note that this is *neither* a pure transposition cipher nor a pure substitution cipher. Thus, it misses the shortcomings of those pure forms. Indeed, many or most 'modern' ciphers are effectively combinations of transposition and substitution ciphers. But the Hill cipher has the weakness of **linearity**, which will be described below.

Exercises

8.1.01 Encrypt 'mydoghasbigfleas' with a Hill cipher of block size 2 and with key

$$\begin{pmatrix} 3 & 17 \\ 1 & 6 \end{pmatrix}$$

8.1.02 A Hill cipher's key is known to be

$$K = \begin{pmatrix} 3 & 17 \\ 1 & 6 \end{pmatrix}$$

A given ciphertext encrypted with this key is XZIIAUCR. What is the plaintext?

8.2 Hill Cipher Attacks

A *chosen-plaintext* attack against a Hill cipher is not difficult. If the block size is known to be N, then encryption of the N character strings (each of length N)

$$(1, 0, 0, \ldots, 0, 0)$$

$$(0, 1, 0, \ldots, 0, 0)$$

$$(0, 0, 1, \ldots, 0, 0)$$

$$\cdots$$

$$(0, 0, 0, \ldots, 1, 0)$$

$$(0, 0, 0, \ldots, 0, 1)$$

(rewritten as 'column vectors') will yield the *rows* of the key K. Indeed, these are exactly the columns of the N-by-N *identity matrix* 1_N. If the block size is not known, longer strings with all '0' but a single '1' can be used to infer the block size, as well.

A *known-plaintext* attack may be a little more complicated. If the block length is known to be N, and if N strings $x^1, \ldots, x^N$ each of length N are given, with known encryptions

$$y^i = E_K(x^i)$$

the goal is to find the key (N-by-N matrix) K. Rewrite each x^i and y^i as a column vector. Then, in terms of matrix multiplication, we have

$$y^i = K \cdot x^i$$

Let X be the N-by-N matrix whose columns are the x^i, and let Y be the N-by-N matrix whose columns are the y^i. Then, because of the way matrix multiplication works, we have

$$Y = K \cdot X$$

Now, *if* only X had a *multiplicative inverse* X^{-1}, we could simply right-multiply the equation by X^{-1} to

$$Y \cdot X^{-1} = K \cdot X \cdot X^{-1} = K$$

which yields the key K. However, the probability is at least 0.75 or so that X will *not* have a multiplicative inverse. The consequence is that the relation $Y = KX$ does not uniquely specify K.

One scenario, then, is that the several possibilities for K must be individually investigated by other means.

Another scenario is that we hope to have more than just N known plaintext strings x^i whose encryptions y^i we know. In that case, there are slightly more sophisticated algebraic methods that can be brought to bear.

One point here is that chosen-plaintext or known-plaintext attacks are relatively easy (even if needing a bit more mathematics), since the encryption and decryption are just matrix multiplication. This means that for two blocks x and x' (written as column vectors)

$$E_K(x + x') = E_K(x) + E_K(x')$$

simply by the fact that for matrices A, B, C of suitable sizes we have the *distributive law*

$$A\,(B + C) = A\,B + A\,C$$

Also, for $c \in \mathbf{Z}/26$,

$$E_K(c\,x) = c\,E_K(x)$$

That is, this cipher is **linear**. This is what makes these attacks work.

A *ciphertext-only* attack on a Hill cipher is more difficult. We'll do an attack where we have a **crib**, that is, a **probable word**. This means that we have confidence that a particular word appears in the plaintext, though we may not know where in the plaintext it appears. In practice it is very reasonable to suppose that an attacker would know *some* fragments of the plaintext, so it's entirely reasonable to think about a probable-word attack rather than a pure ciphertext-only attack. We will do examples with blocks just of size 2, for simplicity.

Suppose that the ciphertext message

$$QAIXP\ XDAFG\ IDYQJ\ S$$

is known to be encrypted with a Hill cipher E_k with block size 2, and is suspected to contain the **probable word** 'butter' (as in 'butter and guns'). We'll decrypt the whole message, even though the whole keyspace has

$$(13^2 - 1)(13^2 - 13)(2^2 - 1)(2^2 - 2) = 157,248$$

possible keys in it (2-by-2 matrices with entries in $\mathbf{Z}/26$ which are multiplicatively invertible): a probable word attack cuts this down to the search of a set about the size of the number of characters in the message.

Remark: Getting that peculiar number that counts the number of keys in the keyspace is a special case of more general assertions. It is not so hard to tell what is true, but it is a bit hard to explain *why* in our present context. Anyway, the number of 2-by-2 matrices with entries in $\mathbf{Z}/p^e$ and with an inverse mod p^e, for p prime, is

$$p^{4(e-1)} \cdot (p^2 - 1)(p^2 - p)$$

The number of n-by-n matrices with entries in $\mathbf{Z}/p$ and with an inverse mod p, for p prime, is

$$(p^n - 1)(p^n - p)(p^n - p^2)(p^n - p^3) \ldots (p^n - p^{n-2})(p^n - p^{n-1})$$

So there are general patterns here, but with explanations not quite accessible yet.

The key here is a 2-by-2 matrix $k = \begin{pmatrix} a & b \\ c & d \end{pmatrix}$, and the encryption of each 2-character block (x_1, x_2) of plaintext is by

$$E_k(x_1, x_2) = \begin{pmatrix} a & b \\ c & d \end{pmatrix} \cdot \begin{pmatrix} x_1 \\ x_2 \end{pmatrix}$$

Suppose, for example, that the block decomposition has the 'bu' and the 'tt' grouped together for encryption. (This will happen if 'butter' occurs after an **even** number of characters in the message.) Suppose that these two blocks are encrypted as

$$E_k(b, u) = (y_1, y_2) \qquad E_k(t, t) = (y_3, y_4)$$

where the y_i are characters of the ciphertext. This means that

$$\begin{pmatrix} a & b \\ c & d \end{pmatrix} \begin{pmatrix} 1 \\ 20 \end{pmatrix} = \begin{pmatrix} y_1 \\ y_2 \end{pmatrix} \qquad \begin{pmatrix} a & b \\ c & d \end{pmatrix} \begin{pmatrix} 19 \\ 19 \end{pmatrix} = \begin{pmatrix} y_3 \\ y_4 \end{pmatrix}$$

or

$$\begin{pmatrix} a & b \\ c & d \end{pmatrix} \begin{pmatrix} b & t \\ u & t \end{pmatrix} = \begin{pmatrix} a & b \\ c & d \end{pmatrix} \begin{pmatrix} 1 & 19 \\ 20 & 19 \end{pmatrix} = \begin{pmatrix} y_1 & y_3 \\ y_2 & y_4 \end{pmatrix}$$

We can then solve this for $\begin{pmatrix} a & b \\ c & d \end{pmatrix}$ by **inverting** the matrix

$$\begin{pmatrix} b & t \\ u & t \end{pmatrix} = \begin{pmatrix} 1 & 19 \\ 20 & 19 \end{pmatrix}$$

modulo 26 and getting the key by

$$\begin{pmatrix} a & b \\ c & d \end{pmatrix} = \begin{pmatrix} y_1 & y_3 \\ y_2 & y_4 \end{pmatrix} \begin{pmatrix} 1 & 19 \\ 20 & 19 \end{pmatrix}^{-1}$$

To do a trial decryption, of course what we really want is the **inverse** of the key. Since the matrices are so little, inversion is easy by the formula

$$\begin{pmatrix} a & b \\ c & d \end{pmatrix}^{-1} = \begin{pmatrix} \frac{d}{det} & \frac{-b}{det} \\ \frac{-c}{det} & \frac{a}{det} \end{pmatrix}$$

So we'll want

$$k^{-1} = \begin{pmatrix} 1 & 19 \\ 20 & 19 \end{pmatrix} \begin{pmatrix} y_1 & y_3 \\ y_2 & y_4 \end{pmatrix}^{-1}$$

Similarly, if 'butter' occurs after an **odd** number of plaintext characters, then the 2-letter blocks 'ut' and 'te' will be grouped together for encryption. Thus, if we know

$$E_k(u,t) = (y_1, y_2), \quad E_k(t,e) = (y_3, y_4)$$

then

$$k \cdot \begin{pmatrix} u & t \\ t & e \end{pmatrix} = \begin{pmatrix} y_1 & y_3 \\ y_2 & y_4 \end{pmatrix}$$

and then

$$k = \begin{pmatrix} y_1 & y_3 \\ y_2 & y_4 \end{pmatrix} \cdot \begin{pmatrix} u & t \\ t & e \end{pmatrix}^{-1} = \begin{pmatrix} y_1 & y_3 \\ y_2 & y_4 \end{pmatrix} \cdot \begin{pmatrix} 20 & 19 \\ 19 & 4 \end{pmatrix}^{-1}$$

The inverse of the key (which is what we would want for attempted decryption) is then

$$k^{-1} = \begin{pmatrix} 20 & 19 \\ 19 & 4 \end{pmatrix} \begin{pmatrix} y_1 & y_3 \\ y_2 & y_4 \end{pmatrix}^{-1}$$

Suppose, for example, that the plaintext is 'butter???....'. That is, suppose that 'butter' comes exactly at the beginning. To encrypt, the plaintext is broken into blocks of length 2:

$$bu \; tt \; er \; ?? \; ?? \; \ldots$$

and converted into numbers mod 26 and multiplied by $\begin{pmatrix} a & b \\ c & d \end{pmatrix}$. If this were the plaintext, then we'd have

$$E_k(b,u) = k \cdot \begin{pmatrix} b \\ u \end{pmatrix} = \begin{pmatrix} Q \\ A \end{pmatrix}, \quad E_k(t,t) = k \cdot \begin{pmatrix} t \\ t \end{pmatrix} = \begin{pmatrix} I \\ X \end{pmatrix}$$

(the ciphertext starts 'QAIX') or

$$k \cdot \begin{pmatrix} b & t \\ u & t \end{pmatrix} = \begin{pmatrix} Q & I \\ A & X \end{pmatrix}$$

and therefore

$$k = \begin{pmatrix} Q & I \\ A & X \end{pmatrix} \begin{pmatrix} b & t \\ u & t \end{pmatrix}^{-1}$$

and, by inverting

$$k^{-1} = \begin{pmatrix} b & t \\ u & t \end{pmatrix} \begin{pmatrix} Q & I \\ A & X \end{pmatrix}^{-1}$$

$$= \begin{pmatrix} 1 & 19 \\ 20 & 19 \end{pmatrix} \begin{pmatrix} 16 & 8 \\ 0 & 23 \end{pmatrix}^{-1}$$

Since $\begin{pmatrix} 16 & 8 \\ 0 & 23 \end{pmatrix}$ has determinant divisible by 2, it cannot be invertible mod 26, so this cannot be a possible key.

If the plaintext were '?butter...', then it would get encrypted in blocks

$$?b\ ut\ te\ r?\ ??\ \ldots$$

Thus, the 2nd and 3rd blocks of ciphertext would come from 'ut' and 'te':

$$E_k(u,t) = k \cdot \begin{pmatrix} u \\ t \end{pmatrix} = \begin{pmatrix} I \\ X \end{pmatrix}, \qquad E_k(t,e) = k \cdot \begin{pmatrix} t \\ e \end{pmatrix} = \begin{pmatrix} P \\ X \end{pmatrix}$$

(since the ciphertext is 'QAIXPX...') or

$$k \cdot \begin{pmatrix} u & t \\ t & e \end{pmatrix} = \begin{pmatrix} I & P \\ X & X \end{pmatrix}$$

and then

$$k = \begin{pmatrix} I & P \\ X & X \end{pmatrix} \begin{pmatrix} u & t \\ t & e \end{pmatrix}^{-1}$$

Inverting:

$$k^{-1} = \begin{pmatrix} u & t \\ t & e \end{pmatrix} \begin{pmatrix} I & P \\ X & X \end{pmatrix}^{-1} = \begin{pmatrix} 20 & 19 \\ 19 & 4 \end{pmatrix} \begin{pmatrix} 8 & 15 \\ 23 & 23 \end{pmatrix}^{-1} = \begin{pmatrix} 11 & 14 \\ 9 & 9 \end{pmatrix}$$

But when we decrypt with this as the supposed (inverse of the) key, we get

$$uoutt\ ehbjv\ avuwn\ j$$

which doesn't look so meaningful.

If the plaintext were '??butter...', then it would get encrypted in blocks

$$??\ bu\ tt\ er??\ \ldots$$

Thus, the 2nd and 3rd blocks of ciphertext would come from 'bu' and 'tt':

$$E_k(u,t) = k \cdot \begin{pmatrix} b \\ u \end{pmatrix} = \begin{pmatrix} I \\ X \end{pmatrix}, \qquad E_k(t,e) = k \cdot \begin{pmatrix} t \\ t \end{pmatrix} = \begin{pmatrix} P \\ X \end{pmatrix}$$

(since the ciphertext is 'QAIXPX...') or

$$k \cdot \begin{pmatrix} b & t \\ u & t \end{pmatrix} = \begin{pmatrix} I & P \\ X & X \end{pmatrix}$$

and then

$$k = \begin{pmatrix} I & P \\ X & X \end{pmatrix} \begin{pmatrix} b & t \\ u & t \end{pmatrix}^{-1}$$

Inverting:

$$k^{-1} = \begin{pmatrix} b & t \\ u & t \end{pmatrix} \begin{pmatrix} I & P \\ X & X \end{pmatrix}^{-1} \begin{pmatrix} 1 & 19 \\ 20 & 19 \end{pmatrix} \begin{pmatrix} 8 & 15 \\ 23 & 23 \end{pmatrix}^{-1} = \begin{pmatrix} 10 & 9 \\ 11 & 14 \end{pmatrix}$$

But when we decrypt with this as the supposed (inverse of the) key, we get

$$eubut\ tehaj\ dauus\ n$$

which doesn't look so meaningful.

If the plaintext were '???butter...', then it would get encrypted in blocks

$$?? \ ?b\ ut\ te\ r?\ ??\ \ldots$$

Thus, the 3nd and 4rd blocks of ciphertext would come from 'ut' and 'te':

$$E_k(u, t) = k \cdot \begin{pmatrix} u \\ t \end{pmatrix} = \begin{pmatrix} P \\ X \end{pmatrix}, \quad E_k(t, e) = k \cdot \begin{pmatrix} t \\ e \end{pmatrix} = \begin{pmatrix} D \\ A \end{pmatrix}$$

(since the ciphertext is 'QAIXPXDA...') or

$$k \cdot \begin{pmatrix} u & t \\ t & e \end{pmatrix} = \begin{pmatrix} P & D \\ X & A \end{pmatrix}$$

and then

$$k = \begin{pmatrix} P & D \\ X & A \end{pmatrix} \begin{pmatrix} u & t \\ t & e \end{pmatrix}^{-1}$$

Inverting:

$$k^{-1} = \begin{pmatrix} u & t \\ t & e \end{pmatrix} \begin{pmatrix} P & D \\ X & A \end{pmatrix}^{-1} = \begin{pmatrix} 20 & 19 \\ 19 & 4 \end{pmatrix} \begin{pmatrix} 15 & 3 \\ 23 & 0 \end{pmatrix}^{-1} = \begin{pmatrix} 15 & 25 \\ 10 & 9 \end{pmatrix}$$

When we decrypt with this as the supposed (inverse of the) key, we get

$$getbu\ ttera\ ndgun\ s$$

which looks good.

Exercises

8.2.01 Suppose a Hill cipher with block size 2 is given, with known plaintext and corresponding encryption

$$E_K(\ \text{'guns'}\ ) = \ \text{'YGJC'}$$

What are the possibilities for the key K?

8.2.02 (*) Viewing a Hill cipher with block size known to be 2 as a substitution cipher on *bigrams*, what are the chances of attacking such a cipher by frequency counts for bigrams (rather than single characters as was done against Vigenere)?

9

Complexity

We won't make any very serious use of complexity theory in the rest of the book, but it is worthwhile to look through the ideas for perspective. Most of the time, in practice, we'll simply distinguish 'fast' from 'slow' algorithms. This will most often mean distinguishing *non-polynomial-time* from *polynomial-time*, in the sense made precise in this chapter. In some cases, with 'slow' algorithms, there is some purpose served in distinguishing 'slow', 'slower', and 'less slow', but again the details won't matter too much for us.

9.1 Big-Oh/Little-Oh Notation

For many purposes, we do not need to know *exactly* how big something is, or how long a process takes. Rather, we only need to know in terms sufficient to compare with other objects or processes. Also, we may not care about *immediate* comparisons, but only *long-term (asymptotic)* comparisons. Here is some very standard notation for this.

If f and g are functions of integer or real-number inputs, and if there is a constant C and a value x_0 so that

$$|f(x)| \leq C \cdot g(x)$$

for all $x \geq x_0$, then write

$$f(x) = O(g(x)) \quad \text{or simply} \quad f = O(g)$$

That is, *eventually* $f(x)$ is bounded by *some* constant multiple of $g(x)$. This notation does not say *what* constant multiple of $g(x)$ is bigger than $f(x)$, nor *how big* the input x must be before this is true.

If

$$\lim_{x \to +\infty} \frac{f(x)}{g(x)} = 0$$

then write

$$f(x) = o(g(x)) \quad \text{or simply} \quad f = o(g)$$

If $f = O(g)$ and $g = O(f)$, then write

$$f \sim g$$

Sometimes this is written as $f = \Theta(g)$ but the latter notation is quite a bit less standard than $f \sim g$ and the big-oh/little-oh notation, so be cautious in using it.

There are several easy-to-verify but still very handy rules for manipulation of the big-oh/little-oh symbols:

Proposition.
- If $f = O(h)$ and $g = O(h)$, then $f + g = O(h)$
- If $f = O(h)$ and $g = O(k)$, then $fg = O(hk)$
- If $f = O(h)$ and $g = O(k)$, then $fg = O(hk)$
- If $f = O(g)$ and $g = O(h)$, then $f = O(h)$

Proof: *We prove just the first assertions.* Suppose that $f = O(h)$ and $g = O(h)$. Let C_1, C_2 be positive constants and x_1, x_2 positive real numbers so that

$$|f(x)| < C_1 \cdot h(x) \quad \text{for } x > x_1$$

$$|g(x)| < C_2 \cdot h(x) \quad \text{for } x > x_2$$

Let x_0 be the larger of x_1, x_2, and put $C = C_1 + C_2$. Then for $x > x_0$ we have

$$|f(x) + g(x)| \le |f(x)| + |g(x)| < C_1 \cdot h(x) + C_2 \cdot h(x) = C \cdot h(x)$$

as desired.   ♣

Many examples from calculus can be put in these terms. Some of these are more elementary than others, but in the worst case L'Hospital's Rule can be used to verify these.

- $5 = O(1)$, and the same is true for any constant c: $c = O(1)$

- $x = o(x^2)$, since $\lim_{x \to +\infty} x/x^2 = 0$

- $1/x = o(1)$, since $\lim_{x \to +\infty} 1/x = 0$

- $x^2 + 3x + 7 = O(x^2)$, since each of the summands is $O(x^2)$

- $6x^2 = O(x^2)$, since $|6x^2| \le 6 \cdot |x^2|$

- $\sin x = O(1)$

- $\ln x = o(x^\varepsilon)$ for any $\varepsilon > 0$

- $x^n = o(e^x)$ for any exponent n (as $x \to +\infty$)

Exercises

9.1.01 Show that $4x^3 + 3x^2 + 5x + 17 = O(x^3)$.

9.1.02 Show that for any integer $n \ge 0$, as $x \to +\infty$, $x^n = O(e^x)$.

9.1.03 Show that $1 + 2 + 3 + 4 + \cdots + (n-1) + n = O(n^2)$.

9.1.04 Show that $1^2 + 2^2 + 3^2 + 4^2 + \cdots + (n-1)^2 + n^2 = O(n^3)$.

9.2 Bit Operations

One fairly good and not-too-inaccurate way of describing how long a computation takes is to tell how many **bit operations** it takes. Such estimates ignore the time spent in *reading and writing*, such as memory access and movement among registers, but this seems not to fatally invalidate the estimates. One important virtue is that these estimates ignore the specifics of the underlying machine. Further, such estimates are reusable even when contemplating parallelizing these algorithms.

In this section we are interested in finding a good approximation for the **complexity** of the basic operations of arithmetic, such as adding and multiplying integers.

The smallest unit of 'action' will be a rather ambiguously defined thing called a **bit operation**. As usual, a **bit** (*'binary digit'?*) is the smallest unit of information and is either 0 or 1. A bit operation has two inputs, each of which is either 0 or 1.

There are two outputs, each of which is either 0 or 1. We do not worry *where* these 0's and 1's are kept, nor how they are moved around.

In this simple model, to describe arithmetic in terms of 0's and 1's it is reasonable to view integers as being written in *binary*, even if we do not plan to actually *do* any computations in binary. In particular, there is no need to worry too much about the *conversion* algorithm to convert from decimal representations of integers to *binary* and back. This conversion seldom plays the dominant role in any serious algorithm anyway. Still, a little reflection upon this conversion is worthwhile, if only so that we think carefully about our notation system for integers.

The 'usual' *decimal* representation expresses integers as sums of multiples (from 0 to 9) of powers of 10, as in

$$1375 = 1375_{10} = 1 \cdot 10^3 + 3 \cdot 10^2 + 7 \cdot 10^1 + 5 \cdot 10^0$$

The subscript is sometimes used if there is ambiguity or need for emphasis. The *binary* representation of the same number (decimal 1375)

$$10101011111 = 10101011111_2 = 2^{10} + 2^8 + 2^6 + 2^4 + 2^3 + 2^2 + 2^1 + 2^0$$

uses powers of 2 rather than 10, and the coefficients are in the corresponding range, simply 0 or 1. Because of the smaller range, we can omit the coefficients entirely if we are so inclined, and also omit the powers of 2 which have coefficient 0. It's fairly clear how to do the analogous thing for other 'bases' than just 10 and 2. Both octal and hexadecimal are commonly used, and our system of time, which is base-60 for minutes and seconds, shows the influence of the ancient Babylonians' (and others!) enthusiasm for other choices.

The **algorithm** that tells how to obtain the base-b expansion of an integer is fairly straightforward. First, some terminology: given an integer n and positive integer d, the **integer part** of n/d is the largest integer smaller-than-or-equal n/d. Given a positive integer n, to express n in base-b as

$$n = a_0 + a_1 \cdot b + a_2 \cdot b^2 + a_3 \cdot b^3 + \cdots$$

(with each 'digit' a_i in the range $0 \leq a_i < b$), execute the following procedure:

$$a_0 = n \ \% \ b \text{ and replace } n \text{ by the integer part of } n/b$$

$$a_1 = n \ \% \ b \text{ and replace } n \text{ by the integer part of } n/b$$

$$a_2 = n \ \% \ b \text{ and replace } n \text{ by the integer part of } n/b$$

$$\cdots$$

Continue until the integer part of n/b is just 0.

Remark: In the previous procedure, the notational device of 'replacing' n by a new value is very convenient. By contrast, if we insisted upon naming each of the 'new' values of n, we'd have a proliferation of names that served no purpose.

The usual rules for addition and multiplication in binary are very similar to those for decimal, except now the 'single-digit' rules in binary are few in number and much simpler to remember:

- $0 + 0 = 0$, $1 + 0 = 0 + 1 = 1$, $1 + 1 = 10$

- $0 \cdot 0 = 0$, $1 \cdot 0 = 0 \cdot 1 = 0$, $1 \cdot 1 = 1$

Addition of multi-digit binary integers can be done as for decimal integers, digit-wise from right to left, with *carries* when appropriate. Likewise, the common way of multiplying multi-digit binary integers works the same way as for decimal integers.

The operation of *addition* of two single-digit binary integers is an example of a bit operation: one of the output bits is the ones-place part of the sum of the two input bits, and the other output bit is the carry digit, if any. Likewise, the operation of *multiplication* of two single-digit binary integers is a bit operation: in this case we only use one of the output bits, which is the product of the two input bits. (In binary there is never any 'carrying' in multiplication of single-digit integers.)

We say that an integer x is an **n-bit** integer if in binary representation it takes n digits. That is, the n-bit integers x are those in the range $2^n - 1 \le x < 2^{n+1}$. Because $\log_{10} 2 \approx .30103 \approx 3/10$, the number of binary digits is always about $10/3$ the number of decimal digits.

Proposition.

- Comparison of two n-bit integers (to determine which is larger, or whether they're equal) takes $O(n)$ bit operations.

- Addition of two n-bit integers takes $O(n)$ bit operations.

- Multiplication of an m-bit and an n-bit integer takes $O(mn)$ bit operations.

- Division-with-remainder of an n-bit integer modulo an m-bit integer, with $m \le n$, takes $O(mn)$ bit operations.

Remark: The proofs can be given by tracing through the details of the simple arithmetic algorithms taught in grade school!

A *number* of n bits or fewer is of size 2^n or less. Therefore, if we describe numbers not by the number of their binary digits, but by their *size*, then we can rephrase the last proposition as

Proposition.

- Comparison of two integers $< n$ takes $O(\log_2 n)$ bit operations.

- Addition of two integers $< n$ takes $O(\log_2 n)$ bit operations.

- Multiplication of two integers $< n$ takes $O(\log_2^2 n)$ bit operations.

- Division-with-remainder of an integer $< n$ modulo an integer $< m$, with $m \le n$, takes $O(\log_2 m \, \log_2 n)$ bit operations.

In general
$$\log_{10} 2 \cdot \log_2 n = \log_{10} n$$

and $\log_{10} n$ is roughly the number of *decimal* digits of n. Thus, if some calculation requires
$$O(\log_2^\ell n)$$

bit operations for input integer n, it will require
$$(\log_{10} 2)^\ell \times O(\log_{10}^\ell n) = O(\log_{10}^\ell n)$$

bit operations. Part of the point here is that *it doesn't matter which logarithm is used in such estimates*, since changing from base 2 to base 10 (or base e) does not change the big-oh estimate!

Remark: Especially for large-ish integers, there are several algorithms for multiplication which are considerably faster than the method taught in grade school. However, the speed-ups don't occur until the integers are considerably larger than those used by schoolchildren.

Remark: Note that for *human* use there is a lack of economy in binary representation of numbers: the multiplication and addition tables are *small*, but many more (admittedly simpler) operations must be performed: an n-digit decimal number will have more than $3n$ binary digits, so a binary multiplication (by the naive algorithm) will involve 9 times as many operations, even though each individual operation is simpler. *Memory is underutilized.*

Even though the literal optimization of human execution of these elementary algorithms seems to be waning in importance, time/memory trade-offs are important in computational questions. It seems to be more common to worry about *time* rather than *space*, but there is really more to it than that.

Exercises

9.2.01 Estimate the number of bit operations necessary to add up (in the most naive way) the first 2^{10} integers.

9.2.02 Estimate the number of bit operations necessary to add up (in the naive way) the first 2^{10} integers *reduced modulo* 101.

9.2.03 Estimate the number of bit operations necessary to compute (in the naive way) the factorial 100!.

9.2.04 Estimate the number of bit operations necessary to compute (in the naive way) 100! mod 103.

9.2.05 Estimate the number of bit operations necessary to compute (by repeatedly computing $2^{n+1} = 2^n \cdot 2$) 2^{100}.

9.2.06 Estimate the number of bit operations necessary to compute (by repeatedly computing $2^{n+1} = 2^n \cdot 2$) 2^{100} % 117.

9.2.07 Estimate the number of bit operations necessary to run the Euclidean algorithm on an m-bit and an n-bit number, with $m \leq n$.

9.2.08 Estimate the number of bit operations necessary to test an n-bit number for primality by the naive primality test.

9.3 Probabilistic Algorithms

For many people, the idea that an algorithm could have random elements in it comes as a surprise. An even bigger surprise is that for some important problems there are *much* faster probabilistic algorithms than deterministic ones. Here is some terminology:

A **Monte Carlo** algorithm *always* gives an answer (in polynomial time), but it has only some *probability* of being correct. More precisely, it is **yes-biased** if a 'yes' answer is only true with some probability, but a 'no' answer is always correct. (Likewise we can have **no-biased** Monte Carlo algorithms.) Thus, a geniune Monte Carlo algorithm is either yes-biased or no-biased, so 'half' its answers are *certain*.

A **Las Vegas** algorithm only runs in *expected* polynomial time, so may not give any answer at all, but if it *does* give an answer for a particular input, then the answer is *correct*.

A slightly less standard usage is that an **Atlantic City** algorithm gives a correct answer at least 3/4 of the time, and runs in polynomial time. (The number 3/4 can be replaced with any probability above 1/2.)

The Atlantic City algorithms are the *two-sided* versions of Monte Carlo algorithms.

9.4 Complexity

The simplest measure of the complexity of an algorithm is just *how long it runs* as a function of the size of the input. Since we worry mainly about what happens for large-ish inputs, we will use the big-oh/little-oh notation, thereby not worrying about subtler details.

An *algorithm* that finishes in time $O(n^r)$ for an input of length n, for *some* real number r is said to run in **polynomial time**. Such algorithms are generally considered to be **good**. Note that in this time estimate the implicit constant must be independent of what n is. This means that *even in the worst-case scenario* (for possibly tricky or nasty inputs) the estimate must hold. It is entirely possible that most often even less time is used, but the worst-case scenario must be accounted for.

A *question* with an algorithm to answer it that runs in polynomial time is said to be in **class** $\mathcal{P}$.

If the *correctness of a guess* at an answer to a question can be proven or disproven in polynomial time, then the question is in **class** $\mathcal{NP}$. This class of questions certainly contains the class $\mathcal{P}$.

It is widely believed that the class $\mathcal{P}$ is strictly smaller than the class $\mathcal{NP}$, but this is the main open question in complexity theory. Problems in $\mathcal{P}$ are considered **easy**, and those in $\mathcal{NP}$ but not in $\mathcal{P}$ are considered **hard**. Ironically, since we don't have a proof that $\mathcal{P}$ is strictly smaller than $\mathcal{NP}$, for now we have no proof that there are *any* hard problems in this sense.

Of course, in any case we are ignoring the constants when we use the asymptotic big-oh/little-oh notation. Thus, if for an input of length n the worst-case runtime is less than or equal

$$10^{1000} \times n^2$$

then we have polynomial runtime, but the constant in front is so huge that the thing will never finish. *Such possibilities are not really taken into account here!*

One question A is *reducible* to another question B (in polynomial time) if there is a polynomial-time algorithm to answer question A (for a given input) from an answer to question B (with related input). In this context, an unknown and unspecified process to answer B is called an **oracle** for question B. Intuitively, A is no more difficult than B. Surprisingly, it has been shown that there are problems C in $\mathcal{NP}$ so that *any* problem in $\mathcal{NP}$ can be reduced to to C in polynomial time. Such problems are **NP-hard** or **NP-complete**. (Finer distinctions can be made which make these two phrases mean different things, unlike our usage.)

Other classes of questions are those answerable in polynomial time with use of **randomization**. The class $\mathcal{ZPP}$ consists of those questions answerable by a Las Vegas algorithm running in polynomial time. The class $\mathcal{RP}$ consists of those questions answerable in polynomial time by a Monte Carlo method. Questions answerable by polynomial-time Atlantic City algorithms are in $\mathcal{BPP}$. While the notations $\mathcal{P}$ and $\mathcal{NP}$ are completely standard, these $\mathcal{ZPP}$, $\mathcal{RP}$, and $\mathcal{BPP}$ are somewhat less standard.

If an algorithm does not (in its worst case) run in polynomial time, then (by default) we say it runs in **exponential time**. Note that this is measured in terms of input size.

Thus, for example, recall that the naive trial-division test for primality of a number N uses roughly $\sqrt{N}$ steps to prove that N is prime (if it is). The *size* n of N as input is $n = \log_2 N$, and

$$\sqrt{N} = 2^{\log_2 N/2} = 2^{n/2}$$

This grows faster than any polynomial in n. By contrast, even the usual naive algorithms for addition and multiplication of integers *do* run in polynomial time.

We pointedly want to make run-time estimates that are independent of the sort of machine on which the algorithm runs, and of the language in which the program is written. Of course, this must mean only *as independent as is reasonable to expect*, since a faster machine will run most algorithms faster than a slower machine. One way to make this hypothesis a little more precise is to postulate that for (non-parallel!) 'reasonably good' computers

Hypothesis: *The runtime of an algorithm depends only upon the number of* **bit operations** *it requires, and upon the* **speed of the machine,** *by a formula*

$$\textbf{runtime} \; = \; \frac{\text{number of bit operations}}{\text{machine speed}}$$

Remark: What this means, roughly, is that machines may be faster or slower, but not really 'cleverer' in any way that allows greater and greater speed-up of execution. Work of E. Post, Kurt Gödel, Alan Turing, and Alonzo Church showed that if we only consider machines that are not ridiculously primitive, and execute instructions in a sequence, then this supposition is true. On the other hand, **infinitely-parallelized** algorithms on **infinitely parallel** computers such as **quantum computers** (if and when they ever exist!) fall outside this class, so *can* do things 'better'.

Remark: The issue of whether there could be more to 'smartness' than simply speed is interesting. *Algorithm quality* certainly plays a role: a fast machine using a slow algorithm might be at a disadvantage in comparison to a slow machine using a good algorithm. *Memory access* (including organization) plays a very visible role in human function, as it does in computer function. It might be amusing to reflect upon those characteristics that usually pass for 'smartness' for a human, in terms of machine function.

9.5   Subexponential Algorithms

In general, an algorithm is considered *good* only if it is *polynomial-time*, meaning that its runtime is polynomial in the size of the input. However, at this point, the best algorithms for factoring integers into primes, for computing discrete logarithms, and for other important computations are not polynomial-time, but are nevertheless significantly faster than exponential-time. For practical purposes this can make a decisive difference. We can quantify distinctions among the speed of algorithms that are slower than polynomial-time, yet faster than genuinely exponential-time.

The class of algorithms $L(a, b)$ is the class of algorithms whose runtime for input of size n is

$$O\left(e^{(b+o(1)) \,\cdot\, n^a \,(\ln n)^{1-a}} \right)$$

with $b \geq 0$, $0 \leq a \leq 1$. Here $o(1)$ denotes some function which goes to 0 as $n \to \infty$. The union

$$\bigcup_{0 < a < 1, \, 0 < b} L(a, b)$$

of these spaces for all $0 < a < 1$, $0 < b$, is the collection of **subexponential algorithms**.

As one extreme case, for any $b \geq 0$, $L(0, b)$ is the collection of polynomial-time algorithms with runtimes $O(n^b)$. At the other extreme, each $L(1, b)$ consists of exponential-time algorithms with runtimes $O(e^{bn})$.

As it happens, the best algorithms currently known for *factoring* and the best algorithms for *computing discrete logarithms* in $\mathbf{Z}/p^e$ (p prime) are conjecturally in a class

$$L(\frac{1}{3}, 1.923)$$

See [Coppersmith 1993] for factoring and [Adleman 1994] for discrete logs in $\mathbf{Z}/p^e$. Note that these run-time estimates are only *conjectural*, since they rely upon plausible but unproven hypotheses on the distributions of various special sorts of integers. Also, it is peculiar that the two conjectural runtime estimates are *the same*. It is important to note that this discrete logarithm runtime estimate is valid only in the simplest finite fields, $\mathbf{Z}/p$. For general finite fields the best estimate seems to be of the form $L(\frac{1}{2}, b)$. Further, for more abstract discrete logarithm problems, such as on *elliptic curves*, no runtime this low is known.

9.6 Kolmogorov Complexity

Relatively recently, Solomonoff, Chaitin, and Kolmogorov (independently) developed a version of *complexity* which emphasizes *program length* (in characters) rather than *program runtime*. This viewpoint also affords a different viewpoint on *random numbers* and on probability more generally. *Information theory* and issues about *compression* are also clarified by thinking in such terms.

The idea is that a rather special string of characters such as

101010101010101010101010101010101010101010101010101010

can be described much more briefly than by listing the characters, for example as '26 copies of 10'. By contrast, the string

10111011101000001010000011011010011111110110000000110

admits no obvious simpler description than to just list all the characters directly.

From a probabilistic viewpoint, sometimes we pretend that every string of (for example) 56 0's and 1's is equally likely to be chosen at random. Of the two strings above, the second is plausibly 'random', and we would not be suspicious if we were told that it was indeed chosen at random. However, the first one of the two is 'too structured', so we would tend to doubt that it 'could have been' chosen at random. A traditional objection is that, out of 2^{56} strings of 0's and 1's, the probability that the 26 copies of '10' would be chosen is very tiny, 2^{-56}, supposedly proving the unlikeliness that this string would be chosen at random. However, from that viewpoint *the second one is just as unlikely*, yet we do not object to it!

We can modify our notion of 'random string of characters of length n' to *include* the idea that a *truly random object* should not have a description any simpler (or shorter) than the thing itself. This makes more legitimate our objection to the 26 10's, since it *has* a shorter description, while still admitting the other string as 'random', since no simpler description springs to mind.

A first informal definition of the **Kolmogorov complexity** of an object is that it is the *length of the shortest complete description of the object*. Here 'the object itself' counts as a description of itself. And of course there are pointlessly long-winded descriptions of a thing. The issue in general is whether there is a significantly *shorter* description of it than just it itself.

It can be proven (after making things more precise!) that 'most' strings of characters of a given length n have no description shorter than n, so that the shortest description of them is achieved just by listing them.

Certainly a necessary preliminary to a serious treatment of this subject is proof that program length only depends in a rather shallow manner upon the specific machine and programming language.

To illustrate the need for some care (and precise formalization) in use of this idea, let's define a positive integer n by

$$n = \text{the first integer } not \text{ describable in } < 60 \text{ characters}$$

The paradox is that we have apparently just used fewer than 60 characters to describe it. One way to try to escape the paradox is to claim that *every* integer is describable in fewer than 60 characters. But this is an untenable claim: since there are only *finitely many* strings of fewer than 60 characters (using the finite collection of letters a–z, numerals 0–9, blanks, and punctuation). The real objection probably has to be that the meaning of 'describable' must be made more precise.

A thorough introduction to many facets of this subject is M. Li and P.M.B. Vitanyi's *Introduction to Kolmogorov Complexity and its Applications*, Springer, 1997 (second edition), ISBN 0387948686.

9.7 Linear Complexity

Determination of the Kolmogoroff complexity of a finite sequence of 0's and 1's cannot be done in polynomial time, in general. One might interpret this as asserting that asking about the Kolmogoroff complexity of objects is too strenuous and general a question. Going to a different extreme, instead of producing (finite but long) sequences of 0's and 1's by arbitrary procedures, one might ask about producing sequences of 0's and 1's by **linear feedback shift registers**, or LFSRs. We will discuss these in more detail later, but for the moment we can describe such things in sufficient detail for our immediate purpose.

A LFSR of **length** N is a sequence $c = (c_0, \ldots, c_{N-1})$ of 0's and 1's. We also need an initial state $s = (s_0, s_1, s_2, s_3, s_{N-1})$. Then we recursively define, for $n + 1 \geq N$,

$$s_{n+1} = c_0\, s_n + c_1\, s_{n-1} + c_2\, s_{n-2} + \cdots + c_{N-1}\, s_{n-3} \ \% \ 2$$

This is a vastly simpler mechanism than the completely arbitrary procedures allowed in Kolmogoroff complexity.

The **linear complexity** of a finite sequence

$$x = (x_0, x_1, \ldots, x_t)$$

is the smallest N so that there is a linear feedback shift register of length N which for some choice of initial data $s = (s_0, s_1, s_2, s_3, s_{N-1})$ produces the sequence x. That is, instead of asking for the smallest description of *any* sort which will produce the sequence, we sharply restrict the class of production mechanisms, to just LFSRs. So, of course, it is entirely possible that the linear complexity of a sequence would be high despite its having a lower complexity from the Kolmogoroff viewpoint. Certainly if a sequence has low linear complexity it has low Kolmogoroff complexity.

In marked contrast to the Kolmogoroff situation, there is a relatively simple algorithm to determine the linear complexity of a finite sequence, that is, to determine the smallest LFSR which will produce the sequence. This algorithm, due to Massey and Berlekamp, will determine the coefficients of an LFSR of length N after sampling only $2N$ contiguous terms in the sequence.

Later we will see that there are LFSRs of length N which can produce sequences of length $2^N - 1$ before repeating themselves, which invites (mistakenly!) their use for cryptographic purposes. The key point is that the Massey and Berlekamp algorithm shows that despite the long time before repeating, the linear complexity is too low for cryptographic use.

9.8 Worst-Case versus Expected

Another distinction to keep in mind in discussion of runtimes of algorithms is the contrast between the *worst-case scenario* and the *expected* runtime. This is relevant to *construction* of ciphers, since neither encrypting nor decrypting should be too hard. The distinction is relevant to (possibly hostile) *cryptanalysis*, since whatever case one has at hand may not be 'average', nor may it be the worst case.

Further, proof of the 'average' security of a cipher does not prevent particular instances of it from being successfully attacked. This is true both of asymmetric (public-key) and symmetric ciphers. For example, there is the issue of **weak keys**: it is quite common that in the use of an otherwise quite good cipher certain choices of keys must be avoided, because it is known that the cipher is much more breakable when such keys are used.

This distinction must be kept in mind when referring to much of the traditional complexity literature, as well, since it is standard to treat only the worst-case scenario. Thus, many of the theorems or other results of traditional complexity theory can give an inappropriate impression about their applicability to cryptological issues.

10

Public-Key Ciphers

This chapter introduces public-key (asymmetric) ciphers. Much of the rest of the book will be devoted to filling in details, providing explanations, and studying techniques which might be interpreted as *attacks* on such ciphers.

The alternative terminology 'asymmetric' reveals a little of what these ciphers are about. First, by contrast, all classical ciphers, as well as certain contemporary ciphers such as DES and AES, are *symmetric* in the sense that knowledge of the decryption key is equivalent to, or often exactly equal to, knowledge of the encryption key. By contrast, knowledge of encryption and decryption keys for asymmetric ciphers are not equivalent (by any feasible computation). That is, one or the other of the encryption/decryption keys might be kept secret, while the other is made public, allowing many different people to encrypt, but only one person to decrypt.

This asymmetry is the crucial point in understanding the new possibilities that arise once we know about public-key ciphers.

The Diffie–Hellman key exchange, the RSA cipher, the ElGamal cipher, and the knapsack cipher are well-known, standard, and relatively elementary. Adi Shamir's attack on the knapsack cipher, and subsequent defenses to this attack, are too complicated to explain here without going far away from our main themes. We have included a new and quite promising cipher, the NTRU cipher, whose mechanism is less elementary, and whose security depends upon more sophisticated things. The section on the NTRU cipher is somewhat harder to read than the earlier ones but still mostly based on things we've already covered or will cover a bit later. The last and most sophisticated discussion, which probably should be skipped entirely on a first reading, concerns the Arithmetica cipher and the Hughes-Tannenbaum attack on it.

Until about 1975, the only kinds of ciphers in existence were **symmetric ciphers**, meaning that knowledge of the encryption key would easily give knowledge of the decryption key, and vice versa. These are also commonly called **secret-key ciphers**, since *all* of the keys involved have to be kept secret.

By contrast, a **public-key** or **asymmetric** cipher system is one in which knowledge of the encryption key gives essentially no clue as to the decryption key. Looking at all the classical symmetric ciphers certainly gives no inkling that a public-key cipher is even *possible*.

After some highly original (and unappreciated) work by Ralph Merkle, the general idea of a public-key cipher was first publicly proposed in [Diffie, Hellman 1976]. (In fact, some people in the British secret service came up with very similar ideas in the mid 1960s. This came to light only in the late 1990s.) A public-key system based on the **knapsack problem** appeared in [Merkle, Hellman 1978]. The latter system was 'cracked', and even though it has now been 'fixed', the loss of confidence in the knapsack problem seems irreversible. One of the most popular public-key systems is *RSA*, named after the authors [Rivest, Shamir, Adleman 1978]. The security of RSA is based upon the difficulty of prime factorizations. The ElGamal system [ElGamal 1985] is a relative latecomer to the scene, appearing in 1985.

The possibility of public-key cipher systems gives rise to applications that were previously inconceivable. We will look at some of these **protocols** later.

A simple example of the use of public-key ciphers is in a **communications network**. For N people to communicate among each other using an *asymmetric* cipher such as RSA requires only N triples (e, d, n): each individual publishes their public key, so to communicate securely with them *anyone* simply encrypts with the corresponding public key. That is, the whole communication network only requires one batch of information (e, d, n) *per person*. By contrast, a *symmetric* cipher would require a key *per pair of people*, which would require $N(N-1)/2$ for N people. Thus, using asymmetric ciphers greatly reduces the number of keys required to maintain a communications network. Using the $N(N-1)/2$ keys for a symmetric cipher set-up for a communication network involving N people, in which every *pair* of people has an encryption/decryption key pair, is not good. First, each person in the network must remember $N-1$ keys. Second, there are altogether $N(N-1)/2$ key pairs, which have to be created and distributed.

Because the encryption and decryption algorithms for asymmetric ciphers are considerably slower than those for symmetric ciphers, in practice the asymmetric ciphers are used to securely exchange a **session key** for a symmetric cipher to be used for the actual communication. That is, the only plaintext encrypted with the asymmetric cipher is the key for a symmetric cipher, and then the faster-running symmetric cipher is used for encryption of the actual message.

The trick of using *session keys* is by now very common in real uses of cryptography. That is, a *public*-key system is used to establish a shared key (the session key) for a (faster) *private*-key system, through which the bulk of the communication will occur. After the message is sent, the session key is discarded and not reused. Thus, in encryption for secrecy, the advantages of public-key ciphers can be realized while at the same time benefiting from the speed of symmetric ciphers. Further, in applications to new 'exotic' protocols there is no replacement for public-key ciphers.

10.1 Trapdoors

Each asymmetric (public-key) cipher depends upon the *practical irreversibility* of some process, usually referred to as the **trapdoor**. At present, all the asymmetric ciphers believed to be reasonably secure make use of tasks from *number theory*, although in principle there are many other possibilities.

The RSA cipher uses the fact that, while it is not hard to compute the product $n = pq$ of two large primes p, q (perhaps $\approx 10^{80}$ or larger), to *factor* a very large integer $n \approx 10^{160}$ into its prime factors seems to be essentially impossible.

The El Gamal cipher uses the fact that, while exponentiation modulo large moduli m is not hard, computation of *discrete logs* is prohibitively difficult. That is, given x, e, p (with p prime) all $\approx 10^{140}$ or so, to compute $y = x^e \% p$ is not too hard. But, going the other direction, to compute the exponent e (the *discrete logarithm* of y base x modulo p) given y, x, p seems to be hard.

Note the qualifications in the last two paragraphs: we say that the tasks *seem to be* hard. At this time there is no *proof* that factorization into primes is *intrinsically* terribly hard. On the other hand, there is a great deal of practical evidence that this is a hard task: people have been thinking about this issue for hundreds of years, and more recently more intensely so because of its relevance to cryptology. The same is true of the discrete-logarithm problem.

The earliest public-key cipher, that of Hellman-Merkle, had the opposite problem: while based upon a *provably* hard problem, the so-called *knapsack problem*, the modification necessary to make decoding possible fatally altered the problem so as to make it no longer hard!

In 1978, McEliece proposed a cipher based on algebraic coding theory. This used a *Goppa code* made to appear as a general *linear code*. The decoding problem for general linear codes is *provably* difficult ('NP-complete'), while the decoding problem for Goppa codes is 'easy'. This cipher does not seem to have been broken, but it is not as popular as RSA and ElGamal. The idea of 'hiding' an easier problem inside an NP-complete problem is similar to the trick in Hellman-Merkle, which seems to have made some people nervous and suspicious of the security of the McEliece cipher.

So, in the end, although the problems haven't been *proven* hard, the *apparent practical difficulty* (after very intense scrutiny) of the problems of factoring and taking discrete logs make RSA and ElGamal the most popular public-key ciphers for now. The recently publicized **elliptic-curve ciphers** are abstract variants of discrete-logarithm ciphers. A real description of them requires considerable further preparation.

10.2 The RSA Cipher

The idea of this cipher is due to [Rivest, Shamir, Adleman 1978]. The key point is that factoring large numbers into primes is difficult. Perhaps surprisingly, merely testing large numbers for primality, without trying to find factors, is much easier.

The hard task here is *factorization of large integers into primes.* Essential tasks which are *relatively* easy are:

- exponentiation $x^e \% n$ modulo n for $n > 10^{160}$ and for large exponents e

- finding many large primes $p > 10^{80}$

As we will see, the contrast in apparent difficulties of these tasks is the basis for the security of the RSA cipher.

The difficulty of factoring large integers into primes is intuitively clear, although this itself is no proof of its difficulty. By contrast, it is surprising that *we can test large numbers for primality without looking for their factors.* The issue of efficiently evaluating large powers x^e of large integers x reduced modulo large integers n is more elementary. And keep in mind that the relevant sizes $n > 10^{160}$ and $p > 10^{80}$ will have to be increased somewhat as computing speeds increase, even if no improvements in algorithms occur.

Description of encryption and decryption. There are two keys, e and d. Auxiliary information, which is not secret, consists of a large-ish integer n. (The nature of n, and the relation of e, d to each other and to n, will be described below.) A plaintext x is *encoded* first as a positive integer which we still call x, and for present purposes we require that $x < n$. Then the **encoding** step is

$$E_{n,e}(x) = x^e \% n$$

where $z \% n$ denotes the **reduction** of z modulo n. This produces a ciphertext $y = x^e \% n$ which is also a positive integer in the range $0 < y < n$. The **decryption** step is simply

$$D_{n,d}(y) = y^d \% n$$

Example: We'll use artificially small numbers for simplicity. Alice chooses $p = 71$, $q = 59$, so $n = 4189$. Both p and q are congruent to 3 mod 4. Alice decides to use $e = 3$ as the public key. She publishes $n = 4189$ and $e = 3$ and keeps p, q secret. Further, to have the decryption exponent, she needs to find the multiplicative inverse of $e = 3$ modulo $(p - 1)(q - 1)$, which she can do by using the Euclidean algorithm, to obtain:

$$d = e^{-1} \bmod 4060 = 2707$$

(or by brute force if the numbers are small). Whenever Bob wants to send Alice a secure message, for example, $x = 1234$, he computes the plaintext

$$y = x^e \; \% \; n = 1234^3 \; \% \; 4189 = 229 \bmod 4189$$

He transmits this to Alice. When Alice receives such a message, she decrypts by computing

$$x = y^d = 229^{2707} \; \% \; 4189 = 1234$$

Thus, indeed, she found the plaintext.

Of course, for the decryption step to *really decrypt*, the two keys e, d must have the property that

$$(x^e)^d \equiv x \bmod n$$

for all integers x (at least in the range $0 < x < n$). **Euler's theorem** (below) asserts in general that if $\gcd(x, n) = 1$, then

$$x^{\varphi(n)} \equiv 1 \bmod n$$

where $\varphi(n)$ is the Euler phi-function evaluated at n, defined to be the number of integers ℓ in the range $0 < \ell \leq n$ with $\gcd(\ell, n) = 1$. Thus, the relation between e and d is that they are mutually **multiplicative inverses modulo** $\varphi(n)$, meaning that

$$d \cdot e \equiv 1 \bmod \varphi(n)$$

For integers n of the form $n = p \cdot q$ with $p \neq q$ there is a simple expression for the value of this function (which we will understand better later):

$$\varphi(p \cdot q) = (p - 1)(q - 1)$$

This explains the appearance of the expression $(p - 1)(q - 1)$ above. In that case, we can verify that the encryption and decryption really work for $\gcd(x, n) = 1$.

$$D_{n,d}(E_{n,e}(x)) = (x^e \; \% \; n)^d \; \% \; n = (x^e)^d \; \% \; n$$

since by now we know that reduction modulo n can be done whenever we feel like it, or *not*, in the course of an arithmetic calculation whose answer will be reduced modulo n at the end. By properties of exponents,

$$(x^e)^d \; \% \; n = x^{e \cdot d} \; \% \; n$$

Since $ed \equiv 1 \bmod \varphi(n)$, there is an integer ℓ so that

$$ed = 1 + \ell\varphi(n)$$

Then
$$x^{ed} = x^{1+\ell\varphi(n)} = x^1 \cdot (x^{\varphi(n)})^\ell \equiv x \cdot 1^\ell \equiv x \bmod n$$

by invoking Euler's theorem. Note that Euler's theorem requires that the plaintext x is **prime to** n. Since n is the product of the two primes p and q, being relatively prime to n means *not* being divisible by either p or q. The probability that a 'random' integer x in the range $0 \le x \le n$ would be divisible by p or q is

$$\frac{1}{p} + \frac{1}{q} - \frac{1}{pq}$$

This is a very tiny number, so we *just ignore this possibility*. In fact, here Euler's theorem works without assuming $\gcd(x, n) = 1$.

The encryption exponent e (and decryption exponent d) must be prime to $\varphi(n) = (p-1)(q-1)$ so that it will have a multiplicative inverse modulo $\varphi(n)$, which will be the decryption exponent d.

A common chain of events is the following. Alice picks two large primes p and q (with $p \neq q$), both congruent to 3 modulo 4, and puts $n = pq$. The primes p and q must be kept secret. She then further picks the encryption and decryption exponents e and d so that $e \cdot d \equiv 1 \bmod \varphi(n)$. *She publishes the encryption exponent e on her web page, along with the modulus n.* Her decryption exponent d is kept secret also. Then anyone who wants to send email to Alice encrypted so that only Alice can read it can encrypt plaintext x by

$$E_{n,e}(x) = x^e \,\%\, n$$

Alice is the only person who knows the decryption exponent d, so she is the only one who can recover the plaintext by

$$x = D_{n,d}(E_{n,e}(x))$$

Since in this situation she can make the encryption key *public*, often the encryption key e is called the **public key** and the decryption key d is called the **private key**.

Remark: Integers n of the form $n = pq$ with p and q distinct primes, both congruent to 3 modulo 4, are called **Blum integers**, or sometimes **RSA moduli**.

Remark: It is clear that Alice must be able to compute large powers of integers modulo 4189. (Her choice of encryption exponent 3 means that encryptors will not need to worry about this.) We'll see later that there is a very good algorithm to do this exponentiation.

Elementary aspects of security of RSA. The security of RSA more or less depends upon the *difficulty of factorization of integers into primes*. This seems to be a genuinely difficult problem. But, more precisely, security of RSA depends upon a much more *special* problem, the difficulty of factoring numbers of the special form $n = pq$ (with p, q prime) into primes. It is conceivable that the more special problem could be solved by special methods not applicable to the general one. But for now the specialness of the problem seems not to have allowed any particularly good specialized factorization attacks.

The reason that difficulty of factorization makes RSA secure is that for n the product of two big primes p, q (with the primes kept secret), it seems hard to compute $\varphi(n)$ when only n is given. Of course, once the prime factorization $n = p \cdot q$ is known, then it is *easy* to compute $\varphi(n)$ via the standard formula

$$\varphi(n) = \varphi(pq) = (p-1)(q-1)$$

If an attacker learns $\varphi(n)$, then the decryption exponent d can be relatively easily computed from the encryption exponent e, by using the **Euclidean algorithm**, since the decryption exponent is just the multiplicative inverse of e modulo n.

In fact, we can prove that for numbers n of this special form, knowing both n and $\varphi(n)$ *gives* the factorization $n = p \cdot q$ (with very little computation). The trick is based on the fact that p, q are the roots of the equation

$$x^2 - (p+q)x + pq = 0$$

Already $pq = n$, so if we can express $p + q$ in terms of n and $\varphi(n)$, we will have the coefficients of this equation expressed in terms of n and $\varphi(n)$, giving an easy route to p and q separately.

Since

$$\varphi(n) = (p-1)(q-1) = pq - (p+q) + 1 = n - (p+q) + 1$$

we can rearrange to get

$$p + q = n - \varphi(n) + 1$$

Therefore, p and q are the roots of the equation

$$x^2 - (n - \varphi(n) + 1)x + n = 0$$

Therefore, the two roots

$$\frac{-(n - \varphi(n) + 1) \pm \sqrt{(n - \varphi(n) + 1)^2 - 4n}}{2}$$

are p and q.

And we must note that it is conceivable there is some other way to obtain the plaintext, or some portion of it, without factoring n.

It might seem that knowledge of the encryption and decryption exponents e, d would not yield the prime factorization $n = p \cdot q$. Thus, it might *seem* that even if the pair e, d is *compromised*, the utility of the number $n = p \cdot q$ is not gone. However, we will see later that *disclosure of the private (decryption) key compromises the cipher*. Specifically, there is a Las Vegas algorithm that runs 'quickly' which will yield the factorization $n = pq$.

The *users* of a system with modulus n (the product of two secret primes p, q), public key e, and private key d *do not need to know the primes* p, q. Therefore, it would be possible for a **central agency** to use the same modulus $n = pq$ over and over. However, as just noted, compromise of one key pair compromises the others.

Speed of encryption/decryption algorithms. If done naively, raising large numbers to large powers takes a long time. Such exponentiation is required by both encryption and decryption in the RSA, so from a naive viewpoint it may be unclear why the algorithms themselves are any easier to execute than a hostile attack. But, in fact, the required exponentiation can be arranged to be much faster than prime factorizations for numbers in the relevant range (with a hundred or more digits). Even so, at this time it seems that the RSA encryption and decryption algorithms (and *most* asymmetric cipher algorithms) run considerably more slowly than the best *symmetric* cipher algorithms.

Typically the primes p, q are chosen to have a hundred digits or so. Therefore, even if the encryption exponent e is chosen to be relatively small, perhaps just a few decimal digits, the multiplicative inverse (the decryption key) will be about as large as n. Thus, the task of computing large powers of integers, modulo a large n, must be executable relatively quickly by comparison to the task of *factoring n*.

There is an important elementary speed-up of exponentiation we'll describe below, which allows us to consider exponentiation 'easy'. This algorithm is useful for computing powers of numbers or other algebraic entities even more generally. That is, to compute x^e we do *not* compute all of $x^1, x^2, x^3, x^4, x^5, \ldots, x^{e-1}, x^e$.

Key generation and management. To set up a modulus $n = pq$ from secret primes p, q, and to determine a key pair e, d with $ed \equiv 1$ mod $\varphi(n)$, requires first of all two large primes p, q, at least $> 10^{80}$, for example. Since the security of RSA is based upon the intractability of factoring, it is very lucky that *primality testing is much easier than factorization into primes*. That is, we are able to obtain many 'large' primes $p, q > 10^{80}$ *cheaply*, despite the fact that we cannot generally factor 'large' numbers $n = pq > 10^{160}$ into primes (even with good algorithms).

The *decryption* (or *private*) key d can be chosen first, after p, q. For there to be a corresponding *encryption* key e it must be that d is relatively prime to $(p-1)(q-1)$, and then the Euclidean algorithm gives an efficient means to compute e.

One way to obtain d relatively prime to $(p - 1)(q - 1)$ is simply by *guessing and checking*, as follows. Note that since $p - 1$ and $q - 1$ themselves are large we may not have their prime factorizations! We pick a random large *prime d*, and then use the Euclidean algorithm to find the greatest common divisor of this d and $(p - 1)(q - 1)$. If the *gcd* is > 1 we just guess again. Since d was a large random *prime*, the heuristic probability is very high that there first guess itself will already be relatively prime to $(p - 1)(q - 1)$. We'll expand on this and related points later.

Further technical notes:

- Sometimes the *encryption* exponent is taken to be 3, with primes p, q *not* 1 modulo 3.

- For technical reasons, some people have more recently recommended $2^{16} + 1 = 65537$ (which is prime) as encryption exponent. Then take the primes p, q *not* congruent to 1 modulo 65537.

- Both $p - 1$ and $q - 1$ should have at least one very large prime factor, since there are factorization attacks against $n = pq$ that are possible if $p - 1$ or $q - 1$ have only smallish prime factors (Pollard's $p - 1$ attack).

- The primes p and q should not be 'close' to each other, since there are factorization attacks on n that succeed in this case (Fermat, and so on).

- The ratio p/q should not be 'close' to a rational number with smallish numerator and denominator, since then D. H. Lehmer's Continued Fraction factorization attack on $n = pq$ will succeed.

We'll look at various *factorization attacks* later.

Report on attacks on RSA. At present, it seems that attacks on RSA will succeed only when RSA is **improperly implemented**, for example, with too-small modulus. That is, it seems that there exist exploitable weaknesses when certain **avoidable mistakes** are made. Of course, ironically, in some cases the fact that a choice is a 'mistake' is only discovered after someone finds an attack to exploit that choice.

Of course, the key size (meaning the size of the RSA modulus $N = pq$, with secret primes p, q) must not be too small, or a brute-force attempt to factor n may succeed in a time smaller than one would want. For example, in late spring of 1999, Adi Shamir designed a specialized computer 'Twinkle', partly analogue and partly digital, which speeded up execution of sophisticated factorization attacks by a factor of 100 or 1000. This makes a 512-bit RSA modulus N (about 160 decimal digits, made from two 80-digit primes) look too small for high-security purposes.

Again, as always, the practical question is not about the *absolute* unbreakability of a cipher, but about *how long* it would take to break it. A speed-up by a factor of 1000 means that a cipher that was secure for 10 years is now secure only for 3 days. But a cipher that was previously secure for 10^{30} years is still secure for 10^{27} years.

Let's quickly review the basic set-up of RSA: make a secret choice of two large primes p, q, both congruent to 3 mod 4. The **RSA modulus** $N = p \cdot q$ is public. Make a public choice of encryption exponent e, relatively prime to N. Often $e = 3$, but maybe better $e = 2^{16} + 1 = 65,537$. By Euclidean algorithm easily compute secret decryption exponent $d = e^{-1} \bmod (p - 1)(q - 1)$. A message is broken into blocks x which are viewed as integers in the range $1 < x < N$. The encryption step is

$$E_{N,e}(x) = x^e \ \% \ N$$

This can be executed by anyone, since e, N are publicly known. The decryption step is

$$D_{N,d}(y) = y^d \ \% \ N$$

The secret decryption exponent d is used to execute this. The pair (N, e) is the **public key** and (N, d) is the **private key**.

- To break the **RSA function** means to invert the function

$$x \to x^e \; \% \; N$$

  without being given the decryption exponent d in advance. That is, one tries to describe the eth-**root-taking** function mod N.

- To break the **RSA cipher** means something with more possibilities than breaking the RSA *function*. It means to recover a plaintext *or part of a plaintext* without being given the decryption exponent. Unbreakability of the cipher, rather than of the function, is sometimes called **semantic security**.

- Certainly if the factorization $N = pq$ is known, then the quantity $(p-1)(q-1)$ can be computed, and the decryption exponent d can be found, which is **one way** that we can describe the eth-**root-taking** function.

- It seems to be unknown at this time whether being able to take eth roots mod N with $e \geq 3$ allows factorization of N. (By contrast, if we can take **square roots** mod N, then we have a good probabilistic algorithm to factor N.)

- To use the Euclidean algorithm to efficiently find the decryption exponent from the encryption exponent using the quantity $(p-1)(q-1)$, the latter quantity must be known. Knowing both quantities $Q = (p-1)(q-1)$ and $N = pq$ allows one to find the primes p, q by solving the quadratic equation

$$x^2 - (N - Q + 1)x + N = 0$$

  Thus, **factoring** N is equivalent (by efficient algorithms) to computing the decryption exponent d via the Euclidean algorithm.

- Thus, one obvious attack on RSA is to try to factor the modulus N.

- By 1999 standards, to permanently (!?) thwart a factorization attack, N should be a 1024-bit number, about 309 decimal digits. So both p, q should be 512-bit numbers, or about 154 decimal digits.

- If quantum computers ever become a reality, 1993 work of Peter Shor shows that there is a fast *quantum* algorithm to factor large numbers. This will/would change many things!

- Also, p, q should be **strong primes**.

Remark: The notion of 'strong prime' seems to vary depending on who's saying it and depending on the circumstances. The first *minimal* version of **strong prime** is a prime p so that $p-1$ is divisible by a 'large' prime. It is said that $p-1$ is **not smooth**. This property thwarts **Pollard's** $p-1$ **attack** (which we'll look at later). A very common refinement of the definition of **strong prime** is to require further that $p+1$ is also divisible by a large prime. That is, neither $p-1$ nor $p+1$ is **smooth**. This also thwarts a variant of Pollard's $p-1$ attack which uses small factors of $p+1$ instead. Further strengthenings of the definition of **strong prime** are: a prime p so that $p-1$ is divisible by a 'large' prime r, and $p+1$ is also divisible by a large prime, *and* $r-1$ is divisible by a large prime. And so on.

- For now it does not appear that direct factorization attacks against the RSA function are feasible, assuming that the prime factors are large enough and are *strong*.

- The best contender for general-purpose factoring of very large integers is the **Number Field Sieve**, whose asymptotic running time to factor n-bit integers appears to be

$$e^{2 \, n^{1/3} \, \log^{2/3} n}$$

  This is **subexponential**, but not **polynomial**, as a function of n. Adi Shamir's newly invented (1999) gadget 'Twinkle' was designed to run the number field sieve much faster than previous general-purpose computers could. Even though Shamir's device speeds up things by as much as 1000 times, this does not *qualitatively* change things, since it's easy to get back that factor by using slightly larger moduli.

Forward search attack. If the collection of all possible messages is known, and is relatively small, then the attacker need only encrypt all the messages until a match is found. For example, if the message is known to be either "yes" or "no", then only one encryption need be computed to know which is the plaintext. Therefore, especially in the case of small messages, messages should be **padded** by adding random bits at front and/or back.

Common modulus attack. Note that the authorized decryptor does not need to know the factorization $N = pq$ of the RSA modulus. This may lead to an attempt at economy by using the same modulus for several parties, and merely varying the encryption (and decryption) keys. This is a mistake. Knowing N and any encryption/decryption pair e, d allows factorization of N, from which any other decryption keys can be obtained. Therefore, an RSA modulus should never be used by more than one person.

Small decryption exponent attack. To save some computation time, one might try to arrange so that the decryption exponent is relatively small. (Of course, not so small as to make the system vulnerable to a brute force attack.) But if $d < \frac{1}{3} N^{1/4}$, then there is an efficient algorithm to recover this decryption exponent! See [Wiener 1990]. The argument uses the classical number theory of **continued fractions** and the manner in which best rational approximations to quadratic irrational numbers are found. That is, for 1024-bit moduli, the decryption exponent should be at least 256 bits, which creates complications for very cramped implementations. Further, [D. Boneh, G. Durfee, preprint] report that this result can be 'improved' to give fast breaking even for larger decryption exponents. In [Boneh 1999] it is speculated that using a decryption modulus less than $\sqrt{N}$ may be vulnerable to such attacks.

Small public exponent attacks. Using encryption exponent $e = 2^{16} + 1 = 65537$ (a Fermat prime!) avoids some attacks that $e = 3$ allows. Using $e = 2^{16}+1 = 65537$ means that encryption requires 17 exponentiations for 1024-bit RSA modulus, by contrast to just 2 for $e = 3$, which is annoying. (Still, 17 exponentiations is in contrast to about 1000 exponentiations for 'random' encryption exponent.) But there are some attacks against small encryption exponents. The first is:

Suppose that Alice wishes to send the same secret message to several different people. The obvious thing is to encrypt the message using each of their public keys, and send. Eve, listening on the insecure channel that Alice uses, can collect all the encrypted messages. Suppose that the message fits into a single RSA block for all the intended recipients. **If the number of messages is greater than or equal the encryption exponent e, then Eve can recover the message.** For example, if $e = 3$ and if the message is small enough to fit into a single block, then just 3 different encryptions are sufficient to recover the message.

To defend against this, one might imagine **padding** the message by some random stuff. This is a good idea. Of course, it would be easiest to use rather simply determined padding, varying in a simple way for different recipients. But it turns out that the **padding must be random**, or else such padding doesn't really help:

Some more sophisticated attacks of this sort are **Hastad's broadcast attack** and **Coppersmith's short pad attack**. But if the larger $e = 2^{16+1} = 65537$ is used, the vulnerability in this direction seems to be essentially eliminated.

Further, when the (public) encryption exponent is small, **partial disclosure** of the decryption key completely breaks RSA, as reported in [Boneh 1999]. In [Boneh, Durfee, Frankel 1998] it is shown that given the $n/4$ least significant bits of the (private) decryption key d, the entire decryption key can be recovered in time linear in $e \log_2 e$, where e is the encryption exponent. This is strongly related to a factorization result: **Given either the $n/4$ highest or $n/4$ lowest bits of p, one can efficiently factor N** [Coppersmith 1998].

Implementation attacks. Especially in situations such as smart cards where an adversary may have virtually unlimited opportunities to do known-plaintext attacks, naive forms of RSA are vulnerable to **timing attacks**, where the adversary *times* the computation, thereby finding the number of exponentiations occuring in a decryption, thereby getting information on the decryption exponent [Kocher 1996].

Exercises

10.2.01 An RSA cipher is set up with modulus 12091 and encryption key 3. The plaintext is '2107' (converted from text to an integer in some manner that we don't care about). Encrypt it.

10.2.02 An RSA cipher is set up with modulus 210757 and encryption key 3. The plaintext is '12345' (converted from text to an integer in some manner that we don't care about). Encrypt it.

10.2.03 An RSA cipher is set up with modulus 210757 and encryption key 3. The plaintext is '54321' (converted from text to an integer in some manner that we don't care about). Encrypt it.

10.2.04 An RSA cipher is set up with modulus 12091 and encryption key 3. Find the decryption key.

10.2.05 An RSA cipher is set up with modulus 14659 and encryption key 3. Find the decryption key.

10.2.06 An RSA cipher is set up with modulus 15943 and encryption key 3. Find the decryption key.

10.2.07 An RSA cipher is set up with modulus $1019 \cdot 1031$ and encryption key 3. Find the decryption key.

10.2.08 An RSA cipher is set up with modulus 12091 and encryption key 3. The ciphertext is '9812'. Decrypt it (just as an integer, which we presume is encoded from text in some unknown but irrelevant manner).

10.3 Diffie–Hellman Key Exchange

This is both the original public-key idea and an important mechanism in current use. The practical point is that symmetric ciphers are generally much faster than asymmetric ones (both for hardware and software reasons), so the public-key cipher is merely used to set up a private key, a **session key**, intended to be used only for a single conversation.

This protocol makes use of the particulars involving discrete logarithms, and of course of the relative difficulty of *computing* discrete logarithms. Therefore, it not only works in the $\mathbf{Z}/p$ discrete-logarithm situation, but also generalizes to arbitrary finite fields, elliptic curves, or any other group structure where logarithms make sense.

First, Alice and Bob agree on a large prime m, and a primitive root g modulo m. These need not be kept secret and can be shared by a group of users. Alice chooses a large random integer x, privately computes $X = g^x \% m$, and sends X to Bob by the possibly insecure channel. Meanwhile, Bob similarly chooses a large random integer y, privately computes $Y = g^y \% m$, and sends Y to Alice across the possibly insecure channel.

Then Alice privately computes $k = Y^x \% m$, and Bob symmetrically computes $k' = X^y \% m$. In fact, $k = k' \bmod m$, seen as follows: computing modulo m, we have

$$k' = X^y = (g^x)^y = g^{xy} = (g^y)^x = k \bmod m$$

since the properties of exponents are enjoyed by integers modulo m. But no one else on the network can obtain k unless they can compute discrete logarithms. Then the key k $(= k')$ can be used directly or indirectly as a key for a symmetric cipher.

For security, the prime modulus m should be large, of course. And m should probably be a *strong prime*, meaning foremost that $m - 1$ should be divisible by a relatively large prime. One might imagine that it would be optimal for m to be a **Sophie Germain prime**, meaning that $(m - 1)/2$ is also prime. However, these primes are rather sparse by comparison to primes as a whole. They are roughly as rare as **twin primes**, meaning primes p so that $p + 2$ is also prime. It is not known whether there are infinitely many Sophie Germain primes (nor whether there are infinitely many twin primes).

In fact, the protocol does not really require that g be a primitive root, only (for security reasons) that it generate a large subgroup of $\mathbf{Z}/n^\times$, so that adversaries cannot compute the relevant 'logarithm'.

As with many of these protocols, this first version of the protocol is vulnerable to a **man-in-the-middle attack** by an active adversary: an active eavesdropper who can intercept the messages from Alice to Bob and Bob to Alice and who can replace these messages with their own messages can (in effect) do a Diffie–Hellman exchange separately with Bob and with Alice, and maintain the illusion for Alice and Bob that they are communicating directly with each other. If Alice and Bob really have had no prior contact, and therefore no other way of verifying each other's identity, it is hard to prevent various kinds of masquerades.

This protocol, and elaborations upon it, was patented by Public Key Partners, but the patent expired on April 29, 1997.

10.4 ElGamal Cipher

This idea appeared in [ElGamal 1985]. It is a little more complicated than RSA, but still essentially elementary. The idea of the ElGamal cipher also lends itself to certain technical generalizations more readily than does RSA. For example, the elliptic-curve cryptosystems are analogues of the ElGamal cipher.

The hard task. The hard task here is **computation of discrete logs**. This means the following. Fix a modulus m and integers b, c. An integer solution x to the equation

$$b^x \equiv c \bmod m$$

is a **(discrete) logarithm base** b of c **modulo** m. It is important to know that for random m, b, and c there *may be no such* x. But for prime modulus p and good choice of base b there *will* exist a discrete logarithm for any c not divisible by p. (These theoretical aspects will be clarified later.)

Fix a large prime $p > 10^{150}$. For two integers b, c suppose that we know that

$$b^x = c \bmod p$$

for some x. The difficult task is to *compute* x given only b, c, p.

For any positive integer m, an integer b is usually called a **primitive root modulo** p if every integer c relatively prime to p may be expressed in the form

$$c = b^x \bmod m$$

We will see later that there exist primitive roots mod m only for special sorts of integers, including mainly *prime* moduli. For prime modulus p, we will see that a primitive root b mod p has the property that the smallest positive power b^k of b congruent to 1 modulo p is $p - 1$. That is,

$$b^{p-1} \equiv 1 \bmod p$$

and no smaller power will do. More generally, for arbitrary x relatively prime to a modulus divisible by prime m, the **order** or **exponent** of x mod m is the smallest positive integer exponent n so that

$$x^n \equiv 1 \bmod m$$

We will see that primitive roots have *maximal* order.

For ElGamal it is not strictly necessary to have a primitive root modulo p, since we only need the configuration $b^\ell \equiv c \bmod p$, but we must require that the *order* of b mod p is close to the maximum possible, or else the cipher can be too easily broken.

Both the idea of 'discrete logarithm' and the use of the difficulty of computing discrete logarithms to construct a cryptosystem admit further abstraction. The most popular example of such a generalization is the **elliptic curve cipher**, which needs considerable preparation even to *describe*. We will do this later.

Description of encryption and decryption. Fix a large prime $p > 10^{150}$, a primitive root b modulo p (meaning that any y can be expressed as $y = b^L \bmod p$), and an integer c in the range $1 < c < p$. The *key* is the power ℓ (the **discrete logarithm**) so that $b^\ell = c \bmod p$. Only the *decryptor* knows ℓ.

The **encryption step** is as follows. An encryptor knows b, c, p. A plaintext x is encoded as an integer in the range $0 < x < p$. The encryptor chooses an auxiliary random integer r, which is *a temporary secret known only to the encryptor*, and encrypts the plaintext x as

$$y = E_{b,c,p,r}(x) = (x \times c^r) \% p$$

Along with this encrypted message is sent the 'header' b^r. Note that the encryptor needs to know only b, c, p and chooses random r, but does not know the discrete logarithm ℓ.

The decryption step requires knowledge of the discrete logarithm ℓ, but *not* the random integer r. The decryptor knows b, c, p, ℓ. First, from the 'header' b^r the decryptor computes

$$(b^r)^\ell = b^{r \cdot \ell} = (b^\ell)^r = c^r \bmod p$$

Then the plaintext is recovered by multiplying by the multiplicative inverse $(c^r)^{-1}$ of c^r modulo p:

$$D_{b,c,p,r,\ell}(y) = (c^r)^{-1} \cdot y \% p = (c^r)^{-1} \cdot c^r \cdot x \bmod p = x \% p$$

Remark: In fact, b need not be a primitive root, but it should be the case that the smallest positive integer k so that $b^k = 1 \bmod p$ is nearly as large as p. We might call such b a **near-primitive root**.

So, for Alice to set up a discrete-log public-key cipher system so that people can send encrypted messages that only *she* can decrypt, she chooses a large random prime p, chooses a random near-primitive root b mod p, picks a random ℓ in the range $1 < \ell < p - 1$, and computes

$$c = b^\ell \bmod p$$

Thus, rather than actually computing a discrete logarithm, Alice picks the 'logarithm' ℓ first, and computes the quantity c which will have ℓ as its logarithm. She keeps ℓ secret (it is the private/secret key), but publishes b, c, p. Then when anyone else wants to send her a message, they have sufficient information, the (b, c, p), to encrypt. But only Alice can decrypt, since only she knows the discrete logarithm.

Example: We can do an artificially small example to clarify the process. Alice chooses $p = 1009$ as her 'random' prime, and tries $b = 101$ as a 'random' near-primitive root. She chooses the 'random' logarithm $\ell = 237$, and computes

$$101^{237} \% 1009 = 482$$

She publishes the list $(b, c, p) = (101, 482, 1009)$, and keeps $\ell = 237$ secret. Whenever Bob (or anyone else) wants to send Alice the message $x = 559$, he proceeds as follows. He picks 'random' $r = 291$ (though he'd use a different r on a different occasion), and computes

$$c^r = 482^{291} \% 1009 = 378$$

Then Bob transmits to Alice

$$x \cdot c^r \% 1009 = 559 \cdot 378 \% 1009 = 421$$

along with the header

$$b^r \% 1009 = 101^{291} \% 1009 = 661$$

When Alice receives the message/header pair $(421, 661)$, she decrypts as follows. Since Alice knows the discrete log ℓ, from $b^r = 661$ she can compute (all modulo 1009) c^r by

$$c^r = (b^\ell)^r = (b^r)^\ell = 661^{237} = 378 \bmod 1009$$

Alice then computes the multiplicative inverse

$$378^{-1} \bmod 1009 = 670$$

so she finishes the decryption by computing

$$\text{plaintext } = 378^{-1} \cdot 421 \bmod 1009 = 670 \cdot 421 = 559$$

Yes, indeed, she recovered the original message '559'.

Remark: Note that Alice (and Bob) must be able to compute large powers of numbers modulo 1009. There is a good algorithm to accomplish this, which we'll see a bit later.

Elementary aspects of security of ElGamal. The security of this cipher depends upon the difficulty of computing the **discrete logarithm** ℓ of an integer c **base** b, modulo prime p. Again, this is an integer so that

$$b^\ell = c \bmod p$$

There is little tangible connection between these logarithms and logarithms of real or complex numbers, although they share some abstract properties. The naive algorithm to compute a discrete logarithm is simply trial and error. Better algorithms to compute discrete logarithms (to attack the ElGamal cipher, for example) require more understanding of integers modulo p.

To avoid some specialized **logarithm computation attacks** effective in certain cases, we must choose p so that $p - 1$ does not have 'too many' small prime factors. Since $p - 1$ is even, it will always have a factor of 2, but beyond this we hope to avoid small factors. This can be made more precise.

Speed of encryption/decryption algorithms. As with RSA, the speed of encryption and decryption is mainly dependent upon speed of exponentiation modulo n, which can be made reasonably fast. A feature of ElGamal (and related algorithms) is that encryptors need a good supply of random numbers. Thus, availability of high-quality pseudo-random-number generators is relevant to ElGamal.

Comments on key generation and management. The most obvious requirement for this cipher system is a generous supply of large primes p, meaning $p > 10^{160}$ or so. Trial division is completely inadequate for this. Whoever creates the configuration $b^\ell \equiv c \bmod p$ will presumably first choose a large prime p, most likely meeting some further conditions. An especially nice kind of prime, for this and many other purposes, is of the form $p = 2 \cdot p' + 1$ where p' is another prime. In that case, about half the numbers b in the range $1 < b < p - 1$ are primitive roots (so have order $2p'$) and the other half have order p', which is still not so bad. Thus, random selection of b gives good candidates. Choice of a random exponent ℓ and computation of $c = b^\ell \% p$ complete the preparations.

If the prime p is of the special form $2p' + 1$ with p' prime, it is easy to find primitive roots, since (as we will see later) the elements of orders p' (rather than $2p'$, which a primitive root would have) are all **squares** in $\mathbf{Z}/p$. The property of being a square or not is easily computable by using quadratic symbols, as we will see. Thus, it is feasible to require that the number b used in ElGamal be a primitive root for primes $p = 2p' + 1$.

It is plausible to use a single prime modulus p for several key configurations $b^\ell = c \bmod p$, since there are many different primitive roots modulo p, but compromise of one such configuration compromises others.

Also, any encryptor will need a good supply of pseudo-random integers for the encryption process. This is an issue in itself.

Exercises

10.4.01 Given the public information $b = 2$, $c = 58$, $p = 103$ for an ElGamal cipher, use $r = 31$ as auxiliary 'random' number, and encrypt the message '87'. (Presumably '87' is a numerical encoding of text.)

10.4.02 Verify that the discrete log of $c = 58$ base $b = 2$ modulo $p = 103$ (relevant to the previous problem) is $\ell = 47$.

10.4.03 With public information $b = 2$, $c = 58$, $p = 103$ for an ElGamal cipher, using the private/secret key $\ell = 47$, decrypt the ciphertext '79'.

10.5 Knapsack Ciphers

There is no single 'knapsack cipher', but rather a family of ciphers using the same underlying mathematical problem, the *knapsack* or *subset sum problem*. Merkle and Hellman [Merkle, Hellman 1978] first made a cipher of this type. Adi Shamir [Shamir 1982] found a decisive attack. In fact, the progression of attacks and attempts to defeat them is representative of the kind of iterative processes by which real ciphers come into existence. We'll only describe the basic version here and briefly indicate the nature of Shamir's attack. Unfortunately, the number of times that various knapsack ciphers have been found problematical is large enough that many people have lost enthusiasm for them, even though the most improved versions seem not to have been broken.

The **knapsack problem** is: given a list of positive integers $a_1, \cdots, a_n$, and given another integer b, find a subset $a_{i_1}, \cdots, a_{i_k}$ so that

$$a_{i_1} + \cdots + a_{i_k} = b$$

if this is possible. (Each element a_i can be used at most once, although some of the values a_i may be the same.) There are variants of this problem: one is to simply tell, for given a_i's and b, whether or not a solution *exists*. Another is, granting that a solution exists, *find it.* All of these are (provably!) NP-complete, meaning approximately that it is hard to solve them, but easy to verify the correctness of a solution. Certainly a brute-force search adding up all possible 2^n subsets of the a_i's will take a very long time if $n = 300$ or so, even longer for $n = 4096$, for example.

For convenience of discussion, call $a = (a_1, \ldots, a_n)$ the **knapsack vector**, and b the **size** of the knapsack. The a_i's which occur in a solution

$$b = a_{i_1} + \cdots + a_{i_k}$$

are **in the knapsack** of size b. A knapsack vector $a = (a_1, \ldots, a_n)$ of length n can be used to *encrypt* a vector $x = (x_1, \ldots, x_n)$ of bits (0's and 1's) by computing a function that in structure resembles a dot product:

$$b = f_a(x) = x_1 a_1 + \cdots + x_n a_n$$

So this amounts to adding up only those among the a_i's for which the corresponding x_i is 1. Then the knapsack vector a and the size b are transmitted. *Decryption* consists of finding (?) a subset of the knapsack vector entries which add up to the size. Thus, the decryption step amounts to solving a knapsack problem. We noted above that solving a knapsack problem in general is hard. So we are in the ridiculous situation that authorized as well as unauthorized decryption would in general be hard.

Of course, there is the immediate issue of whether there might be more than one possible decryption, which would be bad. So a knapsack vector with the property that for a given size there is *at most one* solution to the knapsack problem is called **injective**. It should not be surprising that with the function

$$f_a(x) = x_1\,a_1 + \cdots + x_n\,a_n$$

mentioned above as the possible decryption function for a string x of n bits, the knapsack vector $a = (a_1, \ldots, a_n)$ is injective if and only if f_a is injective. In particular, this requires that all the a_i's be different.

Based on the NP-completeness of the general knapsack problem, we might be confident of the difficulty of unauthorized decryption of the cipher mentioned above, but as things stand the *authorized* decryptor has the same difficulties. To make it possible for the authorized decryptor to solve an easier problem (to do the decryption), the plan is to arrange things so that the *authorized* decryption amounts to solving a much easier *subproblem*, which we now describe.

A knapsack vector $a = (a_1, \ldots, a_n)$ is **superincreasing** if each a_i is strictly greater than the sum of the preceding elements in the vector, that is, for every index i

$$a_1 + \cdots + a_{i-1} < a_i$$

If the knapsack vector $a = (a_1, \ldots, a_n)$ is superincreasing, then there is a much easier method for solving the knapsack problem with size b:

- If $b < a_n$, then a_n *cannot* be in the knapsack of size b, since it just won't fit.
- If $b \geq a_n$, the a_n *must* be in the knapsack of size b, since by the superincreasing property the other a_i's add up to less than a_n, so certainly cannot add up to b.

In the first case, keep the same size b. In the second case, replace b by $b - a_n$. In either case, replace the knapsack vector by $(a_1, \ldots, a_{n-1})$. This converts the problem into a new knapsack problem with a shorter knapsack vector. Obviously the process terminates when we reach a_1, and the problem will be solved in the affirmative if $a_1 = b$ (with the new value of b at that time), and in the negative if $a_1 \neq b$. This also shows that there is *at most one* solution to a knapsack problem with a superincreasing knapsack vector. Thus, if the authorized decryptor can decrypt by solving a superincreasing knapsack problem, the decryption is acceptably easy.

But if the knapsack were visibly superincreasing, an unauthorized decryptor could do the same. So we imagine that we will *disguise* the superincreasing property in a manner known to the authorized decryptor, but not to adversaries. Even if the list of knapsack items were wildly rearranged, the sorting n things takes only $O(n \log n)$ steps if done just slightly cleverly.

The first idea of hiding an easier problem is by a secret multiplication and reduction for some modulus. Alice chooses a superincreasing knapsack vector $(a_1, \ldots, a_n)$, and chooses an integer (the **modulus**)

$$m > a_1 + \cdots + a_n$$

Choosing m to be larger than the sum of the a_i's is what causes this procedure sometimes to be called **strong modular multiplication**. She chooses another number (the **multiplier**) t relatively prime to m, so that t has a multiplicative inverse modulo m. Then Alice computes

$$c_i = (ta_i) \% m$$

This gives a new knapsack vector $c = (c_1, \ldots, c_n)$, which Alice publishes as her *public key* to the cipher. Alice keeps the t and m (and the inverse of t modulo m) secret. For Bob to encrypt a message so that only Alice can read it, the encryption step is similar to what was done before, encrypting an n-bit message $x = (x_1, \ldots, x_n)$ as

$$b = f_c(x) = c_1 x_1 + \cdots + c_n x_n$$

with the altered knapsack vector c. Bob transmits the ciphertext b to Alice. Alice's decryption procedure is first to compute

$$t^{-1} \cdot b \ \% \ m = t^{-1}(c_1 x_1 + \cdots + c_n x_n)$$

$$= (t^{-1}c_1)x_1 + \cdots + (t^{-1}c_n)x_n = a_1 x_1 + \cdots + a_n x_n \bmod m$$

Since m is larger than the sum of all the a_i's, this equality modulo m is actually an equality of integers, meaning that

$$(t^{-1}b) \ \% \ m = a_1 x_1 + \cdots + a_n x_n$$

Since Alice knows the superincreasing knapsack vector of a_i's, or in any case can compute them from the c_i's by

$$a_i = t^{-1} \cdot b_i \ \% \ m$$

she can easily solve the knapsack problem and decrypt as above. So it would appear that we have a plausible public-key cipher. The legal recipient has a much easier problem to solve than the general knapsack problem, so if an adversary approaches a hostile decryption as a general knapsack problem, it will be hard.

   Problem: It turns out that an adversary need not find *the* secret t and m in order to convert the problem into a superincreasing knapsack problem. (And then certainly the adversary need not solve a general knapsack problem.) After all, if an adversary is lucky enough to find *any* t' and m' so that

$$a' = (t'^{-1}c_1 \ \% \ m', \ldots, t'^{-1}c_n \ \% \ m')$$

is superincreasing, this converts the problem to an easy one. In this vein, Adi Shamir [Shamir 1978] found a way to find a pair (t', m') in polynomial time to convert the published vector to a superincreasing one. This breaks this simplest knapsack cipher.

Remark: Note, too, that as it stood this cipher was completely vulnerable to chosen-plaintext attacks.

10.6 NTRU Cipher

The NTRU cipher, invented in 1995 by J. Hoffstein, J. Pipher, and J. Silverman, [Hoffstein, Pipher, Silverman 1996], is mathematically more complicated than RSA or ElGamal, and because of its complexity and relative youth cannot yet be said to be as thoroughly studied. After all, the problem of factoring numbers into primes is very old, and in particular has been studied by computer scientitsts since the invention of computers, while the type of computation required to understand or attack NTRU has been important only since the late 1800s in the work of Minkowski, and has been studied by computer scientists for only 25 years. But it would be foolish to behave as though invention of new things better than old were impossible. NTRU is patented.

One notable feature of the NTRU cipher is that apparently when compared to RSA or elliptic-curve ciphers ('ECC') it has large advantages in some regards, but disadvantages in others. On the positive side, (with apparent comparable security) NTRU runs many times faster than RSA or ECC, has much faster key generation, and requires less memory. On the negative side, NTRU requres more bandwidth and has larger keysizes than RSA or ECC. For example, at the security level of 1024-bit RSA, the NTRU public key is about twice as large. But the disparity decreases as the security levels increase. If or when the NTRU cipher earns the same level of trust as older ciphers, these performance trade-offs will give the NTRU cipher a marked advantage in many practical applications.

Another feature which may eventually be important is that (as far as we know at this time) NTRU would not be be broken if and when quantum computers become feasible, while RSA and ordinary ElGamal certainly will be broken. Ever since Peter Shor's 1993 [Shor 1996a] discovery of quantum algorithms for fast factorization of large integers, this eventuality has loomed as a future hazard for RSA and ordinary discrete-logarithm ciphers. Of course, it may well be that fast quantum algorithms will be discovered for the 'hard tasks' of other public-key ciphers as well, but for the moment RSA and ElGamal are the most vulnerable.

The description of the setup and operation of the NTRU cipher is much less elementary than that for RSA or ElGamal, although it still uses only very basic abstract algebra and number theory. By comparison, the mathematical sophistication required to understand the use of elliptic-curve discrete-logarithm ciphers is considerably greater.

The hard task. The computational task which is presumed to be difficult, thereby presumed to assure the security of the NTRU cipher, is not as readily described, because it is not as elementary as prime factorization or discrete logarithms. One task which must remain difficult is *finding the smallest vector in a lattice*. (For the present discussion, a 'lattice' is a 'nice' collection of vectors, though probably living in a high-dimensional space.) There is a relatively good algorithm, the LLL (Lenstra-Lenstra-Lovasz) algorithm [Lenstra, Lenstra, Lovasz 1982], improved in [Schnorr, Euchner 1994], which works well in finding a short vector in a *typical* lattice. But when the smallest vector is near to or longer than the 'expected value' of sizes of shortest vectors, the LLL algorithm does not perform well. Parameter choices for NTRU must be made to play upon this effect.

Description of encryption and decryption. Fix positive integer parameters N, p, q, where p, q need not be prime but must be *relatively* prime, and probably $\gcd(N, pq) = 1$. Let R be the set of polynomials in x with integer coefficients and with degree strictly less than N, with the seemingly peculiar multiplication $\star$

$$x^i \star x^j = x^{i+j \,\%\, N}$$

That is,

$$\left(\sum_{0 \le i < N} a_i x^i \right) \star \left(\sum_{0 \le j < N} b_i x^i \right) = \sum_{i,j} a_i b_j \, x^{i+j \,\%\, N}$$

$$= \sum_{0 \le k < N} \left(\sum_{i+j=k \,\%\, N} a_\ell b_k \right) x^k$$

The addition in R is the usual addition of polynomials. From this description it is certainly not clear that this multiplication is commutative, associative, nor that it is distributive with respect to addition, although in fact it has all these properties.

We have some special operations on R, namely reduction mod p and reduction mod q, meaning to reduce the coefficients of polynomials modulo p or q, respectively. Compatibly with our general usage, we will write

$$f \,\%\, p = \text{polynomial } f \text{ with coefficients reduced mod } p$$

$$f \,\%\, q = \text{polynomial } f \text{ with coefficients reduced mod } q$$

Note that there is essentially no connection between the outcomes of the two reductions. We will say that a polynomial f has an **inverse mod** p if there is another polynomial F (the inverse) so that

$$(f \star F) \,\%\, p = 1$$

For Alice to create an NTRU key, she chooses two polynomials f and g of degrees $N - 1$, making sure that f has an inverse F_p mod p and an inverse F_q mod q. Alice's public key is

$$h = (F_q \star g) \,\%\, q$$

Alice's private key is f.

For this cipher, a *message* should be a polynomial of degree $N - 1$ with coefficients reduced mod p (in our current sense, so they lie in the range $(-p/2, p/2]$). For Bob to encrypt a message x for Alice, he randomly chooses a polynomial φ of degree $N - 1$ and computes

$$y = (p\varphi \star h + x) \,\%\, q$$

which he transmits to Alice.

Decryption may may fail occasionally, although this can be corrected systematically by a suitable probabilistic algorithm. For Alice to decrypt the message y, she needs the polynomial F_p which she had computed earlier from f (and could have saved in a secure location). Alice computes

$$a = (f \star y) \ \% \ q$$

Then Alice decrypts by computing

$$x = (F_p \star a) \ \% \ p$$

Remark: It is not at all clear from the description above that the alleged decryption really recovers the original message. Indeed, the parameters should be chosen properly in order to arrange that correct decryption occurs with very high probability.

Remark: In terms of the *ring theory* we will develop later, the collection R of polynomials, with ordinary addition but the peculiar multiplication given above, is an example of a standard construction of a *quotient ring*. In particular, in those terms R is simply

$$R = \mathbf{Z}[x]/(x^N - 1)$$

Similar objects are often used in 'convolution' computations in various fields of mathematics, science, and engineering, often without explicit mention of the idea of a quotient ring. One virtue of this viewpoint is that it provides a systematic way to understand that 'multiplication' operations such as the one introduced above truly will behave 'normally'.

Why does decryption work? The polynomial that Alice computes in the decryption step is

$$
\begin{aligned}
a &= f \star y \\
&= f \star (p\phi \star h + m) \ \% \ q && \text{(by definition of encryption)} \\
&= f \star (p\phi \star F_q \star g + m) \ \% \ q && \text{(by construction of } h\text{)} \\
&= (f \star p\phi \star F_q \star g + f \star m) \ \% \ q && \text{(by distributivity)} \\
&= (f \star F_q \star p\phi \star g + f \star m) \ \% \ q && \text{(by commutativity)} \\
&= (1 \star p\phi \star g + f \star m) \ \% \ q && \text{(by inverse property of } F_q \bmod q\text{)} \\
&= (p\phi \star g + f \star m) \ \% \ q
\end{aligned}
$$

Then Alice shifts the coefficients by subtracting q if necessary to make them all lie in the interval $(-q/2, q/2]$. By careful choices of parameters, it can be arranged that all the coefficients lie in the range $(-q/2, q/2]$ *even before reduction modulo q*, so that reduction mod q causes no loss of information: in that case the coefficients will not change when (the currently normalized version of) a is reduced mod q. Therefore, since the reduction mod q step doesn't do anything, Alice is really computing

$$
\begin{aligned}
(a \ \% \ p) &= (p\phi \star g + f \star m) \ \% \ q \ \% \ p \\
&= (p\phi \star g + f \star m) \ \% \ p \\
&= 0 \star g + f \star h \ \% \ p && \text{(since } p\phi \ \% \ p = 0\text{)} \\
&= f \star m \ \% \ p
\end{aligned}
$$

Then the star-multiplication by F_p recovers the plaintext:

$$
\begin{aligned}
(f \star m) \star F_p \; \% \; p & = (f \star F_p) \star m \; \% \; p \\
& = 1 \star m \\
& = m
\end{aligned}
$$

where again we use the commutativity and associativity of $\star$, as well as the defining property

$$f \star F_p \; \% \; p = 1$$

of F_p.

Parameter settings. In fact, the official description of the algorithm requires/suggests that f, g, and ϕ always be chosen to have only ± 1 and 0 coefficients. Indeed, there are further specific recommendations based on partly heuristic and partly theoretical considerations. Apart from the usual sort of keyspace considerations, the parameters should be chosen to thwart *lattice attacks*, described very roughly just below.

Security. The first point is that fairly standard meet-in-the-middle attacks (playing upon the *birthday paradox* idea) reduce the search space roughly by taking the square root of the size of the actual key space. Thus, to require an attacker to search 10^{100} possibilities it is necessary that f, g, ϕ be chosen from sets with 10^{200} elements.

The most serious type of attack on the NTRU cipher seems to be what are called *lattice attacks*, which view the key f as more or less the shortest vector in a special collection ('lattice') of vectors. The LLL algorithm will quickly find a short vector, unless it is frustrated by having the length of the shortest vector be close to or even larger than the expected value of such length (for suitably 'random' lattice). In order to break NTRU, however, the LLL algorithm would have to find one of the shortest vectors in a lattice where all the 'short' vectors have *moderate* length rather than being short. Suitable parameter settings in NTRU seem to achieve the effect of frustrating LLL: experimental evidence suggests that the runtime can be superexponential in the parameter N. In particular, this suggests that relatively small values of N allow secure implementations of NTRU.

At a lower level, note that the polynomial multiplications in NTRU are often just multiplications of polynomials with coefficients which are 1's, 0's, and -1's. And the parameters p and q are 'normal' integers, *small* by cryptographic standards, so that all operations are done with small/ordinary integers, rather than specially implemented *long* integers. This contributes to the speed of NTRU.

Remark: An unusual feature of NTRU is that it sends roughly $\frac{\ln q}{\ln p}$ bits of ciphertext for each bit of plaintext. Since it is necessary that $q > p$ to avoid losing information, this shows how NTRU uses more bandwidth than the older ciphers.

In a different vein, it bears repeating that at this time (mid 2000) there are no quantum *algorithms* known that would provide speed-up of lattice attacks at a future time when we have operational quantum *computers*. Of course this does not preclude discovery of such algorithms in the future. But this is in sharp contrast to the status of RSA and prime factorization: Shor's quantum algorithm for factorization *would* completely break RSA.

For discussion of relative speeds of encryption/decryption, apparent security, and more details, see NTRU's home page at
http://www.ntru.com/

10.7 Arithmetica Key Exchange

The key exchange mechanism presented here is quite abstract and should probably be skipped on a first reading. But it illustrates the role that contemporary mathematics can play in cryptography.

The Arithmetica key exchange [Anschel, Anschel, Goldfeld 1999] is a new *key exchange mechanism*. It intends to achieve the same effect as the Diffie–Hellman key exchange discussed above, that of establishing a shared secret when the only communication possible is across an insecure channel. By extreme constrast with Diffie–Hellman, it plays upon some sophisticated mathematics to make a plausible claim of security. However, the *length attack* of [Hughes, Tannenbaum 2000] gives a plausible heuristic argument for a class of attacks on this and related ciphers. Both the key exchange and the proposed attack are not easy to explain in down-to-earth terms, but mention of such possibilities seems like a good idea when surveying ciphers and their mechanisms.

The description of the key exchange needs some ideas from *group theory*, which we'll discuss systematically later, but can sketch a little now. It appears that some general ideas about using group theory to make ciphers appeared earlier in [Wagner, Magyarik 1985]. A significant new idea in [Anschel, Anschel, Goldfeld 1999] is use of the braid group, or more generally Artin groups, making use of a new algorithm discovered in [Birman, Ko, Lee 1998]. The Arithmetica key exchange is patented.

Let G be a **group**. Roughly (see later chapters) this means that G is a set with an *operation* on pairs of elements $x, y \in G$ written xy, as though it were ordinary multiplication. It is important to note that we *cannot* presume that the operation is *commutative*. That is, probably $xy \neq yx$. There is also an *identity* element $e \in G$ with the property that $eg = ge = g$ for all $g \in G$. And there are *inverses*. That is, for each $g \in G$ there is $g^{-1} \in G$ so that

$$gg^{-1} = g^{-1}g = e$$

Finally, we require that the operation be *associative*, meaning that

$$(xy)z = x(yz)$$

This is a quite general abstraction, and it is *not* at all clear what all the ramifications of such a general idea may be. Indeed, the notion of 'group' took more than 100 years to develop into this form, from about 1800 to 1920.

As an example 'group' of roughly the right sort, the collection of two-by-two matrices with real entries and nonzero determinant fits these axioms, with

$$e = \begin{pmatrix} 1 & 0 \\ 0 & 1 \end{pmatrix}$$

And we may remember that matrix multiplication is in general not commutative, as simple examples show.

For a fixed set of elements $S = \{s_1, \ldots, s_n\}$ in G, a **word** in S is any expression of the sort

$$s_{i_1}^{k_1} s_{i_2}^{k_2} \ldots s_{i_N}^{k_N}$$

where the exponents k_j are positive or negative integers. For example,

$$s_1 s_2^3 s_1^{-7} s_2$$

is a word in s_1, s_2 and their inverses. Or

$$aabbaba^3 b^{-1}$$

is a word in a, b and their inverses. 'Words' are any expressions that can be obtained by repeated multiplications by the elements and their inverses. The set S **generates** G if *every* element of G is expressible as a word in the elements of S and their inverses.

The **word problem** in a group G with respect to a subset $S = \{s_1, \ldots, s_n\}$ is the question of telling whether two *words* in S are equal, that is, telling whether the two words give the same element of the group G. The **conjugacy problem** in a group G with respect to S is the question of telling, for two words x, y in S, whether or not there is $g \in G$ so that $gxg^{-1} = y$. It is known that in general the word problem is *undecidable*, meaning that there is no algorithm to solve it. The conjugacy problem has a similar status. Even for specific groups where there *is* an algorithm, such as Coxeter groups (see [Garrett 1997]), the algorithm may be 'bad' in that it runs in exponential time in the length of the inputs.

So in general the word problem and conjugacy problem are hard. But in [Birman, Ko, Lee 1998] a class of groups, the *braid groups*, was distinguished in which the word problem has a polynomial-time solution, and seemingly the conjugacy problem does not. If one is thinking in such terms, this is the sort of situation that would suggest making a cipher in which authorized decryption requires solving the word problem, and unauthorized decryption requires solving the conjugacy problem.

A **braid group** with n generators is a group G generated by a set $S = \{s_1, \ldots, s_n\}$ and where we know that

$$s_i s_{i+1} s_i = s_{i+1} s_i s_{i+1}$$

and

$$s_i s_j = s_j s_i \quad \text{for } |i - j| > 1$$

There are no 'hidden' relations, in the sense that any other true equality should be derivable from these. That is, except for elements s_i with adjacent indices, they commute with each other, and the adjacent ones have the funny relationship above. This arose historically in looking at actual 'braids'.

The definition of **Artin group** includes braid groups as a special case where all parameters m_i are 3 (see just below). An Artin group is a group G generated by a set $S = \{s_1, \ldots, s_n\}$ and where we know that

$$\underbrace{s_i s_{i+1} s_i \ldots s_i s_{i+1} s_i}_{m_i \text{ factors}} = \underbrace{s_{i+1} s_i s_{i+1} \ldots s_{i+1} s_i s_{i+1}}_{m_i \text{ factors}}$$

and

$$s_i s_j = s_j s_i \quad \text{for } |i - j| > 1$$

Further, there are no 'hidden' relations, in the sense that any other true equality should be derivable from these. That is, except for elements s_i with adjacent indices, they commute with each other, and the adjacent ones have the relationship above, which for $m_i = 3$ gives the braid group of the previous paragraph. The definition of **Coxeter group** includes groups defined just as Artin groups, but with additional relations

$$s_i^2 = e \quad \text{for all indices } i$$

Remark: Lacking prior experience with such things, this should indeed look mysterious! And, there are genuine complications in understanding such things. Indeed, the conjugacy problem is presumed to be essentially as hard as any computational problem can be, if we arrange things suitably.

The key exchange. Again, the idea of a key exchange is to establish a shared secret in a situation where the only communication takes place over an insecure channel. Here Alice and Bob proceed as follows. The public information is a group G and two lists $S_A = \{a_1, \ldots, a_m\}$, $S_B = \{b_1, \ldots, b_n\}$ of elements of G. Alice chooses a secret word a in S_A, and Bob chooses a secret word b in S_B. (Recall that this means a can be expressed as some product of the elements of S_A and their inverses, and similarly for b.) Alice transmits to Bob the list

$$ab_1 a^{-1}, \ a_2^b a^{-1}, \ \ldots, \ ab_n a^{-1}$$

and Bob transmits to Alice the list

$$ba_1 b^{-1}, \ ba_2 b^{-1}, \ \ldots, \ ba_m b^{-1}$$

(These must be disguised slightly to make this work well.) Then the common key for Alice and Bob will be the expression (called the *commutator* of a and b)

$$\text{common key} = aba^{-1}b^{-1}$$

which they can both compute, as follows.

Let

$$a^{-1} = a_{i_1}^{e_{i_1}} \ldots a_{i_N}^{k_{i_N}}$$

be an expression of the inverse a^{-1} of Alice's secret a in terms of Alice's a_i's. Then it is a basic property of the *conjugation operation* $x \to bxb^{-1}$ that

$$\begin{aligned}
ba^{-1}b^{-1} &= b(a_{i_N}^{e_{i_1}} \ldots a_{i_N}^{k_{i_N}})b^{-1} \\
&= (ba_{i_1}b^{-1})^{e_{i_1}} \ldots (ba_{i_N}b^{-1})^{k_{i_N}}
\end{aligned}$$

Now those expressions ba_jb^{-1} are exactly what Bob had sent to Alice, so she knows what they are. That is, Alice can compute $ba^{-1}b^{-1}$. And then, since she knows her own secret a, she can compute

$$a \cdot (ba^{-1}b^{-1}) = aba^{-1}b^{-1}$$

Symmetrically, Bob can compute aba^{-1}, and since he knows his own secret b (and its inverse b^{-1}), he can compute

$$(aba^{-1}) \cdot b^{-1} = aba^{-1}b^{-1}$$

Thus, Alice and Bob have a shared secret.

Remark: The most obvious attack on such a cipher would depend upon being able to solve the conjugacy problem. At this time the conjugacy problem is not known to have a fast algorithm for braid groups, for example.

Remark: The above description did not depend upon specifics concerning the group G. But for the shared secret $aba^{-1}b^{-1}$ to be unambiguous, it must be convertible to some 'canonical' form. For braid groups this is in effect accomplished in [Birman, Ko, Lee 1998].

Fix a group G and a set S of generators $s_1, \ldots, s_n$ for G. For an element $w \in G$, choose an expression of w in terms of the s_i's that is as *short as possible*:

$$w = s_{i_1}^{k_1} s_{i_2}^{k_2} \ldots s_{i_N}^{k_N}$$

That is, we choose such an expression with minimal

$$|k_1| + |k_2| + \cdots + |k_N|$$

Then the **length** of w (with respect to S) is

$$\text{length } w = \ell(w) = |k_1| + |k_2| + \cdots + |k_N|$$

This definition makes sense in an arbitrary group with generators S, but has tractable properties in types of groups with special generators such as braid groups, Artin groups, and Coxeter groups. In general,

$$\ell(xy) \leq \ell(x) + \ell(y)$$

If some parts of the shortest word expressions for x and y *cancel*, then it can happen that the length of the product xy is *much* less than the sum of the lengths of x and y separately.

In this context, we *very* roughly describe the Hughes-Tannenbaum length attack on such ciphers. Using the notation in the description of the cipher above, the intuitive idea is to compute

$$\ell(a_i^{\pm 1} (at_j a^{-1}) a_i^{\mp 1})$$

and whenever

$$\ell(a_i^{\pm 1}\, (at_j a^{-1})\, a_i^{\mp 1}) < \ell(at_j a^{-1})$$

we imagine that $a_i^{\mp 1}$ is a factor of a on the left with some positive probability. A rough analysis in this direction indicates that the workload will be polynomial in the lengths and numbers of key material.

Remark: This attack is an even newer idea than the cipher itself and has not been worked out fully. It may well be that it is ineffective against such ciphers, but only indicates that parameter choices must be made wisely. It is a subject of ongoing research.

10.8 Quantum Cryptography

Since we don't include an introduction to quantum mechanics here, the descriptions of quantum cryptography and quantum algorithms will be very brief.

First, in reference to quantum effect we do *not* intend to express concern about the ever-decreasing size of conventional computer parts, nor the decades-old use of quantum effects in building transistors and chips. Rather, we will discuss very briefly *novel* applications and exploitation of quantum effects.

It *does* appear that practical **quantum channels** can be and are being used to communicate with absolute security, in a certain qualified sense. In very rough terms, these are channels designed to be very sensitive to quantum effects, such as changes in state due to observation. In particular, the general idea is that if anyone eavesdrops on the channel, this will *change* the message, for reasons of basic quantum mechanics, since 'eavesdropping' would be an 'observation'. That is, *detection* of eavesdropping is certain. Using such channels as the basic mechanism to assure secure communication is one part of **quantum cryptography**. While there are certainly many practical limitations, working models have been made. The downside of this mechanism is that if there *is* an eavesdropper who doesn't mind being detected, then communication is disrupted. And there is no *prevention* mechanism, only detection.

An aspect of quantum cryptography which seems less practical at this point (March 2000) is what is called **quantum teleportation**, which means using the Einstein-Podolsky-Rosen effect [Einstein, Podolsky, Rosen 1935]. This is related to Bell's theorem [Bell 1993]. The rough idea is that if two particles have quantum states which are 'tangled', and then they are separated widely in space, a change of state in one (perhaps caused by an observation being made) *instantly* causes a corresponding change of state in the other. That is, information has traveled faster than light, and without interaction with any intervening medium. If we could really make such things in a reliable fashion, this would be quantum teleportation, and would plausibly provide absolutely secure communication of a really novel (and unbelievable) type.

In a different vein, there does seem to be incremental progress toward building a real *quantum computer*. Although it is true that ordinary transistors and microchips make use of quantum effects in forms used for several decades, mostly designers wish these circuits to behave in a manner entirely compatible with macroscopic objects, so in fact *avoiding* the peculiarities of quantum behavior. But by the 1980s several people had contemplated *exploitation* rather than avoidance of quantum effects. Early on, Richard Feynman noted that it appeared unlikely that classical computers would ever be able to efficiently simulate quantum events.

The discussion of hypothetical quantum computers was somewhat obscure until about 1993, at which time Peter Shor's algorithm for factoring large numbers quickly on a quantum computer [Shor 1996a] decisively illustrated the cataclysmic changes that could occur in computation if and when a functional quantum computer were constructed. For example, the most popular public-key cipher, RSA, would be completely broken.

Although in the early 1990s enthusiasts were optimistic, progress has been slower than hoped. The most recent progress is reported in [Knill, Laflamme, Martinez, Tseng 2000]. That research group had earlier reported successful manipulation of 3 qubits, then 5 qubits, and now 7 qubits. In all cases they used nuclear magnetic resonance (NMR). In their words, 'Our experimental procedure can be used as a reliable and efficient method for creating a standard pseudopure state, the first step for implementing traditional quantum algorithms in liquid state NMR systems.'

On the other hand, even if we optimistically imagine that quantum computers will be constructed some time soon, low-level traditional computational techniques have to be rebuilt or replaced in quantum computers. For example, in the same issue of *Nature*, in [Pati, Braunstein 2000], it is reported that it is impossible to delete a copy of an arbitrary quantum state perfectly. While a classical computer can delete information, and can undo the deletion using a copy, a quantum computer cannot delete quantum information (even irreversibly).

A crucial technical issue which has effectively disappeared for classical computers is that of (internal) *error correction*, and *fault-tolerant* computing. By this point, classical computers are so reliable (in hardware) that almost no internal redundancy is built into them. By contrast, the very nature of the quantum effects exploited by (hypothetical) quantum computers requires a whole new development of quantum-oriented error-correction techniques. Though roughly based on classical error correction, the peculiarities of quantum mechanics demand subtle changes. As a sample, see [Calderbank, Shor 1996].

In summary, people have high hopes, but not much has happened yet. It is still unclear whether or not there will *ever* be quantum computers. It is unclear whether or not ordinary people would be able to afford them if they do exist. It is unclear whether ordinary people would be *allowed* to own them.

Exercises

10.8.01 (**) Build a quantum computer than can factor 6 as 2×3.

10.8.02 (**) Build a quantum computer than can factor 15 as 3×5.

10.9 U.S. Export Regulations

Until the last year or so, encryption products were classified by the U.S. government as *munitions*, whose export required approval from federal agencies. In general, strong encryption products were not exportable at all, although not surprisingly strong encryption products are available worldwide. For years people speculated on the motivations behind this legislation. Some people inferred that it was believed that if the U.S. didn't export it, no one else would have strong crypto. Others perceived that disallowing export would inhibit widespread domestic use of strong crypto, and the F.B.I. certainly has wanted to discourage use of strong crypto.

By 1998, the strict viewpoint was modified slightly: export of RSA software with any keysize was allowed for **authentication** purposes, although it had to be demonstrated that the product in question could not easily be converted to use for encryption. For RSA used for encryption, evidently the keysize allowed for export was limited to 512 bits. Export of encryption for financial use with larger key sizes was sometimes allowed: for example, Cybercash has been allowed to export 768-bit keys for financial transactions.

By late 1999, federal legislation changed the situation, at least in principle. In theory, anything is exportable once certain federal paperwork is done, as long as strong crypto products are not sent to the countries supporting terrorism. It appears that this makes it possible for corporations to export strong crypto products, but does not make clear the status of private individuals. For example, it is not yet clear whether 'free' code for strong crypto can be legally put on web sites. There is the additional issue of whether putting things on the web constitutes export.

In May 2000 the European Union surprised the rest of the world by informally announcing a tentative agreement to completely deregulate export of cryptographic software within the Union and to several other countries including the U.S., Canada, and Japan. This was opposite to the direction of change expected by U.S. government policymakers, and was directly opposed by the U.K. and France. It was presumed that the U.S. government's policy would have to match or somehow exceed the liberality of the E.U.'s policy for U.S. manufacturers to remain competitive. The tentative agreement reached by the E.U. was to be formally ratified and formally announced June 13, 2000 along with other recent policy developments, *but it was not*. No explanation was given. Back to the status quo?

The RSA FAQ is one reasonable reference for the current status of export questions in general, and certainly for practical questions about RSA:

- http://www.rsa.com/rsalabs/newfaq/

11

Prime Numbers

This chapter discusses prime numbers in some detail. With the exception of the first subsection, regarding Euclid's proof of the infinitude of primes, the discussion here is more difficult than many other parts of this book, and it can be skipped without impairing understanding of the rest.

But for a deeper understanding one has to work through the things presented in this chapter, and in more detail than we have space to present here.

11.1 Euclid's Theorem

Our experience probably already suggested that integers have unique factorization into primes, but it is less intuitive that there are *infinitely many primes*. Euclid's 2000-year-old proof of this is not only ingenious, but also is a good example of an indirect proof ('by contradiction').

For this discussion we grant that integers do have *unique factorizations* into primes. (This is a special case of our later result that *all Euclidean rings have unique factorization.*)

Theorem. (*Euclid*) There are infinitely many prime numbers.

Proof: This is a proof by contradiction. Suppose that there were only finitely many primes. Then we could list *all* of them: $p_1, \ldots, p_n$. Then consider the number

$$N = p_1 \cdot p_2 \cdot \ \cdots \ \cdot p_{n-1} \cdot p_n \ + \ 1$$

That is, N is the product of all the primes, plus 1. Since $N > 1$, and since N has a factorization into primes, we can say that there is a prime p dividing N. Then p cannot be in the list $p_1, \ldots, p_n$, since if it *were* in that list, then p would divide

$$N - (p_1 \cdots p_n) = 1$$

which it does not. But the fact that p is not on the list contradicts the hypothesis that we had listed them all. That is, assuming that there were only finitely many primes leads to a contradiction. Thus, there are infinitely many primes.   ♣

Note that this gives no substantial idea of what integers are or are not primes, nor 'how many' primes there may be.

11.2 Prime Number Theorem

By about 1800 Legendre had made conjectures about the distribution of prime numbers, from looking at lists of primes. Gauss also considered the issue, but neither Legendre nor Gauss was able to prove anything precise. It was not until one hundred years later, in 1896, that Hadamard and de la Valleé-Poussin independently proved the result described just below.

The standard counting function for primes is

$$\pi(x) = \text{number of primes less than } x$$

We use the standard notation that

$$f(x) \sim g(x)$$

means

$$\lim_{x \to +\infty} \frac{f(x)}{g(x)} = 1$$

Theorem. *Prime Number Theorem:* As $x \to +\infty$

$$\pi(x) \sim \frac{x}{\ln x}$$

The proof of this is difficult, and we won't give it here. The theorem as it stands does not give any indication whatsoever of how *fast* the expression $(\pi(x)\ln x)/x$ goes to 1, nor what fluctuations if any there are along the way. The next level of work, which continues to this day but which was especially active for the decades immediately following proof of this theorem, addresses the question of this approach to the limit.

11.3 Primes in Sequences

There was a delay of about 1900 years between Euclid's proof that there are infinitely many primes, and the following result of Dirichlet about primes in certain arithmetic progressions.

An arithmetic progression is a set of expressions $an + b$, where $a \neq 0$ and b are fixed integers and $n = 0, 1, 2, 3, 4, \ldots$. For example, with $a = 5$, $b = 3$, we have the arithmetic sequence

$$3, 8, 13, 18, 23, 28, 33, 38, \ldots$$

With $a = 3$, $b = 6$, we have the arithmetic sequence

$$3, 9, 15, 21, 27, 33, 39, \ldots$$

In the first of these two there are several primes, and if we were to continue we would find more and more. In the second of these two the first element, 3, is the only prime. Indeed, we see that every element in the second sequence will be divisible by 3, so surely not prime (after the very beginning). So the second sequence certainly does *not* contain infinitely many primes, but for a reason which is not subtle at all. Thus, taking a lesson from this example, we would surely *not* expect infinitely many primes in an arithmetic sequence $\{an+b : n = 0, 1, 2, \ldots\}$ unless $\gcd(a, b) = 1$. The happy result is that this simple and understandable condition is enough:

Theorem. (*Dirichlet*) Let $\gcd(a, b) = 1$. Then there are infinitely many primes in the arithmetic sequence

$$b, \ a + b, \ 2a + b, \ 3a + b, \ 4a + b, \ \ldots$$

(*Proof omitted: too hard for us.*)

Remark: There *is* an accessible proof in the case that $b = 1$, using cyclotomic polynomials, which we'll see later.

Almost immediately after the proof in 1896 of the Prime Number Theorem, that idea was combined with Dirichlet's earlier ideas about primes in arithmetic progressions, to prove a corresponding statement:

Theorem. Let $\gcd(a, b) = 1$. Let $\pi_{a,b}(x)$ be the number of primes in the arithmetic sequence

$$b, \; a + b, \; 2a + b, \; 3a + b, \; 4a + b, \; \ldots$$

below the bound x. Let $\varphi(a)$ be the Euler phi-function of a. Then

$$\lim_{x \to \infty} \frac{\pi_{a,b}(x)}{x/\varphi(a) \, \ln x} = 1$$

(Proof omitted: too hard for us.)

The occurrence of the factor of $\varphi(a)$ in the latter theorem is a manifestation of the fact that *no* primes will occur in any such arithmetic sequence if b has a common factor with a, so for fixed a there are only $\varphi(a)$ arithmetic sequences that have primes in them (not counting sequences as different if they start at integers differing by multiples of a). We would say that the primes are **equidistributed** among the congruence classes $b \bmod a$, where b is prime to a.

11.4 Chebycheff's Theorem

In 1851 Chebycheff made a breakthrough toward proving the Prime Number Theorem. Although what he proved was weaker than the conjectured result, it was the first real progress beyond collecting statistics and making lists. His proof is more or less accessible in terms of things we know, so we'll do it here:

Theorem.   *(Chebycheff)* There are positive constants c and C so that eventually (for large-enough x)

$$c \cdot \frac{x}{\ln x} \leq \pi(x) \leq C \cdot \frac{x}{\ln x}$$

Proof: We need to define standard auxiliary functions

$$\theta(x) = \sum_{p \text{ prime: } p < x} \ln p$$

$$\psi(x) = \sum_{p \text{ prime: } k \in \mathbf{Z}, \; p^k < x} \ln p$$

That is, in words, $\theta(x)$ is the sum of the natural logarithms of all primes less than x, and $\psi(x)$ is the sum of $\ln p$ for every *prime power* p^k less than x. The easiest estimates arise in terms of θ and ψ, so at the end we will return to see what these say about the prime-counting function π. The first thing necessary is to see that, for purposes of our asymptotic estimates, θ and ψ are not far apart. After that come two rather clever lemmas due to Chebycheff.

Lemma.
$$0 \leq \psi(x) - \theta(x) \leq x^{1/2}(\ln x)^2$$

(Proof left to the reader: there's nothing delicate about this comparison!)

Lemma. *(Chebycheff)* $\theta(x) = O(x)$.

Proof: For $m = 2^e$ with positive integer e, consider the binomial coefficient

$$N = \binom{m}{m/2}$$

Since

$$2^m = (1+1)^m = \sum_{0 \leq k \leq m} \binom{m}{k} 1^{m-k} 1^k = \sum_{0 \leq k \leq m} \binom{m}{k}$$

it is clear that $\binom{m}{m/2}$ is a *positive integer* and is less than 2^m. On the other hand, from the expression

$$\binom{m}{m/2} = \frac{m!}{(m/2)!\,(m/2)!}$$

we can see that each prime p in the range $\frac{m}{2} < p \leq m$ divides $\binom{m}{m/2}$. Thus,

$$\prod_{(m/2) < p \leq m} p \leq \binom{m}{m/2}$$

The natural logarithm function is **monotone increasing**, meaning that $x < y$ implies $\ln(x) < \ln(y)$. Therefore, taking natural logarithms of both sides of the last displayed inequality, we have

$$\theta(m) - \theta(m/2) \leq m \ln 2$$

That is,

$$\theta(2^e) - \theta(2^{e-1}) \leq m \ln 2 = 2^e \ln 2$$

Therefore, applying this repeatedly, we have

$$\begin{aligned}
\theta(2^e) &= (\theta(2^e) - \theta(2^{e-1})) + \theta(2^{e-1}) \\
&\leq 2^e \ln 2 + (\theta(2^{e-1}) - \theta(2^{e-2})) + \theta(2^{e-2}) \\
&\leq 2^e \ln 2 + 2^{e-1} \ln 2 + \theta(2^{e-2}) \\
&\leq 2^e \ln 2 + 2^{e-1} \ln 2 + 2^{e-2} \ln 2 + \theta(2^{e-3})
\end{aligned}$$

which, by repeating further, is

$$\begin{aligned}
&\leq 2^e \ln 2 + 2^{e-1} \ln 2 + 2^{e-2} \ln 2 + \cdots + 2^1 \ln 2 + \ln 2 \\
&= 2^{e+1} \ln 2 - 1 \leq 2^{e+1} \ln 2
\end{aligned}$$

So for $2^{e-1} \leq x \leq 2^e$, we have

$$\theta(x) \leq \theta(2^e) = 2^{e+1} \ln 2 = 2 \cdot 2^e \ln 2 \leq 4 \cdot x \ln 2 = (4 \ln 2) \cdot x$$

This proves the lemma.   ♣

Lemma.   *(Chebycheff)* There are positive constants c, C so that

$$cx \leq \psi(x) \leq Cx$$

Proof: Consider

$$I = \int_0^1 x^n (1-x)^n \, dx$$

Multiplying out the $(1-x)^n$ and integrating term-by-term, no term has a denominator larger than $2n + 1$, so if we multiply out by the least common multiple of $1, 2, 3, \ldots, 2n + 1$, the result is an integer:

$$I \times \operatorname{lcm}(1, 2, 3, \ldots, 2n, 2n + 1) \in \mathbf{Z}$$

Thus,

$$1 \leq I \times \operatorname{lcm}(1, 2, 3, \ldots, 2n, 2n + 1)$$

or

$$\frac{1}{I} \leq \operatorname{lcm}(1, 2, 3, \ldots, 2n, 2n + 1)$$

On the other hand, the maximum of $x(1-x)$ on the interval $[0, 1]$ is $1/4$, so the integrand is at most $(1/4)^n$, and

$$I \leq \left(\frac{1}{4}\right)^n$$

which can be rearranged to

$$4^n \leq \frac{1}{I}$$

Thus, putting these inequalities together, we have

$$4^n \leq \operatorname{lcm}(1, 2, 3, \ldots, 2n, 2n + 1)$$

Taking logarithms,

$$(\ln 4) \cdot n \leq \ln \operatorname{lcm}(1, 2, 3, \ldots, 2n + 1)$$

Now we are happy, because of the following essentially elementary observation (which, of course, was the real reason that Chebycheff introduced ψ in the first place):

Lemma.
$$\psi(n) = \ln \operatorname{lcm}(1, 2, 3, \ldots, 2n+1)$$

(Proof left to the reader: it's not too hard!)

Finally we can return to the counting function $\pi(x)$ rather than the auxiliary functions θ and ψ. We have a **Riemann-Stieljes integral**

$$\pi(x) = \int_{3/2}^{x} \frac{1}{\ln t} \, d\theta(t)$$

Integrating by parts, this gives

$$\pi(x) = \frac{\theta(x)}{\ln x} + \int_{3/2}^{x} \frac{\theta(x)}{t \ln^2 t} \, dt$$

Using the fact that $\theta(x) = O(x)$, this gives

$$\pi(x) = \frac{\theta(x)}{\ln x} + \int_{3/2}^{x} \frac{O(x)}{t \ln^2 t} \, dt = \frac{\theta(x)}{\ln x} + O(\frac{x}{\ln^2 x})$$

Since we know by now that
$$cx \le \theta(x) \le Cx$$

for some positive constants c, C,

$$\frac{cx}{\ln x} \le \overset{\pi(x)}{\theta(x)} \le \frac{Cx}{\ln x}$$

This finishes the proof of the theorem.   ♣

11.5 Sharpest Asymptotics

The sharpest known assertion about asymptotic distribution of primes is somewhat sharper than the simple statement of the Prime Number Theorem, since it gives an *error term*. This result comes from work of I. Vinogradov and Korobov, but was finished in all details by A. Walfisz and H.-E. Rickert. See [Walfisz 1963]. A reasonable exposition in English of this and related results is in [Karatsuba 1990].

The **logarithmic integral** is defined to be

$$\operatorname{li}(x) = \int_{2}^{x} \frac{1}{\ln t} \, dt \quad \left(\sim \frac{x}{\ln x} \right)$$

The sharpest assertion proven concerning the distribution of primes (in 1997) seems to be: *there exists a positive constant c so that*

$$\pi(x) = \operatorname{li}(x) + O \left(\frac{x}{e^{c(\ln x)^{3/5} (\ln \ln x)^{-1/5}}} \right)$$

To simplify a little for clarity, we can weaken this statement to assert

$$\pi(x) = \frac{x}{\ln x} + O\left(\frac{x}{\ln^2 x}\right)$$

Since $\mathrm{li}(x)$ is monotone increasing, it has an inverse function. Write

$$\mathrm{li}^{-1}(x)$$

for the *inverse function* (*not* for $1/\mathrm{li}(x)$). Then the nth prime p_n is estimated by

$$p_n = \mathrm{li}^{-1}(n) + O\left(\frac{n}{e^{(\ln n)^{3/5}\,(\ln \ln n)^{-1/5}}}\right)(\sim n \ln n)$$

11.6   Riemann Hypothesis

Even though the Prime Number Theorem was not proven until 1896, already by 1858 B. Riemann had seen the connection between error terms in the distribution of primes and the subtle behavior of a special function, the **zeta function**, defined below.

For a complex number s with real part > 1, the series

$$\zeta(s) = \sum_{n \geq 1} \frac{1}{n^s}$$

is absolutely convergent and defines a function of s. This is the **zeta function**, often called **Riemann's** because G. Riemann (about 1858) was the first to see that analytical properties of $\zeta(s)$ are intimately related to delicate details concerning the distribution of primes. Other people (for example, L. Euler) had seen that there were general connections. Already Euler had observed the **Euler product expansion**: for complex s with real part > 1

$$\zeta(s) = \prod_{p \text{ prime}} \frac{1}{1 - \frac{1}{p^s}}$$

To give this function meaning when the real part of s is less than or equal to 1 is already an issue, but this was resolved more than 140 years ago by Riemann, if not already by Euler.

For a real number r in the range $\frac{1}{2} < r < 1$, let PNT_r be the statement

$$\pi(x) = \frac{x}{\ln x} + O(x^{r+\varepsilon}) \quad \text{for all } \varepsilon > 0$$

It is important to realize that there is presently no proof that any such assertion is true: the **error term** in this assertion is asymptotically smaller than any error term that anyone has proven to hold. (See above.)

On the other hand, again for a real number r in the range $\frac{1}{2} < r < 1$, let RH_r be the statement

$$\zeta(s) \neq 0 \quad \text{when the real part of } s \text{ is } > r$$

No one has been able to prove any such statement for any $r < 1$. At the same time, it is known that there are *infinitely many* complex numbers ρ with real part $\frac{1}{2}$ so that $\zeta(\rho) = 0$.

Theorem. *(Sketched by Riemann)* For each $\frac{1}{2} < r < 1$, the assertion PNT_r is **equivalent** to RH_r.

In particular, the **Riemann Hypothesis** is that $\zeta(s) \neq 0$ for complex s with real part $> \frac{1}{2}$.

Thus, the *best possible error term* in the description of the asymptotic distribution of primes would be obtained if the Riemann Hypothesis were known to be true. But essentially nothing is known in this direction, although the accumulation of numerical evidence strongly supports the truth of the Riemann Hypothesis. *If the Riemann Hypothesis is true, in fact (as H. von Koch has proven)*

$$\pi(x) = \text{li}(x) + O(\sqrt{x}\,\ln x)$$
$$n\text{th prime } = \text{li}^{-1}(n) + O(\sqrt{n}\,(\ln n)^{5/2})$$

Then there is the **Extended Riemann Hypothesis** which is a similar assertion about the zeros of a wider class of functions than just the zeta function. And the **Generalized Riemann Hypothesis** is a comparable assertion about the zeros of a yet wider class. All these hypotheses, if true, would give the best possible error estimates on the distribution of primes and generalizations of primes. Unfortunately, essentially nothing is known about these things, apart from numerical evidence in favor of all of them.

12

Roots mod p

More than 350 years ago Pierre de Fermat made many astute observations regarding prime numbers, factorization into primes, and related aspects of number theory (not to mention other parts of mathematics and science as well). About 300 years ago, Leonhard Euler systematically continued Fermat's work. Most of these things were prototypes for 'modern' mathematical ideas, and at the same time remain very much relevant to contemporary number theory and its applications.

This chapter applies several ideas of Fermat. The so-called Fermat Little Theorem is a prototype for many later results, and has immediate applications in factorization tricks as well as formulas for roots modulo primes.

The fact that there are often relatively easy ways to compute powers and roots in $\mathbf{Z}/p$ will be used constantly in the rest of this book.

12.1 Fermat's Little Theorem

This little result is over 350 years old. It is basic in elementary number theory itself and is the origin of the first *probabilistic* primality test. It is possible to prove Fermat's Little Theorem with very minimal prerequisites, as we'll do now.

Theorem. Let p be a prime number. Then for any integer x

$$x^p \equiv x \bmod p$$

Proof: We will first prove that prime p divides the binomial coefficients

$$\binom{p}{i}$$

with $1 \le i \le p - 1$, keeping in mind that the 'extreme' cases $i = 0$ and $i = p$ can't possibly also have this property, since

$$\binom{p}{0} = 1 \qquad \binom{p}{p} = 1$$

Indeed, from its definition,
$$\binom{p}{i} = \frac{p!}{i!\,(p-i)!}$$

Certainly p divides the numerator. Since $0 < i < p$, the prime p divides none of the factors in the factorials in the denominator. By unique factorization into primes, this means that p does not divide the denominator at all.

From the binomial theorem,

$$(x+y)^p = \sum_{0 \le i \le p} \binom{p}{i} x^i\, y^{p-i}$$

In particular, since the coefficients of the left-hand side are integers, the same must be true of the right-hand side. Thus, all the binomial coefficients are *integers*. (We did not use the fact that p is prime to reach *this* conclusion.)

Thus, the binomial coefficients with $0 < i < p$ are *integers* expressed as fractions whose numerators are divisible by p and whose denominators are *not* divisible by p. Thus, when all cancellation is done in the fraction, there must remain a factor of p in the numerator. This proves the desired fact about binomial coefficients.

Now we prove Fermat's Little Theorem (for *positive* x) by induction on x. First, certainly $1^p \equiv 1 \bmod p$. For the induction step, suppose that we already know for some particular x that

$$x^p \equiv x \bmod p$$

Then

$$(x + 1)^p = \sum_{0 \le i \le p} \binom{p}{i} x^i \, 1^{p-i} = x^p + \sum_{0 < i < p} \binom{p}{i} x^i + 1$$

All the coefficients in the sum in the middle of the last expression are divisible by p. Therefore,

$$(x + 1)^p \equiv x^p + 0 + 1 \equiv x + 1 \bmod p$$

since our induction hypothesis is that $x^p \equiv x \bmod p$. This proves the theorem for positive x.

   To prove the theorem for $x < 0$ we use the fact that $-x$ is then *positive*. For $p = 2$ we can just treat the two cases $x \equiv 0 \bmod 2$ and $x \equiv 1 \bmod 2$ separately and directly. For $p > 2$ we use the fact that such a prime is *odd*. Thus,

$$x^p = -(-x)^p \equiv -(-x) \bmod p = x \bmod p$$

by using the result for positive integers.   ♣

Exercises

12.1.01 Compute $2^{1000} \% 17$ easily.

12.1.02 Compute $3^{1000} \% 17$ easily.

12.1.03 Compute $2^{1000} \% 23$ easily.

12.1.04 Compute $3^{1000} \% 23$ easily.

12.1.05 Compute $2^{1,000,000} \% 17$ easily.

12.1.06 Compute $3^{1,000,000} \% 17$ easily.

12.1.07 Show that if $\gcd(x, p) = 1$ with p prime, then a multiplicative inverse of x modulo p is $x^{p-2} \% p$.

12.1.08 (*) Which is easier, computing multiplicative inverses by the Euclidean algorithm, or by the formula of the previous exercise?

12.2 Factoring Special Expressions

Using Fermat's Little Theorem, we can follow in his footsteps and speed up certain *special* factorizations by a significant factor. First we prove a lemma that looks too good to be true:

   Lemma. Let $b > 1$. Then for any two positive integers m, n,

$$\gcd(b^m - 1, \, b^n - 1) = b^{\gcd(m,n)} - 1$$

Remark: From elementary algebra we should remember the identity

$$x^N - 1 = (x - 1)(x^{N-1} + x^{N-2} + \cdots + x^2 + x + 1)$$

for positive integers N. For a positive divisor d of n, letting $x = b^d$ and $N = n/d$, we obtain

$$b^n - 1 = (b^d)^N - 1 = (b^d - 1)((b^d)^{N-1} + (b^d)^{N-2} + \cdots + (b^d)^2 + (b^d) + 1$$

Thus, for simple reasons $b^d - 1$ divides $b^n - 1$ for $d|n$.

Proof: First, note that if $m = n$, then the assertion of the proposition is certainly true. The rest of the proof is by induction on the larger of m, n. We may suppose that $m \leq n$ (reversing the roles of m, n if necessary). In the case that $n = 1$, the assertion would be that the gcd of $b - 1$ and $b - 1$ is $b - 1$, which is certainly true. Now the induction step. We may suppose that $m < n$, since the $m = n$ case has been treated already. Note that

$$(b^n - 1) - b^{n-m}(b^m - 1) = b^{n-m} - 1$$

We claim that

$$\gcd(b^m - 1, b^n - 1) = \gcd(b^m - 1, b^{n-m} - 1)$$

On one hand, if $d|b^n - 1$ and $d|b^m - 1$, then $d|(b^n - 1) - b^{n-m}(b^m - 1)$, and then $d|b^{n-m} - 1$. Thus, any common divisor d of $b^n - 1$ and $b^m - 1$ also is a divisor of $b^{n-m} - 1$. On the other hand, from the rearranged expression

$$b^n - 1 = b^{n-m}(b^m - 1) + b^{n-m} - 1$$

any common divisor of $b^m - 1$ and $b^{n-m} - 1$ divides the right-hand side, so divides $b^n - 1$. This proves the claim.

Thus, invoking the induction hypothesis, we have

$$\gcd(b^m - 1, b^n - 1) = \gcd(b^m - 1, b^{n-m} - 1) = b^{\gcd(m, n-m)} - 1$$

So we should show that $\gcd(m, n) = \gcd(m, n - m)$: this follows the same standard idea as the proof of the last claim: On one hand, certainly if d is a common divisor of m and n, then $d|n - m$. On the other hand, using $n = m + (n - m)$, if d is a common divisor of m and $n - m$, then $d|n$ as well.   ♣

Corollary. Fix a positive integer b. Let n be a positive integer. If a prime p divides $b^n - 1$, then either $p|b^d - 1$ for some divisor d of n with $d < n$, or $p \equiv 1 \bmod n$.

Proof: Suppose that p divides $b^n - 1$. By Fermat's Little Theorem, $b^{p-1} \equiv 1 \bmod p$, so p divides $b^{p-1} - 1$. Therefore, by the lemma, p divides $b^{\gcd(n, p-1)} - 1$.

If $d = \gcd(n, p-1) < n$, then certainly $d < n$ is a positive divisor of n with $p | b^d - 1$. If $\gcd(n, p-1) = n$, then $n | p - 1$, which is to say that $p \equiv 1 \bmod n$.   ♣

Remark: The latter corollary shows that divisors of numbers of the form $b^n - 1$ are considerably restricted. Further, for *odd* primes p and *odd* n, since $\gcd(n, 2) = 1$, if $n | p - 1$, then from $2 | p - 1$ we can conclude that $2n | p - 1$, so $p \equiv 1 \bmod 2n$.

12.3 Mersenne Numbers

The restriction on the possible prime factors of numbers of the form $b^n - 1$ noted above reduces by a significant factor the time to factor (by otherwise naive methods) Mersenne numbers $2^n - 1$.

Example: Factor $127 = 2^7 - 1$: Since 7 is prime, the corollary shows that the only possible prime factors p of this number must satisfy $p \equiv 1 \bmod 14$. On the other hand, $\sqrt{127} < 12$, so we need only attempt division by primes under 12. But there aren't any such things that are also congruent to 1 modulo 14, so $2^7 - 1$ must be prime.

Remark: Even though we could easily test primality of 127 by hand anyway, it is pretty cute that we can also do it 'by pure thought' (meaning *without computing very much*).

Example: Factor $255 = 2^8 - 1$: The composite exponent yields many factors: from $2^2 - 1 = 3$ we get 3, from $2^4 - 1 = 15 = 3 \cdot 5$ we get 5. Dividing, we have

$$255/(3 \cdot 5) = 17$$

which is prime. So $2^8 - 1 = 3 \cdot 5 \cdot 17$.

Example: Factor $511 = 2^9 - 1$: The composite exponent gives a factor $2^3 - 1 = 7$. Then $511/7 = 73$, which is prime. So $2^9 - 1 = 7 \cdot 73$.

Example: Factor $1023 = 2^{10} - 1$: First, since the exponent is *composite*, this Mersenne number is certainly composite. We note that the (positive) divisors of 10 less than 10 are $1, 2, 5$, so we have divisors $3 = 2^2 - 1$ and $31 = 2^5 - 1$ of $2^{10} - 1$. The corollary then tells us that any *other* primes dividing $2^{10} - 1$ must be congruent to 1 modulo 10. First try 11: indeed

$$1023/11 = 93 = 3 \cdot 31$$

So

$$1023 = 3 \cdot 11 \cdot 31$$

Of course, since $2^{10} - 1$ has the small factor 3, $1023/3 = 341$ is probably already small enough that we might not mind continuing its factorization by hand. Especially after being handed the factor of $31 = 2^5 - 1$, and computing $341/31 = 11$, there's nothing left to the imagination.

Example: Factor $2047 = 2^{11} - 1$: Now we don't have any 'cheap' factors, since 11 is prime. If this number were to turn out to be prime, then it would be a **Mersenne prime**. The corollary above assures us that any prime p dividing 2047 must satisfy $p \equiv 1 \bmod 11$. Since also p must be *odd*, as noted above we can in fact assert that such p satisfies $p \equiv 1 \bmod 22$. So we attempt division of 2047 by $23 = 22 + 1$, and find that $2047/23 = 89$. (Since $89 < 100$, trial division by merely $2, 3, 5, 7$ shows that 89 is prime.) So $2047 = 23 \cdot 89$.

Example: Factor $4095 = 2^{12} - 1$: The exponent is so composite that we have many easy prime factors arising from the factors $2^d - 1$ with $d < 12$ dividing 12. That is, we can first look at the prime factors of $2^2 - 1 = 3$, $2^3 - 1 = 7$, $2^4 - 1 = 15 = 3 \cdot 5$, and $2^6 - 1 = 63 = 3^2 \cdot 7$. Thus, 4095 is divisible by $3^2 \cdot 5 \cdot 7$. Dividing, we are left with
$$4095/(3^2 \cdot 5 \cdot 7) = 13$$
So the whole factorization is $4095 = 3^2 \cdot 5 \cdot 7 \cdot 13$.

Example: Factor $8191 = 2^{13} - 1$. The exponent 13 is prime, so there are no obvious factors. If this number were to turn out to be prime, then it would be a **Mersenne prime**. Since $\sqrt{8191} \approx 90.5$, we need only do trial division by primes under 90. The corollary above says that we need only consider primes $p \equiv 1 \bmod 26$. First, $26 + 1 = 27$ is not prime, so we need not attempt division by it. Second, $2 \cdot 26 + 1 = 53$ *is* prime, but $8191 \% 53 = 29$. Then $3 \cdot 26 + 1 = 79$ is prime, but $8191 \% 79 = 54$. So 8191 is prime.

Example: Factor $16383 = 2^{14} - 1$. We look at $2^2 - 1 = 3$ and $2^7 - 1 = 127$ first. We saw above that 127 is prime. So we can take out prime factors of 3 and 127, leaving
$$16383/(3 \cdot 127) = 43$$
which we recognize as being prime.

Example: Factor $32767 = 2^{15} - 1$: From $2^3 - 1 = 7$ and $2^5 - 1 = 31$ we find prime factors 7 and 31. Dividing out, we have

$$32767/(7 \cdot 31) = 151$$

We could attack this by hand, or invoke the corollary to restrict our attention to primes p with $p \equiv 1 \bmod 30$ which are less than $\sqrt{151} < 13$. Since there aren't any such primes, we can conclude for *qualitative* reasons that 151 is prime. Therefore, the prime factorization is $2^{15} - 1 = 7 \cdot 31 \cdot 151$.

Example: Factor $65535 = 2^{16} - 1$: From $2^2 - 1 = 3$, $2^4 - 1 = 15 = 3 \cdot 5$, $2^8 - 1 = 255 = 3 \cdot 5 \cdot 17$ (from above), we obtain prime factors 3, 5, and 17.

Dividing, we get

$$65535/(3 \cdot 5 \cdot 17) = 257$$

Now we invoke the corollary to restrict our attention to potential prime factors p with $p \equiv 1$ mod 16. At the same time, $\sqrt{257} < 17$. This excludes all candidates, so 257 is prime, and the prime factorization is

$$2^{16} - 1 = 3 \cdot 5 \cdot 17 \cdot 257$$

Example: Factor $131071 = 2^{17} - 1$: Since 17 is prime, we only look for prime factors p with $p \equiv 1$ mod 34, and also $p \leq \sqrt{131071} < 362.038$. First, $34 + 1 = 35$ is not prime. Next, $2 \cdot 34 + 1 = 69$ is divisible by 3, so is not prime. Next, $3 \cdot 34 + 1 = 103$ *is* prime, but $131071 \% 103 = 55$. Next, $4 \cdot 34 + 1 = 137$ is prime, but $131071 \% 137 = 99$. Next, $5 \cdot 34 + 1 = 171$, which is divisible by 3. Next, $6 \cdot 34 + 1 = 205$, visibly divisible by 5. Next, $7 \cdot 34 + 1 = 239$, which is prime (testing prime divisors $2, 3, 5, 7, 11, 13$ all $\leq \sqrt{239} < 16$). But $131071 \% 239 = 99$. Next, $8 \cdot 34 + 1 = 273$, which is divisible by 3. Next, $9 \cdot 34 + 1 = 307$, which is prime (testing prime divisors $\leq \sqrt{307} < 18$). But $131071 \% 307 = 289$. Next, $19 \cdot 34 + 1 = 341$, which is divisible by 11. Since this is the last candidate prime below the bound 362, it must be that $131071 = 2^{17} - 1$ is prime.

Example: It turns out that $524287 = 2^{19} - 1$ is prime. To verify this in the most naive way, we would have to look for possible prime divisors $\leq \sqrt{524287} < 725$, If we did this in the *most* naive way it would require about $725/2 \approx 362$ trial divisions to verify the primality. But if we invoke the lemma and restrict our attention to primes p with $p \equiv 1$ mod 38, we'll only need about $725/38 \approx 19$ trial divisions.

Example: Factor $8388607 = 2^{23} - 1$: By the corollary, we need only look at primes p with $p \equiv 1$ mod 46. And, by luck 47 divides this number. Divide, to obtain $8388607/47 = 178481$. Anticipating (!?) that this is a prime, we note that we must attempt division by primes $\leq \sqrt{178481} < 422.5$. Looking only at these special primes, we have about $422/46 \approx 9$ trial divisions to do, rather than the $422/2 \approx 211$ in the most naive approach.

Example: Factor $536870911 = 2^{29} - 1$: Any possible prime factors p satisfy $p \equiv 1$ mod 58, and if this number is not prime, then it has such a factor $\leq \sqrt{536870911} \approx 23170$. Looking at 59, 117 (not prime), 175 (not prime), 233, ..., by luck it happens that 233 divides 536870911. Divide:

$$536870911/233 = 2304167$$

The latter is not divisible by 233. We know that if 2304167 is not prime then it has a prime divisor $\leq \sqrt{2304617} < 1518$. After 14 more trial divisions, we would find that the prime $19 * 58 + 1 = 1103$ divides 2304167. Dividing, we have $2304167/1103 = 2089$. If 2089 were not prime, then it would have a prime factor $\leq \sqrt{2089} < 46$, but also $\equiv 1$ mod 58. There aren't any such things, so 2089 is prime. Therefore,

$$536870911 = 233 \cdot 1103 \cdot 2089$$

12.4 More Examples

We continue with more examples using Fermat's observation about factors of special numbers of the form $b^n - 1$.

Every number $3^n - 1$ (for $n > 1$) has the obvious factor $3 - 1$, so is not prime. But this is a rather weak statement, since we might want the whole prime factorization, or at least be curious whether or not $(3^n-1)/(3-1)$ is prime. Fermat's trick is helpful in investigating this, in the same way that it was helpful in looking at Mersenne numbers.

The trick we have in mind here asserts that if a prime p divides $b^n - 1$ then either $p|(b^d - 1)$ for some $d|n$ with $d < n$, or else $p \equiv 1 \bmod n$. And in case n is odd then $p \equiv 1 \bmod 2n$. Thus, in rough terms, the number of primes p to attempt to divide into $b^n - 1$ is reduced by a factor of n or $2n$.

First, $3^2 - 1 = 8 = 2^3$.

Next, $(3^3 - 1)/2 = 26/2 = 13$. Fermat's trick indicates that a prime dividing $3^3 - 1$ and not dividing $3^1 - 1$ should be congruent to 1 mod $2 \cdot 3 = 6$, which is the case with 13.

Next, $3^4 - 1 = (3^2 - 1)(3^2 + 1)$. We factored $3^2 - 1$ above. The factor $3^2 + 1$ is still certainly divisible by 2, and then $(3^2 + 1)/2 = 5$, which is indeed a prime congruent to 1 modulo 4.

Next, $3^5 - 1 = 242$. Taking out the factor $3 - 1$ leaves 121. By Fermat's trick, any prime dividing this must be congruent to 1 modulo $2 \cdot 5 = 10$. Trying $10 + 1 = 11$, we see that in fact (as we really probably knew all along) $121 = 11^2$.

Next, $3^6 - 1 = (3^3 - 1)(3^3 + 1) = (3^3 - 1)(3 + 1)(3^2 - 3 + 1)$. We already understand all the factors except $3^2 - 3 + 1 = 7$. Indeed, this is a prime congruent to 1 modulo 6.

Next, $3^7 - 1 = 2186$. Taking out the factor of $3 - 1 = 2$ leaves 1093. By Fermat's trick, we know that any prime factor of this must be congruent to 1 mod $2 \cdot 7 = 14$. Since $14 + 1 = 15$ is not prime, the first prime we try to divide into 1093 is $2 \cdot 14 + 1 = 29$, and we find that $1093 \% 29 = 20$. Now $\sqrt{1093} \approx 33.06 < 34$, so we know in advance that we need not test potential divisors for 1093 larger than 33. But 29 is the only prime < 34 and congruent to 1 modulo 14, so we're done: 1093 is prime.

Next $3^8 - 1 = (3^4 - 1)(3^4 + 1)$. After taking the factor of $3 - 1 = 2$ out of $3^4 + 1$, we have $(3^4 + 1)/2 = 41$. Fermat's trick assures us that any prime not dividing $3^4 - 1 = 80 = 2^4 \cdot 5$ and dividing $3^8 - 1$ will be congruent to 1 modulo 8. Since there are no primes congruent to 1 mod 8 and $\leq \sqrt{41} < 7$, it follows that 41 is prime. (Yes, we already knew that anyway.)

Next, $(3^9 - 1)/(3^3 - 1) = 3^6 + 3^3 + 1 = 757$. From Fermat, 757 must be divisible only by primes congruent to 1 modulo $2 \cdot 9 = 18$. Also, if 757 is not prime then it will have a prime divisor $\leq \sqrt{757} < 28$. The only prime in this range is $18 + 1 = 19$, but $757 \% 19 = 16$, so 757 is prime.

Next, $(3^{10} - 1)/(3^5 - 1) = 244$. Taking out the factor of 2^2, this is 61. This has no prime factors dividing $3^2 - 1 = 8$ or $(3^5 - 1)/2 = 11^2$, so any prime factors of it must be congruent to 1 modulo 10. There are no such primes $\leq \sqrt{61} < 8$, so 61 is prime. (Yes, we knew that already.)

Next $(3^{11} - 1)/2 = 88,573$. Any prime dividing this must be congruent to 1 modulo 22. Attempting division by the first such, 23, gives a quotient of 3851 with no remainder. Trying again, $3851 \% 23 = 10$, so 23 does not divide 3851. If 3851 is not prime, it has a prime divisor $\leq \sqrt{3851} \approx 62.06 < 63$. The next candidate, $23 + 22 = 45$, is not prime. The next candidate is $45 + 22 = 67$, which is prime but is too large already. Therefore, 3851 is prime.

It turns out that $(3^{13} - 1)/2 = 797,161$ is prime, but even with Fermat's speed-up, this would still take about 35 trial divisions. This is plausible to do 'by hand', certainly better than the over 400 trial divisions that the most naive primality test would require.

Skipping ahead a little, let's look at $3^{15} - 1$. The quotient $(3^{15} - 1)/(3^5 - 1) = 59,293$ has prime factors either dividing $3^3 - 1 = 2 \cdot 13$ or congruent to 1 modulo $2 \cdot 15 = 30$. Trying 13, we get $59,293/13 = 4561$. (And 13 does not divide 4561.) The only prime divisors of *this* are congruent to 1 modulo 30. Also, if 4561 is not prime, it must have a factor $\leq \sqrt{4561} \approx 67.54 < 68$. Trying 31, we find $4561 \% 31 = 4$. Trying 61, we find $4561 \% 61 = 47$. Thus, 4561 is prime.

Exercises

12.4.01 (*) Show that Fermat's trick also applies to expressions $a^n - b^n$ for relatively prime a, b. That is, prove that for a prime p dividing $a^n - b^n$ either $p | a^d - b^d$ for some divisor d of n smaller than n, or $p = 1 \bmod n$.

12.4.02 Using the previous exercise, factor $3^n - 2^n$ into primes for $1 \leq n \leq 16$.

12.4.03 Using the first exercise, factor $4^n - 3^n$ into primes for $1 \leq n \leq 16$.

12.4.04 Easily (for example, by a very short hand computation) show that $15^3 - 14^3 = 631$ is prime.

12.4.05 Easily (for example, by a short hand computation) show that $11^5 - 10^5 = 61,051$ is prime.

12.4.06 Easily (for example, by hand) show that the factor 6553 of $242,461 = 4^9 - 3^9$ is prime.

12.5 Exponentiation Algorithm

The most naive version of exponentiation, in which to compute x^n one computes x^2, then $x^3 = x \cdot x^2$, then $x^4 = x \cdot x^3$, ..., $x^n = x \cdot x^{n-1}$, is very inefficient. Here we note a very simple but much faster improvement upon this, which has been known for at least 3000 years. This improvement is especially relevant for exponentiation modulo m.

The idea is that to compute x^e we express e as a *binary* integer

$$ e = e_0 + e_1 \cdot 2^1 + e_2 \cdot 2^2 + ... + e_n \cdot 2^n $$

with each e_i equal to 0 or 1, and compute power-of-two powers of x **by squaring**:

$$x^2 = x \cdot x$$
$$x^4 = (x^2)^2$$
$$x^8 = (x^4)^2$$
$$x^{2^4} = (x^8)^2$$
$$x^{2^5} = (x^{2^4})^2$$

$$\cdots$$

Then

$$x^e = x^{e_0} (x^2)^{e_1} (x^4)^{e_2} (x^8)^{e_3} (x^{2^4})^{e_4} \cdots (x^{2^n})^{e_n}$$

Again, the e_i's are just 0 or 1, so in fact this notation is clumsy: we *omit* the factor x^{2^k} if $e_k = 0$ and *include* the factor x^{2^k} if $e_k = 1$.

A fairly good way of implementing this is the following. To compute x^e, we will keep track of a triple (X, E, Y) which initially is $(X, E, Y) = (x, e, 1)$. At each step of the algorithm:

- If E is odd, then replace Y by by $X \times Y$ and replace E by $E - 1$

- If E is even, then replace X by $X \times X$ and replace E by $E/2$.

- When $E = 0$ the value of Y at that time is x^e.

Remark: This algorithm takes at most $2 \log_2 E$ steps (although of course the numbers involved grow considerably!).

For our purposes, this pretty fast exponentiation algorithm is of special interest when combined with reduction modulo m: the rewritten algorithm is: to compute $x^e \% m$, we will keep track of a triple (X, E, Y) which initially is $(X, E, Y) = (x, e, 1)$. At each step of the algorithm:

- If E is odd, then replace Y by by $X \times Y \% m$ and replace E by $E - 1$

- If E is even, then replace X by $X \times X \% m$ and replace E by $E/2$.

When $E = 0$, the value of Y at that time is $x^e \% m$.

Again, this algorithm takes at most $2 \log_2 E$ steps. When the exponentiation is done modulo m, the numbers involved stay below m^2, as well. Thus, for example, to compute something like

$$2^{1000} \% 1,000,001$$

would require no more than $2 \log_2 1000 \approx 2 \cdot 10 = 20$ multiplications of 6-digit numbers. Generally, we have

Proposition. The above algorithm for evaluation of $x^e \% m$ uses $O(\log e \log^2 n)$ bit operations.

For example, let's directly evaluate 2^{1000} mod 89. Setting this up as indicated just above, we have

X	E	output	
2	1000	1	initial state
4	500	1	'E' was even: square 'X' mod 89
16	250	1	'E' was even: square 'X' mod 89
78	125	1	'E' was even: square 'X' mod 89
78	124	78	'E' was odd: multiply 'out' by 'X' mod 89
32	62	78	'E' was even: square 'X' mod 89
45	31	78	'E' was even: square 'X' mod 89
45	30	39	'E' was odd: multiply 'out' by 'X' mod 89
67	15	39	'E' was even: square 'X' mod 89
67	14	32	'E' was odd: multiply 'out' by 'X' mod 89
39	7	32	'E' was even: square 'X' mod 89
39	6	2	'E' was odd: multiply 'out' by 'X' mod 89
8	3	2	'E' was even: square 'X' mod 89
8	2	16	'E' was odd: multiply 'out' by 'X' mod 89
64	1	16	'E' was even: square 'X' mod 89
64	0	45	'E' was odd: multiply 'out' by 'X' mod 89

We conclude that
$$2^{1000} \% 89 = 45$$

Exercises

12.5.01 Compute $2^{56} \% 1001$ by the fast exponentiation algorithm.

12.5.02 Compute $3^{59} \% 1001$ by the fast exponentiation algorithm.

12.5.03 Compute $2^{62} \% 1003$ by the fast exponentiation algorithm.

12.5.04 Compute $3^{70} \% 1003$ by the fast exponentiation algorithm.

12.5.05 Find the multiplicative inverse of 2 mod 59 by computing $2^{57} \% 59$. Explain why this works.

12.5.06 Find the multiplicative inverse of 7 mod 59 by computing $7^{57} \% 59$. Explain why this works.

12.5.07 Find the multiplicative inverse of 23 mod 521 by computing $23^{519} \% 521$. Explain why this works.

12.5.08 Find the multiplicative inverse of 29 mod 521 by computing $29^{519} \% 521$. Explain why this works.

12.5.09 Execute the fast exponentiation algorithm to compute the 17th power of the matrix $\begin{pmatrix} 1 & 2 \\ 2 & 5 \end{pmatrix}$.

12.5.10 Estimate the number of bit operations necessary to compute 2^{100} by the fast exponentiation algorithm.

12.5.11 Define the Fibonacci numbers as usual by the initial data

$$F_0 = 0, \quad F_1 = 1$$

and the *recurrence relation*

$$F_i = F_{i-1} + F_{i-2} \quad \text{for } i > 1$$

Let

$$F = \begin{pmatrix} 0 & 1 \\ 1 & 1 \end{pmatrix}$$

Prove by induction that

$$F^n = \begin{pmatrix} F_{n-1} & F_n \\ F_n & F_{n+1} \end{pmatrix}$$

12.5.12 Using the result of the previous exercise, easily compute $F_{128} \% 10$ (for example, by hand).

12.6 Square Roots mod p

In the case that a prime p satisfies $p = 3 \bmod 4$ we can also give a *formula* for the square root of a square modulo p prime. Since we have a good algorithm for exponentiation, this formula should be viewed as reasonably good for finding square roots. Note that it only applies if the prime modulus p is congruent to 3 modulo 4, and only if the given number *really is a square mod p*. (Otherwise, the formula can be evaluated but the output is not a square root of the number.)

>   **Theorem.** Let p be a prime satisfying $p = 3 \bmod 4$. Then for an integer y which is a square-modulo-p,
>
> $$x = y^{(p+1)/4} \bmod p$$
>
>   is a square-root-mod-p of y. That is, $x^2 = y \bmod p$. This called is the **principal square root** of y.

Remark: Unfortunately, if y is *not* a square modulo p, the formula can be evaluated but does *not* give a square root of y modulo p. Also, unfortunately, for $p = 1 \bmod 4$ there is no simple formula for square roots analogous to this.

Proof: First note that the expression $(p + 1)/4$ is not an integer unless $p = 3 \bmod 4$. Suppose that $y = x^2$. Let's check that $z = y^{(p+1)/4}$ has the property that $z^2 = y \bmod p$. (Note that we do *not* assert that $z = x$.) Then

$$(y^{(p+1)/4})^2 = y^{(p+1)/2} = (x^2)^{(p+1)/2} = x^{p+1} = x^p\, x^1 = x \cdot x = y$$

where we get $x^p = x \bmod p$ from Fermat's Little Theorem.   ♣

Remark: This **principal square root** can be characterized in another way, too, independent of this theorem: modulo a prime $p = 3 \bmod 4$, if y is a nonzero square mod p with $x^2 = y \bmod p$, y certainly has **two** square roots $\pm x \bmod p$, one of which is a square mod p and the other *not* a square mod p. (There's no way to know which is which just from looking at the $\pm$ itself.) The square root which is itself a square is the principal square root. We can verify that the formula of the theorem gives a square root which is itself a square: let $x^2 = y \bmod p$ and $p = 4k - 1$. Then

$$y^{(p+1)/4} = (x^2)^{(4k-1+1)/4} = x^{2k} = (x^k)^2 \bmod p$$

That is, the principal square root given by the formula of the theorem is the square of x^k modulo p.

Exercises

12.6.01 Find the principal square root of 2 modulo 19.

12.6.02 Find the principal square root of 6 modulo 19.

12.6.03 Find the principal square root of 2 modulo 71.

12.6.04 Find the principal square root of 50 modulo 71.

12.6.05 Find the principal square root of 2 modulo 103.

12.6.06 Find the principal square root of 2 modulo 1039.

12.6.07 Find the principal square root of 892 modulo 1039.

12.6.08 Find the principal square root of 3 modulo 107.

12.6.09 Find the principal square root of 9 modulo 107.

12.6.10 Find the principal square root of 4 modulo 107.

12.6.11 Find the principal square root of 2 modulo 1000039.

12.7 Higher Roots mod p

Generalizing the square-root case above, in certain circumstances we have a formula to find nth roots modulo p. A nonzero y modulo p is an nth-**power** (or, in archaic terminology, nth-**power residue**) modulo p if there is x so that $x^n = y \bmod p$. (If there is no such x, then y is an nth-**power non-residue**.)

Theorem. Let p be a prime. If n is relatively prime to $p - 1$, then *every y* has an nth root modulo p. In particular, letting r be a multiplicative inverse for n modulo $p - 1$, an nth root of y mod p is $y^r \% p$.

Proof: We check that $(y^r)^n = y \bmod p$. For $p|y$, so that $y = 0 \bmod p$, this is easy. So now suppose that p does not divide y. Since $rn = 1 \bmod p - 1$, there is a positive integer ℓ so that $rn = 1 + \ell(p-1)$. Then

$$(y^r)^n = y^{rn} = y^{1+\ell(p-1)} = y^1 \cdot y^{\ell(p-1)} = y \cdot (y^{(p-1)})^\ell = y \cdot 1^\ell = y \bmod p$$

since Fermat's Little Theorem gives $y^{p-1} = 1 \bmod p$.   ♣

Having treated the case that $\gcd(n, p-1) = 1$, we will ignore the intermediate cases where $1 < \gcd(n, p-1) < n$ and treat the other extreme where $\gcd(n, p-1) = n$: We have a computationally effective way to compute nth roots modulo primes p with $n | (p-1)$ as long as $\gcd(n, \frac{p-1}{n}) = 1$:

Theorem. Let p be a prime so that $p = 1 \bmod n$, but so that $\gcd(n, \frac{p-1}{n})$ is 1. Let r be a multiplicative inverse of n modulo $(p-1)/n$. *If y is an nth power then an nth root of y mod p is $y^r \% p$.*

Proof: The basic mechanism of the argument is the same as the previous proof, with a few complications. We check that $(y^r)^n = y \bmod p$. For $p | y$, so that $y = 0 \bmod p$, this is easy. So now suppose that p does not divide y. Since $rn = 1 \bmod (p-1)/n$, there is a positive integer ℓ so that $rn = 1 + \ell(p-1)/n$. Also, since we are assuming that y has an nth root, we can express y as $y = x^n \bmod p$. Then

$$(y^r)^n = ((x^n)^r)^n = x^{n \cdot rn} = x^{n \cdot (1 + \frac{\ell(p-1)}{n})} = x^n \cdot x^{\ell \cdot (p-1)}$$
$$= x^n \cdot (x^{p-1})^\ell = x^n \cdot 1^\ell = x^n = y \bmod p$$

where we invoke Fermat's Little Theorem to know that $x^{p-1} = 1 \bmod p$.   ♣

Remark: The formula in the latter theorem yields *garbage* if y is *not* an nth power! But, of course, it is not necessary to know whether or not y is an nth power before doing the computation. Rather, apply the formula, and *check* whether or not the nth power of the result is the original y. If it is, then obviously y *is* an nth power. If it is not the original y, then y is *not* an nth power.

Remark: If $\gcd(n, \frac{p-1}{n}) > 1$, then computation of roots is more complicated.

Remark: The difference between the two formulas for the nth roots for the two cases in the two theorems just above is very important. Application of either one in the *other* situation yields garbage.

Exercises

12.7.01 Find a cube root of 2 modulo 101 gracefully.

12.7.02 Find a cube root of 46 modulo 101 gracefully.

12.7.03 Find a cube root of 97 modulo 101 gracefully.

12.7.04 Find a cube root of 14 modulo 103 gracefully.

12.7.05 Find a cube root of 61 modulo 103 gracefully.

12.7.06 Find an 11th root of 2 modulo 101 gracefully.

12.7.07 Find an 11th root of 58 modulo 199 gracefully.

13

Roots Mod Composites

Now we do some computations with *composite* moduli, reducing some problems to the case of *prime* moduli. One important use of this is to understand the structure of $\mathbf{Z}/n$, and the differences in this structure depending upon whether or not n is prime. This is relevant to primality tests and factorization attacks, as well as to understanding the general security of many public-key ciphers.

One notable feature of such computations is visible in the section on square-root oracles. There we see that for large integers n which are products of just two distinct primes p, q both congruent to 3 mod 4, being able to find square roots mod n gives a (probabilistic) algorithm to find the factors p, q of n. That is, a square-root *oracle* can be employed to obtain certain factorizations.

Some of the the proofs in this section are incomplete, since they depend on the existence of *primitive roots* modulo primes, which we can only later prove to exist. Nevertheless, these results illustrate the relevance of the later more abstract results.

As the direct intellectual successor to Fermat, Leonhard Euler systematically continued Fermat's work in number theory and its applications. For example, as you'd guess from their names, Euler's theorem, and the Euler criterion for integers to have nth roots mod m, are basic results due to Euler.

13.1 Sun Ze's Theorem

The result of this section is sometimes known as the **Chinese Remainder Theorem**, mainly because the earliest results (including and following Sun Ze's) were obtained in China. Sun Ze's result was obtained before 450, and the statement below was obtained by Chin Chiu Shao about 1250. Such results, with virtually the same proofs, apply to much more general 'numbers' than the integers $\mathbf{Z}$.

Let $m_1, \ldots, m_n$ be nonzero integers such that for any pair of indices i, j with $i \neq j$ the integers m_i and m_j are relatively prime. We say that the integers m_i are **mutually relatively prime**. Let

$$\mathbf{Z}/m_1 \times \mathbf{Z}/m_2 \times \cdots \times \mathbf{Z}/m_n$$

denote (as usual) the collection of ordered n-tuples with the ith item lying in $\mathbf{Z}/m_i$. Define a map

$$f : \mathbf{Z}/(m_1 \cdots m_n) \to \mathbf{Z}/m_1 \times \mathbf{Z}/m_2 \times \cdots \times \mathbf{Z}/m_n$$

by

$$f(x\text{-mod-}(m_1 \cdots m_n)) = (x\text{-mod-}m_1, \, x\text{-mod-}m_2, \cdots, \, x\text{-mod-}m_n)$$

Theorem. *(Sun Ze)* For $m_1, \ldots, m_n$ mutually relatively prime, this map

$$f : \mathbf{Z}/(m_1 \cdots m_n) \to \mathbf{Z}/m_1 \times \mathbf{Z}/m_2 \times \cdots \times \mathbf{Z}/m_n$$

is a *bijection*.

Proof: First, we consider the case that there are just two different relatively prime moduli m, n, and show that the corresponding map

$$f : \mathbf{Z}/mn \to \mathbf{Z}/m \times \mathbf{Z}/n$$

given by

$$f(x\text{-mod-}mn) = (x\text{-mod-}m, \, x\text{-mod-}n)$$

is a bijection. First, we prove *injectivity*: if $f(x) = f(y)$, then $x \equiv y \bmod m$ and $x \equiv y \bmod n$. That is, $m|x - y$ and $n|x - y$. Since m, n are relatively prime (!), this implies that $mn|x - y$, so $x \equiv y \bmod mn$.

At this point, since $\mathbf{Z}/mn$ and $\mathbf{Z}/m \times \mathbf{Z}/n$ are *finite* sets with the same number of elements (namely mn), any injective map must be surjective. So we could stop now and say that we know that f is surjective (hence bijective).

But it is worthwhile to understand the surjectivity more tangibly, to see once more where the relative prime-ness of m, n enters. Since m, n are relatively prime, there are integers s, t so that

$$sm + tn = 1$$

(We can find these s, t via the Euclidean algorithm if we want, but that's not the point just now.) Then we claim that given integers a and b,

$$f((b(sm) + a(tn))\text{-mod-}mn) = (a\text{-mod-}m, b\text{-mod-}n)$$

Indeed,

$$b(sm) + a(tn) \equiv b(sm) + a(1 - sm) \equiv a \bmod m$$

and similarly

$$b(sm) + a(tn) \equiv b(1 - tn) + a(tn) \equiv b \bmod n$$

This proves the surjectivity, and thus the bijectivity, of the function f in the case of just two moduli.

Now consider an arbitrary number of (mutually relatively prime) moduli m_1, $\ldots$, m_n. We'll do induction on the number n of moduli involved. The case $n = 2$ was just treated, and if $n = 1$ there is nothing to prove. So take $n > 2$. By induction on n, the map

$$f_0 : \mathbf{Z}/m_2 \cdots m_n \to \mathbf{Z}/m_2 \times \mathbf{Z}/m_3 \times \cdots \times \mathbf{Z}/m_n$$

defined by

$$f_0(x\text{-mod-}m_2 \cdots m_n) = (x\text{-mod-}m_2, x\text{-mod-}m_3, \cdots, x\text{-mod-}m_n)$$

is a bijection. Thus, the map

$$f_1 : \mathbf{Z}/m_1 \times \mathbf{Z}/m_2 \cdots m_n \to \mathbf{Z}/m_1 \times \mathbf{Z}/m_2 \times \mathbf{Z}/m_3 \times \cdots \times \mathbf{Z}/m_n$$

defined by

$$f_1(x\text{-mod-}m_1, x\text{-mod-}m_2 \cdots m_n)$$
$$= (x\text{-mod-}m_1, x\text{-mod-}m_2, x\text{-mod-}m_3, \ldots, x\text{-mod-}m_n)$$

is a bijection.

At the same time, invoking unique factorization (!), m_1 and the product $m_2 m_3 \cdots m_n$ are relatively prime, so the case $n = 2$ gives the bijectivity of the map

$$f_2 : \mathbf{Z}/m_1(m_2 \cdots m_n) \to \mathbf{Z}/m_1 \times \mathbf{Z}/m_2 \cdots m_n$$

defined by

$$f_2(x\text{-mod-}m_1(m_2 \cdots m_n)) = (x\text{-mod-}m_1, x\text{-mod-}m_2 \cdots m_n)$$

Therefore, the composite map

$$f = f_2 \circ f_1$$

is also a bijection.   ♣

Exercises

13.1.01 Show that $x = 2 \bmod 6$ and $x = 3 \bmod 4$ have *no* simultaneous solution.

13.1.02 Show that $x = 2 \bmod 6$ and $x = 0 \bmod 4$ *do* have a simultaneous solution.

13.2 Special Systems

Now we paraphrase the theorem above in terms of solving several congruences simultaneously. There are some similarities to the more elementary discussion of systems of linear *equations*, but there are critical differences, as well.

To start with, let's take the smallest non-trivial systems, of the form

$$\begin{cases} x \equiv a \bmod m \\ x \equiv b \bmod n \end{cases}$$

where m, n are *relatively prime*, a, b are arbitrary integers, and we are to find all integers x which satisfy this system.

Notice that there are *two* congruences but just one *unknown*, which in the case of *equations* would probably lead to non-solvability immediately. But systems of congruences behave slightly differently. Our only concession is: **We'll only consider the case that the moduli m and n are** *relatively prime*, **that is, where** $\gcd(m, n) = 1$.

Using the Euclidean algorithm again, there are integers s, t so that

$$sm + tn = 1$$

since we supposed that $\gcd(m, n) = 1$. And this can be rearranged to

$$tn = 1 - sm$$

for example. **Here comes the trick:** the claim is that **the single congruence**

$$x_0 = a(tn) + b(sm) \bmod mn$$

is equivalent to (has the same set of solutions) as the *system* of congruences above.

Let's check: modulo m, we have

$$\begin{aligned} x_0 &\equiv (a(tn) + b(sm)) \bmod m \equiv a(tn) + 0 \bmod m \\ &\equiv a(tn) \bmod m \equiv a(1 - sm) \bmod m \\ &\equiv a(1) \bmod m \equiv a \bmod m \end{aligned}$$

The discussion of the congruence modulo n is nearly identical, with roles reversed. Let's do it:

$$x_0 \equiv (a(tn) + b(sm)) \bmod n \equiv 0 + b(sm) \bmod m$$
$$\equiv b(sm) \bmod n \equiv b(1 - tn) \bmod n$$
$$\equiv b(1) \bmod n \equiv b \bmod n$$

Thus, anything congruent to this x_0 modulo mn is a solution to the system.

On the other hand, suppose x is a solution to the system, and let's prove that it is congruent to x_0 modulo mn. Since $x \equiv a \bmod m$ and $x \equiv b \bmod n$, we have

$$x - x_0 \equiv a - a \equiv 0 \bmod m$$

and

$$x - x_0 \equiv b - b \equiv 0 \bmod n$$

That is, both m and n divide $x - x_0$. Since m and n are *relatively prime*, we can conclude that mn divides $x - x_0$, as desired.

Note that the process of sticking the solutions together via the goofy formula above uses the Euclidean algorithm in order to be computationally effective (rather than just theoretically *possible*).

For example, let's solve the system

$$\begin{cases} x \equiv 2 \bmod 11 \\ x \equiv 7 \bmod 13 \end{cases}$$

To 'glue' these congruences together, we execute the Euclidean Algorithm on 11 and 13, to find

$$6 \cdot 11 - 5 \cdot 13 = 1$$

Thus, using the goofy formula above, the single congruence

$$x \equiv 2(-5 \cdot 13) + 7(6 \cdot 11) \bmod 11 \cdot 13$$

is equivalent to the given system. In particular, this gives the solution

$$x \equiv -2 \cdot 5 \cdot 13 + 7 \cdot 6 \cdot 11 \equiv 332 \bmod 11 \cdot 13$$

Quite generally, consider a system

$$\begin{cases} x \equiv b_1 \bmod m_1 \\ x \equiv b_2 \bmod m_2 \\ x \equiv b_3 \bmod m_3 \\ \quad \cdots \\ x \equiv b_n \bmod m_n \end{cases}$$

We'll only consider the scenario that m_i and m_j are relatively prime (for $i \neq j$). We solve it in steps: first, just look at the subsystem

$$\begin{cases} x \equiv b_1 \bmod m_1 \\ x \equiv b_2 \bmod m_2 \end{cases}$$

and use the method above to turn this into a single (equivalent!) congruence of the form

$$x \equiv c_2 \bmod m_1 m_2$$

Then look at the system

$$\begin{cases} x \equiv c_2 \bmod m_1 m_2 \\ x \equiv b_2 \bmod m_3 \end{cases}$$

and use the method above to combine these two congruences into a single equivalent one, say

$$x \equiv c_3 \bmod m_1 m_2 m_3$$

and so on.

Remark: Yes, this procedure is just a paraphrase of the proof of the previous section.

The solution of one of these rather special types of systems of linear congruences can be restated in a form that is conceptually a little cleaner:

Theorem. Let $m_1, \ldots, m_n$ be mutually relatively prime, and consider the system of simultaneous congruences

$$\begin{cases} x \equiv b_1 \bmod m_1 \\ x \equiv b_2 \bmod m_2 \\ x \equiv b_3 \bmod m_3 \\ \qquad \cdots \\ x \equiv b_n \bmod m_n \end{cases}$$

Let M be the product $M = m_1 \cdot \; \cdots \cdot m_n$ and let $M_i = M/m_i$. Let $T_i = M_i^{-1} \bmod m_i$. (This exists since by hypothesis M_i and m_i are relatively prime.) Then

$$x = T_1 M_1 b_1 + \cdots + T_n M_n b_n \bmod M$$

is the unique solution modulo M to this system.

Proof: We show that the latter formula gives a solution to $x = b_i \bmod m_i$, for all i. Indeed, for $j \neq i$, $m_i | M_j$, so

$$T_j M_j b_j = T_j \cdot 0 \cdot b_j = 0 \bmod m_i \quad \text{for } j \neq i$$

And

$$T_i M_i = 1 \bmod m_i$$

That is, all the summands but the ith are 0 modulo m_i, and the ith is b_i modulo m_i. Thus, the expression gives a solution modulo m_i for all indices i. The uniqueness modulo M of the solution of such a system was already proven in Sun Ze's theorem, so we're done.   ♣

Exercises

13.2.01 Find an integer x so that $x = 1$ mod 12 and $x = 1$ mod 35.

13.2.02 Find an integer x so that $x = 1$ mod 13 and $x = 1$ mod 36.

13.2.03 Find an integer x so that $x = 1$ mod 12 and $x = 8$ mod 35.

13.2.04 Find an integer x so that $x = 5$ mod 12 and $x = 19$ mod 35.

13.2.05 Find an integer x so that $x = 0$ mod 12 and $x = 1$ mod 35.

13.2.06 Find an integer x so that $x = 1$ mod 12 and $x = 0$ mod 35.

13.2.07 Find an integer x so that $x = 5$ mod 48 and $x = 3$ mod 35.

13.3 Composite Moduli

In general, to solve a congruence such as $x^2 \equiv b$ mod m with *composite* modulus $m = m_1 m_2$ (with m_1 and m_2 relatively prime), it is faster to solve the congruence modulo m_1 and m_2 *separately* and use Sun Ze's theorem to glue the solutions together into a solution modulo m, rather than trying to solve modulo m. This is especially true if the prime factorization of m is known.

For example, let's try to solve

$$x^2 \equiv -1 \bmod 13 \cdot 17 \cdot 29$$

by hand (so that a brute-force search is unreasonable, since we would not want to search through any significant fraction of $13 \cdot 17 \cdot 29 = 6409$ possibilities by hand!). We observe that Sun Ze's theorem asserts that the collection of integers x modulo 6409 satisfying $x^2 \equiv -1$ mod 6409 is in bijection with the set of triples (x_1, x_2, x_3) where $x_1 \in \mathbf{Z}/13$, $x_2 \in \mathbf{Z}/17$, and $x_3 \in \mathbf{Z}/29$ and

$$x_1^2 \equiv -1 \bmod 13, \qquad x_2^2 \equiv -1 \bmod 17 \qquad x_3^2 \equiv -1 \bmod 13$$

The bijection is

$$x\text{-mod-}6409 \longrightarrow (x\text{-mod-}13, x\text{-mod-}17, x\text{-mod-}29)$$

Further, the discussion above tells how to go in the other direction, that is, how to get back from $\mathbf{Z}/13 \times \mathbf{Z}/17 \times \mathbf{Z}/29$.

In this example, since the numbers 13, 17, 29 are not terribly large, a brute-force search for square roots of -1 modulo 13, 17, and 29 won't take very long. Let's describe such a search in the case of modulus 29. First, $-1 = 28$ modulo 29, but 28 is not a square. Next, add 29 to 28: 57 is not a square. Add 29 to 57: 86 is not a square. Add 29 to 86: 115 is not a square. Add 29 to 115: $144 = 12^2$. Thus, ± 12 are square roots of -1 modulo 29. Similarly, we find that ± 5 are square roots of -1 modulo 13, and ± 4 are square roots of -1 modulo 17.

To use Sun Ze's theorem to get a solution modulo $6409 = 13 \cdot 17 \cdot 29$ from this, we first need integers s, t so that $s \cdot 13 + t \cdot 17 = 1$. The theoretical results about gcd's guarantee that there are such s, t, and Euclid's algorithm finds them:

$$17 - 1 \cdot 13 = 4$$
$$13 - 3 \cdot 4 = 1$$

Going back:

$$1 = 13 - 3 \cdot 4$$
$$= 13 - 3 \cdot (17 - 1 \cdot 13)$$
$$= 4 \cdot 13 - 3 \cdot 17$$

Therefore, from the square root 5 of -1 modulo 13 and square root 4 of -1 modulo 17 we get a square root of -1 modulo $13 \cdot 17$:

$$4(4 \cdot 13) - 5(3 \cdot 17) = -47 \bmod 13 \cdot 17$$

Proceeding further, now we need integers s, t so that

$$s \cdot (13 \cdot 17) + t \cdot 29 = 1$$

Apply Euclid's algorithm, noting that $13 \cdot 17 = 221$:

$$221 - 7 \cdot 29 = 18$$
$$29 - 1 \cdot 18 = 11$$
$$18 - 1 \cdot 11 = 7$$
$$11 - 1 \cdot 7 = 4$$
$$7 - 1 \cdot 4 = 3$$
$$4 - 1 \cdot 3 = 1$$

Going back, we get

$$1 = 4 - 1 \cdot 3$$
$$= 4 - 1 \cdot (7 - \cdot 4)$$
$$= 2 \cdot 4 - 1 \cdot 7$$
$$= 2 \cdot (11 - 7) - 7$$
$$= 2 \cdot 11 - 3 \cdot 7$$
$$= 2 \cdot 11 - 3(18 - 11)$$
$$= 5 \cdot 11 - 3 \cdot 18$$
$$= 5(29 - 18) - 3 \cdot 18$$
$$= 5 \cdot 29 - 8 \cdot 18$$
$$= 5 \cdot 29 - 8(221 - 7 \cdot 29)$$
$$= 61 \cdot 29 - 8 \cdot 221$$

Therefore, from the square root -47 of -1 modulo $221 = 13 \cdot 17$ and the square root 12 of -1 modulo 29 we get the square root

$$12(-8 \cdot 221) + (-47)(61 \cdot 29) = -104359 = 4594 \bmod 6409$$

Further, the most tedious part of the above procedure doesn't need to be repeated to find the other 7 (!) square roots of -1 modulo $13 \cdot 17 \cdot 29$, since we already have the numbers 's, t' in our possession.

Exercises

13.3.01 Find an integer x so that $3x \equiv 2 \bmod 5$ and $4x \equiv 5 \bmod 7$.

13.3.02 Find an integer x so that $7x \equiv 11 \bmod 5$ and $3x \equiv 22 \bmod 35$.

13.3.03 Find four integers x which are distinct modulo $5 \cdot 7$ and so that $x^2 \equiv 1 \bmod 5$ and $x^2 \equiv 1 \bmod 7$. That is, find 4 *different* square roots of 1 modulo 35.

13.3.04 Find four integers x which are distinct modulo $7 \cdot 11$ and so that $x^2 \equiv 1 \bmod 7$ and $x^2 \equiv 1 \bmod 11$. That is, find 4 *different* square roots of 1 modulo 77.

13.3.05 Find four integers x which are distinct modulo $13 \cdot 17$ and so that $x^2 \equiv 1 \bmod 13$ and $x^2 \equiv 1 \bmod 17$. That is, find 4 *different* square roots of 1 modulo 221.

13.3.06 Find four different square roots of 2 modulo $7 \cdot 23$.

13.3.07 Explain why there are eight different square roots of 1 modulo $3 \cdot 5 \cdot 7 = 105$.

13.4 Hensel's Lemma

In many cases, solving a polynomial equation $f(x) \equiv 0 \bmod p$ modulo a prime p suffices to assure that there are solutions modulo p^n for powers p^n of p, and also to find such solutions efficiently. And, funnily enough, the procedure to do so is exactly parallel to Newton's method for numerical approximation to roots, from calculus. In particular, we will use a purely algebraic form of Taylor expansions to prove the result.

First we'll do a numerical example to illustrate the idea of the process to which Hensel's Lemma refers. Suppose we want to find x so that $x^2 \equiv 2 \bmod 7^3$. Noting that a solution mod 7^3 certainly must give a solution mod 7, we'll start by finding a solution mod 7. This is much easier, since there are only 7 things in $\mathbf{Z}/7$, and by a very quick trial-and-error hunt we see that $(\pm 3)^2 = 9 = 2 \bmod 7$.

Now comes the trick: being optimists, we imagine that we can simply *adjust* the solution 3 mod 7 to obtain a solution mod 7^2 by adding (or subtracting) some multiple of 7 to it. That is, we imagine that for some $y \in \mathbf{Z}$

$$(3 + 7 \cdot y)^2 \equiv 2 \bmod 49$$

Multiplying out, we have

$$9 + 21y + 49y^2 \equiv 2 \bmod 49$$

(handwritten: $42y$ above $21y$)

Happily, the y^2 term disappears (modulo 49), because its coefficient is divisible by 49. Rearranging, this is

$$7 + 42y \equiv 0 \bmod 49$$

Dividing through by 7 gives

$$1 + 6y \equiv 0 \bmod 7$$

Since the coefficient (namely, 6) of y is invertible modulo 7, with inverse 6, we find a solution $y = (6^{-1})(-1) = 6 \cdot (-1) = 1 \bmod 7$. Thus,

$$3 + 7 \cdot 1 = 10$$

is a square root of 2 modulo 7^2.

Continuing in our optimism: Now we hope that we can *adjust* the solution 10 mod 7^2 by adding some multiple of 7^2 to it in order to get a solution mod 7^3. That is, we hope to find y so that

$$(10 + 7^2 y)^2 \equiv 2 \bmod 7^3$$

Multiplying out and simplifying, this is

$$294y \equiv -98 \bmod 7^3$$

Dividing through by 7^2 gives

$$6y \equiv -2 \bmod 7$$

Again, the inverse of 6 mod 7 is just 6 again, so this is

$$y \equiv 6(-2) \equiv 2 \bmod 7$$

Therefore,

$$10 + 7^2 \cdot 2 = 108$$

satisfies

$$108^2 \equiv 2 \bmod 7^3$$

This was considerably faster than brute-force hunting for a square root of 2 mod 7^3 directly.

To prepare for a more general assertion of Hensel's Lemma, we need to give a purely algebraic description of the **derivative** of a polynomial. That is, we don't want the definition to require taking any limits. Let

$$f(x) = c_n x^n + \cdots + c_0$$

with the coefficients in Z. Simply *define* another polynomial f' by

$$f'(x) = nc_n x^{n-1} + (n-1)c_{n-1}x^{n-2} + \cdots + 2c_2 x + c_1 + 0$$

Remark: Of course, we have *defined* this derivative by the formula that we know is 'correct' *if* it were defined as a limit.

Proposition. Using the purely algebraic definition of derivative, for polynomials f, g with coefficients in Z, and for $r \in Z$, we have

$$
\begin{array}{rcll}
(rf)' & = & rf' & \text{(constant-multiple rule)} \\
(f+g)' & = & f'+g' & \text{(sum rule)} \\
(fg)' & = & f'g+fg' & \text{(product rule)} \\
(f \circ g)' & = & f' \circ g \cdot g & \text{(chain rule)}
\end{array}
$$

Proof: We know from calculus that these assertions hold, even though we didn't mention limits here. ♣

Theorem. *(Hensel's Lemma)* Let f be a polynomial with coefficients in **Z**. Let p be a prime number, and suppose that $x_n \in \mathbf{Z}$ satisfies

$$ f(x_n) \equiv 0 \bmod p^n $$

with $n > 0$. *Suppose* that $f'(x_n) \not\equiv 0 \bmod p$. Let $f'(x_1)^{-1}$ be an integer which is a multiplicative inverse to $f'(x_1)$ modulo p. Then

$$ x_{n+1} = x_n - f(x_n) f'(x_1)^{-1} $$

satisfies

$$ f(x_{n+1}) \equiv 0 \bmod p^{n+1} $$

Further, from this construction,

$$ x_{n+1} = x_n \bmod p^n $$

In particular, for every index,

$$ x_n = x_1 \bmod p $$

Remark: Note that the quantity $f'(x_1)^{-1} \bmod p$ does not need to be recomputed each cycle of the iteration, but only once at the beginning.

Proof: First, let's check that if f has integer coefficients, then for every positive integer k the quotient $f^{(k)}/k!$ has integer coefficients, where $f^{(k)}$ is the kth derivative of f. To prove this it suffices to look at $f(x) = x^n$, since every polynomial with integer coefficients is a sum of multiples of such things. In this case, $f^{(k)}/k! = \binom{n}{k} x^{n-k}$. Since $\binom{n}{k}$ appears as a coefficient in $(x+1)^n$, which has integer coefficients (!), this proves what we wanted.

Now we can almost prove the theorem. Let $y = -f(x_n)f'(x_n)^{-1} \bmod p^{n+1}$. Note that this expression uses $f'(x_n)^{-1} \bmod p^{n+1}$ instead of $f'(x_1)^{-1} \bmod p$. We'll have to come back at the end and take care of this adjustment.

We have $y \equiv 0 \bmod p^n$. Since f is a polynomial, a Taylor expansion for it about *any* point is finite, and converges to f. Thus,

$$f(x_n + y) = f(x_n) + \frac{f'(x_n)}{1!}y + \frac{f''(x_n)}{2!}y^2 + \frac{f^{(3)}(x_n)}{3!}y^3 + \cdots$$

(The sum is finite!) Each $f^{(i)}(x_n)/i!$ is an integer, and p^{2n} divides $y^2, y^3, y^4, \ldots$, so

$$p^{2n} \text{ divides } \frac{f^{(2)}(x_n)}{2!}y^2 + \frac{f^{(3)}(x_n)}{3!}y^3 + \cdots$$

Replacing y by its definition from above, we have

$$f(x_n) + \frac{f'(x_n)}{1!}y = f(x_n) + \frac{f'(x_n)}{1!}(-f(x_n)f'(x_n)^{-1})$$

Since $f'(x_n)^{-1}$ is a multiplicative inverse of $f'(x_n)$ modulo p, there is an integer t so that

$$f'(x_n) \cdot f'(x_n)^{-1} = 1 + tp$$

Then

$$f(x_n) + \frac{f'(x_n)}{1!}y$$

$$= f(x_n) + \frac{f'(x_n)}{1!}(-f(x_n)f'(x_n)^{-1})$$

$$= f(x_n) - f(x_n)(1 + tp) = f(x_n) \cdot tp$$

Since $f(x_n) \equiv 0 \bmod p^n$, and we have picked up one further factor of p, this is 0 modulo p^{n+1}, as claimed.

Further, regarding the last assertions of the theorem, note that the quantity $f(x_n)/f'(x_n)$ by which we adjust x_n to get x_{n+1} is a multiple of p^n.

Finally, we need to check that

$$f(x_n)f'(x_n)^{-1} = f(x_n)f'(x_1)^{-1} \bmod p^{n+1}$$

where $f'(x_1)^{-1}$ is just an inverse mod p, not mod p^{n+1}. Since $x_n = x_1 \bmod p$, and since f' has integer coefficients, it is not so hard to check that

$$f'(x_n) = f'(x_1) \bmod p$$

Therefore,

$$f'(x_n)^{-1} = f'(x_1)^{-1} \bmod p$$

Further, by hypothesis p^n divides $f(x_n)$, so, multiplying through by $f(x_n)$ gives

$$f(x_n)f'(x_n)^{-1} = f(x_n)f'(x_1)^{-1} \bmod p \cdot p^n$$

This verifies that we don't need to compute $f'(x_n)^{-1} \bmod p^{n+1}$, but just the single quantity $f'(x_1)^{-1}$. ♣

Remark: We could give purely algebraic proofs of the differentiation formulas and the representability of polynomials by their Taylor expansions, but this can be done later in greater generality anyway, so we'll be content with the calculus-based argument here.

Exercises

13.4.01 Find $\sqrt{2} \bmod 7^5$ via Hensel's Lemma.

13.4.02 Find $\sqrt{5} \bmod 11^6$ via Hensel's Lemma.

13.4.03 Find $\sqrt{3} \bmod 11^6$ via Hensel's Lemma.

13.4.04 Find $\sqrt{-1} \bmod 5^6$ via Hensel's Lemma.

13.4.05 Find $\sqrt{-1} \bmod 13^3$ via Hensel's Lemma.

13.4.06 (*) Discuss the failure of the quadratic formula to solve the equation $x^2 + x + 1 \equiv 0 \bmod 2$.

13.5 Square-Root Oracles

Recall that an *oracle* is a 'black box' that can answer certain questions, although we don't necessarily know *how* it does this. This idea of 'oracle' is an important abstraction in discussion of *relative* complexity and feasibility of many computations, which then is certainly connected to questions about the security of ciphers whose security depends upon the difficulty of various tasks. Here we'll consider a special but very typical situation of an oracle.

Theorem. Let p, q be large primes, both congruent to 3 modulo 4. Let $n = pq$. Then an *oracle* that can take square roots modulo n (without knowing the separate factors p and q) can be used to make a probabilistic algorithm to find the factors p, q of n.

Remark: This situation is that of the construction of an RSA modulus, for example.

Remark: Of course, we want to *see* what this algorithm is, not merely know that it exists. So, the proof of the theorem consists of describing the algorithm.

Suppose that we have $n = pq$ as above, and that we have an oracle that finds square roots (of squares, of course) modulo n, without knowledge of the factors p and q of n. We repeatedly do the following: pick a random x, compute $x^2 \% n$, and feed the result to the oracle, which returns a square root y of x^2 modulo n.

Since there are exactly two square roots of any nonzero square modulo a prime, by Sun Ze's theorem there are exactly 4 square roots of any square modulo $n = pq$, and $\pm x$ are just 2 of them. Let the other two be $\pm x'$. Assuming that the original x really was chosen 'randomly', the probability is $1/2$ that the oracle will return $\pm x'$ as y. If it does return $\pm x'$, then n does not divide either of $x \pm y$ (since

$y \neq \pm x \bmod n$), but nevertheless n divides $x^2 - y^2$ (since $x^2 = y^2 \bmod n$). So p divides one of $x \pm y$ and q divides the other of the two. Therefore, $\gcd(x - y, n)$ is either p or q (and we don't care which). *This completes the description of a single step of the probabilistic algorithm.*

Since the oracle can be called repeatedly, each time it is called there is probability $1/2$ that a factorization will be obtained. So the probability that after ℓ calls to the oracle we *won't* obtain a factorization is $(1/2)^\ell$. This goes to 0 quite fast as ℓ goes to infinity. For example, the probability that it will take as many as 10 calls to the oracle to obtain a factorization is

$$\text{prob(10 calls needed)} = (1/2)^{10} \approx 0.001$$

This is unlikely.

In fact, we can compute the *expected number* of calls to the oracle before a factorization of n is obtained: the probability is $1/2$ that the very first call gives the factorization. The probability is $1/2$ that we fail on the first try, and $1/2$ that we succeed on the second, so the probability is $1/4$ that it takes 2 calls to the oracle. Similarly, the probability is $(1/2)^2$ that we fail twice, and then $1/2$ that we succeed on the third try, so $1/8$ that it takes 3 tries. In general, the probability is $(1/2)^n$ that we fail $n - 1$ times and then succeed in obtaining a factorization. So the expected number of oracle calls needed is

expected number of calls to oracle

$$= \sum_{n=1}^{\infty} n \cdot (1/2)^n$$

We can evaluate this by using *generating functions*: consider

$$f(x) = \sum_{n=1}^{\infty} n \cdot x^n$$

'As usual' when using generating functions, since

$$x \cdot \frac{d}{dx} x^n = n \cdot x^n$$

we notice that our big sum is

$$f(x) = x \cdot \frac{d}{dx} \sum_{n=1}^{\infty} x^n$$

Remembering how to sum geometric series

$$\sum_{n=1}^{\infty} x^n = \frac{1}{1 - x} \quad \text{(for } |x| < 1\text{)}$$

we obtain

$$f(x) = x \cdot \frac{d}{dx} \frac{1}{1-x} = \frac{x}{(1-x)^2}$$

Evaluating this when $x = 1/2$ gives $f(1/2) = 2$, so the expected number of oracle calls to get a factorization is just 2.

Example: Let's take $p = 103$ and $1 = 107$, both congruent to 3 modulo 4, and $n = pq = 11021$. The oracle we'll use will not be mysterious; rather, internally it will make use of knowledge of p and q to compute *principal* square roots modulo n by the formulas derived from Fermat's Little Theorem, and then stick them together by using Sun Ze's theorem. To set up the oracle, either by guessing-and-checking or by using the Euclidean algorithm, we find

$$(-27) \cdot 103 + (26) \cdot 107 = 1$$

The oracle will compute the (principal) square root of (a square) y mod p and mod q by the formulas

$$\text{square root of } y \bmod p \ = y^{(p+1)/4} \bmod p = y^{26} \bmod 103$$

$$\text{square root of } y \bmod q \ = y^{(q+1)/4} \bmod p = y^{27} \bmod 107$$

Then these solutions will be stuck together by

$$\text{square root of } y \bmod n \ = -27 \cdot y^{27} \cdot 103 + 26 \cdot y^{26} \cdot 107 \bmod 11021$$

(where, of course, in computing these powers we can reduce modulo 11021 whenever we want).

To run the probabilistic algorithm trying to factor n, pick a 'random' integer x: let's take $x = 50$. Then we feed $50^2 = 2500$ to the oracle, which will return

$$-27 \cdot (2500)^{27} \cdot 103 + 26 \cdot (2500)^{26} \cdot 107 \bmod 11021 = 2625 \bmod 11021$$

Using the oracle's output, we use the Euclidean algorithm to compute the relevant greatest common divisor $\gcd(2625 - 50, 11021)$:

$$
\begin{aligned}
11,021 - 4 \cdot 2575 &= 721 \\
2575 - 3 \cdot 721 &= 412 \\
721 - 1 \cdot 412 &= 309 \\
412 - 1 \cdot 309 &= 103 \\
309 - 3 \cdot 103 &= 0
\end{aligned}
$$

so we look at the last nonzero entry on the right-hand side, which is 103, which is indeed a proper factor of 11,021. So in this example the oracle enabled us to find a proper factor in just one try.

Exercises

13.5.01 (*) If $n = pqr$ with distinct primes p, q, and r, and you have an oracle that takes square roots modulo n, can you use the oracle to make a probabilistic algorithms to factor n?

13.5.02 (*) Let p and q be 'secret' primes both congruent to 4 mod 9, and let $n = p \cdot q$. Suppose we have an oracle that takes cube roots mod n. Can you use the oracle to make a probabilistic algorithm to factor n?

13.6 Euler's Theorem

Here we *state* Euler's Theorem generalizing Fermat's Little Theorem. An intelligent proof of Euler's Theorem is best given as a corollary of some basic *group theory*, but we can give a more elementary (if less illuminating) proof right here also.

For a positive integer n, the **Euler phi-function** $\varphi(n)$ is the number of integers b so that $0 < b < n$ and $\gcd(b, n) = 1$.

Theorem. *(Euler)* For x relatively prime to a positive integer n,

$$x^{\varphi(n)} = 1 \bmod n$$

Remark: The special case that n is prime is just Fermat's Little Theorem, since for prime p we easily see that $\varphi(p) = p - 1$.

Proof: Let G be the collection of integers-mod-n which have multiplicative inverses (mod n, of course). We first note that the product

$$P = \prod_{g \in G} g = \text{product of all elements of } G$$

is again in G. Indeed, let $g_1, \ldots, g_t$ be a listing of all elements in G, so $P = g_1 \ldots g_t$. Then it should not be surprising that the inverse of $P = g_1 \ldots g_t$ is obtained by inverting the factors (and reversing the order!?):

$$(g_1 g_2 \ldots g_t) \cdot (g_t^{-1} \ldots g_2^{-1} g_1^{-1}) = 1 \bmod n$$

That is, P has a multiplicative inverse mod n, although we aren't trying to identify it.

Let x be an element of G. Then we claim that the map $f : G \to G$ defined by

$$f(g) = xg$$

is a bijection of G to itself. First, we should check that f really maps G to itself: indeed, for x and g both invertible mod n,

$$(xg)(g^{-1}x^{-1}) = 1 \bmod n$$

so $f(g) = xg$ is again in G. Next, check injectivity: if $f(g) = f(h)$, then by definition of f we have $xg = xh \bmod n$. Multiply this equality by $x^{-1} \bmod n$ to obtain $g = h \bmod n$, proving injectivity. Last, check surjectivity: given $g \in G$, let's find $h \in G$ so that $f(h) = g$. That is, find $h \in G$ so that $xh = g$. Well, taking $h = x^{-1}g$ works. This proves that f is a bijection as claimed.

Finally we get to the computational part of the argument. Again let P be the product of all elements of G. Then

$$P = \prod_{g \in G} g = \prod_{g \in G} f(g)$$

since the map f merely mixes around the elements of G. Then

$$P = \prod_{g \in G} f(g) = \prod_{g \in G} xg = x^{\varphi(n)} \prod_{g \in G} g = x^{\varphi(n)} \cdot P$$

where $\varphi(n)$ is the Euler phi-function of n. Since, as shown above, P is invertible mod n, we multiply through by $P^{-1} \bmod n$ to get

$$1 = x^{\varphi(n)} \bmod n$$

This proves Euler's Theorem.   ♣

Remark: On one hand, this argument might hint that it is a mere shadow of some more systematic general approach. This is indeed the case. On the other hand, there are other equally important techniques toward which this little proof gives no hint.

Exercises

13.6.01 From the definition, find $\varphi(30)$, $\varphi(15)$, and $\varphi(24)$.

13.6.02 From the definition, find $\varphi(36)$, $\varphi(18)$, and $\varphi(28)$.

13.6.03 By direct computation, check that 2 is *not* a primitive root modulo 17, but that 3 *is*.

13.7 Facts about Primitive Roots

In this section we simply *explain* what a *primitive root* is supposed to be, and state what is true. The *existence* of primitive roots *modulo primes* will be used just below to prove the 'hard half' of Euler's criteria for whether or not things have square roots (or nth roots) modulo primes. The proofs of *existence* (and non-existence) of primitive roots require more preparation.

Let n be a positive integer. An integer g is a **primitive root modulo** n if the smallest positive integer ℓ so that $g^\ell = 1 \bmod n$ is $\varphi(n)$.

Note that Euler's Theorem assures us that in any case for g relatively prime to n no exponent ℓ larger than $\varphi(n)$ is necessary.

For 'most' integers n there is *not* primitive root modulo n. The precise statement about when there is or isn't a primitive root modulo m is

Theorem. The only integers n for which there is a primitive root modulo n are those of the forms

- $n = p^e$ with an odd prime p, and $e \geq 1$

- $n = 2p^e$ with an odd prime p, and $e \geq 1$

- $n = 2, 4$

This will be proven later. In particular, the most important case is that there *do* exist primitive roots modulo *primes*.

It is useful to make clear one important property of primitive roots:

Proposition. Let g be a primitive root modulo n. Let ℓ be an integer so that $g^\ell = 1 \bmod n$ Then $\varphi(n)$ divides ℓ.

Proof: Using the division algorithm, we may write $\ell = q \cdot \varphi(n) + r$ with $0 \leq r < \varphi(n)$. Then

$$1 = g^\ell = g^{q \cdot \varphi(n) + r} = (g^{\varphi(n)})^q \cdot g^r = 1^q \cdot g^r = g^r \bmod n$$

Since g is a primitive root, $\varphi(n)$ is the least positive exponent so that g raised to that power is 1 mod n. Thus, since $1 = g^r \bmod n$, it must be that $r = 0$. That is, $\varphi(n) | \ell$.   ♣

Exercises

13.7.01 Show that 2 is not a primitive root modulo 23.

13.7.02 Show that 3 is not a primitive root modulo 23.

13.7.03 Granting that 2 is not a primitive root mod 23, show *gracefully* that 4 is not a primitive root modulo 23.

13.7.04 From the definition, compute $\varphi(11)$.

13.7.05 From the definition, compute $\varphi(13)$.

13.7.06 From the definition, compute $\varphi(10)$.

13.7.07 From the definition, compute $\varphi(12)$.

13.7.08 From the definition, compute $\varphi(14)$.

13.7.09 From the definition, compute $\varphi(24)$.

13.7.10 From the definition, compute $\varphi(101)$.

13.7.11 From the definition, compute $\varphi(103)$.

13.8 Euler's Criterion

There is a efficient criterion (due to Euler) for whether or not an integer y can be an nth power modulo a prime p, when $p \equiv 1 \bmod n$. By contrast, we've already seen that when $\gcd(n, p-1) = 1$, *everything* is an nth power mod p. In the case of square roots a little more can be said, which is important in later discussion of *quadratic symbols* and the theorem on quadratic reciprocity. (This presumes that we are acquainted with a fast exponentiation algorithm.) To prove Euler's criterion we must grant the existence of **primitive roots** modulo primes, which will be proven only later.

Given y, a **square root** of y modulo m (with m not necessarily prime) is an integer x so that
$$x^2 \equiv y \bmod m$$
If there is such an x, then y is a **square mod** m, or, in archaic terminology, a **quadratic residue mod m**. If there is no such x, then y is a **non-square mod** m, or, in archaic terminology, a **quadratic non-residue mod** m.

Remark: As with multiplicative inverses, there is essentially no *tangible* connection between these square roots and square roots which may exist in the real or complex numbers. Thus, the expressions '$\sqrt{y}$' or '$y^{1/2}$' have no intrinsic meaning for $y \in \mathbf{Z}/m$.

Example: Since $2^2 = 4 = -1 \bmod 5$, 2 is a square root of -1 modulo 5. We would write
$$2 = \sqrt{-1} \bmod 5$$
Note that the fact that there is no *real* number which is a square root of -1 is no argument against the existence of a square root of -1 modulo 5.

Example: Since $4^2 = 16 = 5 \bmod 11$,
$$4 = \sqrt{5} \bmod 11$$

Example: There is *no* $\sqrt{2}$ modulo 5: to be sure of this, we compute 5 cases:
$$0^2 = 0 \neq 2 \bmod 5$$
$$1^2 = 1 \neq 2 \bmod 5$$
$$2^2 = 4 \neq 2 \bmod 5$$
$$3^2 = 9 = 4 \neq 2 \bmod 5$$
$$4^2 = 16 = 1 \neq 2 \bmod 5$$

Since $\mathbf{Z}/5$ consists of just the 5 congruence classes $\bar{0}, \bar{1}, \bar{2}, \bar{3}, \bar{4}$, we don't need to check any further to know that there is no square root of 2 modulo 5.

From a naive viewpoint, it would appear that the only way to check whether the square root of y modulo m exists is by *brute force*, squaring each element of

$\mathbf{Z}/m$ in turn to see if by chance the value y appears among the squares. From this viewpoint, it would be especially laborious to be sure that something had *no* square root, since all of $\mathbf{Z}/m$ would have to be searched. Fermat's Little Theorem (together with the *fast exponentiation* algorithm) gives some help here. But at present we can only prove *half* the following theorem:

Again, a nonzero y modulo p is an nth-**power** (or, in archaic terminology, nth-**power residue**) modulo p if there is x so that $x^n \equiv y$ mod p. (If there is no such x, then y is an nth-**power non-residue**.)

Theorem. *(Euler's Criterion)* Let p be a prime with $p \equiv 1$ mod n. Let y be relatively prime to p. Then y is an nth power mod p if and only if $y^{(p-1)/n} \equiv 1$ mod p. As a special case, for odd primes p, for p not dividing y, y is a *nonzero* square mod p, if and only if $y^{(p-1)/2} \equiv 1$ mod p.

Remark: This is a reasonable test for *not* being a square mod p. Apparently Euler was the first to observe this, about 300 years ago. Also, later *quadratic reciprocity* will give another mechanism to test whether or not something is a square modulo p. The criterion for nth powers has no simpler replacement.

Proof: Easy half: Suppose that $y = x^n$ mod p. Then, invoking Fermat's Little Theorem,

$$y^{(p-1)/n} = (x^n)^{(p-1)/n} = x^{p-1} = 1 \text{ mod } p$$

as claimed.

Hard half: Now suppose that $y^{(p-1)/n} = 1$ mod p, and show that y is an nth power. Let g be a *primitive root* modulo p, and let ℓ be a positive integer so that $g^\ell = y$. We have

$$(g^\ell)^{(p-1)/n} = 1 \text{ mod } p$$

From the discussion of primitive roots above, this implies that

$$(p-1) \,|\, \ell \cdot (p-1)/n$$

(since $\varphi(p) = p - 1$ for prime p). By unique factorization in the ordinary integers, the only way that this can happen is that ℓ be divisible by n, say $\ell = kn$ for some integer k. Then

$$y = g^\ell = g^{kn} = (g^k)^n \text{ mod } p$$

That is, y is the nth power of g^k.   ♣

Corollary. *(Euler's Criterion)* Let p be an odd prime. Let y be relatively prime to p. Then

$$y^{(p-1)/2} \equiv 1 \text{ mod } p \text{ if } y \text{ is a square mod } p$$

and

$$y^{(p-1)/2} \equiv -1 \text{ mod } p \text{ if } y \text{ is a non-square mod } p$$

Proof: The only new thing to prove is that, if y is a non-square, then $y^{(p-1)/2}$ is -1 mod p. Since by Fermat's Little Theorem $y^{p-1} = 1$ mod p, certainly

$$(y^{(p-1)/2})^2 = 1 \bmod p$$

That is, $y^{(p-1)/2}$ mod p satisfies $x^2 = 1$ mod p, and it is not 1. Certainly -1 is one other solution to the equation $x^2 = 1$ mod p. If we can show that there are no other solutions to this equation than ± 1, then we'll be done. Suppose x is an integer so that $x^2 = 1$ mod p. Then, by definition, $p|(x-1)(x+1)$.

We recall that since p is prime, if $p|ab$ then either $p|a$ or $p|b$. It might be good to review why this is true: suppose that $p|ab$ but p does not divide a, and aim to show that $p|b$. Let $ab = kp$. Since p is prime, $\gcd(p, a) = 1$, so there are integers s, t so that $sp + ta = 1$. Then

$$b = b \cdot 1 = b \cdot (sp + ta) = bsp + tab = bsp + tkp = p \cdot (bs + tk)$$

Thus, $p|b$, as claimed.

Therefore, in the case at hand, if $p|(x-1)(x+1)$, then either $p|(x-1)$ or $p|(x+1)$. That is, as claimed, $x = \pm 1$ mod p. This completes the proof that $y^{(p-1)/2} = -1$ mod p if and only if y is a non-square mod p (and relatively prime to p). ♣

Exercises

13.8.01 Is 2 a square modulo 101?

13.8.02 Is 14 a square modulo 101?

13.8.03 Is 69 a square modulo 101?

13.8.04 Is 2 a square modulo 109?

13.8.05 Is 5 a cube modulo 109?

13.8.06 Is 69 a cube modulo 109?

13.8.07 Is 2 a cube modulo 109?

13.8.08 Is 68 a cube modulo 109?

13.8.09 Is 105 a 144th power modulo 1009?

14

Weak Multiplicativity

14.1 Weak Multiplicativity

Many functions occurring naturally in number theory and other parts of mathematics have the property known as **weak multiplicativity** (defined just below). This idea lends itself to simplification of many computations and proofs. As a special and important case, we prove a formula for the Euler phi-function evaluated at n in terms of the prime factorization of n.

Let f be a function on the *positive integers*. This function can be complex-valued, for example, or simply integer-valued: the nature of the values is not too important. Such a function is **multiplicative** if always

$$f(mn) = f(m) \cdot f(n)$$

Although such a condition is important in its own right, it turns out that this strong condition is too restrictive for application to things that turn up in number theory. Thus, we weaken this a bit and say that f is **weakly multiplicative** if

$$f(mn) = f(m) \cdot f(n) \quad \text{for } m, n \text{ relatively prime}$$

Worth noting is that the value $f(1)$ of a weakly multiplicative function f at 1 is either 0 or 1, since $m = 1$ and $n = 1$ are relatively prime, and we compute

$$f(1) = f(1 \cdot 1) = f(1) \cdot f(1)$$

so $f(1)$ is a solution to the equation

$$x = x^2$$

which has only solutions $0, 1$. (This argument applies to weakly multiplicative functions taking values in the integers, rational numbers, real numbers, or complex numbers. More exotic values may require modification of the conclusion.)

The most standard family of (relatively elementary) weakly multiplicative functions (that are not actually *multiplicative*) are the **sums of powers of divisors** functions

$$
\begin{array}{lll}
\sigma_0(n) & = s_0(n) & = \quad \text{number of positive divisors of } n \\
\sigma_1(n) & = s_1(n) & = \quad \text{sum of positive divisors of } n \\
\sigma_k(n) & = s_k(n) & = \quad \text{sum of } k\text{th powers of divisors of } n
\end{array}
$$

(The index k can be any complex number, in fact.)

The proof that s_k is weakly multiplicative depends upon *unique factorization* in the integers. Let m, n be relatively prime. The key point is that, because of unique factorization and the relative coprime-ness of m and n, every positive divisor of the product mn is a product de of two positive divisors d of m and e of n, *and* can be written in only one way as such. Therefore,

$$s_k(mn) = \sum_{D|mn, D>0} D^k = \sum_{d|m, e|n,\, d,e>0} (de)^k = \sum_{d|m, d>0} d^k \sum_{e|n, e>0} e^k = s_k(m) \cdot s_k(n)$$

as claimed.

Another important weakly multiplicative function is the **Möbius function**, μ, defined by

$$\mu(n) = \begin{cases} (-1)^\ell & \text{if } n \text{ is divisible by exactly } \ell \text{ distinct prime factors} \\ 0 & \text{if } n \text{ is divisible by the square of any prime} \end{cases}$$

The weak multiplicativity is a consequence of unique factorization.

A somewhat subtler example is **Euler's phi-function**

$$\varphi(n) = \text{number of integers } i \text{ relatively prime to } n \text{ and } 0 < i \le n$$

Proposition. The Euler phi-function is weakly multiplicative. That is, for $\gcd(m, n) = 1$

$$\varphi(mn) = \varphi(m)\,\varphi(n)$$

Proof: From the theoretical aspects of the *gcd*, an integer y has a multiplicative inverse modulo m if and only if $gcd(y, m) = 1$, since from an expression $ay + bm = 1$ we see that a is a multiplicative inverse of y modulo m. Thus,

$$\varphi(n) = \text{number of multiplicatively invertible elements of } \mathbf{Z}/m$$

Further, multiplicative invertibility of y modulo m means that the congruence

$$xy \equiv 1 \bmod m$$

is solvable for x. Sun Ze's theorem shows that when $m = m_1 m_2$ is a factorization into relatively prime factors m_1, m_2, the solvability of $xy \equiv 1 \bmod m$ is equivalent to the simultaneous solvability of

$$\begin{cases} xy & \equiv 1 \bmod m_1 \\ xy & \equiv 1 \bmod m_2 \end{cases}$$

Since $\varphi(m_1)$ and $\varphi(m_2)$ count the number of solutions in $\mathbf{Z}/m_1$ and $\mathbf{Z}/m_2$ of these equations, we have

$$\varphi(m_1 m_2) = \varphi(m_1) \cdot \varphi(m_2)$$

for m_1 and m_2 relatively prime, as claimed.   ♣

Corollary. Let $p_1 < p_2 < \cdots < p_k$ be primes and $e_1, e_2, \ldots, e_n$ positive integers. Then

$$\varphi(p_1^{e_1} \ldots p_k^{e_k}) = (p_1 - 1)p_1^{e_1 - 1}\,(p_2 - 1)p_2^{e_2 - 1} \cdots (p_k - 1)p_k^{e_k - 1}$$

Proof: Since we know that φ is weakly multiplicative, it suffices to prove the formula

$$\varphi(p^e) = (p - 1)p^{e-1}$$

for a prime p and positive integer e. In this case, $\varphi(p^e)$ counts the integers ℓ with $0 < \ell \le p^e$ that are relatively prime to p. Since p is prime, this means simply that p doesn't divide ℓ. To count the integers ℓ' in that range *divisible* by p is easy: $1/p$ of them are divisible by p, so the total is p^e/p. Thus, subtracting,

$$\varphi(p^e) = p^e - p^e/p = p \cdot p^{e-1} - p^{e-1} = (p - 1)p^{e-1}$$

as asserted.   ♣

Exercises

14.1.01 Compute the number of positive divisors of 1000.

14.1.02 Compute the number of the positive divisors of

$$999 = 3 \cdot 3 \cdot 3 \cdot 37$$

14.1.03 Compute the sum of the positive divisors of 1000.

14.1.04 Compute the sum of the positive divisors of

$$999 = 3 \cdot 3 \cdot 3 \cdot 37$$

14.1.05 Compute the sum of the squares of the divisors of 1,000,000.

14.1.06 Compute the number of divisors of 10^{100}.

14.2 Arithmetic Convolutions

Here we note a process to build up more complicated weakly multiplicative functions from simpler ones. This **(arithmetic) convolution product** occurs frequently in number theory.

Proposition. Let f be a weakly multiplicative function on positive integers. Define another function F by

$$F(n) = \sum_{d|n,\, d>0} f(d)$$

Then F is also weakly multiplicative.

Proof: Let m, n be relatively prime. Then

$$F(mn) = \sum_{D|mn,\, D>0} f(D) = \sum_{d|m, d>0,\, e|n, e>0} f(d \cdot e)$$

since positive divisors of mn are uniquely expressible as products de, where d is a positive divisor of m and e is a positive divisor of n. Since $\gcd(m, n) = 1$, necessarily such d and e are relatively prime. Therefore, $f(de) = f(d)f(e)$, and this is

$$= \sum_{d|m, d>0} f(d) \sum_{e|n, e>0} f(e) = F(m) \cdot F(n)$$

as claimed.

♣

The construction of this last proposition is a standard procedure for obtaining new weakly multiplicative functions from old ones. A construction generalizing the previous proposition is the **convolution product**:

Proposition.   Let f and g be weakly multiplicative functions on positive integers. Define another function F, sometimes called the **arithmetic convolution** of f and g, by

$$F(n) = \sum_{d|n,\, d>0} f(d)\, g\left(\frac{n}{d}\right)$$

Then F is also weakly multiplicative.

Proof: Let m, n be relatively prime. Then

$$F(mn) = \sum_{D|mn,\, D>0} f(D)g\left(\frac{mn}{D}\right) = \sum_{d|m,d>0,\, e|n,e>0} f(d \cdot e)g\left(\frac{mn}{ed}\right)$$

since positive divisors of mn are uniquely expressible as products de, where d is a positive divisor of m and e is a positive divisor of n. Further, since m and n are relatively prime, m/d and m/e are relatively prime. And since $gcd(m, n) = 1$, necessarily such d and e are relatively prime. Therefore, $f(de) = f(d)f(e)$ and $g(mn/de) = g(m/d)g(n/e)$. Therefore, the expression for $F(mn)$ becomes

$$= \sum_{d|m,d>0} f(d)g(m/d) \sum_{e|n,e>0} f(e)g(n/e) = F(m) \cdot F(n)$$

as claimed.   ♣

Remark: The first proposition is a special case of the second proposition, by taking $g(n) = 1$ (for all n), which is not only *weakly* multiplicative, but just plain *multiplicative*.

Exercises

14.2.01 Let $f(n)$ be the number of positive divisors of n, and let $g(n)$ be the sum of the divisors of n. Let

$$h(n) = \sum_{0<d|n} f(d)\, g(n/d)$$

(where, as indicated, d ranges over positive divisors of n). Compute $h(1000)$.

14.2.02 (*) Can you identify the function h of the previous exercise in more elementary or intuitive terms?

14.3 Möbius Inversion

The version of the *Möbius inversion formula* here is a peculiar sort of formula, which comes in very handy throughout elementary number theory. Other versions of Möbius inversion appear throughout mathematics. We apply this to prove a peculiar identity for Euler's phi-function which will be useful later. Keep in mind that $\mu(n)$ denotes the Möbius mu-function of n.

Theorem. Let f be a weakly multiplicative function on positive integers, and

$$F(n) = \sum_{d|n, d>0} f(d)$$

Then

$$f(n) = \sum_{d|n, d>0} F(d)\mu(\frac{n}{d})$$

Symmetrically, if we let

$$G(n) = \sum_{d|n, d>0} f(d)\mu(\frac{n}{d})$$

then we have

$$f(n) = \sum_{d|n, d>0} G(d)$$

Proof: First consider the assertion regarding F. This can be simplified by realizing that the expression that we're claiming is $f(n)$ is in any case the *convolution* of F and μ. By results just above, in the first place F is weakly multiplicative, since f was, and the convolution of F and μ is then weakly multiplicative as well, since μ is. Therefore, to prove that the convolution of F and μ is equal to the weakly multiplicative function f, it suffices to consider $n = p^e$ for prime p and non-negative integer e. The simplest case is

$$F(1) = \sum_{d|1, d>0} f(d) = f(1)$$

and

$$\sum_{d|1, d>0} F(d)\mu(\frac{1}{d}) = F(1)\mu(1) = F(1) = f(1)$$

So we have proven the assertion about F for the input 1.

We've simplified enough now to just start computing: let e be a positive integer, and p a prime:

$$\sum_{d|p^e, d>0} F(d)\mu(\frac{p^e}{d}) = \sum_{0 \le i \le e} F(p^i)\mu(p^{e-i})$$

From its definition,

$$\mu(p^{e-i}) = \begin{cases} 1 & \text{if } e-i = 0 \\ -1 & \text{if } e-i = 1 \\ 0 & \text{if } e-i > 1 \end{cases}$$

Thus, the sum over i may as well be just over the two values $i = e - 1$ and $i = e$, and the whole thing simplifies a bit to

$$\sum_{0 \le i \le e} F(p^i)\mu(p^{e-i}) = \sum_{i=e-1,e} F(p^i)\mu(p^{e-i}) = \begin{cases} -F(p^{e-1}) + F(p^e) & \text{if } e > 0 \\ F(1) & \text{if } e = 0 \end{cases}$$

Now replace F by *its* definition in terms of f:

$$= - \sum_{d|p^{e-1},d>0} f(d) + \sum_{d|p^e,d>0} f(d)$$

Now notice that the only positive divisor of p^e whose summand in the second sum is not cancelled by the corresponding summand in the first sum is that corresponding to $d = p^e$. Therefore, this is

$$-F(p^{e-1}) + F(p^e) = - \sum_{d|p^{e-1},d>0} f(d) + \sum_{d|p^e,d>0} f(d) = f(p^e)$$

This proves that the two weakly multiplicative functions agree on prime powers p^e, so agree for all inputs.

For G, the argument is similar but with some details changed, so we'll give it. Again, since f is weakly multiplicative, so is G, since G is the convolution of f and μ. Likewise, the function

$$H(n) = \sum_{d|n,d>0} G(d)$$

is weakly multiplicative. To prove that the two weakly multiplicative functions H and f are equal it suffices to prove that they agree for prime power inputs. Let p be a prime and e a non-negative integer. Then

$$G(p^e) = \sum_{d|p^e,d>0} f(d)\mu(\frac{p^e}{d}) = \sum_{0 \le i \le e} f(p^i)\mu(p^{e-i})$$

The indicated value of μ is 0 unless $e - i$ is just 0 or 1, so this is

$$G(p^e) = \begin{cases} f(p^e) - f(p^{e-1}) & \text{for } e > 0 \\ f(1) & \text{for } e = 0 \end{cases}$$

Then

$$H(p^e) = \sum_{d|p^e,d>0} G(d) = G(1) + \sum_{d|p^e,d>1} G(d) = G(1) + \sum_{1 \le i \le e} G(p^i)$$

$$= f(1) + \sum_{1 \le i \le e} f(p^i) - f(p^{i-1})$$

$$= f(1) + \big(f(p) - f(1)\big) + \big(f(p^2) - f(p)\big) + \cdots + \big(f(p^e) - f(p^{e-1})\big)$$

$$= f(p^e)$$

by 'telescoping' the sum.

♣

Corollary. The Euler phi-function satisfies

$$\sum_{d|n, d>0} \varphi(d) = n$$

for positive integers n.

Proof: Note that the function $f(n) = n$ on positive integers is weakly multiplicative. By Möbius inversion, the claim of this corollary is equivalent to the claim that

$$\varphi(n) = \sum_{d|n, d>0} f(d)\mu\left(\frac{n}{d}\right)$$

And, by the weak multiplicativity of everything in sight, it suffices to prove the latter identity for $n = p^e$ with p prime and e a positive integer. (The case $n = 1$ can be checked directly.) That is, we want to verify that

$$\varphi(p^e) = \sum_{0 \le i \le e} f(p^i)\mu(p^{e-i})$$

As above, $\mu(p^{e-i}) = 0$ unless $e - i$ is 0 or 1, so what we want to verify simplifies to

$$\varphi(p^e) = f(p^e) - f(p^{e-1}) = p^e - p^{e-1}$$

Indeed, p^e is the number of integers ℓ in the range $0 < \ell \le p^e$, and p^{e-i} is the number of such which are *divisible* by p, so this difference is the number relatively prime to p. This proves the corollary.

♣

Exercises

14.3.01 Let μ be the Möbius function. Compute $\mu(100)$.

14.3.02 Let μ be the Möbius function. Compute $\mu(144)$.

14.3.03 Let μ be the Möbius function. Compute $\mu(35)$.

14.3.04 Let μ be the Möbius function. Compute $\mu(105)$.

14.3.05 Let μ be the Möbius function. Compute $\mu(1000000)$.

14.3.06 Let μ be the Möbius function. Compute the sum of $\mu(d)$ as d ranges over all positive divisors of 10^{20}.

15

Quadratic Reciprocity

The algorithm here for fast computation of 'quadratic symbols' is fundamental to many algorithms. Perhaps second in importance only to the Euclidean algorithm, this is another of the *good* algorithms we have. It is important to note that *the algorithm here is significantly faster than Euler's criterion* for determination of whether or not a given integer b is a square modulo a prime p.

Even from a non-computational viewpoint, the theorem on *quadratic reciprocity* should be quite striking, as it relates two things which have no obvious relationship. Thus, sometimes the importance of quadratic reciprocity for computation is overlooked.

Unfortunately, the proof that quadratic symbols work the way they do is too complicated for us, so is omitted.

15.1 Square Roots

Solving equations modulo m has many features in common with the techniques for solving equations involving rational, real, or complex numbers. However, some of our intuition which has been developed by dealing almost exclusively with real and complex numbers needs *refinement* in order to be accurate in more general situations.

For a given modulus n and a given number b, the question is whether b has a square root *modulo n* or not. That is, is the equation

$$x^2 \equiv b \bmod n$$

solvable, or not?

For example,

$$x^2 \equiv 2 \bmod 7$$

has the solutions $x = 3, 4$, since

$$3^2 = 9 \equiv 2 \bmod 7$$

$$4^2 = 16 \equiv 2 \bmod 7$$

On the other hand, as a different example, the congruence $x^2 \equiv 5 \bmod 7$ has *no* solution, as can be verified by squaring 0, 1, 2, 3, 4, 5, 6 (at worst) and seeing that none of the resulting squares is congruent to 5 modulo 7.

Note that the presence of these solutions is *unrelated* to the fact that there is no *integer* x so that $x^2 = 2$. These solutions are also unrelated to the *real number* approximating a square root of 2:

$$\sqrt{2} = 1.4142135623731\ldots$$

In fact, from a completely naive viewpoint the presence or not of square roots modulo m is inexplicable. At least our prior experience with square roots of real numbers or complex numbers seems of little relevance.

As another example, consider

$$x^2 = -1 \bmod 5$$

By now we might have been conditioned to respond that there can be no *real* number with a negative square, so there certainly can't be an *integer* whose square is negative (or something like that). However, both 2 and 3 are square roots of -1 mod 5:

$$2^2 = 4 = -1 \bmod 5$$
$$3^2 = 9 = -1 \bmod 5$$

From a naive viewpoint, the only way to tell whether $x^2 = c$ is solvable mod m is by trial and error, squaring $1, 2, \ldots, m - 1$ and seeing whether we get c mod m or not. At least this procedure has the virtue that *if* there is a square root then we'll not only know of its *existence* but actually *find it*.

For prime moduli p congruent to 3 mod 4, we have derived the formula

$$\text{square root of } y \text{ mod } p \ = y^{(p+1)/4} \text{ mod } p$$

for square roots. For arbitrary primes we don't have a formula, although there does exist a probabilistic algorithm for square roots. But to invoke these formulas or algorithms requires that we know the *factorization* of the modulus. By now we are aware that this might be burdensome.

15.2 Quadratic Symbols

Here we introduce standard notation, and change the issues a little bit to fit better into the theorem on *quadratic reciprocity*.

For an odd prime p, the **quadratic symbol** or **Legendre symbol** $(b/p)_2$ (or sometimes simply (b/p), dropping the subscript) is defined by

$$\left(\frac{b}{p}\right)_2 = \begin{cases} 0 & \text{if } \gcd(b, p) > 1 \\ 1 & \text{if } x^2 = b \text{ mod } p \text{ has a solution } x \text{ and } \gcd(b, p) = 1 \\ -1 & \text{if } x^2 = b \text{ mod } p \text{ has no solution } x \text{ and } \gcd(b, p) = 1 \end{cases}$$

Note that

$$\text{if } b \equiv b' \text{ mod } p \quad \text{then} \quad \left(\frac{b}{p}\right)_2 = \left(\frac{b'}{p}\right)_2$$

Remark: For notational emphasis, we will use that subscript '2' on the quadratic symbol even though we won't use any symbols $(x/p)_r$ with $r \neq 2$. These other symbols would tell whether or not x was an rth power modulo a prime p. We don't use them here, and they have more subtleties than quadratic symbols.

Then for arbitrary integers n which factor as

$$n = 2^{e_0} p_1^{e_1} \ldots p_k^{e_k}$$

with odd primes p_i, the **extended quadratic symbol** or **Jacobi symbol** is defined as

$$\left(\frac{b}{n}\right)_2 = \left(\frac{b}{p_1}\right)_2^{e_1} \cdots \left(\frac{b}{p_k}\right)_2^{e_k}$$

For p prime the quadratic (Legendre) symbol $(b/p)_2$ tells whether or not b is a square modulo p. This is the whole reason for this discussion. However, this is *not* the case for non-prime n. That is, for n not necessarily prime the value of the (Jacobi) symbol $(b/n)_2$ does not directly indicate whether or not $x^2 = b$ can be solved modulo n.

Thus, the Jacobi symbol is of interest mostly as an **auxiliary** gadget, useful in computation of Legendre symbols. Its utility in this auxiliary role is due to the fact that Jacobi symbols *can be computed quickly* using quadratic reciprocity (below).

15.3 Multiplicative Property

If we grant ourselves Euler's criterion for things being squares modulo primes, we can prove the important basic multiplicative property of quadratic symbols. We had earlier stated the following theorem:

Theorem. *(Euler's Criterion)* For prime $p > 2$, for integer b,

$$\left(\frac{b}{p}\right)_2 \equiv b^{(p-1)/2} \bmod p$$

Corollary.

$$\left(\frac{-1}{p}\right)_2 = (-1)^{(p-1)/2}$$

(This is a special case of the theorem, using the fact that we don't need to reduce modulo p when taking powers of -1.)

Now we have the **multiplicative property** of quadratic symbols:

Corollary. For prime p and integers a, b,

$$\left(\frac{ab}{p}\right)_2 = \left(\frac{a}{p}\right)_2 \cdot \left(\frac{b}{p}\right)_2$$

Proof: Granting the theorem, the proof of this is not too hard: computing modulo p

$$\left(\frac{ab}{p}\right)_2 = (ab)^{(p-1)/2} = a^{(p-1)/2}\, b^{(p-1)/2} = \left(\frac{a}{p}\right)_2 \cdot \left(\frac{b}{p}\right)_2 \bmod p$$

Remark: The least obvious part of this is the implicit assertion that if both a and b are *non-squares* modulo a prime p, then the product ab is a *square* mod p.

The general version of the **multiplicative property** is:

Corollary. For arbitrary odd integer n, and for a and b relatively prime to n,

$$\left(\frac{ab}{n}\right)_2 = \left(\frac{a}{n}\right)_2 \cdot \left(\frac{b}{n}\right)_2$$

Proof: Let the prime factorization of n be

$$n = p_1^{e_1} \dots p_k^{e_k}$$

Then, by definition of this extended quadratic symbol (that is, with not-necessarily-prime lower input)

$$\left(\frac{a}{n}\right)_2 = \left(\frac{a}{p_1}\right)_2^{e_1} \dots \left(\frac{a}{p_k}\right)_2^{e_k}$$

Then

$$\left(\frac{a}{n}\right)_2 \cdot \left(\frac{a}{n}\right)_2 = \left(\frac{a}{p_1}\right)_2^{e_1} \dots \left(\frac{a}{p_k}\right)_2^{e_k} \cdot \left(\frac{b}{p_1}\right)_2^{e_1} \dots \left(\frac{b}{p_k}\right)_2^{e_k} = \left(\frac{ab}{p_1}\right)_2^{e_1} \dots \left(\frac{ab}{p_k}\right)_2^{e_k}$$

by the previous corollary. Then, winding this back up, it is

$$= \left(\frac{ab}{n}\right)_2$$

which proves the corollary.   ♣

15.4 Quadratic Reciprocity

Now we *state* the theorem called **the Law of Quadratic Reciprocity**. This is the first result of *modern* number theory. Its truth had been conjectured in the late 18th century, but it was not proven until about 1796, by C. F. Gauss. From a naive viewpoint, there is absolutely no reason why any such thing should be true. But, by now, 200 years later, this result has been well assimilated and is understood as the simplest representative of a whole family of *reciprocity laws*, which themselves are part of what is called *classfield theory*, which itself has been assimilated into the so-called *Langlands program*.

The use of the word 'reciprocity' refers to the first (and most important) assertion of the theorem, which asserts a *reciprocity* between the issue of p being a square mod q and q being a square mod p. The proof of this will be delayed a bit.

Theorem. *(Gauss' Quadratic Reciprocity)* Let p, q be distinct odd primes. Then

$$\left(\frac{p}{q}\right)_2 = (-1)^{(p-1)\cdot(q-1)/4} \left(\frac{q}{p}\right)_2$$

The expression $(-1)^{(p-1)\cdot(q-1)/4}$ appearing in this formula only depends upon p and q modulo 4. Also

$$\left(\frac{-1}{p}\right)_2 = (-1)^{(p-1)/2}$$

$$\left(\frac{2}{p}\right)_2 = (-1)^{(p^2-1)/8}$$

In particular, $\left(\frac{-1}{p}\right)_2$ only depends upon p modulo 4, and $\left(\frac{2}{p}\right)_2$ only depends upon p modulo 8.

Note that this result refers only to the Legendre symbol, not the more general Jacobi symbol.

Thus, granting this result, we have an algorithm for telling whether $x^2 = c \bmod p$ is solvable or not, although this does not *find* the square root if it exists.

Remark: The difference between *proving existence* of the square root and the harder task of *finding it* are entirely in parallel to the difference between proving that a number *fails to be prime* and actually *finding a proper factor*.

For example, let's see whether

$$x^2 \equiv 19 \bmod 101$$

is solvable or not. We have

$$\left(\frac{19}{101}\right)_2 = (-1)^{(19-1)(101-1)/4}\left(\frac{101}{19}\right)_2$$

by quadratic reciprocity. Looking at 19 and 101 modulo 4, it is easy to see that the power of -1 has value 1, so the right-hand side simplifies to

$$\left(\frac{101}{19}\right)_2 = \left(\frac{6}{19}\right)_2 = \left(\frac{2}{19}\right)_2 \cdot \left(\frac{3}{19}\right)_2$$

since

$$101 \% 19 = 6$$

and by invoking the corollary to Euler's theorem above. We continue to evaluate each of the last two quadratic symbols separately. For the first, from quadratic reciprocity we have

$$\left(\frac{2}{19}\right)_2 = (-1)^{(19^2-1)/8} = (-1)^{(20\cdot 18)/8} = (-1)^{5\cdot 9} = -1$$

Continuing to apply quadratic reciprocity, the other quadratic symbol is

$$\left(\frac{3}{19}\right)_2 = (-1)^{(3-1)(19-1)/4}\left(\frac{19}{3}\right)_2 = -\left(\frac{19}{3}\right)_2 = -\left(\frac{1}{3}\right)_2 = -1$$

by reducing 19 mod 3. Therefore, in summary,

$$\left(\frac{19}{101}\right)_2 = \left(\frac{6}{19}\right)_2 = \left(\frac{2}{19}\right)_2 \cdot 319 = (-1)(-1) = 1$$

Therefore, 19 is a square modulo 101.

But, in fact, apart from taking out powers of 2, there is no reason to factor into primes the inputs to these quadratic symbols! This becomes especially relevant for large integers.

Corollary. *(Quadratic Reciprocity for Jacobi symbols)* Let m, n be odd positive integers. Then, using the extended Jacobi symbols rather than merely the Legendre symbols, we have

$$\left(\frac{m}{n}\right)_2 = (-1)^{(m-1)(n-1)/4} \left(\frac{n}{m}\right)_2$$

Proof: Of course, we use Gauss' theorem on quadratic reciprocity to prove this. Let

$$m = p_1^{e_1} \dots p_k^{e_k}$$
$$n = q_1^{f_1} \dots q_\ell^{f_\ell}$$

be the prime factorizations of m and n. Then the Jacobi symbol $\left(\frac{m}{n}\right)_2$ is expressed in terms of the more basic Legendre symbols as

$$\left(\frac{m}{n}\right)_2 = \prod_j \left(\frac{m}{q_j}\right)_2^{f_j}$$

By the corollary to Euler's theorem above, we have

$$\left(\frac{m}{q_j}\right)_2 = \prod_i \left(\frac{p_i}{q_j}\right)_2^{e_i}$$

Therefore, altogether, we have

$$\left(\frac{m}{n}\right)_2 = \prod_{i,j} \left(\frac{p_i}{q_j}\right)_2^{e_i f_j}$$

Now we apply quadratic reciprocity to each $\left(\frac{p_i}{q_j}\right)_2$, obtaining

$$\left(\frac{m}{n}\right)_2 = \prod_{i,j} (-1)^{e_i f_j (p_i-1)(q_j-1)/4} \left(\frac{q_j}{p_i}\right)_2^{e_i f_j}$$

$$= \left(\prod_{i,j} (-1)^{(p_i-1)(q_j-1)/4}\right) \left(\frac{n}{m}\right)_2$$

In order to prove the corollary, we have to show that

$$\prod_{i,j} (-1)^{e_i f_j (p_i-1)(q_j-1)/4} = (-1)^{(m-1)(n-1)/4}$$

Since we are talking about powers of -1, all we really need to show is

$$\sum_{i,j} \frac{(p_i-1)(q_j-1)}{4} e_i f_j \equiv \frac{(m-1)(n-1)}{4} \bmod 2$$

Multiplying out the denominator 4, this is equivalent to requiring

$$\sum_{i,j} (p_i - 1)(q_j - 1)\, e_i\, f_j \equiv (m - 1)(n - 1) \bmod 8$$

Being a little optimistic, it would suffice to prove that for any *odd* integers a, b, c we have

$$(ab - 1)(c - 1) \equiv (a - 1)(c - 1) + (b - 1)(c - 1) \bmod 8$$

Instead of symbols a, b, c for the three odd integers, let's use $2a + 1$, $2b + 1$, and $2c + 1$ for the three odd integers. Then what we want is

$$((2a + 1)(2b + 1) - 1)((2c + 1) - 1)$$

$$\equiv ((2a + 1) - 1)((2c + 1) - 1) + ((2b + 1) - 1)((2c + 1) - 1) \bmod 8$$

Multiplying everything out and doing a little cancelling, what we are wanting is

$$(4ab - 2a - 2b)(2c) = (4ac) + (4bc) \bmod 8$$

Taking out the common factors of 4, this last congruence is equivalent to

$$2abc - ac - bc \equiv ac + bc \bmod 2$$

Moving everything to the left-hand side, this is equivalent to

$$2abc - 2ac - 2bc \equiv 0 \bmod 2$$

The latter is certainly true. Since the truth of this is equivalent to the assertion we need for the corollary to be true, we have proven the corollary (invoking the theorem on quadratic reciprocity).   ♣

Accompanying the previous corollary, which extends the most important case of quadratic reciprocity to apply to Jacobi symbols, we also need the corresponding results for $\left(\frac{2}{n}\right)_2$ and $\left(\frac{-1}{n}\right)_2$.

Corollary. For an odd positive integer n, we can evaluate Jacobi symbols

$$\left(\tfrac{-1}{n}\right)_2 = (-1)^{(n-1)/2}$$
$$\left(\tfrac{2}{n}\right)_2 = (-1)^{(n^2-1)/8}$$

In particular, $\left(\frac{-1}{n}\right)_2$ only depends on what n is modulo 4, and $\left(\frac{2}{n}\right)_2$ only depends on what n is modulo 8.

Proof: Let $n = p_1^{e_2} \dots p_k^{e_k}$ be the prime factorization of n. Again from the definition of the Jacobi symbols in terms of Legendre symbols, we have

$$\left(\frac{-1}{n}\right)_2 = \prod_i \left(\frac{-1}{p_i}\right)_2^{e_i}$$

which we know has value

$$\prod_i (-1)^{e_i(p-1)/2}$$

To prove that this is equal to

$$(-1)^{(n-1)/2}$$

as in the proof of the previous corollary, it suffices to prove for odd integers a and b that

$$\frac{a-1}{2} + \frac{b-1}{2} \equiv \frac{ab-1}{2} \bmod 2$$

Replacing a by $2a+1$ and b by $2b+1$, and multiplying through by the denominator 2, this is equivalent to showing that

$$(2a+1) - 1 + (2b+1) - 1 = (2a+1)(2b+1) - 1 \bmod 4$$

Multiplying out, this is equivalent to

$$2a + 2b \equiv 4ab + 2a + 2b \bmod 4$$

which is certainly true. This proves the assertion about $\left(\frac{-1}{n}\right)_2$.

For $\left(\frac{2}{n}\right)_2$, the argument is the same if we have the confidence to just push it through. The definition of the Jacobi symbol gives

$$\left(\frac{2}{n}\right)_2 = \prod_i \left(\frac{2}{p_i}\right)_2^{e_i}$$

which by quadratic reciprocity is

$$\prod_i (-1)^{e_i(p_i^2-1)/8}$$

To prove that this is equal to

$$(-1)^{(n^2-1)8}$$

it suffices, as before, to prove the more general assertion that for any two odd numbers a, b

$$(-1)^{((ab)^2-1)/8} = (-1)^{(a^2-1)/8}(-1)^{(b^2-1)/8}$$

To prove this assertion about powers of -1 is equivalent, as before, to proving for odd integers a, b that

$$\frac{(ab)^2 - 1}{8} \equiv \frac{a^2 - 1}{8}\frac{b^2 - 1}{8} \bmod 2$$

Multiplying through by the denominator 8 and replacing a by $2a+1$ and b by $2b+1$, this is equivalent to

$$[(2a+1)(2b+1)]^2 - 1 \equiv (2a+1)^2 - 1 + (2b+1)^2 - 1 \bmod 16$$

Simplifying, this is equivalent to

$$(4a^2 + 4a + 1)(4b^2 + 4b + 1) - 1 \equiv 4a^2 + 4a + 4b^2 + 4b \bmod 16$$

or

$$16a^2b^2 + 16a^2b + 16ab^2 + 16ab + 4a^2 + 4b^2 + 4a + 4b \equiv 4a^2 + 4a + 4b^2 + 4b \bmod 16$$

If we ignore multiples of 16 and cancel summands appearing on both sides, we are left with the equivalent congruence $0 \equiv 0 \bmod 16$, which is true.

Finally, let's check that the values of the quadratic symbols $\left(\frac{-1}{n}\right)_2$ and $\left(\frac{2}{n}\right)_2$ depend only upon the values of n modulo 4 or 8. This is straightforward. For a positive integer ℓ,

$$\left(\frac{-1}{n+4\ell}\right)_2 = (-1)^{(n+4\ell-1)/2} = (-1)^{2\ell}(-1)^{(n-1)/2} = (-1)^{(n-1)/2} = \left(\frac{-1}{n}\right)_2$$

For $\left(\frac{2}{n}\right)_2$, we compute

$$\left(\frac{2}{n+8\ell}\right)_2 = (-1)^{((n+8\ell)^2-1)/8} = (-1)^{8\ell^2+2\ell n}(-1)^{(n^2-1)/8}$$

as required.   ♣

15.5 Fast Computation

For reasons quite similar to the reasons for efficiency of the Euclidean algorithm, the extended form of quadratic reciprocity for Jacobi symbols gives us a good algorithm to compute quadratic symbols. Note that by using the Jacobi symbol we *avoid* having to factor numbers into primes, which is a great time-saver.

We'll do two examples here in order to illustrate the method. The first is relatively simple, and we'll do it in detail. In the second case, using significantly larger numbers, we'll omit the smaller details in order to see that the algorithm really does proceed quite efficiently. At the end we give a somewhat more formal description of the algorithm.

Let's compute $\left(\frac{1237}{4327}\right)_2$ without any odd prime factorization. (The number 4327 *is* prime.) We have

$$\left(\frac{1237}{4327}\right)_2 = (-1)^{\frac{(1237-1)(4327-1)}{4}} \left(\frac{4327}{1237}\right)_2 = \left(\frac{4327}{1237}\right)_2$$

by quadratic reciprocity. Note that we neither know nor care whether or not 1237 is prime. Reducing 4327 modulo 1237, this is equal to

$$\left(\frac{616}{1237}\right)_2$$

Taking out factors of 2 from the top, this is equal to

$$\left(\frac{2}{1237}\right)_2 \left(\frac{308}{1237}\right)_2 = \left(\frac{2}{1237}\right)_2 \left(\frac{2}{1237}\right)_2 \left(\frac{154}{1237}\right)_2$$

$$= \left(\frac{2}{1237}\right)_2 \left(\frac{2}{1237}\right)_2 \left(\frac{2}{1237}\right)_2 \left(\frac{77}{1237}\right)_2$$

$$= \left(\frac{2}{1237}\right)_2 \left(\frac{77}{1237}\right)_2$$

since always

$$\left(\frac{m}{n}\right)_2^2 = 1$$

for m, n relatively prime. To evaluate $\left(\frac{2}{1237}\right)_2$ we may reduce 1237 modulo 8, so

$$\left(\frac{2}{1237}\right)_2 = \left(\frac{2}{5}\right)_2 = (-1)^{(5^2-1)/8} = (-1)^3 = -1$$

Saving the latter result, we compute

$$\left(\frac{77}{1237}\right)_2 = (-1)^{(77-1)(1237-1)/4} \left(\frac{1237}{77}\right)_2 = \left(\frac{1237}{77}\right)_2 = \left(\frac{5}{77}\right)_2$$

$$= (-1)^{(77-1)(5-1)/4} \left(\frac{77}{5}\right)_2 = \left(\frac{77}{5}\right)_2 = \left(\frac{2}{5}\right)_2$$

And again (by coincidence the same computation as in the last paragraph!)

$$\left(\frac{2}{5}\right)_2 = (-1)^{(5^2-1)/8} = (-1)^3 = -1$$

Combining and summarizing these results,

$$\left(\frac{1237}{4327}\right)_2 = \left(\frac{4327}{1237}\right)_2 = \left(\frac{616}{1237}\right)_2 = \left(\frac{2}{1237}\right)_2 \left(\frac{77}{1237}\right)_2$$

$$= (-1) \left(\frac{1237}{77}\right)_2 = (-1) \left(\frac{5}{77}\right)_2 = (-1) \left(\frac{77}{5}\right)_2 = (-1) \left(\frac{2}{5}\right)_2 = (-1)(-1) = 1$$

Thus, we conclude that 1237 is a square modulo 4327.

Now let's do a larger example: compute

$$\left(\frac{123456791}{987654323}\right)_2$$

where, incidentally, 987654323 is prime. Using quadratic reciprocity, noting that both these numbers reduce modulo 4 to 3, this is

$$\left(\frac{123456791}{987654323}\right)_2 = -\left(\frac{987654323}{123456791}\right)_2 = -\left(\frac{123456786}{123456791}\right)_2$$

(At this point we could be slightly clever and save a step, but let's not and see that it works out nicely anyway.) Taking out powers of 2, this is

$$-\left(\frac{2}{123456791}\right)_2\left(\frac{61728393}{123456791}\right)_2 = -\left(\frac{2}{7}\right)_2\left(\frac{61728393}{123456791}\right)_2 = -\left(\frac{61728393}{123456791}\right)_2$$

Since $61728393 \% 4 = 1$, this is

$$-\left(\frac{123456791}{61728393}\right)_2 = -\left(\frac{5}{61728393}\right)_2 = -\left(\frac{61728393}{5}\right)_2 = -\left(\frac{3}{5}\right)_2$$

$$= -\left(\frac{5}{3}\right)_2 = -\left(\frac{2}{3}\right)_2 = -(-1) = 1$$

Therefore, 123456791 is a square modulo 987654323.

Of course, in the last example we were a bit lucky that the algorithm terminated so quickly. In general, by a similar estimate as for the Euclidean algorithm, one can verify that there are at most $2\log_2 n$ *steps* necessary in evaluation of $\left(\frac{x}{n}\right)_2$ with $1 < x < n$. However, the factors of 2 that appear require some extra treatment, and at the beginning the 'steps' involve large-ish numbers.

Exercises

15.5.01 Compute the value of the quadratic symbol $(-1/1009)_2$. Is -1 a square modulo 1009?

15.5.02 Compute the value of the quadratic symbol $(-1/1033)_2$. Is -1 a square modulo 1009?

15.5.03 Compute the value of the quadratic symbol $(2/1009)_2$. Is 2 a square modulo 1009?

15.5.04 Compute the value of the quadratic symbol $(2/1033)_2$. Is 2 a square modulo 1033?

15.5.05 Compute the value of the quadratic symbol $(3/1009)_2$. Is 3 a square modulo 1009?

15.5.06 Compute the value of the quadratic symbol $(-5/1009)_2$. Is -5 a square modulo 1009?

15.5.07 Compute the value of the quadratic symbol $(119/1009)_2$. Is 119 a square modulo 1009?

15.5.08 Compute the value of the quadratic symbol $(-1/2009)_2$. Is -1 a square modulo 2009?

15.5.09 Compute the value of the quadratic symbol $(-1/2033)_2$. Is -1 a square modulo 2033?

15.5.10 Compute the value of the quadratic symbol $(-1/2041)_2$. Is -1 a square modulo 2041?

15.5.11 Compute the value of the quadratic symbol $(2/2009)_2$. Is 2 a square modulo 2009?

15.5.12 Compute the value of the quadratic symbol $(3/2009)_2$. Is 3 a square modulo 2009?

15.5.13 Compute the value of the quadratic symbol $(-5/2009)_2$. Is -5 a square modulo 2009?

15.5.14 Compute the value of the quadratic symbol $(119/2009)_2$. Is 119 a square modulo 2009?

15.5.15 (*) Which is faster and/or better to determine whether x is a square modulo a prime p, using Euler's criterion, or using quadratic reciprocity?

16
Pseudoprimes

The simplest test for primality, the **trial division** method, may require roughly $\sqrt{n}$ steps to prove that n is prime. This already takes several minutes on a 200-MHz machine when $n \approx 10^{18}$, so it would take about 10^{16} years for $n \approx 10^{60}$. Yet modern ciphersystems need *many* primes at least 10^{60}, if not larger.

The first compromise is that we can gain enormously in *speed* if we sacrifice *certainty*. That is, we can quickly prove that very large numbers are *likely* to be prime, but will not have the absolute certainty of primality that traditional computations would give. But, since those traditional computations could never be completed, perhaps the idea that something is being 'sacrificed' is incorrect.

Numbers which are not truly known to be prime, but which have passed various probabilistic tests for primality, are called **pseudoprimes** (of various sorts) or **probable primes**. Sometimes the word 'pseudoprime' is used to indicate a *non-prime* which has nevertheless passed a probabilistic test for primality. For us, though, a pseudoprime is simply a number (which may or may not really be prime) which has passed some sort of probabilistic primality test.

Each of these yet-to-be-specified probabilistic primality tests to be performed upon a number n makes use of one or more auxiliary numbers b, chosen 'at random' from the range $1 < b < n$. If a particular auxiliary b tells us that 'n is likely prime', then b is a **witness** to the primality of n. The problem is that a significant fraction of the numbers b in the range $1 < b < n$ may be **false witnesses** (sometimes called **liars**), meaning that they tell us n is prime when it's *not*. Thus, part of the issue is to be sure that a large fraction of the numbers b in the range $1 < b < n$ are ('true') witnesses to either the primality or compositeness of n. The fatal flaw in the Fermat pseudoprime test is that there are composite numbers n for which there are *no* witnesses. These are called **Carmichael numbers**. The other two primality tests have no such flaw.

In all cases, the notion of *probability* that we use in saying something such as 'n is prime with probability 2^{-10}' is a fundamentally *heuristic* one, based on the doubtful hypothesis that among n possibilities *which we don't understand* each has probability $1/n$ of occurring. (This sort of pseudo-probabilistic reasoning has been rightfully disparaged for over 200 years.)

On the other hand, these probabilistic primality tests can be converted to *deterministic* tests if the **Extended Riemann Hypothesis** is true. Many mathematicians believe that the Extended Riemann Hypothesis is true, and there is no simple evidence to the contrary (as of mid 2000), but it seems that no one has any idea how to *prove* it, either. The question has been open for about 140 years, with no real progress on it. Assuming that the Extended Riemann Hypothesis is true, it would follow that there is a universal constant C so that for any number n, if n is composite, then there is an *Euler witness* (and also a *strong witness*) b with

$$1 < b < C \cdot (\log n)^2$$

That is, we wouldn't have to look too far to find a (truthful) witness if n is composite. Ironically, even with refined versions of this result, and even granting the Extended Riemann Hypothesis, to test primality of large numbers *with certainty* would require hundreds or thousands of times the number of Miller–Rabin tests that the probabilistic version requires. That is, even if we *had* a deterministic version available, the probabilistic version would run much faster. This should cause us to ask how much we're willing to 'pay' to have absolute certainty rather than 99.9999999% probability of primality.

16.1 Fermat Pseudoprimes

This section gives a heuristic test for primality. It has several weaknesses and in the end is not what we will use, but it illustrates two very interesting points: first, that *probabilistic* algorithms may run much faster than deterministic ones, and, second, that we simply can't expect to provide proofs for everything which seems to be true.

On one hand, Fermat's so-called *Little Theorem* asserts that for any prime number p and integer b

$$b^p = b \bmod p$$

Equivalently, for p not dividing b, we have

$$b^{p-1} = 1 \bmod p$$

This is a special case of Euler's theorem, which asserts that for b prime to an integer n,

$$b^{\varphi(n)} = 1 \bmod n$$

where φ is Euler's phi-function. (Euler's theorem is best proven using a little *group theory*, and we will do this later.)

An integer n is called a **Fermat pseudoprime** or **ordinary pseudoprime** or simply **pseudoprime** if

$$2^{n-1} = 1 \bmod n$$

No, there is no assurance that n's being a Fermat pseudoprime implies that n is prime, since there is no converse to Fermat's Little Theorem. Yet, *in practice* it is 'very unusual' that $2^n = 2 \bmod n$ and yet n is not prime. Specifically, $341 = 11 \times 31$ is not prime, and is the first non-prime number which is a Fermat pseudoprime: $2^{341} = 2 \bmod 341$. The next few non-prime Fermat pseudoprimes are

$$561, 645, 1105, 1387, 1729, 1905, 2047, 2465$$

There are only 5597 non-prime Fermat pseudoprimes below 10^9.

It *is* true that if an integer n *fails* the Fermat test, meaning that $2^{n-1} \neq 1 \bmod n$, then n is certainly *not* a prime (since, if it *were* prime, then $2^{n-1} = 1 \bmod p$, after all).

Since the fast exponentiation algorithm provides an economical method for computing $b^{n-1} \bmod p$, *we can test whether an integer n is a Fermat pseudoprime much faster than we can test it for primality by trial division.*

We can make a more stringent condition: an integer n is a **Fermat pseudoprime base b** if

$$b^{n-1} = 1 \bmod n$$

If $b^{n-1} \neq 1 \bmod n$, then n is certainly *not* a prime. On the other hand, even if $b^{n-1} = 1 \bmod n$ for all b relatively prime to n, we have no assurance that n is prime.

An integer b in the range $1 < b < n-1$ so that $b^{n-1} = 1 \bmod n$ is a **(Fermat) witness** for the primality of n. If n isn't actually prime, then that b is a (Fermat) **false witness** or (Fermat) **liar**.

And the behavior of a non-prime can be different with respect to different bases. For example, the non-prime $91 = 7 \cdot 13$ is *not* a Fermat pseudoprime (base 2), but *is* a Fermat pseudoprime base 3.

Again, in practice, it is very unusual for an integer to be a pseudoprime base b for one or more bases b and yet fail to be a prime. Nevertheless, there are infinitely many integers which are pseudoprimes to all bases (relatively prime to them) and yet are not prime. These are called **Carmichael numbers**. The Carmichael numbers under 10,000 are

$$561, \ 1105, \ 1729, \ 2465, \ 2821, \ 6601, \ 8911$$

There are 'only' 2163 Carmichael numbers below 10^9, and 8241 Carmichael numbers below 10^{12}, $19,279$ up to 10^{13}, $44,706$ up to 10^{14}, and $105,212$ up to 10^{15} (see [Pinch 1993]).

Later, we will show that *a Carmichael number must be odd, square-free, and divisible by at least 3 primes*. This result is also necessary to understand why the *better* versions of 'pseudoprime' and corresponding probabilistic primality tests (below) do not have failings analogous to the presence of Carmichael numbers.

It was an open problem for more than 80 years to determine whether there are or are not infinitely many Carmichael numbers. Rather recently, it was proven that there are infinitely many: in fact, there is a constant C so that the number of Carmichael numbers less than x is $\geq C \cdot x^{2/7}$. See [Alford, Granville, Pomerance 1994].

Exercises

16.1.01 Show that the composite number 45 is a Fermat pseudoprime base 17.

16.1.02 Show that the composite number 49 is a Fermat pseudoprime base 18.

16.1.03 Show that the composite number 51 is a Fermat pseudoprime base 35.

16.1.04 Show that the composite number 55 is a Fermat pseudoprime base 21.

16.1.05 Show that the composite number 57 is a Fermat pseudoprime base 20.

16.1.06 Show that the composite number 65 is a Fermat pseudoprime base 14.

16.1.07 Verify that the numbers 341, 561, 645, 1105 are the smallest Fermat pseudoprimes base 2 which are not prime. Which of these false primes are detected by Fermat's test base 3? Base 5?

16.1.08 Show that if n is a Fermat pseudoprime base 2 and base 3, then it is a Fermat pseudoprime base 6.

16.2 Non-Prime Pseudoprimes

It happens to be relatively easy to show that, for fixed base b, if there is *one* non-prime Fermat pseudoprime base b, then we can explicitly manufacture *infinitely many* more such. In fact, better than this, there is an explicit construction of infinitely many non-prime Fermat pseudoprimes base b. These ideas go back to A. Korselt in 1899, E. Malo in 1903, M. Cipolla in 1904, and R.D. Carmichael in 1912.

The first proposition assumes that we already have a non-prime Fermat pseudoprime base b, from which we can produce a rapidly growing infinite sequence of such.

Proposition. Suppose that $b^{n-1} = 1 \bmod n$ but n is a composite number and $\gcd(b - 1, n) = 1$. Then

$$N = \frac{b^n - 1}{b - 1}$$

has the same property: $b^{N-1} = 1 \bmod N$ but N is composite and relatively prime to $b - 1$. Thus, from a non-prime Fermat pseudoprime n base b we can make another, N.

Proof: First,

$$N - 1 = \frac{b^n - 1}{b - 1} - 1 = \frac{b^n - 1 - b + 1}{b - 1} = b\frac{b^{n-1} - 1}{b - 1}$$

Since n and $b - 1$ have no common factor, and by hypothesis n divides $b^{n-1} - 1$, then still n divides $\frac{b^{n-1}-1}{b-1}$. So there is an integer ℓ so that

$$\frac{b^{n-1} - 1}{b - 1} = n\ell$$

That is, we have

$$N - 1 = b\frac{b^{n-1} - 1}{b - 1} = bn\ell$$

Then

$$b^{N-1} - 1 = b^{bn\ell} - 1 = (b^n)^{b\ell} - 1$$

which by basic algebra is a multiple of $b^n - 1$, so is surely a multiple of $N = (b^n - 1)/(b - 1)$. Finally, to verify that N and $b - 1$ are relatively prime, recall Fermat's observation that for $b > 1$

$$\gcd(b^m - 1, b^n - 1) = b^{\gcd(m,n)} - 1$$

Thus, $\gcd(b - 1, b^n - 1) = b - 1$ and $\gcd(b - 1, (b^n - 1)/(b - 1)) = 1$. This finishes the proof.   ♣

The next proposition produces a denser collection of infinitely many non-prime Fermat pseudoprimes base b.

Proposition. Let $b \geq 2$, and $p > 2$ a prime *not* dividing $b(b - 1)(b + 1)$. Then

$$N = \frac{b^p - 1}{b - 1} \cdot \frac{b^p + 1}{b + 1}$$

is a non-prime Fermat pseudoprime base b.

Proof: Since $b \geq 2$ and $p > 2$ is odd, both $(b^p - 1)/(b - 1)$ and $(b^p + 1)/(b + 1)$ are integers greater than 1, so N is surely not prime. Then

$$\frac{b^p - 1}{b - 1} \cdot \frac{b^p + 1}{b + 1} - 1 = \frac{b^2((b^2)^{p-1} - 1)}{b^2 - 1}$$

Since p is prime and does not divide b, p divides $(b^2)^{p-1} - 1$. Since p does not divide $b^2 - 1$, in fact p divides

$$\frac{(b^2)^{p-1} - 1}{b^2 - 1}$$

Also, regardless of the parity of b, the quantity

$$\frac{b^2((b^2)^{p-1} - 1)}{b^2 - 1}$$

is *even*. So write

$$\frac{b^2((b^2)^{p-1} - 1)}{b^2 - 1} = 2\ell p$$

for some integer ℓ. Then

$$b^{\frac{b^p - 1}{b - 1} \cdot \frac{b^p + 1}{b + 1} - 1} - 1 = b^{2\ell p} - 1$$

which is a multiple of $b^{2p} - 1$ by elementary algebra. Thus, surely, this is a multiple of $N = (b^{2p} - 1)/(b^2 - 1)$. Thus, N is a non-prime Fermat pseudoprime base b. ♣

Remark: By contrast, it is much harder to prove that there are infinitely many *Carmichael numbers*, meaning non-prime numbers n so that $b^{n-1} = 1 \mod n$ for *all* b relatively prime to n. This was accomplished only in 1994 in [Alford, Granville, Pomerance 1994].

Exercises

16.2.01 Find 5 different non-prime Fermat pseudoprimes base 2.

16.2.02 Find 5 different non-prime Fermat pseudoprimes base 3.

16.2.03 Find 6 different non-prime Fermat pseudoprimes base 7.

16.2.04 (*) Find 5 different non-prime numbers which are nevertheless Fermat pseudoprimes base 2 and base 3.

16.3 Euler Pseudoprimes

We can improve our probabilistic primality test, successfully excluding some non-primes which nevertheless are (Fermat) pseudoprimes. This requires a little additional set-up. The Solovay-Strassen test was the first fully legitimate general probabilistic primality test, discovered in 1976. The fact that it is a reasonably fast algorithm is dependent upon the fact that Quadratic Reciprocity allows efficient evaluation of (Jacobi) quadratic symbols. A number which is assessed as being 'likely prime' according to the Solovay-Strassen test (but which may or may not actually be prime) is called an **Euler pseudoprime**. It is important to note that there is no analogue of the Carmichael numbers for Euler pseudoprimes.

For a given modulus n and a given number b, the question is whether b has a square root *modulo n* or not. That is, is the equation

$$x^2 = b \bmod n$$

solvable, or not?

For an odd prime p, the **quadratic symbol** or **Legendre symbol** $(b/p)_2$ (or sometimes simply (b/p), dropping the subscript) is defined by

$$\left(\frac{b}{p}\right)_2 = \begin{cases} 0 & \text{if } gcd(b,p) > 1 \\ 1 & \text{if } x^2 = b \bmod p \text{ has a solution } x \text{ and } gcd(b,p) = 1 \\ -1 & \text{if } x^2 = b \bmod p \text{ has no solution } x \text{ and } gcd(b,p) = 1 \end{cases}$$

Then for arbitrary integers n which factor as

$$n = 2^{e_0} p_1^{e_1} \ldots p_k^{e_k}$$

with odd primes p_i, the **extended quadratic symbol** or **Jacobi symbol** is defined as

$$\left(\frac{b}{n}\right)_2 = \left(\frac{b}{p_1}\right)_2^{e_1} \ldots \left(\frac{b}{p_k}\right)_2^{e_k}$$

It is important to realize that, while for p prime the quadratic symbol $(b/p)_2$ really does tell whether or not b is a square modulo p, this is *not* the case for non-prime n. That is, the value of $(b/n)_2$ does not directly indicate whether or not $x^2 = b$ can be solved modulo n. However, for present purposes the point of the Jacobi symbol is that *it can be computed quickly*. (If $(b/n)_2 = -1$, then b is definitely *not* a square, but if the value is $+1$, it's still only 50-50 whether b is a square or not.)

Euler proved (as we will do a little later) that for *prime p*

$$\left(\frac{b}{p}\right)_2 = b^{\frac{p-1}{2}} \bmod p$$

By contrast, if n is *not* prime, then the values of $b^{(n-1)/2}$ for varying b seem to be random.

Making the same unreasonable leap as with Fermat pseudoprimes, we declare an integer n to be an **Euler pseudoprime base** b if

$$\left(\frac{b}{n}\right)_2 = b^{(n-1)/2} \bmod n$$

Since the values of the quadratic symbol are ± 1 and 0, we can see that *an Euler pseudoprime base b is a Fermat prime base b*. After all, the thing we need to compute to apply the Fermat criterion is the square modulo n of what we compute to apply the Euler criterion.

Of course, to make this criterion at all worthwhile we must be able to compute $b^{(n-1)/2} \bmod n$ quickly and also compute the Jacobi symbol quickly. The fast exponentiation algorithm does the former, and **quadratic reciprocity** provides a fast algorithm for the latter.

An integer b so that $b^{(n-1)/2} = \left(\frac{b}{n}\right)_2$ is an **Euler witness** to the primality of n. If this equality holds but n is not prime, then b is a **false (Euler) witness**, or **liar**.

Happily, we will see later that *there are no Euler-pseudoprime analogues of Carmichael numbers.* That is, if a number n is *not* prime then at least half the numbers b in the range $0 < b < n$ are *witnesses* to this fact. The problem remains that we don't have any good information on the *distribution* of the witnesses.

16.4 Solovay–Strassen Test

This test was the first probabilistic primality test, being discovered in 1976. When applied to a number n it tests whether n is an *Euler pseudoprime* base b for several different bases b. The fact that it is a reasonably fast algorithm is dependent upon the fact that quadratic reciprocity allows efficient evaluation of (Jacobi) quadratic symbols. It is clunkier to program than the Miller–Rabin, test, however, and *in real life* it is the Miller–Rabin test which is used. (On the other hand, it's a little harder to understand why the Miller–Rabin test works at all!)

It must be noted that the Solovay–Strassen test is obsolete for practical purposes, since the Miller–Rabin test is simpler and gives a better result. However, the mechanism is worth studying, as it introduces important issues and concepts for later use.

The Solovay–Strassen test can prove compositeness with *certainty*, but proves primality only with a certain *heuristic probability*.

We will describe just the *operation* of the Solovay–Strassen algorithm. To explain *why* it works will require more preparation.

Let n be a positive odd integer. Choose k 'random' integers b in the range $1 < b < n - 1$. For each b in the list, compute both

$$b^{(n-1)/2} \% n$$

and the (Jacobi) quadratic symbol

$$\left(\frac{b}{n}\right)_2$$

If for any b in the list the two computed values are not the same, *stop:* the number n is not prime. If the two expressions are equal for every b in the list, then we imagine that n is prime with probability at least

$$1 - 2^{-k}$$

The idea is that if n *is* composite then at least half the integers b in the range $1 < b < n - 1$ are *witnesses* to this fact, meaning that for such n and b

$$b^{(n-1)/2} \% n \neq \left(\frac{b}{n}\right)_2$$

Again, such a witness b is called an **Euler witness** to the compositeness of n.

For each b, one can check that each of the computations takes $O(\log_2^3 n)$ bit operations.

It is important to be sure that for any composite n at least half the numbers b in the range $1 < b < n$ are witnesses. We can prove this when we understand primitive roots (and related matters such as quadratic reciprocity).

It is certainly not easy to see why the Solovay–Strassen test should work at all, or why the probabilities should be as asserted.

Exercises

16.4.01 Find the smallest Euler (Solovay–Strassen) witnesses to the compositeness of the 3 smallest Carmichael numbers 561, 1105, 1729.

16.5 Strong Pseudoprimes

Continuing with the use of square roots to test primality, we can go a bit further than Euler's criterion. Here the underlying idea is that if p is a prime, then $\mathbf{Z}/p$ should have only 2 square roots of 1, namely ± 1.

Let n be an *odd* number, and factor

$$n - 1 = 2^s \cdot \ell$$

with ℓ odd. Then n is a **strong pseudoprime** base b if

$$\text{either} \quad b^\ell = 1 \bmod n \quad \text{or} \quad b^{2^r \cdot \ell} = -1 \bmod n \quad \text{for some } 0 \le r < s$$

On the face of it, it is certainly hard to see how this is related to primality. And despite the remark just above about this test being related to the presence of 'false' square roots of 1, it's certainly not so clear why or how that works, either.

Nevertheless, granting fast exponentiation, the algorithm runs pretty fast. We'll address the *how* and *why* issues later.

16.6 Miller–Rabin Test

The Miller–Rabin probabilistic primality test hunts for *strong pseudoprimes*. When applied to a number n it tests whether n is an *strong pseudoprime* base b for several different bases b. This test is easy to implement, so gets used in real life. The fact that makes it reasonably fast is that exponentiation modulo n is reasonably fast.

The *idea* of the test is that for non-prime n there will be at least 2 elements x of $\mathbf{Z}/n$ with the property that $x^2 = 1$ but $x \ne \pm 1$. That is, there will be more square roots of 1 than there should be. As with the Solovay–Strassen test, much further explanation is needed to see *why* it works, etc. The *operation* of the Miller–Rabin test itself is quite simple, though, even simpler than that of the Solovay–Strassen test.

As with the Solovay–Strassen test, this test can prove compositeness with *certainty*, but proves primality only with a certain *probability*. For this reason, sometimes the Miller–Rabin algorithm is referred to as a **compositeness test**.

Let n be a positive odd integer. Find the largest power 2^r dividing $n-1$, and write $n-1 = 2^r \cdot m$. (So m is odd.) In order to discover either

- n is composite *with certainty*

or

- n is prime with probability $\geq 1 - (1/4)^k$

choose k 'random' integers b in the range $1 < b < n-1$. For each b in the list, do the following:

- Compute $b_o = b^m \% n$.

- If $b_o = \pm 1 \bmod n$, stop: this b is a witness that n is prime with probability $\geq 3/4$.

- Otherwise continue: while $s < r$, compute $b_s = (b_{s-1})^2 \% n$. If $b_s = -1 \bmod n$, stop: n is prime with probability $\geq 3/4$. If $b_s = 1 \bmod n$ (with $s > 1$), the whole algorithm terminates: n is definitely composite.

- If *none* of $b_1, b_2, b_3, \ldots, b_{r-1}$ is -1, again the whole algorithm terminates: n is definitely composite.

- If for *every* b in the list this procedure indicates that n is prime with probability $3/4$, then we imagine that n is *prime* with probability $> 1 - (1/4)^k$, by hypothesizing that the tests corresponding to the varying b's are probabilistically independent.

The idea (from which the probabilities come) is that if n *is* composite, then at least $3/4$ the integers b in the range $1 < b < n-1$ are *witnesses* to this fact. As with the Solovay–Strassen test, to demonstrate the presence of so many witnesses requires preparation, so we postpone it.

Exercises

16.6.01 Show that the composite number 1281 is a strong pseudoprime base 41.

16.6.02 Show that the composite number 1729 is a strong pseudoprime base 10.

16.6.03 Show that the composite number 3073 is a strong pseudoprime base 1146.

16.6.04 Show that the composite number 3201 is a strong pseudoprime base 1163.

16.6.05 Show that the composite number 3585 is a strong pseudoprime base 434.

16.6.06 Show that the composite number 5377 is a strong pseudoprime base 848.

16.6.07 Find the smallest strong (Miller–Rabin) witnesses to the compositeness of the Carmichael numbers 2465, 2821.

17
Groups

Here we encounter the first instance of *abstract algebra* rather than the *tangible algebra* studied in high school. One way to think of the point of this is that it is an attempt to study the *structure* of things directly, without reference to irrelevant particular details.

This does achieve amazing efficiency (in the long run, anyway), since it turns out that the same underlying structures occur over and over again in mathematics. Thus, a careful study of these basic structures is amply rewarded by allowing a much simpler and more unified mental picture of otherwise seemingly-different phenomena.

17.1 Groups

The simplest (but maybe not most immediately intuitive) object in abstract algebra is a *group*. This idea is pervasive in modern mathematics. Many seemingly elementary issues seem to be merely secret manifestations of facts about groups. This is especially true in elementary number theory, where it is *possible* to give 'elementary' proofs of many results, but only at the cost of having everything be complicated and so messy that it can't be remembered.

A **group** G is a set with an operation $g * h$, with a special element e called **the identity**, and with properties:

- The property of the identity: for all $g \in G$, $e * g = g * e = g$.

- Existence of **inverses**: for all $g \in G$ there is $h \in G$ (the **inverse** of g) so that $h * g = g * h = e$.

- Associativity: for all $x, y, z \in G$, $x * (y * z) = (x * y) * z$.

If the operation $g * h$ is *commutative*, that is, if $g * h = h * g$ then the group is said to be **abelian** (named after N. H. Abel, born on my birthday but 150 years earlier). In that case, often, but not always, the operation is written as *addition*. And if the operation is written as addition, then the identity is often written as 0 instead of e.

And in many cases the group operation is written as multiplication

$$g * h = g \cdot h = gh$$

This does not *preclude* the operation being abelian, but rather suggests only that there is no *presumption* that the operation is abelian. If the group operation is written as multiplication, then often the identity is written as 1 rather than e. Especially when the operation is written simply as *multiplication*, the **inverse** of an element g in the group is written as

$$\text{inverse of } g = g^{-1}$$

If the group operation is written as *addition*, then the inverse is written as

$$\text{inverse of } g = -g$$

This notation would be inappropriate except that we could prove that *each group element has exactly one inverse*.

In each of the following examples, it is easy to verify the properties necessary for the things to qualify as *groups*: we need an *identity* and we need *inverses*, not to mention *associativity*.

- The integers $\mathbf{Z}$ with operation the usual addition $+$. The identity is 0 and the inverse of x is $-x$. This group is *abelian*.

- The *even* integers $2\mathbf{Z}$ with the usual addition $+$. The identity is 0 and the inverse of x is $-x$. This group is *abelian*.

- The set $7\mathbf{Z}$ of multiples of 7 among integers, with the usual addition $+$. The identity is 0 and the inverse of x is $-x$. This group is *abelian*.

- The set $\mathbf{Z}/m$ of integers-mod-m, with addition-mod-m as the operation. The identity is 0-mod-m and the inverse of x-mod-m is $(-x)$-mod-m. This group is *abelian*.

- The set $\mathbf{Z}/m^\times$ of integers mod m *relatively prime to m*, with multiplication-mod-m as the operation. The identity is 1-mod-m. In this example, one unacquainted with arithmetic mod m would not realize that *there are multiplicative inverses*. We can compute them via the Euclidean algorithm. So this is the first 'non-trivial' example. This group is *abelian*.

- The collection of vectors in real n-space $\mathbf{R}^n$, with operation vector addition. The identity is just the 0 vector. Inverses are just negatives. (Note that we are literally *forgetting* the fact that there is a scalar multiplication.)

- The set $GL(2,\mathbf{R})$ of invertible two-by-two real matrices, with group law matrix multiplication. Here the identity is the matrix

$$\begin{pmatrix} 1 & 0 \\ 0 & 1 \end{pmatrix}$$

The existence of inverses is just part of the definition. The fact that matrix multiplication is *associative* is not obvious from the definition, but this can either be checked by hand or inferred from 'higher principles'. The fact that the product of two invertible matrices is invertible is interesting: suppose that g, h both have inverses, g^{-1} and h^{-1}, respectively. Then you can check that $h^{-1}g^{-1}$ is an inverse to gh. This group is certainly not abelian.

- Permutations of a set form a group, with operation being *composition* (as functions) of permutations. The do-nothing permutation is the identity. The associativity follows because permutations are *mappings*. If there are more than two elements in the set, the group of permutations of it is certainly non-abelian.

- The collection of all bijective functions from a set S to itself form a group, with the operation being composition of functions. The identity is the function e which maps every element just back to itself, that is, $e(s) = s$ for all $s \in S$. (This example is just a more general paraphrase of the previous one about permutations!)

Exercises

17.1.01 Prove that in any group G for any elements $h, x, y \in G$ we have $h(xy)h^{-1} = (hxh^{-1})(hyh^{-1})$.

17.1.02 Prove (by induction) that in any group G for any elements $g, h \in G$ and for any integer n $hg^n h^{-1} = (hgh^{-1})^n$.

17.1.03 Make an addition table for $\mathbf{Z}/4$ and a multiplication table for $\mathbf{Z}/5^\times$.

17.1.04 Why isn't $\{1, 2, 3, 4, 5\}$ with operation *multiplication modulo* 6 a group?

17.1.05 Prove by induction that in an *abelian* group G we have $(gh)^n = g^n h^n$ for all $g, h \in G$, and for all positive integers n.

17.1.06 Show that $(gh)^2 = g^2 h^2$ in a group if and only if $gh = hg$.

17.1.07 Prove that $(gh)^{-1} = h^{-1} g^{-1}$.

17.1.08 Prove that $(gh)^{-1} = g^{-1} h^{-1}$ if and only if $gh = hg$.

17.2 Subgroups

Subgroups are subsets of groups which are groups 'in their own right'. A subset H of a group G is said to be a **subgroup** if, with the same operation as that used in G, it is a group.

That is, if H contains the identity element $e \in G$, if H contains inverses of all elements in it, and if H contains products of any two elements in it, then H is a subgroup. (The associativity of the operation is assured, since the operation was *assumed* associative for G itself to be a group.)

Another paraphrase: if $e \in H$, and if for all $h \in H$ the inverse h^{-1} is also in H, and if for all $h_1, h_2 \in H$, the product $h_1 h_2$ is again in H, then H is a subgroup of G.

Another cute paraphrase is: if $e \in H$, and if for all $h_1, h_2 \in H$, the product $h_1 h_2^{-1}$ is again in H, then H is a subgroup of G. (If we take $h_1 = e$, then the latter condition assures the existence of inverses! And so on.)

In any case, one usually says that H is **closed under inverses** and **closed under the group operation**.

For example, the collection of all *even* integers is a subgroup of the additive group of integers. More generally, for fixed integer m, the collection H of all multiples of m is a subgroup of the additive group of integers. To check this: first, the identity 0 is a multiple of m, so $0 \in H$. And for any two integers x, y divisible by m, write $x = ma$ and $y = mb$ for some integers a, b. Then using the 'cute' paraphrase, we see that

$$x - y = ma - mb = m(a - b) \in H$$

so H is *closed under inverses and under the group operation*. Thus, it is a subgroup of $\mathbf{Z}$.

Exercises

17.2.01 Check that $H = \{0\text{-mod-}8, 2\text{-mod-}8, 4\text{-mod-}8, 6\text{-mod-}8\}$ is a subgroup of the group $\mathbf{Z}/8$-with-addition.

17.2.02 Check that the collection of powers of 2 modulo 7 is a subgroup of $\mathbf{Z}/7^\times$.

17.2.03 Prove that the intersection $H \cap K$ of two subgroups H, K of a group G is again a subgroup of G.

17.2.04 Show that in an *abelian* group G, for a fixed positive integer n, the set X_n of elements g of G so that $g^n = e$ is a subgroup of G.

17.2.05 Find all 5 of the distinct subgroups of the group $\mathbf{Z}/16$ (with addition). (List each subgroup only once!)

17.2.06 Find all 8 of the distinct subgroups of the group $\mathbf{Z}/24$ (with addition). (List each subgroup only once!)

17.2.07 There are 8 subgroups of the group $\mathbf{Z}/30^\times$. Find them all. (List each subgroup only once!)

17.2.08 Check that the collection of matrices g in $GL(2, \mathbf{Q})$ of the form $g = \begin{pmatrix} a & 0 \\ 0 & d \end{pmatrix}$ (that is, with lower left and upper right entries 0) is a *subgroup* of $GL(2, \mathbf{Q})$.

17.2.09 Check that the collection of matrices g in $GL(2, \mathbf{Q})$ of the form $g = \begin{pmatrix} a & b \\ 0 & d \end{pmatrix}$ (that is, with lower left entry 0) is a *subgroup* of $GL(2, \mathbf{Q})$.

17.3   Lagrange's Theorem

The theorem of this section is the simplest example of the use of group theory as *structured counting*. Although the discussion of this section is completely abstract, it gives the easiest route to (the very tangible) Euler's theorem proven as a corollary below. A **finite group** is simply a group which is also finite. The **order** of a finite group is the number of elements in it. Sometimes the order of a group G is written as $|G|$. Throughout this section we will write the group operation simply as though it were ordinary multiplication.

> **Theorem.**   *(Lagrange)* Let G be a *finite* group. Let H be a subgroup of G. Then the order of H *divides* the order of G.

For the proof we need some other ideas which themselves will be reused later. For subgroup H of a group G, and for $g \in G$, the **left coset** of H by g or **left translate** of H by g is

$$gH = \{gh : h \in H\}$$

The notation gH is simply shorthand for the right-hand side. Likewise, the **right coset** of H by g, or **right translate** of H by g, is

$$Hg = \{hg : h \in H\}$$

Proof: First, we will prove that the collection of all left cosets of H is a *partition* of G, meaning that every element of G lies in *some* left coset of H, and if two left cosets xH and yH have non-empty intersection, then actually $xH = yH$. (Note that this need not imply $x = y$.)

Certainly $x = x \cdot e \in xH$, so every element of G lies in a left coset of H.

Now suppose that $xH \cap yH \neq \phi$ for $x, y \in G$. Then for some $h_1, h_2 \in H$ we have $xh_1 = yh_2$. Multiply both sides of this equality on the right by h_2^{-1} to obtain

$$(xh_1)h_2^{-1} = (yh_2)h_2^{-1}$$

The right-hand side of this is

$$
\begin{aligned}
(yh_2)h_2^{-1} &= y(h_2 h_2^{-1}) && \text{(by associativity)} \\
&= y \cdot e && \text{(by property of inverse)} \\
&= y && \text{(by property of } e\text{)}
\end{aligned}
$$

Let $z = h_1 h_2^{-1}$ for brevity. By associativity in G,

$$y = (xh_1)h_2^{-1} = x(h_1 h_2^{-1}) = xz$$

Since H is a *subgroup*, $z \in H$.

Then

$$yH = \{yh : h \in H\} = \{(xz)h : h \in H\} = \{x(zh) : h \in H\}$$

On one hand, since H is closed under multiplication, for each $h \in H$ the product zh is in H. Therefore,

$$yH = \{x(zh) : h \in H\} \subset \{xh' : h' \in H\} = xH$$

Thus, $yH \subset xH$. But the relationship between x and y is completely symmetrical, so also $xH \subset yH$. Therefore $xH = yH$. (In other words, we have shown that the left cosets of H in G really do *partition* G.)

Next, we will show that the cardinalities of the left cosets of H are *all the same*. To do this, we show that there is a *bijection* from H to xH for any $x \in G$. In particular, define

$$f(g) = xg$$

(It is clear that this really does map H to xH.) Second, we prove *injectivity*: if $f(g) = f(g')$, then

$$xg = xg'$$

Left-multiplying by x^{-1} gives

$$x^{-1}(xg) = x^{-1}(xg')$$

Using associativity gives

$$(x^{-1}x)g = (x^{-1}x)g'$$

Using the property $x^{-1}x = e$ of the inverse x^{-1} gives

$$eg = eg'$$

Since $eg = g$ and $eg' = g'$, by the defining property of the identity e, this is

$$g = g'$$

which is the desired injectivity. For *surjectivity*, we simply note that by its very definition the function f was arranged so that

$$f(h) = xh$$

Thus, any element in xH is hit by an element from H. Thus, we have the bijectivity of f, and all left cosets of H have the same number of elements as does H itself.

So G is the union of all the different left cosets of H (no two of which overlap). Let i be the number of different left cosets of H. We just showed that every left coset of H has $|H|$ elements. Then we can count the number of elements in G as

$$|G| = \text{sum of cardinalities of cosets } = i \times |H|$$

Both sides of this equation are integers, so $|H|$ divides $|G|$, as claimed.   ♣

Exercises

17.3.01 Suppose a finite group G has subgroups H, K of orders 16 and 35, respectively. Show that $H \cap K = \{1\}$.

17.3.02 Show that a group of order 101 has no subgroups except $\{1\}$ and itself.

17.3.03 Show that a group of order 1009 has no subgroups except $\{1\}$ and itself.

17.4 Index of a Subgroup

Having introduced the idea of a *coset* in the proof of Lagrange's theorem, we can now define the *index* of a subgroup. Let G be a group, and H a subgroup of G. The **index** of H in G, denoted

$$[G : H]$$

is the number of (left) cosets of H in G.

Corollary. *(of Lagrange's theorem)* For a finite group G and subgroup H,

$$|G| = [G : H] \cdot |H|$$

Proof: This is just a recapitulation of the counting done in proving Lagrange's theorem: we show that G is the disjoint union of the left cosets of H, and that each such coset has $|H|$ elements. Thus, the statement of this corollary is an assertion that counting the elements in G in two ways gives the same result.   ♣

A closely related counting or divisibility principle is the following **multiplicative property** of indices of subgroups:

Proposition. Let G be a finite group, let H, I be subgroups of G, and suppose that $H \supset I$. Then

$$[G : I] = [G : H] \cdot [H : I]$$

Proof: The group G is a disjoint union of $[G : I]$ left cosets of I. Also, G is the disjoint union of $[G : H]$ left cosets of H. If we can show that any left *coset* of H is a disjoint union of $[H : I]$ left cosets of I, then the assertion of the proposition will follow.

Let

$$gH = \{gh : h \in H\}$$

be a left coset of H. And express H as a (disjoint) union of $[H : I]$ left cosets of I by

$$H = h_1 I \cup h_2 I \cup \ldots \cup h_{[H:I]} I$$

Then

$$gH = g\left(h_1 I \cup h_2 I \cup \ldots \cup h_{[H:I]} I\right) = gh_1 I \cup gh_2 I \cup \ldots \cup gh_{[H:I]} I$$

which is certainly a union of left cosets of I. We might want to check that $h_i I \cap h_j I = \phi$ (for $i \neq j$) implies that

$$gh_i I \cap gh_j I = \phi$$

Suppose that $g \in gh_i I \cap gh_j I$. Then for some $i_1 \in I$ and $i_2 \in I$ we have

$$gh_i i_1 = x = gh_j i_2$$

Left-multiplying by g^{-1} gives

$$h_i i_1 = h_j i_2$$

The left-hand side is (by hypothesis) an element of $h_i I$, and the right-hand side is an element of $h_j I$. But we had assumed that $h_i I \cap h_j I = \phi$, so this is impossible. That is, we have proven that $gh_i I \cap gh_j I = \phi$ if $h_i I \cap h_j I = \phi$. This certainly finishes the proof of the multiplicative property of subgroup indices. ♣

17.5 Laws of Exponents

It should be emphasized that the so-called *laws of exponents* are not 'laws' at all, but are *provable properties* of the exponential notation. And the exponential notation itself is basically nothing more than an abbreviation for repeated multiplication.

Of course, we must be sure to be explicit about this *exponential notation* g^n for integer n, where g is an element of a group G. This is, after all, merely an abbreviation: first,

$$g^0 = e$$

and

$$g^n = \underbrace{g \cdot g \cdot \; \cdots \; \cdot g}_{n} \qquad \text{(for } n \geq 0)$$

$$g^n = \underbrace{g^{-1} \cdot g^{-1} \cdot \; \cdots \; \cdot g^{-1}}_{|n|} \qquad \text{(for } n \leq 0)$$

A more precise though perhaps less intuitive way of defining g^n is by **recursive definitions:**

$$g^n = \begin{cases} e & \text{for } n = 0 \\ g \cdot g^{n-1} & \text{for } n > 0 \\ g^{-1} \cdot g^{n+1} & \text{for } n < 0 \end{cases}$$

These are the definitions that lend themselves both to computation and to proving things.

While we're here, maybe we should check that the so-called *laws of exponents* really do hold:

Proposition. *(Laws of Exponents)* For g in a group G, for integers m, n

- $g^{m+n} = g^m \cdot g^n$

- $g^{mn} = (g^m)^n$

Proof: The least obvious thing to prove is that

$$(g^{-1})^{-1} = g$$

Note that we absolutely cannot simply pretend to invoke 'laws of exponents' to prove this! Instead, to prove this, we must realize that the way one checks that y is an inverse of x is to compute xy and yx and see that they are both just e. So to prove that x is the inverse of x^{-1}, we must compute both $x^{-1}x$ and xx^{-1}. And, indeed, by the property of x^{-1} these both are e.

This also invokes the *uniqueness* of the inverse of x, which we can prove now since it is relevant. Suppose y and z were elements which had properties of an inverse of x, namely $yx = e$ and $xz = e$. Right-multiply the equation $yx = e$ by z to obtain $(yx)z = ez = z$. Using associativity and the fact that $xz = e$, this gives $ye = z$, and then $y = z$.

We could make the proof of properties of exponents an exercise in *induction,* but that would be a bit tedious, and nothing exciting would happen. Instead, let's indicate heuristically why these 'laws' should be true. For example, let's see why

$$g^{m+n} = g^m \cdot g^n$$

for m and n non-negative integers.

$$
\begin{aligned}
g^m \cdot g^n &= \underbrace{(g \cdot \cdots \cdot g)}_{m} \cdot \underbrace{(g \cdot \cdots \cdot g)}_{n} \\
&= \underbrace{(g \cdot \cdots \cdot g)}_{m+n} \\
&= g^{m+n}
\end{aligned}
$$

Keep in mind that we are implicitly using associativity many times in this manipulation. Thus, this 'law' of exponents is mostly a property of the notation. To see why $(g^m)^n = g^{mn}$ should hold:

$$
\begin{aligned}
(g^m)^n &= \underbrace{g^m \cdot \cdots \cdot g^m}_{n} \\
&= \underbrace{\underbrace{(g \cdots g)}_{m} \cdots \underbrace{(g \cdots g)}_{m}}_{n} \\
&= \underbrace{g \cdots g}_{mn} \\
&= g^{mn}
\end{aligned}
$$

Dealing with combinations of positive and negative exponents is messier, but follows the same ideas.   ♣

17.6 Cyclic Subgroups

For an element g of a group G, let

$$
\langle g \rangle = \{g^n : n \in \mathbf{Z}\}
$$

This is called the **cyclic subgroup of G generated by** g.

The smallest positive integer n (if it exists!) so that

$$
g^n = e
$$

is the **order** or **exponent** of g. The order of a group element g is often denoted by $|g|$. Yes, we are reusing the terminology 'order', but it will turn out that these uses are compatible (just below).

Corollary. *(of laws of exponents)* For g in a group G, the sub*set* $\langle g \rangle$ of G really is a sub*group* of G.

Proof: The associativity is *inherited* from G. The *closure* under the group operation and the closure under taking inverses both follow immediately from the laws of exponents, as follows. First, the inverse of g^n is just g^{-n}, since

$$
g^n \cdot g^{-n} = g^{n+(-n)} = g^0 = e
$$

And

$$g^m \cdot g^n = g^{m+n}$$

certainly verifies closure under multiplication.   ♣

Theorem.   Let g be an element of a finite group G. Let n be the order of g. Then the order of g (as group *element*) is equal to the order of $\langle g \rangle$ (as *subgroup*). Specifically,

$$\langle g \rangle = \{g^0, g^1, g^2, \ldots, g^{n-1}\}$$

Generally, for arbitrary integers i, j,

$$g^i = g^j \quad \text{if and only if} \quad i \equiv j \bmod n$$

Proof: The last assertion easily implies the first two, so we'll just prove the last. On one hand, if $i \equiv j \bmod n$, then write $i = j + \ell n$ and compute (using laws of exponents):

$$g^i = g^{j+\ell n} = g^j \cdot (g^n)^\ell = g^j \cdot e^\ell = g^j \cdot e = g^j$$

On the other hand, suppose that $g^i = g^j$. Without loss of generality, exchanging the roles of i and j if necessary, we may suppose that $i \leq j$. Then $g^i = g^j$ implies $e = g^{j-i}$. Using the reduction/division algorithm, write

$$j - i = q \cdot n + r$$

where $0 \leq r < n$. Then

$$e = g^{j-i} = g^{qn+r} = (g^n)^q \cdot g^r = e^q \cdot g^r = e \cdot g^r = g^r$$

Therefore, since n is the least positive integer so that $g^n = e$, it must be that $r = 0$. That is, $n | (j - i)$, which is to say that $i \equiv j \bmod n$ as claimed.   ♣

Corollary.   The order $|g|$ of an element g of a finite group G divides the order of G.

Proof: We just proved that $|g| = |\langle g \rangle|$. By Lagrange's theorem, $|\langle g \rangle|$ divides $|G|$, which yields this corollary.   ♣

Exercises

17.6.01 Let g, h be elements of a group G, and $|g| = 30$ while $|h| = 77$. Show that $\langle g \rangle \cap \langle h \rangle = \{e\}$.

17.6.02 Prove that a group element and its inverse have the same order.

17.6.03 Without computing, show that in the group $\mathbf{Z}/100$ (with addition) the elements $1, 99$ have the same order, as do $11, 89$.

17.6.04 Suppose that $x^e = 1$ mod n for a positive integer e. Show that x^{-1} mod n is x^{e-1} mod n.

17.6.05 Find the orders of the following elements g, h of the group $GL(2, \mathbf{R})$ of two-by-two real matrices with nonzero determinant:

$$g = \begin{pmatrix} 0 & -1 \\ 1 & 0 \end{pmatrix}, \quad h = \begin{pmatrix} 0 & 1 \\ -1 & -1 \end{pmatrix}$$

Compute the product gh, compute $(gh)^n$ for integers n, and then show that gh is necessarily of *infinite order* in the group.

17.6.06 Let G be a finite group. Let N be the *least common multiple* of the orders of the elements of G. Show that for all $g \in G$ we have $g^n = e$.

17.6.07 (*) Let G be an *abelian* group. Let m, n be relatively prime positive integers. Let g be an element of order m and let h be an element of order n. Show that $|gh| = mn$.

17.6.08 Let x be an element of a group G and suppose that $x^{3 \cdot 5} = e$ and $x^3 \neq e$. Show that the order of x is either 5 or 15.

17.6.09 Show that any integer i so that $1 \leq i < 11$ is a generator for the additive group $\mathbf{Z}/11$ of integers modulo 11.

17.6.10 Check that $\mathbf{Z}/8^\times$ cannot be generated by a single element.

17.6.11 Prove that if an element g of a group G has order n and if d is a divisor of n, then $g^{n/d}$ has order d. (Equivalently, g^d has order n/d.)

17.7 Euler's Theorem

Now we return to number theory and give a clean and conceptual proof of Euler's identity, as a corollary of Lagrange's theorem and the discussion of laws of exponents and cyclic subgroups. Further, we can give a slightly refined form of it.

Let $\varphi(n)$ be Euler's phi-function, counting the number of integers ℓ in the range $0 < \ell \leq n$ which are relatively prime to n. The proof we give of this is simply the abstracted version of Euler's original argument.

Theorem. Let n be a positive integer. For $x \in \mathbf{Z}$ relatively prime to n,

$$x^{\varphi(n)} \equiv 1 \bmod n$$

Proof: The set $\mathbf{Z}/n^\times$ of integers-mod-n which are relatively prime to n has $\varphi(n)$ elements. By Lagrange's theorem and its corollaries just above, this implies that the order k of $g \in \mathbf{Z}/n^\times$ divides $\varphi(n)$. Therefore, $\varphi(n)/k$ is an integer, and

$$g^{\varphi(n)} = (g^k)^{\varphi(n)/k} = e^{\varphi(n)/k} = e$$

Applied to x-mod-n this is the desired result.   ♣

Remark: This approach also gives another proof of Fermat's theorem, dealing with the case that that n is prime, without mention of binomial coefficients.

Further, keeping track of what went into the proof of Euler's theorem in the first place, we have

Theorem. Let n be a positive integer. For $x \in \mathbf{Z}$ relatively prime to n, the smallest positive exponent ℓ so that

$$x^{\ell} \equiv 1 \bmod n$$

is a divisor of $\varphi(n)$. That is, the order of x in the multiplicative group $\mathbf{Z}/n^{\times}$ is a divisor of $\varphi(n)$.

Proof: The proof is really the same: the order x is equal to the order of the subgroup $\langle x \rangle$, which by Lagrange's theorem is a divisor of the order of the whole group $\mathbf{Z}/n^{\times}$.   ♣

17.8 Exponents of Groups

The idea of Euler's theorem can be made more precise and abstracted. For a group G, the smallest positive integer ℓ so that for every $g \in G$

$$g^{\ell} = e$$

is the **exponent** of the group G. It is not clear from the definition that there really is such a positive integer ℓ. Indeed, for *infinite* groups G there may not be. But for *finite* groups the mere finiteness allows us to characterize the exponent:

Proposition. Let G be a finite group. Then the exponent of G exists, and in particular

$$\text{exponent of } G = \text{least common multiple of } |g| \text{ for } g \in G$$

Proof: If $g^k = e$, then we know from discussion of cyclic subgroups above that $|g|$ divides k. And, on the other hand, if $k = m \cdot |g|$, then

$$g^k = g^{m \cdot |g|} = (g^{|g|})^m = e^m = e$$

Since G is finite, every element of it is of finite order. And, since there are only finitely many elements in G, the least common multiple M of their orders exists. From what we've just seen, surely $g^M = e$ for any g. Thus, G does have an exponent. And, if $g^k = e$ for all $g \in G$, then k is divisible by the orders of all elements of G, so by their least common multiple. Thus, the exponent of G really is the least common multiple of the orders of its elements.   ♣

And Lagrange's theorem gives a limitation on what we can expect the exponent to be:

Corollary. Let G be a finite group. Then the exponent of G divides the order $|G|$ of G.

Proof: From the proposition, the exponent is the least common multiple of the orders of the elements of G. From Lagrange's theorem, each such order is a divisor of $|G|$. The least common multiple of any collection of divisors of a fixed number is certainly a divisor of that number.   ♣

18

Sketches of Protocols

In this only very introductory and very informal discussion of protocols, it is important to keep in mind that there are several gradations of adversaries: at the very least a distinction can be made between *passive* eavesdroppers and *active* eavesdroppers. Almost all the time in this book we are thinking only in terms of *passive* eavesdroppers, who may listen but do not actively disrupt communications, and in particular do not attempt to impersonate sender or receiver or both. And a further important qualifying question about active eavesdroppers is *how powerful they are.* **Passive eavesdroppers** are not powerful enough to actually disrupt the protocols or destroy messages, but they listen to communications not intended for them. Also, there are **cheaters**, parties directly involved in the communication who for various reasons act to deceive. Cheaters can also be **passive cheaters** or **active cheaters** with varying degrees of power. As with active eavesdroppers, it is even more difficult to defend against very powerful active cheaters.

Most protocols can only guarantee (even informally) successful defense against relatively passive eavesdroppers.

And in all cases there can be a distinction made between **prevention** and **detection**. Often it is much harder to prevent eavesdropping or cheating entirely than just to detect it, so any real system must include plans for what to do when a compromise is detected, rather than simply pretending that it will be prevented.

18.1 Basic Public-Key Protocol

This is what people think of as the basic idea of public-key cryptography, but (as indicated just below) it needs much enhancement in order to be usable. The set-up sketched here applies both to RSA and to ElGamal-type public-key systems.

Alice publishes her public key K_{pub}. Then anyone who wants to generate a plaintext x decryptable only by Alice generates a ciphertext y by

$$y = E_{K_{\mathrm{pub}}}(x)$$

Then the message can be sent by an insecure channel to Alice. Presumably no one else but Alice has the (private) decryption key, and presumably the key size is large enough (and has no weaknesses!) so that only Alice can decrypt. To decrypt, Alice uses her private key.

One immediate flaw with this set-up is that senders can masquerade as someone else, without Alice's having any easy way to detect it. Since her public key and modulus are published, while only Alice can *read* encrypted messages, anyone can *send* a message. What is needed to prove the identity of the sender is a **signature**, meaning some unforgeable thing that shows that no one else could have sent it.

Another flaw exists in the possibility that Eve can **impersonate** Alice in the first place, meaning to usurp the setup itself, and publish a public key whose corresponding private key is possessed by Eve, not Alice. Then, if Eve can intercept mail intended for Alice, she can decrypt it and respond as if she were Alice. At the same time Eve does *not* allow Alice to see the mail, or, even better, falsifies some plausible mail so that Alice will not become suspicious. In the resent documents Eve could falsify a public key for the sender, thus enabling herself to intercept and decrypt return encrypted messages from Alice to the sender. That is, Eve short-circuits the actual communications between Alice and Bob, and to Alice impersonates Bob, and to Bob impersonates Alice. This is one type of **man-in-the-middle attack**.

Yet further, the whole issue might come down to a contest between Alice and Eve in which each tries to 'prove' that they are the *true Alice*. Indeed, the senders of messages might know Alice only as an on-line persona, and Eve's publication of a false public key for Alice might be indistinguishable from a 'true' publication of such by Alice.

One way of **certifying** public keys is by use of **certificate authorities**, trusted entities who supposedly won't lie, and who will adequately check that the public keys really belong to the entities that they appear to. Certainly this is an imprecise notion! Still, most web browsers currently are shipped with the addresses of several such authorities already listed, and so-called secure transactions rely upon these certificates, among other things.

Another type of active eavesdropping involves **timing**: an active adversary might intercept a message and resend it at a later time. Or, similarly, a message might be copied and **replayed** one or more times later. These problems motivate inclusion of a **timestamp** in messages so that the recipient can *detect* these attacks. But the general unpredictability of networks makes this less simple than one would hope.

So a basic public key protocol by itself is insufficient. The certificate-authority solution is only a patch, but maybe nothing better can be done.

18.2 Diffie–Hellman Key Exchange

This is both the original public-key idea and an important mechanism in current use. The practical point is that symmetric ciphers are generally much faster than asymmetric ones (both for hardware and software reasons), so the public-key cipher is merely used to set up a private key, a **session key**, intended to be used only for a single conversation.

This protocol makes use of the particulars involving discrete logarithms, and of course of the relative difficulty of *computing* discrete logarithms. Therefore, it not only works in the $\mathbf{Z}/p$ discrete-logarithm situation, but also generalizes to arbitrary finite fields, elliptic curves, or any other group structure where logarithms make sense.

First, Alice and Bob agree on a large prime m, and a primitive root g modulo m. These need not be kept secret and can be shared by a group of users. Alice chooses a large random integer x, privately computes $X = g^x \% m$, and sends X to Bob by the possibly insecure channel. Meanwhile, Bob similarly chooses a large random integer y, privately computes $Y = g^y \% m$, and sends Y to Alice across the possibly insecure channel.

Then Alice privately computes $k = Y^x \% m$, and Bob symmetrically computes $k' = X^y \% m$. In fact, $k = k' \bmod m$, seen as follows: computing modulo m, we have

$$k' = X^y = (g^x)^y = g^{xy} = (g^y)^x = k \bmod m$$

since the properties of exponents are enjoyed by integers modulo m. But no one else on the network can obtain k unless they can compute discrete logarithms. Then the key k ($= k'$) can be used directly or indirectly as a key for a symmetric cipher.

For security, the prime modulus m should be large, of course. And m should probably be a *strong prime*, meaning foremost that $m - 1$ should be divisible by a relatively large prime. One might imagine that it would be optimal for m to be a **Sophie Germain prime**, meaning that $(m - 1)/2$ is also prime. However, these primes are rather sparse by comparison to primes as a whole. They are roughly as rare as **twin primes**, meaning primes p so that $p + 2$ is also prime. It is not known whether there are infinitely many Sophie Germain primes (nor whether there are infinitely many twin primes).

In fact, the protocol does not really require that g be a primitive root, only (for security reasons) that it generate a large subgroup of $\mathbf{Z}/n^\times$, so that adversaries cannot compute the relevant 'logarithm'.

As with many of these protocols, this first version of the protocol is vulnerable to a **man-in-the-middle attack** by an active adversary: an active eavesdropper who can intercept the messages from Alice to Bob and Bob to Alice and who can replace these messages with their own messages can (in effect) do a Diffie–Hellman exchange separately with Bob and with Alice, and maintain the illusion for Alice and Bob that they are communicating directly with each other. If Alice and Bob really have had no prior contact, and therefore no other way of verifying each other's identity, it is hard to prevent various kinds of masquerades.

This protocol, and elaborations upon it, was patented by Public Key Partners, but the patent expired on April 29, 1997.

18.3 Secret Sharing

This section presents a mathematical mechanism which a protocol could use to create a circumstance in which a secret can be uncovered only if sufficiently many, but not necessarily *all*, the members of a group agree. A mechanism to accomplish this is called a **threshold scheme**.

The problem presented here, which in real implementation would be addressed by a suitably designed protocol probably involving public-key algorithms and related devices, is: given a **secret** x to be k-**shared** among t people $A_1, A_2, \ldots, A_t$, give A_i a blob of information a_i so that

- A_i knows a_i (but not a_j for $j \neq i$).

- *No part* of the secret x can be recovered from any $k-1$ of the blobs a_i.

- The secret x can easily be computed from any k of the a_i's.

That is, the t entities involved **share the secret** in the sense that at least k of them must cooperate in order to recover the secret. For a given number t and a given secret x, a list of $a_1, \ldots, a_n$ which accomplish the objectives above is a (k, t)-**threshold scheme**. The simplest example of such a scheme uses Sun Ze's theorem (the Chinese Remainder Theorem), as follows.

Let $m_1, \ldots, m_t$ be mutually relatively prime integers greater than 1. Let $a_1, \ldots, a_t$ be integers. Let $M = m_1 \ldots m_t$, $M_i = M/m_i$, and let $n_i = M_i^{-1} \bmod m_i$. (Since m_i is relatively prime to m_j for $j \neq i$, m_i is also relatively prime to M_i, by unique factorization, since M_i is the product of integers prime to m_i. Thus, the multiplicative inverse N_i exists and is nicely computable via Euclid's algorithm.) In this situation, as an explicit form of Sun Ze's theorem, the family of simultaneous congruences

$$x = a_i \bmod m_i \quad \text{for all } i$$

is equivalent to the single congruence

$$x = \sum_{i=1}^{t} a_i \, M_i \, n_i \mod M$$

Fix k with $1 < k \leq t$. Let H_k be the *smallest* product of k different m_i's, and let h_{k-1} be the *largest* product of $k-1$ different m_i's. For example, if $m_1 < m_2 < \ldots < m_t$, then

$$H_k = m_1 m_2 \ldots m_{k-1} m_k$$

and

$$h_{k-1} = m_{t-k+2} m_{t-k+3} \ldots m_{t-1} m_t$$

We must assume that H_k is much larger than h_{k-1}: in particular, we assume that

$$H_k \geq (N+1) \cdot h_{k-1}$$

for some very large positive integer N.

Theorem. For any **secret** x represented as a number in the range

$$h_k < x < H_k$$

let $a_i = x \mathbin{\%} m_i$. Then the set $\{a_1, \ldots, a_t\}$ is a (k, t) threshold scheme for x.

Remark: The security is best if the moduli m_i are large and relatively close together. This is visible in detail in the proof.

Proof: Suppose that $a_1, \ldots, a_k$ are known. Let $M' = a_1 \ldots a_k$, and $M_i' = M'/m_i$ for $1 \leq i \leq k$. Let $n_i' = M_i'^{-1} \mod m_i$ for $1 \leq i \leq k$. Let

$$x' = \sum_{i=1}^{k} a_i \, M_i' \, n_i \mod M'$$

Then (as in Sun Ze's theorem)

$$x' = x \mod M'$$

Now since $M' \geq H_k > x$, the secret x is already reduced modulo M', so the secret x can be computed by

$$x = x' \mathbin{\%} M'$$

(This argument does not assume that $m_1 < \ldots < m_t$.)

On the other hand, suppose that only $a_1, \ldots, a_{k-1}$ are known. Then let $M' = a_1 \ldots a_{k-1}$, and $M_i' = M'/m_i$ for $1 \leq i \leq k-1$. Let $n_i' = M_i'^{-1} \mod m_i$ for $1 \leq i \leq k-1$. Let

$$x' = \sum_{i=1}^{k-1} a_i \, M_i' \, n_i \mod M'$$

As before, since $M' = m_1 \ldots m_{k-1}$,

$$x' = x \bmod m_1 m_2 \ldots m_{k-1}$$

We know that $m_1 m_2 \ldots m_{k-1} \le h_{k-1}$. Since $h_{k-1} < x < H_k$ and (by hypothesis)

$$(H_k - h_{k-1})/h_{k-1} > N$$

there are at least N possibilities for $y \bmod M$, so that

$$x' = y \bmod M'$$

Thus, knowledge of only $k - 1$ of the a_i's is certainly insufficient to discover the secret x.   ♣

To set up a situation in which to use this mathematical mechanism, we might suppose that there is a **trusted central agency** which has the secret x, which knows the moduli m_i, which computes the threshold scheme data $a_1, \ldots, a_n$, and which communicates a_i to the entity A_i by secure means. What remains is to set up a protocol for k among the t entities to share their information without anyone cheating, or at least without cheating going undetected. This is a non-trivial problem in itself.

18.4 Oblivious Transfer

Here we look at some protocols which are necessary if there is no mutually trusted referee, as is certainly the case very often. A simple version of the goal here is that Alice has a secret which she wishes to communicate to Bob in such a manner that, after the protocol is complete, Alice herself does not know whether Bob actually received the secret, but Bob knows.

A more purposeful and more complicated version of this is that Alice has *several* secrets, and wishes to transfer one of them to Bob in such manner that only Bob knows which secret was actually communicated. This would be relevant if Bob does not want to embarrass himself by directly confessing that he is ignorant of one or more of the secrets.

For the simpler case, we'll assume that the single secret is the factorization $n = pq$ of a large integer n which is the product of two large primes p, q with $p = 3 \bmod 4$ and $q = 3 \bmod 4$. This is effectively completely general, because any other secret could be encrypted via RSA using modulus n, so that knowing the factorization allows decryption, revealing the secret. For a slightly more complicated version we'll use the intractability of computation of discrete logarithms, instead.

We also use the fact that **knowing** $x, y \bmod n$ **so that** $x^2 = y^2 \bmod n$ **but** $x \ne \pm y$ **allows factorization of** n, proven as follows: from $x^2 - y^2 = 0 \bmod n$ we get $(x - y)(x + y) = 0 \bmod n$. Yet since $x \ne \pm y \bmod n$, neither $x - y$ nor $x + y$ is $0 \bmod n$. That is, n divides the product $(x - y)(x + y)$, but does not divide either $x - y$ or $x + y$. On the other hand, since p divides the product $(x - y)(x + y)$ it must divide one or the other (or both) of $x - y$ and $x + y$. The same applies to the prime q. Since n does not divide the separate factors $x - y$ and $x + y$, it must be that p divides exactly one of the factors while q divides the other. Therefore, using the Euclidean algorithm to compute $\gcd(n, x - y)$ will give either p or q: indeed, whatever this gcd is, it is not divisible by n but is divisible by either p or q. Since p and q are primes and $n = pq$, there's nothing else that can happen, by unique factorization. This proves that knowing $x, y \bmod n$ so that $x^2 = y^2 \bmod n$ but $x \neq \pm y$ allows factorization of n. ♣

The first protocol allows Alice to transfer a secret to Bob without knowing whether or not Bob really got it. The secret is the factorization of a large integer n which is the product of two large primes p, q with $p = 3 \bmod 4$ and $q = 3 \bmod 4$.

- Bob chooses a random number x in the range $0 < x < n$, computes $z = x^2 \bmod n$ and sends this to Alice.

- Alice easily computes the principal square root w_1 of $z \bmod p$ and the principal square root of w_2 of $z \bmod q$ via the formulas

$$w_1 = z^{(p+1)/4} \bmod p$$

$$w_2 = z^{(q+1)/4} \bmod q$$

coming from Fermat's Little Theorem. Choosing $\pm$'s randomly, Alice lets y_1 be one of $\pm w_1$, lets y_2 be one of $\pm w_2$, and uses Sun Ze's theorem (with the Euclidean algorithm) to stick these square roots together to make a square root y of z modulo $n = pq$ so that $y = y_1 \bmod p$ and $y = y_2 \bmod q$. She sends y back to Bob.

- If Bob's original x had the property that $x = \pm y \bmod n$, then Bob cannot easily factor n, but if

$$x = y_1 \bmod p \quad \text{and} \quad x = -y_2 \bmod q$$

or

$$x = -y_1 \bmod p \quad \text{and} \quad x = y_2 \bmod q$$

then Bob can compute $\gcd(n, x - y)$ to find one of the primes p, q.

We know that a quadratic equation $y^2 = z \bmod p$ has at most 2 solutions for prime p, by unique factorization of polynomials in one variable with coefficients in a field. Therefore, by Sun Ze's theorem (Chinese Remainder Theorem) $y^2 = z \bmod pq$ with distinct primes p, q has at most 4 solutions. In the case that there are 2 solutions both mod p and mod q, there are 4 solutions altogether. Thus, in Bob's situation, the two solutions $\pm x \bmod n$ are 2 of the 4 total, and Alice has equal probability of delivering any one of the 4. Thus, after Alice's information is provided, Bob has 50% chance of being able to factor n. But there is also 50% chance that he will *not* be able to factor n.

Remark: That is, after a single such transaction Alice only knows probabilities for Bob's knowing or not knowing the secret, although in fact Bob either does or does not know it. The point is that only Bob knows whether he knows, and Alice does not know whether Bob knows or not.

Now suppose that Alice has two secrets and wants to transfer them to Bob so that Bob gets just one of them, but so that Alice does not know which of the two he got. We assume intractability of computation of discrete logs modulo a large prime p. And note that from knowledge of the modulus p, a primitive root g mod p, and the values g^x mod p and g^y mod p, the value g^{xy} mod p *cannot* be easily computed: to compute g^{xy} mod p from the values g^x mod p and g^y mod p seems to require knowing the discrete logarithms x and y. We will assume that the secrets are two integers s_1, s_2. By padding the shorter one if necessary, we may assume that when expanded in binary they have the same length.

- A large prime p is chosen randomly and publicly, a primitive root g for **Z** mod p is chosen at random, and a random number c is chosen in the range $1 < c < p - 1$.

- Bob sets up an ElGamal-style public key by picking a random bit i and random $1 < x < p - 1$ and computing

$$
\begin{aligned}
b_i &= g^x \bmod p \\
b_{1-i} &= c \cdot g^{-x} \bmod p
\end{aligned}
$$

where we note that whichever of $0, 1$ the bit i is, the bit $1 - i$ is the other one of the two. Bob uses the ordered pair (b_0, b_1) as his public encryption key and keeps (i, x) secret.

- Alice checks that $b_0 b_1 = c \bmod p$.

- Alice randomly picks y_0, y_1 in the interval $[2, p - 2]$ and computes

$$
a_0 = g^{y_0} \quad t_0 = b_0^{y_0} \quad m_0 = s_0 \oplus t_0
$$

$$
a_1 = g^{y_1} \quad t_1 = b_1^{y_1} \quad m_1 = s_1 \oplus t_1
$$

She sends a_0, a_1, m_0, m_1 to Bob.

- With the random bit i that is not publicly known, Bob acquires the secret s_i by computing (all mod p)

$$
a_i^x = (g^{y_i})^x = (g^x)^{y_i} = b_i^{y_i} = t_i
$$

and then

$$
s_i = m_i \oplus t_i
$$

Remark: Since the logarithm of c base g mod p is not obtainable by Bob, he cannot determine the discrete logs of *both* b_0 and b_1. The random bit i prevents public knowledge of which of b_0, b_1 Bob knows the discrete logarithm. Bob cannot acquire both s_0 and s_1, since he cannot compute the discrete log of c.

18.5 Zero-Knowledge Proofs

As a simple case, we look at a protocol for Peter to convince Vera that he knows the factorization of a large integer n which is the product of two large primes p, q, but without imparting to Vera the factorization itself.

Suppose that Peter knows the factorization $n = pq$ with large primes p, q both congruent to 3 mod 4.

- Vera chooses a random integer x and sends $x^4 \% n$ to Peter.

- Peter computes the principal square root $y_1 = (x^4)^{(p+1)/2}$ of x^4 mod p and principal square root $y_2 = (x^4)^{(q+1)/2}$ of x^4 mod q, and uses Sun Ze's theorem (and the Euclidean algorithm) to compute y so that $y = y_1$ mod p and $y = y_2$ mod q. Peter sends this value back to Vera.

Remark: This formula for square roots modulo primes congruent to 3 mod 4 returns the *principal* square root, which is itself a square. Indeed, for a prime $p = 3$ mod 4 and for $a = b^2$ mod p, the two square roots are $\pm b$ mod m, and exactly one of $\pm b$ is itself a square, since -1 is a non-square and $\mathbf{Z}/p^\times$ is cyclic.

Remark: Since Vera already can compute x^2, Peter has certainly imparted no new information to Vera.

Remark: Vera *should* be convinced that there is no *other* way for Peter to have found this square root than by knowing the factors p, q, because in any case being able to take square roots modulo n gives a probabilistic algorithm for factoring n (when n is of the special form $n = pq$ with distinct primes p, q), as follows. If we have an **oracle** (meaning some otherwise unexplained mechanism) which computes square roots mod n, we repeatedly do the following: pick a random x, compute $x^2 \% n$, and feed the result to the oracle, which returns a square root y of x^2 modulo n. As remarked above in discussion of other protocol ideas, since there are exactly two square roots of any nonzero square modulo a prime, by Sun Ze's theorem there are exactly 4 square roots of any square modulo $n = pq$, and $\pm x$ are just 2 of them. Let the other two be $\pm x'$. Assuming that the original x really was chosen 'randomly', the probability is 1/2 that the oracle will return $\pm x'$ as y. If so, then n does not divide either of $x \pm y$ (since $y \neq \pm x$ mod n), but nevertheless n divides $x^2 - y^2$ (since $x^2 = y^2$ mod n). So p divides one of $x \pm y$ and q divides the other of the two. Therefore, $\gcd(x - y, n)$ is either p or q, which could be easily computed. Since the oracle can be called repeatedly, at each invocation there is probability 1/2 that a factorization will be obtained. So the probability that after ℓ invocations we *won't* obtain a factorization is $(1/2)^\ell$. This goes to 0 quite briskly as ℓ goes to infinity, which we construe as an indication that we *will* obtain a factorization in a reasonable time.

18.6 Authentication

This section is different from the previous ones in this chapter. Now we ignore issues of *secrecy* and look briefly at related but different goals concerning *reliability* of communication in a possibly hostile environment. Indeed, one can imagine scenarios in which the obstacles to communication are more serious than mere loss of confidentiality. In the current state of things, we cannot pretend to definitively *answer* these questions, but can only point out the problems. As with encryption in practice, both public-key and private-key techniques are used to address (with varying degrees of success) the issues raised here.

Message authentication is any procedure to verify that messages come from the alleged source and have not been altered. It should be possible, further, to verify that messages are received in the correct order, that they are received roughly at the time they are sent, that none are missing, and so on. Altogether, for any message(s) sent across a hostile network of any sort, apart from issues of secrecy, one might care about verifying:

- Origin of messages

- Content of messages

- Sequence of messages

- Timing of messages

- Receipt of messages

- Non-repudiation of messages

Origin. One would not want attackers to be able to send messages to your correspondents while pretending to be you. And you would not want third parties to be able to pose as one of your trusted correspondents and send you false messages. As an important example of this hazard: in many email systems it is very easy to send mail in the local network with whatever return address one wishes.

Content. Even if the content of a message need not be secret, you would not want an adversary to be able to *alter* the content.

Sequence. You would not want an adversary to delete some of a sequence of messages, or reorder a sequence of messages.

Timing. An adversary should not be able to **replay** one or more old messages as if they were new, or be able to **delay** messages to make them appear that they were sent later than they actually were.

Receipt. You would not want an adversary to be able to falsely report that a was lost, or to report falsely that it was received.

Non-repudiation. You would not want a sender to be able to deny that they sent a message to you. This idea begins a discussion of circumstances in which one does not entirely trust one's correspondents.

Of course, in all cases there are two possibilities: **prevention** of an attack, and **detection** of an attack (with corresponding adaptation). Prevention would be ideal, but for these issues at the present time (lacking quantum channels) it seems that *detection* is a practical goal. Likewise, given the vagaries of networks, messages can get out of order or be delayed not due to hostile acts, but merely due to random events. Thus, verifying sequence and timing is often more complicated than verifying origin and content.

Although there are no absolute distinctions to be made, there are three somewhat distinct types of mechanisms used in message authentication:

- **message encryption**

- **message authentication codes** ('MAC')

- **hash functions**

Message encryption. In this approach to message authentication, one encrypts the whole message using a cipher that the authorized recipient can decrypt, and sends the ciphertext. Then the authorized recipient decrypts the ciphertext. That is, the ciphertext is the **authenticator** of itself, because we presume that no unauthorized party could create a message that would decrypt properly.

Message authentication codes. These are many-to-one functions which produce a 'small' piece of authentication material by using a public function of the message and of a secret key. This small piece of data, often called *the MAC*, is sent along with the plaintext. The *authenticator object* in this case is the value of the MAC. The recipient of the message recomputes the MAC of the received message and checks that it matches the MAC value sent along with it.

Hash functions. These are message authentication codes without keys. Just as MACs do, hash functions produce a 'small' piece of authenticating data by using a public function of the message. While, of course, lack of key material changes the situation, and might seem undesirable, there are scenarios in which it would not be possible (or would be inconvenient) to have arranged a shared secret key.

When the **encrypted message is used as the authenticator**, the reasoning is that the authorized sender is the only person who could create a ciphertext decrypting (with the key possessed by the authorized recipient) to a coherent plaintext. But this is a little tricky: the input to the decryption can be *anything*, so, if the legitimate messages can be fairly arbitrary strings of 0's and 1's, then the decryption will give a supposed plaintext whose legitimacy will be hard to check. On the other hand, if the plaintext is expected to be English, then it should be hard to make a bogus ciphertext without having the true encryption key.

With 'binary' messages an additional structure can be imposed in a way that can be easily recognized by the authorized decryptor but not duplicated or simulated without possession of the encryption key. For example, the sender can append a **checksum** (also called **frame check sequence**, or FCS) of the whole message to itself before encryption. That this is the protocol must be known to both authorized sender and receiver. Then the decryptor decrypts the whole, removes the checksum from the tail of the alleged plaintext, and computes the checksum value of the remaining alleged plaintext to see whether it matches the checksum. One imagines that it would be difficult for an interloper to generate a fake ciphertext which would decrypt to plaintext-plus-checksum unless the interloper had the encryption key. This still does not prevent *replay attacks*. Note that in any case it is essential that the checksum (or any other structure) be added **before** encryption.

Encryption itself does not prevent *replay* of old messages which had been over-heard and copied by an eavesdropper. To avoid having old messages be *replayed*, the time of generation of a message should be included as a part of the message itself, as a **timestamp**. The timestamp should be added to the message before any other authentication code of the message is computed, and likewise before encryption.

Leaving messages unencrypted but computing a keyed MAC and appending the MAC is less computationally intensive than fully encrypting everything, and also allows the recipient a choice of whether or not to verify, based on circumstances. The secret-key material used in computing the MAC prevents unauthorized interceptors from altering the message and creating a matching MAC value.

While it sounds like a good thing, the very concept of *verification of receipt* of messages creates some difficulties, since if such a protocol were implemented, then by sending uninvited email one could obtain information about other people without their permission. The 'finger' protocol already allows something of this sort, with the pursuant privacy problems, even if one is not allowed to check last login times. For this reason 'finger' is often disabled, and so there is not yet any widespread receipt-verification protocol in use.

Finally, non-repudiation is tricky. Someone can send you an encrypted message, but later claim that their key had been compromised prior to that time, so they are not responsible for the content of the message. There seems to be no simple solution to this.

18.7 e-Money, e-Commerce

We may notice that mention of the 'information superhighway' has given way to 'e-commerce' and 'e-banking'. It should not be surprising that commercial interests would try to exploit communication by networked computers. But there are difficulties well beyond the first practical matter of securing servers on which credit-card numbers are stored, or establishing encrypted connections by which to communicate. In this section we point out some problems that arise in this context which are still far from a satisfactory solution.

The issue of *non-repudiation* of messages arises in the context of signing contracts or authorizing actions over the Internet. This also exposes the issue of *identity*: Who are you, in terms of the Internet, and how do you prove it? And can you maintain different identities for different purposes?

Data privacy has captured attention because of concern over medical records, credit records, and records of actions taken on the Internet (often embodied in *cookies* on one's browser). This concern raises questions such as: *How can one execute a transaction on the Internet without exposing more information than desired?* On the other hand, from the viewpoint of merchants, some information must be divulged in order to establish sufficient trust to justify shipping a product. Ideally, the buyer should be able to give just enough information, no more, to the seller, in order to convince the seller to complete the transaction. Similarly, in light of a number of scams run on the Internet, the seller also may need to establish trust.

An incidental technical issue which is nevertheless of basic importance in discussion of electronic transactions is *failure mode*: what happens if an electronic transaction is interrupted before completion? Is your money withdrawn from your bank, or not? Perhaps it is withdrawn from your account, but doesn't make it to your hands? Protocols and software and hardware ensuring *atomicity* of transactions are important.

A true electronic abstraction of 'money' is still in the future. A drawback to use of conventional credit cards, as opposed to paper money, is that the credit card's value exists only insofar as it is connected to your identity. But then your transactions are traceable. By contrast, paper money has value in itself, and in particular has no connection to your identity, so cannot yield information about other transactions. Current electronic banking has the same problem as credit cards, in that *someone* knows quite a lot about your financial transactions, where you are when they are made, and your general spending patterns.

Ideally, *e-money* would have (by convention) a value independent of the possessor's identity, would be *divisible*, would be *transferable*, would *not* be *reusable* (meaning that you couldn't spend the same dollar twice), would *not* depend upon a *central authority*, and transactions could take place *offline*.

As yet we are not close to achieving these goals.

19

Rings, Fields, Polynomials

The notions of *ring* and *field*, defined below, are (in part) abstractions of various notions of *number*. The motivation to understand things in abstraction is partly the motivation of efficiency, since we don't want to repeat ourselves unnecessarily. But also a common abstraction can suggest using ideas from one realm in another, sometimes yielding important insights.

These abstractions arose gradually, beginning about 1800 in the number theory work of Legendre, Gauss, Eisenstein, and others, as well as in Galois' and Abel's work in the theory of equations. Initially, the notions were not at all abstract, and were firmly imbedded in computation. By 1900 enough separate phenomena had been witnessed and catalogued so that the idea of abstraction as unification made sense.

19.1 Rings, Fields

The idea of **ring** generalizes the idea of 'numbers', among other things, so maybe it is a little more intuitive than the idea of **group**. A **ring** R is a set with two operations, $+$ and $\cdot$, and with a special element 0 (**additive identity**) with most of the usual properties we expect or demand of 'addition' and 'multiplication':

- The addition is **associative**: $a + (b + c) = (a + b) + c$ for all $a, b, c \in R$.

- The addition is **commutative**: $a + b = b + a$ for all $a, b \in R$.

- For every $a \in R$ there is an **additive inverse** denoted $-a$, with the property that $a + (-a) = 0$.

- The zero has the property that $0 + a = a + 0 = a$ for all $a \in R$.

- The multiplication is **associative**: $a(bc) = (ab)c$ for all $a, b, c \in R$.

- The multiplication and addition have left and right **distributive** properties: $a(b + c) = ab + ac$ and $(b + c)a = ba + ca$ for all $a, b, c \in R$.

When we write this multiplication, just as in high school algebra, very often we omit the dot, and just write

$$ab = a \cdot b$$

Very often, a particular ring has some additional special features or properties:

- If there is an element 1 in a ring with the property that $1 \cdot a = a \cdot 1$ for all $a \in R$, then 1 is said to be **the (multiplicative) identity** or **unit** in the ring, and the ring is said to **have an identity** or **have a unit** or be a **ring with unit**. And 1 is **the unit** in the ring. We also demand that $1 \neq 0$ in a ring.

- If $ab = ba$ for all a, b in a ring R, then the ring is said to be a **commutative ring**. That is, a ring is called *commutative* if and only if the *multiplication* is commutative.

Most often, but not always, our rings of interest will have units '1'. The condition of commutativity of multiplication is often met, but, for example, *matrix multiplication is not commutative*.

- In a ring R with 1, for a given element $a \in R$, if there is $a^{-1} \in R$ so that $a \cdot a^{-1} = 1$ and $a^{-1} \cdot a = 1$, then a^{-1} is said to be a **multiplicative inverse** for a. If $a \in R$ *has* a multiplicative inverse, then a is called **a unit** in R. The collection of all units in a ring R is denoted $R^{\times}$ and is called **the group of units in** R.

- A commutative ring in which every nonzero element is a *unit* is called a **field**.

- A not-necessarily commutative ring in which every nonzero element is a unit is called a **division ring**.

- In a ring R an element r so that $r \cdot s = 0$ or $s \cdot r = 0$ for some nonzero $s \in R$ is called a **zero divisor**. A commutative ring *without* nonzero zero-divisors is an **integral domain**.

- A commutative ring R has the **cancellation property** if, for any $r \neq 0$ in R, if $rx = ry$ for $x, y \in R$, then $x = y$. Most rings with which we're familiar have this property.

Remark: There is indeed an inconsistency in the use of the word *unit*. But that's the way the word is used. So *the* unit is 1, while *a* unit is merely something which has a multiplicative inverse. Of course, there are *no* multiplicative inverses unless there is a unit (meaning that there is a 1). *It is almost always possible to tell from context what is meant.*

It is very important to realize that the notations $-a$ for an additive inverse and a^{-1} for multiplicative inverse are meant to *suggest* 'minus a' and 'divide-by-a', but that at the moment we are *not justified* in believing any of the 'usual' high school algebra properties. *We have to prove that all the 'usual' things really do still work in this abstract situation.*

If we take a ring R with 0 and with its addition, then we get an abelian group, called **the additive group of** R.

The group of units $R^\times$ in a ring with unit certainly is a group. Its identity is the unit 1. This group is abelian if R is commutative.

In somewhat more practical terms: as our examples above show, very often a *group* really is just the *additive group* of a ring, or is the *group of units* in a ring. There are many examples where this is not really so, but many fundamental examples are of this nature.

The integers $\mathbf{Z}$ with usual addition and multiplication form a ring. This ring is certainly *commutative* and has a multiplicative identity '1'. The group of units $\mathbf{Z}^\times$ is just $\{\pm 1\}$. This ring is an integral domain.

The *even* integers $2\mathbf{Z}$ with the usual addition and multiplication form a commutative ring *without* unit. Just as this example suggests, very often the lack of a unit in a ring is somewhat artificial, because there is a 'larger' ring it sits inside which *does* have a unit. There are no units in this ring.

The integers mod m, denoted $\mathbf{Z}/m$, form a commutative ring with identity. *As the notation suggests,* the group of units really is $\mathbf{Z}/m^\times$: notice that we used the group-of-units notation in this case before we even introduced the terminology.

Take p a prime. The ring of integers mod p, denoted $\mathbf{Z}/p$, is a *field* if p is *prime*, since all positive integers less than p have a multiplicative inverse modulo p for p prime (computable by the Euclidean algorithm!). The group of units really is $\mathbf{Z}/p^\times$.

The collection of n-by-n real matrices (for fixed n) is a ring, with the usual matrix addition and multiplication. Except for the silly case $n = 1$, this ring is *non-commutative*. The group of units is the group $GL(n, \mathbf{R})$.

The rational numbers $\mathbf{Q}$, the real numbers $\mathbf{R}$, and the complex numbers $\mathbf{C}$ are all examples of *fields*, because all their nonzero elements have multiplicative inverses.

Just as in the beginning of our discussion of *groups*, there are some things which we might accidentally take for granted about how rings behave. In general these presumptions are reasonable, based on all our previous experience with numbers, etc. But it is certainly better to give the 'easy' little proofs of these things and to be conscious of what we believe, rather than to be unconscious.

Let R be a ring. We will prove the following fundamental properties:

- *Uniqueness of additive identity:* If there is an element $z \in R$ and another $r \in R$ so that $r + z = r$, then $z = 0$. (Note that we need this condition only for *one* other $r \in R$, not for *all* $r \in R$.)

- *Uniqueness of additive inverses:* Fix $r \in R$. If there is $r' \in R$ so that $r + r' = 0$, then actually $r' = -r$, the additive inverse of r.

- *Uniqueness of multiplicative identity:* Suppose that R has a unit 1. If there is $u \in R$ so that for all $r \in R$ we have $u \cdot r = r$, then $u = 1$. Or, if for all $r \in R$ we have $r \cdot u = r$, then $u = 1$. Actually, all we need is that *either* $1 \cdot u = 1$ *or* $u \cdot 1 = 1$ to assure that $u = 1$.

- *Uniqueness of multiplicative inverses:* If $r \in R$ has a multiplicative inverse r^{-1}, and if $r' \in R$ is such that $r \cdot r' = 1$, then $r' = r^{-1}$. Or, assuming instead that $r' \cdot r = 1$, we still conclude that $r' = r^{-1}$.

- For $r \in R$, we have $-(-r) = r$. That is, the additive inverse of the additive inverse of r is just r.

Proof: *(of uniqueness of additive identity).* If there is an element $z \in R$ and $r \in R$ so that $r + z = r$, add $-r$ to both sides of this equation to obtain

$$(r + z) - r = r - r = 0$$

by definition of additive inverse. Using the commutativity and associativity of addition, the left-hand side of this is

$$(r + z) - r = (z + r) - r = z + (r - r) = z + 0 = z$$

also using the property of the 0. That is, putting this together, $z = 0$, proving what we wanted.   ♣

Proof: *(of uniqueness of additive inverses).* Fix $r \in R$. If there is $r' \in R$ so that $r + r' = 0$, then add $-r$ to both sides to obtain

$$(r + r') - r = 0 + (-r)$$

Using the commutativity and associativity of addition, the left-hand side of this is

$$(r + r') - r = (r' + r) - r = r' + (r - r) = r' + 0 = r'$$

Since the right-hand side is $0 + (-r) = -r$, we have $r' = -r$, as claimed.   ♣

Proof: *(of uniqueness of multiplicative identity).* Suppose that *either* $1 \cdot u = 1$ *or* $u \cdot 1 = 1$ to assure that $u = 1$. Well, let's just do one case, since the other is identical apart from writing things in the opposite order. Suppose that $u \cdot 1 = 1$. Then, since $u \cdot 1 = u$ by the property of the multiplicative identity 1, we have $u = 1$, which is the desired uniqueness. ♣

Proof: *(of uniqueness of multiplicative inverses).* Assume that $r \in R$ has a multiplicative inverse r^{-1}, and that $r' \in R$ is such that $r \cdot r' = 1$. Then multiply that latter equation by r^{-1} on the left to obtain

$$r^{-1} \cdot (r \cdot r') = r^{-1} \cdot 1 = r^{-1}$$

by the property of 1. Using the associativity of multiplication, the left-hand side is

$$r^{-1} \cdot (r \cdot r') = (r^{-1} \cdot r) \cdot r' = 1 \cdot r' = r'$$

by property of multiplicative inverses and of the identity. Putting this together, we have $r' = r^{-1}$ as desired. ♣

The proof that $-(-r) = r$ (that is, that the additive inverse of the additive inverse of r is just r) is identical to the argument given for *groups* that the inverse of the inverse is the original thing.

There are several 'slogans' that we all learned in high school or earlier, such as 'minus times minus is plus,' and 'zero times anything is zero.' It may be interesting to see that from the axioms for a ring we can *prove* those things. (We worried over the so-called 'laws of exponents' already a little earlier.)

These things are a little subtler than the 'obvious' things above, insofar as they involve the interaction of the multiplication and addition. These little proofs are good models for how to prove simple general results about rings.

Let R be a ring.

- For any $r \in R$, $0 \cdot r = r \cdot 0 = 0$.

- Suppose that there is a 1 in R. Let -1 be the additive inverse of 1. Then for any $r \in R$ we have $(-1) \cdot r = r \cdot (-1) = -r$, where as usual $-r$ denotes the additive inverse of r.

- Let $-x, -y$ be the additive inverses of $x, y \in R$. Then $(-x) \cdot (-y) = xy$.

Proof: Throughout this discussion, keep in mind that to prove that $b = -a$ means to prove just that $a + b = 0$.

Let's prove that 'zero times anything is zero': Let $r \in R$. Then

$$\begin{aligned} 0 \cdot r &= (0 + 0) \cdot r &&\text{(since } 0 + 0 = 0\text{)} \\ &= 0 \cdot r + 0 \cdot r &&\text{(distributivity)} \end{aligned}$$

Then, adding $-(0 \cdot r)$ to both sides, we have

$$0 = 0 \cdot r - 0 \cdot r = 0 \cdot r + 0 \cdot r - 0 \cdot r = 0 \cdot r + 0 = 0 \cdot r$$

That is, $0 \cdot r$. The proof that $r \cdot 0 = 0$ is nearly identical.

Let's show that $(-1) \cdot r = -r$. That is, we are asserting that $(-1)r$ is the additive inverse of r, which by now we know is unique. So all we have to do is check that

$$r + (-1)r = 0$$

We have

$$r + (-1)r = 1 \cdot r + (-1) \cdot r = (1 - 1) \cdot r = 0 \cdot r = 0$$

by using the property of 1, using distributivity, and using the result we just proved, that $0 \cdot r = 0$. We're done.

Last, to show that $(-x)(-y) = xy$, we prove that $(-x)(-y) = -(-(xy))$, since we know generally that $-(-r) = r$. We can get halfway to the desired conclusion right now: we claim that $-(xy) = (-x)y$: this follows from the computation

$$(-x)y + xy = (-x + x)y = 0 \cdot y = 0$$

Combining these two things, what we want to show is that

$$(-x)(-y) + (-x)y = 0$$

Well,

$$(-x)(-y) + (-x)y = (-x)(-y + y) = (-x) \cdot 0 = 0$$

using distributivity and the property $r \cdot 0 = 0$. This proves that $(-x)(-y) = xy$.

Exercises

19.1.01 Check that the congruence class $\bar{1}$ of 1 modulo m really is the multiplicative identity '1' in the ring $\mathbf{Z}/m$.

19.1.02 Check that the subset $\{\bar{0}, \bar{3}\}$ of $\mathbf{Z}/6$ is a ring, and that $\bar{3}$ is the multiplicative identity '1'.

19.1.03 Check that $\{\bar{0}, \bar{2}, \bar{4}, \bar{6}, \bar{8}\} \subset \mathbf{Z}/10$ is a ring, and that $\bar{6}$ is the multiplicative identity '1' in this ring.

19.1.04 Check that $\{\bar{0}, \bar{3}, \bar{6}, \bar{9}, \bar{12}\} \subset \mathbf{Z}/15$ is a ring, and that $\bar{6}$ is the multiplicative identity '1' in this ring.

19.1.05 Find the group of units in the rings $\mathbf{Z}/4$, $\mathbf{Z}/5$, $\mathbf{Z}/6$.

19.1.06 Find the group of units in the ring $\mathbf{Z}/12$

19.1.07 Check that the collection $2\mathbf{Z}$ of all even integers is a ring, although *without* unit.

19.1.08 Check that $\mathbf{Z}/n$ has nonzero zero divisors if n is composite.

19.1.09 Check that if p is prime then $\mathbf{Z}/p$ is an integral domain.

19.1.10 Show that a multiplicatively invertible element in a ring can never be a zero-divisor. (Recall that $1 \neq 0$.)

19.1.11 Let R be the collection of numbers of the form $a + bi$ where $a, b \in \mathbf{Q}$ and $i = \sqrt{-1}$. Just to keep in practice, check that R is 'closed' under multiplication and addition. Then, granting that R is a ring (meaning not to worry about associativity, etc.) show that R is a *field*. (*Hint:* Remember 'rationalizing denominators'?)

19.1.12 Let R be the collection of numbers of the form $a+b\sqrt{2}$ where $a, b \in \mathbf{Q}$. Check that R is 'closed' under multiplication and addition. Then, granting that R is a ring (meaning not to worry about associativity, etc.) show that R is a *field*. (*Hint:* 'Rationalizing denominators.')

19.1.13 Let R be the collection of numbers $a + bi$ with $a, b \in \mathbf{Z}$ and $i = \sqrt{-1}$. Check that R is 'closed' under multiplication and addition. Granting that it is a ring, then, find the *group of units*.

19.1.14 Let R be the collection of numbers $a + b\sqrt{-5}$ with $a, b \in \mathbf{Z}$. Check that R is 'closed' under multiplication and addition. Granting that it is a ring, then, find the *group of units*.

19.1.15 Show that in a ring the equation $r + r = r$ can hold only for $r = 0$.

19.1.16 Find several examples of *nonzero* elements x, y in the ring $\mathbf{Z}/15$ whose product is nevertheless 0.

19.1.17 Find several examples of *nonzero* elements x, y in the ring $\mathbf{Z}/21$ whose product is nevertheless 0.

19.1.18 Find several examples of *nonzero* elements x, y in the ring $\mathbf{Z}/16$ whose product is nevertheless 0.

19.1.19 Find several examples of *nonzero* elements x, y in the ring $\mathbf{Z}/21$ whose product is nevertheless 0.

19.2 Divisibility

Before trying to prove that various commutative rings 'have unique factorization', we should make clear what this should mean. To make *this* clear, we need to talk about *divisibility* again. In this section we presume that any ring in question is *commutative* and has a *unit*.

The very first thing to understand is the potential failure of the possibility of the *cancellation property*, and its connection with the presence of nonzero zero divisors:

> **Theorem.** A commutative ring R has the *cancellation property* if and only if it is an *integral domain*.

Proof: Suppose that R has the cancellation property, and suppose that $r \cdot s = 0$. Since $r \cdot 0 = 0$ for any $r \in R$, we can write $r \cdot s = r \cdot 0$. For $r \neq 0$ we can cancel the r and obtain $s = 0$. Similarly, if $s \neq 0$, then $r = 0$. This shows that the cancellation property implies that there are no nonzero zero divisors.

On the other hand, suppose that R has no nonzero zero divisors. Suppose that $ra = rb$ with $r \neq 0$. Then, subtracting, $r(a - b) = 0$. Since $r \neq 0$, it must be that $a - b = 0$, or $a = b$. This is the desired cancellation property. ♣

In a commutative ring R, say that $x \in R$ **divides** $y \in R$ if there is $z \in R$ so that $y = zx$. And also say then that y is a **multiple** of x. And just as for the ordinary integers we may write

$$x|y$$

to say that x divides y. And then x is a **divisor** of y. If $xz = y$ and neither x nor z is a unit, then say that x is a **proper divisor** of y.

Keep in mind that, since $r \cdot 0 = 0$, *anything* divides 0. But for the same reason 0 divides only *itself* and nothing else. On the other hand, if $u \in R$ is a *unit* in R (meaning that it has a multiplicative inverse in R), then u divides *everything*: let $r \in R$ be anything, and then we see that

$$r = r \cdot 1 = r \cdot (u^{-1} \cdot u) = (r \cdot u^{-1}) \cdot u$$

making clear that r is a multiple of u.

An element p in R is **irreducible** if p itself is *not* a unit in R, but if $xy = p$ (with both $x, y \in R$), then either x or y is a *unit* in R. A paraphrase of this is: an element is irreducible if and only if it has *no proper divisors*.

- If d is a *proper* divisor of a nonzero element r in an integral domain R, then

$$R \cdot r \subset R \cdot d$$

but

$$R \cdot r \neq R \cdot d$$

Proof: Since d is a divisor of r, there is $x \in R$ so that $xd = r$. Then

$$R \cdot r = R(xd) = (Rx)d \subset R \cdot d$$

since R is closed under multiplication, after all. Suppose that $R \cdot r = R \cdot d$. Then

$$d = 1 \cdot d \in R \cdot d = R \cdot r$$

so there is $s \in R$ so that $d = s \cdot r$. But then

$$r = xd = x(sr) = (xs)r$$

which gives $r(1 - xs) = 0$. Since $r \neq 0$ and R is an integral domain, $1 - xs = 0$ or $xs = 1$. That is, x is a unit, contradicting the assumption that $xd = r$ is a *proper* factorization of r.   ♣

Two prime elements $p, q \in R$ are **associate** if there is a unit u in R so that $q = up$. (Since the inverse of a unit is, of course, a unit as well, this condition is symmetrical, being equivalent to the existence of a unit v, so that $p = vq$.)

The idea is that, for purposes of *factorization into primes*, two *associate* prime elements will be viewed as being essentially the same thing.

Exercises

19.2.01 Show that in the ring $\mathbf{Z}/35$ the so-called *cancellation law* fails: that is, for such n, find (*nonzero*) elements $a, b, c \in \mathbf{Z}/35$ so that $ca = cb$ but $a \neq b$.

19.2.02 Show that in the ring $\mathbf{Z}/77$ the so-called *cancellation law* fails: that is, for such n, find (*nonzero*) elements $a, b, c \in \mathbf{Z}/77$ so that $ca = cb$ but $a \neq b$.

19.2.03 Show that in the ring $\mathbf{Z}/n$ with n a *composite* (that is, not prime) number, the so-called *cancellation law* fails: that is, for such n, find (*nonzero*) elements $a, b, c \in \mathbf{Z}/n$ so that $ca = cb$ but $a \neq b$.

19.2.04 Let u be a unit in a commutative ring R. Show that no non-unit in R can *divide* u.

19.2.05 Show that in a ring, if $x = yu$ with a unit u, then $y = xu'$ for some unit u'.

19.2.06 Let R be an *integral domain* with unit 1, and suppose that $Rx = Ry$ for two elements x, y of R. Show that there is a unit $u \in R^{\times}$ so that $y = ux$.

19.2.07 Suppose that in an integral domain R we have $xy = z$, where neither x nor y is a unit. Show that $Rz \subset Rx$ but $Rz \neq Rx$.

19.3 Polynomial Rings

Another important and general construction of rings is **polynomial rings**: let R be a *commutative ring with unit*, and define

$$R[x] = \{\text{polynomials with coefficients in } R\}$$

Then we use the usual addition and multiplication of polynomials. We will be especially interested in polynomials whose coefficients lie in a *field k*. By default, we might imagine that k is $\mathbf{Q}$ or $\mathbf{R}$ or $\mathbf{C}$, although we should also admit the possibility that the field k is a finite field such as $\mathbf{Z}/p$ for p prime.

Let R be a commutative ring with unit 1. Let x be the thing we usually think of as a 'variable' or 'indeterminate'. The **ring of polynomials in x with coefficients in R** is what it sounds like: the collection of all polynomials using indeterminate x and whose coefficients are in the ring R. This is also called the ring of polynomials in x **over** R. The notation for this is very standard: using *square brackets*:

$$R[x]$$

denotes the ring of polynomials over k. With the usual addition and multiplication of polynomials, this $R[x]$ is a *ring*.

We are most accustomed to polynomials with real numbers or complex numbers as coefficients, but there is nothing special about this.

When a polynomial with **indeterminate** x is written out as

$$P(x) = c_n x^n + c_{n-1} x^{n-1} + \cdots + c_3 x^3 + c_2 x^2 + c_1 x + c_0$$

the **coefficients** are the 'numbers' $c_n, \ldots, c_0$ in the ring R. The **constant coefficient** is c_0. If $c_n \neq 0$, then $c_n x^n$ is called **the highest-order term** or **leading term** and c_n is the **highest-order coefficient** or **leading coefficient**.

We refer to the summand $c_i x^i$ as the **degree i term**. Also sometimes i is called the **order** of the summand $c_i x^i$. The order of the highest nonzero coefficient is the **degree** of the polynomial.

Remark: Sometimes people write a polynomial in the form above but *forget* to say whether c_n is definitely nonzero or not. Sometimes, also, people *presume* that if a polynomial is written in this fashion then c_n is nonzero, but that's not safe at all.

A polynomial is said to be **monic** if its *leading* or *highest-order* coefficient is 1.

Remark: Sometimes polynomials are thought of as simply being a kind of *function*, but that is too naive generally. Polynomials *give rise to* functions, but they are more than just that. It *is* true that a polynomial

$$f(x) = c_n x^n + c_{n-1} x^{n-1} + \cdots + c_1 x + c_0$$

with coefficients in a ring R *gives rise to* functions on the ring R, writing as usual

$$f(a) = c_n a^n + c_{n-1} a^{n-1} + \cdots + c_1 a + c_0$$

for $a \in R$. That is, as usual, we imagine that the 'indeterminate' x is replaced by a everywhere (or 'a is substituted for 'x'). This procedure gives functions from R to R.

But polynomials themselves have features which may become invisible if we mistakenly think of them as just being functions. For example, suppose that we look at the polynomial $f(x) = x^3 + x^2 + x + \bar{1}$ in the polynomial ring $(\mathbf{Z}/2)[x]$, that is, with coefficients in $\mathbf{Z}/2$. Then

$$f(\bar{0}) = \bar{0}^3 + \bar{0}^2 + \bar{1} + \bar{1} = \bar{0}$$

$$f(\bar{1}) = \bar{1}^3 + \bar{1}^2 + \bar{1} + \bar{1} = \bar{0}$$

That is, the *function* attached to the polynomial is the 0-function, but the polynomial is visibly not the zero polynomial. As another example, consider $f(x) = x^3 - x$ as a polynomial with coefficients in $\mathbf{Z}/3$. Once again, $f(\bar{0})$, $f(\bar{1})$, $f(\bar{2})$, are all $\bar{0}$, but the polynomial is certainly not the zero polynomial.

Exercises

19.3.01 Find the two roots of $x^2 + 3x + 2 = 0$ in $\mathbf{Z}/5$.

19.3.02 Find the two roots of $x^2 + 3x + 2 = 0$ in $\mathbf{Z}/7$.

19.3.03 Find the two roots of $x^2 + 1 = 0$ in $\mathbf{Z}/5$.

19.3.04 Find the two roots of $x^2 + 1 = 0$ in $\mathbf{Z}/13$.

19.3.05 Verify that $x^2 + x + 1 = 0$ has no roots in $\mathbf{Z}/2$.

19.3.06 Let p be a prime. Verify that $x^p - x + a = 0$ has no roots in $\mathbf{Z}/p$.

19.3.07 Find all 4 roots of $x^2 - 1 = 0$ in $\mathbf{Z}/8$.

19.3.08 Find all 4 roots of $x^2 - 2 = 0$ in $\mathbf{Z}/161$.

19.3.09 Find all 8 roots of $x^2 - 1 = 0$ in $\mathbf{Z}/105$.

19.3.10 Find another way to factor $x^2 - 1$ as a polynomial with coefficients in $\mathbf{Z}/15$ besides the obvious $(x - 1)(x + 1)$. (Keep in mind that 1 and 16 and -14, etc., do *not* count as being different modulo 15.)

19.3.11 Find two different ways to factor $x^2 - 2$ into monic linear factors, as a polynomial with coefficients in $\mathbf{Z}/161$ (keeping in mind that $(x - a)(x - b)$ counts as different from $(x - c)(x - d)$ only if a, b and c, d are different *modulo* 161).

19.3.12 Let $k[x]$ be the polynomial ring in one variable x over a field k. What is the group of units $k[x]^\times$?

19.3.13 Let $R[x]$ be the polynomial ring in one variable x over a commutative ring R with unit 1. What is the group of units $R[x]^\times$?

19.3.14 (*) Why does the quadratic formula fail to find roots in the example of trying to solve $x^2 + x + 1 = 0$ in $\mathbf{Z}/2$?

19.4 Euclidean Algorithm

In a polynomial ring $k[x]$ with k a *field*, there is a **division algorithm** and (therefore) there is a **Euclidean algorithm** nearly identical *in form* to the analogous algorithms in the ordinary integers $\mathbf{Z}$. The division algorithm is just the usual *division of one polynomial by another*, with remainder, as we all learned in high school or earlier. It takes just a moment's reflection to see that the procedure we all learned does *not* depend upon the nature of the field that the coefficients are in, and that the degree of the remainder is indeed less than the degree of the divisor!

For example: let's reduce $x^3 + 1$ modulo $x^2 + 1$:

$$(x^3 + 1) - x \cdot (x^2 + 1) = x - 1$$

We're done with the reduction because the degree of $x - 1$ is (strictly) less than the degree of $x^2 + 1$. Reduce $x^5 + 1$ modulo $x^2 + 1$, in stages:

$$\begin{aligned}(x^5 + 1) - x^3 \cdot (x^2 + 1) &= -x^3 + 1 \\ (-x^3 + 1) + x \cdot (x^2 + 1) &= x + 1\end{aligned}$$

which, summarized, gives the reduction step

$$(x^5 + 1) - (x^3 - x) \cdot (x^2 + 1) = x + 1$$

Next, since the division algorithm works for polynomials with coefficients in a field, it is a *corollary* that we have a Euclidean algorithm: the crucial thing in having the Euclidean algorithm work is that at each step the division algorithm gives progressively smaller numbers at each step.

With coefficients in $\mathbf{Z}/2$ (the simplest case!), divide

$$x^7 + x^6 + x^5 + x^4 + x^3 + x^2 + 1$$

by $x^3 + x + 1$. Written out in full:

$$
\begin{array}{r}
x^4 \quad +x^3 \quad +0 \quad +x^1 \quad +0 \quad \text{R} \ x^1 +x^0 \\
x^3 \quad +0 \quad +x^1 \quad +x^0 \, \big| \, \overline{x^7 \quad +x^6 \quad +x^5 \quad +x^4 \quad +x^3 \quad +x^2 \quad +0 \quad +x^0} \\
x^7 \quad +0 \quad +x^5 \quad +x^4 \quad +0 \quad +0 \quad +0 \quad +0 \\
\hline
x^6 \quad +0 \quad +0 \quad +x^3 \quad +x^2 \quad +0 \quad +x^0 \\
x^6 \quad +0 \quad +x^4 \quad +x^3 \quad +0 \quad +0 \quad +0 \\
\hline
x^4 \quad +0 \quad +x^2 \quad +0 \quad +x^0 \\
x^4 \quad +0 \quad +x^2 \quad +x^1 \quad +0 \\
\hline
x^1 \quad +x^0
\end{array}
$$

So as a single line this would be

$$
\begin{aligned}
&(x^7 + x^6 + x^5 + x^4 + x^3 + x^2 + 1) \\
&\quad -(x^4 + x^3 + x)(x^3 + x + 1) \quad = \quad x + 1
\end{aligned}
$$

If the field is not simply $\mathbf{Z}/2$, it can easily happen that a divisor D is not **monic**, that is, has leading (nonzero) coefficient c_n not 1. In that case, the polynomial $c_n^{-1}D$ *is* monic, and we divide by $c_n^{-1}D$ instead. Then from an expression

$$F = Q \cdot (c_n^{-1}D) + R$$

for the division algorithm with divisor $c_n^{-1}D$ we immediately get

$$F = (Qc_n^{-1}) \cdot D + R$$

which is the division algorithm mod D, as desired.

The number of operations performed to divide by a non-monic polynomial is the same as the approach just indicated, but (especially when executed by a human) the approach of the previous paragraph seems to help avoid errors.

Factoring, testing irreducibility. As in the naive primality/factoring approach for ordinary integers, for small-degree polynomials over a small finite field we can use a **naive** primality and factorization algorithm. Analogous to the fact that for ordinary integers

$$|xy| = |x| \cdot |y|$$

we need the fact for polynomials with coefficients in a field that

$$\deg(P \cdot Q) = \deg P + \deg Q$$

where deg is degree. The truth of this assertion depends upon the fact that there are no zero divisors in a field: let

$$
\begin{aligned}
P(x) &= a_m x^m + a_{m-1} x^{m-1} + \cdots + a_2 x^2 + a_1 x + a_0 \\
Q(x) &= b_n x^n + b_{n-1} x^{n-1} + \cdots + b_2 x^2 + b_1 x + b_0
\end{aligned}
$$

where the *apparent* leading coefficients a_m and b_n *really are* nonzero. Then in the product $P \cdot Q$ the highest-degree term is x^{m+n}, which occurs only in one way, as the product of the leading terms from P and Q, so it has coefficient $a_m \cdot b_n$. Since neither of these is 0, and since the product of nonzero elements of a field is nonzero, the coefficient of x^{m+n} is nonzero. This proves that the **degree of the product is the sum of the degrees.**

- Thus, for a proper divisor D of a polynomial F

$$0 < \deg D < \deg F$$

Further, if F has a proper divisor, then it has a proper divisor F with

$$0 < \deg D \leq \frac{1}{2} \deg F$$

Proof: If a proper divisor D of F has degree $\geq \frac{1}{2} \deg F$, then F/D has degree less than or equal to $\frac{1}{2} \deg F$.   ♣

More facts:
- Every linear polynomial is irreducible, since there is no value of 'degree' between 1 and 0.
- If a quadratic polynomial factors properly, then it must be the product of two linear factors.
- If a cubic polynomial factors properly, then it must have at least one linear factor.
- If a quartic or higher-degree polynomial factors properly, it may nevertheless fail to have a linear factor.
- A polynomial $F(x)$ with coefficients in a field k has a linear factor $x - a$ (with $a \in k$) if and only if $F(a) = 0$.

Proof: If $x - a$ is a factor, then $F(x) = (x - a)G(x)$ for some G, and

$$F(a) = (a - a)G(a) = 0 \cdot G(a)$$

On the other hand, suppose that $F(a) = 0$. Use the division algorithm to write

$$F(x) = Q(x) \cdot (x - a) + R$$

Since $\deg R < \deg(x - a) = 1$, R must be a constant. Evaluate both sides at a:

$$0 = F(a) = Q(a) \cdot (a - a) + R = Q(a) \cdot 0 + R = R$$

Therefore, $R = 0$, and so $x - a$ divides $F(x)$.   ♣

Remark: This gives a slightly more economical way to test for linear factors.

There is only one degree 0 polynomial in $\mathbf{Z}/2[x]$, namely the constant 1. The 0 polynomial is more aptly said to have degree $-\infty$.

There are just two linear polynomials in $\mathbf{Z}/2[x]$, namely x and $x+1$. Since every linear polynomial is irreducible, they are irreducible.

For **quadratic** polynomials, there are 2 choices for the linear coefficient and 2 choices for the constant coefficient, so $2 \cdot 2 = 4$ quadratic polynomials in $\mathbf{Z}/2[x]$. Testing for irreducibility: here the algebra is easy...

- Obviously $x^2 = x \cdot x$.

- Obviously $x^2 + x = x \cdot (x+1)$.

- Less obviously $x^2 + 1 = (x+1)^2$. Here use the fact that $2 = 0$, so that we have the simplification $(x+1)^2 = x^2 + 2x + 1 = x^2 + 0 + 1 = x^2 + 1$.

- $x^2 + x + 1$: Now it's a little easier to see whether or not this is 0 when values 0 and 1 are plugged in, respectively:

$$0^2 + 0 + 1 = 1 \neq 0$$

$$1^2 + 1 + 1 = 1 \neq 0$$

So $x^2 + x + 1$ is irreducible in $\mathbf{Z}/2[x]$. It's the **only** irreducible quadratic polynomial in $\mathbf{Z}/2[x]$.

For **cubic** polynomials with coefficients in $\mathbf{Z}/2$, there are 2 choices for quadratic coefficient, 2 for linear coefficient, and 2 for constant, so 8 altogether. If we are looking only for irreducible ones, we should exclude those with constant coefficient 0, because they'll have value 0 for input 0 (equivalently, they'll have a linear factor x). Also, those with an even number of nonzero coefficients will have value 0 for input 1, so will have a linear factor $x+1$. Keep in mind that if a cubic is not irreducible, then it has at least one linear factor.

We conclude that a cubic polynomial in $\mathbf{Z}/2$ with constant coefficient 1 and with an odd total number of nonzero coefficients is necessarily irreducible. Thus, the only two irreducible cubics in $\mathbf{Z}/2[x]$ are

$$x^3 + x^2 + 1$$

$$x^3 + x + 1$$

There are $2^4 = 16$ choices for cubic, quadratic, linear, and constant coefficients in $\mathbf{Z}/2[x]$. If the constant term is 0, or if the total number of nonzero coefficients is even, then there is a linear factor x or $x+1$.

This leaves 4 possibilities for irreducible quartics:

$$x^4 + x^3 + x^2 + x + 1$$
$$x^4 + x^3 + 1$$
$$x^4 + x^2 + 1$$
$$x^4 + x + 1$$

None of these has a **linear** factor in $\mathbf{Z}/2[x]$. But we must look for (irreducible!) **quadratic** factors. From above, the only irreducible quadratic in $\mathbf{Z}/2[x]$ is x^2+x+1, so the only reducible quartic without linear factors **must** be

$$x^4 + x^2 + 1 = (x^2 + x + 1)^2$$

This leaves 3 irreducible quartics in $\mathbf{Z}/2[x]$: $x^4 + x^3 + x^2 + x + 1$, $x^4 + x^3 + 1$, and $x^4 + x + 1$.

There are $2^5 = 32$ quintics in $\mathbf{Z}/2[x]$. Excluding those with 0 constant coefficient (and therefore divisible by x) leaves $2^4 = 16$. Excluding those with an even total number of nonzero coefficients (divisible by $x + 1$) leaves

$$\binom{4}{3} + \binom{4}{1} = 4 + 4 = 8$$

This 8 is the number of quintics with no linear factors. The only way a quintic with no linear factors can be obtained as a product of lower-degree polynomials is

irreducible quadratic $\cdot$ irreducible cubic

For example, if there were 2 irreducible quadratic factors, then that would leave room only for a linear factor, which we've assumed away. We've already found out that there is only one irreducible quadratic in $\mathbf{Z}/2[x]$, and just 2 irreducible cubics, so there are exactly 2 reducible quintics without linear factors. They are

$$\begin{array}{rcl}
(x^2 + x + 1) \cdot (x^3 + x^2 + 1) & = & x^5 + x + 1 \\
(x^2 + x + 1) \cdot (x^3 + x + 1) & = & x^5 + x^4 + 1
\end{array}$$

That leaves 6 irreducible quintics in $\mathbf{Z}/2[x]$, which we obtain by listing anything not noted above to be reducible: they must have constant coefficient 1, an odd number of nonzero coefficients, and not be $x^5 + x + 1$ nor $x^5 + x^4 + 1$. With exactly 5 nonzero coefficients: these are all irreducible:

$$\begin{array}{l}
x^5 + 0 + x^3 + x^2 + x + 1 \\
x^5 + x^4 + 0 + x^2 + x + 1 \\
x^5 + x^4 + x^3 + 0 + x + 1 \\
x^5 + x^4 + x^3 + x^2 + 0 + 1
\end{array}$$

With exactly 3 nonzero coefficients, avoiding the two reducible ones noted above:

$$\begin{array}{l}
x^5 + x^3 + 1 \\
x^5 + x^2 + 1
\end{array}$$

Before anyone imagines that RSA could be implemented using the difficulty of factorization in $\mathbf{Z}/p[x]$ (instead of in $\mathbf{Z}$), **forget it!** There is a fast algorithm due to Berlekamp which factors these polynomials.

Exercises

19.4.01 Find the greatest common divisor of $x^5 + x^4 + x^3 + x^2 + x + 1$ and $x^4 + x^2 + 1$, viewed as elements in the ring $\mathbf{Q}[x]$ of polynomials over $\mathbf{Q}$.

19.4.02 Find the greatest common divisor of $x^9 + x^6 + x^3 + 1$ and $x^{10} + x^8 + x^6 + x^4 + x^2 + 1$, viewed as elements in the ring $\mathbf{Q}[x]$ of polynomials over $\mathbf{Q}$.

19.4.03 Find the greatest common divisor of $x^6 + x^3 + 1$ and $x^2 + x + 1$, viewed as elements in the ring $\mathbf{F}_3[x]$ of polynomials over the finite field $\mathbf{F}_3$ with 3 elements.

19.4.04 Find the greatest common divisor of $x^6 + x^4 + x^2 + 1$ and $x^8 + x^6 + x^4 + x^2 + 1$, viewed as elements in the ring $\mathbf{F}_2[x]$ of polynomials over the finite field $\mathbf{F}_2$ with 2 elements.

19.4.05 Find the greatest common divisor of $x^5 + x^4 + 1$ and $x^5 + x + 1$, viewed as elements in the ring $\mathbf{F}_2[x]$ of polynomials over the finite field $\mathbf{F}_2$ with 2 elements.

19.4.06 Find the greatest common divisor of the two polynomials $x^7 + x^5 + x^4 + x^2 + 1$ and $x^8 + x^7 + x^4 + x^3 + 1$ which have coefficients in $\mathbf{F}_2$.

19.4.07 Find the greatest common divisor of the two polynomials in $\mathbf{F}_2[x]$:

$$x^{14} + x^{13} + x^{11} + x^{10} + x^9 + x^7 + x^5 + x^4 + x^3 + 1$$

$$x^{14} + x^{12} + x^8 + x^7 + x^4 + x^3 + x + 1$$

19.4.08 Find the greatest common divisor of the two polynomials $x^7 + x^6 + x^4 + x^3 + 1$ and $x^8 + x^7 + x^5 + x^3 + x^2 + x + 1$ which have coefficients in $\mathbf{F}_2$.

19.4.09 Factor into irreducibles the polynomial $x^{12} + x^{10} + x^7 + x^6 + 1$ from $\mathbf{F}_2[x]$.

19.4.10 Factor into irreducibles the polynomial $x^{12} + x^9 + x^8 + x^7 + x^6 + x^5 + 1$ from $\mathbf{F}_2[x]$.

19.4.11 Factor into irreducibles the polynomial $x^{12} + x^{10} + x^9 + x^8 + x^7 + x^5 + x^4 + x^3 + 1$ from $\mathbf{F}_2[x]$.

19.5   Euclidean Rings

Based on the important examples of rings with a *division algorithm* and therefore with a *Euclidean algorithm*, the ordinary integers and polynomials over a field, we abstract the property which makes this work. The goal is to prove that *Euclidean rings have unique factorization*. This reasoning applies to the integers as well, so we will have *proven* what had been taken for granted, that the integers have unique factorizations.

An **absolute value** on a commutative ring R is a real-valued function usually denoted $|r|$ of elements $r \in R$ having the properties

- *Multiplicativity:* For all $r, s \in R$, we have $|rs| = |r| \cdot |s|$.

- *Triangle inequality:* For all $r, s \in R$, we have $|r + s| \le |r| + |s|$.

- *Positivity:* If $|r| = 0$ then $r = 0$.

If an absolute value on a ring R has the property that *any non-empty subset S of R has an element of least positive absolute value* (among the collection of absolute values of elements of S), then we say the absolute value is **discrete**.

A commutative ring R with unit is **Euclidean** if there is a *discrete* absolute value on it, denoted $|r|$, so that for any $x \in R$ and for any $0 \neq y \in R$ there are $q, r \in R$, so that

$$x = yq + r \quad \text{with } |r| < |y|$$

The idea is that *we can divide and get a remainder strictly smaller than the divisor.*

The hypothesis that the absolute value be *discrete* in the above sense is critical. Sometimes it is easy to see that this requirement is fulfilled. For example, if $|\ |$ is *integer-valued*, as is the case with the usual absolute value on the ordinary integers, then the usual Well-Ordering Principle assures the 'discreteness'.

The most important examples of Euclidean rings are the ordinary integers $\mathbf{Z}$ and any polynomial ring $k[x]$ where k is a field. The absolute value in $\mathbf{Z}$ is just the usual one, while we have to be a tiny bit creative in the case of polynomials. Define

$$|P(x)| = 2^{\text{degree } P}$$

and define $|0| = 0$. Here the number 2 could be replaced by any other number bigger than 1, and the absolute value obtained would work just as well.

- A Euclidean ring R is an *integral domain.*

Proof: We must show that R has no (nonzero) *zero-divisors*, that is, we must show that if $xy = 0$, then either x or y is 0. Well, if $xy = 0$, then

$$0 = |0| = |xy| = |x| \cdot |y|$$

by the multiplicative property of the norm. Now $|x|$ and $|y|$ are non-negative real numbers, so for their product to be 0, one or the other of $|x|$ and $|y|$ must be 0. And then by the positivity property of the norm it must be that one of x, y themselves is 0, as claimed.   ♣

- In a Euclidean ring R, if $r \in R$ has $|r| < 1$, then $r = 0$.

Proof: Since $|ab| = |a| \cdot |b|$, we have $|r^n| = |r|^n$. If $r \neq 0$, the powers $|r|^n$ form a set of values of the absolute value which have no *least* value: they form a decreasing sequence with limit 0 but not *containing* 0. Thus, $r = 0$.   ♣

- In a Euclidean ring R, an element $u \in R$ is a *unit* (that is, has a multiplicative inverse) if and only if $|u| = 1$. In particular, $|1| = 1$.

Proof: First, since $1 \cdot 1 = 1$, by taking absolute values and using the multiplicative property of the absolute value, we have

$$|1| = |1 \cdot 1| = |1| \cdot |1|$$

The only real numbers z with the property that $z = z^2$ are 0 and 1, and since $1 \neq 0$, we have $|1| \neq 0$, so necessarily $|1| = 1$. If $uv = 1$, then, by taking absolute values, we have $1 = |uv| = |u| \cdot |v|$. Since the only ring element with absolute value strictly smaller than 1 is 0 (from just above), we conclude that both $|u|$ and $|v|$ are ≥ 1. Therefore, since their product is 1, they must both be 1. So the absolute value of a unit is 1. On the other hand, suppose $|u| = 1$. Then, applying the division algorithm, we reduce 1 itself to get

$$1 = q \cdot u + r$$

with $|r| < |u|$. Since $|u| = 1$, $|r| < 1$. But from above we know that this implies $r = 0$. So $1 = qu$, and q is the multiplicative inverse to u. So anything with absolute value 1 is a unit.   ♣

Theorem.   For x, y in a Euclidean ring R, an element of the form $sx + ty$ (for $s, t \in R$) with smallest absolute value is a *gcd* of x, y.

Proof: The discreteness hypothesis on the absolute value assures that among the *nonzero* values $|sx + ty|$ there is one which is minimal. Let $g = sx + ty$ be such. We must show that $g|x$ and $g|y$. Using the division/reduction algorithm, we have

$$x = q(sx + ty) + r$$

with $|r| < |sx + ty|$. Rearranging the equation, we obtain

$$r = (1 - qs)x + (-qt)y$$

So r itself is of the form $s'x + t'y$ with $s', t' \in R$. Since $sx + ty$ had the smallest nonzero absolute value of any such thing, and since $|r| < |sx + ty|$, it must be that $r = 0$. So $sx + ty$ divides x. Similarly, $sx + ty$ must divide y. This proves that $sx + ty$ is a divisor of both x and y. On the other hand, if both $d|x$ and $d|y$, then certainly $d|(sx + ty)$, so this value $sx + ty$ is divisible by every common divisor of x and y.   ♣

Proposition.   In a Euclidean ring R, an element $p \in R$ is prime if $d|p$ implies $|d| = 1$ or $|d| = |p|$. That is, a *proper* divisor d of $r \in R$ has the property that $1 < |d| < |r|$.

Proof: Recall that the definition of a prime element p in a commutative ring R is that if $ab = p$, then either a or b is a unit. To prove both statements of the proposition, it suffices to prove that if $ab = n$ with *neither* a nor b a unit, then $1 < |a| < |n|$. On one hand, if $1 < |a| < |n|$, then, because $|n| = |ab| = |a| \cdot |b|$, we have $|n| > |b| > 1$. Thus, since the units of R are exactly those elements with absolute value 1, neither a nor b is a unit. On the other hand, if $ab = n$ and neither a nor b is a unit, then $1 < |a|$ and $1 < |b|$. Since $|n| = |ab| = |a| \cdot |b|$, it follows that also $|a| < |n|$ and $|b| < |n|$.   ♣

Lemma.   Let p be a prime element in a Euclidean ring R. If $p|ab$, then $p|a$ or $p|b$. Generally, if a prime p divides a product $a_1 \ldots a_n$ then p must divide one of the factors a_i.

Proof: It suffices to prove that if $p|ab$ and $p \nmid a$, then $p|b$. Since $p \nmid a$, and since p is prime, the *gcd* of p and a is just 1. Therefore, there are $s, t \in R$ so that

$$1 = sa + tp$$

Then

$$b = b \cdot 1 = b \cdot (sa + tp) = s(ab) + (bt)p$$

Since $p|ab$, surely p divides the right-hand side. Therefore, $p|b$, as claimed.

Generally, if p divides $a_1 \ldots a_n$, rewrite this as $(a_1)(a_2 \ldots a_n)$. By the first part, either $p|a_1$ or $p|a_2 \ldots a_n$. In the former case we're done. In the latter case, we continue: rewrite $a_2 \ldots a_n = (a_2)(a_3 \ldots a_n)$. So either $p|a_2$ or $p|a_3 \ldots a_n$. Continuing (induction!), we find that p divides at least one of the factors a_i.   ♣

> **Theorem.** In a Euclidean ring R, every element $r \in R$ can be factored into primes as $r = up_1^{e_1} \ldots p_m^{e_m}$ where u is a unit, the p_i are distinct primes, and the e_i are positive integers. If $r = vq_1^{f_1} \ldots q_n^{f_n}$ is another such factorization, with unit v and primes q_i, then $m = n$, and we can reorder and relabel the q_i's so that $q_i = p_i \times u_i$ for some unit u_i, for all indices i. And $e_i = f_i$. That is, the factorization into primes is **essentially unique.**

Proof: First we prove the *existence* of factorizations into primes. Suppose that some $r \in R$ did not have a factorization. Then, invoking the discreteness, there is an $r \in R$ without a factorization and with $|r|$ *smallest* among all elements lacking a prime factorization. If r is prime, then of course it has a factorization, so such r can't be prime. But then r has a proper factorization $r = ab$. Just above, we saw that this means that $1 < |a| < |r|$ and $1 < |b| < |r|$. Since $|a| < |r|$ and $|b| < |r|$, by the minimality of r it must be that both a and b have prime factorizations. Then a prime factorization of r would be obtained by multiplying together the prime factorizations for a and b. (The product of two units is again a unit!)

Now we prove uniqueness of the factorization. Suppose that

$$r = u \cdot p_1^{e_1} \ldots p_m^{e_m}$$

and also

$$r = v \cdot q_1^{f_1} \ldots q_n^{f_n}$$

with primes p_i and q_i. By induction, we could assume that m is the *smallest* integer for which there is a *different* factorization. Since p_1 divides $vq_1^{f_1} \ldots q_n^{f_n}$ and p is prime, by the Key Lemma above p_1 must divide one of the q_i. By relabelling the q_i's, we may suppose that $p_1|q_1$. Since these are both prime, they must differ by a unit, that is, there is a unit u_1 so that $q_1 = u_1 \cdot p_1$. Replacing q_1 by $u_1 p_1$, we get

$$up_1^{e_1} \ldots p_m^{e_m} = vu_1^{f_1} \cdot p_1^{f_1} q_2^{f_2} q_3^{f_3} \ldots q_n^{f_n}$$

Note that $vu_1^{f_1}$ is still a unit. Since $e_1 \geq 1$ and $f_1 \geq 1$, we can *cancel* at least one factor of p_1 from both sides. (We have already proven that a Euclidean ring is an integral domain.)

By induction, since we assumed that m was the smallest integer occurring in an expression of some $r \in R$ in two different ways, after removing the common factor of p_1 the remaining factorizations must be essentially the same. That is, after adjusting the primes by units if necessary, they and their exponents all match.   ♣

One might notice that we didn't use the triangle inequality at all in these proofs. That is indeed so, but in practice anything which is a reasonable candidate for an 'absolute value' in the axiomatic sense suggests itself mostly because it *does* behave like an absolute value in a more down-to-earth sense, which includes a triangle inequality.

20

Cyclotomic Polynomials

Now we will prove the basic results about primitive roots, as corollaries of properties of factors of the simple polynomials $x^N - 1$. These results are of fundamental importance in many parts of mathematics and its applications.

The cyclotomic polynomials occur at first only as auxiliary objects, but they are also of fundamental importance in understanding the algebraic mechanisms at play in $\mathbf{Z}/m$ and in finite fields generally.

20.1 Characteristics

Let k be a field. The **characteristic** char k of k is the smallest positive integer n (if there *is* one) so that

$$\underbrace{1_k + 1_k + \cdots + 1_k}_{n} = 0_k$$

where 1_k is the unit in k and 0_k is the zero. As usual, we abbreviate

$$\ell \cdot 1_k = \underbrace{1_k + 1_k + \cdots + 1_k}_{\ell}$$

.

for positive integers ℓ.

If there is *no* such positive integer n, then the characteristic is said to be 0. Thus,

$$\text{char } \mathbf{Q} = 0$$

By contrast,

$$\text{char } (\mathbf{Z}/p) = p$$

Proposition. The characteristic of a field is a prime number, if it is nonzero. For a field of characteristic p with p prime, if for some positive integer n

$$\underbrace{1_k + 1_k + \cdots + 1_k}_{n} = 0_k$$

then p divides n.

Proof: Suppose that

$$\underbrace{1_k + 1_k + \cdots + 1_k}_{n} = 0_k$$

with n *minimal* to achieve this effect, and that n has a factorization

$$n = a \cdot b$$

with positive integers a and b. Then

$$\underbrace{(1_k + 1_k + \cdots + 1_k)}_{a} \cdot \underbrace{(1_k + 1_k + \cdots + 1_k)}_{b} = \underbrace{1_k + 1_k + \cdots + 1_k}_{n} = 0_k$$

Since a field has no proper zero-divisors, it must be that either $a \cdot 1_k = 0$ or $b \cdot 1_k = 0$. By the hypothesis that n was minimal, if $a \cdot 1_k = 0$ then $a = n$, and similarly for b. Thus, the factorizaton $n = a \cdot b$ was not *proper*. Since n has no proper factorization, it is prime.

Suppose that $n \cdot 1_k = 0_k$. By the division algorithm, we have $n = qp + r$ with $0 \leq r < p$. Then

$$0_k = n \cdot 1_k = q(p \cdot 1_k) + r \cdot 1_k = 0_k + r \cdot 1_k$$

From this, $r \cdot 1_k = 0_k$. Since $r < p$ and p was the least positive integer with $p \cdot 1_k = 0_k$, it follows that $r = 0$ and p divides n.   ♣

Fields with positive characteristic p have a peculiarity which is at first counterintuitive, but which plays an important role in both theory and applications:

Proposition. Let k be a field of positive characteristic p. Then for any polynomial

$$f(x) = a_n x^n + a_{n-1} x^{n-1} + \cdots + a_2 x^2 + a_1 x + a_0$$

in $k[x]$ we have

$$f(x)^p = a_n^p x^{pn} + a_{n-1}^p x^{p(n-1)} + \cdots + a_2^p x^{2p} + a_1^p x^p + a_0^p$$

Proof: Recall that p divides binomial coefficients $\binom{p}{i}$ with $0 < i < p$. Therefore, for $0 < i < p$,

$$\binom{p}{i} \cdot 1_k = 0 \cdot k$$

Thus, for $a_n \in k$ and any polynomial $g(x)$ with coefficients in k,

$$(a_n x^n + g(x))^p = (a_n x^n)^p + \sum_{0<i<p} \binom{p}{i} (a_n x^n)^{p-i} g(x)^i + g(x)^p$$

All the middle terms have a coefficient

$$\binom{p}{i} \cdot 1_k = 0_k$$

so they disappear. Thus,

$$(a_n x^n + g(x))^p = a_n^p x^{pn} + g(x)^p$$

The same assertion applies to $g(x)$ itself. Take

$$g(x) = a_{n-1} x^{n-1} + h(x)$$

Then

$$g(x) = a_{n-1}^p x^{p(n-1)} + h(x)^p$$

Continuing (that is, doing an induction), we obtain the result for f.   ♣

For example, with coefficients in $k = \mathbf{Z}/p$ with p prime, we have

$$(x+1)^p = x^p + \sum_{0 < i < p} \binom{p}{i} x^i + 1 = x^p + 1$$

Also

$$\begin{array}{rcl} (x^2 + 1)^p & = & x^{2p} + 1 \\ (x^2 + x + 1)^p & = & x^{2p} + x^p + 1 \end{array}$$

and such things.

20.2 Multiple Factors

There is a very simple device to detect repeated occurrence of a factor in polynomials (with coefficients in a field). This is very useful both theoretically and in computational situations. Let k be a *field*. For a polynomial

$$f(x) = c_n x^n + \cdots c_1 x + c_0$$

with coefficients c_i in k, we *define*

$$f'(x) = n c_n x^{n-1} + (n-1) c_{n-1} x^{n-2} + \cdots + 3 c_3 x^2 + 2 c_2 x + c_1$$

Remark: Note that we simply *define* a 'derivative' this way, purely algebraically, without taking any limits. Of course (!) this formula is still supposed to yield a thing with familiar properties, such as the product rule. So we've simply used our calculus experience to make a 'good guess'.

Lemma. For two polynomials f, g in the ring $k[x]$ of polynomials in x with coefficients in k, and for $r \in k$,

- $(r \cdot f)' = r \cdot f'$
- $(f + g)' = f' + g'$
- $(fg) = f'g + fg'$

Proof: The first assertion is easy: let $f(x) = a_m x^m + \cdots + a_0$, and compute

$$(r \cdot (a_m x^m + \cdots + a_0))' = (r a_m x^m + r a_{m-1} x^{m-1} + \cdots + r a_0)'$$

$$= m \cdot (r a_m) x^{m-1} + (m-1) \cdot (r a_{m-1}) x^{m-2} + \cdots + r a_1 + 0$$

$$= r(m \cdot (a_m) x^{m-1} + (m-1) \cdot (a_{m-1}) x^{m-2} + \cdots + a_1 + 0) = r \cdot f'(x)$$

The second assertion is also not hard: let $f(x) = a_m x^m + \cdots + a_0$ and $g(x) = b_n x^n + \cdots + b_0$. Padding the one of smaller degree with terms of the form $0 \cdot x^\ell$, we can suppose without loss of generality that $m = n$. (This simplifies notation considerably!) Then

$$(f(x) + g(x))' = ((a_n + b_n)x^n + \cdots + (a_1 + b_1)x + (a_0 + b_0)x^0)'$$

$$= n(a_n + b_n)x^{n-1} + (n-1)(a_{n-1} + b_{n-1})x^{n-2} + \cdots + 1(a_1 + b_1)x^0 + 0 \cdot x^0$$

$$= \left(na_n x^{n-1} + (n-1)a_{n-1}x^{n-2} + \cdots + 1 \cdot a_1 x^0\right)$$

$$+ \left(nb_n x^{n-1} + \cdots + (n-1)b_{n-1}x^{n-2} + \cdots + 1 \cdot b_1 x^0\right)$$

$$= f'(x) + g'(x)$$

For the third property, let's first see what happens when f and g are *monomials*, that is, are simply $f(x) = ax^m$, $g(x) = bx^n$. On one hand, we have

$$(fg)' = (ax^m \cdot bx^n)' = (abx^{m+n})' = ab(m+n)x^{m+n-1}$$

On the other hand,

$$f'g + fg' = amx^{m-1} \cdot bx^n + ax^m \cdot bnx^{n-1} = ab(m+n)x^{m+n-1}$$

after simplifying. This proves the product rule for monomials.

To approach the general product rule, let

$$f(x) = a_m x^m + \cdots + a_0$$

$$g(x) = b_n x^n + \cdots + b_0$$

The coefficient of x^ℓ in the product $f(x)g(x)$ is

$$\sum_{i+j=\ell} a_i \cdot b_j$$

Then the coefficient of $x^{\ell-1}$ in the derivative of the product is

$$\ell \sum_{i+j=\ell} a_i \cdot b_j$$

On the other hand, the coefficient of $x^{\ell-1}$ in $f'g$ is

$$\sum_{i+j=\ell} (ia_i) \cdot b_j$$

and the coefficient of $x^{\ell-1}$ in fg' is

$$\sum_{i+j=\ell} a_i \cdot jb_j$$

Adding these two together, we find that the coefficient of $x^{\ell-1}$ in $f'g + fg'$ is

$$\sum_{i+j=\ell} a_i \cdot b_j \cdot (i+j) = \ell \sum_{i+j=\ell} a_i \cdot b_j$$

which matches the coefficient in $(fg)'$. This proves the product rule.   ♣

Proposition.   Let f be a polynomial with coefficients in a field k. Let P be a polynomial with coefficients in k. On one hand, if P^2 divides f, then P divides $\gcd(f, f')$. On the other hand, if the characteristic p of k is positive, if P is irreducible, if every element $a \in k$ has a pth root in k, and if P divides $\gcd(f, f')$, then P^2 divides f. (Note that the latter condition holds, for example, for finite fields $\mathbf{Z}/p$ with p prime.)

Proof: On one hand, suppose $f = P^2 \cdot g$. Then, using the product rule,

$$f' = 2PP' \cdot g + P^2 \cdot g' = P \cdot (2P'g + Pg')$$

which is certainly a multiple of P. This half of the argument did not use the irreducibility of P. On the other hand, suppose that P divides both f and f' (and show that actually P^2 divides f). Dividing f/P by P, we obtain $f/P = Q \cdot P + R$ with the degree of R less than that of P. Then $f = QP^2 + RP$. Taking the derivative, we have

$$f' = Q'P^2 + 2QPP' + R'P + RP'$$

By hypothesis P divides f'. All the terms on the right-hand side except possibly RP' are divisible by P, so P divides RP'. Since P is irreducible and it divides the product RP', it must divide either R or P'. If it divides R, then we've shown that P^2 divides f, so we're done.

If P fails to divide R, then P must divide P'. Since P' is of lower degree than P, if P divides it, then P' must be the zero polynomial. Let's see that this is impossible for P irreducible. Let

$$P(x) = a_n x^n + a_{n-1} x^{n-1} + \cdots + a_2 x^2 + a_1 x + a_0$$

Then

$$P'(x) = n a_n x^{n-1} + (n-1) a_{n-1} x^{n-2} + \cdots + 2 a_2 x^1 + a_1 + 0$$

For this to be the zero polynomial it must be that

$$\ell \cdot a_\ell = 0$$

for all indices ℓ. That is, for any index ℓ with $a_\ell \neq 0$ it must be that $\ell \cdot 1_k = 0_k$. Since at least one coefficient of P is nonzero, this implies that the *characteristic* of k is not 0, so from above is some prime p. From above, $\ell \cdot 1_k = 0_k$ implies that p divides ℓ. That is, the characteristic p divides ℓ if the coefficient a_ℓ is nonzero. So we can write

$$f(x) = a_{pm} x^{pn} + a_{p(m-1)} x^{p(m-1)} + a_{p(m-2)} x^{p(m-2)} + \cdots + a_{2p} x^{2p} + a_p x^p + a_0$$

Let b_i be a pth root of a_i in k. From above, the latter expression is the pth power of

$$b_{pm}x^n + b_{p(m-1)}x^{(m-1)} + b_{p(m-2)}x^{(m-2)} + \cdots + b_{2p}x^2 + b_p x + b_0$$

But if P is a pth power, it is certainly not irreducible. Therefore, for P irreducible it cannot be that P' is the zero polynomial. Therefore, above it must have been that $R = 0$, which is to say that P^2 divides f, as claimed.   ♣

Exercises

20.2.01 The polynomial $x^4 + x^2 + 1$ in $\mathbf{F}_2[x]$ has a repeated factor. Find it.

20.2.02 The polynomial $x^6 + x^4 + x^2 + 1$ in $\mathbf{F}_2[x]$ has a repeated factor. Find it.

20.2.03 The polynomial $x^8 + x^7 + x^6 + x^4 + x^3 + x + 1$ in $\mathbf{F}_2[x]$ has a repeated factor. Find it.

20.2.04 The polynomial $x^9 + x^8 + x^6 + x^5 + x^4 + x^3 + 1$ in $\mathbf{F}_2[x]$ has a repeated factor. Find it.

20.2.05 The polynomial $x^8 + x^7 + x^5 + x^4 + x^2 + x + 1$ in $\mathbf{F}_2[x]$ has a repeated factor. Find it.

20.3 Cyclotomic Polynomials

For b in a field k, the **exponent** of b is the smallest positive integer n (if it exists at all) so that $b^n = 1$. That is, $b^n = 1$ but $b^d \neq 1$ for $0 < d < n$. In other words, b is a root of the polynomial $x^n - 1$ but not of $x^d - 1$ for any smaller d. What we'll do here is describe the polynomial φ_n, the nth **cyclotomic polynomial**, of which b must be a root in order to have exponent n.

Fix a field k, and an integer n *not* divisible by the characteristic of k. (If the characteristic is 0, then this is no condition at all.)

Lemma. For m, n two integers (divisible by the characteristic or not)

$$\gcd(x^m - 1, x^n - 1) = x^{\gcd(m,n)} - 1$$

$$\operatorname{lcm}(x^m - 1, x^n - 1) = x^{\operatorname{lcm}(m,n)} - 1$$

Proof: We do induction on the maximum of m and n. First, if by chance $m = n$, then $x^m - 1 = x^n - 1$ and we are certainly done. Second, if $m > n$, doing a fragment of a division, we have

$$x^m - 1 - x^{m-n} \cdot (x^n - 1) = x^{m-n} - 1$$

So if D is a polynomial, dividing both $x^m - 1$ and $x^n - 1$, then D divides $x^{m-n} - 1$ as well. By induction,

$$\gcd(x^{m-n} - 1, x^n - 1) = x^{\gcd(m-n,n)} - 1$$

But
$$\gcd(m, n) = \gcd(m - n, n)$$

and
$$x^m - 1 = x^{m-n} \cdot (x^n - 1) + x^{m-n} - 1$$

so
$$\gcd(x^m - 1, x^n - 1) = \gcd(x^{m-n} - 1, x^n - 1)$$

If $m < n$, we reverse the roles of m and n: let's repeat the argument. Doing a fragment of a division:

$$x^n - 1 - x^{n-m} \cdot (x^m - 1) = x^{n-m} - 1$$

So if D is a polynomial dividing both $x^m - 1$ and $x^n - 1$, then D divides $x^{n-m} - 1$ as well. By induction,

$$\gcd(x^{n-m} - 1, x^n - 1) = x^{\gcd(n-m,n)} - 1$$

But
$$\gcd(m, n) = \gcd(n - m, n)$$

and
$$x^n - 1 = x^{n-m} \cdot (x^m - 1) + x^{n-m} - 1$$

so
$$\gcd(x^m - 1, x^n - 1) = \gcd(x^{n-m} - 1, x^m - 1)$$

This completes the induction step. (The discussion of the least common multiple is essentially identical, and also follows from this discussion.)   ♣

Lemma.   Let n be a positive integer not divisible by the characteristic of the field k. Then the polynomial $x^n - 1$ has no repeated factors.

Proof: From above, it suffices to check that the *gcd* of $x^n - 1$ and its derivative nx^{n-1} is 1. Since the characteristic of the field does not divide n, $n \cdot 1_k$ has a multiplicative inverse t in k. Then, doing a division with remainder,

$$(x^n - 1) - (tx) \cdot (nx^{n-1}) = -1$$

Thus, the *gcd* is 1.   ♣

Now suppose that n is not divisible by the characteristic of the field k, and define the nth **cyclotomic polynomial** $\varphi_n(x)$ (with coefficients in k) by

$$\varphi_n(x) = \frac{x^n - 1}{lcm \text{ of all } x^d - 1 \text{ with } 0 < d < n,\ d \text{ dividing } n}$$

where the least common multiple is taken to be *monic*.

Theorem. Let m and n be integers neither of which is divisible by the characteristic of the field k. Then

- φ_n is monic.

- $\gcd(\varphi_m, \varphi_n) = 1$.

- The degree of φ_n is $\varphi(n)$ (Euler's phi-function).

- There is a more efficient description of $\varphi_n(x)$:

$$\varphi_n(x) = \frac{x^n - 1}{\prod_{1 \leq d < n, d \mid n} \varphi_d(x)}$$

- The polynomial $x^n - 1$ factors as

$$x^n - 1 = \prod_{1 \leq d \leq n, d \mid n} \varphi_d(x)$$

Proof: First, we really should check that the least common multiple of the $x^d - 1$ with $d < n$ and $d \mid n$ divides $x^n - 1$. We know that $d \mid n$ (and $d > 0$) implies that $x^d - 1$ divides $x^n - 1$ (either by high school algebra or from the lemma above). Therefore, using *unique factorization* of polynomials with coefficients in a field, it follows that the least common multiple of a collection of things each dividing $x^n - 1$ will also divide $x^n - 1$.

Next, the assertion that φ_n is *monic* follows from its definition, since it is the quotient of the monic polynomial $x^n - 1$ by the monic *lcm* of polynomials.

Next, to determine the *gcd* of φ_m and φ_n, first observe that φ_m divides $x^m - 1$ and φ_n divides $x^n - 1$, so

$$\gcd(\varphi_m, \varphi_n) \text{ divides } \gcd(x^m - 1, x^n - 1)$$

In the lemma above we computed that

$$\gcd(x^m - 1, x^n - 1) = x^{\gcd(m,n)} - 1$$

But from its definition, φ_m divides

$$\frac{x^m - 1}{x^{\gcd(m,n)} - 1}$$

so $\gcd(\varphi_m, \varphi_n)$ also divides this. Since n is not divisible by the characteristic, the lemma above shows that $x^n - 1$ has no repeated factors. Therefore, from the fact that $\gcd(\varphi_n, \varphi_m)$ divides $x^{\gcd(m,n)} - 1$ and also divides $(x^n - 1)/(x^{\gcd(m,n)} - 1)$ we conclude that $\gcd(x^m - 1, x^n - 1) = 1$.

Next, we use induction to prove that

$$x^n - 1 = \prod_{1 \leq d \leq n, \, d \mid n} \varphi_d(x)$$

For $n = 1$ the assertion is true. From the definition of φ_n, we have

$$x^n - 1 = \varphi_n(x) \cdot \text{lcm}\{x^d - 1 : d|n, 0 < d < n\}$$

By induction, for $d < n$

$$x^d - 1 = \prod_{0 < e < d, e|d} \varphi_e(x)$$

Since we have already shown that for $m \neq n$ the *gcd* of φ_m and φ_n is 1, we have

$$\text{lcm}\{x^d - 1 : d|n, 0 < d < n\} = \prod_{d|n, d<n} \varphi_d(x)$$

Thus,

$$x^n - 1 = \varphi_n(x) \cdot \prod_{d|n, d<n} \varphi_d(x)$$

as claimed.

The assertion about the degree of φ_n follows from the identity proven earlier for Euler's phi-function:

$$\sum_{d|n, d>0} \varphi(d) = n$$

This completes the proof of the theorem.   ♣

Exercises

20.3.01 Determine the cyclotomic polynomials φ_2, φ_3, φ_4, φ_5, φ_6, φ_8, φ_9, φ_{12}.

20.3.02 Use a bit of cleverness to avoid working too much, and determine the cyclotomic polynomials φ_{14}, φ_{16}, φ_{18}, φ_{20}, φ_{24}, φ_{25}.

20.3.03 Use some cleverness as well as perseverance to determine the cyclotomic polynomials φ_{15}, φ_{21}.

20.3.04 (*) Find a cyclotomic polynomial that has coefficients other than $0, +1, -1$.

20.4 Primitive Roots

Now we can prove that the multiplicative group $k^\times$ of the any finite field k is a *cyclic group*. A generator of $k^\times$ is sometimes called a *primitive root* for k. This property of $k^\times$ is essential for the working of modern primality tests and modern factorization algorithms.

Theorem. Let k be a finite field. Then $k^\times$ is a cyclic group.

Proof: Let q be the number of elements in k. The group of units $k^\times$ is a group. Since k is a field, any $b \neq 0$ has a multiplicative inverse in k. So the order of $k^\times$ is $q - 1$. Thus, by corollaries to Lagrange's theorem, for $b \neq 0$,

$$b^{q-1} = 1$$

That is, any nonzero element of k is a root of the polynomial $f(x) = x^{q-1} - 1$. On the other hand, by the Fundamental Theorem of Algebra, this polynomial has at most $q - 1$ roots in k. Therefore, it has *exactly* $q - 1$ (distinct) roots in k.

Let p be the characteristic of k. Certainly p cannot divide $q - 1$, since if it did then the derivative of $f(x) = x^{q-1} - 1$ would be zero, so $\gcd(f, f') = f$, and f would have multiple roots. We have just noted that f has $q - 1$ distinct roots, so this doesn't happen.

Since the characteristic of k does not divide $q - 1$, we can apply the results from just above concerning cyclotomic polynomials. Thus,

$$x^{q-1} - 1 = \prod_{d|q-1} \varphi_d(x)$$

Since $x^{q-1} - 1$ has $q - 1$ roots in k, and since the φ_d's here are relatively prime to each other, each φ_d with $d|q - 1$ must have number of roots (in k) equal to its degree. Thus, φ_d for $d|q - 1$ has $\varphi(d) > 0$ roots in k (Euler's phi-function).

Finally, the roots of $\varphi_{q-1}(x)$ are those field elements b so that $b^{q-1} = 1$ and no smaller positive power than $q - 1$ has this property. The primitive roots are exactly the roots of $\varphi_{q-1}(x)$. The cyclotomic polynomial φ_{q-1} has $\varphi(q - 1)$ roots. Therefore, there are $\varphi(q - 1) > 0$ primitive roots. That is, the group $k^\times$ has a generator, that is, is cyclic.   ♣

20.5 Primitive Roots mod p

Now we can verify that the multiplicative group $\mathbf{Z}/p^\times$ of the finite field $\mathbf{Z}/p$ with p elements is a *cyclic group*. Any generator of it is called a *primitive root* for $\mathbf{Z}/p$. This property of $\mathbf{Z}/p$ (and other finite fields) is essential in primality tests and factorization algorithms.

Theorem. The group of units $\mathbf{Z}/p^\times$ is a cyclic group for p prime.

Proof: As corollary of our study of cyclotomic polynomials, we've already proven that the multiplicative group $k^\times$ of any finite field k is cyclic. Therefore, all we need do is check that $\mathbf{Z}/p$ is a field. That is, we must check that any nonzero element $b \in \mathbf{Z}/p$ has a multiplicative inverse.

Let's repeat the explanation of why there is a multiplicative inverse, even though we've given it before in other contexts. Indeed, since p is prime, if $b \neq 0 \bmod p$, then $\gcd(p, b) = 1$. Thus, there are integers s, t so that $sp + tb = 1$. Then, looking at the latter equation modulo p, we see that t is a multiplicative inverse to b modulo p.   ♣

Exercises

20.5.01 Find primitive roots modulo 11 and 13.

20.5.02 Find primitive roots modulo 17.

20.5.03 Explain why it is relatively easy to tell that 2 is not a primitive root modulo 7, modulo 17, and modulo 31.

20.5.04 Show that neither 2 nor 3 is a primitive root modulo 23, but that 5 is a primitive root.

20.5.05 Show that none of $2, 3, 4, 5$ is a primitive root modulo 41, but that 6 is a primitive root.

20.5.06 Show that no integer smaller than 19 is a primitive root modulo 191, but that 19 is a primitive root.

20.6 Prime Powers

To prove that there is a primitive root in $\mathbf{Z}/p^e$ for p an odd prime is not difficult, once we know that there is a primitive root for $\mathbf{Z}/p$. A minor adaption of this applies as well to $\mathbf{Z}/2p^e$.

> **Theorem.** For an odd prime p, $\mathbf{Z}/p^e$ and $\mathbf{Z}/2p^e$ have primitive roots. That is, the multiplicative groups $\mathbf{Z}/p^{e\times}$ and $\mathbf{Z}/2p^{e\times}$ are *cyclic*.

> **Corollary.** In fact, for an integer g which is a primitive root mod p, either g is a primitive root mod p^e and mod $2p^e$ for all $e \geq 1$, or else $(1+p)g$ is. In particular, if $g^{p-1} \neq 1 \bmod p^2$, then g is a primitive root mod p^e and mod $2p^e$ for all $e \geq 1$. Otherwise, $(1+p)g$ is.

The following proposition is of interest in its own right, and is necessary to prove the theorem on primitive roots. Its point is that understanding the order of *certain* types of elements in $\mathbf{Z}/p^{e\times}$ is much more elementary than the trouble we went through to show that $\mathbf{Z}/p$ has a primitive root. We'll prove this proposition before proving the theorem and corollary on primitive roots.

> **Proposition.** Let p be an odd prime. For integers $1 \leq k \leq e$, and for an integer x with $p \nmid x$, the order of an element $1 + p^k x$ in $\mathbf{Z}/p^{e\times}$ is p^{e-k}. In particular, for $p \nmid x$ and $k \geq 1$,
> $$(1 + p^k x)^{p^\ell} = 1 + p^{k+\ell} y$$

with $y = x \bmod p$.

Proof: The main trick here is that a prime p divides the binomial coefficients
$$\binom{p}{1}, \binom{p}{2}, \ldots, \binom{p}{p-2}, \binom{p}{p-1}$$
Also, the hypothesis that $p > 2$ is essential.

Let's first compute
$$(1 + p^k x)^p = 1 + \binom{p}{1}p^k x + \binom{p}{2}p^{2k}x^2 + \cdots + \binom{p}{p-1}p^{(p-1)k}x^{p-1} + p^{pk}x^p$$

$$= 1 + p^{k+1} \cdot \underbrace{\left(x + \binom{p}{2} p^{2k-(k+1)} x^2 + \cdots + p^{pk-(k+1)} x^p \right)}_{y}$$

Since p divides those binomial coefficients, the expression y differs from x by a multiple of p. Looking at the very last term, $p^{pk-(k+1)} x^p$, we see that it is necessary that $pk - (k+1) \geq 1$ for this to work. Since all we know about k is that $k \geq 1$, it must be that $p > 2$, or this inequality could fail. This explains why the argument fails for the prime 2. So we have proven that

$$(1 + p^k x)^p = 1 + p^{k+1} y$$

with $y = x \bmod p$. Repeating this argument (that is, doing an induction), we get

$$(1 + p^k x)^{p^\ell} = 1 + p^{k+\ell} y$$

with $y = x \bmod p$. This is the formula asserted in the proposition.

Now let's see that this formula gives the assertion about orders. First we must see what the order in $\mathbf{Z}/p^{e\times}$ of elements of the form $1 + px$ can be. To do this we will invoke Lagrange's theorem. So we have to count the number of elements of $\mathbf{Z}/p^{e\times}$ expressible as $1 + px$. In the first place, for any integer x the integer $1 + px$ is relatively prime to p, so gives an element of $\mathbf{Z}/p^{e\times}$. On the other hand, if

$$1 + px = 1 + px' \bmod p^e$$

then $p^e | (1 + px - 1 - px')$. That is, $p^{e-1} | x - x'$. So the integers $1 + px$ and $1 + px'$ give the *same* element of $\mathbf{Z}/p^{e\times}$ only if $x = x' \bmod p^{e-1}$. Thus, the p^{e-1} integers $x = 0, 1, 2, \ldots, p^{e-1} - 1$ give all the elements of $\mathbf{Z}/p^{e\times}$ expressible as $1 + px$.

By Lagrange's theorem, the order of any element $1 + px$ in $\mathbf{Z}/p^{e\times}$ must divide p^{e-1}.

This limitation allows our computation of $(1 + p^k x)^{p^\ell}$ to give a definitive answer to the question of order: for $p \nmid x$,

$$(1 + p^k x)^{p^\ell} = 1 + p^{k+\ell} y$$

with $y = x \bmod p$, so this is not $1 \bmod p^e$ unless $k + \ell \geq e$. (And if $k + \ell \geq e$, it *is* $1 \bmod p^e$.) Thus,

$$\text{(multiplicative) order of } 1 + p^k x \bmod p^e \text{ is } p^{e-k}$$

This proves the proposition.   ♣

Proof: The assertion of the corollary is stronger than the theorem, so it certainly suffices to prove the more specific assertion of the corollary in order to prove the theorem.

Before the most serious part of the proof, let's see why an integer g which is a primitive root for $\mathbf{Z}/p^e$ will also be a primitive root for $\mathbf{Z}/2p^{e\times}$. The main point is that for an odd prime p

$$\varphi(2p^e) = (2-1)(p-1)p^{e-1} = (p-1)p^{e-1} = \varphi(p^e)$$

Let g be a primitive root modulo p^e. Then $\ell = \varphi(p^e)$ is the smallest exponent so that $g^\ell = 1 \bmod p^e$. Thus, surely there is no *smaller* exponent ℓ so that $g^\ell = 1 \bmod 2p^e$, since $p^e | 2p^e$. Therefore, a primitive root mod p^e also serves as a primitive root mod p^e.

Now for the central case, that of primitive roots for $\mathbf{Z}/p^e$. That is, we want to show that the multiplicative group $\mathbf{Z}/p^{e\times}$ is of the form $\langle g \rangle$ for some g. Let g_1 be a primitive root mod p, which we already know exists for *other* reasons. The plan is to 'adjust' g_1 suitably to obtain a primitive root mod p^e, somewhat in the spirit of Hensel's lemma. But it turns out that at most a single adjustment is necessary altogether, so in some regards the situation is *simpler* than a Hensel's lemma application.

If (by good luck?)

$$g_1^{p-1} = 1 + px$$

with $p \nmid x$, then let's show that g_1 is already a primitive root mod p^e for any $e \geq 1$. By Lagrange's theorem, the order of g_1 in $\mathbf{Z}/p^{e\times}$ is a divisor of $\varphi(p^e) = (p-1)p^{e-1}$. Since $p-1$ is the smallest positive exponent ℓ so that $g_1^\ell = 1 \bmod p$, $p-1$ divides the order of g_1 in $\mathbf{Z}/p^{e\times}$ (from our discussion of cyclic subgroups). Thus, the order of g_1 is in the list

$$p-1, \ (p-1)p, \ (p-1)p^2, \ \ldots, \ (p-1)p^{e-1}$$

Thus, the question is to find the smallest positive ℓ so that

$$g_1^{(p-1)p^\ell} = 1 \bmod p^e$$

We are assuming that

$$g_1^{p-1} = 1 + px$$

with $p \nmid x$, so the question is to find the smallest positive ℓ so that

$$(1 + px)^{p^\ell} = 1 \bmod p^e$$

From the proposition, the smallest positive ℓ with this property is $\ell = e - 1$. That is, we have proven that g_1 is a primitive root mod p^e for *every* $e \geq 1$.

Now suppose that

$$g_1^{p-1} = 1 + px$$

with $p | x$. Then consider

$$g = (1 + p)g_1$$

Certainly g is still a primitive root mod p, because $g = g_1 \bmod p$. And we compute

$$(1+p)^{p-1} = 1 + \binom{p-1}{1}p + \binom{p-1}{2}p^2 + \cdots + \binom{p-1}{p-2}p^{p-2} + p^{p-1}$$

$$1 + p \cdot \underbrace{\left(\binom{p-1}{1} + \binom{p-1}{2}p + \binom{p-1}{3}p^2 + \cdots\right)}_{y} = 1 + py$$

Since

$$\binom{p-1}{1} = p - 1$$

we see that

$$y = p - 1 \bmod p$$

so $p \nmid y$. Thus,

$$g^{p-1} = ((1+p)g_1)^{p-1} = (1+py)(1+px) = 1 + p(y + x + pxy)$$

Since $p|x$, we have

$$y + x + pxy = y \bmod p$$

In particular, $p \nmid y + x + pxy$. Thus, by adjusting the primitive root a bit, we have returned to the first case above, that g^{p-1} is of the form $g^{p-1} = 1 + pz$ with $p \nmid z$. In that case we already saw that such g is a primitive root mod p^e for any $e \geq 1$.

This finishes the proof of existence of primitive roots in $\mathbf{Z}/p^e$ for p an odd prime. ♣

20.7 Counting Primitive Roots

After proving *existence* of primitive roots, it is at least equally interesting to have an idea *how many* there are.

Theorem. If $\mathbf{Z}/n$ has a primitive root, then there are exactly

$$\varphi(\varphi(n))$$

primitive roots mod n. (Yes, that is Euler's *phi* of Euler's *phi* of n.) For example, there are

$$\varphi(\varphi(p^e)) = \varphi(p-1) \cdot (p-1)p^{e-2}$$

primitive roots mod p^e for an odd prime p.

Proof: The hypothesis that $\mathbf{Z}/n$ has a primitive root is that the multiplicative group $\mathbf{Z}/n^\times$ is *cyclic*. That is, for some element g (the 'primitive root')

$$\mathbf{Z}/n^\times = \langle g \rangle$$

Of course, the order $|g|$ of g must be the order $\varphi(n)$ of $\mathbf{Z}/n^\times$. From general discussion of cyclic subgroups, we know that

$$g^0, g^1, g^2, g^3, \ldots, g^{\varphi(n)-1}$$

is a complete list of all the different elements of $\langle g \rangle$. And

$$\text{order of } g^k = \frac{\text{order of } g}{\gcd(k, |g|)}$$

So the generators for $\langle g \rangle$ are exactly the elements

$$g^k \text{with } 1 \leq k < |g| \text{ and } k \text{ relatively prime to } |g|$$

By definition of Euler's φ-function, there are $\varphi(|g|)$ of these. Thus, since $|g| = \varphi(n)$, there are $\varphi(\varphi(n))$ primitive roots. ♣

Corollary. For an odd prime p, the fraction $\varphi(p-1)/p$ of the elements of $\mathbf{Z}/p^{e\times}$ consists of primitive roots.

Proof: From the theorem just proven the ratio of primitive roots to all elements is

$$\frac{\varphi(\varphi(p^e))}{\varphi(p^e)} = \frac{\varphi(p-1) \cdot (p-1)p^{e-2}}{(p-1)p^{e-1}} = \frac{\varphi(p-1)}{p}$$

as claimed. ♣

Remark: Thus, there are relatively *many* primitive roots modulo p^e.

20.8 Non-Existence

For *generic* integers n, there is *no* primitive root in $\mathbf{Z}/n$.

Theorem. If n is *not* 2, 4, nor of the forms p^e, $2p^e$ for p an odd prime (and e a positive integer), then there is *no* primitive root modulo n.

Proof: First, let's look at $\mathbf{Z}/2^e$ with $e \geq 3$. Any $b \in \mathbf{Z}/2^{e\times}$ can be written as $b = 1 + 2x$ for integer x. Then

$$(1 + 2x)^2 = 1 + 4x + 4x^2 = 1 + 4x(x + 1)$$

The peculiar feature here is that for any integer x, the expression $x(x+1)$ is divisible by 2. Indeed, if x is even, surely $x(x+1)$ is even, and if x is odd, then $x+1$ is even and $x(x+1)$ is again even. Thus,

$$(1 + 2x)^2 = 1 \bmod 8$$

(rather than merely modulo 4). And from the pattern

$$(1 + 2^k x)^2 = 1 + 2^{k+1} x + 2^{2k} x^2$$

we can prove by induction that

$$(1 + 8x)^{2^{e-3}} = 1 \bmod 2^e$$

Putting this together, we see that

$$(1 + 2x)^{2^{e-2}} = 1 \bmod 2^e$$

But $2^{e-2} < 2^{e-1} = \varphi(2^e)$. That is, there cannot be a primitive root modulo 2^e with $e > 2$.

Now consider n not a power of 2. Then write $n = p^e m$ with p an odd prime not dividing m. By Euler's theorem, we know that

$$b^{\varphi(p^e)} = 1 \bmod p^e$$

$$b^{\varphi(m)} = 1 \bmod m$$

Let $M = \mathrm{lcm}(\varphi(p^e), \varphi(m))$. Then (as usual)

$$b^M = (b^{\varphi(p^e)})^{M/\varphi(p^e)} = 1^{M/\varphi(p^e)} = 1 \bmod p^e$$

and

$$b^M = (b^{\varphi(m)})^{M/\varphi(m)} = 1^{M/\varphi(m)} = 1 \bmod m$$

Thus, certainly

$$b^M = 1 \bmod p^e m$$

But a primitive root g would have the property that no smaller exponent ℓ than $\varphi(p^e m)$ has the property that $g^\ell = 1 \bmod p^e m$. Therefore, unless

$$\gcd(\varphi(p^e), \varphi(m)) = 1$$

we'll have

$$\mathrm{lcm}(\varphi(p^e), \varphi(m)) < \varphi(p^e)\, \varphi(m) = \varphi(p^e m)$$

which would deny the possibility that there be a primitive root.

Thus, we need $\varphi(m)$ relatively prime to $\varphi(p^e) = (p - 1)p^{e-1}$. Since $p - 1$ is even, this means that $\varphi(m)$ must be odd. If an odd prime q divides m, then $q - 1$ divides $\varphi(m)$, which would make $\varphi(m)$ even, which is impossible. Thus, no odd prime can divide m. Further, if any power of 2 greater than just 2 itself divides m, again $\varphi(m)$ would be even, and no primitive root could exist.

Thus, except for the cases where we've already proven that a primitive root *does* exist, there is no primitive root mod n. ♣

20.9 Search Algorithm

If we know the factorization of $p - 1$ for a prime p, then there is a reasonable algorithm to *find* a primitive root modulo p, since we'll have an efficient criterion to *check* whether or not a candidate b is a primitive root modulo p.

Lemma.   Let p be a prime. An integer b is a primitive root modulo p if and only if $b^{(p-1)/q} \neq 1 \bmod p$ for all primes q dividing $p - 1$.

Proof: If b is a primitive root, certainly the conditions of the lemma are met. On the other hand, suppose that the conditions of the lemma are fulfilled for a particular b. Let q^e be the exact power of q dividing $p - 1$, and let t be the order of q in $\mathbf{Z}/p^\times$. Then $t | p - 1$ by Fermat's Little Theorem. If q^e did not divide t, then still t would divide $(p - 1)/q$. But by hypothesis t does not divide $(p - 1)/q$. Therefore, $q^e | t$. Since this is true for every prime q dividing $p - 1$, the least common multiple m of all these prime powers *also* divides t, by unique factorization of integers. Of course, the least common multiple of all prime powers dividing any number $p - 1$ is that number itself. Thus, $m = p - 1$, and $p - 1$ divides t. Since t divides $p - 1$, this gives $t = p - 1$. That is, b is a primitive root modulo p.   ♣

Remark: Note that the number of primes dividing $p - 1$ is well below $\log_2 p$.

Remark: Recall that the number of primitive roots modulo p (for p prime) is $\varphi(p-1)$, which is typically above $(p-1)/4$. Thus, choosing primitive-root candidates at random has at least a $1/4$ chance of success. Thus, as a heuristic, we should usually expect to find a primitive root after about 2 or 3 tries.

The algorithm to find a primitive root b modulo a prime p, using knowledge of the factorization of $p - 1$, is as follows:

- Pick a random b.

- For each prime q dividing $p - 1$, compute $b^{(p-1)/q} \bmod p$.

- If *any* of these values is $1 \bmod p$, reject b and try a different candidate.

- If *none* of these values is $1 \bmod p$, then b is a primitive root modulo p.

Remark: Again, as roughly a quarter or more of the elements of $\mathbf{Z}/p^\times$ are primitive roots, random guessing will succeed in finding a primitive root quickly. The lemma above justifies the fairly efficient procedure to test whether or not a candidate is a primitive root. It is taken for granted that we use an efficient exponentiation algorithm.

Remark: Very often 2 or 3 is a primitive root. Among the 168 primes under 1000, only 60 have the property that neither 2 nor 3 is a primitive root. Among the 168 primes under 1000, only the 7 moduli 191, 311, 409, 439, 457, 479, and 911 have the property that none of 2, 3, 5, 6, 7, 10, 11 is a primitive root.

21

Random Number Generators

Any sequence of numbers generated by a deterministic process, meaning that the output is completely determined by the input, cannot be *random* in any real sense. And, while we may have an intuition for what we mean by 'random number,' it is quite difficult to make this idea precise.

To obtain 'truly random' sequences of numbers the best sources seem to be radioactive materials. Popular and often-used sources such as **keyboard latency** (that is, time lags between keyboard actions) have enough structure to them to make them inappropriate for the most serious cryptographic purposes if used for high-volume production of random numbers.

Since we won't be generating *truly* random numbers (even if we could figure out what we mean by that), we will refer to **pseudo-random number generators,** or **pRNGs**.

One interesting use of pRNGs is to create fake one-time pads, as discussed a little further below. But it is very hard to make pRNGs of good enough quality for this use: the key issue is whether or not an attacker could predict future elements in the keystream from knowledge of past ones. In particular, the linear feedback shift registers (LFSRs) we'll look at here are most definitely *not* good enough, because the Massey-Berlekamp algorithm shows that the future elements can easily be predicted from knowledge of a quite small number of past elements. Still, many fancier (and better-quality) pRNGs use LFSRs as their raw material.

Another use of pseudo-random numbers is for **simulation**. For such purposes the requirements are not so stringent as for the most serious cryptographic demands.

In either case, while a deterministic process cannot produce truly random numbers, in practice the criterion does not address randomness itself. Rather, the operational criterion is that it must be 'hard' (for an adversary?) to **predict** the *next* number in the sequence from knowledge of the previous ones, *without* knowing the *key*. But we've traded one problem for another: what does 'predict' mean, anyway?

A little more precisely, a pRNG should accept as input a **seed**, or **key**, and then produce a stream of bits or numbers determined completely by the seed.

The linear congruential, linear feedback shift register, and related generators are **not** good enough for cryptological purposes but *with care* can be used for simulation. Some related generators called *lagged Fibonacci generators* have extremely long periods but are nevertheless insecure. To substantiate the claim that these are weak pRNGs, we should describe effective *attacks* on them.

By contrast, the Blum–Blum–Shub generator is believed to be relatively secure, since its security is (nearly) provably equivalent to the existence of a fast algorithm for quadratic residues modulo a composite number whose factorization is not known, which is *believed to be* 'hard'. The problem is that production of each random bit by the BBS algorithm is relatively expensive by comparison to other (less provably secure) algorithms. We briefly describe this algorithm here for comparison.

21.1 Fake One-Time Pads

The general idea in what are called *asynchronous stream ciphers* is that a *modest-sized* **key** produces a *very long random-looking* **keystream**

$$S = (s_0, s_1, s_2, s_3, \ldots)$$

of integers modulo m by a chosen pRNG (for some modulus m) to use as a key for a fake one-time pad.

That is, the keystream s is simply *added* (modulo m) to the plaintext $x = (x_0, x_1, \ldots)$:

$$E_k(x) = (x_0 + s_0, x_1 + s_1, x_2 + s_2, \ldots)$$

Decryption is the corresponding subtraction. The reason this is a *fake* one-time pad is that the keystream does not clearly meet the requirement of 'true randomness' that makes the one-time pad truly secure. (There are other problems, too, but let's not worry.)

If it were feasible to generate a fake one-time pad from relatively small keys, then such a system would simplify the **key management** for one-time pads: instead of having to distribute huge keys for one-time pads, just the (much smaller) key to *generate* the keystream would have to be distributed. The key for the next message could be included at the end of each message, for example.

In this context, presumably the main cryptological issue would be a ciphertext-only attack. Notice that if by some chance the keystream is *periodic*, meaning that it repeats itself, then the cipher degenerates into a *Vigenere cipher*, which is very vulnerable to attack based on letter frequencies. Therefore, the very first imperative for pseudo-random number generators is to try to assure that the **period length is as long as possible**.

21.2 Period of a pRNG

The very first condition on a pseudo-random number generator is that (for a given value of the seed) the sequence produced should not repeat itself very often. There is a notion of **period** for any sequence. This notion is defined as follows. A sequence

$$s_0, s_1, s_2, s_3, \ldots$$

is said to be **periodic** with **period** p if

$$s_{i+p} = s_i \qquad \text{(for all indices } i)$$

This is a little too restrictive, however. More generally, say that a sequence

$$s_0, s_1, s_2, s_3, \ldots$$

is **(eventually) periodic** with **period** p if there is an index i_0 so that

$$s_{i+p} = s_i \qquad \text{(for all indices } i \text{ with } i \geq i_0)$$

Thus, we allow some irregular behavior at the beginning, but eventually the behavior is periodic.

Certainly not every sequence is periodic, but sequences produced by simple mechanisms by 'finite-state' machines tend to be so. The first issue is to make the period as large as possible for a given size of 'mechanism'. The precise meaning of this depends upon the context and will be clarified later in various examples.

21.3 Congruential Generators

Linear congruential generators are *not* adequate by themselves for use in secret ciphers but *are* useful for other things, such as simulation. Even though they are *not* good for cryptographic purposes, as with many other failed systems it is worthwhile to understand *how* they fail.

The very simplest version of **linear congruential generator** is obtained by specifying a modulus m and an integer a which is invertible modulo m. For a **seed** s_0 in $\mathbf{Z}/m$, the stream of pseudorandom numbers produced is

$$
\begin{aligned}
s_1 &= a \cdot s_0 \ \% \ m \\
s_2 &= a \cdot s_1 \ \% \ m \\
s_3 &= a \cdot s_2 \ \% \ m \\
&\cdots \\
s_{n+1} &= a \cdot s_n \ \% \ m
\end{aligned}
$$

More generally, fix a modulus m, an integer a which is invertible modulo m, and another integer b. Take a **seed** $s_0 \in \mathbf{Z}/m$. The stream of pseudorandom numbers produced from this data is defined by

$$s_1 = as_0 + b \ \% \ m$$

$$s_2 = as_1 + b \ \% \ m$$

$$s_3 = as_2 + b \ \% \ m$$

$$\cdots$$

$$s_{n+1} = as_n + b \ \% \ m$$

Obviously the simpler first version is obtained by taking $b = 0$.

For example, take $m = 17$, $a = 2$, $b = 7$, so that the way that the next element of a stream is generated from the previous is

$$s_{n+1} = 2 \cdot s_n + 7 \ \% \ 17$$

With seed $s_0 = 1$, the stream produced (including the seed value 1) is

$$1, 9, 8, 6, 2, 11, 12, 14, 1, 9, 8, 6, 2, 11, 12, 14, 1, 9, \ldots$$

Note that if at any point an earlier value occurs again, then the sequence starts repeating itself. This is clear since the next value is completely determined by the previous.

In this example, notice that the **period** is 8 and that (necessarily) *not* every element of $\mathbf{Z}/17$ occurs, but only 8 of them.

As another example, take $m = 17$, $a = 7$, $b = 1$, so that the way the next element of a stream is generated from the previous is

$$s_{n+1} = 7 \cdot s_n + 1 \% 17$$

With seed $s_0 = 1$, the stream produced (including the seed value 1) is

$$1, 8, 6, 9, 13, 7, 16, 11, 10, 3, 5, 2, 15, 4, 12, 0, 1, 8, \ldots$$

Again, once an earlier value occurs again, then the sequence starts repeating itself. This is clear since the next value is completely determined by the previous. In this example, with the same modulus as before, the period is 16. All values mod 17 other than 14 occur.

And notice what happens it we use seed 14: the stream obtained is just

$$14, 14, 14, 14, 14, 14, \ldots$$

which is not too random looking.

Whichever parts of the data a, b, m, s_0 are taken to be 'secret', it turns out that they are all easy to recover from a small number of values $s_1, s_2, \ldots$. Indeed, we should know by now that having an enormous keyspace is necessary, but definitely not sufficient, to make a cipher secure. An example of this is the Vigenere cipher.

Especially in the context of the Vigenere cipher, we have an obvious important question: how long before the sequence *repeats*? That is, *how long is the period?* That is, what is the smallest n so that $s_n = s_0$? Note that if $s_n = s_0$, then $s_{n+1} = s_1$, $s_{n+2} = s_2$, etc. If the period is much shorter than the length of the message, then this cipher is effectively a Vigenere cipher, which is vulnerable to Friedman's index-of-coincidence attack. The question of period length will be answered after a bit of technical preparation.

There are other criteria that should be satisfied besides having a long period. Without explaining them, we can still mention a linear congruential generator which is 'good' in the sense that it meets many of these yet-to-be-named criteria. It appeared in *Comm. of ACM*, vol. 31, 1988, pp. 1192-1201. Take

$$\begin{aligned} \text{modulus } m &= 2147483647 \\ \text{multiplier } a &= 16807 \end{aligned}$$

(So here the 'b' above is just 0.) Given a seed s_0, the pseudorandom stream produced is

$$s_0, \quad (a \cdot s_0) \% m, \quad (a^2 \cdot s_0) \% m, \quad (a^3 \cdot s_0) \% m, \quad \ldots$$

The modulus m is prime, and a is a primitive root modulo m. In particular, the modulus is the Mersenne prime

$$2147483647 = 2^{31} - 1$$

The smallest primitive root modulo m is 7, and

$$a = 16807 = 7^5$$

And 5 (the exponent that just appeared) does not divide $m - 1$, so 7^5 is still a primitive root modulo m. Finally, $a = 7^5$ is fairly close to the square root of m, slightly above it in fact, which might give us intuitive encouragement that multiplication by a will 'mix' well.

Exercises

21.3.01 Consider the form of recursion

$$s_{n+1} = c\, s_n \,\%\, 26$$

where c is a fixed integer modulo 26. Show (treating examples, if nothing else) that the largest possible period of a keystream generated by such a recursion is 12.

21.3.02 Consider a linear congruential generator L defined by

$$x_{n+1} = L(x_n) = 7 \cdot x_n + 2 \bmod 13$$

with initial data $x_0 = 6$. What is the smallest index n so that x_n returns to the value $x_0 = 6$? Does the length of period really depend on the initial data, do you think? Find the single 'bad' initial value x_{bad} with the property that $L(x_{\text{bad}}) = x_{\text{bad}}$.

21.3.03 Consider a linear congruential generator L defined by

$$x_{n+1} = L(x_n) = 6 \cdot x_n + 9 \bmod 11$$

with initial data $x_0 = 4$. What is the smallest index n so that x_n returns to the value $x_0 = 4$? Does the length of period really depend on the initial data, do you think? Find the single 'bad' initial value x_{bad} with the property that $L(x_{\text{bad}}) = x_{\text{bad}}$.

21.3.04 Consider a linear congruential generator L defined by

$$x_{n+1} = L(x_n) = 7 \cdot x_n + 2 \bmod 11$$

with initial data $x_0 = 6$. What is the smallest index n so that x_n returns to the value $x_0 = 6$? Does the length of period really depend on the initial data, do you think? Find the single 'bad' initial value x_{bad} with the property that $L(x_{\text{bad}}) = x_{\text{bad}}$.

21.4 Feedback Shift Generators

Now we look at another mechanism which is *not* adequate by itself for direct use in secret ciphers but *is* useful for other things, and which in any case we must study enough to see *why* it is inadequate.

Fix a size N, a modulus m (often $m = 2$), and choose **coefficients** $c = (c_0, \ldots, c_{N-1})$. Also choose a **seed** or **initial state** $s = (s_0, s_1, s_2, s_3, \ldots, s_{N-1})$. This will be the beginning of the keystream, as well. Then we recursively define, for $n + 1 \geq N$,

$$s_{n+1} = c_0\, s_n + c_1\, s_{n-1} + c_2\, s_{n-2} + \cdots + c_{N-1}\, s_{n-N+1} \,\%\, m$$

The kind of recursive definition used to define the keystream here can be written in terms of matrices. For simplicity, let's just suppose that $N = 4$. From coefficients $c = (c_0, c_1, c_2, c_3)$, we make a matrix

$$C = \begin{pmatrix} c_0 & c_1 & c_2 & c_3 \\ 1 & 0 & 0 & 0 \\ 0 & 1 & 0 & 0 \\ 0 & 0 & 1 & 0 \end{pmatrix}$$

and the recursion relation can be written as

$$\begin{pmatrix} s_{n+1} \\ s_n \\ s_{n-1} \\ s_{n-2} \end{pmatrix} = C \cdot \begin{pmatrix} s_n \\ s_{n-1} \\ s_{n-2} \\ s_{n-3} \end{pmatrix} \qquad \text{(all modulo } m)$$

For example, suppose that the modulus is $m = 2$ and the coefficients are $c_0 = 1$, $c_1 = 0$, $c_2 = 0$, $c_3 = 1$. Then the output stream is produced by

$$\begin{aligned} s_{i+1} &= c_0 \cdot s_i + c_1 \cdot s_{i-1} + c_2 \cdot s_{i-2} + c_3 \cdot s_{i-3} \\ &= 1 \cdot s_i + 0 \cdot s_{i-1} + 0 \cdot s_{i-2} + 1 \cdot s_{i-3} \\ &= s_i + s_{i-3} \end{aligned}$$

With seed $(s_0, s_1, s_2, s_3) = (1, 1, 0, 0)$, the whole stream produced (including the initial $(1, 1, 0, 0)$) is

$$1, 1, 0, 0, 1, 0, 0, 0, 1, 1, 1, 1, 0, 1, 0, 1, 1, 0, 0, 1, 0, 0, 0, \ldots$$

In this case, if an earlier-occuring pattern of 4 consecutive bits recurs, then the stream will repeat itself, since the four previous values completely determine the next one. Here the initial $(1, 1, 0, 0)$ recurred after 15 steps.

The possibility of expressing the computation of the output stream in terms of matrices is convenient both for computations and as an exploitable vulnerability for cryptanalytic attacks.

It is possible that for *some* choices of seed the keystream has a large period, but for other choices it has a short period, both with the same coefficients c. For this reason, in some scenarios the coefficients $c_0, c_1, c_2, \ldots$ should be chosen carefully, and only the seed $(s_0, s_1, s_2, \ldots)$ chosen 'at random'. Further technical preparation is necessary in order to study the issue of *period length*.

Exercises

21.4.01 Consider a linear feedback shift register which generates a keystream by the recursion

$$s_{n+1} = s_n - s_{n-1}$$

with *real* numbers s_i. Show that for *any* choice of seed $s = (s_0, s_1)$ this gives a periodic keystream with period 6 (or a divisor of 6).

21.4.02 Find a constant a_0 so that recursion

$$s_{n+1} = a_0 \, s_n + s_{n-1} \; \% \; 26$$

generates a keystream with period longer than 6 for *some* initial fragment s_0, s_1.

21.4.03 Find the period of the LFSR with initial state $(x_0, x_1, x_2, x_3) = (0, 1, 0, 0)$ defined by

$$x_{n+1} = x_n + x_{n-1} + x_{n-2} + x_{n-3}$$

21.4.04 Let L be a linear feedback shift register with coefficients (in ascending order) 0 0 1 0 1. Let the initial data be 1 0 0 0 0 (in ascending order). How many cycles until L returns to its original state? Speculate on how different initial data would affect the number of cycles before the initial state recurs.

21.4.05 Let L be a linear feedback shift register with coefficients (in ascending order) 1 1 1 0 1. Let the initial data be 0 1 0 0 0 (in ascending order). How many cycles until L returns to its original state? Speculate on how different initial data would affect the number of cycles before the initial state recurs. Do you suppose this has to do with the primality of the Mersenne number $2^5 - 1$? What about the fact that if you use the shift register coefficients as the lower coefficients of a quintic polynomial (with leading term x^5), the resulting quintic is irreducible? Coincidence?

21.5 Blum–Blum–Shub Generator

In contrast to the linear congruential generators, linear feedback shift registers, and other related non-secure pRNGs, the Blum–Blum–Shub generator is *provably secure*, assuming that it is hard to factor large numbers into primes. See [Blum, Blum, Shub 1986]. The proof of this relative security is rather long and difficult, so we don't include it here.

Choose two very large (secret) primes p, q, both congruent to 3 mod 4, and compute the product $n = p \cdot q$. This modulus can be made public and can be reused. For a given **seed** s_0, compute the sequence $s_1, s_2, s_3, \ldots$ by the recursive formula

$$s_{i+1} = s_i^2 \; \% \; n$$

From this sequence of numbers in the range $0, 1, 2, \ldots, n-1$, we create a sequence of pseudo-random bits by

$$b_i = s_i \; \% \; 2$$

Since the prime p is congruent to 3 modulo 4, for z a square modulo p the formula

$$y = z^{(p+1)/4} \bmod p$$

computes a square root of z, called the **principal square root** of z because it is the one of the two square roots of $z \bmod p$ which is itself a square. From this, some reflection might show that the squaring map is a **permutation** of the set of squares-mod-p. The same is true for q, so (by Sun Ze's theorem) the squaring map is a permutation of the set of squares-mod-n.

A careful analysis, which is a little too long to include here, can show that (in rough terms) if a sequence of bits produced by a BBS generator modulo n can be distinguished from a sequence of *random* bits, then there is a fast probabilistic algorithm to find square roots modulo n, which then gives a fast probabilistic algorithm to factor n into its factors $n = p \cdot q$.

For moduli n of size somewhat above 512 bits (about 170 decimal digits) there is no algorithm that will factor n in reasonable time (less than some large number of years), which is interpreted as evidence that the Blum–Blum–Shub generator is secure.

(Again, in mid-1999 Adi Shamir, the 'S' in RSA, designed a specialized, partly analogue, partly digital computer 'Twinkle' that can run factorization attacks from 100 to 1000 times faster than previously. This makes 512-bit RSA moduli significantly less secure than before, since if anyone *really* cared and had the resources, they could now factor your 512-bit RSA modulus in a few hours, rather than 10 years.)

21.6 Naor–Reingold Generator

The Naor–Reingold pseudo-random number generator [Naor, Reingold 1995], is relatively new. As with the Blum–Blum–Shub algorithm, of which it is something of a descendant, it is provably secure *assuming* the infeasibility of factoring integers $N = p \cdot q$, where p and q are sufficiently large primes (both probably congruent to 3 mod 4). This generator is defined as follows.

Fix a size n, and choose two random n-bit primes p and q, and let $N = pq$. Choose a random integer g which is a square mod N. Let

$$a = (a_{1,0}, a_{1,1}, a_{2,0}, a_{2,1}, \ldots, a_{n,0}, a_{n,1})$$

be a random sequence of $2n$ values in $\{1, 2, \ldots, N\}$. Let $r = (r_1, \ldots, r_n)$ be a random sequence of 0's and 1's. For any integer t of at most $2n$ bits, let $\beta_{2n}(t)$ denote the vector of binary expansion 'digits' of t, padding it out as necessary on the left to make it have length $2n$. For example, with $2n = 6$ and $t = 13$, in binary we have $13 = 1101_2$, and so

$$\beta_6(13) = (0, 0, 1, 1, 0, 1)$$

The two 0's on the left end are padding. For two such binary vectors

$$v = (v_1, \ldots, v_n), \qquad w = (w_1, \ldots, w_n)$$

with v_i's and w_i's all 0's or 1's, define a sort of dot product modulo 2 by

$$v \cdot w = (v_1, \ldots, v_n) \cdot (w_1, \ldots, w_n) = (\sum_{1 \leq i \leq n} v_i w_i) \ \% \ 2$$

Then for any n-tuple $x = (x_1, \ldots, x_n)$ of 0's and 1's, define the $\{0, 1\}$-valued function

$$f(x) = f_{N,g,a,r}(x) = r \cdot \beta(g^{a_1,x_1 + a_2,x_2 + a_3,x_3 + \cdots + a_n,x_n} \ \% \ N)$$

Then

Theorem.   (Naor–Reingold) Assuming that it is infeasible to factor N, the output of the function $f = f_{N,g,a,r}$ is indistinguishable from random bits, meaning that the sequence

$$f(1), f(2), f(3), \ldots, f(t)$$

with t much smaller than N, is indistinguishable from a sequence of random bits.

Remark: The proof is somewhat easier than for Blum–Blum–Shub but still a bit too long for us to include here.

Remark: The use of 'random' in the previous discussion means chosen under the assumption that a probability is assigned to possible choices so that all choices have the same probability. That is, the probability distribution is *uniform*. And it must be assumed that whatever device is used to choose the primes p and q to give the Blum integer N is sufficiently random in some sense or other so that factoring N is infeasible.

Remark: The issues involved in *distinguishing* 'random bits' from 'not random bits' also merit much more discussion than we give them here.

21.7 Periods of LCGs

A little linear algebra is all it takes to completely understand the period of a linear congruential generator. For simplicity we'll only consider *prime* moduli. Fix a *prime* modulus p, take $a \in \mathbf{Z}/p^\times$ and $b \in \mathbf{Z}/p$. First consider the case that $b = 0$, which is very easy. Consider the linear congruential generator described by

$$s_{i+1} = a \cdot s_i \ \% \ p$$

Theorem.   The **period** of the linear congruential generator $s_{i+1} = a \cdot s_i \ \% \ p$ is the *order* of a in the multiplicative group $\mathbf{Z}/p^\times$, as long as the seed s_0 is nonzero modulo p. In particular, this order is always a divisor of $p - 1$, and the maximum possible value $p - 1$ is obtained exactly when a is a primitive root modulo p. (We know that such primitive roots exist and that there are $\varphi(p - 1)$ of them.)

Proof: Since the seed s_0 is presumed nonzero (or else all s_i in the stream are 0), none of the $s_i = a^i \cdot s_0 \bmod p$ in the stream is 0 mod p. Consider the condition for the period to be ℓ:

$$s_{i+\ell} = s_i \text{ (for all sufficiently large } i)$$

In terms of the particulars here, this is

$$a^{i+\ell} \cdot s_0 = a^i \cdot s_0 \bmod p$$

or, dividing by $s_0 \bmod p$,

$$a^{i+\ell} = a^i \bmod p$$

Cancel the a^i: the condition is

$$a^\ell = 1 \bmod p$$

By Lagrange's theorem (or even by more elementary computations based on Fermat's Little Theorem) this gives

$$\ell \text{ divides } p - 1$$

That is, the period of the LCG is equal to the order of a in $\mathbf{Z}/p^\times$. And by now we have proven that primitive roots exist, so we know that the maximum possible period is $p - 1$.   ♣

Now consider the slightly more general linear congruential generator specified by

$$s_{i+1} = a \cdot s_i + b \% p$$

That is, now we allow the additive constant b to be nonzero. Also assume that $a \neq 1 \bmod p$.

Theorem. The **period** of the linear congruential generator

$$s_{i+1} = a \cdot s_i + b \% p$$

is the *order* of a in the multiplicative group $\mathbf{Z}/p^\times$, as long as the seed value s_0 is **not** equal to the single **bad seed value**

$$s_{\text{bad}} = -(a - 1)^{-1} \cdot b \bmod p$$

In particular, this order is always a divisor of $p-1$, and the maximum possible value $p-1$ is obtained exactly when a is a primitive root modulo p. (We know that such primitive roots exist and that there are $\varphi(p - 1)$ of them.)

Proof: Such a generator is better described in terms of two-by-two matrices:

$$\begin{pmatrix} s_{n+1} \\ s_n \end{pmatrix} = \begin{pmatrix} a & b \\ 0 & 1 \end{pmatrix} \begin{pmatrix} s_n \\ s_{n-1} \end{pmatrix}$$

Iterating this, we have

$$\begin{pmatrix} s_{n+k} \\ s_{n+k-1} \end{pmatrix} = \begin{pmatrix} a & b \\ 0 & 1 \end{pmatrix}^k \begin{pmatrix} s_n \\ s_{n-1} \end{pmatrix}$$

To understand the behavior of the matrix

$$L = \begin{pmatrix} a & b \\ 0 & 1 \end{pmatrix}$$

we look for its **eigenvalues** and **eigenvectors**. That is, we look for numbers λ (eigenvalues) and 2-by-1 matrices (eigenvectors) v so that

$$Lv = \lambda \cdot v$$

That is, we look for vectors on which the action of multiplication is as simple as possible, namely, as though it were simply a scalar multiplication.

If we had good guesses for the eigenvalues, then corresponding eigenvectors can be found by solving the system of linear equations

$$Lv = \lambda \cdot v$$

for the components of v.

The Cayley–Hamilton theorem tells how to find eigenvalues of an n-by-n matrix M, as follows. Let I be the n-by-n identity matrix (that is, with 1's down the upper-left to lower-right diagonal, 0's off this diagonal). Let x be an indeterminate, and compute the determinant

$$P_M(x) = \det(xI - M)$$

This polynomial is the **characteristic polynomial** of M. The Cayley–Hamilton theorem says that the roots of the **characteristic equation**

$$P_M(x) = 0$$

are the eigenvalues of M.

Of course throughout this discussion all computations are done modulo p.

In the case at hand, let I be the 2-by-2 identity matrix, and we compute

$$\begin{aligned} P_L(x) &= \det(\begin{pmatrix} x & 0 \\ 0 & x \end{pmatrix} - \begin{pmatrix} a & b \\ 0 & 1 \end{pmatrix}) \\ &= \det \begin{pmatrix} x - a & -b \\ 0 & x - 1 \end{pmatrix} = (x - a)(x - 1) \end{aligned}$$

Note that this does not depend at all upon the value of b. Thus, the characteristic equation is

$$(x - a)(x - 1) = 0$$

which has roots $a, 1$.

To find an eigenvector $v = \begin{pmatrix} x \\ y \end{pmatrix}$ with eigenvalue a, solve

$$\begin{pmatrix} a & b \\ 0 & 1 \end{pmatrix} \begin{pmatrix} x \\ y \end{pmatrix} = a \cdot \begin{pmatrix} x \\ y \end{pmatrix}$$

This simplifies to the system

$$\begin{cases} a \cdot x + b \cdot y &= a \cdot x \\ 0 \cdot x + y &= a \cdot y \end{cases}$$

In the first equation, the ax terms cancel, leaving the condition $by = 0$. The second of the two equations simplifies to $(a - 1)y = 0$, which implies $y = 0$, since $a \neq 1$. Thus, certainly $by = 0$ also. Thus, we may take $\begin{pmatrix} 1 \\ 0 \end{pmatrix}$ as eigenvector with eigenvalue a.

To find an eigenvector $v = \begin{pmatrix} x \\ y \end{pmatrix}$ with eigenvalue 1, solve

$$\begin{pmatrix} a & b \\ 0 & 1 \end{pmatrix} \begin{pmatrix} x \\ y \end{pmatrix} = 1 \cdot \begin{pmatrix} x \\ y \end{pmatrix}$$

This simplifies to the system

$$\begin{cases} a \cdot x &+& b \cdot y &=& x \\ 0 \cdot x &+& y &=& y \end{cases}$$

The second equation simplifies to $0 = 0$, which is always met. The first equation (and thus the whole system) simplifies to

$$(a - 1)x + by = 0$$

Since $a - 1 \neq 0$,

$$x = -(a - 1)^{-1} by$$

That is, x is uniquely determined by y. We may take

$$\begin{pmatrix} -(a - 1)^{-1}b \\ 1 \end{pmatrix}$$

as eigenvector with eigenvalue 1.

The utility of this is that (in fortuitous situations) every vector can be written as a sum of scalar multiples of eigenvectors and thereby have its behavior under matrix multiplication understood in more elementary terms.

For example, we should express the initial state vector $\begin{pmatrix} s_0 \\ 1 \end{pmatrix}$ in the form

$$\begin{pmatrix} s_0 \\ 1 \end{pmatrix} = c \begin{pmatrix} 1 \\ 0 \end{pmatrix} + d \begin{pmatrix} -(a - 1)^{-1}b \\ 1 \end{pmatrix}$$

for some scalars c, d (in $\mathbf{Z}/p$). By looking at the second component, it is clear that $d = 1$, and then we solve for c by looking at the first component:

$$s_0 = c - (a - 1)^{-1}b$$

so

$$c = s_0 + (a - 1)^{-1}b$$

Now we have the payoff:

$$
\begin{aligned}
L^k \begin{pmatrix} s_0 \\ 1 \end{pmatrix} &= L^k \left((s_0 + (a - 1)^{-1}b) \begin{pmatrix} 1 \\ 0 \end{pmatrix} + \begin{pmatrix} -(a - 1)^{-1}b \\ 1 \end{pmatrix} \right) \\
&= a^k(s_0 + (a - 1)^{-1}b) \begin{pmatrix} 1 \\ 0 \end{pmatrix} + \begin{pmatrix} -(a - 1)^{-1}b \\ 1 \end{pmatrix}
\end{aligned}
$$

(since the second eigenvalue is just 1).

Note that the second summand in the previous expression does not change, because it corresponds to the eigenvalue 1. Thus, the stream of values is *constant* if the first summand is 0 by accident. That bad case (in which case the stream is *constant*) occurs if and only if

$$s_0 = -(a - 1)^{-1}b$$

21.8 Primitive Polynomials

The idea of **primitive polynomial** is necessary in many applications.

Definition: A polynomial P of degree N in $\mathbf{Z}/p[x]$ is **primitive** if P divides $x^N - 1$ but does not divide $x^t - 1$ for any integer t with $0 < t < N$.

Equivalently, a polynomial P of degree N is primitive if and only if

$$x^N = 1 \bmod P$$

but

$$x^t \neq 1 \bmod P \text{ for } 0 < t < N$$

Theorem.   A polynomial P of degree N is primitive if and only if if

$$x^N = 1 \bmod P$$

but

$$x^t \neq 1 \bmod P \text{ for } 0 < t < N \text{ and } t \text{ dividing } N$$

Remark: The point is that we don't need to check *all* smaller exponents than N, but only possible exponents from among the *divisors* of the degree N.

Proof: It suffices to prove that if $x^N = 1 \bmod P$ and $x^t = 1 \bmod P$ for some $0 < t < N$ then $x^d = 1 \bmod P$ for some divisor d of N with $0 < d < N$. Let a, b be the integers so that

$$\gcd(t, N) = aN + bt$$

Then

$$x^{\gcd(N,t)} = x^{aN+bt} = (x^N)^a \cdot (x^t)^b = 1^a \cdot 1^b = 1 \bmod P$$

Note that for negative exponents we need to know that x is invertible mod P, and this is true since $x^N = 1 \bmod P$ implies

$$x \cdot x^{N-1} = 1 \bmod P$$

That is, x^{N-1} is an inverse of $x \bmod P$. In any case, we see that $x^{\gcd(N,t)} = 1 \bmod P$, which proves the proposition. ♣

Quite a bit later, we will prove

Theorem. A polynomial P in $\mathbf{F}_p[x]$ of degree n is primitive if and only if it divides the $(p^n - 1)$th cyclotomic polynomial. Conversely, every irreducible factor of the $(p^n - 1)$th cyclotomic polynomial in $\mathbf{F}_p[x]$ is of degree n and is a primitive polynomial. *(Proof postponed.)*

Remark: Note that the latter theorem asserts that all the irreducible factors of the $(p^N - 1)$th cyclotomic polynomial in $\mathbf{Z}/p[x]$ are of degree N. This is certainly not obvious.

Then there would be the interesting corollary counting primitive polynomials:

Corollary. The number of primitive polynomials of degree n in $\mathbf{F}_p[x]$ is

$$\varphi(p^n - 1)/n$$

where φ is Euler's phi-function.

Proof: Assuming that we know the last theorem to be true, the $(p^n - 1)$th cyclotomic polynomial has irreducible factors which are exactly the primitive polynomials of degree n. On the other hand, by now we know that the degree of the tth cyclotomic polynomial is $\varphi(t)$, so the degree of the $(p^n - 1)$th cyclotomic polynomial is $\varphi(p^n - 1)$. By the theorem, this cyclotomic is evidently a product of irreducible polynomials of degree n. Since the degree of a product is the sum of the degrees, it must be that there are $\varphi(p^n - 1)/n$ irreducible factors of the $\varphi(p^n - 1)$th cyclotomic polynomial. As already noted, these factors are exactly the primitive polynomials of degree n. ♣

By the theorem above, primitive polynomials are irreducible. Thus, while we are counting primitives we might be interested in counting irreducible polynomials of a given degree. An integer is usually said to be **square-free** if it is not divisible by the square of any prime number. Recall that the Möbius function μ is defined on positive integers by

$$\mu(n) = \begin{cases} (-1)^t & \text{if } n \text{ is square-free, divisible by exactly } t \text{ primes} \\ 1 & \text{if } n = 1 \\ 0 & \text{if } n \text{ is divisible by the square of some prime} \end{cases}$$

Theorem. The number of irreducible monic polynomials in $\mathbf{F}_p[x]$ of degree n is

$$\frac{1}{n} \sum_{1 \le d \le n,\ d|n} \mu(d)\, p^{n/d}$$

That is, this number is

$$\frac{1}{n} \cdot \left(p^n - \sum_{p_1|n} p^{n/p_1} + \sum_{p_1,p_2|n} p^{n/p_1p_2} - \sum_{p_1,p_2,p_3|n} p^{n/p_1p_2p_3} + \cdots \right)$$

where the sums are over collections of *distinct* prime divisors of n. (*Proof postponed.*)

The most interesting special case of the theorem is

Corollary. If $n = p_1$ is prime, then there are

$$\frac{p^{p_1} - p}{p_1}$$

irreducible monic polynomials of degree n in $\mathbf{F}_p[x]$.

Proof: See what the mu-function does in this special case.   ♣

In particular, if we believe these theorems, then we can see that for degree n so that $p^n - 1$ is *prime*, all irreducible polynomials are primitive. This requires of course that $p = 2$, or else $p - 1$ is a proper factor.

Corollary. Let n be such that $2^n - 1$ is prime. Then every irreducible polynomial in $\mathbf{F}_2[x]$ of degree n is primitive.

Proof: The theorem on primitives implies that every primitive polynomial of degree n is irreducible. The number of irreducibles of degree n in this case is

$$\text{number of monic irreducibles} = \frac{2^n - 2}{n}$$

by the formula above for counting irreducibles. On the other hand, the formula above for counting monic primitive polynomials gives

$$\text{number of monic primitives} = \frac{\varphi(2^n - 1)}{n}$$

Since $2^n - 1$ is assumed prime,

$$\varphi(2^n - 1) = (2^n - 1) - 1 = 2^n - 2$$

Thus, in this special, case the two counting formulas give the same number. Since the primitives are a subset of the irreducibles, this counting argument implies that the two sets must be identical.   ♣

21.9 Periods of LFSRs

Linear feedback shift registers (LFSRs) can also be completely analyzed by linear algebra. The notion of **primitive polynomial** is necessary here. Let c_0, c_1, ..., c_{N-1} be the coefficients of an LFSR which has recursion

$$s_{n+1} = c_0 s_n + c_1 s_{n-1} + c_2 s_{n-2} + \cdots + c_{N-1} s_{n-N+1}$$

Theorem. If the polynomial

$$x^N - c_0 x^{N-1} - c_1 x^{N-2} - c_2 x^{N-3} - \cdots - c_{N-1}$$

in $\mathbf{Z}/p[x]$ is primitive, then the linear feedback shift register with coefficients c_0, ..., c_{N-1} has period $p^N - 1$ for *any* initial state $s_0, s_1, \ldots, s_{N-1}$ (other than all 0's).

Remark: If that polynomial is *not* primitive, then the period will be less, *and* there will be several 'bad' initial states which will cause the LFSR to have a much smaller period.

Proof: As in the earlier example define the corresponding matrix L by

$$L = \begin{pmatrix} c_0 & c_1 & c_2 & \ldots & c_{N-2} & c_{N-1} \\ 1 & 0 & 0 & \ldots & 0 & 0 \\ 0 & 1 & 0 & \ldots & 0 & 0 \\ 0 & 0 & 1 & \ldots & 0 & 0 \\ & & \ldots & & & \\ 0 & 0 & \ldots & 0 & 1 & 0 \end{pmatrix}$$

That is, the top row consists of the coefficients (note the ordering of them!) and everything else is 0 except for the 1's on the subdiagonal. Then

$$L \cdot \begin{pmatrix} s_n \\ s_{n-1} \\ \ldots \\ s_{n-N+2} \\ s_{n-N+1} \end{pmatrix} = \begin{pmatrix} s_{n+1} \\ s_n \\ \ldots \\ s_{n-N+1} \\ s_{n-N} \end{pmatrix}$$

As in the much simpler case of the basic linear congruential generator, the *idea* is to express the initial state

$$\begin{pmatrix} s_{N-1} \\ s_{N-2} \\ \cdots \\ s_1 \\ s_0 \end{pmatrix}$$

as a **linear combination**

$$\begin{pmatrix} s_{N-1} \\ s_{N-2} \\ \cdots \\ s_1 \\ s_0 \end{pmatrix} = a_1 \cdot v_1 + \cdots + a_n \cdot v_n$$

of **eigenvectors** v_i of L with corresponding eigenvalue λ_i, thereby being easily able to evaluate L^k:

$$L^k \begin{pmatrix} s_{N-1} \\ s_{N-2} \\ \cdots \\ s_1 \\ s_0 \end{pmatrix} = \lambda_1^k a_1 \cdot v_1 + \cdots + \lambda_n^k a_n \cdot v_n$$

If you understand how determinants work, then you can see that the **characteristic polynomial** of a matrix of the special form that L has is just

$$P_L(x) = x^N - c_0 x^{N-1} - c_1 x^{N-2} - c_2 x^{N-3} - \cdots - c_{N-1}$$

But we cannot expect to 'solve' high-degree polynomial equations explicitly, so we cannot proceed as directly as in the LCG case.

Instead of being so explicit, we could demand that all the eigenvalues λ_i have the largest possible order(s). That is, the smallest positive integer ℓ so that λ_i^ℓ is as large as possible.

Remark: A possible problem here is that if we've discussed only the finite fields $\mathbf{Z}/p$ and no others, then we don't know where to look to find these eigenvalues, since we probably *cannot* solve the characteristic equation in $\mathbf{Z}/p$! We need to understand finite fields more generally to understand what's going on with LFSRs, even though we don't mention finite fields in the definition of LFSR! But let's not worry too much right now.

Assuming (as we did) that P_L is irreducible, these eigenvalues lie in the finite field F_{p^N} (since P_L is of degree N). In the discussion of primitive roots, we actually showed that the multiplicative group of *any* finite field is cyclic, so $F_{p^N} \times$ is cyclic, of order $p^N - 1$. That is, every nonzero element of F_{p^N} satisfies

$$x^{p^N - 1} - 1 = 0$$

But we want to exclude elements with smaller orders (so, by Lagrange's theorem, having order *proper* divisors of P_L). That is, we want to look at the polynomial

that's left after removing from $x^{p^N-1} - 1 = 0$ all its common factors with polynomials $x^d - 1$, where d is a proper divisor of $p^N - 1$. From the discussion of cyclotomic
polynomials, what remains after such common factors are removed is exactly the
$(p^N - 1)$th **cyclotomic polynomial**.

Therefore the hypothesis that P_L is irreducible and divides the $(p^N - 1)$th
cyclotomic polynomial assures that the order of each eigenvalue is $p^N - 1$.

Then look at the periodicity condition

$$\lambda_1^{i+\ell} a_1 \cdot v_1 + \cdots + \lambda_n^{i+\ell} a_n \cdot v_n = \lambda_1^i a_1 \cdot v_1 + \cdots + \lambda_n^i a_n \cdot v_n$$

This simplifies to

$$(\lambda_1^{i+\ell} - \lambda_1^i)v_1 + \cdots + (\lambda_N^{i+\ell} - \lambda_N^i)v_N = 0$$

or

$$(\lambda_1^\ell - 1)\lambda_1^i v_1 + \cdots + (\lambda_N^\ell - 1)\lambda_N^i v_N = 0$$

Certainly if $p^N - 1$ divides ℓ, then the quantities in parentheses are all 0, so the
sum is 0.

To prove the other half, that this vector sum's being zero implies that every
$\lambda_i^\ell - 1 = 0$, we need a bit more information about eigenvectors. First, in this
situation we know that P_L has **distinct roots**, since P_L is a divisor of the (p^N-1)th
cyclotomic polynomial, which we know to have distinct roots. Now we claim that
for an N-by-N matrix M with *distinct* eigenvalues $\lambda_1, \ldots, \lambda_N$, any relation

$$a_1 v_1 + \cdots + a_N v_N = 0$$

among corresponding eigenvectors v_i must have all coefficients a_i equal to 0. To
prove this, make the clever hypothesis that we have such a relation, and that among
all such relations it is has the fewest nonzero a_i's. Apply M to both sides of that
relation, obtaining

$$\lambda_1 a_1 v_1 + \cdots + \lambda_N a_N v_N = 0$$

Multiplying the first relation by λ_j and subtracting from the second gives a vector
relation

$$(\lambda_1 - \lambda_j)a_1 v_1 + \cdots + (\lambda_N - \lambda_j)a_N v_N = 0$$

This has the effect of getting rid of the jth term. Note that since the eigenvalues
are all distinct, none of the quantities $\lambda_i - \lambda_j$ is 0 except for $i = j$. Thus, we can
obtain a relation with fewer nonzero coefficients by using this trick to kill off some
nonzero coefficient. Contradiction.

Thus, in the case at hand,

$$(\lambda_1^\ell - 1)\lambda_1^i v_1 + \cdots + (\lambda_N^\ell - 1)\lambda_N^i v_N = 0$$

if and only if *all* coefficients $(\lambda_i^\ell - 1)\lambda_i$ are 0. Since $\lambda_i^{p^N-1} = 1$, λ_i is nonzero itself,
so the condition is that

$$\lambda_i^\ell - 1 = 0 \text{ (for all } i)$$

Since every λ_i has order $p^N - 1$, this holds if and only if ℓ divides $p^N - 1$. That is, we've proven that the order of such an LFSR is $p^N - 1$.

Remark: We did *not* prove that every vector can be expressed as a linear combination

$$v = a_1 v_1 + \cdots + a_N v_N$$

of eigenvectors v_i. Since the eigenvalues are all different from each other, this *is* true, but we'll not prove it here.

21.10 Examples of Primitives

As concrete examples, let's determine the primitive polynomials in $\mathbf{F}_2[x]$ of degree 8 or less. We'll use the criterion that primitive polynomials of degree n in $\mathbf{F}_2[x]$ are the irreducible divisors of the $(2^n - 1)$th cyclotomic polynomials. This criterion is simple and conceptually helpful for small-degree polynomials. A little later we'll look at a more appropriate computational criterion for large-degree polynomials.

A **linear** polynomial in $\mathbf{F}_2[x]$ is primitive if it is irreducible and divides the $(2^1 - 1)$th cyclotomic polynomial, which is

$$\varphi_1 = x - 1 = x + 1$$

This directly shows that the linear polynomial $x + 1$ *is* primitive, while the linear polynomial x is *not*.

A **quadratic** polynomial in $\mathbf{F}_2[x]$ is primitive if it is irreducible and divides the $(2^2 - 1)$th cyclotomic polynomial, which is

$$\varphi_{2^2-1} = \varphi_3 = \frac{x^3 - 1}{x - 1} = x^2 + x + 1$$

which is by coincidence quadratic itself. It's easy to check (by trial division) that $x^2 + x + 1$ is irreducible, so $x^2 + x + 1$ is the only primitive quadratic polynomial mod 2.

A **cubic** polynomial in $\mathbf{F}_2[x]$ is primitive if it is irreducible and divides the $(2^3 - 1)$th cyclotomic polynomial, which is

$$\varphi_{2^3-1} = \varphi_7 = \frac{x^7 - 1}{x - 1} = x^6 + x^5 + x^4 + x^3 + x^2 + x + 1$$

By trial division we know that the irreducible cubics mod 2 are exactly

$$x^3 + x^2 + 1, \qquad x^3 + x + 1$$

Just checking, multiply out

$$(x^3 + x^2 + 1) \cdot (x^3 + x + 1) = x^6 + x^5 + x^4 + x^3 + x^2 + x + 1$$

We conclude that both the irreducible cubics are primitive.

A **quartic** polynomial in $\mathbf{F}_2[x]$ is primitive if it is irreducible and divides the $(2^4 - 1)$th cyclotomic polynomial, which is

$$\varphi_{2^4-1} = \varphi_{15} = \frac{x^{15}-1}{(x^2+x+1)(x^5-1)}$$

$$= x^8 + x^7 + x^5 + x^4 + x^3 + x + 1$$

By trial division we know that the irreducible quartics mod 2 are exactly the 3

$$x^4 + x^3 + x^2 + x + 1, \quad x^4 + x^3 + 1, \quad x^4 + x + 1$$

If we make a lucky (?!) guess that the second two are the primitive ones (since they are somewhat related to each other), then we check:

$$(x^4 + x^3 + 1) \cdot (x^4 + x + 1) = x^8 + x^7 + x^5 + x^4 + x^3 + x + 1$$

Yes, these two are the primitive quartics mod 2. So 2 out of 3 irreducible quartics are primitive. Note that we might have recognized that $x^4 + x^3 + x^2 + x + 1$ is not primitive by the fact that it is in fact exactly φ_5. That implies that every root of it has order 5 rather than 15.

A **quintic** polynomial in $\mathbf{F}_2[x]$ is primitive if it is irreducible and divides the $(2^5 - 1)$th cyclotomic polynomial, which is

$$\varphi_{2^5-1} = \varphi_{31} = \frac{x^{31} - 1}{x - 1}$$

This is of degree 30. Since it is exactly the product of the primitive quintics, there should be $30/5 = 6$ of them. In fact we already saw (by trial division) that there are exactly six irreducible quintics,

$$x^5 + 0 + x^3 + x^2 + x + 1$$
$$x^5 + x^4 + 0 + x^2 + x + 1$$
$$x^5 + x^4 + x^3 + 0 + x + 1$$
$$x^5 + x^4 + x^3 + x^2 + 0 + 1$$
$$x^5 + x^3 + 1$$
$$x^5 + x^2 + 1$$

Since there are six irreducible quintics, and six irreducible (necessarily quintic) factors of the 31st cyclotomic polynomial, they must be the same six irreducible quintics. If one cared, one could check that the product of these is φ_{31} directly by multiplying out.

A **sextic** polynomial in $\mathbf{F}_2[x]$ is primitive if it is irreducible and divides the

$$(2^6 - 1)\text{th} = 63\text{rd} = (3 \cdot 3 \cdot 7)\text{th}$$

cyclotomic polynomial, which is of degree

$$\varphi(2^6 - 1) = \varphi(3 \cdot 3 \cdot 7) = (3 - 1)3(7 - 1) = 42$$

is

Since it i exactly the product of the primitive sextics, then there should be $42/6 = 7$ of them. How many irreducible sextics are there mod 2? We will show later that there are

$$\frac{2^6 - 2^3 - 2^2 + 2^1}{6} = \frac{54}{6} = 9$$

three

So *two* irreducible sextics are *not* primitive. Which two? It's hard to say without doing larger computations.   *See   21.11.01*

A **septic** polynomial in $\mathbf{F}_2[x]$ is primitive, by definition, if it is irreducible and divides the

$$(2^7 - 1)\text{th} = 127\text{th}$$

cyclotomic polynomial, which is of degree

$$\varphi(2^7 - 1) = 127 - 1 = 2 \cdot 3 \cdot 3 \cdot 7$$

(since 127 is prime). So if we imagine that it's exactly the product of the primitive septics, then there should be $126/7 = 18$ of them. How many irreducible septics are there mod 2? It turns out that there are

$$\frac{2^7 - 2^1}{7} = \frac{126}{7} = 18$$

So *all* irreducible septics mod 2 are primitive.

An **octic** polynomial in $\mathbf{F}_2[x]$ is primitive, by definition, if it is irreducible and divides the

$$(2^8 - 1)\text{th} = 255\text{th} = (3 \cdot 5 \cdot 17)\text{th}$$

cyclotomic polynomial, which is of degree

$$\varphi(2^8 - 1) = (3 - 1)(5 - 1)(7 - 1) = 24 \cdot 6 = 48$$

So if we anticipate that it's exactly the product of the primitive octics, then there should be $48/8 = 6$ of them. How many irreducible octics are there mod 2? From the general formula we'll prove later, there are

$$\frac{2^8 - 2^4}{8} = 2^5 - 2 = 30$$

So only 6 of the 30 irreducible octics are primitive.

Exercises

21.10.01 Find the two primitive monic quadratic polynomials over $\mathbf{F}_3$.

21.10.02 Find the four primitive monic quadratic polynomials over $\mathbf{F}_5$.

21.10.03 Find the four primitive monic cubic polynomials over $\mathbf{F}_3$.

21.10.04 (*) Find the two non-primitive irreducible sextic polynomials in $\mathbf{F}_2[x]$.

21.10.05 (*) Find at least one primitive octic in $\mathbf{F}_2[x]$.

21.11 Testing for Primitivity

For large degree d, we need to be as efficient as possible in testing for primitivity of polynomials in $\mathbf{Z}/p[x]$. To that end, we further refine the criterion for primitivity. Several examples are given.

> **Theorem.** Let P be an polynomial of degree n in $\mathbf{Z}/p[x]$. Let $N = p^n - 1$. Then P is primitive if and only if
>
> $$x^N = 1 \bmod P$$
>
> and
>
> $$x^{N/q} \neq 1 \bmod P$$
>
> for every prime number q dividing N.

Proof: We already saw that P is primitive if and only if $x^N = 1 \bmod P$ but $x^d \neq 1 \bmod P$ for every divisor d of N with $0 < d < N$. Suppose that $x^d = 1 \bmod P$ for some divisor d of P with $0 < d < N$. Then $N/d > 1$, so has a prime divisor q. Then

$$x^{N/q} = x^{d \cdot (N/dq)} = (x^d)^{N/dq} = 1^{N/dq} = 1 \bmod P$$

Note that N/dq is an integer, since q divides N/d. This proves what we want. ♣

Remark: As usual, the way we test whether a polynomial f is 1 **mod P** is to divide-with-remainder f by P, and see whether or not the remainder is 1.

Remark: Of course, we should use the fast exponentiation algorithm here.

Remark: The fast exponentiation algorithm in $\mathbf{Z}/2[x]$ runs especially fast, since all that is necessary to square such a polynomial is to double the exponents (of terms which actually occur). For example, in $\mathbf{Z}/2[x]$,

$$(x^5 + x^4 + x + 1)^2 = x^{10} + x^8 + x^2 + 1$$

Example: Let's verify that the nonic $1 + x^4 + x^9$ is primitive, while the nonic $1 + x + x^9$ is irreducible but not primitive. In both cases, we'll take the irreducibility for granted. Also, for brevity, let's express polynomials in $\mathbf{Z}/2[x]$ as arrays of non-negative integers, where an integer i occurs if and only if x^i occurs in the polynomial. (Of course this trick is special to the case that the coefficients are in $\mathbf{Z}/2$.)

First, note that

$$2^9 - 1 = 7 \cdot 73$$

so (by Lagrange's theorem, and so on) it might be that

$$x^7 = 1 \bmod \text{irred nonic}$$

or

$$x^{73} = 1 \bmod \text{irred nonic}$$

if the nonic is not primitive. In the first case, x^7 is already reduced modulo any nonic polynomial, so it cannot be that $x^7 = 1$ modulo any nonic. Next, compute $x^{73} \bmod 1 + x^4 + x^9$ via fast exponentiation algorithm:

$[1]$	73	$[0]$
$[1]$	72	$[1]$
$[2]$	36	$[1]$
$[4]$	18	$[1]$
$[8]$	9	$[1]$
$[8]$	8	$[0,4]$
$[2,6,7]$	4	$[0,4]$
$[0,3,5,7]$	2	$[0,4]$
$[1,4,6]$	1	$[0,4]$
$[1,4,6]$	0	$[4,6,8]$

Thus,

$$x^{73} = x^4 + x^6 + x^8 \bmod 1 + x^4 + x^9$$

which is not $1 \bmod 1 + x^4 + x^9$.

Just to check, let's verify that $x^{511} = 1 \bmod 1 + x^4 + x^9$. Of course, taking advantage of the power-of-2 situation, it would be smarter to verify that $x^{512} = x \bmod 1 + x^4 + x^9$:

$[1]$	512	$[0]$
$[2]$	256	$[0]$
$[4]$	128	$[0]$
$[8]$	64	$[0]$
$[2,6,7]$	32	$[0]$
$[0,3,5,7]$	16	$[0]$
$[1,4,6]$	8	$[0]$
$[2,3,7,8]$	4	$[0]$
$[0,2,5,7]$	2	$[0]$
$[1]$	1	$[0]$
$[1]$	0	$[1]$

so that $x^{512} = x \bmod 1 + x^4 + x^9$, as it should.

Remark: If for some nonic P it happened that

$$x^{2^9} \neq x \bmod P$$

then we would know that the nonic P was **reducible**. (Why?) For example, with

$$
\begin{aligned}
P(x) &= 1 + x^9 = (1 + x^3)(1 + x^3 + x^6) \\
&= (1 + x)(1 + x + x^2)(1 + x^3 + x^6)
\end{aligned}
$$

we compute x^{512} mod P (here there is an unusual shortcut):

$$x^{512} = x^{9 \cdot 56 + 8} = (x^9)^{56} \cdot x^8$$
$$= 1 \cdot x^8 = x^8 \bmod x^9 + 1$$

which is not x mod $x^9 + 1$, so we have proven indirectly that $x^9 + 1$ is not irreducible.

On the other hand, let's look at the second nonic mentioned above, $1 + x + x^9$. Compute x^{73} mod $1 + x + x^9$ by fast exponentiation, with the abbreviation used above:

$[1]$	73	$[0]$
$[1]$	72	$[1]$
$[2]$	36	$[1]$
$[4]$	18	$[1]$
$[8]$	9	$[1]$
$[8]$	8	$[0,1]$
$[7,8]$	4	$[0,1]$
$[5,6,7,8]$	2	$[0,1]$
$[1,2,3,4,5,6,7,8]$	1	$[0,1]$
$[1,2,3,4,5,6,7,8]$	0	$[0]$

That is,

$$x^{73} = 1 \bmod 1 + x + x^9$$

which proves that $1 + x + x^9$ is *not* primitive.

Just to check, let's compute x^{512} mod $1 + x + x^9$:

$[1]$	512	$[0]$
$[2]$	256	$[0]$
$[4]$	128	$[0]$
$[8]$	64	$[0]$
$[7,8]$	32	$[0]$
$[5,6,7,8]$	16	$[0]$
$[1,2,3,4,5,6,7,8]$	8	$[0]$
$[1,3,5,7]$	4	$[0]$
$[1,5]$	2	$[0]$
$[1]$	1	$[0]$
$[1]$	0	$[1]$

Thus, $x^{512} = x$ modulo $1 + x + x^9$, as it should because $1 + x + x^9$ is irreducible. (Why?)

Exercises

21.11.01 Verify that the polynomial $x^6 + x^3 + 1$ in $\mathbf{F}_2[x]$ is not primitive.

21.11.02 Verify that the polynomial $x^8 + x^4 + x^3 + x + 1$ in $\mathbf{F}_2[x]$ is not primitive.

21.11.03 Verify that the polynomial $x^8 + x^7 + x^4 + x^3 + x^2 + x + 1$ in $\mathbf{F}_2[x]$ is not primitive.

21.11.04 (*) Show that if $2^d - 1$ is prime, then any irreducible polynomial in $\mathbf{F}_2[x]$ of degree d is necessarily primitive.

22

More on Groups

We can make further use of the 'group' concept to get a better understanding of our earlier formulas for square roots, cube roots, and so on, in $\mathbf{Z}/p$ for prime p. In the context of Fermat's Little Theorem, these may have appeared as lucky guesses, but in a larger context they can be seen as fairly inevitable.

22.1 Group Homomorphisms

A *function* (or *map*)

$$f : G \to H$$

from one group G to another one H is a **group homomorphism** if

$$f(g_1 g_2) = f(g_1)\, f(g_2)$$

for all $g_1, g_2 \in G$.

Let e_G be the identity in G and e_H the identity in H. The **kernel** of such a group homomorphism f is

$$\text{kernel of } f \; = \ker f = \{g \in G : f(g) = e_H\}$$

The **image** of f is just like the image of any function:

$$\text{image of } f \; = \operatorname{im} f = \{h \in H : \text{there is } g \in G \text{ so that } f(g) = h\}$$

Let $f : G \to H$ be a group homomorphism. Let e_G be the identity in G and let e_H be the identity in H.

- Necessarily f carries the identity of G to the identity of H: $f(e_G) = e_H$.

- For $g \in G$, $f(g^{-1}) = f(g)^{-1}$.

- The *kernel* of f is a subgroup of G.

- The *image* of f is a subgroup of H.

- A group homomorphism $f : G \to H$ is *injective* if and only if the kernel is *trivial* (that is, is the trivial subgroup $\{e_G\}$).

Proof: The image $f(e_G)$ under f of the identity e_G in G has the property

$$f(e_G) = f(e_G \cdot e_G) = f(e_G) \cdot f(e_G)$$

using the property of the identity in G and the group homomorphism property. Left-multiplying by $f(e_G)^{-1}$ (whatever this may be!), we get

$$f(e_G)^{-1} \cdot f(e_G) = f(e_G)^{-1} \cdot (f(e_G) \cdot f(e_G))$$

Simplifying and rearranging a bit, this is

$$e_H = (f(e_G)^{-1} \cdot f(e_G)) \cdot f(e_G) = e_H \cdot f(e_G) = f(e_G)$$

This proves that the identity in G is mapped to the identity in H.

To check that the image of an inverse is the image of an inverse, we simply compute

$$f(g^{-1}) \cdot f(g) = f(g^{-1} \cdot g)$$

by the homomorphism property, and this is

$$= f(e_G) = e_H$$

by the inverse property and by the fact (just proven) that the identity in G is mapped to the identity in H by a group homomorphism. Likewise, we also compute that

$$f(g) \cdot f(g^{-1}) = e_H$$

so the image of an inverse is the inverse of the image, as claimed.

To prove that the kernel of a group homomorphism $f : G \to H$ is a subgroup of G, we must prove three things. First, we must check that the identity lies in the kernel: this follows immediately from the fact just proven that $f(e_G) = e_H$. Next, we must show that if g is in the kernel, then g^{-1} is also. Happily (by luck?) we just showed that $f(g^{-1}) = f(g)^{-1}$, so if $f(g) = e_H$, then

$$f(g^{-1}) = f(g)^{-1} = e_H^{-1} = e_H$$

Finally, suppose both x, y are in the kernel of f. Then

$$f(xy) = f(x) \cdot f(y) = e_H \cdot e_H = e_H$$

so the 'product' is also in the kernel.

Now let X be a subgroup of G. Let

$$f(X) = \{f(x) : x \in X\}$$

To show that $f(X)$ is a subgroup of H, we must check the usual three things: presence of the identity, closure under taking inverses, and closure under products. Again, we just showed that $f(e_G) = e_H$, so the image of a subgroup contains the identity. Also, we showed that $f(g)^{-1}) = f(g^{-1})$, so the image of a subgroup is closed under inverses. And $f(xy) = f(x)f(y)$ by the defining property of a group homomorphism, so the image is closed under multiplication.

Finally, let's prove that a homomorphism $f : G \to H$ is injective if and only if its kernel is trivial. First, if f is injective, then at most one element can be mapped to $e_H \in H$. Since we know that at least e_G is mapped to e_H by such a homomorphism, it must be that *only* e_G is mapped to e_H. Thus, the kernel is trivial.

On the other hand, suppose that the kernel is trivial. We will suppose that $f(x) = f(y)$, and show that $x = y$. Left-multiply the equality $f(x) = f(y)$ by $f(x)^{-1}$ to obtain

$$e_H = f(x)^{-1} \cdot f(x) = f(x)^{-1} \cdot f(y)$$

By the homomorphism property, this gives

$$e_H = f(x)^{-1} \cdot f(y) = f(x^{-1}y)$$

Thus, $x^{-1}y$ is in the kernel of f, so (by assumption) $x^{-1}y = e_G$. Left-multiplying this equality by x and simplifying, we get $y = x$. This proves the injectivity.   ♣

If a group homomorphism $f : G \to H$ is *surjective*, then H is said to be a **homomorphic image** of G. If a group homomorphism $f : G \to H$ is a *bijection*, then f is said to be an **isomorphism**, and G and H are said to be **isomorphic**.

Remark: At least from a theoretical viewpoint, two groups that are *isomorphic* are considered to be 'the same', in the sense that any *intrinsic* group-theoretic assertion about one is also true of the other. In practical terms, however, the *transfer of structure* via the isomorphism may be difficult to *compute*.

Exercises

22.1.01 What is the kernel of the homomorphism $x \to x \mod N$ from $\mathbf{Z}$ (with addition) to $\mathbf{Z}/N$ (with addition modulo N)?

22.1.02 Let M, N be positive integers, with $N|M$. What is the kernel of the map $x \mod M \to x \mod N$ from $\mathbf{Z}/M$ (with addition mod M) to $\mathbf{Z}/N$ (with addition mod N)?

22.1.03 Let $\det : GL(2, \mathbf{Q}) \to \mathbf{Q}^\times$ be the usual determinant

$$\det \begin{pmatrix} a & b \\ c & d \end{pmatrix} = ad - bc$$

Show by computation that det is a group homomorphism.

22.1.04 Show that for any integer n and positive integer N the map $f : \mathbf{Z}/N \to \mathbf{Z}/N$ defined by $f(x) = n \cdot x$ is a group homomorphism (with addition mod N).

22.1.05 Show that for any integer n and positive integer N the map $f : \mathbf{Z}/N^\times \to \mathbf{Z}/N^\times$ defined by $f(x) = x^n$ is a group homomorphism.

22.1.06 Fix a positive integer N. Show that for any group homomorphism $f : \mathbf{Z}/N \to \mathbf{Z}/N$ (with addition mod N) there is an integer n so that $f(x) = n \cdot x$ *Hint:* Try $n = f(1)$, and use the fact that $f(x) = f(\underbrace{1 + \cdots + 1}_{x})$.

22.1.07 Show that the map

$$t \to \begin{pmatrix} 1 & t \\ 0 & 1 \end{pmatrix}$$

is an isomorphism from $\mathbf{Q}$ (with addition) to a subgroup of $GL(2, \mathbf{Q})$.

22.1.08 Show that the map

$$\begin{pmatrix} a & b \\ 0 & d \end{pmatrix} \to a$$

is a *homomorphism* from the group of all matrices $\begin{pmatrix} a & b \\ 0 & d \end{pmatrix}$ in which a, d are *nonzero* rational numbers and b is *any* rational number, to the multiplicative group $\mathbf{Q}^\times$ of nonzero rational numbers. What is its kernel?

22.1.09 Show that

$$\begin{pmatrix} a & b \\ 0 & d \end{pmatrix} \to b$$

is *not* a homomorphism.

22.1.10 Define a map $E : \mathbf{Q} \to GL(2, \mathbf{Q})$ by

$$x \to \begin{pmatrix} 1 & x \\ 0 & 1 \end{pmatrix}$$

Show that E is a group homomorphism from $\mathbf{Q}$ (with addition) to a subgroup of $GL(2, \mathbf{Q})$.

22.1.11 Define a map $E : \mathbf{Q} \to GL(3, \mathbf{Q})$ by

$$x \to \begin{pmatrix} 1 & x & \frac{x^2}{2} \\ 0 & 1 & x \\ 0 & 0 & 1 \end{pmatrix}$$

Show that E is a group homomorphism from $\mathbf{Q}$ (with addition) to a subgroup of $GL(3, \mathbf{Q})$.

22.1.12 Define a map $r : \mathbf{R} \to GL(2, \mathbf{R})$ by

$$x \to \begin{pmatrix} \cos x & \sin x \\ -\sin x & \cos x \end{pmatrix}$$

Show that r is a group homomorphism from $\mathbf{R}$ (with addition) to a subgroup of $GL(2, \mathbf{R})$. What is its kernel?

22.1.13 Let n be an integer. Show that $f : \mathbf{Z} \to \mathbf{Z}$ defined by $f(x) = nx$ is a homomorphism.

22.1.14 Show that a homomorphism $f : G \to H$ always has the property that $f(g^{-1}) = f(g)^{-1}$ for $g \in G$.

22.2 Finite Cyclic Groups

A finite group G is **cyclic** if there is $g \in G$ so that $\langle g \rangle = G$. And such a g is a **generator** of G, and G is said to be **generated by** g. (The case of *infinite* cyclic groups will be considered in the next section.) Finite cyclic groups are the simplest of all groups and can be readily understood, as we'll see here.

Let $N = |G|$. Since $G = \langle g \rangle$, also $N = |g|$. It is important to remember that (as proven a bit earlier)

- The elements $e = g^0, g^1, g^2, \ldots, g^{N-2}, g^{N-1}$ form a complete list of the *distinct* elements of $G = \langle g \rangle$.

- With arbitrary integers i, j, we have $g^i = g^j$ if and only if $i \equiv j \bmod N$.

- Given an integer j, let i be the *reduction of j* mod N. Then $g^j = g^i$.

Then the collections of all *subgroups* and of all *generators* can be completely understood in terms of elementary arithmetic:

- The *distinct* subgroups of G are exactly the subgroups $\langle g^d \rangle$ for all *divisors* d of N.

- For $d | N$ the order of the subgroup $\langle g^d \rangle$ is the order of g^d, which is just N/d.

- The order of g^k with arbitrary integer $k \neq 0$ is $N/\gcd(k, N)$.

- For any integer n we have

$$\langle g^n \rangle = \langle g^{gcd(n,N)} \rangle$$

- The distinct generators of G are the elements g^r, where $1 \le r < N$ and $\gcd(r, N) = 1$. Thus, there are $\varphi(N)$ of them, where φ is Euler's phi-function.

- The number of elements of order n in a finite cyclic group of order N is 0 unless $n|N$, in which case it is N/n.

Remark: Some aspects of this can be paraphrased nicely in words. For example: *Every subgroup of a finite cyclic group is again a finite cyclic group, with order dividing the order of the group. Conversely, for every divisor of the order of the group, there is a **unique** subgroup of that order.*

Proof: Let's prove that that the order of g^k is $N/\gcd(k, N)$. First, if $(g^k)^\ell = e = g^0$, then $k\ell \equiv 0 \bmod N$, from the simpler facts recalled above. That is, $N|k\ell$. That is, there is an integer m so that $k\ell = mN$. Then divide both sides of this equality by $\gcd(k, N)$, obtaining

$$\frac{k}{\gcd(k, N)} \cdot \ell = m \cdot \frac{N}{\gcd(k, N)}$$

Since now $N/\gcd(k, N)$ and $k/\gcd(k, N)$ are relatively prime, by unique factorization we conclude that

$$\frac{N}{\gcd(k, N)} \text{ divides } \ell$$

Therefore, the actual order of g^k is a multiple of $N/\gcd(k, N)$. On the other hand,

$$(g^k)^{N/\gcd(k,N)} = (g^N)^{k/\gcd(k,N)} = e^{k/\gcd(k,N)} = e$$

Note that we use the fact that $N/\gcd(k, N)$ and $k/\gcd(k, N)$ are both integers, so that all the expressions here have genuine content and sense. This finishes the proof that the order of g^k is $N/\gcd(k, N)$.

As a special case of the preceding, if $k|N$ then the order of g^k is $N/\gcd(k, N) = N/k$, as claimed above.

Since we know by now that $|\langle h \rangle| = |h|$ for any h, certainly

$$|\langle g^k \rangle| = |g^k| = N/\gcd(k, N)$$

Given integer k, let's show that

$$\langle g^k \rangle = \langle g^{\gcd(k,N)} \rangle$$

Let $d = \gcd(k, N)$, and let s, t be integers so that

$$d = sk + tN$$

Then

$$g^d = g^{sk+tN} = (g^k)^s \cdot (g^N)^t = (g^k)^s \cdot (e)^t = (g^k)^s \cdot e = (g^k)^s$$

so $g^d \in \langle g^k \rangle$. On the other hand,

$$g^k = (g^d)^{k/d}$$

since $d|k$. Thus, $g^k \in \langle g^d \rangle$. Therefore, since the subgroups $\langle g^k \rangle$ and $\langle g^d \rangle$ are closed under multiplication and under inverses, for any integer ℓ

$$(g^k)^\ell \in \langle g^d \rangle$$

and

$$(g^d)^\ell \in \langle g^k \rangle$$

But $\langle g^d \rangle$ *is* just the set of all integer powers of g^d (and similarly for g^k), so we have shown that

$$\langle g^d \rangle \subset \langle g^k \rangle$$

and vice versa, so we find at last that

$$\langle g^d \rangle = \langle g^k \rangle$$

Therefore, all the *cyclic* subgroups of $\langle g \rangle = G$ are of the form $\langle g^d \rangle$ for some positive d dividing $N = |G| = |g|$. And different divisors d give different subgroups.

Let H be an *arbitrary* subgroup of G. We must show that H is generated by some g^k (so is in fact cyclic). Let k be the smallest positive integer so that $g^k \in H$. We claim that $\langle g^k \rangle = H$. For any other $g^m \in H$, we can write

$$m = q \cdot k + r$$

with $0 \le r < k$. Then

$$g^r = g^{m - q \cdot k} = g^m \cdot (g^k)^q \in H$$

since H is a subgroup. Since k was the smallest positive integer so that $g^k \in H$, and $0 \le r < k$, it must be that $r = 0$. Therefore, m is a multiple of k, and g^k generates H.

As another particular case, notice that $\langle g^k \rangle = \langle g \rangle$ if and only if $\gcd(k, N) = 1$. And we may as well only consider $0 < k < N$, since otherwise we start repeating elements. That is, the distinct generators of $\langle g \rangle$ are the elements g^k with $0 < k < N$ and $\gcd(k, N) = 1$. So there certainly are $\varphi(N)$ of them.

Likewise, since

$$|g^k| = |\langle g^k \rangle| = |\langle g^{\gcd(k,N)} \rangle| = |g^{\gcd(k,N)}|$$

it is not hard to count the number of elements of a given order in $\langle g \rangle$.   ♣

- *A homomorphic image of a finite cyclic group is finite cyclic.*

Proof: This follows by checking that the image of a generator is a generator for the image.   ♣

- A *finite cyclic group of order N is isomorphic to* $\mathbf{Z}/N$. Specifically, for any choice of generator g of the cyclic group G, the map

$$f : n \to g^n$$

describes an isomorphism $f : \mathbf{Z}/N \to G$.

Proof: This is just a paraphrase of some of the other properties above.   ♣

A possibly disturbing issue here is that of proving that the map f as described above is **well defined**. That is, we have some sort of formula which *appears* to describe a map, but there are hidden pitfalls. What we must show is that if $m = n \bmod N$, then $f(m) = f(n)$. (This has *nothing* to do with injectivity!) Well, it turns out that everything is alright, because we've already shown (in discussion of cyclic subgroups) that $g^m = g^n$ if and only if $m = n \bmod N$.

For emphasis, we'll write the group operation in the cyclic group G as $*$ rather than as multiplication or addition. The crucial property which must be demonstrated is the homomorphism property $f(m + n) = f(m) * f(n)$. Indeed,

$$f(m + n) = f((m + n) \,\%\, N) = g^{m+n \,\%\, N} = g^{m+n}$$

since we proved (in the discussion of cyclic subgroups) that $g^i = g^j$ whenever $i = j \bmod N$. And then this is $f(g^m) * f(g^n)$ as desired.

To see that f is injective, suppose that $f(m) = f(n)$ for integers m, n. Then $g^m = g^n$. Again, this implies that $m = n \bmod N$, which says that $m - \mathrm{mod} - N = n - \mathrm{mod} - N$, as desired. So f is injective.

The surjectivity is easy: given $g^n \in \langle g \rangle$, $f(n) = g^n$. Therefore, the map f is a bijective homorphism, so by definition is an isomorphism.

Exercises

22.2.01 List all elements of order 4 in $\mathbf{Z}/8$. List all elements of order 6 in $\mathbf{Z}/72$.

22.2.02 List all elements of order 4 in $\mathbf{Z}/13$.

22.2.03 Show that the subgroups $\langle 3 \rangle$ and $\langle 97 \rangle$ of $\mathbf{Z}/100$ generated by $3, 97$ are the same subgroup.

22.2.04 Suppose that $G = \langle g \rangle$ is a cyclic group of order 30. Compute the orders of the elements g^4, g^8, g^{12}, g^{16} g^{20}, g^{24} g^{28}.

22.2.05 Suppose that G is a finite cyclic group and has just 2 subgroups altogether: itself and the trivial subgroup $\{e\}$. What can you say about the order of G?

22.2.06 Suppose that G is a finite cyclic group and has just 3 subgroups altogether: itself, the trivial subgroup $\{e\}$, and a (*proper*) subgroup of order 13. What is the order of G?

22.2.07 Let p be a prime. Suppose that a group G has p elements. Prove that G is *cyclic*. (*Hint:* Take $g \neq e$ and look at $\langle g \rangle$: Use Lagrange's theorem.)

22.2.08 Let m, n be relatively prime. Let H, K be subgroups of a group G where $|H| = m$ and $|K| = n$. Show that $H \cap K = \{e\}$.

22.3 Infinite Cyclic Groups

There are non-finite cyclic groups, as well, whose nature is also simple, though different from that of the finite cyclic groups. Dropping the assumption that a cylic group is *finite* creates a few complications, but things are still tractable. For example, **Z** with addition is an infinite cyclic group. A group G is **infinite cyclic** if G is an *infinite* group and if there is $g \in G$ so that $\langle g \rangle = G$. Such a g is a **generator** of G, and G is said to be **generated by** g.

It is important to understand the assertions for *infinite* cyclic groups analogous to those for *finite* cyclic groups above:

- The elements $\ldots, g^{-3}, g^{-2}, g^{-1} e = g^0, g = g^1, g^2, g^3, \ldots$ are all *distinct* elements of $G = \langle g \rangle$.

- With integers i, j, we have $g^i = g^j$ if and only if $i = j$.

An infinite cyclic group is isomorphic to **Z**. Specifically, for any generator g of the infinite cyclic group G, the map $g^n \to n$ is an isomorphism $G \to \mathbf{Z}$. Thus, *an infinite cyclic group has just two generators*, since that is true of **Z**.

Then the collections of all *subgroups* and of all *generators* can be completely understood in elementary terms:

- The *distinct* subgroups of G are exactly the subgroups $\langle g^d \rangle$ for all *non-negative* integers d.

- Any subgroup $\langle g^d \rangle$ is *infinite cyclic*, except for the trivial group $\{e\} = \{g^0\} = \langle g^0 \rangle$.

- Each subgroup $\langle g^d \rangle$ has exactly *two* generators, g^d and g^{-d}.

Some aspects of this can be paraphrased nicely in words: *Every non-trivial subgroup of an infinite cyclic group is again an infinite cyclic group.*

Also, about the number of elements of various orders: all elements of an infinite cyclic group are of infinite order except $e = g^0$, which is of order 1.

Exercises

22.3.01 Prove that for any subgroup H of **Z** other than the trivial subgroup $\{0\}$ the *smallest positive element s of H* is a generator for H, which is a cyclic group.

22.4 Roots and Powers in Groups

In a cyclic group $G = \langle g \rangle$ of order n it is possible to reach very clear conclusions about the solvability of the equation $x^r = y$.

Let G be a cyclic group of order n with generator g. Fix an integer r, and define $f : G \to G$ by $f(x) = x^r$.

Theorem. This map f is a group homomorphism of G to itself. If $\gcd(r, n) = 1$, then f is an *isomorphism*. That is, if $\gcd(r, n) = 1$, then every $y \in G$ has an rth root and has *exactly* one such root. Generally,

$$\text{order of kernel of } f \;=\; \gcd(r, n)$$
$$\text{order of image of } f \;=\; n/\gcd(r, n)$$

If an element y has an rth root, then it has exactly $\gcd(r, n)$ of them. There are exactly $n/\gcd(r, n)$ rth powers in G.

Proof: Certainly

$$f(x \cdot y) \;=\; (xy)^r \;=\; x^r\, y^r \quad \text{(since } G \text{ is abelian)}$$
$$= f(x) \cdot f(y)$$

which shows that f is a homomorphism.

We may as well use the fact that G is isomorphic to $\mathbf{Z}/n$ with addition (proven just above). This allows us to directly use things we know about $\mathbf{Z}/n$ and the relatively simple behavior of addition mod n to prove things about arbitrary finite cyclic groups. Thus, converting to the additive notation appropriate for $\mathbf{Z}/n$-with-addition, the map f is

$$f(x) = r \cdot x$$

We already know that if $\gcd(r, n) = 1$, then there is a multiplicative inverse r^{-1} to $r \bmod n$. Thus, the function

$$g(x) = r^{-1} \cdot x$$

gives an inverse function to f. This proves that f is both surjective and injective, so is a bijection, and thus an isomorphism.

For arbitrary r, let's look at the solvability of

$$r \cdot x = y \bmod n$$

for given y. Rewritten in more elementary terms, this is

$$n \,|\, (rx - y)$$

or, for some integer m,

$$mn = rx - y$$

Let $d = \gcd(r, n)$. Then certainly it is *necessary* that $d|y$, or this equation is impossible. On the other hand, suppose that $d|y$. Write $y = dy'$ with some integer y'. Then we want to solve

$$r \cdot x = dy' \bmod n$$

'Dividing through' by the common divisor d, this congruence is equivalent to

$$\frac{r}{d} \cdot x = y' \bmod \frac{n}{d}$$

The removal of the common divisor has made r/d relatively prime to n/d, so there is a multiplicative inverse $(r/d)^{-1}$ to r/d mod n/d, and

$$x = (r/d)^{-1} \cdot y' \bmod (n/d)$$

That is, any integer x meeting this condition is a solution to the original congruence. Letting x_0 be one such solution, the integers

$$x_0, \; x_0 + \frac{n}{d}, \; x_0 + 2 \cdot \frac{n}{d}, \; x_0 + 3 \cdot \frac{n}{d}, \; \ldots, \; x_0 + (d-1) \cdot \frac{n}{d}$$

are also solutions and are distinct mod n. That is, altogether we have d distinct solutions modulo n.

The necessary and sufficient condition $\gcd(r,n)|y$ for the equation

$$rx = y \bmod n$$

to have a solution shows that there are exactly $n/\gcd(r,n)$ integers y mod n which fulfill this condition. That is, there are exactly $n/\gcd(r,n)$ 'rth powers'.

The kernel of f is the collection of x so that $rx = 0 \bmod n$. Taking out the common denominator $d = \gcd(r,n)$, this is $(r/d)x = 0 \bmod n/d$, which means $(n/d)|(r/d)x$. Since now r/d and n/d have no common factor, by unique factorization this implies that n/d divides x. Thus, mod n, there are d different solutions x. That is, the kernel of f has d elements. ♣

Earlier, we saw that for a prime p so that $p = 3 \bmod 4$, it is easy to take square roots (of squares mod p): there is the formula

$$\text{square root of } b = b^{(p+1)/2} \bmod p \qquad b^{\frac{p+1}{4}} \bmod p$$

Of course, this formula gives a square root of b mod p only if b is a square mod p. Otherwise it gives garbage as output. The following theorem is a version of this abstracted to groups.

Theorem. Let G be an *abelian* group of order N, and let n be an integer relatively prime to N. Let r be a multiplicative inverse to n modulo N. For any $x \in G$, there is exactly one nth root of x in G, and it is given by the formula

$$\sqrt[n]{x} = x^r$$

Remark: It is in general unwise to use the notation $\sqrt[n]{x}$ without some assurance in advance that such a thing exists.

Proof: Since r is a multiplicative inverse of n modulo N, we have

$$r \cdot n = 1 + \ell N$$

for some integer ℓ. Then

$$(x^r)^n = x^{rn} = x^{1+\ell N} = x \cdot (x^N)^\ell$$

As a corollary of Lagrange's theorem, we found that the order of any element x is a divisor of the order N of the group, so $x^N = e$. Thus, we can go a little further:

$$(x^r)^n = x^{rn} = x^{1+\ell N} = x \cdot (x^N)^\ell = x \cdot e^\ell = x \cdot e = x$$

This proves that an nth root of x exists and is given by the indicated formula.

To prove uniqueness, suppose that both y and z were nth roots of x. Then

$$(y/z)^n = y^n/z^n = x/x = e$$

It is here that we use the abelian-ness of the group: without it, it is not generally true that $(xy)^k = x^k y^k$. Therefore, the order of the element y/z is a divisor of n. By Lagrange's theorem, this order is also a divisor of N. Therefore, the order of y/z is a common divisor of n and N, so divides $\gcd(n, N) = 1$. Therefore, this order (being a positive integer) is just 1. That is, $y/z = e$, so $y = z$.   ♣

Now we can formulate an **abstract Euler criterion** for nth roots in cyclic groups. This abstracts the concrete case from classical number theory.

Theorem.   Let G be a cyclic group of order N. Let n be an integer dividing N. Let

$$m = N/n$$

A given element $g \in G$ is an nth power in G (that is, there is $h \in G$ so that $h^n = g$) if and only if

$$g^m = e$$

Proof: If g is an nth power of $h = x^\ell$ for a generator x of G, then $g = (x^\ell)^n$, and

$$g^m = ((x^\ell)^n)^m = (x^\ell)^{mn} = (x^\ell)^N = e$$

because (by Lagrange's theorem) the Nth power of any element is e.

For the converse, suppose that $g^m = e$. Then, writing $g = x^\ell$ for some exponent ℓ,

$$e = g^m = (x^\ell)^m = x^{\ell m}$$

Since the order of x is N, this can hold if and only if $N | \ell\, m$. Since $m = N/n$, this implies (by unique factorization) that $n | \ell$. That is,

$$g = x^\ell = x^{n(\ell/n)} = (x^{\ell/n})^n$$

which demonstrates that g is an nth power.   ♣

Exercises

22.4.01 Let p be a prime congruent to 3 modulo 4. Suppose that a is a square in $\mathbf{Z}/p$. Show that $a^{(p+1)/4}$ is a square root of a.

22.4.02 Let p be a prime congruent to 7 mod 9. If a is a cube in $\mathbf{Z}/p$, show that $a^{(p+2)/9}$ is a cube root of a.

22.4.03 Let p be a prime congruent to 4 mod 9. If a is a cube in $\mathbf{Z}/p$, show that $a^{(p+5)/9}$ is a cube root of a.

22.5 Square Root Algorithm

Let G be a *cyclic* group of order N. We consider the case that $2|N$, and we'll look for a general algorithm to find square roots.

First, we must find a non-square g in G. This is the probabilistic part of the algorithm. *At random*, choose an element g_0 of G. Compute $g_0^{N/2}$ (using the fast exponentiation algorithm). If $g_0^{N/2} \neq e$, then take $g = g_0$. On the other hand, if $g_0^{N/2} = e$, then g_0 is a square, and we choose (at random) a different $g_1 \in G$ and try again. Repeat until a non-square g is found.

Remark: We are using the abstract version Euler's criterion for squares in cyclic groups of even order.

Remark: Note that each random choice of $g_i \in G$ has a 50-50 chance of being a non-square: from above, we know that the elements of a cyclic group of even order N generated by x are (without repetition)

$$x^0, \ x^1, \ x^2, \ \ldots, \ x^{N-1}$$

and (from the previous paragraph) that among these the squares are exactly those x^ℓ with $2|\ell$. Thus, the $N/2$ elements $x^0, x^2, \ldots, x^{N-4}, x^{N-2}$ are squares while the $N/2$ elements $x^1, x^3, \ldots, x^{N-3}, x^{N-1}$ are non-squares.

Let 2^s be the largest power of 2 that divides the order N, and put

$$N = 2^s \cdot m$$

with m odd. Let H be the subgroup of G consisting of 2^sth powers. ~~Let H be the subgroup of G consisting of 2^sth powers.~~ By the abstract version of Euler's theorem for cyclic groups, an element h of G is in H if and only if $h^m = 1$. Also, the order of H is m, which is *odd*. Therefore, every $h \in H$ has a unique square root (in H) given by

$$\sqrt{h} = h^{(m+1)/2}$$

Given a square y in G, and given a non-square g, if we can manage to write

$$y = g^e \cdot h$$

for some **even** integer e and for some $h \in H$, then

$$\sqrt{y} = g^{e/2} \cdot h^{(m+1)/2}$$

What we need is a good algorithm to obtain the exponent e. (In effect, we will obtain the exponent e expressed in binary, somewhat as in the fast exponentiation algorithm.)

To compute the square root of a square b mod p with p prime:

- Factor $p - 1 = 2^s \cdot m$ with m odd.

- Find a non-square g mod p.

- Let $B = b^m \bmod p$, $G = g^m \bmod p$. Initialize $E = 0$.

- For $i = 2, \ldots, s$, if $(B \cdot G^E)^{2^{s-i}} \neq 1 \bmod p$, replace E by $E + 2^{i-1}$, or else don't change E.

- Let $F = (p - 1) - E$.

- Then $\sqrt{b} = (b \cdot g^E)^{(m+1)/2} \cdot g^{F/2} \bmod p$.

Example: Compute $\sqrt{11} \bmod 1013$. Let $b = 11$ and $p = 1013$, in the notation above. First find a non-square g mod 1013 by guessing and checking via Euler's criterion: guess 2 as non-square, check

$$2^{(1013-1)/2} = -1 \bmod 1013$$

so $g = 2$ really is a non-square mod 1013. Take out powers of 2 from $1013 - 1$:

$$1013 - 1 = 2^2 \cdot 235$$
$$253$$

So set $s = 2$ and $m = 253$. Compute

$$
\begin{aligned}
B &= b^m &= 11^{253} \% 1013 = 1012 = -1 \bmod 1013 \\
G &= g^m &= 2^{253} \% 1013 = 45 \bmod 1013
\end{aligned}
$$

Let $E = 0$. The range for index i is $i = 2, \ldots, s$, which in this case is just the single index $i = 2$:

$$(B \cdot G^E)^{2^{s-i}} = (-1)^{2^{2-2}} = (-1)^{2^0} = (-1)^1 \neq 1 \bmod 1013$$

so we replace E by

$$E + 2^{i-1} = E + 2^{2-1} = E + 2^1 = E + 2 = 0 + 2 = 2$$

So the final E is $E = 2$. Then put $F = (p-1) - E = 1012 - 2 = 1010$. And modulo 1013

$$
\begin{aligned}
\sqrt{11} &= (b \cdot g^E)^{(m+1)/2} \cdot g^{F/2} \\
&= (11 \cdot 2^2)^{(253+1)/2} \cdot 2^{1010/2} \\
&= 44^{127} \cdot 2^{505} \\
&= 32 \bmod 1013
\end{aligned}
$$

Finally, we can check:

$$32^2 = 1024 = 1024 - 1013 = 11 \bmod 1013$$

so we have indeed found a square root of 11 modulo 1013.

Example: Compute $\sqrt{2} \bmod 48049$. Let $b = 2$ and $p = 48049$, in the notation above. First find a non-square $g \bmod 48049$ by guessing and then checking via Euler's criterion: here 2, 3, 5, 7, 11, 13 are all squares mod 48049, and 17 is the smallest non-square:

$$17^{(48049-1)/2} = -1 \bmod 48049$$

so $g = 17$ really is a non-square mod 48049. Take out powers of 2 from $48049 - 1$:

$$48049 - 1 = 2^4 \cdot 3003$$

So set $s = 4$ and $m = 3003$. Compute

$$B = b^m = 2^{3003} \% 48049 = 23300 \bmod 48049$$

$$G = g^m = 17^{3003} \% 48049 = 12891 \bmod 48049$$

Let $E = 0$. The range for index i is $i = 2, \ldots, s$, which in this case is $i = 2, 3, 4$:

$$B^{2^{s-2}} = (23300)^{2^{4-2}} = 48048 \neq 1 \bmod 48049$$

so we replace E by

$$E + 2^{2-1} = E + 2^{2-1} = E + 2^1 = E + 2 = 0 + 2 = 2$$

For $i = 3$:
$$(B \cdot G^E)^{2^{s-3}} = (23300 \cdot 12891^2)^{2^{4-3}} = 1 \bmod 48049$$

(So at this step E does not change.) The last step is $i = 4$:

$$
\begin{aligned}
(B \cdot G^E)^{2^{s-4}} &= (23300 \cdot 12891^2)^{2^{4-4}} \\
&= (23300 \cdot 12891^2)^1 = 1 \bmod 48049
\end{aligned}
$$

(So at this step as well E does not change.) So the final E is $E = 2$. Then put $F = (p - 1) - E = 48049 - 1 - 2 = 48046$. And modulo 48049

$$
\begin{aligned}
\sqrt{2} &= (b \cdot g^E)^{(m+1)/2} \cdot g^{F/2} \\
&= (2 \cdot 17^2)^{(3003+1)/2} \cdot 17^{48046/2} \\
&= 578^{1502} \cdot 17^{24023} \\
&= 310 \bmod 48049
\end{aligned}
$$

We can check:

$$310^2 = 96100 = 2 \bmod 48049$$

so 310 is indeed a square root of 2 modulo 48049.

Exercises

22.5.01 Find a square root of 2 modulo 17 using the probabilistic algorithm.

22.5.02 Find a square root of 211 modulo 433 using the probabilistic algorithm.

22.5.03 Find a square root of 331 modulo 449 using the probabilistic algorithm.

22.5.04 Find a square root of 123 modulo 521 using the probabilistic algorithm.

22.5.05 Find a square root of 67 modulo 569 using the probabilistic algorithm.

23

Pseudoprimality Proofs

At last we are in a position to prove that our probabilistic primality tests really work. First we prove some relatively straightforward properties of Carmichael numbers. This much is not hard to understand. The other proofs are more difficult, and can be omitted without loss of understanding of later material. On the other hand, these proofs are a good illustration of the utility of the abstract algebra developed so far.

23.1 Lambda Function

To understand Carmichael numbers means to understand how the Fermat pseudo-prime test fails. To understand this mechanism we continue in the spirit of Euler's theorem and Fermat's Little Theorem.

For a positive integer n, define Carmichael's **lambda function**

$$\lambda(n) = \text{exponent of the multiplicative group } \mathbf{Z}/n^\times$$

371

This usage is consistent with the notion of *exponent* of an arbitrary group G. That is, $\lambda(n)$ is the *least* positive integer so that for every $x \in \mathbf{Z}/n^\times$

$$x^{\lambda(n)} = 1 \bmod n$$

We already know (from discussion of cyclic subgroups) that if $x^k = 1 \bmod n$, then the order $|x|$ of x divides k: to recall how the proof of this important fact goes, write $k = q \cdot |x| + r$ with $0 \leq r < |x|$. Then

$$1 = x^k = x^{q \cdot |x| + r} = (x^{|x|})^q \cdot x^r = (1)^q \cdot x^r = x^r \bmod n$$

Since $|x|$ is the smallest *positive* integer so that $x^{|x|} = 1 \bmod n$, it must be that $r = 0$, so $|x|$ indeed divides n.

We also know, from Lagrange's theorem, that the exponent of a finite group divides the order of the group. Thus,

$$\lambda(n) = \text{exponent of } \mathbf{Z}/n^\times \text{divides } \varphi(n)$$

Now we can completely determine $\lambda(n)$. It is *not* weakly multiplicative, but nevertheless behaves in a way that is manageable.

Theorem.
- For m and n relatively prime, the Carmichael lambda function has the property $\lambda(m \cdot n) = \text{lcm}(\lambda(m), \lambda(n))$.

- For an odd prime p, $\lambda(p^e) = \varphi(p^e) = (p-1)p^{e-1}$. Since there is a primitive root mod p^e, there is an element whose order is $\lambda(p^e)$.

- For powers of 2: $\lambda(2) = 1$, $\lambda(4) = 2$, and $\lambda(2^e) = 2^{e-2}$ for $e > 2$. There is an element of $\mathbf{Z}/2^{e\times}$ whose order is $\lambda(2^e)$.

Proof: For m and n relatively prime, by Sun Ze's theorem the system

$$\begin{aligned} x^k &= 1 \bmod m \\ x^k &= 1 \bmod n \end{aligned}$$

is equivalent to the single congruence

$$x^k = 1 \bmod mn$$

Thus, if $x^k = 1 \bmod mn$, certainly $x^k = 1 \bmod m$ and $x^k = 1 \bmod n$. Thus, by the observation just before the statement of the theorem, certainly $\lambda(m)$ and $\lambda(n)$ both divide $\lambda(mn)$. Thus, $\lambda(mn)$ is a common multiple of the two. On the other hand, let M be any common multiple of $\lambda(m)$ and $\lambda(n)$. Write $M = m'\lambda(m)$ and $M = n'\lambda(n)$ for some integers m' and n'. Then

$$x^M = (x^{\lambda(m)})^{m'} = 1^{m'} = 1 \bmod m$$

and

$$x^M = (x^{\lambda(n)})^{n'} = 1^{n'} = 1 \bmod n$$

Thus, by Sun Ze (using the relative primeness of m and n)

$$x^M = 1 \bmod mn$$

That is, if M is divisible by all the orders mod m and by all the orders mod n, it is divisible by all the orders mod mn. This proves that

$$\lambda(m \cdot n) = \mathrm{lcm}(\lambda(m), \lambda(n))$$

For p an odd prime we know that there is a primitive root g modulo p^e. Thus, there is an element of order $(p-1)p^{e-1} = \varphi(p^e)$ in $\mathbf{Z}/p^{e\times}$. Thus, $\varphi(p^e)$ divides $\lambda(p^e)$. By Lagrange's theorem, the order of *any* element in $\mathbf{Z}/p^{e\times}$ divides the order $\varphi(p^e)$ of $\mathbf{Z}/p^{e\times}$. Thus, thinking again of the observation just before the theorem, $\lambda(p^e) = \varphi(p^e)$.

Now consider powers of 2. The group $\mathbf{Z}/2^\times$ has just one element, so its order is necessarily 1. The group $\mathbf{Z}/4^\times$ has order 2, so necessarily has order 2.

In showing that there is *no* primitive root mod 2^e for $e \geq 3$, we already noted that

$$(1 + 2x)^2 = 1 + 4x(1 + x) = 1 \bmod 8$$

for any integer x. And, further, we saw that

$$(1 + 8x)^{2^k} = 1 \bmod 2^{3+k}$$

Therefore,

$$(1 + 2x)^{2^{e-2}} = 1 \bmod 2^e$$

for $e \geq 3$. Thus, the actual order of any element must be a divisor of 2^{e-2}. On the other hand, for $k \geq 2$, and for odd integer x,

$$(1 + 2^k x)^2 = 1 + 2^{k+1}x + 2^{2k}x^2 = 1 + 2^{k+1} \cdot \underbrace{(x + 2^{k-1}x^2)}_{y} = 1 + 2^{k+1}y$$

Since $k \geq 2$, $2^{k-1}x^2$ is even, so $y = x \bmod 2$. Thus, by induction,

$$(1 + 4x)^{2^\ell} = 1 + 2^{2+\ell}y$$

with $y = x \bmod 2$. In particular, this is not 1 mod 2^e unless $2 + \ell \geq e$. Thus, for example, the element $1 + 4$ has order 2^{e-2} in $\mathbf{Z}/2^{e\times}$. Thus,

$$\lambda(2^e) = 2^{e-2} \text{for } e \geq 3$$

This completes the computation of $\lambda(n)$.

♣

23.2 Carmichael Numbers

Even though it is awkward that there are infinitely many Carmichael numbers, there are demonstrable restrictions on what kind of numbers may be Carmichael. These restrictions are used in proving that the more refined Solovay–Strassen and Miller–Rabin tests (probabilistically) *succeed* in detecting compositeness.

Theorem. A positive integer is a Carmichael number if and only if

$$\lambda(n) \text{ divides } n - 1$$

In particular, a Carmichael number is necessarily odd, square-free, and divisible by at least three different primes.

Proof: Suppose n is Carmichael. That is, suppose that for every b relatively prime to n we have

$$b^{n-1} = 1 \bmod n$$

By definition, the Carmichael function $\lambda(n)$ gives the smallest positive integer so that

$$b^{\lambda(n)} = 1 \bmod n$$

for all b prime to n. We have seen that there exists an element whose order is exactly $\lambda(n)$. Let b be such an element. Write $n - 1 = q \cdot \lambda(n) = r$ with $0 \le e < \lambda(n)$. Then

$$1 = b^{n-1} = b^{q \cdot \lambda(n)+r} = (b^{\lambda(n)})^q \cdot b^r \bmod n$$

Since $\lambda(n)$ is the least positive integer so that b raised to that power is 1 modulo n, it must be that $r = 0$, so $\lambda(n)$ divides $n - 1$. From this fact the other particular assertions will follow.

From the general formula for $\lambda(n)$, notice that if $n > 2$, then 2 divides $\lambda(n)$: if n has any prime p factor other than 2, then $p - 1$ divides $\lambda(n)$. On the other hand, if n is a power of 2 larger than 2 itself, then 2 divides $\lambda(n)$.

Therefore, if n is Carmichael, then since 2 divides $\lambda(n)$ and (as we just saw) $\lambda(n)$ divides $n - 1$, it must be that 2 divides $n - 1$. Thus, n is odd.

If for some odd prime p a power p^e divides n with $e > 1$, then p divides $\lambda(n)$. Since $\lambda(n)$ divides $n - 1$, this implies that p divides $n - 1$. But this can't happen when p divides n. Thus, n is square-free.

If n is just the product $n = pq$ of two different odd primes p, q, then

$$\lambda(n) = \lambda(pq) = \operatorname{lcm}(\lambda(p), \lambda(q)) = \operatorname{lcm}(p - 1, q - 1)$$

And $\lambda(n)$ divides $n - 1 = pq - 1$, so we obtain

$$p - 1 \mid pq - 1$$

and

$$q - 1 \mid pq - 1$$

We can rearrange a little:

$$p - 1 \text{ divides } pq - 1 = (p - 1)q + q - 1$$

Therefore, $p - 1$ divides $q - 1$. Symmetrically, $q - 1$ divides $p - 1$. But since $p \neq q$, this is impossible. Thus, n must be divisible by at least three different primes.   ♣

23.3 Euler Witnesses

Now we prove the *existence* of Euler witnesses to the compositeness of non-prime numbers, in contrast to the fact that Carmichael numbers have no *Fermat* witnesses to their compositeness. Also we prove that there are *many* Euler witnesses for composite numbers, in the sense that at least half the numbers b in the range $1 < b < n$ are Euler witnesses to the compositeness of n.

> **Proposition.**   An Euler witness to the primality of n is also a Fermat witness to the primality of n. In the other direction, a Fermat witness to the compositeness of n is an Euler witness to the compositeness. In other words, a *false* Euler witness to primality is a *false* Fermat witness to primality. In particular, if there were a composite number n with no Euler witnesses to its compositeness, then n would have to be a Carmichael number.

Proof: What we assert is that if

$$b^{(n-1)/2} = \left(\frac{b}{n} \right)_2 \mod n$$

for b relatively prime to n, then

$$b^{n-1} = 1 \mod n$$

Indeed, squaring both sides of the first equation, we get

$$b^{n-1} = \left(\frac{b}{n} \right)_2^2 \mod n$$

Since b is relatively prime to n, the quadratic symbol has value ± 1, so its square is unavoidably just 1. Thus, the Euler witness b is certainly a Fermat witness.

So if n were a composite number so that nevertheless for all b relatively prime to n

$$b^{(n-1)/2} = \left(\frac{b}{n} \right)_2 \mod n$$

then also $b^{n-1} = 1 \mod n$ for all such b, and n is Carmichael.   ♣

Remark: Thus, we might say

$$\{\text{Euler pseudoprimes }\} \subset \{\text{Fermat pseudoprimes }\}$$

Or, more precisely,

$$\{\text{Euler pseudoprimes base } b \} \subset \{\text{Fermat pseudoprimes base } b \}$$

Now we prove existence of Euler witnesses to compositeness:

Theorem.   *Existence of Euler witnesses:* Assume that n is a positive composite integer. Then there is at least one integer b in the range $1 < b < n$ and with $\gcd(b, n) = 1$ so that

$$b^{(n-1)/2} \neq \left(\frac{b}{n}\right)_2$$

That is, there exists an Euler witness.

Proof: If n is not Carmichael, then there is already a Fermat witness b to the compositeness of n, so b is certainly an Euler witness.

So consider a Carmichael number n. From above, this implies that n is square-free and odd. So write $n = pm$ with p prime and p not dividing m. Let b_0 be a quadratic non-residue mod p, and (by Sun Ze) find b so that $b \equiv b_0 \bmod p$ and $b \equiv 1 \bmod m$. Then, on one hand,

$$\left(\frac{b}{n}\right)_2 = \left(\frac{b}{pm}\right)_2 = \left(\frac{b}{p}\right)_2 \left(\frac{b}{m}\right)_2 = \left(\frac{b_0}{p}\right)_2 \left(\frac{1}{m}\right)_2 = (-1)(+1) = -1$$

using the definition

$$\left(\frac{b}{pm}\right)_2 = \left(\frac{b}{p}\right)_2 \left(\frac{b}{m}\right)_2$$

of the Jacobi symbol for composite lower input. On the other hand,

$$b^{(n-1)/2} = 1^{(n-1)/2} = 1 \bmod m$$

so already modulo m we have

$$b^{(n-1)/2} \neq \left(\frac{b}{pm}\right)_2 \bmod m$$

which surely gives

$$b^{(n-1)/2} \neq \left(\frac{b}{pm}\right)_2 \bmod pm$$

Therefore, this b is an Euler witness to the compositeness of $n = pm$.   ♣

Now, invoking Lagrange's theorem, we can prove that there are 'many' Euler witnesses:

Corollary.   For composite n, at least half the numbers b in the range $1 < b < n$ are Euler witnesses to the compositeness of n.

Proof: The idea is to show that the collection L of *false* witnesses (but relatively prime to n) is a *subgroup* of $\mathbf{Z}/n^\times$. Since (by the theorem) there is at least *one* witness, the subgroup of *false* witnesses is a *proper* subgroup. By Lagrange's theorem, the order $|L|$ of L must be a *proper* divisor of the order $\varphi(n)$ of $\mathbf{Z}/n^\times$. Therefore, certainly

$$|L| \le \frac{1}{2}\varphi(n) \le \frac{1}{2}(n-1)$$

So let's prove that the collection L of witnesses to the primality of n is a subgroup of $\mathbf{Z}/n^\times$. Suppose that x, y are witnesses to the primality of n. That is,

$$x^{(n-1)/2} = \left(\frac{x}{n}\right)_2 \bmod n$$

and

$$y^{(n-1)/2} = \left(\frac{y}{n}\right)_2 \bmod n$$

Then

$$(xy)^{(n-1)/2} = x^{(n-1)/2} \cdot y^{(n-1)/2} = \left(\frac{x}{n}\right)_2 \cdot \left(\frac{x}{n}\right)_2 \bmod n$$

We know that

$$\left(\frac{x}{n}\right)_2 \cdot \left(\frac{x}{n}\right)_2 = \left(\frac{xy}{n}\right)_2$$

Thus,

$$(xy)^{(n-1)/2} = x^{(n-1)/2} \cdot y^{(n-1)/2} = \left(\frac{x}{n}\right)_2 \cdot \left(\frac{x}{n}\right)_2 = \left(\frac{xy}{n}\right)_2 \bmod n$$

Thus, xy is again a witness to the primality of n.

Next, we check that the (multiplicative) identity 1 in $\mathbf{Z}/n^\times$ is in L. This is silly:

$$1^{(n-1)/2} = 1 = \left(\frac{1}{n}\right)_2 \bmod n$$

Next, we check that the set L of witnesses is closed under taking multiplicative inverses modulo n. Let $x \in L$, and let x^{-1} denote its inverse modulo n. First, we have

$$\left(\frac{x}{n}\right)_2 \cdot \left(\frac{x^{-1}}{n}\right)_2 = \left(\frac{x \cdot x^{-1}}{n}\right)_2 = \left(\frac{1}{n}\right)_2 = 1$$

Thus,

$$\left(\frac{x^{-1}}{n}\right)_2 \left(\frac{x}{n}\right)_2 = 1$$

Then, using properties of exponents,

$$(x^{-1})^{(n-1)/2} = (x^{(n-1)/2})^{-1} = \left(\frac{x}{n}\right)_2^{-1} = \left(\frac{x^{-1}}{n}\right)_2 \mod n$$

That is, if x is a witness, then so is x^{-1}.

Thus, L is closed under multiplication, closed under inverses, and contains the identity, so is a subgroup of $\mathbf{Z}/n^\times$. Since we showed that for composite n there is at least one b which is *not* a (false!) witness to the primality of n, for composite n the subgroup of (false!) witnesses is a *proper subgroup*. Thus, as indicated at the beginning of the proof, by Lagrange's theorem we conclude that at least half of the numbers in the range $1 < b < n$ will detect the compositeness of composite n. ♣

Thus, we are assured that the Solovay–Strassen primality test 'works'.

23.4 Strong Witnesses

Now we prove that there are strong witnesses, and that in fact for odd composite n at least $3/4$ of the numbers in the range $1 < b < n$ are witnesses to the compositeness of n. Thus, the Miller–Rabin test 'works'. Along the way, we compare strong pseudoprimes and Euler pseudoprimes.

Let n be a fixed odd integer throughout this discussion, and let $n - 1 = 2^s \cdot m$ with m odd. Since n is odd, $s \geq 1$.

Let's review the Miller–Rabin test, using a *single* auxiliary number b. First, choose a 'random' auxiliary number b from the range $1 < b < n$, and compute $c = b^m$. If $c = 1 \mod n$, then stop: b is a **strong witness** to the primality of n. If c is not $-1 \mod n$, then start computing successive squares:

$$c^2, \ c^4 = (c^2)^2, \ c^8 = ((c^2)^2)^2, \ c^{2^4} = (c^8)^2, \ \ldots, \ c^{2^{s-1}}$$

If for any $k < s$ we obtain $c^{2^k} = -1 \mod n$, then stop: b is a **strong witness** to the primality of n. On the other hand, if for some k we obtain $c^{2^k} = 1 \mod n$ but $c^{2^{k-1}} \neq -1 \mod n$, then n is **definitely composite**. And, if *no* $c^{2^k} = 1$, for $0 \leq k \leq s$, then n is **definitely composite**.

Remark: If *no* $c^{2^k} = 1$, for $0 \leq k \leq s$, then $b^{n-1} \neq 1 \mod n$, so already n fails the Fermat pseudoprime base b test.

If auxiliary numbers $b_1, b_2, \ldots, b_k$ are used, and if each is a witness to the primality of n, then we imagine that n is prime with 'probability'

$$1 - \left(\frac{1}{4}\right)^k$$

We should verify that a genuine prime is a strong pseudoprime for any base b. That is, we should verify that a genuine prime will pass any number of rounds of the Miller–Rabin test.

Proposition.   Genuine primes are strong pseudoprimes, and pass the Miller–Rabin test. That is: let $p > 2$ be prime, and $p - 1 = 2^s \cdot m$ with m odd. Let b be any integer not divisible by p. Let t be the smallest non-negative integer so that $(b^m)^{2^t} = 1 \bmod p$. Then either $t = 0$, or

$$(b^m)^{2^{t-1}} = -1 \bmod p$$

Proof: Since p is prime, $\mathbf{Z}/p$ is a *field*, and by the Fundamental Theorem of Algebra, the equation $x^2 - 1 = 0$ has number of roots at most equal to its degree. Thus, $\pm 1 - \bmod - p$ are the only elements of $\mathbf{Z}/p$ whose square is $1 - \bmod - p$. Thus, if $(b^m)^{2^t} = 1 \bmod p$ but $(b^m)^{2^{t-1}} \neq 1 \bmod p$, the only possibility is that $(b^m)^{2^{t-1}} = -1 \bmod p$. Thus, the genuine prime p would pass every such test.   ♣

Now we have a simple argument to show that the Miller–Rabin test is at least as discriminating as the Fermat test. This fact is also a corollary of the fact (already proven) that Euler witnesses are Fermat witnesses, together with the fact (proven below) that strong witnesses are Euler witnesses. But this proposition itself has a much simpler proof:

Proposition.   A strong witness to the primality of n is also a Fermat witness.

Proof: Let b the random number chosen, and let $c = b^m$. First suppose that $c = 1$. Then

$$b^{n-1} = b^{m \cdot 2^s} = c^{2^s} = 1^{2^s} = 1 \bmod n$$

so b is a Fermat witness. Or, if

$$c^{2^t} = -1 \bmod n$$

with $t < s$, then

$$b^{n-1} = b^{m \cdot 2^s} = c^{2^s} = (c^{2^t})^{2^{s-t}} = (-1)^{2^{s-t}} = 1 \bmod n$$

So again in this case b is a Fermat witness.   ♣

Before proving that strong witnesses are Euler witnesses, we need some notation, and a preliminary computation: for positive integer N and an integer k, let

$$\operatorname{ord}_N k = \text{order of } k \text{ in the multiplicative group } \mathbf{Z}/N^\times$$

Lemma.   For integer k and an odd prime p (not dividing k),

$$\operatorname{ord}_{p^e} k / \operatorname{ord}_p = \text{non-negative power of } p$$

Proof: We use the fact that $\mathbf{Z}/p^{e\times}$ is a cyclic group, that is, that there is a primitive root g. Let ℓ be a positive integer so that $g^\ell = k$. From the discussion of cyclic groups and cyclic subgroups,

$$\begin{aligned}
\operatorname{ord}_{p^e} k &= \varphi(p^e)/\gcd(\ell, \varphi(p^e)) \\
\operatorname{ord}_p k &= \varphi(p)/\gcd(\ell, \varphi(p))
\end{aligned}$$

Since $p - 1$ and p^{e-1} are relatively prime,

$$\gcd(\ell, \varphi(p^e)) = \gcd(\ell, (p-1)p^{e-1}) = \gcd(\ell, p-1) \cdot \gcd(\ell, p^{e-1})$$

Thus,

$$\operatorname{ord}_{p^e} k/\operatorname{ord}_p = \frac{\varphi(p^e)/\gcd(\ell, \varphi(p^e))}{\varphi(p)/\gcd(\ell, \varphi(p))} = \frac{(p-1)p^{e-1} \cdot \gcd(\ell, \varphi(p))}{(p-1) \cdot \gcd(\ell, \varphi(p^e))}$$

$$= \frac{p^{e-1}}{\gcd(\ell, p^{e-1}))}$$

This proves the assertion.   ♣

Theorem. A strong witness to the primality of n is also an Euler witness.

Proof: First, if n is prime, then it will pass any number of rounds of either Solovay–Strassen or Miller–Rabin tests.

So consider composite odd n. Let b be the random number chosen, and let $c = b^m$. Let the prime factorization of n be

$$n = p_1^{e_1} \ldots p_N^{e_N}$$

Let b be a strong witness for n, and put $c = b^d$. The hypothesis that b is a strong witness for n is that either

$$\text{(i) } c = 1 \bmod n$$

or

$$\text{(ii) } c^{2^t} = -1 \bmod n \text{ for some } 1 \le t < s$$

Since $c^{2^t} = -1 \bmod p^e$ for each prime power p^e dividing n,

$$\operatorname{ord}_{p^e} c = 2^{t+1}$$

and, therefore,

$$\operatorname{ord}_{p^e} b = 2^{t+1} \times \text{ (odd)}$$

(In the case that $c = 1$, these orders are odd, and 2^0 divides them, etc.)
     By the lemma, also,

$$\operatorname{ord}_p b = 2^{t+1} \times \text{ (odd)}$$

since the only thing that might change is the power of p occurring.

Let 2^{t_i} be the exact power of 2 dividing $p_i - 1$. Thus,

$$t + 1 \le k_i \text{for all } i$$

Let g_i be a primitive root mod p_i, and write $b = g_i^{\ell_i}$ with $\ell_i | p_i - 1$. Then (from discussion of cyclic subgroups)

$$\text{ord}_{p_i} b = \frac{p_i - 1}{\ell_i}$$

Thus, for a given index i, if $t + 1 < k_i$, then b is a square mod p_i. It is only for $t + 1 = k_i$ that b is a non-square mod p_i.

Let M be the number of indices i so that b is a non-square mod p_i, and so that $t + 1 = k_i$. Then

$$\left(\frac{b}{n}\right)_2 = \left(\frac{b}{p_1}\right)_2^{e_1} \cdots \left(\frac{b}{p_N}\right)_2^{e_N} = (-1)^M$$

On the other hand, since $2^{t+1} | p_i - 1$ for each index i, write

$$p_i = 1 + 2^{t+1} x_i$$

for some odd number x_i. Then

$$p_i^2 = 1 + 2 \cdot 2^{t+1} x_i + 2^{2t+2} x^2 = 1 \bmod 2^{t+2}$$

Thus, modulo 2^{t+2}, all the prime powers in n with exponent 2 or higher are just 1. And, modulo 2^{t+2},

$$p_i = 1 + 2^{t+1} \cdot (\text{odd}) \equiv 1 + 2^{t+1} \bmod 2^{t+2}$$

Thus, the prime powers occurring in n with exponent just 1 contribute factors of $1 + 2^{t+1}$ modulo 2^{t+2}. Therefore, modulo 2^{t+2},

$$
\begin{aligned}
n & = p_1^{e_1} \cdots p_N^{e_N} = (1 + 2^{t+1})^M \bmod 2^{t+2} \\
& = 1 + \binom{M}{1} 2^{t+1} + \binom{M}{2} 2^{2t+2} + \binom{M}{3} 2^{3t+3} + \cdots = 1 + M \cdot 2^{t+1} \bmod 2^{t+2}
\end{aligned}
$$

Thus, depending upon whether M is odd or even:

$$
\begin{aligned}
n & = 1 + M \cdot 2^{t+1} = 1 + 2^{t+1} \bmod 2^{t+2} && \text{(for } M \text{ odd)} \\
n & = 1 + M \cdot 2^{t+1} = 1 \bmod 2^{t+2} && \text{(for } M \text{ even)}
\end{aligned}
$$

Therefore, in the case that M is odd, the power of 2 dividing $n - 1$ is *exactly* 2^{t+1}. That is, $s = t + 1$. Therefore,

$$b^{(n-1)/2} = b^{m \cdot 2^{s-1}} = c^{2^{s-1}} = c^{2^t} = -1 \bmod n$$

So for M odd, we have

$$b^{(n-1)/2} = -1 = \left(\frac{b}{n}\right)_2$$

And, therefore, in the case that M is even, the power of 2 dividing $n-1$ is *at least* 2^{t+2}. That is, $s \geq t+2$. Therefore,

$$b^{(n-1)/2} = b^{m \cdot 2^{s-1}} = c^{2^{s-1}} = (c^{2^t})^{2^{s-1}-2^t} = (-1)^{2^{s-1}-2^t} = 1 \bmod n$$

So once again we have

$$b^{(n-1)/2} = 1 = \left(\frac{b}{n}\right)_2$$

This completes the proof that strong witnesses are Euler witnesses.   ♣

Theorem.   If an odd integer n is composite, then at least $3/4$ of the integers b in the range $1 < b < n$ are strong (Miller–Rabin) witnesses to the compositeness of n.

Proof: Let k be the largest non-negative integer so that there is at least one b with $b^{2^k} = -1 \bmod n$. Since $(-1)^{2^0} = -1$, there exists such k. We need:

Lemma. $n = 1 \bmod 2^{k+1}$.

Proof: With $b^{2^k} = -1 \bmod n$, certainly $b^{2^{k+1}} = 1 \bmod n$. Thus, $n | b^{2^{k+1}} - 1$. Thus, by Fermat's observation, for any prime p dividing n, either $p | b^{2^\ell} - 1$ for some $\ell < k+1$, or $p = 1 \bmod 2^{k+1}$. Since by hypothesis $b^{2^k} = -1 \bmod n$ and b^{2^r} is neither $1 \bmod n$ nor $-1 \bmod n$ for $r < k$, it cannot be that $p | b^{2^\ell} - 1$ for some $\ell < k+1$. Thus, for any prime p dividing n we have $p = 1 \bmod 2^{k+1}$. Multiplying any number of such primes together gives a product n which must also be $1 \bmod 2^{k+1}$.   ♣

Now return to the proof of the theorem. Let $\ell = 2^k \cdot m$, with $n-1 = 2^s \cdot m$ and m odd, as above. By the lemma, $2\ell | n - 1$. Define subgroups of $G = \mathbf{Z}/n^\times$:

$$H = \{g \in G : a^{n-1} = 1 \bmod n\}$$
$$I = \{g \in G : g^\ell = \pm 1 \bmod p_i^{e_i} \text{for all } i\}$$
$$J = \{g \in G : g^\ell = \pm 1 \bmod n\} \supset \{\text{strong liars }\}$$
$$K = \{g \in G : a^\ell = 1 \bmod n\}$$

It is not so hard to check that we have inclusions

$$G \supset H \supset I \supset J \supset K$$

(It is very easy to check, from the definition of subgroup, that all these are subgroups of G.)

Lemma.   The *strong liars* (false witnesses to the primality of n) all lie inside the subgroup J.

Proof: First, if $b^m = 1 \bmod n$, then surely $b^\ell = 1 \bmod n$, since $m | \ell$. On the other hand, if

$$b^{m \cdot 2^t} = -1 \bmod n$$

for some $t < s$, then $t \leq k$ by the definition of k. Thus,

$$b^\ell = b^{m \cdot 2^k} = (b^{m \cdot 2^t})^{2^{k-t}} = (-1)^{2^{k-t}} \mod n$$

Thus, indeed, any strong liar is in J.   ♣

Next, except for the special case $n = 9$ which is easy to dispatch directly, we'll show that

$$[G : J] \geq 4$$

Since the strong liars are contained in J, this will show that

number of witnesses to compositeness of n

$$\geq (n - 1) - \frac{1}{4}\varphi(n) \geq (n - 1) - \frac{1}{4}(n - 1) = \frac{3}{4}(n - 1)$$

as desired.

Let

$$f : G \to G$$

be the map

$$f(g) = g^\ell$$

Since G is abelian, this is a group homomorphism.

Lemma. Let

$$S = \{a \in G : a = \pm 1 \mod p_i^{e_i} \text{ for all indices } i\}$$

Every element of S is a (2^k)th power of some element in G. Therefore, every element of S is an ℓth power of some element in G. That is, the group homomorphism $f : G \to S$ is a *surjection*.

Proof: Let x be an integer so that $x = b \mod p_i^{e_i}$ or $x = b^2 \mod p_i^{e_i}$, with possibly different choices for different primes p_i, where b is the special element as above. Then $x^{2^k} = +1 \mod p_i^{e_i}$ if $x = b^2 \mod p_i^{e_i}$, and $x^{2^k} = -1 \mod p_i^{e_i}$ if $x = b \mod p_i^{e_i}$. This proves the first assertion of the lemma. Since m is odd, both $\pm 1 \mod p_i^{e_i}$ are mth powers of themselves. Thus, if

$$g^{2^k} = h$$

with $h \in S$, then

$$g^\ell = g^{2^k \cdot m} = h^m = h \mod p_i^{e_i}$$

for all indices i. This proves that f is surjective.   ♣

We want to claim that K has index 2^N in I. We can get this as a corollary of a lemma that applies much more generally to groups:

Lemma. Let $h : X \to Y$ be a group homomorphism, with finite groups X, Y. Let Z, W be subgroups of Y, with $Z \supset W$, and suppose that Z is contained in the image $f(X)$ of f. Put

$$h^{-1}(Z) = \{g \in G : h(g) \in Z\}$$

$$h^{-1}(W) = \{g \in G : h(g) \in W\}$$

Then we have a formula regarding *indices:*

$$[Z : W] = [h^{-1}(Z) : h^{-1}(W)]$$

Proof: Let V be the kernel of the homomorphism $h : X \to Y$. We will prove that

$$|h^{-1}(Z)| = |V| \cdot |Z|$$

and, similarly,

$$|h^{-1}(W)| = |V| \cdot |W|$$

As soon as we know that these equalities hold, then

$$[Z : W] = \frac{|Z|}{|W|} = \frac{|V| \cdot |Z|}{|V| \cdot |W|} = \frac{|h^{-1}(Z)|}{|h^{-1}(W)|} = [h^{-1}(Z) : h^{-1}(W)]$$

The *inverse image* $h^{-1}(Z)$ of Z is the disjoint union of the *inverse images*

$$h^{-1}(z) = \{x \in X : h(x) = z\}$$

of elements $z \in Z$. If we can prove that

$$\text{number of elements in } h^{-1}(z) = |V|$$

then it will follow that

$$\begin{aligned} |h^{-1}(Z)| &= \text{sum of cardinalities of sets } h^{-1}(z) \text{ for } z \text{ in } Z \\ &= |Z| \cdot |V| \end{aligned}$$

since there are $|Z|$ different sets $h^{-1}(z)$ and we anticipate that each one has cardinality $|V|$.

Thus, the problem is reduced to showing that

$$\text{number of elements in } h^{-1}(z) = |V|$$

for any $z \in Z$. To do this, let's make a bijection

$$b : V \to h^{-1}(z)$$

This would prove that the sets have the same number of elements, without directly counting. Since z is in the image of h, we can find at least one $x_0 \in X$ so that $h(x_0) = z$. With this in hand, let's try

$$b(v) = v \cdot x_0$$

First we have to check that this really maps from V to $h^{-1}(z)$. That is, we must check that

$$h(b(v)) = z \text{for all } v \in V$$

Indeed,

$$h(b(v)) = h(v \cdot x_0) = h(v) \cdot h(x_0) = e_Y \cdot z = z$$

since v is in the kernel V of h. Next, let's check that b is *injective*: suppose that $b(v) = b(v')$ for $v, v' \in V$. That is, we assume that

$$v \cdot x_0 = v' \cdot x_0$$

By right-multiplying by x_0^{-1} and simplifying, we get $v = v'$, so b is indeed injective. Last, check surjectivity: given $q \in h^{-1}(z)$, find $v \in V$ so that $q = b(v)$. Let's check that $q \cdot x_0^{-1} \in V$ hits q:

$$h(q \cdot x_0^{-1}) = h(q) \cdot h(x_0^{-1}) = z \cdot h(x_0)^{-1} = z \cdot z^{-1} = e_Z$$

This finishes the proof that $b : V \to h^{-1}(z)$ is a bijection, proving that the number of elements in $h^{-1}(z)$ is equal to $|V|$. Thus, this finishes the proof of the lemma. ♣

Corollary. We have

$$[I : K] = [f^{-1}(S) : f^{-1}(\{e\})] = [S : \{e\}] = 2^N$$

Proof: From the definition of f as $f(g) = g^\ell$,

$$K = f^{-1}(\{e\})$$

And another lemma above proved that

$$I = f^{-1}(S)$$

By the previous lemma,

$$[f^{-1}(S) : f^{-1}(\{e\})] = [S : \{e\}]$$

which is the same thing as $|S|$. Since S consists of choices of ± 1 for each of the N different primes p_i dividing n, $|S| = 2^N$. This proves the corollary. ♣

Using the last lemma again, we also have:

Corollary. Let $P = \{\pm 1 \bmod n\}$, and $E = \{e_G\}$. We have

$$[J : K] = [f^{-1}(P) : f^{-1}(E)] = [P : E] = 2$$

Now we are in the situation that $I \supset J \supset K$ and $[I : K] = 2^N$ and $[J : K] = 2$. In the original discussion of group indices, we proved the multiplicative property

$$[I : J] \cdot [J : K] = [I : K]$$

Thus,

$$[I : J] = [I : K]/[J : K] = 2^{N-1}$$

Since also $[G : J] = [G : I] \cdot [I : J]$, surely

$$[G : J] \geq [I : J] = 2^{N-1}$$

Since the strong (Miller–Rabin) liars are all contained in J, we see that

$$\frac{\text{number of liars}}{|G|} \leq \frac{1}{2^{N-1}}$$

If the number N of distinct prime factors of n is at least 3, then we have

$$\frac{\text{number of liars}}{|G|} \leq \frac{1}{4}$$

If the number N of distinct prime factors is 2, then we know by now that n cannot be a Carmichael number. That is, the group denoted H above is a *proper* subgroup of $G = \mathbf{Z}/n^\times$. That is, by Lagrange's theorem, $[G : H] \geq 2$. Then from the multiplicative property of subgroup indices (applied repeatedly) we have in this case

$$[G : J] = [G : H] \cdot [H : I] \cdot [I : J] \geq [G : H] \cdot [I : J] \geq 2 \cdot 2^1 = 4$$

Thus, also in this case, we conclude that the liars make up less than $1/4$ of all the elements of G.

Finally, suppose that $n = p^e$, a power of a single prime p. (This is the case $N = 1$.) In this case we know from the existence of primitive roots that $\mathbf{Z}/p^{e\times}$ is *cyclic*. The group H in this case becomes

$$H = \{g \in \mathbf{Z}/p^{e\times} : g^{p^e - 1} = 1 \bmod p^e\}$$

From our discussion of cyclic groups, to determine $|J|$ we can use the *isomorphism* of the multiplicative group $\mathbf{Z}/p^{e\times}$ with the additive group $\mathbf{Z}/\varphi(p^e)$. Converting to additive notation, we want to know the number of solutions x to the equation

$$(p^e - 1) \cdot x = 0 \bmod \varphi(p^e)$$

This is

$$(p^e - 1) \cdot x = 0 \bmod (p-1)p^{e-1}$$

We have solved such congruences before: taking out the common factor, this is equivalent to

$$\frac{p^e - 1}{p - 1} \cdot x = 0 \bmod p^{e-1}$$

Now the coefficient of x is relatively prime to the modulus, so has a multiplicative inverse, and this is equivalent to

$$x = 0 \bmod p^{e-1}$$

Since x is an integer modulo p^e, we see that we get exactly $p-1$ different solutions mod $\varphi(p^e)$.

Thus,

$$[G : J] = [G : H] \cdot [H : J] \geq [G : H] = \frac{\varphi(p^e)}{p - 1} = p^{e-1}$$

Except for the case $p = 3$ and $e = 2$ we obtain the necessary $[G : J] \geq 4$. From this we conclude again in this case that at most $1/4$ of the possible candidates are liars.

The remaining special case of $n = 9$ can be treated directly. There are just two strong liars, ± 1, and $2/(9 - 1) = 1/4$.

At long last, this finishes the proof of the theorem, demonstrating that the Miller–Rabin test works.   ♣

24

Factorization Attacks

Trying to *factor* a large integer is a much harder problem than testing whether or not it's prime. And *proving* that a pseudoprime is *truly* prime is more difficult than verifying its pseudoprimality.

In any case, it is usually wise from the viewpoint of efficiency to do a certain amount of trial division by small primes before any more sophisticated tests are used.

And it is wise to check that an integer n *fails* a pseudoprimality test before trying to factor it, since the more sophisticated factorization methods all have possibility of failure, which is unfortunately indistinguishable from the reasonable failure to factor due to n being prime. That is, it is important to know that any failure in attempting factorization of n is due to bad luck in the algorithm rather than n being prime, so that we can make adjustments and try again. Thus, unfortunately, most sophisticated factorization methods are *not* good for testing primality, due to their failure modes! So we will only discuss factorization of large integers *known to be composite* (probably by Fermat or Miller–Rabin tests).

Likewise, primality *proof* methods should only be attempted after a number is known to be a *pseudoprime* (that is, a **probable prime**).

And, from a practical viewpoint, whenever it is helpful we can assume that all 'small' prime factors have already been removed, perhaps simply by trial division. (The precise meaning of 'small' depends upon the context.)

The two factorization methods we show here are *not* the state of the art but have the virtue that they are relatively easy to explain, to understand, and to implement. Further, the *rho method* make a charming use of the birthday-paradox idea. The $p-1$ method is important because in public key cryptosystems the primes used must be chosen to avoid vulnerability to this and related attacks.

24.1 Pollard's Rho Method

Pollard's rho method quickly finds relatively small factors of composite numbers. It is a very simple factorization method which already runs several times faster than trial division for numbers whose smallest prime factor is about $1,000,000$. Further, it has the practical virtue that if a number has a small prime factor, then the method finds such a factor faster than it would find a large factor. On the other hand, it has the minor disadvantage of being probabilistic, so that one must always be alert to occurrence of 'bad cases'. Finally, it has a peculiar disadvantage that it is difficult to *prove* that it works as well as it does: On one hand, from an experimental viewpoint this may be perceived as being of no consequence. On the other hand, in applications where correctness really matters this is obviously a fatal flaw. This method was first described in [Pollard 1975].

The description of the algorithm is simple. Given integer n, initialize by setting $x = 2$, $y = x^2 + 1$.

- Compute $g = \gcd(x - y, n)$

- If $1 < g < n$, stop: g is a proper factor of n

- If $g = 1$, replace x by $x^2 + 1$ and y by $(y^2 + 1)^2 + 1$ and repeat.

- If $g = n$, we have *failure*, and the algorithm needs to be reinitialized. This rarely occurs.

Remark: Playing upon the birthday paradox, the number of cycles necessary to find a factor p of n should be roughly of the order of $\sqrt{p}$. If n is composite, then there is a prime factor $p \leq \sqrt{n}$, so this algorithm takes on the order of $\sqrt[4]{n}$ cycles to find a proper factor. (See further comments below.)

Remark: As described, we haven't imposed a limit on the number of cycles to run through. If the number n is known to be composite, this is most likely (!?) acceptable, since the worst thing that will happen is that this algorithm will take as much time as trial division. The most problematical case is the case where $g = n$, which fortunately seems to occur with small probability (difficult to estimate!).

Remark: In implementing this algorithm, probably a limit should be imposed upon the number of cycles to run through before making some adjustments, for which there are several choices. $\sqrt{n}$ steps is too many, and in any case would be no faster than trial division. At the other extreme, $\sqrt[4]{n}$ is probably not enough to allow for 'bad' cases. In practice, $100\sqrt[4]{n}$ cycles seems to be enough to find a proper factor. Still, it is quite reasonable to simply let the algorithm run to either success or the 'failure' state for numbers n *known* to be composite, both because it appears to run fast and without failure, and because it seems hard to give rigorous estimates for a good limitation to put on the number of cycles to allow. For a rare rigorous result about Pollard's rho method, see [Bach 1991].

Remark: Since, as just noted, the worst-case scenario for this algorithm is complete failure, it would be unwise to test primality by this algorithm, since failure can occur for composite numbers. Thus, in practice, before using Pollard's rho one should first apply a primality test to n. The Fermat test can be used here, since for n *failing* the Fermat test n, is definitely composite. Or the Miller–Rabin test can be used.

Remark: In H. Cohen, *A Course in Computational Algebraic Number Theory*, Springer-Verlag, 1993, it is asserted that the best response to the 'failure' state is to use a function other than the $x \to x^2 + 1$ above. The choices $f(y) = y^2 + c$ are computationally simplest, although the values $c = 0, -2$ are bad. (Why?) That source asserts that simply changing the initial value of x from the $x = 2$ above to something else is not wise.

Remark: There is no guarantee that a proper factor g found by this method will be prime, although in practice that tends to be the case. But finding a non-prime proper factor is perfectly fine progress toward factorization in any case.

Why does this work? The clearest explanation is unfortunately not at all rigorous, and attempts to be more rigorous do not succeed. Perhaps this is part of the charm of this algorithm. In any case, there are two key ingredients: the probabilistic idea involved in the birthday paradox, and the Floyd cycle-detection method, which is used to make exploitation of the birthday-paradox idea practical.

So suppose that n is a positive integer with proper divisor d. It does not matter whether d is prime or not, but only that d is much smaller than n. From the birthday paradox, we know that if we have more than $\sqrt{d}$ integers $x_1, x_2, \ldots, x_t$, then the probability is greater than $1/2$ that two of these will be the same modulo d. The idea of Pollard's rho method is that $\sqrt{d}$ is much smaller than $\sqrt{n}$, so we should expect that if we choose a 'random sequence' of integers $x_1, x_2, \ldots$, there will be two the same modulo d long before there are two the same modulo n. That is, supposing that $x_i = x_k \bmod d$ but not already knowing what d is, we can (often) *find* d by computing

$$g = \gcd(x_i - x_j, n)$$

(Keep in mind that computation of gcd's via the Euclidean algorithm is relatively cheap.) More precisely, if $x_i = x_k \bmod d$ but $x_i \neq x_k \bmod n$, then this gcd will be a multiple of d, and will be a divisor of n strictly smaller than n itself. This counts as good progress toward factorization of n.

A too-naive implementation of this as a means of hunting for proper factors of n is to compute the greatest common divisors $\gcd(x_i - x_j, n)$ as we go along, for *all* $i < j$. This is a bad idea: if we hope that we need about $\sqrt{d}$ random integers in order to find the proper factor d, then we will have had to make on the order of

$$\frac{1}{2}(\sqrt{d})^2 = \frac{1}{2}d$$

computations of *gcd*s. That is, we could as well have found d by *trial division*. (Each step in trial division is cheaper than a Euclidean algorithm execution.)

So we need a clever way of taking advantage of the birthday paradox. It is here that we make use of the specific manner in which Pollard's rho algorithm creates the supposedly random integers. First, we are having to pretend that the function $f(x) = x^2 + 1 \% n$ used in the algorithm is a **random map** from $\mathbf{Z}/n$ to itself. Since it appears that no one can prove much of anything in this direction, we won't try to say precisely what this might mean. But in any case if we make a sequence of supposedly random numbers by

$$
\begin{aligned}
x_0 &= 2 \\
x_1 &= f(x_0) \\
x_2 &= f(x_1) \\
x_3 &= f(x_2) \\
&\cdots
\end{aligned}
$$

then each element in the sequence determines the next one completely. That is, if ever $x_j = x_i \bmod d$ with $i < j$, then also inevitably $x_{j+1} = x_{i+1}$, $x_{j+2} = x_{i+2}$, $x_{j+3} = x_{i+3}$, and so on. modulo d. In particular, for all $t \geq j$,

$$x_t = x_{t-(j-i)} \bmod d$$

Further, for the same reason,

$$x_t = x_{t-(j-i)} = x_{t-2(j-i)} = x_{t-3(j-i)} = \ldots = x_{t-\ell(j-i)} \bmod d$$

as long as $t - \ell(j - i) \geq i$. That is, there is more structure here than if we merely had a growing *set* of random numbers.

Keep in mind that we don't necessarily care about the very *first* case that some $x_i = x_j$, but only about a *relatively early* case. **Floyd's cycle-detection method** is the following efficient way of looking for matches. First, we do not keep in memory the whole list of x_i's, as this would be needlessly inefficient. Rather, we just remember the last one computed. But at the same time we separately compute a sequence

$$
\begin{aligned}
y_1 &= x_2 \\
y_2 &= x_4 \\
y_3 &= x_6 \\
y_4 &= x_8 \\
&\cdots \\
y_i &= x_{2i}
\end{aligned}
$$

The efficient way to compute the sequence of y_i's is by noting that

$$y_{i+1} = (y_i^2 + 1)^2 + 1 \% n$$

And we only remember the last y_i computed.

At each step we only remember the last x_t and y_t computed, and consider $\gcd(x_t - y_t, n)$. Why will this most likely find a proper factor? Let j be the first index so that $x_j = x_i \bmod d$ for some $i < j$. As noted above, this means that

$$x_t = x_{t-\ell(j-i)} \bmod d$$

whenever $t - \ell(j - i) \geq i$. So, taking $t = 2s$:

$$y_s = x_{2s} = x_{2s-\ell(j-i)} \bmod d$$

for all s with $2s - \ell(j - i) \geq i$. So when $s = \ell(j - i)$ with $\ell(j - i) \geq i$ (which of course holds for ℓ sufficiently large)

$$y_s = x_{2s} = x_{2s-\ell(j-i)} = x_{2s-s} = x_s \bmod d$$

whenever $s = 2s - \ell(j - i) \geq i$. This proves that the trick used above really does succeed in finding x_i and x_j which are the same mod d, *assuming that there are such*.

Remark: Again, the latter heuristic discussion assumes that the function $x \to x^2 + 1$ behaves 'randomly', and we have no assurance that this is so. Also, assuming the randomness of this map, it is possible to do a more precise analysis of the *expected* number of cycles before a match occurs. This analysis is related to but more sophisticated than what we said above.

Exercises

24.1.01 Use Pollard's rho method to find a proper factor of 1133.

24.1.02 Use Pollard's rho method to find a proper factor of 1313.

24.1.03 Use Pollard's rho method to find a proper factor of 1649.

24.2 Pollard's $p - 1$ method

This method is specialized, working well only to find prime factors p so that $p - 1$ is divisible only by 'small' factors, and not working particularly well outside those cases. Still, application of this test is relatively simple, so to *prevent* factorization attacks it must be taken into account.

Fix an integer B. An integer n is B-**smooth** if all its prime factors are less than or equal B. In this context B is a **smoothness bound**. An integer n is B-**power smooth** if all its prime *power* factors are less than or equal B.

Given an integer n, Pollard's $p-1$ algorithm finds a prime factor p of n such that $p-1$ is B-smooth, in $O(B \ln n / \ln B)$ multiplications modulo n.

Remark: Keeping B small is obviously desirable. It should certainly be *much* smaller than $\sqrt{n}$, or nothing is gained over doing trial division. On the other hand, a too-small value of B will cause the algorithm to fail to find factors. In practice, because the value of B must be kept too small to find all possible factors, this algorithm is used 'just a little' on the chance that we are lucky and some $p-1$ has all small prime factors, for a prime divisor p of the large integer in question.

Remark: The serious question of how large we should expect the prime factors of a randomly chosen number to be is not trivial and does not have a simple answer.

Given an integer n known to be composite, but **not a prime power**, and given a smoothness bound B, choose a random integer b with $2 \le b \le n-1$. Compute $g = \gcd(b, n)$. If $g \ge 2$, then g is a proper factor, and stop. Otherwise, let $p_1, p_2, \ldots, p_t$ be the primes less than or equal B. For $i = 1, 2, 3, \ldots, t$: let $q = p_i$, and

- Compute $\ell = \mathrm{floor}(\ln n / \ln p_i)$.

- Replace b by b^{q^ℓ}.

- Compute $g = \gcd(b-1, n)$.

- If $1 < g < n$: stop, g is a proper factor.

- Else if $g = 1$: continue.

- Else if $g = n$: stop, failure.

Remark: If B is relatively large, some time can be saved by not computing all the primes $p_1, \ldots, p_t$ at the beginning, but only as needed, hoping that a factor is found well before they're all used. On the other hand, if several numbers are being tested, it is pointless to delay computing the list of primes.

Why does this work? Well, if we can arrange that for some integer b we have $1 < \gcd(b-1, n) < n$, then certainly we have found a proper factor $g = \gcd(b-1, n)$ of n. In this algorithm, let

$$p = 1 + p_1^{e_1} \ldots p_t^{e_t}$$

be a prime factor of n such that $p-1$ is B-smooth, with some integer exponents e_i. For any integer b prime to p by Fermat's Little Theorem

$$b^{p-1} = 1$$

That is,

$$b^{p_1^{e_1} \ldots p_t^{e_t}} = 1 \bmod p$$

The quantity

$$\ell_i = \mathrm{floor}(\ln n / \ln p_i)$$

is larger than or equal e_i. Let

$$T = p_1^{\ell_1} \dots p_t^{\ell_t}$$

Then $p_1^{e_1} \dots p_t^{e_t}$ divides T, so certainly

$$b^T = 1 \bmod p$$

for any integer b prime to p. That is,

$$p | \gcd(b^T - 1, n)$$

Note that the actual algorithm given above computes *gcd*'s more often than indicated in the last paragraph. This provides some opportunities to avoid the cases that $\gcd(b^T - 1, n) = n$.

Failure of this algorithm can occur for two different sorts of reasons. One is that there are *no* prime factors p of n so that $p - 1$ is B-smooth. In that case the *gcd* computed is 1 all the time. The other failure mode is that *all* the prime factors q of n have $q - 1$ being B-smooth. In this case $\gcd(b^T - 1, n) = n$. It is for this reason that the algorithm written above computes additional *gcd*'s. Even if all the *gcd*'s computed are either 1 or n, so long as there is at least one occurrence of n among the *gcd*'s there is hope that this algorithm can succeed: simply start with a different initial random b.

Example: Factor $9991 = 97 \cdot 103$ by the $p-1$ method. Note that $97 - 1 = 2^5 \cdot 3$, so $97 - 1$ is $\{2, 3\}$-smooth. Initialize $b = 3$. The integer part of $\log_2 9991$ is 13, so first compute

$$b^{2^{13}} \% 9991 = 229$$

and assign that value to b. Using the Euclidean algorithm (not shown), compute

$$\gcd(9991, 229 - 1) = 1$$

so we fail to find a factor of 9991 on this round. Next, the integer part of $\log_3 9991$ is 8, so compute

$$b^{3^8} \% 9991 = 3202$$

and assign that value to b. Using the Euclidean algorithm, compute

$$\gcd(9991, 3202 - 1) = 97$$

Thus, the algorithm found the factor 97.

Example: Factor $3801911 = 1801 \cdot 2111$. The factor 1801 is $\{2, 3, 5\}$-smooth:

$$1801 - 1 = 2^3 \cdot 3^2 \cdot 5^2$$

Initialize $b = 3$. The integer part of $\log_2 3801911$ is 21, so first compute

$$b^{2^{21}} \% 3801911 = 3165492$$

and assign that value to b. Using the Euclidean algorithm (not shown), compute

$$\gcd(3801911, 3165492 - 1) = 1$$

so we fail to find a factor of 3801911 on this round. Next, the integer part of $\log_3 3801911$ is 13, so compute

$$b^{3^{13}} \% 3801911 = 2431606$$

and assign that value to b. Using the Euclidean algorithm, compute

$$\gcd(3801911, 2431606 - 1) = 1$$

Again we've failed to find a proper factor. Last the integer part of $\log_5 3801911$ is 9, so compute

$$b^{5^9} \% 3801911 = 2604247$$

and assign that value to b. Using the Euclidean algorithm, compute

$$\gcd(3801911, 2604247 - 1) = 1801$$

Thus, we find the proper factor 1801 of 3801911.

Remark: In fact, the computation of *gcd*s at intermediate stages can be skipped. These intermediate computations merely serve to avoid some relatively unlikely coincidences.

Example: Factor $54541557732143 = 54001 \cdot 1010010143$. The prime 54001 is $\{2, 3, 5\}$-smooth. Initialize $b = 3$. Let's skip the intermediate *gcd* computations this time. The exponent for 2 is 45, the exponent for 3 is 28, and the exponent for 5 is 19. Compute

$$b^{2^{45}} \% 54541557732143 = 1333741139152$$

and assign this value to b. Next, compute

$$b^{3^{28}} \% 54541557732143 = 22167690980770$$

and assign this value to b. Then compute

$$b^{5^{19}} \% 54541557732143 = 2268486536233$$

and assign this value to b. Last, compute (by the Euclidean algorithm)

$$\gcd(54541557732143, 2268486536233 - 1) = 54001$$

Thus, we find the proper factor 54001 of 54541557732143.

Exercises

24.2.01 Use Pollard's $p - 1$ method with factor base $B = \{2\}$ to find a factor p of 901 so that $p - 1$ is B-smooth.

24.2.02 Use Pollard's $p - 1$ method with factor base $B = \{2, 3\}$ to find a factor p of 11009 so that $p - 1$ is B-smooth.

24.2.03 Use Pollard's $p - 1$ method with factor base $B = \{2, 3\}$ to find a factor p of 11227 so that $p - 1$ is B-smooth.

24.2.04 Use Pollard's $p - 1$ method with factor base $B = \{2, 3\}$ to find a factor p of 11663 so that $p - 1$ is B-smooth.

24.3 Pocklington–Lehmer Criterion

This is a specialized technique which is especially useful to test primality of numbers N so that the factorization of $N - 1$ is known. This is most often applied to numbers of special forms, such as Fermat numbers $2^{2^n} + 1$. A more sophisticated variant of it gives the Lucas-Lehmer test for primality of Mersenne numbers $2^n - 1$, among which are the largest explicitly known primes. This test is *not* probabilistic, so it gives *proofs* of primality when it is applicable. This idea originates in work of Eduard Lucas in 1876 and 1891, and is a sort of *true* converse to Fermat's Little Theorem.

This technique applies to *prove* primality of integers N, or to cut down the search space for proper factors, when the factorization of $N - 1$ is known.

Lemma. Let N be a positive integer, q a prime divisor of $N - 1$. Let b be an integer so that $b^{N-1} = 1 \bmod N$ but $\gcd(b^{(N-1)/q} - 1, N) = 1$. Let q^e be the exact power of q dividing $N - 1$. Then *any* positive divisor d of N satisfies

$$d = 1 \bmod q^e$$

Proof: Let d be a positive divisor of N. Since we can write d as a product of primes $d = \prod_i p_i^{e_i}$, if we can prove that $p_i = 1 \bmod q^e$, then certainly $d = 1 \bmod q^e$, since multiplication modulo q^e behaves nicely. So it suffices to consider the case of prime divisors $p = d$ of N.

The hypothesis of the lemma gives

$$b \cdot b^{N-2} = 1 \bmod N$$

so b is multiplicatively invertible modulo N, so is relatively prime to N. So b is relatively prime to p as well.

Let t be the order of b in the multiplicative group $\mathbf{Z}/p^\times$: that is, $b^t = 1 \bmod p$ but no smaller positive exponent will do. Fermat's Little Theorem gives $b^{p-1} = 1 \bmod p$, so $t | p - 1$. On the other hand, since $\gcd(b^{(N-1)/q} - 1, N) = 1$, certainly

$\gcd(b^{(N-1)/q} - 1, p) = 1$, so p does *not* divide $b^{(N-1)/q} - 1$, and

$$b^{(N-1)/q} \neq 1 \bmod p$$

That is, $t \nmid (N-1)/q$. Also, since $b^{N-1} = 1 \bmod N$, certainly $b^{N-1} = 1 \bmod p$, so $t | N - 1$.

From $t | N - 1$, and $t \nmid (N-1)/q$ we conclude that $q^e | t$. Since $t | p - 1$ and $q^e | t$, we conclude that $q^e | p - 1$. That is, $p = 1 \bmod q^e$ as asserted.   ♣

Theorem. Let $N - 1 = K \cdot U$, where K and U are relatively prime, the factorization of K is known, and $K > \sqrt{N}$.

- If for each prime q dividing K there is b so that $b^{N-1} = 1 \bmod N$ but $\gcd(b^{(N-1)/q} - 1, N) = 1$, then N is prime.

- If N is prime, then for each prime q dividing K there is b so that $b^{N-1} = 1 \bmod N$ but $\gcd(b^{(N-1)/q} - 1, N) = 1$.

Proof: If N is prime, then $\mathbf{Z}/N$ has a primitive root b, which fulfills the condition.

Now suppose that the conditions of the corollary are fulfilled, and show that N is prime. Suppose that for each q dividing K there is b so that $b^{N-1} = 1 \bmod N$ but $\gcd(b^{(N-1)/q} - 1, N) = 1$. Then from the lemma all divisors of N are congruent to 1 modulo K. If N were not prime, then it would have a (prime) factor d in the range $1 < d < \sqrt{N}$. But the condition $d = 1 \bmod K$, with $K > \sqrt{N}$, contradicts this inequality. Thus, N is prime.   ♣

A specialization of this gives a very efficient test for the primality of special types of numbers:

Corollary. ([Proth 1878]) Let $N = u2^n + 1$, where $u < 2^n$ and u is odd. Suppose that there is b so that $b^{(N-1)/2} = -1 \bmod N$. Then N is prime.

Proof: We have $N - 1 = 2^n \cdot u$. Since $u < 2^n$, $2^n > \sqrt{N}$, which is the inequality needed to apply the previous corollary with $K = 2^n$ and $U = u$. And $b^{(N-1)/2} = -1 \bmod N$ implies $b^{(N-1)/2} - 1 = -2 \bmod N$, so $\gcd(b^{(N-1)/2} - 1, N)$ divides $\gcd(-2, N)$, which is 1, since N is odd.   ♣

And there is a further improvement possible, given by the following theorem. Note that the seemingly peculiar condition that the unfactored part have no prime divisors $\leq B$ for some given bound B is a practical one, since in practice small prime divisors of $N - 1$ are readily removed by trial division and Pollard's rho method.

Theorem. Suppose that $N - 1 = K \cdot U$, where the factorization of K is known, $\gcd(K, U) = 1$, and all the prime factors of the unfactored part U are greater than a bound B. Suppose that $B \cdot K \geq \sqrt{N}$. Suppose that for each prime q dividing K there is b (depending upon q) so that $b^{N-1} = 1 \bmod N$ but $\gcd(b^{(N-1)/q} - 1, N) = 1$. *And* suppose that there is b_0 so that $b_0^{N-1} = 1 \bmod N$ and $\gcd(b_0^K - 1, N) = 1$. Then N is prime. Conversely, if N is prime, then these conditions are met.

Proof: This parallels the proof of the lemma. Let p be a prime divisor of N. From the lemma above, $p = 1 \bmod K$. Let t be the exact order of b_0 in $\mathbf{Z}/p^\times$, so $t|p-1$ (by Fermat's Little Theorem). Also $t|N-1$ and $t \nmid K$ by the last hypothesis. Keep in mind that $K = (N-1)/U$. It cannot be that t is relatively prime to U, since $t \nmid K$ and $t|K\cdot U$. Since U has all prime factors greater than B, $\gcd(t,U) > B$. Since K and U are relatively prime, from $t|p-1$ and $K|p-1$, by unique factorization $\mathrm{lcm}(t,K)|p-1$. In particular, $\gcd(t,U) \cdot K$ divides $p-1$. Since $\gcd(t,U) > B$ and $K \cdot B > \sqrt{N}$, this gives $p-1 > B \cdot K > \sqrt{N}$. Thus, N has no prime divisor $\leq \sqrt{N}$, so is prime.   ♣

As a special application of this, we can test the primality of the **Fermat numbers**

$$N = F_n = 2^{2^n} + 1$$

The previous corollary gives only a *sufficient* condition for primality, but if we allow ourselves to invoke quadratic reciprocity, we can prove a *necessary and sufficient* condition in the special case of Fermat numbers:

Corollary. (*Pepin's test*) The nth Fermat number $F_n = 2^{2^n} + 1$ is prime if and only if

$$3^{(F_n-1)/2} = -1 \bmod F_n$$

Proof: This is the case $k = 1$ of the previous corollary: on one hand, if the congruence holds then F_n is prime. The converse is trickier. Suppose F_n is prime. Then we can compute the **quadratic symbol** by using quadratic reciprocity:

$$\left(\frac{3}{F_n}\right)_2 = (-1)^{(3-1)(F_n-1)/4} \cdot \left(\frac{F_n}{3}\right)_2 = \left(\frac{F_n}{3}\right)_2$$

Modulo 3 we compute

$$F_n = 2^{2^n} + 1 = (2^{2^n-1})^2 + 1$$

$\left(2^{2^{n-1}}\right)^2 + 1$

Since 2^{2^n-1} is nonzero modulo 3, it is ± 1 modulo 3, so its square is 1. Therefore, modulo 3

$$F_n = 2^{2^n} + 1 = (2^{2^n-1})^2 + 1 = 1 + 1 = 2 \bmod 3$$

And 2 is not a square mod 3, so

$$\left(\frac{F_n}{3}\right)_2 = \left(\frac{2}{3}\right)_2 = -1$$

And we can compute this as well by Euler's criterion:

$$\left(\frac{3}{F_n}\right)_2 = 3^{(F_n-1)/2} \bmod F_n$$

Thus, if F_n is prime, we can invoke quadratic reciprocity and Euler's criterion to obtain the asserted congruence.   ♣

Remark: It seems that only the first 5 Fermat numbers,

$$2^{2^0} + 1 = 3$$
$$2^{2^1} + 1 = 5$$
$$2^{2^2} + 1 = 17$$
$$2^{2^3} + 1 = 257$$
$$2^{2^4} + 1 = 65,537$$

are known to be prime. These were known by Fermat. It is known that the next 19 Fermat numbers are composite. Fermat claimed that the next Fermat number

$$2^{2^5} + 1 = 4294967297$$

is prime, but 100 years later Euler found the proper factor 641:

$$4294967297 = 641 \cdot 6700417$$

Euler did not use brute force, but instead first sharply reduced the search space for factors by proving and using the following lemma, whose proof resembles Fermat's observation on possible prime factors of $b^n - 1$. This achieved a search speed-up by a factor of 128.

Lemma. Every prime factor p of $2^{2^n} + 1$ satisfies

$$p = 1 \bmod 2^{n+2}$$

(Proof below.)

Thus, to look for factors of $2^{2^5} + 1$, one only looks among primes of the form $k \cdot 2^7 + 1$: these are 257, 641, etc. While 257 does not divide $2^{2^5} + 1$, it is easy to check that 641 does. This is much easier than trial division by the 116 primes starting with 2,3, and continuing up through 641.

Remark: Note that this speed-up trick becomes less and less effective in finding divisors of $2^{2^n} + 1$ as n grows. For example, the sixth Fermat number

$$F_6 = 2^{2^6} + 1 = 18446744073709551617$$

is composite by Pepin's criterion, executed in a few seconds on a desktop computer in an interpreted (rather than compiled) language. This is too large to attempt trial division on, but if we use Euler's speed-up the factor 274117 is found in a few seconds, although all we know in advance is that there might be as many as

$$\sqrt{18446744073709551617}/128 \approx 33554432$$

trial divisions before finding a factor. Also, Pollard's rho method finds the factorization

$$F_6 = 274,177 \cdot 67280421310721$$

in a few seconds. The Miller–Rabin test using bases 2, 3, 5, 7, 11, 13, 17, 19 indicates that 67280421310721 is a probable prime (in less than a second). But the latter is a bit too big to verify its primality by trial division in reasonable time: it takes a few *minutes*. Still, if we use Euler's speed-up to trial division, and only attempt division by numbers $d = 1 \bmod 128$ (since $2^{6+2} = 128$), this will require only about

$$\sqrt{67280421310721}/128 \approx 64081$$

trial divisions. The latter approach verifies the primality of 67280421310721 in a few seconds. The seventh Fermat number

$$F_7 = 340282366920938463463374607431768211457$$

is composite, by Pepin's test. However, trial division would take an exorbitant amount of time to find a factor, even with Euler's speed-up, and Pollard's rho does not find a factor within several minutes (under the same conditions): we might need

$$\sqrt{\sqrt{340282366920938463463374607431768211457}} \approx 4294967296$$

cycles to find a factor near the square root of F_7.

   Proof: *(of Euler's lemma)* If p divides $2^{2^n} + 1$, then $2^{2^n} = -1 \bmod p$. Then $2^{2^{n+1}} = 1 \bmod p$, and we conclude that the *order* of 2 in $\mathbf{Z}/p^\times$ is exactly 2^{n+1}. By Fermat's Little Theorem $2^{p-1} = 1 \bmod p$, so the order of 2 divides $p - 1$. That is, $2^{n+1}|p-1$. This nearly gives the result, but we can sharpen the conclusion further, as follows. For $n \geq 2$, this implies that $p = 1 \bmod 8$, so by quadratic reciprocity $\left(\frac{2}{p}\right)_2 = 1$. That is, 2 is a square modulo p. By Euler's criterion, $2^{(p-1)/2} = 1 \bmod p$. Therefore, in fact, the order of 2 in $\mathbf{Z}/p^\times$ divides $(p-1)/2$. From this we reach the conclusion of the lemma.   ♣

Remark: Without using quadratic reciprocity, we reach a somewhat weaker conclusion, that p dividing $2^{2^n} + 1$ is of the form $1 + k \cdot 2^{n+1}$ for some integer k.

Remark: The special argument for testing primality of Fermat numbers can be generalized a bit to treat numbers of the form $u2^n + 1$, as well.

Remark: Euler's condition on prime factors of $2^{2^n} + 1$ easily generalizes (omitting the invocation of quadratic reciprocity) to the assertion that any prime factor $p > 2$ of $b^n + 1$ is of the form

$$p = 1 \bmod 2n$$

Again, this is very similar to Fermat's observation on divisors of $b^n - 1$, but is in fact simpler.

Remark: A somewhat more sophisticated discussion using larger finite fields leads to the **Lucas-Lehmer test** for the primality of Mersenne numbers $2^n - 1$: define the sequence

$$u_0 = 4, \quad u_1 = u_0^2 - 2, \quad u_2 = u_1^2 - 2, \quad \ldots, \quad u_{n-2} = u_{n-3}^2 - 2$$

For $n > 2$, this number is prime if and only if n is prime, and

$$u_{n-2} = 0 \bmod 2^n - 1$$

For n in the list 3, 5, 7, 13, 17, 19, 31, 61, 89, 107, 127, 521, 607, 1279, 2203, 2281, 3217 the Mersenne number $2^n - 1$ is prime. All these values are small enough so that a desktop computer can easily run the Lucas-Lehmer test to verify the primality. On the other hand, the later Mersenne numbers indicated on this list are certainly too large to *prove* prime by any more generic method. For example, already

$$2^{127} - 1 = 170141183460469231731687303715884105727$$

has 39 digits. This was apparently the largest known prime in 1947. And

$$2^{3217} - 1 =$$

2591170860132026277762467679224415309418
1888755312542730397492316187401926658636
2086201209516800483406550695241733194177
4416895092388070174103777095975120423130
6662408291635351795231118615486226560454
7691127595848775610568757931191017711408
8262521538490358304011850721164247474618
2303147139834022928807454567790794103728
8235820705892351068433882986888616658650
2809276920803396058693087905004095037098
7590211901837199162099400256893511313654
8829739112656797303241986517250116412703
5097054277734779723498216764434466683831
1932254009964899405179024162405651905448
3690809616061625743042361721863339415852
4264312087372665919620617535357488928945
9962919518308262186085340093793283942026
1866586142503251450773096274235376822938
6494071277008460771242118230808041392980
8705750471382526457144837937112503208182
6126566649084251699453951887789613650248
4057393785945994443352311882801236604062
6246860921215034993758478229223714433962
8858485938215738821232393687046160677362
909315071

has 970 digits. The largest known prime as of late 1998 is the Mersenne prime

$$2^{3021377} - 1$$

Remark: [Fellows, Koblitz 1992] gives a **deterministic polynomial-time algorithm which factors** N, assuming we are given the factorization of $N - 1$.

Exercises

24.3.01 Use the Pocklington–Lehmer criterion in the special case of Proth's corollary to prove the primality of 193. That is, write 193 in the form $193 = u2^k + 1$ with odd u, etc.

24.3.02 Use the Pocklington–Lehmer criterion in the special case of Proth's corollary to prove the primality of 241.

24.3.03 Use the Pocklington–Lehmer criterion in the special case of Proth's corollary to prove the primality of 353.

24.4 Strong Primes

A **strong prime** p is supposed to be a prime p which, if it occurs as a factor of a larger integer n, makes the factorization of n relatively difficult. The actual meaning therefore depends upon thinking of specific factorization attacks to which presence of p should present the *worst-case scenario*.

In reality, the notion of 'strong prime' presumably will change with time, as the state of the art of factorization changes, and as the size of the relevant numbers increases, as key sizes go up, as machine speeds go up. (And as algorithms improve?)

Precisely, a **strong prime** is a prime p so that

- $p - 1$ has a 'large' prime factor r.

- $p + 1$ has a 'large' prime factor.

- $r - 1$ has a 'large' prime factor.

The first condition assures that if an integer n has a factor p, then n resists the Pollard $p - 1$ factorization method. That is, p is not very *smooth*. The second condition is a requirement of resistance to an analogous attack on n which would try to use any possible smoothness of $p + 1$ for a prime factor p of n. The third condition is a bit more complicated to explain but is of the same nature.

Remark: Formerly, the condition that a large prime factor s of $p + 1$ should itself have a large prime factor was imposed on 'strong primes'. But this condition is no longer imposed, since apparently it is believed that the factorization attack this guarded against has become less effective as sizes have increased. In a similar manner, the large prime factor s of $r - 1$ could be required to be such that $s - 1$ has a large prime factor. But the 'smoothness' attack against which this protects is ineffective with numbers of the relevant size.

The following rough algorithm needs some tuning to achieve the above objectives exactly. For the sake of specificness, we'll discuss finding 256-bit strong primes. Do note that throughout the process there are parameters that we don't really specify, but which would need to be chosen wisely.

- Pick a random odd 256-bit integer r.

- Test r, $r+2$, $r+4$, $r+6$, $r+8$, $r+10$, ... for strong pseudoprimality using Miller–Rabin. (Do a little trial division on each candidate first, to avoid exponentiating when there is an 'obvious' small prime factor.)

- Let p_1' be the (strong pseudo-) prime found.

- From the Prime Number Theorem, heuristically it will take about $\frac{1}{2}\log r \approx$ 89 attempts before a (pseudo-) prime is found. Each step moves by 2, so

$$p_1 \approx r + 2 \cdot \frac{1}{2}\log r = r(1 + \frac{\log r}{r})$$

from which

$$\log_2 p_1 \approx \log_2 r + \log_2(1 + \frac{\log r}{r}) \approx \log_2 r = 256$$

So we expect that p_1' will most likely be a 256-bit (pseudo-) prime.

- Then test $2p_1' + 1$, $4p_1' + 1$, $6p_1' + 1$, $8p_1' + 1$, and $10p_1' + 1$, for strong pseudoprimality (with a little preliminary trial division).

- Let p_1 be the (pseudo-) prime found.

- From Dirichlet's theorem on primes in arithmetic progressions, as a heuristic we imagine that it will take about $\frac{1}{2}\log p_1' \approx 91$ attempts before a prime is found, so p_1 will have about

$$256 + \log_2(2\frac{1}{2}\log(p_1')) \approx 256 + \log_2(\frac{1}{2}2^{256}) \approx 256 + 6.5 \approx 263 \text{ bits}$$

- Find p_2 in a manner similar to the way in which p_1' was found: pick a random 256-bit odd integer r, and test r, $r+2$, $r+4$, $r+6$, $r+8$, $r+10$, ... for strong pseudoprimality until a (pseudo-) prime is found.

- Let p_2 be the (pseudo-) prime so found. By the Prime Number Theorem we anticipate about $\frac{1}{2}\log r \approx 89$ attempts before finding a prime.

$$p_2 \approx r + 2 \cdot \frac{1}{2}\log r = r(1 + \frac{\log r}{r})$$

from which

$$\log_2 p_2 \approx \log_2 r + \log_2(1 + \frac{\log r}{r}) \approx \log_2 r = 256$$

and p_2 will most likely be a 256-bit prime.

- Now use the Euclidean algorithm to efficiently find an integer t so that

$$\begin{cases} t & = & 1 \bmod p_1 \\ t & = & -1 \bmod 4p_2 \end{cases}$$

(That is, we use the algorithmic rather than purely existential version of Sun Ze's theorem.) We throw the factor of '4' into the modulus just to make sure that t is odd and $t = 3 \bmod 4$.

- Given one solution t, any quantity $t \pm \ell 4p_1p_2$ is also a solution. So we can adjust t so that (without loss of generality)

$$4p_1p_2 < t < 8p_1p_2$$

- Then test

$$t + 4p_1p_2, \quad t + 8p_1p_2, \quad t + 12p_1p_2, \quad t + 16p_1p_2, \quad t + 20p_1p_2, \quad \ldots$$

for strong pseudoprimality via Miller–Rabin. Again by Dirichlet's theorem on primes in an arithmetic progression, we imagine that there will be about

$$\frac{1}{2}\log(t) \approx \frac{1}{2}\log(4p_1p_2) \approx \frac{1}{2}(2 + \log p_1 + \log p_2) \approx 180$$

attempts before a prime is found.

- Let p be the first (pseudo-) prime found. So we anticipate, invoking Dirichlet's theorem again, that

$$p \approx t + 180 \cdot 4p_1p_2 \approx 724p_1p_2 \approx 2^{528.5}$$

The point is that the prime produced may be a bit larger than we really want. So this algorithm needs some tweaking in two ways:

- Try to compensate in advance for the fact that the numbers get bigger by a roughly estimable amount.

- Be prepared to reject pseudoprimes which are simply too large. This is necessary since the invocations of the prime number theorem and Dirichlet's theorem are only **heuristics**: the theorems are true, but they don't really say what we pretend they do.

That is, it is only a *heuristic* that

- Near x, about $1/\log x$ of the numbers are primes.

- Near x, about $\frac{1}{\varphi(N)\log x}$ of the numbers are primes congruent to b modulo N, for b relatively prime to N.

24.5 Primality Certificates

Even though *proof* of primality can be laborious for numbers not of special forms, strangely enough it is sometimes possible to provide easily verifiable **certificates of primality**, using the Pocklington–Lehmer criterion. This amounts to giving information which puts the recipient in a position to verify the primality with only a modest amount of work, that is, *in polynomial time*.

Remark: In all but the last example given below, in fact we start from scratch to *find* the data to provide the primality certificate. The very last example is contrived to show that primality of *selected* numbers may be provable even where *generic* methods fail.

For example, by the first (and simpler) Lucas–Pocklington–Lehmer theorem above, to *prove* that N is prime, it suffices to factor

$$N - 1 = K \cdot U$$

- where the factorization of K is completely known,
- $K > \sqrt{N}$,
- for each prime q dividing K find b_q so that $b_q^{N-1} = 1 \bmod N$ but $\gcd(b_q^{(N-1)/q} - 1, N) = 1$.

Or, using the second version, it suffices to factor

$$N - 1 = K \cdot U$$

- where the factorization of K is completely known,
- where no prime factor of the unfactored part U is $\leq B$ for some bound B,
- $B \cdot K > \sqrt{N}$,
- for each prime q dividing K find b_q so that $b_q^{N-1} = 1 \bmod N$ but $\gcd(b_q^{(N-1)/q} - 1, N) = 1$,
- find b_0 so that $b_0^{N-1} = 1 \bmod N$ but $\gcd(b_0^K - 1, N) = 1$.

In either version, the factorization of K, the list of the b's, and the primes q to which they're attached together comprise a **certificate of primality** for N.

Of course, this certificate must include certificates of primality for the smaller primes q which occur in the factorization of K, which requires certificates for the primes occurring in *these* certificates, and so on.

For example, consider $N = 1000000033$. By applying Miller–Rabin with bases 2, 3, 5, 7, 11 we see that this is a probable prime. It is easy to remove several small factors from $N - 1$:

$$N - 1 = 2 \cdot 2 \cdot 2 \cdot 2 \cdot 2 \cdot 3 \cdot 127 \cdot 82021$$

where we can easily verify the primality of 2, 3, and 127 directly. Also, presuming that we do this by trial division, we would know that the remaining $U = 82021$ has no prime factor ≤ 127. That is, in the notation above, $B = 127$. Taking

$$K = 2 \cdot 2 \cdot 2 \cdot 2 \cdot 2 \cdot 3 \cdot 127 = 12192$$

we see that the condition

$$K \cdot B \approx 1548384 > \sqrt{N} \approx 31623$$

Now we hunt for the b's for the primes dividing $N - 1$, and also for the leftover unfactored part U. Anticipating that N is prime, it should be easy to satisfy the condition $b^{N-1} = 1 \bmod N$. The more difficult will be the requirements that $\gcd(b^{(N-1)/q} - 1, N) = 1$. First, with divisor $q = 2$ of $N - 1$,

$$2^{(N-1)/2} = 1 \bmod N$$

$$3^{(N-1)/2} = 1 \bmod N$$

so neither 2 nor 3 will work here, but

$$5^{(N-1)/2} = -1 \bmod N$$

so $b_2 = 5$ will work. (Since N is odd, if $A = -1 \bmod N$, then $A - 1 = -2 \bmod B$, and A is necessarily relatively prime to B.) For the prime $q = 3$ dividing $N - 1$, we may as well try 5 again:

$$5^{(N-1)/3} = 566663896 \bmod N$$

and the Euclidean algorithm shows that

$$\gcd(5^{(N-1)/3} - 1, N) = 1$$

Thus, $b_3 = 5$ also works. For the prime $q = 127$ dividing $N - 1$,

$$5^{(N-1)/127} = 915796555 \bmod N$$

and the required gcd is checked to be 1. Thus, $b_{127} = 5$ works.

Finally, since we are using the slightly improved version, we need to find b_0 so that $b_0^{N-1} = 1 \bmod N$ but $\gcd(b_0^K - 1, N) = 1$. Let's try 5 again, since we already know the first condition to be fulfilled: the Euclidean algorithm shows that

$$\gcd(5^K - 1, N) = 1$$

Thus, the data

$$K = 2 \cdot 2 \cdot 2 \cdot 2 \cdot 2 \cdot 3 \cdot 127 = 12192$$

$$b_2 = b_3 = b_{127} = b_0 = 5$$

is a **primality certificate** for

$$N = 1000000033$$

Remark: Once given this information, all the checking that needs to be done can be accomplished efficiently (that is, in *polynomial time*). That is, a primality certificate may leave some work to the viewer, but that remaining work must be polynomial-time work rather than something burdensome like trial division of a large number, etc.

Remark: In this example, in fact it did not require much (machine) work to find the data to make up the certificate. But there might be circumstances where this is not so.

Remark: Note that in this example, we did not care about the fact that $U = 82021$ was prime, but only that it had no prime factors ≤ 127. Here this saved 75 further trial divisions.

As a more substantial example, consider

$$N = 3^{53} - 2^{53} = 19383245658672820642055731$$

The Miller–Rabin test indicates that this is a probable prime. We will use the Pocklington theorem to give a primality certificate for it. It is most likely unreasonable to attempt to completely factor $M - 1$, so we only search for factors among primes under 10,000:

$$N - 1 = 2 \cdot 3 \cdot 5 \cdot 7 \cdot \cdot 53 \cdot 263 \cdot 6621792797417598667$$

Using Miller–Rabin base 2, we find that the latter number

$$t = 6621792797417598667$$

is definitely composite (though evidently with no prime factor under 10,000). It is small enough so that Pollard's rho should be effective: we easily find (after only 592 cycles)

$$t = 906043 \cdot 7308475201969$$

It is easy to check (by machine) that 906043 is prime. Miller–Rabin indicates that the larger factor $u = 7308475201969$ is a probable prime. We want to use Pocklington to verify this, as well: factor $u - 1$ as

$$u - 1 = 2 \cdot 2 \cdot 2 \cdot 2 \cdot 3 \cdot 83 \cdot 17539 \cdot 104593$$

and all these factors are readily verified (by machine) to be prime. To prove that the factor u of $N - 1$ is prime, we try to meet the conditions of Pocklington–Lehmer, but 2, 3, 5, 7 fail as b_2, and the first success comes with 11:

$$11^{u-1} = 1 \bmod u$$

$$\gcd(11^{(u-1)/2} - 1, u) = 1$$

which means that (in the notation above) $b_2 = 11$ will work. But

$$\gcd(3^{(u-1)/3} - 1, u) = 1$$

(and $3^{u-1} = 1 \bmod u$) so we can use $b_3 = 3$. Likewise,

$$\begin{aligned}
\gcd(3^{(u-1)/5} - 1, u) &= 1 \\
\gcd(3^{(u-1)/7} - 1, u) &= 1 \\
\gcd(3^{(u-1)/53} - 1, u) &= 1 \\
\gcd(3^{(u-1)/263} - 1, u) &= 1
\end{aligned}$$

Thus, we've verified that u is prime. Going back, we have

$$N - 1 = 2 \cdot 3 \cdot 5 \cdot 7 \cdot \cdot 53 \cdot 263 \cdot 906043 \cdot 7308475201969$$

and now we know that all these factors are prime. Now using the Pocklington–Lehmer criterion on N: $2^{N-1} = 1 \bmod N$, and

$$\gcd(2^{(N-1)/2} - 1, N) = 1$$

so $b_2 = 2$ works for N. But 2 fails as candidate for b_3, as does 3. But then 5 works: $5^{N-1} = 1 \bmod N$, and

$$\begin{aligned}
\gcd(5^{(N-1)/3} - 1, N) &= 1 \\
\gcd(5^{(N-1)/5} - 1, N) &= 1 \\
\gcd(5^{(N-1)/7} - 1, N) &= 1 \\
\gcd(5^{(N-1)/53} - 1, N) &= 1 \\
\gcd(5^{(N-1)/263} - 1, N) &= 1 \\
\gcd(5^{(N-1)/906043} - 1, N) &= 1 \\
\gcd(5^{(N-1)/7308475201969} - 1, N) &= 1
\end{aligned}$$

Thus, 5 succeeds as b_3, b_5, b_7, b_{53}, b_{263}, b_{906043}, and $b_{7308475201969}$. (In earlier notation, the latter might also have been denoted b_0.) Thus, with this data,

$$N = 1938324565867282064205573 1$$

is certified prime.

Finally, we can do an example arranged to be inaccessible by generic methods: we'll find a large integer N so that $N - 1$ has several large prime factors, which would cause difficulties in factoring $N-1$ if we didn't know these factors in advance. We'll use the prime N of the previous paragraph, and we need one more large prime. Choosing somewhat randomly just above N, let

$$M = 1938324565867283064205576 7$$

This was picked out as being a probable prime by Miller–Rabin. But we should *prove* that it is prime before proceeding. By trial division by primes under 10,000 we find

$$M - 1 = 2 \cdot 11 \cdot 41 \cdot 47 \cdot 307 \cdot 653 \cdot 2280712525657409$$

Using $B = 10000$, the product of the small factors additionally multiplied by B is above the square root of M, and after the trial division we know that U has no prime factors below B. We find that $2^{M-1} = 1 \bmod M$, and

$$\gcd(2^{(M-1)/2} - 1, M) = 1$$

so $b_2 = 2$ works here. Also, by good luck,

$$\begin{aligned}
\gcd(2^{(M-1)/11} - 1, M) &= 1 \\
\gcd(2^{(M-1)/41} - 1, M) &= 1 \\
\gcd(2^{(M-1)/47} - 1, M) &= 1 \\
\gcd(2^{(M-1)/307} - 1, M) &= 1 \\
\gcd(2^{(M-1)/653} - 1, M) &= 1 \\
\gcd(2^{(M-1)/2280712525657409} - 1, M) &= 1
\end{aligned}$$

This proves that M is prime.

Now we'll make our *big* prime. With M, N as above, we look in the **arithmetic sequence**

$$n = 2MN + 1, \quad 4MN + 1, \quad 6MN + 1, \quad 8MN + 1, \quad \ldots$$

until a number n satisfies Miller–Rabin, and then we'll try to use Pocklington–Lehmer to *prove* the primality of n. The trick here is that by the special form of the numbers n we know in advance that $n - 1$ will have factors M and N, and we hope that the other factors are not too terrible. The trick is that if we *didn't* know in advance that M and N were factors, it would be rather hard to *find* them. We find that

$$n = 2 \cdot 78 \cdot M \cdot N + 1 = 5861079311325559501040468592518951272085175 2536305613$$

is a probable prime. Happily, (actually, by design)

$$n - 1 = 2 \cdot 78 \cdot M \cdot N$$

so we easily factor $n - 1$ into primes as

$$n - 1 = 2 \cdot 2 \cdot 3 \cdot 13 \cdot M \cdot N$$

Further, we are fortunate that 2 works as b_2, b_3, b_{13}, b_M, and b_N. Thus, this number is prime.

Remark: And we found that 2 is a primitive root modulo the n of the last example.

Remark: All the computations above were done on a 200-MHz machine in the interpreted language Python, and all the indicated computations took almost no perceptible time. Since running an interpreted language is probably 10 times slower than running a fully compiled version on the same machine, the computations would be even *more* accessible with more computing power. On the other hand, even on a very good machine a naive brute force approach to proving the primality of the number n of the last example is doomed: it has 54 digits, so at least

$$10^{27}/(27 \ln 10) \approx 10^{25}$$

trial divisions would be necessary. (Here the division by $27 \ln 10$ is a heuristic estimate coming from the Prime Number Theorem.) Even if we could do a trillion trial divisions every second, it would take 100 million years to do all the trial divisions necessary to prove primality in this example.

Further, if we used the Pocklington–Lehmer approach but without knowledge of the large primes M, N, we would need to factor

$$M \cdot N \approx 10^{52}$$

which by trial division would take 10 million years at the rate of a trillion trial division per second.

Even the reasonable classical factoring methods such as Pollard's rho would take a long time to factor $n - 1$ in this example.

25

Modern Factorization Attacks

The quadratic sieve factoring algorithm is the most elementary of 'modern' factorization methods, and when suitably optimized is competitive with even more sophisticated methods such as elliptic curve factorization or the number field sieve. As usual, there is a probabilistic element to this algorithm, but once a proper factor of a large number is found, the fact that it really *is* a factor of that number can be verified with certainty.

The quadratic sieve is the result of several refinements to the basic idea of the **random square factorization** method, which itself originates in methods used by Fermat. In terms of current standards: the quadratic sieve is comparable to the **elliptic curve sieve** (and often faster). The quadratic sieve is slower than the **number field sieve** for integers with more than 115 or 120 digits. Description of these other two factorization methods would require more preparation.

The first section below explains a bit of linear algebra, namely **Gaussian elimination**, which is essential in the operation of even the most primitive forms of the quadratic sieve.

25.1 Gaussian Elimination

Gaussian elimination is an efficient algorithm for finding **linear dependency relations** among vectors in vectorspaces over arbitrary computationally accessible fields. For present purposes we are mostly interested in vectors which are n-tuples of elements of the finite field $\mathbf{F}_2 = \mathbf{Z}/2$ with two elements.

Remark: Often this algorithm is studied in contexts in which floating-point real numbers are used. In that setting, the issue of loss of precision is critical. But in the present scenario, as well as when computing with 'numbers' from arbitrary finite fields, we effectively have *infinite precision*, so we need not worry about round-off error, etc. This avoids many of the technical worries which require lengthy consideration in the floating-point case.

The problem we need to solve is the following: let

$$
\begin{aligned}
v_1 &= (v_{11}, v_{12}, \ldots, v_{1,n}) \\
v_2 &= (v_{21}, v_{22}, \ldots, v_{2,n}) \\
v_3 &= (v_{31}, v_{32}, \ldots, v_{3,n}) \\
&\cdots \\
v_m &= (v_{m1}, v_{m2}, \ldots, v_{m,n})
\end{aligned}
$$

be n-tuples of elements of a field k. The field k may be the rational numbers $\mathbf{Q}$, the real numbers $\mathbf{R}$, finite fields $\mathbf{F}_p = \mathbf{Z}/p$ (with p prime), or any other field. We will operate as though we knew the numbers **exactly** or, as some would say, **with infinite precision**. This hypothesis is usually not fulfilled if the numbers are real numbers which arise from measurements, but for our applications this hypothesis *will* hold. The question is to find elements $c_1, \ldots, c_m$ in k, not all 0, so that

$$
c_1 v_1 + \cdots + c_m v_m = 0
$$

where the indicated multiplications are scalar multiplication

$$
c \cdot (x_1, x_2, \ldots, x_n) = (cx_1, cx_2, \ldots, cx_m)
$$

and the 0 on the right-hand side is the **zero vector**

$$
0 = \underbrace{(0, \ldots, 0)}_{n}
$$

of size n. Expressions of the form

$$
c_1 v_1 + \cdots + c_m v_m
$$

are **linear combinations** of the **vectors** v_i, with **coefficients** c_i, and any relation of the form

$$c_1 v_1 + \cdots + c_m v_m = 0$$

(with not all coefficients 0) is a **linear dependency relation**. The **dimension** of vectors represented as n-tuples is (as expected) n.

Remark: In a systematic development of basic linear algebra, one of the first results proven would be that *if the number of vectors is greater than the dimension, then there is a linear dependency relation.* We will not directly use this fact, except to verify that the algorithm we present does what it claims to do.

First, we form an m-by-n matrix from the components of the vectors: let

$$M = \begin{pmatrix} v_{11} & v_{12} & \cdots & v_{1,n} \\ v_{21} & v_{22} & \cdots & v_{2,n} \\ v_{31} & v_{32} & \cdots & v_{3,n} \\ & & \cdots & \\ v_{m1} & v_{m2} & \cdots & v_{m,n} \end{pmatrix}$$

Then form a larger matrix by sticking an m-by-m identity matrix onto its right end: from now on we look at the matrix

$$\tilde{M} = \begin{pmatrix} v_{11} & v_{12} & \cdots & v_{1,n} & 1 & 0 & 0 & \cdots & 0 \\ v_{21} & v_{22} & \cdots & v_{2,n} & 0 & 1 & 0 & \cdots & 0 \\ v_{31} & v_{32} & \cdots & v_{3,n} & 0 & 0 & 1 & \cdots & 0 \\ & & \cdots & & & & & & \\ v_{m1} & v_{m2} & \cdots & v_{m,n} & 0 & 0 & 0 & \cdots & 1 \end{pmatrix}$$

That identity matrix (or, really, what it turns into subsequently) will keep track of the operations we perform.

The legal operations here, called **elementary row operations** are

- interchange of two rows,

- multiplication of row by nonzero constant,

- subtraction of multiple of one row from another.

The goal is to do elementary row operations until the matrix M (as a part of the larger matrix $\tilde{M}$) has one or more rows which are all 0's. (The identity matrix stuck onto M on the right can never have this property.) That is, the leftmost m entries of one or more rows of $\tilde{M}$ should be 0.

The way to use elementary row operations to do this is as follows. Starting in the leftmost column, if the top entry is 0, but if there is *some* entry in the first column that is nonzero, interchange rows to put the nonzero entry at the top. Divide through by the leftmost entry in the (new) first row so that the leftmost entry is now 1. Let a_{i1} be the leftmost entry in the ith row. Then for $i > 1$ subtract a_{i1} times the top row from all other rows. This has the effect of making all entries in the first column 0 except for the top entry. (If the leftmost or any other column is all 0's, just ignore it.)

Next look at the second column. If necessary, interchange the second row with another row below it in order to arrange that the second entry of the second row is not 0. (The first entries of all rows below the top one have already been made 0.) Divide through the second row by the second entry, so that the second row starts $0, 1$. Let a_{i2} be the ith entry from the top in the second column. Then subtract a_{i2} times the second row from all other rows (including the top one).

Continue this with the third, fourth, up to mth columns, or until any remaining among the first m columns are all zeros. Let A be the new m-by-m matrix on the right end of the matrix obtained by this process. Let $w_1, \ldots, w_m$ be the left n entries of the rows of the new matrix (so these are length-n row vectors). Then what we have is

$$A \begin{pmatrix} v_1 \\ v_2 \\ \cdots \\ v_m \end{pmatrix} = \begin{pmatrix} w_1 \\ w_2 \\ \cdots \\ w_m \end{pmatrix}$$

If $m > n$, then at least the last $m - n$ of the w_i's will be the zero vector. For example w_m will certainly be the length-n zero vector. That is, we have

$$a_{m1}v_1 + a_{m2}v_2 + a_{m3}v_3 + \cdots + a_{mm}v_m = (0, \ldots, 0)$$

It is important that (due to the way we obtained the matrix A) for each index i at least one a_{ij} is nonzero.

In other words, we have found a linear combination of the vectors v_i which is zero. (And not all the coefficients in the linear combination are zero.)

25.2 Random Squares Factoring

This first stage in the development of the quadratic sieve is the **random squares** factorization method. This is based on ideas already used by Fermat 350 years ago. As we present it here, it is *not* a usable algorithm, since we don't have a tangible procedure to carry out some of the necessary steps. However, this discussion is part of the explanation of the operation of the more refined forms given subsequently.

The first idea is that, in looking for factors of an integer n, if $x^2 = y^2 \bmod n$ but $x \neq \pm y \bmod n$, then $\gcd(x - y, n)$ is a proper divisor of n. Indeed, the hypothesis here is that $n | (x - y)(x + y)$, but that $n \nmid (x - y)$ and $n \nmid (x + y)$. That is, n divides the product $(x - y)(x + y)$ but neither of the factors. Therefore, $\gcd(x - y, n) \neq n$ and $\gcd(x + y, n) \neq n$. Yet ~~these~~ neither of these greatest common divisors can be just 1, or else n couldn't divide the product. Thus, the question becomes that of systematically and efficiently finding such x and y for a given n.

Next, let's observe that for $x^2 = y^2 \bmod n$, then there is a good chance that $x \neq \pm y \bmod n$. Specifically, let k be the number of distinct primes > 2 dividing n, and suppose that n is *odd*. (We can always easily detect and remove factors of 2, after all.) Then we claim that for a square $b = x^2 \bmod n$, there are 2^k different square roots of b modulo n. Indeed, let $n = p_1^{e_1} \ldots p_k^{e_k}$. Then the single congruence

$$x^2 = b \bmod n$$

is equivalent, by Sun Ze's theorem, to the system of k simultaneous congruences

$$\begin{cases} x^2 & = & b \bmod p_1^{e_1} \\ & \cdots & \\ x^2 & = & b \bmod p_k^{e_k} \end{cases}$$

Let $\pm a$ be square roots of $b \bmod n$, then the system is equivalent to

$$\begin{cases} x & = & \pm a \bmod p_1^{e_1} \\ & \cdots & \\ x & = & \pm a \bmod p_k^{e_k} \end{cases}$$

An important point is that these plus-or-minuses can be chosen *independently* of each other. That is, since there are k different choices of $\pm$, there are 2^k different systems, each of which has a solution modulo n by Sun Ze's theorem. Then only 2 out of 2^k are the *obvious* solutions $\pm a$, so the probability that two solutions x and y of this system are in the relation $x = \pm y \bmod n$ is only $2/2^k$.

Thus, the question reduces to that of finding *enough* pairs x, y with $x^2 = y^2 \bmod n$ to make the probability high that some x_0, y_0 has $x_0^2 = y_0^2 \bmod n$ but $x_0 \neq \pm y_0 \bmod n$. This idea will be developed below.

25.3 Dixon's Algorithm

The simplest usable form of the quadratic sieve is **Dixon's algorithm**, which we introduce here. This introduces the notion of **factor base**, which is relevant to other problems as well.

We begin with the idea of a *factor base*, which is simply the set of the first t primes

$$S = \{p_1, \ldots, p_t\}$$

(That is, $p_1 = 2$, $p_2 = 3$, etc.) (The question of how to be suitably clever in choosing t will be addressed below.) Then we choose integers a_1, a_2, ... and reduce them modulo n, letting $b_i = a_i^2 \% n$. We demand that each b_i so occurring is **smooth** with respect to the factor basis S, meaning that all the prime factors of b_i are in the set S. That is, we demand that b_i is p_t-**smooth**. (See below for means to do this.) We then find a subset of the b_is whose product is a perfect square in $\mathbf{Z}$. The latter step is accomplished as follows. Write out the factorizations

$$b_i = \prod_{j=1}^{t} p_j^{e_{ij}}$$

Suppose that we have $t + 1$ of these a_i's with $b_i = a_i^2 \% n$ having all factors in S. Let v_i be the **vector** in $\mathbf{F}_2^{t+1}$ which consists of the exponents from the prime factorization of b_i, reduced modulo 2:

$$v_i = (e_{i1} \% 2, e_{i2} \% 2, e_{i3} \% 2, \ldots, e_{it} \% 2)$$

Since there are $t+1$ of these vectors in a t-dimensional space, they are **linearly dependent** over $\mathbf{F}_2$. That is, there are $c_1, \ldots, c_t$ in $\mathbf{F}_2$ so that

$$c_1 v_1 + \cdots + c_t v_t = (0, \ldots, 0) \in \mathbf{F}_2^{t+1}$$

Use *Gaussian elimination* to find such a relation. Then

$$\prod_{i=1}^{t+1} b_i^{c_i} = \prod_{i=1}^{t+1} (\prod_{j=1}^{t} p_j^{e_{ij}})^{c_i} = \prod_{j=1}^{t} \prod_{i=1}^{t+1} p_j^{c_i e_{ij}} = \prod_{j=1}^{t} p_j^{\Sigma_i c_i e_{ij}}$$

has *even* exponents $\sum_i c_i e_{ij}$, so is the square of an integer.

In this scenario, take

$$x = \prod_{i=1}^{t+1} a_i^{c_i} \qquad y = \prod_{j=1}^{t} p_i^{(\Sigma_i c_i e_{ij})/2}$$

Our discussion shows that

$$x^2 = y^2 \bmod n$$

as desired. Thus, assuming that n really is composite (and not a prime power), and assuming that things are sufficiently 'random', we have at least a 50-50 chance that

$$1 < \gcd(x - y, n) < n$$

and we obtain a proper factor of n.

If by mischance $x = \pm y \bmod n$, then we won't get a proper factor. In that case, compute one or more new values $b_i = a_i^2 \% n$ and repeat the Gaussian elimination step just above.

Remark: Upon more careful analysis of the way things work in the vector space $\mathbf{F}_2^t$, it becomes clear that there are several linear dependency relations among the vectors v_i, and then the probability is quite high (assuming that otherwise everything is suitably random) that at least one of them will yield $x \neq \pm y \bmod n$.

The problem has been reduced to two things: a good determination of the number t of primes in the factor base $S = \{p_1, \ldots, p_t\}$, and efficient choice of the a_i's so that $b_i = a_i^2 \% n$ factors into primes lying in the factor base. **Dixon's algorithm** is the process in which the a_i are chosen randomly, and **trial division** by primes in S is attempted to see whether $b_i = a_i^2 \% n$ is p_t-smooth. This requires on the order of t trial divisions, so if t can be kept small, this testing may not be too inefficient. If b_i is not p_t-smooth, simply reject a_i and choose another. This is the basic form of Dixon's algorithm, but we'll make some little improvements before we do examples.

Remark: It is both intuitively clear and provable quantitatively that the smaller the bound B, the greater the fraction of numbers b satisying $2 \leq b \leq B$ which are p_t-smooth. But, on the other hand, if B is too small it may take too long to find sufficiently many *random* a_is so that $b_i = a_i^2 \% n$ is B-smooth. Thus, we want devices which somehow choose a_i's with the resulting $b_i = a_i^2 \% \; n$ relatively small. The most efficient such device known at this time is the **quadratic sieve**, described a bit later.

Remark: **Avoiding prime powers:** If the integer n should happen to be a power of a single (odd) prime, this method will fail entirely, since Hensel's lemma can be used to show that there are at most two square roots of integers modulo such n. Thus, not only should the Miller–Rabin test be run to be sure that n is composite, but a little additional testing must be done to assure that n is not a power of a single prime. And, of course, there should be a special method to factor numbers which we detect as being powers of a single prime.

Remark: The optimal choice of t for a given n is approximately

$$t = e^{\frac{1}{2} \sqrt{\ln n} \sqrt{\ln \ln n}}$$

This comes from further detailed information about the smoothness of integers near $\sqrt{n}$. This, together with use of **sieving** as replacement for trial division as test for smoothness in the quadratic sieve algorithm, gives a runtime heuristically estimated as

$$O\left(e^{(1+o(1))\sqrt{\ln n}\sqrt{\ln \ln n}}\right)$$

Further, this runtime estimate is independent of the size of the prime factors.

25.4 Non-Sieving Quadratic Sieve

This first real version of the **quadratic sieve** actually does no **sieving** in the sense of the word which will be explained a little later. But it does make use of other optimizations in choice of the a_i's, enough so that this form is already usable. It is the same as Dixon's algorithm, except that the pairs (a_i, b_i) are chosen a little more cleverly, and the factor basis $S = \{2, 3, \ldots, p_t\}$ is 'improved' in two ways.

   Again, suppose we are trying to factor an integer n and have chosen a **factor base**

$$S = \{2, 3, 5, 7, 11, \ldots, p_t\}$$

The a_i's (in the sense above) will be chosen to be just above the square root of n. Then for a just above the square root of n, take

$$b = a^2 \% \; n$$

As in any random squares factoring method we **accept** the pair (a, b) if b is S-smooth, and discard it otherwise.

Remark: If a is sufficiently close to the square root of n, then the corresponding b can be computed in a special way. Let $m = \text{floor}(\sqrt{n})$, that is, the largest integer so that $m \leq \sqrt{n}$. Then

$$b = ((a_i - m) + m)^2 - n = (a_i - m)^2 + 2 \cdot (a_i - m) \cdot m + m^2 - n$$

and

$$b_i \% n = (a_i - m)^2 + 2 \cdot (a_i - m) \cdot m + m^2 - n$$

for $a_i - m$ sufficiently small by comparison to m. This offers some further shortcuts when it is applicable.

Remark: If the b's are computed in special ways to achieve greater efficiency, for example so that b's may be negative, -1 should be included in the factor base S in order to make things work right.

Example: As a very small illustration, let us factor $n = 143$ by this method, using factor base $B = \{2, 3, 5\}$. We should start with an integer just above the square root of n, so take $a_1 = 12$. Then compute $b_1 = a_1^2 \% 143 = 1$. We are lucky: this value is itself both B-smooth and is a square. So here take $x = a_1 = 12$ and $y = 1$ (the positive square root of b_1). We have the relation

$$12^2 = 1^2 \bmod 143$$

so we compute $\gcd(12 - 1, 143)$ and $\gcd(12 + 1, 143)$. The former is 11 and the latter is 13, so we have found proper factors of 143.

Example: As another small illustration, let us factor $n = 1739 = 37 \cdot 47$ using factor base $B = \{2, 3, 5\}$. We start choosing a values at 42, just above the square root of n. By luck $b_1 = a_1^2 \% 1739 = 25$ is B-smooth and is a square. Thus, we compute $\gcd(42 - 5, 1739) = 37$ and $\gcd(42 + 5, 1739) = 47$, thereby finding proper factors.

Example: As a small illustration of the issue of choosing the factor base, let us factor $n = 3071 = 37 \cdot 83$ using factor base $B = \{2, 3, 5\}$. We start with $a = 56$, just above the square root of 3071, but the first case where we obtain a B-smooth square (reduced modulo 3071) is $a_1 = 96$, and $b_1 = a_1^2 \% 3071 = 3$. The next B-smooth case doesn't occur until $a_2 = 125$, and $b_2 = a_2^2 \% 3071 = 270$. The next case is $a_3 = 157$ with $b_3 = a_3^2 \% 3071 = 81$. By accident the latter is a square, so we short-circuit the algorithm and compute $\gcd(157 - 9, 3071) = 37$ and $\gcd(157 + 9, 3071) = 83$. The problem here was that we computed about 100 squares and reduced modulo 3071 before anything happened that gave us the factors. It would have been much faster to use trial division.

Remark: Since the a values became large by comparison to the square root of n, we altered the algorithm to *reduce* modulo n.

Example: Let us try $n = 3071 = 37 \cdot 83$ again using the slightly bigger factor base $B = \{2, 3, 5, 7\}$. Again we start with $a = 56$. Here the first B-smooth case is $a_1 = 96$, which is so far above the initial 56 that we cannot stay with the idea of just computing $a^2 - 55$, but rather must reduce modulo 3071. In fact, $a_2 = 97$ gives a perfect square:

$$b_2 = a_2^2 \% 3071 = 196 = 14^2$$

Thus, we find proper factors $\gcd(97 - 14, 3071) = 83$ and $\gcd(97 + 14, 3071) = 37$. This still took too many steps.

Example: Let us try $n = 3071 = 37 \cdot 83$ one more time using the yet bigger factor base $B = \{2, 3, 5, 7, 11\}$. Again we start with $a = 56$. Here the first B-smooth case is $a_1 = 79$. Again, this is quite a lot above the initial value, and bodes ill because we are spending more time than trial division would have required.

Example: With $n = 8383 = 83 \cdot 101$, we start with $a = 92$, and by luck already $92^2 \% 8383 = 81$ is a square. So $\gcd(92 - 9, 8383) = 83$ and $\gcd(92 + 9, 8383) = 101$.

Example: Let's factor $n = 66887 = 211 \cdot 317$ using the choice of factor base $B = \{2, 3, 5, 7, 11\}$. We start at $a = 259$, but do not find a smooth case until $a_1 = 368$, which again is too far above the square root of n for us to use the simpler evaluation form. Nevertheless, we proceed:

$$b_1 = a_1^2 \% 66887 = 1650 = 2 \cdot 3 \cdot 5^2 \cdot 7^0 \cdot 11$$

The next smooth case is $a_2 = 382$, and

$$b_2 = a_2^2 \% 66887 = 12150 = 2 \cdot 3^5 \cdot 5^2 \cdot 7^0 \cdot 11^0$$

Then there is no smooth case for a while, until $a_3 = 697$, which gives

$$b_3 = a_3^2 \% 66887 = 17600 = 2^6 \cdot 3^0 \cdot 5^2 \cdot 7^0 \cdot 11$$

Again there is a little bit of a short-circuit here, because the sum of the respective exponent vectors $(1, 1, 2, 0, 1)$, $(1, 5, 2, 0, 0)$, and $(6, 0, 2, 0, 1)$ is $(8, 6, 6, 0, 2)$, which has even entries. Therefore, dividing all these even entries by 2, we take

$$y = 2^4 \cdot 3^3 \cdot 5^3 \cdot 7^0 \cdot 11^1 \% 66887 = 58904$$

And take x to be $a_1 \cdot a_2 \cdot a_3 \% n$:

$$x = \sqrt{1650 \cdot 12150 \cdot 17600} \% 66887 = 58904$$

We have had bad luck, since $x = y$. To continue with the algorithm we should find more B-smooth values $a^2 \% n$, but we have already spent considerably more time than trial division would have required.

Example: Let's factor $n = 2043221 = 1013 \cdot 2017$ with factor base $B = \{2, 3, 5, 7, 11\}$. We find smooth outcomes:

$$
\begin{array}{rcrcl}
1439^2 \% 2043221 & = & 27500 & = & 2^2 \cdot 3^0 \cdot 5^4 \cdot 7^0 \cdot 11^1 \\
2878^2 \% 2043221 & = & 110000 & = & 2^4 \cdot 3^0 \cdot 5^4 \cdot 7^0 \cdot 11^1 \\
3197^2 \% 2043221 & = & 4704 & = & 2^5 \cdot 3^1 \cdot 5^0 \cdot 7^2 \cdot 11^0 \\
3199^2 \% 2043221 & = & 17496 & = & 2^3 \cdot 3^7 \cdot 5^0 \cdot 7^0 \cdot 11^0 \\
3253^2 \% 2043221 & = & 365904 & = & 2^4 \cdot 3^3 \cdot 5^0 \cdot 7^1 \cdot 11^2 \\
\end{array}
$$

Once again, our choice of things precludes the simpler evaluation style, but nevertheless things are going well. The first two vectors of exponents have a sum which has even entries, but the same problem occurs as in the previous example: $x = y$. But also the sum of the third and fourth vectors of exponents is even:

$$(5, 1, 0, 2, 0) + (3, 7, 0, 0, 0) = (8, 8, 0, 2, 0)$$

so we try

$$y = 2^4 \cdot 3^4 \cdot 5^0 \cdot 7 \cdot 11^0 \ \% \ 2043221 = 9072$$

by using the halves of the exponents in the vector. Then also take x to be the product of the corresponding a_3 and a_4:

$$x = (3197 \cdot 3199) \ \% \ 2043221 = 11098$$

Then we compute greatest common divisors

$$
\begin{aligned}
\gcd(x - y, n) &= \gcd(11098 - 9072, 2043221) &= 1013 \\
\gcd(x + y, n) &= \gcd(11098 + 9072, 2043221) &= 2017
\end{aligned}
$$

This is slower than trial division, but that's because the numbers are artificially small, and because we're using a rather small factor base.

Further, note that if we *are* able to keep a very close to the square root of n, then for a prime p which divides some b_i

$$b_i^2 = n \bmod p$$

That is, this can happen only for p so that n is a square modulo p. By quadratic reciprocity, this is about *half* the primes in any given range. Thus, for fixed n, the factor base S only needs to include primes p so that $(n/p)_2 = 1$. With larger examples this can substantially reduce the computational load, but we can't quite take advantage of it in our smaller examples.

Example: To factor $n = 20000900009 = 100003 \cdot 200003$, we hope that we can use a's close to the square root of n, so that we can omit from a factor basis primes p so that n is not a square mod p. In this case, $n \ \% \ 3 = 2$, which is a non-square mod 3, so we can ignore 3. Also $n \ \% \ 7 = 6$, which is a non-square. And $n \ \% \ 11 = 2$, which is a non-square mod 11. Further, $n \ \% \ 23 = 5$, which is a non-square mod 23. Thus, if we had been contemplating the factor basis $B = \{2, 3, 5, 7, 11, 13, 17, 19, 23, 29\}$, the latter discussion assures us that we should simplify to

$$B = \{2, 5, 13, 17, 19, 29\}$$

Indeed, for $a = 141427, 145023, 150003, 167565,$ and 178547 we obtain smooth values $b = a^2 \ \% \ n$. In fact, by luck,

$$150003^2 \ \% \ 2000090009 = 2500000000 = 50000^2$$

is already a square. And then

$$\gcd(150003 - 50000, 20000900009) = 100003$$

$$\gcd(150003 + 50000, 20000900009) = 200003$$

which gives us the two proper factors.

25.5 The Quadratic Sieve

This refined version of the **quadratic sieve** really does do what is called **sieving** in its choice of the a_i's. This becomes worthwhile when the numbers are very large.

Let everything be as above. First we have to explain an underlying mechanism which motivates the sieving itself, which is described afterward. Note that if p is an odd prime in the factor base S and p divides $q(x)$ for some x, then p also divides $q(x + \ell p)$ for every integer ℓ. Thus, from the one or two different solutions x to the quadratic equation $q(x) = 0 \bmod p$ we get two sequences of other solutions, by letting ℓ vary.

The **sieving** is as follows. For a large number M we make an array A indexed by x in the range $-M \leq x \leq M$. The xth entry is initially set equal to floor($\lg|q(x)|$), where $\lg$ is logarithm base 2, and floor(t) is the greatest integer less than or equal to t. Let x_1, x_2 be the two solutions to the quadratic equation $q(x) = 0 \bmod p$ for an odd prime p in the factor base S.

Now we do the **sieving**: The quantity floor($\lg p$) is subtracted from those entries $A[x]$ of the array A for which $x = x_1 \bmod p$ or $x = x_2 \bmod p$. Repeat this for each odd prime p in the factor base S. (The cases $p = 2$ and prime *powers* are treated in the obviously parallel manner.) After doing this for everything in the factor base S, the array entries $A[x]$ with values 'near' 0 are most likely to be p_t-smooth. This can be *verified* by factoring $q(x)$ by trial division or other deterministic means.

Remark: Yes, round-off errors must be taken into account. Still, by comparison to comparable high-end use of the elliptic curve algorithm, much less precision is required in the quadratic sieve.

25.6 Other Improvements

Several further improvements and optimizations are possible, but it is difficult to explain the rationale for some of them.

Remark: Again, the optimal choice of t for a given n is approximately

$$t = O(e^{\frac{1}{2} \sqrt{\ln n} \sqrt{\ln \ln n}})$$

which comes from detailed information about the smoothness of integers near $\sqrt{n}$. This, together with use of **sieving** as replacement for trial division as test for smoothness in the quadratic sieve algorithm, gives a runtime

$$L[\frac{1}{2}, 1] = O(e^{(1+o(1))\,\sqrt{\ln n}\,\sqrt{\ln \ln n}})$$

and this runtime estimate is independent of the size of the size of the prime factors.

Remark: The **multiple quadratic polynomial sieve** uses several quadratic polynomials rather than the single one as above. This reduces the size of the sieving interval. The asymptotic runtime is still

$$L[\frac{1}{2}, 1] = O(e^{(1+o(1))\,\sqrt{\ln n}\,\sqrt{\ln \ln n}})$$

This seems to be the version used in many implementations.

Remark: The quadratic sieve is very amenable to **parallelization** in the multiple form: each processor uses a different (suitably chosen) quadratic polynomial, and only appropriate pairs a_i, b_i are reported to the central processor. One solves for the pair x, y after sufficiently many a_i, b_i's have been found.

26

Finite Fields

While we are certainly accustomed to (and entitled to) think of the *fields* of rational numbers, real numbers, and complex numbers as 'natural' collections of numbers, it is important to realize that there are *many* other important *fields*. Perhaps unexpectedly, there are many *finite* fields. For example, for a prime number p, the quotient $\mathbf{Z}/p$ is a *field* (with p elements).

After seeing what the proof of the latter fact entails, this ought not seem so surprising: We can already grant ourselves that $\mathbf{Z}/p$ is a *commutative ring with unit*, being the quotient of $\mathbf{Z}$ by the ideal $p\mathbf{Z}$. So the issue is only to check that *every nonzero element has a multiplicative inverse*. Let $x \in \mathbf{Z}/p$ be nonzero: that means that $x = y + p\mathbf{Z}$ for some integer y not divisible by p. Then, for example, computing via the Euclidean algorithm, there are integers s, t so that $sy + tp = gcd(y, p) = 1$. Then $sy \equiv 1 \bmod p$. Therefore, $s + p\mathbf{Z}$ will be a multiplicative inverse of $y + p\mathbf{Z} = x$. That is, any nonzero element has a multiplicative inverse, so $\mathbf{Z}/p$ is a *field*.

In particular, we see that for each prime number p there is indeed a (finite!) field with p elements.

On the other hand, for example, *there is no finite field with 6 or with 10 elements.* (Why?)

While it turns out that there *are* finite fields with, for example, 9 elements, 128 elements, or *any prime-power* number of elements, it requires a bit more preparation to 'find' them.

The simplest finite fields are the rings $\mathbf{Z}/p$ with p prime. For many different reasons, we want *more* finite fields than just these. One immediate reason is that for machine implementation (and for other computational simplifications) it is optimal to use fields *of characteristic 2*, that is, in which $1 + 1 = 2 = 0$. Among the fields $\mathbf{Z}/p$ only $\mathbf{Z}/2$ satisfies this condition. At the same time, for various reasons, we might want the field to be *large*. If we restrict our attention to the fields $\mathbf{Z}/p$, we can't meet both these conditions simultaneously.

26.1 Making Finite Fields

Construction of finite fields, and computations in finite fields, are based upon upon polynomial computations. For brevity, write $\mathbf{F}_q$ for the finite field with q elements. Of course, for a prime p, $\mathbf{Z}/p = \mathbf{F}_p$. Another notation often seen is

$$\mathrm{GF}(q) = \mathbf{F}_q$$

Here *GF* stands for **Galois field**.

For a polynomial P (not necessarily irreducible), and for two other polynomials f, g, all with coefficients in $\mathbf{F}_p$, write

$$f = g \bmod P$$

if P divides $f - g$. This is completely analogous to congruences for ordinary integers. And, continuing with that analogy, define

$$\mathbf{F}_p[x]/P = \{\text{congruence classes} \bmod P\}$$

where the **congruence class** $\bar{f} \bmod P$ of a polynomial f is

$$\bar{f} = \{g \in \mathbf{F}_p[x] : g = f \bmod P\}$$

Usually one just writes 'f' rather than '$\bar{f}$'.

A polynomial f is **reduced mod** P if

$$\deg f < \deg P$$

Via the division algorithm in the polynomial ring $\mathbf{F}_p[x]$, every polynomial in $\mathbf{F}_p[x]$ is equal-mod-P to a reduced polynomial mod P: indeed, given f, by division-with-remainder we obtain polynomials Q and R with $\deg R < \deg P$ and so that

$$f = Q \cdot P + R$$

That is,

$$f - R = Q \cdot P$$

which is to say that $f = R \bmod P$.

Proposition. Two polynomials f, g which are reduced mod P are equal modulo P if and only if they are equal (in $\mathbf{F}_p[x]$).

Theorem. For an irreducible polynomial P of degree n, the ring

$$\mathbf{F}_p[x] \bmod P = \mathbf{F}_p[x]/P$$

of polynomials mod P is a **field**, with p^n elements. The element x-mod-P is a root in $\mathbf{F}_p[x]/P$ of the equation $P(x) = 0 \bmod P$.

It is often desirable in $\mathbf{F}_p[x]/P$ to express anything in **reduced form**, since then it is easy to test two things for equality: just compare their coefficients.

Let k be a field. Another field K containing k is called an **extension field** of k, and k is a **subfield** of K. The **degree** of the extension K of k is the degree of the polynomial P used in the construction of $K = k[x]/P$.

Remark: In this situation, thinking of

$$\alpha = x\text{-mod-}P$$

as existing in its own right now, and being a root of the equation $P(x) = 0 \bmod P$, we say that we have **adjoined** a root of $P(x) = 0$ to k, and write

$$k[\alpha] = k[x]/P$$

Exercises

26.1.01 Show that there is no element $x \in \mathbf{F}_{13}$ so that $x^5 = 1$ except $x = 1$.

26.1.02 Verify that $x^2 + x + 1$ is the only irreducible quadratic polynomial in $\mathbf{F}_2[x]$.

26.1.03 Verify that $x^3 + x + 1$ and $x^3 + x^2 + 1$ are the two irreducible cubics in $\mathbf{F}_2[x]$.

26.1.04 Verify that $x^5 + x + 1$ is irreducible in $\mathbf{F}_2[x]$.

26.1.05 Verify that in $\mathbf{F}_2[x]$ we have the peculiar identity

$$(x^{\ell_1} + \cdots + x^{\ell_k})^2 = x^{2\ell_1} + \cdots + x^{2\ell_k}$$

26.1.06 Verify that, for prime p, in $\mathbf{F}_p[x]$ we have the peculiar identity

$$(x^{\ell_1} + \cdots + x^{\ell_k})^p = x^{p\ell_1} + \cdots + x^{p\ell_k}$$

26.2 Examples of Field Extensions

Now we'll do some specific numerical examples of field extensions, using the set-up of the previous section.

Example: Let's see how to 'make' the complex numbers $\mathbf{C}$ as a **field extension** of the real number $\mathbf{R}$, *not* by presuming that there is a mysterious $\sqrt{-1}$ already existing 'out there somewhere'.

First, let's prove that $x^2 + 1 \in \mathbf{R}[x]$ is irreducible. Since the square of any real number is non-negative, the equation

$$x^2 + 1 = 0$$

has no roots in $\mathbf{R}$. Since the polynomial $x^2 + 1 \in \mathbf{R}[x]$ is quadratic, if it were to factor in $\mathbf{R}[x]$ it would have to factor into two linear factors (since the degree of the product is the sum of the degrees of the factors). But if $x^2 + 1$ had a linear factor, then $x^2 + 1 = 0$ would have a root in $\mathbf{R}$, which it does not. Thus, in the polynomial ring $\mathbf{R}[x]$ the polynomial $x^2 + 1$ is irreducible, as claimed.

Then, from above we know that $\mathbf{R}[x]$ mod I is a field, inside which we can view $\mathbf{R}$ as sitting. Also,

$$x^2 = -1 \bmod x^2 + 1$$

so x-mod-$(x^2 + 1)$ is a $\sqrt{-1}$.

We also showed that any element β of the extension is expressible uniquely in the form $\beta = a + b\alpha$ for $a, b \in \mathbf{R}$. Of course, we usually would write 'i' for the image of x in that extension field, rather than 'α'.

Example: Let's adjoin a square root of 2 to the field $\mathbf{Z}/5$. First, note that there is no a in $\mathbf{Z}/5$ so that $a^2 = 5$. Thus, the quadratic polynomial $x^2 - 2$ does not factor in $\mathbf{Z}/5[x]$ (since if it did it would have a root in $\mathbf{Z}/5$, which it doesn't). Then $\mathbf{Z}/5[x]$ mod $x^2 - 2$ is a field, inside which we can view $\mathbf{Z}/5$ as sitting. And

$$x^2 = 2 \bmod x^2 - 2$$

so x-mod-$(x^2 - 2)$ is a square root of 2. Of course, we usually would write '$\sqrt{2}$' for x-mod-$(x^2 - 2)$, rather than 'α'.

Remark: Yes, these constructions might be viewed as anticlimactic, since the construction 'makes' roots of polynomials in a manner that seemingly is not as tangible as one would like. But in fact it's *good* that the construction is fairly straightforward, since that partly means that *it works well*.

Example: Let's adjoin a cube root of 2 to $\mathbf{Z}/7$. First, note that there is no cube root of 2 in $\mathbf{Z}/7$. (Check by brute force. Or, by noting that $\mathbf{Z}/7^\times$ is cyclic of order 6, from our basic facts about cyclic groups $\mathbf{Z}/7^\times$ will have only two third powers, which we can directly observe are ± 1, so (by exclusion) 2 can't be a cube.)

Thus, the cubic polynomial $x^3 - 2$ is irreducible in $\mathbf{Z}/7[x]$, since if it were *reducible*, then it would have to have a linear factor, and then $x^3 - 2 = 0$ would have to have a root in $\mathbf{Z}/7$, which it doesn't.

From this discussion, $(\mathbf{Z}/7)[x]$-mod-$(x^3 - 2)$ is a field, and x-mod-$(x^3 - 2)$ is a cube root of 2. And every element β of this field extension of $\mathbf{Z}/7$ can be uniquely expressed in the form

$$\beta = a_0 + a_1\alpha + a_2\alpha^2$$

where we use α as an abbreviation for x-mod-$(x^3 - 2)$.

Exercises

26.2.01 There is no cube root of 2 in $\mathbf{Z}/7$. There is also no square root of 3 in $\mathbf{Z}/7$, so the polynomial $x^2 - 3$ in $\mathbf{F}_7[x]$ is irreducible. Make a model of $\mathbf{F}_{49}$ as $\mathbf{F}_7[x]/(x^2 - 3)$. Find a cube root of 2 in this model of $\mathbf{F}_{49}$.

26.2.02 There is no cube root of 2 in $\mathbf{Z}/103$. There is also no square root of 3 in $\mathbf{Z}/103$, so the polynomial $x^2 - 3$ in $\mathbf{F}_{103}[x]$ is irreducible. Make a model of $\mathbf{F}_{103^2}$ as $\mathbf{F}_{103}[x]/(x^2 - 3)$. Find a cube root of 2 in this model of $\mathbf{F}_{103^2}$.

26.2.03 Use the model $\mathbf{F}_{49} = \mathbf{F}_7[x]/(x^2 - 3)$. Let α be x mod $x^2 - 3$. Is α a cube in $\mathbf{F}_{49}$? Is $\alpha + 1$ a cube in $\mathbf{F}_{49}$?

26.2.04 Use the model $\mathbf{F}_{49} = \mathbf{F}_7[x]/(x^2 - 3)$. Let α be x mod $x^2 - 3$. Find a fifth root of α in $\mathbf{F}_{49}$.

26.2.05 Let $P(x) = x^2 - 3$. There is no square root of 3 mod 5, so this polynomial has no roots in $\mathbf{Z}/5$, so is irreducible in $\mathbf{F}_5[x]$. Let $K = \mathbf{F}_5[x]/P(x)$, and let α be x mod $P(x)$, so α is a square root of 3 in this field extension of $\mathbf{F}_5$. Find a root of $x^2 + x + 1 = 0$ in K.

26.2.06 Let K be as in the previous example. Find a root of $x^4 + 1 = 0$ in K.

26.2.07 Let $P(x) = x^2 + 1$. There is no square root of -1 mod 7, so this polynomial has no roots in $\mathbf{Z}/7$, so is irreducible in $\mathbf{F}_7[x]$. Let $K = \mathbf{F}_7[x]/P(x)$, and let α be x mod $P(x)$, so α is a square root of -1 in this field extension of $\mathbf{F}_7$. Find a root of $x^2 - 5 = 0$ in K.

26.2.08 Let K be as in the previous example. Find a root of $x^{16} - x^8 + 1 = 0$ in K. (This is the 48th cyclotomic polynomial.)

26.3 Addition mod P

Addition in a finite field is just addition of polynomials, which itself is structurally identical to vector addition.

Addition in $\mathbf{F}_p[x]/P$ is easy: just add the corresponding coefficients of polynomials. Since the degree of a sum of polynomials is less than or equal to the max of their degrees, the sum of two *reduced* polynomials is still reduced.

For example, in $\mathbf{F}_2[x]/(x^4 + x + 1)$, adding $x^3 + x + 1$ and $x^2 + x + 1$ gives

$$(x^3 + x + 1) + (x^2 + x + 1) = x^3 + x^2 + 2x + 2 = x^3 + x^2 \bmod x^4 + x + 1$$

since $2 = 0$.

26.4 Multiplication mod P

For computational purposes, multiplication in $\mathbf{F}_p[x]/P$ is ordinary multiplication of polynomials followed by reduction modulo P. Much as in the case of multiplication in $\mathbf{Z}/m$, multiplication in $\mathbf{F}_p[x]$ actually has a more intrinsic and meaningful definition, which is indispensable in proving theorems, but the present version is all we need for computations.

Example: In $\mathbf{F}_2[x]/(x^4 + x + 1)$, multiplying $x^3 + x + 1$ and $x^2 + x + 1$ gives

$$
\begin{aligned}
(x^3 + x + 1) \cdot (x^2 + x + 1) &= x^5 + x^4 + 2x^3 + 2x^2 + 2x + 1 \\
&= x^5 + x^4 + 1 \\
&= x^2 \bmod x^4 + x + 1
\end{aligned}
$$

since $2 = 0$ and

$$(x^5 + x + 1) - (x)(x^4 + x + 1) = x^2 + 1$$

is the way that the reduction mod $x^4 + x + 1$ of $x^5 + x^4 + 1$ is computed.

Again: to multiply modulo P, multiply polynomials in the ordinary way and then reduce modulo P.

Exercises

26.4.01 In the field $K = (\mathbf{F}_2)[x]/(x^2 + x + 1)$ let α be the image of x, and compute in reduced form $(1 + \alpha) \cdot \alpha$.

26.4.02 In the field $K = (\mathbf{F}_2)[x]/(x^2 + x + 1)$ let α be the image of x, and compute in reduced form α^5.

26.4.03 In the field $K = (\mathbf{F}_2)[x]/(x^3 + x + 1)$ let α be the image of x, and compute in reduced form α^6.

26.4.04 In the field $K = (\mathbf{F}_2)[x]/(x^5 + x^2 + 1)$ let α be the image of x, and compute in reduced form $(1 + \alpha + \alpha^2) \cdot (1 + \alpha^3)$.

26.5 Multiplicative Inverses mod P

This is the most complicated operation, requiring use either of the Euclidean algorithm or a fast exponentiation algorithm.

Here it is important that the modulus P be *irreducible*. To find the multiplicative inverse of f modulo P for $f \neq 0 \mod P$, use the extended Euclidean algorithm to find polynomials S, T so that

$$S \cdot f + T \cdot P = 1$$

Then

$$S \cdot f - 1 = T \cdot P$$

so by the definition of equality-mod-P

$$S \cdot f = 1 \mod P$$

That is,

$$f^{-1} = S \mod P$$

Because f is not $0 \mod P$, and because P is irreducible, it must be that the *gcd* of the two is 1, so such S, T do exist.

For example, to find the multiplicative inverse of x in $\mathbf{F}_2[x]/(x^2 + x + 1)$, first do Euclid (which is very quick here)

$$(x^2 + x + 1) - (x + 1)(x) = 1$$

Thus, already we have the desired expression

$$(x + 1)(x) + (1)(x^2 + x + 1) = 1$$

from which

$$(x + 1)(x) = 1 \mod x^2 + x + 1$$

In other words,

$$x^{-1} = x + 1 \mod x^2 + x + 1$$

To find the multiplicative inverse of $x^2 + x + 1$ in $\mathbf{F}_2[x]/(x^4 + x + 1)$, first do Euclid

$$(x^4 + x + 1) - (x^2 + x)(x^2 + x + 1) = 1$$

Thus, already we have the desired expression

$$(x^2 + x)(x^2 + x + 1) + (1)(x^4 + x + 1) = 1$$

from which

$$(x^2 + x)(x^2 + x + 1) = 1 \mod x^4 + x + 1$$

In other words,

$$(x^2 + x + 1)^{-1} = x^2 + x \mod x^2 + x + 1$$

Exercises

26.5.01 In the field $K = \mathbf{F}_2[x]/(x^2 + x + 1)$ let α be the image of x, and compute in reduced form $(1 + \alpha)^{-1}$.

26.5.02 In the field $K = \mathbf{F}_2[x]/(x^2 + x + 1)$ let α be the image of x, and compute in reduced form α^{-1}.

26.5.03 In the field $K = \mathbf{F}_2[x]/(x^3 + x + 1)$ let α be the image of x, and compute in reduced form $(1 + \alpha + \alpha^2)^{-1}$.

26.5.04 Verify that the polynomial $x^4 + x + 1$ in $\mathbf{F}_2[x]$ is irreducible. Let α be a root of $x^4 + x + 1 = 0$. Express $(\alpha^2 + 1)^{-1}$ as a polynomial in α.

26.5.05 The polynomial $x^6 + x^3 + 1$ in $\mathbf{F}_2[x]$ is irreducible. (Do not bother to verify this.) Let α be a root of $x^6 + x^3 + 1 = 0$. Find a multiplicative inverse of $1 + \alpha + \alpha^3$ expressed as a polynomial in α.

26.5.06 The polynomial $x^6 + x^5 + x^4 + x^2 + 1$ in $\mathbf{F}_2[x]$ is irreducible. (Do not bother to verify this.) Let α be a root of $x^6 + x^5 + x^4 + x^2 + 1 = 0$. Find a multiplicative inverse of $1 + \alpha + \alpha^3$ expressed as a polynomial in α.

27
Discrete Logs

Recall that the **discrete logarithm** of a base b modulo p is the integer L (if it exists at all) so that

$$a = b^L \bmod p$$

We write

$$L = \log_b a$$

with reference to the modulus understood from context. This L is sometimes called the *index* of a base b modulo p to make clear that it is not an 'ordinary' logarithm. We have seen that for p prime there is a *primitive root* b mod p. Therefore, with b a primitive root modulo prime p, any nonzero a mod p does have a discrete logarithm base b. This idea is readily abstracted by replacing the primitive root b in $\mathbf{Z}/p^\times$ by a generator for a *cyclic group*. Such abstractions have been found useful, because the fastest algorithms for computing discrete logs apply only to the simpler cases such as $\mathbf{Z}/p^\times$, but not to fancier ones (such as *elliptic curves*).

The naive way to compute a discrete logarithm in a group is by *brute force*, simply trying candidates until a successful one is found. That is, to compute $\log_b a$ in $\mathbf{Z}/p$, for a primitive root b mod p, compute (all mod p) b^1, b^2, b^3, b^4, ... until one of these powers of b (mod p) is the target a. This takes $O(p)$ trials. For p large enough for cryptographic purposes (100 digits or more) this naive approach is completely infeasible, much as trial division quickly becomes infeasible as a method for factoring integers.

27.1 Baby-step Giant-step

The baby-step giant-step algorithm to compute discrete logarithms works in any cyclic group G, assuming that computation of the group operation is not too expensive. The runtime is of the order of the square root of $|G|$. That is, the runtime is $O(\sqrt{|G|})$. On the other hand, this algorithm uses $O(\sqrt{|G|})$ memory, as well. Thus, it affords an example of a runtime/memory trade. It is deterministic.

Let G be a cyclic group with generator b. We want to compute the discrete logarithm of some other element $a \in G$ base b. Let n be the order $|G|$ of G, and let

$$m = \text{floor}(\sqrt{n})$$

So m is an integer just less than $\sqrt{n}$. When $\ell = \log_b a$, we can of course write

$$\ell = m \cdot i + j$$

where

$$0 \le i < m$$
$$0 \le j < m$$

The equation

$$a = b^{mi+j}$$

can be rearranged to

$$a(b^{-m})^i = b^j$$

Thus, we first compute the m quantities b^j, $0 \le j < m$ and put them in some type of sorted look-up table. Then begin to compute successively the m quantities a, $a \cdot b^{-m}$, $a \cdot b^{-2m}$, ..., $a \cdot b^{-mi}$, ... At the ith step, compare $a \cdot b^{-mi}$ and b^j. If they are equal, then

$$\log_b a = mi + j$$

Remark: Construction of the list of b^j's takes $\sqrt{n}$ steps initially. Each of the $O(\sqrt{n})$ comparisons of $a \cdot b^{-mi}$ to the b^j's must be done in much less than $O(\sqrt{n})$ time, or else the total number of steps will be $O(n)$, which is no better than brute force. Therefore, the list of the b^j's must be sorted and ordered in a fashion so that testing whether or not an element $a \cdot b^{-mi}$ is on the list is very fast. For example, in simple cases this testing can be done with only $\log_2 m$ comparisons.

Although this algorithm makes sense in any group, the necessary sorting of the b^j's is easiest to describe in a tangible class of examples, such as $\mathbf{Z}/p^\times$, for prime p. Let b be a primitive root mod p. The order n of the group $G = \mathbf{Z}/p^\times$ is $n = p - 1$.

Let m be the greatest integer not greater than $\sqrt{p-1}$. To compute $\log_b a$ in G, first compute

$$(1, b^1 \% p)$$

$$(0, b^0 \% p), (2, b^2 \% p), (3, b^3 \% p), \ldots, (m-1, b^{m-1} \% p)$$

We *sort* these ordered pairs by *size* of their second components, so that testing whether some $g \in G$ is in the list will take only $\log_2 m$ comparisons. Then (to be a little smart about the computations)

- Compute $c = b^{-m} \bmod p$.

- Initialize $x = a$.

- For $i = 0$ to $i = m - 1$: if x is the element b^j in the list $b^0, \ldots, b^{m-1}$, then

$$\log_b a = mi + j$$

Otherwise, replace x by $x \cdot c \bmod p$ and $i = i + 1$.

Remark: Again, a notion of *size* or other simple numerical identifier of the elements of the group G is necessary to make this work efficiently.

Example: Let's compute $\log_2 3$ modulo 29. So $p = 29$, $a = 3$, and $b = 2$. Then $m = \text{floor}(\sqrt{29 - 1}) = 5$. Thus, we compute $(0, b^0), \ldots, (4, b^4 \% 29)$: this list is

$$(0, 1), \ (1, 2), \ (2, 4), \ (3, 8), \ (4, 16)$$

Because the example is artificially small, the second entries are already sorted by size. Also, $c = 2^{-5} \bmod 29 = 10$. Then initialize $x = a = 3$. This is not on the list. Continuing, replace x by $x \cdot c$, which is $3 \cdot 10 \% 29 = 1$, which *is* on the list. That is,

$$3 \cdot 2^{-5} = 2^0$$

Rearranging as planned, this gives

$$\log_2 3 = 5 \cdot 1 + 0 = 5 \ \text{ in } \mathbf{Z}/29^\times$$

Example: Let's compute $\log_2 3$ modulo 101. So $p = 101$, $a = 3$, and $b = 2$. Then $m = \text{floor}(\sqrt{101 - 1}) = 10$. Thus, we compute $(0, b^0), \ldots, (9, b^9 \% 101)$: this list is

$$(0, 1), \ (1, 2), \ (2, 4), \ (3, 8), \ (4, 16), \ (5, 32), \ (6, 64), \ (7, 27), \ (8, 54), \ (9, 6)$$

Sorting by size of the second element, the list is

$$(0, 1), \ (1, 2), \ (2, 4), \ (9, 6), \ (3, 8), \ (4, 16), \ (7, 27), \ (5, 32), \ (8, 54), \ (6, 64)$$

[handwritten top margin: $m = 10$, $C = 2^{-10} \% 101 = 65$]

Also, $c = 2^{-9} \bmod 101 = 29$. Then initialize $x = a = 3$. This is not on the list. Continue, replacing x by $x \cdot c$ and continuing as long as x is not on the list:

$$
\begin{aligned}
3 \cdot 29 \;\% \;101 &= 87 \\
87 \cdot 29 \;\% \;101 &= 99 \\
99 \cdot 29 \;\% \;101 &= 43 \\
43 \cdot 29 \;\% \;101 &= 35 \\
35 \cdot 29 \;\% \;101 &= 5 \\
5 \cdot 29 \;\% \;101 &= 44 \\
44 \cdot 29 \;\% \;101 &= 64
\end{aligned}
$$

[handwritten right column:]
$3 \cdot 65 \% 101 = 94$
$94 \cdot 65 \% 101 = 50$
$50 \cdot 65 \% 101 = 18$
$18 \cdot 65 \% 101 = 59$
$59 \cdot 65 \% 101 = 98$
$98 \cdot 65 \% 101 = 7$

That is,

$$3 \cdot (2^{-9})^7) = 64 = 2^6 \bmod 101$$

[handwritten:]
$3 \cdot (2^{-10})^6 = 7 = 2^9 \% 101$
$\log_2 3 = 10 \cdot 6 + 9 = 69$

Rearranging as planned, this gives

$$\log_2 3 = 9 \cdot 7 + 6 = 69 \quad \text{in } \mathbf{Z}/101^{\times}$$

Exercises

27.1.01 Using the baby-step giant-step algorithm, in $\mathbf{Z}/29$ find $\log_2 3$.

27.1.02 Using the baby-step giant-step algorithm, in $\mathbf{Z}/29$ find $\log_2 5$.

27.1.03 Using the baby-step giant-step algorithm, in $\mathbf{Z}/29$ find $\log_2 7$.

27.1.04 Using the baby-step giant-step algorithm, in $\mathbf{Z}/29$ find $\log_2 11$.

27.1.05 Using the baby-step giant-step algorithm, in $\mathbf{Z}/53$ find $\log_2 3$.

27.1.06 Using the baby-step giant-step algorithm, in $\mathbf{Z}/53$ find $\log_2 5$.

27.1.07 Using the baby-step giant-step algorithm, in $\mathbf{Z}/53$ find $\log_2 7$.

27.1.08 Using the baby-step giant-step algorithm, in $\mathbf{Z}/53$ find $\log_2 11$.

27.1.09 Using the baby-step giant-step algorithm, in $\mathbf{Z}/227$ find $\log_2 3$.

27.1.10 Using the baby-step giant-step algorithm, in $\mathbf{Z}/227$ find $\log_2 5$.

27.1.11 Using the baby-step giant-step algorithm, in $\mathbf{Z}/227$ find $\log_2 7$.

27.1.12 Using the baby-step giant-step algorithm, in $\mathbf{Z}/227$ find $\log_2 11$.

27.2 Pollard's Rho Method

The idea of Pollard's rho algorithm for factoring has an analogue for computation of discrete logs in any group. As in the case of factorization, the rho method achieves a significant speedup over the naive approach, but is not polynomial-time. This rho algorithm is intrinsically probabilistic in nature, depending upon the birthday 'paradox'. In this regard it is exactly parallel to the rho algorithm for factoring.

Remark: This algorithm works for computing discrete logarithms in arbitrary finite cyclic groups, not only $\mathbf{Z}/p$ or other relatively simple cases. For example, it applies to discrete log computation in elliptic curves.

Remark: This algorithm is simplest to present when the order of the cyclic group in question is *prime*. Thus, for example, rather than looking at the multiplicative group $\mathbf{Z}/59^\times$, which is of order 58 with generator 2, to use the simple version of the algorithm we would need to look at the cyclic subgroup G of order 29, generated by $b = 4 = 2^2$. Then we'd compute discrete logs only of elements of $\mathbf{Z}/59^\times$ which happened to lie in the smaller set G. (This subgroup G consists of the *squares* in $\mathbf{Z}/59^\times$.)

Let G be a cyclic group with generator b and identity e. For $a \in G$, we will compute $\log_b a$ in G, meaning that we'll find the smallest positive integer L so that

$$b^L = a$$

Break G into three disjoint pieces S_1, S_2, and S_3, with $e \notin S_2$. Define a 'random' function

$$f : G \to G$$

by the rule

$$f(X) = \begin{cases} a \cdot X & \text{if } X \in S_1 \\ X^2 & \text{if } X \in S_2 \\ b \cdot X & \text{if } X \in S_3 \end{cases}$$

Choose two random integers m_0 and n_0 (possibly both simply 0), and define a sequence of elements $X_i \in G$ recursively by taking the initial element X_0 to be $X_0 = a^{m_0} \cdot b^{n_0}$, and defining

$$X_{i+1} = f(X_i)$$

The same probabilistic mechanism that worked for the rho factoring method works here: assuming that the sequence X_0, X_1, ... is 'random', the probability is at least $1/2$ that for N greater than the square root $\sqrt{|G|}$ of the order $|G|$ of the group G,

$$X_i = X_j$$

for some $i \neq j$, with $i, j \leq N$.

As with the rho factoring method, we use Floyd's cycle-detection trick to avoid using a lot of memory and to avoid making a huge number of comparisons. To achieve this (at the same time that we compute the sequence of X_i's) we compute another sequence Y_0, Y_1, Y_2, ..., defined by $Y_0 = X_o$ and

$$Y_{i+1} = f(f(Y_i))$$

Thus,

$$Y_i = X_{2i}$$

Then for N just a little larger than $\sqrt{|G|}$, the probability is greater than $\frac{1}{2}$ that $Y_i = X_i$, so $X_{2i} = X_i$.

By construction, each X_{i+1} is expressible as a product of powers of a and b (in at least one way), since the function f is described entirely in terms of multiplications by a or b, and by squaring. To have a notation for this, for $i = 0, 1, 2, \ldots$ let m_i and n_i be positive integers so that

$$X_i = a^{m_i} b^{n_i}$$

with m_0 and n_0 chosen at the outset. (As remarked before, $m_0 = 0$ and $n_0 = 0$ is a reasonable choice.) If we spell out how the m_i's and n_i's are determined recursively from the definition of f, it is

$$m_{i+1} = \begin{cases} m_i + 1 & \text{if } X_i \in S_1 \\ 2 \cdot m_i & \text{if } X_i \in S_2 \\ m_i & \text{if } X_i \in S_3 \end{cases}$$

$$n_{i+1} = \begin{cases} n_i & \text{if } X_i \in S_1 \\ 2 \cdot n_i & \text{if } X_i \in S_2 \\ n_i + 1 & \text{if } X_i \in S_3 \end{cases}$$

Then when $X_{2i} = X_i$, we have

$$a^{m_{2i}} b^{n_{2i}} = a^{m_i} b^{n_i}$$

from which we obtain

$$b^{n_{2i} - n_i} = a^{m_i - m_{2i}}$$

Taking logs base b (in G) of both sides gives

$$(\log_b a) \cdot (m_{2i} - m_i) = (n_i - n_{2i}) \bmod |G|$$

since $|b| = |G|$ (by definition of *generator*). Unless by mischance $m_{2i} - m_i$ is *not* relatively prime to the order $|G|$, we can efficiently find a multiplicative inverse t to $m_{2i} - m_i$ modulo $|G|$, and then

$$\log_b a = t \cdot (n_i - n_{2i}) \bmod |G|$$

Thus, the algorithm needs to keep track of the six quantities

$$(X_i, m_i, n_i, Y_i, m_{2i}, n_{2i})$$

for $i = 0, 1, 2, \ldots$, and terminates when $X_i = Y_i$. To describe the process more suitably for execution, define a function

$$F : G \times \mathbf{Z} \times Z \to G \times \mathbf{Z} \times Z$$

by

$$F(X, m, n) = \begin{cases} (a \cdot X, m+1, n) & \text{if } X_i \in S_1 \\ (X^2, 2m, 2n) & \text{if } X_i \in S_2 \\ (b \cdot X, m, n+1) & \text{if } X_i \in S_3 \end{cases}$$

Making the notation more succinct, the algorithm proceeds as follows:

- Choose random integers m_0, n_0.
- Initialize

$$(X, m_X, n_X, Y, m_Y, n_Y) = (a^{m_0} b^{n_0}, m_0, n_0, a^{m_0} b^{n_0}, m_0, n_0)$$

- Repeat until $X = Y$: replace (X, m_X, n_X) by $F(X, m_X, n_X)$ and replace (Y, m_Y, n_Y) by $F(F(Y, m_Y, n_Y))$.
- When $X = Y$, try to solve

$$(\log_b a) \cdot (m_Y - m_X) = (n_X - n_Y) \bmod |G|$$

The algorithm will *fail* if $m_Y - m_X$ is *not* relatively prime to the order $|G|$. Now the assumption that $|G|$ is prime becomes convenient: if we imagine that the integer $m_{2i} - m_i$ is 'random', then the probability that it has a common factor with the prime number $|G|$ is about $1/|G|$, which is 'negligible' for large $|G|$. In the unlikely event that there *is* failure, the algorithm should be run again with a new choice of m_0 and n_0.

Remark: When the order $|G|$ of the group G is not prime, especially if it has a small prime factor p, the probability of failure of the algorithm by having

$$\gcd(m_Y - m_X, |G|) = p > 1$$

is (heuristically) at least $1/p$, which is significant. (Again we imagine that $m_Y - m_X$ is roughly 'random'.) But this can be dealt with (heuristically) by running the algorithm several times with varying random seeds m_0 and n_0.

Remark: The sets S_i must be chosen in a manner so that the test to see which subset S_i a given element X of G lies in is very efficient.

Example: Let G be the subgroup of $\mathbf{Z}/59^\times$ consisting of squares mod 59. By general results about cyclic groups, since 2 is a primitive root mod 59, 4 is a generator for the group G. That is, any nonzero square mod 59 has a discrete log base 4. Further, this subgroup G has prime order $|G| = 29$. We know that 9 is a square mod 59, so it lies in G. Let's compute

$$\log_4 9$$

We must tell how to determine the sets S_1, S_2, and S_3. One common approach is to take

$$
\begin{aligned}
S_1 &= G \cap \{1, 4, 7, 10, \ldots, 55, 58\} \\
S_2 &= G \cap \{2, 5, 8, 11, \ldots, 56\} \\
S_3 &= G \cap \{3, 6, 9, 12, \ldots, 57\}
\end{aligned}
$$

Choose $m_0 = n_0 = 0$, so $X_0 = Y_0 = 1 \bmod 59$. Thus, initialize,

$$(X, m_X, n_X) = (1, 0, 0)$$

$$(Y, m_Y, n_Y) = (1, 0, 0)$$

and $a = 9$, $b = 4$. Starting the iterative steps, the pair of triples are, in succession,

X	m_X	n_X	Y	m_Y	n_Y
1	0	0	1	0	0
9	1	0	36	1	1
36	1	1	27	2	4
26	1	2	28	3	5
27	2	4	26	5	5
49	2	5	49	10	11

So in five steps we find

$$8^{-1} = 11$$

$$(\log_4 9) \cdot (10 - 2) = 5 - 11 \bmod 29$$

(note that we solve this modulo $29 = (59 - 1)/2$, not modulo 59). Then in $\mathbf{Z}/59^\times$

$$\log_4 9 = 21$$

Example: With the same choice of the sets S_i, let's compute a discrete logarithm modulo 227. We choose this modulus because both it and $113 = (227 - 1)/2$ are prime. It happens that 2 is a primitive root modulo 227, so $4 = 2^2$ generates a cyclic subgroup G of $\mathbf{Z}/227^\times$ of order 113, which is prime. Thus, we can compute the logarithm base 4 of any nonzero square modulo 227. For example, $17^2 \% 227 = 62$, so 62 will have a discrete logarithm base 4 modulo 227. Make the simplest choice of seeds $m_0 = n_0 = 0$, so $X_0 = Y_0 = 1 \bmod 227$. Thus, initialize,

$$(X, m_X, n_X) = (1, 0, 0)$$

$$(Y, m_Y, n_Y) = (1, 0, 0)$$

and $a = 62$, $b = 4$. Starting the iterative steps, the pair of triples are, in succession,

X	m_X	n_X	Y	m_Y	n_Y
1	0	0	1	0	0
62	1	0	212	2	0
212	2	0	219	4	1
225	4	0	99	4	3
219	4	1	36	5	4
195	4	2	122	5	6
99	4	3	62	10	13
169	4	4	225	40	52
36	5	4	195	40	54
144	5	5	169	40	56
122	5	6	144	41	57
129	10	12	129	82	116

taking eleven steps. Then solve

$$\log_4 62 \cdot (82 - 10) = 12 - 116 \bmod 113$$

from which we conclude that in $\mathbf{Z}/227^\times$

$$\log_4 62 = 99$$

For further examples, we need a model of a finite field. The polynomial $P(X) = X^5 + X^2 + 1$ in $\mathbf{F}_2[X]$ is irreducible, as is readily verified by trial division: we need only attempt division by irreducible polynomials of degrees not greater than half the degree of P. Here this requires trial divisionx by X, $X + 1$, and $X^2 + X + 1$, none of which divide P. Therefore, $K = \mathbf{F}_2[X]/P$ is a finite field with 2^5 elements (since P) is of degree 5). Since P is of degree 5, and since $2^5 - 1 = 31$ is prime, necessarily $X \bmod P$ is a primitive root in K. Thus, we can compute logarithms base $X \bmod P$ in K. Note that we're using uppercase 'X' for the indeterminate in polynomials, to distinguish it from the 'x' used in the notation for the rho algorithm.

Remark: Note that we were lucky that $31 = 2^5 - 1$ is *prime*, so that the straightforward version of the rho algorithm applies.

Example: With P as above, let's compute the discrete logarithm of $X + 1$ in $K = \mathbf{F}_2[x]/P$ base $X \bmod P$. We need to choose the three sets S_1, S_2, and S_3 from the 31 nonzero elements of K in a manner so that it is easy to test which set a polynomial modulo P is in. Trying to simulate a 'random' choice of subsets:

- Take S_1 to consist of polynomials of degree not more than five whose x^2 coefficient is equal to its x^4 coefficient.

- Take S_2 to consist of polynomials of degree not more than five whose x^3 coefficient is equal to the sum of its constant coefficient and linear coefficient.

- Take S_3 to consist of polynomials of degree not more than five not lying either of in the sets S_1, S_2.

In the notation above, $b = x$, $a = x + 1$. For arbitrary polynomial X define

$$F(X, m, n) = \begin{cases} ((x + 1) \cdot X, m + 1, n) & \text{if } X \in S_1 \\ (X^2, 2 \cdot m, 2 \cdot n) & \text{if } X \in S_2 \\ (x \cdot X, m, n + 1) & \text{if } X \in S_3 \end{cases}$$

Take the simplest choice $m_0 = 0$, $n_0 = 0$. Initialize

$$(X, m_X, n_X, Y, m_Y, n_Y) = (1, 0, 0, 1, 0, 0)$$

and apply F to (X, m_X, n_X) and $F \circ F$ to (Y, m_Y, n_Y) until $X = Y$:

1	0	0	1	0	0
$1 + x$	1	0	$1 + x^2$	2	0
$1 + x^2$	2	0	$x^2 + x^3$	8	0
$1 + x^4$	4	0	$1 + x^4$	16	1

Since the two polynomials in the last step are equal, we solve

$$\log_x (x+1) \cdot (16 - 4) = 0 - 1 \bmod 31$$

from which we see that (modulo $1 + x^2 + x^5$)

$$\log_x (x+1) = 18$$

Remark: With 'less random' choices of subsets S_i, or, equivalently, with less 'random' function f, it may take much longer to achieve the equality $X = Y$.

Example: Take everything to be the same as the previous example except take the sets S_i to be

- Take S_1 to consist of polynomials of degree not more than five whose x^2 coefficient is equal to its x^4 coefficient.

- Take S_2 to consist of polynomials of degree not more than five whose x^3 coefficient is equal to the sum of its constant coefficient and linear coefficient.

- Take S_3 to consist of polynomials of degree not more than five not lying either of in the sets S_1, S_2.

Then the algorithm runs as

1	0	0	1	0	0
x	0	1	$x + x^2$	1	1
$x + x^2$	1	1	$x + x^2 + x^3 + x^4$	3	1
$x + x^3$	2	1	$1 + x^2 + x^4$	8	2
$x + x^2 + x^3 + x^4$	3	1	$1 + x + x^2 + x^3 + x^4$	16	6
$1 + x + x^2$	4	1	$1 + x + x^4$	33	12
$1 + x^2 + x^4$	8	2	$x^3 + x^4$	67	24
$1 + x + x^2 + x^3$	8	3	$x + x^3 + x^4$	68	25
$1 + x + x^2 + x^3 + x^4$	16	6	$1 + x + x^2 + x^3$	138	50
$x + x^4$	32	12	$x + x^4$	552	200

So while we reach the same conclusion (that the logarithm in question is 18), it takes 9 steps instead of 3.

Example: With the same model of the finite field $GF(2^5)$, let's compute

$$\log_x (x^2 + x + 1) \bmod P$$

Use the same sets S_i as in the first finite-field example.

1	0	0	1	0	0
$1 + x + x^2$	1	0	$1 + x^2 + x^4$	2	0
$1 + x^2 + x^4$	2	0	x^3	3	1
x^2	3	0	$1 + x^3 + x^4$	5	1
x^3	3	1	$x + x^3$	6	2
$1 + x^2 + x^3 + x^4$	4	1	x^3	14	4
$1 + x^3 + x^4$	5	1	$1 + x^3 + x^4$	16	4

Thus, solve
$$\log_x(x^2 + x + 1) \cdot (16 - 5) = 1 - 4 \bmod 31$$
and thus, modulo P,
$$\log_x(x^2 + x + 1) = 11$$

Exercises

27.2.01   Use the rho method to find the log of 3 base 2 in $\mathbf{Z}/23^\times$.

27.2.02   Use the rho method to find the log of 6 base 2 in $\mathbf{Z}/23^\times$.

27.2.03   Use the rho method to find the log of 13 base 2 in $\mathbf{Z}/23^\times$.

27.2.04   Use the rho method to find the log of 12 base 2 in $\mathbf{Z}/23^\times$.

27.2.05   Use the rho method to find the log of 9 base 2 in $\mathbf{Z}/47^\times$.

27.2.06   Use the rho method to find the log of 3 base 2 in $\mathbf{Z}/47^\times$.

27.2.07   Use the rho method to find the log of 6 base 2 in $\mathbf{Z}/47^\times$.

27.2.08   Use the rho method to find the log of 21 base 2 in $\mathbf{Z}/47^\times$.

27.2.09   Use the rho method to find the log of 10 base 3 in $\mathbf{Z}/2027^\times$.

27.2.10   Use the rho method to find the log of 4 base 3 in $\mathbf{Z}/2027^\times$.

27.2.11   Use the rho method to find the log of 12 base 3 in $\mathbf{Z}/2027^\times$.

27.2.12   Use the rho method to find the log of $x^3 + x^2 + x + 1$ base x modulo $x^5 + x^2 + 1$.

27.2.13   Use the rho method to find the log of $x^4 + x + 1$ base x modulo $x^5 + x^2 + 1$.

27.2.14   Use the rho method to find the log of $x^4 + x^3 + x^2 + x + 1$ base x modulo $x^5 + x + 1$.

27.2.15   Use the rho method to find the log of $x^4 + x^3 + x + 1$ base x modulo $x^5 + x^2 + 1$.

27.2.16   Use the rho method to find the log of $x + 1$ base x modulo $x^7 + x^3 + x + 1$.

27.2.17   Use the rho method to find the log of $x^2 + 1$ base x modulo $x^7 + x^3 + x + 1$.

27.2.18   Use the rho method to find the log of $x^5 + x^4 + x^3 + x^2 + x + 1$ base x modulo $x^7 + x^3 + x + 1$.

27.2.19   Use the rho method to find the log of $x^5 + x^4 + 1$ base x modulo $x^7 + x^3 + x + 1$.

27.3 The Index Calculus

The method of this section, the **index calculus**, is the best known method for computing discrete logarithms in cyclic groups G. This algorithm cannot be applied effectively to all cyclic groups, but when it *can* be applied it is a subexponential-time algorithm. It is probabilistic.

Remark: At the outset a disclaimer is necessary. That is, the subset S of G used in the algorithm, the so-called **factor basis**, must be chosen well. Unfortunately, it is not generally clear how to make a good choice, or even that there *is* a good choice of factor basis. Tuning of the algorithm amounts to adjustment of the choice of factor basis, but in general there may be no choice good enough to achieve subexponential runtime.

Let b be a generator of a cyclic group G of order $n = |G|$. Let a be another element of G, whose logarithm base b we want to compute.

- Choose a factor base: Choose a 'small' subset S of G, the **factor basis**:

$$S = \{p_1, \ldots, p_t\}$$

- Collect relations: Choose random integers k in the range $0 \le k \le n - 1$ and try to express b^k as a product of elements of S. If such a relation

$$b^k = p_1^{k_1} \cdot \, \cdots \, p_t^{k_t}$$

exists, take logarithms of both sides to obtain

$$k = k_1 \cdot \log_b p_1 + \cdots + k_t \cdot \log_b p_t \bmod n$$

Repeat this until there are somewhat more than t relations.

- Find logarithms $\log_b p_i$: solve the system of relations to find the logarithms base b of the elements of the factor basis. If the system is indeterminate, go back and generate more relations.

- Finding other logarithms: Given $a \in G$, pick a random integer k and try to express $a \cdot b^k$ in the form

$$a \cdot b^k = p_1^{k_1} \cdot \, \cdots \, p_t^{k_t}$$

If successful, solve for

$$\log_b a = (k_1 \cdot \log_b p_1 + \cdots + k_t \cdot \log_b p_t) - k \bmod n$$

If unsuccesful, choose a different k and repeat.

Remark: Certainly the precomputation of logarithms of elements of the factor basis need not be repeated for computation of varying elements of the group.

Remark: As examination of the algorithm makes clear, the factor basis S must be chosen so that 'many' elements of G are expressed as products of powers of elements of S with 'small' exponents. Of course, this idea and its effects must be quantified to optimize the algorithm in any particular case.

Remark: When the cyclic group in question is $G = \mathbf{Z}/p^\times$, for prime p, the factor basis should be the first t primes. Of course, determining a wise choice of t is the issue. Testing whether a randomly-produced group element is a product of elements from the factor basis (with *small* positive integer exponents) can be done very quickly by trial division by elements of the factor basis.

Example: Let $G = \mathbf{Z}/29^\times$. The order of the group is $n = 28$. Use the primitive root $b = 11$. Try a factor basis $S = \{2, 3, 5\}$. Start generating relations, by considering 'random' powers of b modulo 29. Bear in mind that we want to solve the system of relations modulo $n = 28$.

$$
\begin{aligned}
b^2 \; \% \; 29 &= 11^2 \; \% \; 29 &&= \quad 5 \\
b^3 \; \% \; 29 &= 11^3 \; \% \; 29 &&= \quad 26 &&\text{(failure)} \\
b^5 \; \% \; 29 &= 11^5 \; \% \; 29 &&= \quad 14 &&\text{(failure)} \\
b^6 \; \% \; 29 &= 11^6 \; \% \; 29 &&= \quad 9 &&= \quad 3^2 \\
b^7 \; \% \; 29 &= 11^7 \; \% \; 29 &&= \quad 12 &&= \quad 2^2 \cdot 3 \\
b^9 \; \% \; 29 &= 11^9 \; \% \; 29 &&= \quad 2
\end{aligned}
$$

Solving the system modulo 28 to obtain the logarithms of the factor base happens to be easy in this case. From the first relation, we obtain directly that

$$\log_{11} 5 = 2$$

The fourth relation above gives

$$6 = 2 \cdot \log_{11} 3 \bmod 28$$

which does not uniquely determine the log of 3, since the coefficient in front of it (namely, 2) has a common factor with the modulus 28. But the last of the relations gives

$$\log_{11} 2 = 9$$

and then we can use the next-to-last relation

$$7 = 2 \cdot \log_{11} 2 + \log_{11} 3 \bmod 28$$

to obtain

$$\log_{11} 3 = 17$$

This finishes the precomputation for the factor basis $S = \{2, 3, 5\}$. To compute $\log_{11} 7$, for example, multiply the target $a = 7$ by 'random' powers of $b = 11$ (mod 29) and look for results expressible in terms of the factor basis.

$$
\begin{aligned}
a \cdot b \; \% \; 29 &= 7 \cdot 11 \; \% \; 29 &&= \quad 19 &&\text{(failure)} \\
a \cdot b^2 \; \% \; 29 &= 7 \cdot 11 \; \% \; 29 &&= \quad 6 &&= \quad 2 \cdot 3
\end{aligned}
$$

Therefore,

$$\log_{11} 7 = \log_{11} 2 + \log_{11} 3 - 2 = 9 + 17 - 2 = 24$$

Remark: This algorithm becomes noticeably more efficient than the earlier ones only for considerably larger groups.

28

Elliptic Curves

Elliptic curves over finite fields, which we'll define shortly, give examples of *groups* whose structure is even less simple than the structure of $\mathbf{Z}/p^\times$. This gives the opportunity to make ciphers which **abstract** the idea of the ElGamal cipher, which uses *discrete logarithms* in the group $\mathbf{Z}/p^\times$.

The elliptic curve cipher from this family of discrete log ciphers currently seems to be optimal in terms of resistance to attack versus key size, for example by comparison to ElGamal ciphers using groups $\mathbf{Z}/p^\times$. This *may* change as people develop better algorithms pertaining to elliptic curves.

It also seems to be the case that elliptic curve (discrete log) ciphers give better resistance per key size than does RSA. This also *may* change as people develop better algorithms for elliptic curves.

There are also **factorization attacks** based upon the idea that the formula for the group operation will 'blow up' at various points if $\mathbf{Z}/n$ is not actually a **field**, that is, if n is not a prime. For certain ranges of large numbers, this factorization attack is very good, although currently seems not as good as the quadratic sieve in its optimal range, nor as good as the number field sieve for really big integers. Nevertheless, in practice the elliptic curve sieve is widely used.

This chapter only gives the merest introduction to the structure of elliptic curves, which is a subject in its own right. A recent book which explains computational issues on elliptic curves relevant to cryptography (and other computational issues as well) is [Blake, Seroussi, Smart 2000]. From a less computational viewpoint, emphasizing more a systematic application of algebraic geometry, [Silverman 1986] gives a serious systematic introduction to the general theory of elliptic curves, using a substantial but appropriate amount of higher algebra and algebraic geometry.

28.1 Abstract Discrete Logarithms

The simplest case is where we know that $G = \langle b \rangle$, so that there is no doubt that everything in G has a discrete logarithm.

A silly case is $G = \mathbf{Z}/n$ with addition mod n, and let b be anything relatively prime to n. Since the group operation is 'addition', the exponentiation (repeated group operation) is just multiplication. Thus, discrete logarithms here are

$$\log_b x = \ell \ \text{ so that } \ \ell \cdot b = x$$

It is easy to find the discrete logarithm of x in this silly scenario:

$$\log_b x = b^{-1} \cdot x$$

We are interested in cases where it is **hard** to compute discrete logarithms.

The case of discrete logarithms that was first used was where the group is $\mathbf{Z}/p^\times$ (with multiplication modulo p), with p prime. As base we'd take a **primitive root** $b \bmod p$, which is known to exist: that is, b is such that every nonzero element x of $\mathbf{Z}/p^\times$ is a power of b. In fact, $\varphi(p-1)$ of the elements of $\mathbf{Z}/p^\times$ are primitive roots, where φ is Euler's ϕ-function.

(In some scenarios the base b doesn't have to be a primitive root, because we'd know for some other reason that anything we wanted to take a log of was a power of b.)

Roughly, given a 'large' prime p and b, $x \bmod p$, it appears to be as hard to compute $\log_b x$ as it is to factor an integer N of the same size as p.

28.2 Discrete Log Ciphers

These are abstracted versions of the **ElGamal cipher**. First, recall how ElGamal works: Fix a large prime $p > 10^{150}$, a primitive root b modulo p (meaning that any y can be expressed as $y = b^L \bmod p$), and an integer c in the range $1 < c < p$. The *secret* is the power ℓ (the **discrete logarithm**) so that $b^\ell = c \bmod p$. Only the *decryptor* knows ℓ: the decryptor chooses ℓ and then computes c^ℓ.

The **encryption step** is as follows. A plaintext x is encoded as an integer in the range $0 < x < p$. The encryptor chooses an auxiliary random integer r, which is *a temporary secret known only to the encryptor*, and encrypts the plaintext x as

$$y = E_{b,c,p,r}(x) = (x \times c^r) \% p$$

Along with this encrypted message is sent the 'header' b^r. Note that the encryptor only needs to know b, c, p and chooses random r, but does not know the discrete logarithm ℓ.

The decryption step requires knowledge of the discrete logarithm ℓ, but not the random integer r. First, from the 'header' b^r the decryptor computes

$$(b^r)^\ell = b^{r \cdot \ell} = (b^\ell)^r = c^r \bmod p$$

Then the plaintext is recovered by multiplying by the multiplicative inverse $(c^r)^{-1}$ of c^r modulo p:

$$D_{b,c,p,r,\ell}(y) = (c^r)^{-1} \cdot y = (c^r)^{-1} \cdot c^r \cdot x = x \bmod p$$

Abstract version. Now we abstract ElGamal so that it takes place in an arbitrary group. Let G be a group, and fix an element $b \in G$. It need **not** be the case that G is cyclic generated by b.

Pick a *secret* integer ℓ, and let $c = b^\ell$. Only the *decryptor* knows ℓ, which is the **discrete log** of c base b in G.

Remark: We do *not* pick c and then compute the discrete logarithm!

The **encryption step** is as follows. A plaintext x is encoded as an element $x \in G$. The encryptor chooses an auxiliary random integer r, which is *a temporary secret known only to the encryptor*, and encrypts the plaintext x as

$$y = E_{b,c,p,r}(x) = x \cdot c^r \quad \text{(all operations in } G)$$

Along with this encrypted message is sent the 'header' $b^r \in G$. Note that the encryptor only needs to know b, c, G and chooses random $r \in \mathbf{Z}$, but does not know the discrete logarithm $\ell \in \mathbf{Z}$.

The (authorized) **decryption step** requires knowledge of the discrete logarithm ℓ, but not the random integer r. First, from the 'header' $b^r \in G$ the decryptor computes

$$(b^r)^\ell = b^{r \cdot \ell} = (b^\ell)^r = c^r$$

Then the plaintext is recovered by multiplying by the inverse $(c^r)^{-1}$ of c^r in G:

$$D_{b,c,p,r,\ell}(y) = (c^r)^{-1} \cdot y = (c^r)^{-1} \cdot c^r \cdot x = x \in G$$

Remark: The security of a discrete log cipher in a group G certainly depends upon the difficulty of computing discrete logs in G. That is, given b and c in G, and given the assurance that there **exists** some $\ell \in \mathbf{Z}$ so that

$$b^\ell = c$$

it must be the case that it is hard to actually **find** ℓ.

Recall that writing a group operation as 'multiplication' or 'addition' is merely a notational device. Being more formal for a moment, let the group operation be denoted '$*$'. Then 'exponentiation' really means repeated operation by $*$, that is,

$$b^\ell = \underbrace{b * b * \ldots * b}_{\ell}$$

In particular, if the group operation is 'addition', then 'exponentiation' is really just multiplication:

$$\text{‘ } b^\ell \text{ ’} = \underbrace{b + b + \cdots + b}_{\ell} = \ell \cdot b$$

Thus, in the case that G is integers mod n with **addition**, it is very easy to compute 'discrete logarithms', in part because 'exponentiation' is really just multiplication mod n. So to solve for ℓ in an equation

$$\text{‘ } b^\ell \text{ ’} = c \text{ (where group operation is } + \text{ mod } n)$$

is really to solve

$$\ell \cdot b = c$$

which is

$$\ell = b^{-1} \cdot c \bmod n$$

Of course, in a different universe it might have been hard to find multiplicative inverses modulo n, but in *this* universe we can easily find $b^{-1} \bmod n$ via the **Euclidean algorithm**. So **not all** discrete logarithms are difficult to evaluate. By contrast, for the moment, all available evidence seems to indicate that it **is** difficult to evaluate discrete logarithms in the group $\mathbf{Z}/p^\times$. That is, although for obvious reasons discrete logarithms in the group $\mathbf{Z}/p$-with-**addition** are easy to evaluate, discrete logarithms in the group $\mathbf{Z}/p^\times$-with-multiplication are **hard** to evaluate. There is no known theorem which **proves** that discrete logarithms in $\mathbf{Z}/p^\times$ are hard to evaluate, just as there is no known theorem which proves that big numbers are hard to factor. Nevertheless, all available heuristic evidence indicates that evaluating discrete logs in $\mathbf{Z}/p^\times$ for large p is roughly of the same difficulty as factoring large integers n.

Still, just as we saw some 'not-so-bad' algorithms that do better jobs of factoring than crude trial division, we also saw 'not-so-bad' algorithms for computing discrete logs. But those algorithms are still not fast enough to be counted as 'fast'.

28.3 Elliptic Curves

For simplicity, let's start with the case of elliptic curves over $\mathbf{Z}/p$ with $p \neq 2, 3$. Fix $a, b \in \mathbf{Z}/p$ so that the equation

$$x^3 + ax + b = 0$$

has no repeated roots in $\mathbf{Z}/p$. (We know how to check this no-repeated-roots condition by computing the greatest common divisor of $x^3 + ax + b$ with its 'formal' derivative, $3x^2 + a$.) With such a, b, an **elliptic curve** is a set of points (really, a set of pairs of elements of $\mathbf{Z}/p$)

$$E = \{(x, y) \in \mathbf{Z}/p \times \mathbf{Z}/p : y^2 = x^3 + ax + b\}$$

The same construction works for $\mathbf{Z}/2$, $\mathbf{Z}/3$, as well as **any finite field $\mathbf{F}_q = GF(q)$**, except that the most general form one must consider (when the characteristic is possible 2 or 3, *excluded* above) is

$$y^2 + (c + x)y = x^3 + ax^2 + b \quad \text{(characteristic 2)}$$

$$y^2 = x^3 + ax^2 + bx + c \quad \text{(characteristic 3)}$$

The same construction also makes sense when the underlying field (as $\mathbf{Z}/p$ above) is $\mathbf{R}$ or $\mathbf{C}$. In that case, we can also draw somewhat meaningful pictures.

Remark: It is certainly *not* clear that there is any reasonable way to make this into a group, much less that there is any *natural* group structure on this thing. Indeed, the fact that there is such a natural group structure was observed only as a by-product of seemingly unrelated work in complex analysis.

Now we'll define a **group operation on an elliptic curve**. Consider the elliptic curve $E = \{y^2 = x^3 + ax + b\}$. For a moment we'll talk about a mythical **point at infinity**, traditionally denoted **O**, without explaining yet how to make it legitimate. The group operation here will be denoted $+$.

- For two distinct points $\mathbf{P}, \mathbf{Q}$ on the curve, neither **O**, and with **different x-coordinates**, let L be the line through $\mathbf{P}$ and $\mathbf{Q}$. It will be verified that L intersects E in exactly 3 points. Two of these points are $\mathbf{P}, \mathbf{Q}$. Let the third be (x, y). Then the definition of **addition** on E is

$$\mathbf{P} + \mathbf{Q} = (x, -y)$$

- If $\mathbf{P}, \mathbf{Q}$ have the **same** x-coordinate, but $\mathbf{P} \neq \mathbf{Q}$, then the definition is

$$\mathbf{P} + \mathbf{Q} = \mathbf{O}$$

- If $\mathbf{P} = \mathbf{Q} = (x_0, y_0)$ with $y_0 \neq 0$, then let L be the line **tangent** to E at $\mathbf{P}$, and let (x, y) be the third point of intersection of L with E. Then define

$$\mathbf{P} + \mathbf{P} = (x, -y)$$

- If $\mathbf{P} = (x, 0)$ is a point on E, then define

$$\mathbf{P} + \mathbf{P} = \mathbf{O}$$

- For any point $\mathbf{P}$ on the curve, $\mathbf{P} + \mathbf{O} = \mathbf{O} + \mathbf{P} = \mathbf{P}$.

- For any point $\mathbf{P} = (x, y)$ on the curve (other than $\mathbf{O}$), $-\mathbf{P} = (x, -y)$. And $-\mathbf{O} = \mathbf{O}$.

There are several questions that might occur to someone thinking critically about this situation:

- Why is this operation right?

- How is it computed?

- Why is it associative (for example)?

- How would one get the idea of this?

Unfortunately, none of these questions has an easy answer. Our goal here is only to make the case that these questions are important enough to merit the further study they would require.

Remark: While the seemingly geometric language certainly makes some sense if we're graphing curves in the usual 'plane', it is not at all so clear what 'tangent' means if the underlying field is *finite*, for example. The point is that the idea of 'line' certainly must be translated entirely into algebra, rather than depending upon any 'geometric intuition'. In that context, we would further need to explain why a 'line' apparently intersect such a 'cubic curve' in 3 points. Would a 'line' intersect an nth-degree curve in n points?

Now we'll derive the **formula for the sum** of two points on an elliptic curve. Let the elliptic curve E be the set of points (x, y) so that $y^2 = x^3 + ax + b$. Given two points $\mathbf{P}_1 = (x_1, y_1)$ and $\mathbf{P}_2 = (x_2, y_2)$, let's suppose that $y_1 \neq y_2$, and compute the 'sum' $\mathbf{P} + \mathbf{Q}$.

The line L through two points (x_1, y_1) and (x_2, y_2) is the set of points (x, y) so that

$$\frac{y - y_1}{x - x_1} = \frac{y_2 - y_1}{x_2 - x_1}$$

from equating the slope of the segment from (x_1, y_1) to (x_2, y_2) and to (x, y). Rewrite this by solving for y:

$$y = y_1 + \frac{y_2 - y_1}{x_2 - x_1}(x - x_1)$$

which simplifies to

$$y = \frac{y_2 - y_1}{x_2 - x_1} x + \frac{x_2 y_1 - y_2 x_1}{x_2 - x_1}$$

For brevity, let's write this as

$$y = Ax + B$$

and then substitute this expression for y in the cubic equation:

$$(Ax + B)^2 = x^3 + ax + b$$

This rearranges to a cubic equation for x:

$$x^3 - A^2 x^2 + (-2AB + a)x + (b - B^2) = 0$$

For any cubic equation with leading coefficient 1, the coefficient of the x^2 term is the negative of the sum of the roots. This is easy to check by multiplying out:

$$(x - \alpha)(x - \beta)(x - \gamma) = x^3 - (\alpha + \beta + \gamma)x^2 + (\alpha\beta + \beta\gamma + \gamma\alpha)x - \alpha\beta\gamma$$

Therefore, in the cubic for the x-coordinate of the third point, the negative of the coefficient of x^2 is the unknown x-coordinate x_{sum} plus x_1 and x_2: in the notation above,

$$A^2 = x_1 + x_2 + x_{\text{sum}}$$

Writing out what A was, this is

$$x_{\text{sum}} = A^2 - x_1 - x_2 = \left(\frac{y_2 - y_1}{x_2 - x_1}\right)^2 - x_1 - x_2$$

Then, substituting back into the equation for the line, we get

$$Ax_{\text{sum}} + B = \frac{y_2 - y_1}{x_2 - x_1} x_{\text{sum}} + \frac{x_2 y_1 - y_2 x_1}{x_2 - x_1}$$

Taking the negative (by definition) gives the y-coordinate of the sum:

$$y_{\text{sum}} = -\frac{y_2 - y_1}{x_2 - x_1} x_{\text{sum}} - \frac{x_2 y_1 - y_2 x_1}{x_2 - x_1}$$

For practical use (thinking in terms of execution of the fast exponentiation algorithm, for example) it is certainly necessary to have the formula for $2 \cdot \mathbf{P} = \mathbf{P} + \mathbf{P}$ as well.

That is, given $\mathbf{P} = (x_1, y_1)$ on the elliptic curve E, we let L be the tangent line (!?) to E at (x_1, y_1), find the *other* point of intersection of this line with the curve, and negate the y-coordinate to get $(x_{\text{sum}}, y_{\text{sum}})$. The slope of the curve is dy/dx, which we compute by implicit differentiation:

$$2y \cdot \frac{dy}{dx} = 3x^2 + a$$

so

$$\frac{dy}{dx} = \frac{3x^2 + a}{2y}$$

and the value at (x_1, y_1) is

$$\frac{dy}{dx}\Big|_{(x_1, y_1)} = \frac{3x_1^2 + a}{2y_1}$$

Thus, the tangent line is

$$y - y_1 = \frac{3x_1^2 + a}{2y_1}(x - x_1)$$

or

$$y = y_1 + \frac{3x_1^2 + a}{2y_1}(x - x_1)$$

Again substitute this value for y in the relation $y^2 = x^3 + ax + b$ and rearrange this as a cubic equation to be solved for x:

$$\left(y_1 + \frac{3x_1^2 + a}{2y_1}(x - x_1)\right)^2 = x^3 + ax + b$$

or

$$x^3 - \left(\frac{3x_1^2 + a}{2y_1}\right)^2 x^2 + (\text{linear and constant terms}) = 0$$

Thus, since the sum of the roots of a cubic is the negative of the quadratic coefficient, and since the tangent line in effect gives **two** intersections, so two roots,

$$x_{\text{new}} + x_1 + x_1 = \left(\frac{3x_1^2 + a}{2y_1}\right)^2$$

from which

$$x_{\text{new}} = \left(\frac{3x_1^2 + a}{2y_1}\right)^2 - 2x_1$$

Substituting back into the equation of the line gives

$$y_1 + \frac{3x_1^2 + a}{2y_1}(x_{\text{new}} - x_1)$$

of which we take the **negative** (by definition) to get the sum coordinate:

$$y_{\text{sum}} = -y_1 - \frac{3x_1^2 + a}{2y_1}(x_{\text{new}} - x_1)$$

These are the formulas for the coordinates of the **double** of a point $\mathbf{P} = (x_1, y_1)$ on the elliptic curve. Note that this 'exotic' group operation is evaluated via a handful of operations of addition, multiplication, and inversion.

Why does this make an elliptic curve a group? The serious part of this question is **why is it associative?** The commutativity is readily verifiable by looking at the formulas. There are three versions of an answer to the general question, none of which is simple.

- From **complex analysis**, one would learn that an elliptic curve *over the complex numbers* has a group law arising because it is a **quotient group** of the complex plane **C** (which with its usual addition is certainly a group). This only *suggests* that there should be a group law when the underlying field is something else. Traditionally, someone learning mathematics would have studied complex analysis enough to learn about elliptic curves in *that* setting before worrying about elliptic curves over finite fields.

- There is a peculiar and hard-to-understand but seemingly elementary proof of the associativity from **projective geometry** (in the archaic sense of the word). From a contemporary viewpoint this is an overspecialized and not very wholesome way to try to understand the group law on an elliptic curve. Still, depending on how it's set up, this might give a *proof*, as opposed to a mere *heuristic*.

- The technically most difficult approach, but which in the long run gives the clearest viewpoint, has its origins in the (relatively) modern theory of algebraic curves, and in particular in the important and subtle **Riemann-Roch theorem**. This viewpoint really does give a *proof* that an elliptic curve is a group, and gives some idea of what happens with other types of curves, etc.

Now we'll do some sample computations on an elliptic curve. Let E be the elliptic curve $y^2 = x^3 + x$ over the field $\mathbf{F}_{17}$. By trial and error, we find a point $(1, 6)$ on this curve:

$$6^2 = 1^3 + 1 \bmod 17$$

Use the group law on the curve to compute $(1,6) + (1,6) = 2 \cdot (1,6)$: The sum point has x-coordinate

$$x_{\text{sum}} = \left(\frac{3 \cdot 1^2 + 1}{2 \cdot 6} \right)^2 - 2 \cdot 1 = (\frac{1}{3})^2 - 2 = 6^2 - 2 = 0 \bmod 17$$

and y-coordinate

$$y_{\text{sum}} = -6 - \left(\frac{3 \cdot 1^2 + 1}{2 \cdot 6} \right)(0 - 1) = 0 \bmod 17$$

That is,

$$(1,6) + (1,6) = 2 \cdot (1,6) = (0,0)$$

Remark: This is **not** vector addition, nor scalar multiplication, even though it may look like it.

Continuing on the same elliptic curve $y^2 = x^3 + x \bmod 17$,

$$3 \cdot (1,6) = (1,6) + 2 \cdot (1,6) = (1,6) + (0,0)$$

by what we just computed. Then apply the formula

$$x_{\text{sum}} = \left(\frac{0-6}{0-1}\right)^2 - 1 - 0 = 1 \bmod 17$$

$$y_{\text{sum}} = -\left(\frac{0-6}{0-1}\right) \cdot 1 - \frac{0 \cdot 6 - 0 \cdot 1}{0-1} = 11 \bmod 17$$

Therefore,

$$3 \cdot (1,6) = (1,6) + 2 \cdot (1,6) = (1,6) + (0,0) = (1,11)$$

Continuing: if we try to add $(1,6) + (1,11)$, then the general definition of the group law says that we get the **point at infinity O**. That is, it turns out that the point $\mathbf{P} = (1,6)$ is of **order** 4 in the group E.

By trial and error, on the curve E given by

$$\{(x,y) : y^2 = x^3 + x \bmod 17\}$$

we find a total of 16 points if we are sure to include the point at infinity **O**:

$$(0,0)$$
$$(1,\pm 6)$$
$$(3,\pm 8)$$
$$(4,0)$$
$$(6,\pm 1)$$
$$(11,\pm 4)$$
$$(13,0)$$
$$(14,\pm 2)$$
$$(16,\pm 7)$$

By Lagrange's theorem, the only possible orders of elements of E are 1, 2, 4, 8, 16. The only element of order 1 is **O**. The 3 points with y-coordinate 0, namely $(0,0)$, $(4,0)$, and $(13,0)$, are (from the definition) the only points of order 2.

By trial and error, we find that

$$
\begin{array}{rcl}
2 \cdot (1,\pm 6) & = & (0,0) \\
2 \cdot (3,\pm 8) & = & (13,0) \\
2 \cdot (6,\pm 1) & = & (13,0) \\
2 \cdot (11,\pm 4) & = & (4,0) \\
2 \cdot (6,\pm 1) & = & (13,0) \\
2 \cdot (14,\pm 2) & = & (4,0) \\
2 \cdot (16,\pm 7) & = & (0,0)
\end{array}
$$

so all the other points are of order 4. So there are no points of order 8, nor are there any of order 16.

28.4 Points at Infinity

To make the **point at infinity** more reasonable, we can enlarge the plane legitimately, in a manner that fits together well with the study of polynomial equations and algebraic curves, as follows. Let k be any field, including $\mathbf{C}$ and $\mathbf{R}$ and also finite fields $\mathbf{F}_q$. Let k^n be the space of ordered n-tuples of elements from k. This is **affine n-space**.

Let
$$\Omega = \{(x,y,z) \in k^3 : \text{not all } x,y,z \text{ are } 0 \}$$

That is, Ω is k^3 with the origin removed. Define an **equivalence relation** $\sim$ on Ω by
$$(x,y,z) \sim (x',y',z') \text{ if, for some } \lambda \in k^\times, \quad (x,y,z) = (\lambda x', \lambda y', \lambda z')$$

Then the **projective plane** $\mathbf{P}^2$ (over k) is defined to be the set of $\sim$-equivalence classes in Ω:
$$\mathbf{P}^2 = \Omega/\sim$$

The coordinates (x,y,z) are **homogeneous coordinates** for points in $\mathbf{P}^2$.

For example, with $k = \mathbf{Q}$, using homogeneous coordinates on $\mathbf{P}^2$,

$$(1,2,3) \sim (4,8,12) \sim (-1,-2,-3)$$

$$(0,2,0) \sim (0,1,0) \sim (0,-1,0)$$

The **affine plane** k^2 embeds into $\mathbf{P}^2$ nicely by

$$(x,y) \to (x,y,1)$$

Note that $(x,y,1) \sim (x',y',1)$ if and only if $(x,y) = (x',y')$.

Thus, for example, the point $(3,4)$ in the (affine) plane is identified with $(3,4,1)$ in homogeneous coordinates on the projective plane $\mathbf{P}^2$.

The **line at infinity** is the set of points (x,y,z) in $\mathbf{P}^2$ with $z = 0$. Note that no such point lies in the embedded copy of the (affine) plane k^2, so whatever they are, they really do lie outside the usual plane.

Curves in projective space. One motivation to introduce $\mathbf{P}^2$ is to smooth out and symmetrize statements in elementary geometry. For example, in the usual plane $\mathbf{R}^2$, any two (distinct) lines intersect in exactly one point *unless they are parallel*. This is a little unsymmetrical, but we can fix it. After all, there are pictorial motivations for saying that two **parallel lines meet at infinity**. As it stands, of course this has no content. However, we can make sense of it by using $\mathbf{P}^2$.

From the equation of a straight line L

$$ax + by + c = 0$$

in the usual coordinates on k^2 (with not both a, b zero), we create the **associated homogenized equation**

$$ax + by + cz = 0$$

This now has the property that if (x, y, z) satisfies this, then so does $(\lambda x, \lambda y, \lambda z)$ for any $\lambda \in k^\times$. That is, the homogenized equation defines a **curve** $\tilde{L}$ in **projective space P**. And it has the desirable property that under the embedding of k^2 into $\mathbf{P}^2$ the original line L is mapped to a subset of $\tilde{L}$.

What **points at infinity** are there on the extended version $\tilde{L}$ of L? This amounts to looking for solutions to $ax + by + cz = 0$ with $z = 0$: That means $ax + by = 0$. Since not both a, b are zero, without loss of generality we may suppose that $b \neq 0$ and get $y = (-a/b)x$. Thus, we get points

$$(x, -ax/b, 0) \sim (1, -a/b, 0)$$

on $\tilde{L}$. That is, these are just different homogenous coordinates for the same point: there is a single point at infinity lying on a given line.

Then we have the smoothed-out symmetrical assertion:

Theorem. Any two (distinct) lines in the projective plane $\mathbf{P}^2$ intersect in exactly one point.

Proof: Let the two lines in $\mathbf{P}^2$ be, in homogeneous coordinates,

$$
\begin{aligned}
ax + by + cz &= 0 \\
a'x + b'y + c'z &= 0
\end{aligned}
$$

The assumption that they are distinct can be checked to be that (a, b, c) is not a scalar multiple of (a', b', c') (and, equivalently, (a', b', c') is not a scalar multiple of (a, b, c)). We must solve this system of equations for (x, y, z).

Suggested by basic linear algebra, we might view this as hunting for a vector (x, y, z) so that

$$
\begin{aligned}
(x, y, z) \cdot (a, b, c) &= 0 \\
(x, y, z) \cdot (a', b', c') &= 0
\end{aligned}
$$

with the usual **dot product**. Suggested by basic linear algebra over the real numbers, we might anticipate that the **cross product** of $(a, b, c,)$ and (a', b', c') is a solution: try

$$(x, y, z) = (bc' - b'c, -ac' + a'c, ab' - a'b)$$

Indeed,

$$
\begin{aligned}
a(bc' - b'c) + b(-ac' + a'c) + c(ab' - a'b) &= 0 \\
a'(bc' - b'c) + b'(-ac' + a'c) + c'(ab' - a'b) &= 0
\end{aligned}
$$

Note that it is the fact that (a, b, c) and (a', b', c') are not scalar multiples of each other that makes this expression not be $(0, 0, 0)$.

A little more work would show that the collection of all solutions is exactly the collection of scalar multiples of this solution. Thus, modulo the equivalence relation from which $\mathbf{P}^2$ is made, there is a unique solution.   ♣

28.5 Projective Elliptic Curves

An elliptic curve E with equation $y^2 = x^3 + ax + b$ has **homogeneous form**

$$y^2 z = x^3 + axz^2 + bz^3$$

The point is that we insert factors of z into each term, so that each term is of degree 3. This has the effect that if (x, y, z) satisfies the homogenized equation, then so does $(\lambda x, \lambda y, \lambda z)$ for any $\lambda \in k^\times$.

One point of interest is to see what **points at infinity** lie on the extended elliptic curve: set $z = 0$ and solve.

$$0 \cdot y^2 = x^3 + 0^2 \cdot ax + 0^3 \cdot c$$

or

$$0 = x^3$$

Therefore, the only point at infinity is given by the homogeneous coordinates $(0, 1, 0)$. This is the point **O** which is the **identity** for the group law on the elliptic curve.

Now we'll obtain the elliptic curve group law in projective coordinates. Consider an elliptic curve E given in homogeneous coordinates by

$$y^2 z = x^3 + axz^2 + bz^3$$

Given distinct points (x, y, z) and (x', y', z') on the extended elliptic curve, let (a, b, c) be coefficients of the line $\tilde{L}$ passing through both: determine these coefficients by

$$ax + by + cz = 0$$
$$ax' + by' + cz' = 0$$

Since (x, y, z) and (x', y', z') are distinct points in $\mathbf{P}^2$, all solutions (a, b, c) of this system are scalar multiplies of each other, so give a single line $\tilde{L}$ in $\mathbf{P}^2$.

The intersection of $\tilde{L}$ with the elliptic curve is a single point (x_s, y_s, z_s) (computed as before). Then define the **sum** by negating the second coordinate:

$$(x, y, z) + (x', y', z') = (x_s, -y_s, z_s)$$

The general formula for $2 \cdot \mathbf{P}$ is obtained similarly.

29

More on Finite Fields

Our discussion of finite fields and polynomials with coefficients in such fields is adequate for many computational purposes up to this point, but is a bit short on explanation. A stable and operationally effective perspective for longer-term purposes requires more. In this chapter we put our finite field constructions in a slightly larger and more abstract perspective. This is not absolutely necessary, but it may help us in seeing the patterns that exist, rather than perceiving things as more chaotic than they really are.

As it is, these 'theoretical' developments are just the minimum we need. The *field theory* we develop here is specialized to the case of finite fields, and is quite limited. On the other hand, a truly general version of field theory would demand much more time and space.

29.1 Ideals in Commutative Rings

The concept of **ideal** in a commutative ring is a sort of generalization of the concept of *number*. In fact, originally there was a closely related notion of *ideal number* which extended the usual notion of number. This phrase has since been shortened simply to 'ideal'.

Let R be a commutative ring with unit 1. An **ideal** in R is a subset I of R so that

- For all $r \in R$ and $i \in I$ we have $r \cdot i \in I$. (Closure under multiplication by ring elements.)

- For all $i, j \in I$ we have $i + j \in I$. (Closure under addition.)

- For all $i \in I$ we have $-i \in I$. (Closure under additive inverse.)

- $0 \in R$.

The second, third, and fourth conditions can be capsulized as requiring that I-with-addition be a subgroup of the additive group R-with-addition. The first condition may seem a little peculiar. For one thing, it is a stronger requirement than that I be a *subring* of R, since we require that I be closed under multiplication by elements of R, not merely by elements of I itself.

Example: The basic example is the following. In the ring $\mathbf{Z}$, for any fixed n, the set $n \cdot \mathbf{Z}$ consisting of all multiples of n is an ideal. Indeed, if $x = mn$ is a multiple of n, and if $r \in \mathbf{Z}$, then $r \cdot x = r(mn) = (rm)n$ is still a multiple of n. Likewise, 0 is contained in $n\mathbf{Z}$, it's closed under sums and closed under additive inverses.

Example: Let $R = k[x]$ be the ring of polynomials in one variable x with coefficients in a field k. Fix a polynomial $P(x)$, and let $I \subset R$ be the set of all polynomial multiples $M(x) \cdot P(x)$ of $P(x)$. Verification that I is an ideal is identical in form to the previous example.

Example: Abstracting the previous two examples: let R be any commutative ring with unit 1, and fix $n \in R$. Then the set $I = n \cdot R = \{rn : r \in R\}$ consisting of all multiples of m is an ideal, called the **principal ideal generated by** n. The same argument proves that it is an ideal. Such an ideal is called a **principal ideal**.

Example: In any ring, the **trivial ideal** is just the set $I = \{0\}$. Consistent with typical usage in mathematics, an ideal I is **proper** if it is neither the trivial ideal $\{0\}$ nor the whole ring R (which is also an ideal).

The following proposition is an important basic principle.

Proposition. Let I be an ideal in a commutative ring R with unit 1. If I contains any element $u \in R^{\times}$, then $I = R$.

Proof: Suppose I contains $u \in R^\times$. The fact that u is a unit means that there is a multiplicative inverse u^{-1} to u. Then, for any $r \in R$,

$$r = r \cdot 1 = r \cdot (u^{-1} \cdot u) = (r \cdot u^{-1}) \cdot u$$

That is, r is a multiple of u. Since I is an ideal, it must contain every multiple of u, so I contains r. Since this is true of every element $r \in R$, $R = I$.   ♣

Corollary. Let I be an ideal in a polynomial ring $k[x]$, where k is a field. If I contains any nonzero 'constant' polynomial, then $I = k[x]$.

Proof: This will follow from the previous proposition, if we check that nonzero constant polynomials are units (that is, have multiplicative inverses). Indeed, for $a \in k$ with $a \neq 0$, since k is a field, there is $a^{-1} \in k \subset k[x]$. Thus, certainly a is invertible in the polynomial ring $k[x]$.   ♣

We can recycle the notation we used for cosets to write about ideals in a more economical fashion. For two subsets X, Y of a *ring R*, write

$$
\begin{aligned}
X + Y &= && \{x + y : x \in X,\ y \in Y\} \\
X \cdot Y &= & XY = &\{\text{finite sums } \textstyle\sum_i x_i\, y_i : x_i \in X,\ y_i \in Y\}
\end{aligned}
$$

Note that in the context of *ring* theory the notation $X \cdot Y$ has a different meaning than it does in *group* theory. Then we can say that *an ideal I in a commutative ring R is an additive subgroup so that $RI \subset I$.*

Proposition. Every ideal I in $\mathbf{Z}$ is *principal*, that is, of the form $I = n \cdot \mathbf{Z}$. In particular, the integer n so that this is true is the least positive element of I unless $I = \{0\}$, in which case $n = 0$.

Proof: If $I = \{0\}$, then certainly $I = \mathbf{Z} \cdot 0$, and we're done. So suppose I is nonzero. Since I is closed under taking additive inverses, if I contains $x < 0$ then it also contains $-x > 0$. So a non-trivial ideal I does indeed contain *some* positive element. Let n be the least element of I. Let $x \in I$, and use the division algorithm to get $q, r \in \mathbf{Z}$ with $0 \leq r < n$ and

$$x = q \cdot n + r$$

Certainly qn is still in I, and then $-qn \in I$ also. Since $r = x - qn$, we conclude that $r \in I$. Since n was the smallest positive element of I, it must be that $r = 0$. Thus, $x = qn \in n \cdot \mathbf{Z}$, as desired.   ♣

Proposition. Let k be a field. Let $R = k[x]$ be the ring of polynomials in one variable x with coefficients in k. Then every ideal I in R is principal, that is, is of the form $I = k[x] \cdot P(x)$ for some polynomial P. In particular, $P(x)$ is the monic polynomial of smallest degree in I, unless $I = \{0\}$, in which case $P(x) = 0$.

Proof: If $I = \{0\}$, then certainly $I = k[x] \cdot 0$, and we're done. So suppose I is nonzero. Suppose that $Q(x) = a_n x^n + \cdots + a_0$ lies in I with $a_n \neq 0$. Since k is a field, there is an inverse a_n^{-1}. Then, since I is an ideal, the polynomial

$$P(x) = a_n^{-1} \cdot Q(x) = x^n + a_n^{-1} a_{n-1} x^{n-1} + \cdots + a_n^{-1} a_0$$

also lies in I. That is, there is indeed a *monic* polynomial of lowest degree of any element of the ideal. Let $x \in I$, and use the division algorithm to get $Q, R \in k[x]$ with $\deg R < \deg P$ and

$$x = Q \cdot P + R$$

Certainly $Q \cdot P$ is still in I, and then $-Q \cdot P \in I$ also. Since $R = x - Q \cdot P$, we conclude that $R \in I$. Since P was the monic polynomial in I of smallest degree, it must be that $R = 0$. Thus, $x = Q \cdot P \in n \cdot k[x]$, as desired.   ♣

Remark: The proofs of these two propositions can be abstracted to prove that every ideal in a *Euclidean ring* is *principal*.

Example: Let R be a commutative ring with unit 1, and fix two elements $x, y \in R$. Then

$$I = R \cdot x + R \cdot y = \{rx + sy : r, s \in R\}$$

is an ideal in R. This is checked as follows. First,

$$0 = 0 \cdot x + 0 \cdot y$$

so 0 lies in I. Second,

$$-(rx + sy) = (-r)x + (-s)y$$

so I is closed under inverses. Third, for two elements $rx + sy$ and $r'x + s'y$ in I (with $r, r', s, s' \in R$) we have

$$(rx + sy) + (r'x + s'y) = (r + r')x + (s + s')y$$

so I is closed under addition. Finally, for $rx + sy \in I$ with $r, s \in R$, and for $r' \in R$,

$$r' \cdot (rx + sy) = (r'r)x + (r's)y$$

so $R \cdot I \subset I$ as required. Thus, this type of I is indeed an ideal. The two elements x, y are the **generators** of I.

Example: Similarly, for fixed elements $x_1, \ldots, x_n$ of a commutative ring R, we can form an ideal

$$I = R \cdot x_1 + \cdots + R \cdot x_n$$

Example: To construct new, larger ideals from old, smaller ideals we can proceed as follows. Let I be an ideal in a commutative ring R. Let x be an element of R. Then let

$$J = R \cdot x + I = \{rx + i : r \in R, \ i \in I\}$$

Let's check that J is an ideal. First

$$0 = 0 \cdot x + 0$$

so 0 lies in J. Second,

$$-(rx + i) = (-r)x + (-i)$$

so J is closed under inverses. Third, for two elements $rx + i$ and $r'x + i'$ in J (with $r, r' \in R$ and $i, i' \in I$) we have

$$(rx + i) + (r'x + i') = (r + r')x + (i + i')$$

so J is closed under addition. Finally, for $rx + i \in J$ with $r \in R$, $i \in I$, and for $r' \in R$,

$$r' \cdot (rx + i) = (r'r)x + (r'i)$$

so $R \cdot J \subset J$ as required. Thus, this type of set J is indeed an ideal.

Remark: In the case of rings such as $\mathbf{Z}$, where we know that every ideal is principal, the previous construction does not yield any more general type of ideal.

Remark: In some rings R, it is definitely the case that *not* every ideal is principal. That is, there are some ideals that cannot be expressed as $R \cdot x$. The simplest example is the following. Let

$$R = \{a + b\sqrt{-5} : a, b \in \mathbf{Z}\}$$

It is not hard to check that this is a ring. Let

$$I = \{x \cdot 2 + y \cdot (1 + \sqrt{-5}) : x, y \in R\}$$

With just a little bit of cleverness, one can show that this ideal is not principal. This phenomenon is closely related to the *failure of unique factorization* into primes in this ring. For example, we have two apparently different factorizations

$$2 \cdot 3 = 6 = (1 + \sqrt{-5}) \cdot (1 - \sqrt{-5})$$

(All the numbers 2, 3, $1 + \sqrt{-5}$, $1 - \sqrt{-5}$ are 'prime' in the naive sense that they cannot be further factored in the ring R.) These phenomena are not of immediate relevance, but they did provide considerable motivation in the historical development of algebraic number theory.

Remark: In rings R that are not necessarily commutative, there are *three different kinds* of ideals. A **left ideal** I is an additive subgroup so that $R\,I \subset I$, a **right ideal** I is an additive subgroup so that $I\,R \subset I$, and a **two-sided ideal** I is an additive subgroup so that $R\,I + I\,R \subset I$. Mostly we'll care only about ideals in *commutative* rings, so we can safely ignore this complication most of the time.

Exercises

29.1.01 Let N be an integer. Prove carefully that $N \cdot \mathbf{Z}$ is an *ideal* in $\mathbf{Z}$.

29.1.02 Find all the ideals in $\mathbf{Z}/6$.

29.1.03 Find all the ideals in $\mathbf{Z}/10$.

29.1.04 Find all the ideals in $\mathbf{Z}/5$.

29.1.05 Let I, J be two ideals in a ring R. Show that $I \cap J$ is also an ideal in R.

29.1.06 Let I, J be two ideals in a ring R. Let

$$I + J = \{i + j : i \in I \quad \text{and} \quad j \in J\}$$

Show that $I + J$ is an ideal.

29.1.07 (*) Show that the polynomial ring $\mathbf{F}_2[x, y]$ in two variables x, y with coefficients in the finite field $\mathbf{F}_2$ is *not* a principal ideal domain.

29.2 Ring Homomorphisms

Quite analogous to *group homomorphisms*, ring homomorphisms are maps from one ring to another which preserve the ring structures. Precisely, a **ring homomorphism** $f : R \to S$ from one ring R to another ring S is a map so that, for all r, r' in R we have

$$
\begin{aligned}
f(r + r') &= f(r) + f(r') \\
f(rr') &= f(r)\, f(r')
\end{aligned}
$$

That is, we would say that f *preserves* or *respects* both addition and multiplication. A ring homomorphism which is a bijection is an **isomorphism**. Two rings which are isomorphic are construed as 'the same' for all ring-theoretic purposes.

As in the case of groups and group homomorphisms, we do not make an attempt to use different notations for the addition and multiplication in the two different rings R and S in this definition. Thus, more properly put, f converts *addition in R* into *addition in S*, and likewise multiplication.

Very much like the case of groups, the **kernel** of a ring homomorphism $f : R \to S$ is

$$\ker f = \{r \in R : f(r) = 0\}$$

where (implicitly) the latter 0 is the additive identity in S.

Example: The most basic example of a ring homomorphism is

$$f : \mathbf{Z} \to \mathbf{Z}/n$$

given by

$$f(x) = x\text{-mod-}n$$

The assertion that this f is a ring homomorphism is the combination of the two assertions

$$(x\text{-mod-}n) + (y\text{-mod-}n) = (x + y)\text{-mod-}n$$

and

$$(x\text{-mod-}n) \cdot (y\text{-mod-}n) = (x \cdot y)\text{-mod-}n$$

Even though it is slightly misleading, this homomorphism is called the **reduction mod** m **homomorphism**.

Now we prove

Proposition.   the kernel of any ring homomorphism $f : R \to S$ is an ideal in R.

Proof: Let x be in the kernel, and $r \in R$. Then

$$f(rx) = f(r)f(x) = f(r) \cdot 0 = 0$$

since by now we've proven that in any ring the product of anything with 0 is 0. Thus, rx is in the kernel of f. And, for x, y both in the kernel,

$$f(x + y) = f(x) + f(y) = 0 + 0 = 0$$

That is, $x + y$ is again in the kernel. And $f(0) = 0$, so 0 is in the kernel. And for x in the kernel $f(-x) = -f(x) = -0 = 0$, so $-x$ is in the kernel.   ♣

Example: Some homomorphisms which are very important in applications are **evaluation homomorphisms** or **substitution homomorphisms**, described as follows. Let R be a commutative ring, and $R[x]$ the polynomial ring in one variable with coefficients in R. Fix $r_0 \in R$. We want to talk about *evaluating* polynomials at r_0, or, equivalently, *substituting* r_0 for x in a polynomial. What is meant by this is that a polynomial

$$P(x) = a_n x^n + a_{n-1} x^{n-1} + \cdots + a_2 x^2 + a_1 x + a_0$$

should be mapped to

$$P(r_0) = a_n r_0^n + a_{n-1} r_0^{n-1} + \cdots + a_2 r_0^2 + a_1 r_0 + a_0$$

Let e_{r_0} denote this map, which is the **evaluation map**.

- The evaluation map $e_{r_0} : R[x] \to R$ is a ring homomorphism from the polynomial ring $R[x]$ to the ring R.

Remark: Before proving this, note that our experience makes us anticipate the fact that such maps really are ring homomorphisms: indeed, we know that to evaluate the product or sum of two polynomials we can evaluate them individually and then multiply/add, or multiply/add first and then evaluate. This is exactly the assertion that evaluation is a ring homomorphism.

Proof: This is mostly just finding an effective notation. Let

$$\begin{aligned} P(x) &= \sum_{0 \le i \le m} a_i x^i \\ Q(x) &= \sum_{0 \le i \le n} b_i x^i \end{aligned}$$

be two polynomials with coefficients in a commutative ring R. First we show that evaluation e_{r_0} at $r_0 \in R$ respects the addition:

$$e_{r_0}(P+Q) = e_{r_0}\left(\sum_j (a_j + b_j)x^j\right) = \sum_j (a_j + b_j)r_0^j$$

$$= \sum_j a_j r_0^j + \sum_j b_j r_0^j = e_{r_0}(P) + e_{r_0}(Q)$$

where without harming anything we put $a_j = 0$ and $b_j = 0$ for any index outside the range for which the coefficients are defined. This proves that evaluation respects sums. For products:

$$e_{r_0}(P \cdot Q) = e_{r_0}(\sum_{i,j}(a_i \cdot b_j)x^{i+j}) = \sum_{i,j}(a_i \cdot b_j)r_0^{i+j} = e_{r_0}(P) \cdot e_{r_0}(Q)$$

This proves that multiplication is respected also by evaluation, so these evaluations really are ring homomorphisms.   ♣

Proposition. Let $f : R \to S$ be a ring homomorphism. Let $0_R, 0_S$ be the additive identities in R, S, respectively. Then $f(0_R) = 0_S$. That is, always the image of an additive identity under a ring homomorphism is the additive identity in the 'target' ring.

Proof: First,
$$f(0_R) + f(0_R) = f(0_R + 0_R)$$

by the defining property of 'group homomorphism'. Then

$$0_R + 0_R = 0_R$$

(by the property of the additive identity in R), so

$$f(0_R + 0_R) = f(0_R)$$

Thus, together, we have

$$f(0_R) + f(0_R) = f(0_R + 0_R) = f(0_R)$$

Add the additive inverse $-f(0_R)$ to both sides:

$$(f(0_R) + f(0_R)) - f(0_R) = f(0_R) - f(0_R) = 0_S$$

where the last equality uses the definition of additive inverse. Using associativity of addition,

$$(f(0_R) + f(0_R)) - f(0_R) = f(0_R) + (f(0_R) - f(0_R)) = f(0_R) + 0_S = f(0_R)$$

where we also use the defining property of 0_S. Putting these together (repeating a little):

$$f(0_R) = f(0_R) + f(0_R) - f(0_R) = f(0_R + 0_R) - f(0_R) = f(0_R) - f(0_R) = 0_S$$

as claimed.   ♣

- Let $f : R \to S$ be a *surjective* ring homomorphism. Suppose that R has a multiplicative identity 1_R. Then S has a multiplicative identity 1_S and

$$f(1_R) = 1_S$$

Remark: Notice that, unlike the discussion about the additive identity, here we need the further hypothesis of surjectivity. Otherwise the assertion is false: see the remark after the proof.

Proof: Given $s \in S$, let $r \in R$ be such that $f(r) = s$. Then

$$f(1_R) \cdot s = f(1_R) \cdot f(r) = f(1_R \cdot r) = f(r) = s$$

Thus, $f(1_R)$ behaves like the unit in S. By the already proven *uniqueness* of units, it must be that $f(1_R) = 1_S$.   ♣

Remark: It is important to note that the image of the *multiplicative* identity 1_R under a ring homomorphism $f : R \to S$ is not necessarily the *multiplicative* identity 1_S of S. For example, define a ring homomorphism

$$f : \mathbf{Q} \to S$$

from the rational numbers $\mathbf{Q}$ to the ring S of two-by-two rational matrices by

$$f(x) = \begin{pmatrix} x & 0 \\ 0 & 0 \end{pmatrix}$$

Then the image of 1 is simply

$$\begin{pmatrix} 1 & 0 \\ 0 & 0 \end{pmatrix}$$

which is certainly not the same as the multiplicative identity

$$\begin{pmatrix} 1 & 0 \\ 0 & 1 \end{pmatrix}$$

in the ring S.

There are also examples in commutative rings where the unit is mapped to something other than the unit. For example, let $R = \mathbf{Z}/3$ and $S = \mathbf{Z}/6$, and define $f : R \to S$ by

$$f(r \bmod 3) = 4r \bmod 6$$

Check that this is well-defined: if $r = r'$ mod 3, then $3|(4r - 4r')$ and $2|(4r - 4r')$ so surely $6|4(r - r')$, so indeed $4r = 4r'$ mod 6. This proves well-definedness. Check that this is a homomorphism:

$$f(x + y) = 4(x + y) = 4x + 4y = f(x) + f(y)$$

This would have worked with *any* number, not just 4. To see that f preserves multiplication, the crucial feature of the situation is that

$$4 \cdot 4 = 4 \text{ mod } 6$$

Then
$$f(x \cdot y) = 4(x \cdot y) = (4 \cdot 4)(x \cdot y) = (4x) \cdot (4y) = f(x) \cdot f(y)$$

Thus, f is a homomorphism. But $f(1) = 4 \neq 1$ mod 6.

Exercises

29.2.01 Fix an integer $N > 1$. Prove carefully that the map $f : \mathbf{Z} \to \mathbf{Z}/N\mathbf{Z}$ given by $f(x) = x + N\mathbf{Z}$ is a ring homomorphism. (We'd really known this all along!)

29.2.02 Let $f : R \to S$ be a *surjective* ring homomorphism (with R, S commutative, for simplicity). Let I be an ideal in R. Show that $J = \{f(i) : i \in I\}$ is an ideal in S.

29.2.03 Let $f : R \to S$ be a ring homomorphism (with R, S commutative, for simplicity). Let J be an ideal in I. Show that $I = \{i \in I : f(i) \in J\}$ is an ideal in S.

29.2.04 (*) Show that the only two two-sided ideals in the ring R of two-by-two rational matrices are $\{0\}$ and the whole ring R itself.

29.3 Quotient Rings

Now we give a construction of new rings from old in a manner that includes as a special case the construction of $\mathbf{Z}/n$ from $\mathbf{Z}$. Let R be a commutative ring with unit 1. Let I be an ideal in R. The **quotient ring** R/I ("R mod I") is defined to be the set of cosets

$$r + I = \{r + i : i \in I\}$$

We define operations of addition and multiplication on R/I by

$$(r + I) + (s + I) = (r + s) + I$$

$$(r + I) \cdot (s + I) = (r \cdot s) + I$$

The zero in this quotient will be $0_{R/I} = 0 + I$, and the unit will be $1_{R/I} = 1 + I$.

Example: The basic example is that $\mathbf{Z}/n$ is the quotient ring $\mathbf{Z}/I$ where the ideal I is $I = n \cdot \mathbf{Z}$.

But, just as we had to check that the operations of addition and multiplication in $\mathbf{Z}/n$ were *well-defined*, we must do so here as well. The point is that the set $r + I$ typically can be named in several different ways, and we want the alleged addition and multiplication operations not to depend on the way the coset is *named*, but only on *what it is*. This is what well-definedness is about.

So suppose $r + I = r' + I$ and $s + I = s' + I$. That is, we have two cosets, each named in two possibly different ways. To prove well-definedness of addition we need to check that

$$(r + s) + I = (r' + s') + I$$

and to prove well-definedness of multiplication we must check that

$$(r \cdot s) + I = (r' \cdot s') + I$$

Since $r' + I = r + I$, in particular $r' = r' + 0 \in r + I$, so r' can be written as $r' = r + i$ for some $i \in I$. Likewise, $s' = s + j$ for some $j \in I$. Then

$$(r' + s') + I = (r + i + s + j) + I = (r + s) + (i + j + I)$$

The sum $k = i + j$ is an element of I. We claim that for any $k \in I$ we have $k + I = I$. Certainly, since I is closed under addition, $k + I \subset I$. On the other hand, for any $x \in I$ we can write

$$x = k + (x - k)$$

with $x - k \in I$, so also $k + I \supset I$. Thus, indeed, $k + I = I$. Thus,

$$(r' + s') + I = (r + s) + I$$

which proves the well-definedness of addition in the quotient ring. Likewise, looking at multiplication:

$$(r' \cdot s') + I = (r + i) \cdot (s + j) + I = (r \cdot s) + (rj + si + I)$$

Since I is an ideal, rj and si are again in I, and then $rj + si \in I$. Therefore, as just observed in the discussion of addition, $rj + si + I = I$. Thus,

$$(r' \cdot s') + I = (r \cdot s) + I$$

and multiplication is well-defined.

The proofs that $0 + I$ is the zero and $1 + I$ is the unit are similar.

And in this situation the **quotient homomorphism**

$$q : R \to R/I$$

is the natural map

$$q(r) = r + I$$

In fact, the discussion just above proves

Proposition. For a commutative ring R and ideal I, the quotient map $R \to R/I$ is a ring homomorphism. ♣

29.4 Maximal Ideals and Fields

Now we see how to make fields from by taking suitable quotients by maximal ideals. This is a fundamental construction. Let R be a commutative ring with unit 1. An ideal M in R is **maximal** if $M \neq R$ and if for any other ideal I with $I \supset M$, it must be that $I = R$. That is, M is a maximal ideal if there is no ideal strictly larger than M (containing M) except R itself.

Proposition. For a commutative ring R with unit, and for an ideal I, the quotient ring R/I is a *field* if and only if I is a *maximal* ideal.

Proof: Let $x + I$ be a nonzero element of R/I. Then $x + I \neq I$, so $x \notin I$. Note that the ideal $Rx + I$ is therefore strictly larger than I. Since I was already maximal, it must be that $Rx + I = R$. Therefore, there are $r \in R$ and $i \in I$ so that $rx + i = 1$. Looking at this last equation modulo I, we have $rx \equiv 1 \bmod I$. That is, $r + I$ is the multiplicative inverse to $x + I$. Thus, R/I is a field.

On the other hand, suppose that R/I is a field. Let $x \in R$ but $x \notin I$. Then $x + I \neq 0 + I$ in R/I. Therefore, $x + I$ has a multiplicative inverse $r + I$ in R/I. That is,

$$(r + I) \cdot (x + I) = 1 + I$$

From the definition of the multiplication in the quotient, this is $rx + I = 1 + I$, or $1 \in rx + I$, which implies that the ideal $Rx + I$ is R. But $Rx + I$ is the smallest ideal containing I and x. Thus, there cannot be any proper ideal strictly larger than I, so I is maximal. ♣

Exercises

29.4.01 Show that the ideal generated by x in the polynomial ring $\mathbf{Z}[x]$ in one variable over $\mathbf{Z}$ is *not* maximal, by showing that it doesn't contain the prime 2.

29.4.02 Show that the ideal generated by x and a fixed prime number p in the polynomial ring $\mathbf{Z}[x]$ in one variable over $\mathbf{Z}$ is maximal, by showing that the quotient is a field.

29.4.03 Show that the ideal generated by $x^2 + 1$ and the prime number 7 in the polynomial ring $\mathbf{Z}[x]$ in one variable over $\mathbf{Z}$ is maximal, by showing that the quotient is a field.

29.4.04 Show that the ideal generated by x in the polynomial ring $\mathbf{F}_2[x, y]$ in two variables over $\mathbf{F}_2$ is *not* maximal, by showing that it doesn't contain y.

29.4.05 Show that the ideal generated by x and y together in the polynomial ring $\mathbf{F}_2[x, y]$ in two variables over $\mathbf{F}_2$ is maximal, by showing that the quotient is a field.

29.5 More on Field Extensions

Now we'll make the construction above more concrete, making 'bigger' fields by taking quotients of polynomial rings with coefficients in 'smaller' fields. This is just a slight abstraction of the style of our earlier discussion of finite fields, and is basic. Let k be a field. Another field K containing k is called an **extension field** of k, and k is a **subfield** of K.

> **Theorem.** Let k be a field and $P(x)$ an irreducible polynomial in $k[x]$ (other than the zero polynomial). Then the principal ideal $I = k[x] \cdot P(x)$ is *maximal*. Thus, the quotient ring $k[x]/I$ is a *field*. Further, the composite map
> $$k \to k[x] \to k[x]/I$$
> is *injective*, so we may consider the field k as a subset of the field $k[x]/I$. Last, let $\alpha = x + I$ be the image in $k[x]/I$ of the indeterminate x. Then (in the quotient $k[x]/I$)
> $$P(\alpha) = 0$$

Last, any element $\beta \in k[x]/I$ can be *uniquely* expressed in the form

$$\beta = R(\alpha)$$

where R is a polynomial with coefficients in k and of degree strictly less than the degree of P.

Remark: The **degree** of the extension K of k is the degree of the polynomial P used in the construction.

Remark: In this situation, thinking of α as 'existing' now, and being a root of the equation $P(x) = 0$, we say that we have **adjoined** a root of $P(x) = 0$ to k, and write

$$k[\alpha] = k[x]/I$$

Remark: As a notational convenience, often a quotient

$$k[x]/k[x] \cdot P(x)$$

is written as

$$k[x]/P(x)$$

where it is meant to be understood that the quotient is by the *ideal* generated by $P(x)$. This is entirely consistent with the notation $\mathbf{Z}/n$ for $\mathbf{Z}/\mathbf{Z} \cdot n$.

Remark: An element β of $k[x]/I$ expressed as a polynomial $R(\alpha)$ with R of degree less than the degree of P is **reduced**. Of course, since $k[x]/I$ is a ring, *any* polynomial $R(\alpha)$ in α gives something in $k[x]/I$. But everything can be expressed by a polynomial of degree less than that of P, and *uniquely* so. This is exactly analogous to the fact that every equivalence class in the quotient ring $\mathbf{Z}/n$ has a unique representative among the integers reduced modulo n, namely $\{0, 1, 2, \ldots, n-1\}$.

Proof: Let J be a polynomial not in the ideal $I = k[x] \cdot P$. We want to show that the ideal $k[x] \cdot J + I$ is $k[x]$, thereby proving the maximality of I. Since P is irreducible, the *gcd* of J and P is just 1. Therefore, by the Euclidean algorithm in $k[x]$, there are polynomials A, B in $k[x]$ so that

$$A \cdot P + B \cdot J = 1$$

That is, $k[x] \cdot J + I$ contains 1. Let C, D be polynomials so that

$$1 = C \cdot J + D \cdot P$$

Then for *any* polynomial M we have

$$M = M \cdot 1 = M \cdot (C \cdot J + D \cdot P) = (M \cdot C) \cdot J + (M \cdot D) \cdot P$$

which lies in $k[x] \cdot J + k[x] \cdot P$. That is, M is in the ideal $k[x] \cdot J + k[x] \cdot P$, so the latter ideal is the whole ring $k[x]$. This proves the maximality of $k[x] \cdot J + k[x] \cdot P$.

Next, we show that the composite map

$$k \to k[x] \to k[x]/k[x] \cdot P$$

is an injection. Let $I = k[x] \cdot P$. The first map $k \to k[x]$ is the obvious one, which takes $a \in k$ to the 'constant' polynomial a. Suppose $a, b \in k$ so that $a + I = b + I$. Then, by subtracting, $(a - b) + I = 0 + I$, which gives

$$a - b = (a - b) + 0 \in (a - b) + I = I$$

so $a - b \in I$.

Next, we prove that $P(\alpha) = 0$. Let $q : k[x] \to k[x]/I$ be the quotient homomorphism. Write out P as

$$P(x) = a_n x^n + a_{n-1} x^{n-1} + \cdots + a_2 x^2 + a_1 x + a_0$$

To show that $P(\alpha) = 0$ in the quotient, we compute

$$
\begin{aligned}
P(\alpha) &= a_n \alpha^n + a_{n-1} \alpha^{n-1} + \cdots + a_2 \alpha^2 + a_1 \alpha + a_0 \\
&= a_n q(x)^n + a_{n-1} q(x)^{n-1} + \cdots + a_2 q(x)^2 + a_1 \alpha + a_0 \\
&= q(a_n x^n + a_{n-1} x^{n-1} + \cdots + a_2 x^2 + a_1 x + a_0) \ = \ q(P(x))
\end{aligned}
$$

since q is a ring homomorphism, and since the 'constants' in k are essentially unchanged in mapping to the quotient. Since $P(x) \in I$, the image $q(P(x))$ of it under q is 0. That is, we have proven that $P(\alpha) = 0$.

Finally, we prove that any element of the quotient $k[x]/I$ is uniquely expressible as a polynomial in $\alpha = x + I$, of degree less than the degree of P. Indeed, given $\beta \in k[x]/I$ there is some polynomial J so that $q(J(x)) = \beta$. Using the division algorithm for polynomials in one variable over a field, we have

$$J(x) = Q(x) \cdot P(x) + R(x)$$

where $\deg R < \deg P$. Then, under the homomorphism q we have

$$\beta = q(J(x)) = q(Q(x)) \cdot q(P(x)) + q(R(x)) = q(Q(x)) \cdot 0 + R(q(x)) = R(\alpha)$$

since $q(P(x)) = P(\alpha) = 0$, and of course using the ring homormorphism properties. This is the desired result.   ♣

Corollary.   When the field k is finite with q elements, for an irreducible polynomial P of degree n, the field extension $K = k[x]/P(x)$ with has q^n elements.

Proof: Let α be the image of x in K. We use the fact that every element of K has a unique expression as $R(\alpha)$ for a polynomial R of degree less than n. There are q choices for each of the n coefficients (for powers of α ranging from 0 to $n-1$), so there are q^n elements altogether.   ♣

Remark: A field extension $k[x]/P(x)$ with irreducible polynomial P is called **quadratic** if P is quadratic, **cubic** if P is cubic, **quartic** if P is quartic, **quintic** if P is quintic, and so on.

29.6 Frobenius Automorphism

One essential higher-level structural feature of finite fields is the presence of **Frobenius maps**, which play a central technical role. Several basic theorems about finite fields, which don't mention the Frobenius maps directly, nevertheless make use of the Frobenius maps in their proofs. In this section we will think about finite fields more abstractly, and rely less upon specific models of them depending upon choices of irreducible polynomials. In fact, this more abstract study will be used to give proofs of the counting assertions about irreducible and primitive polynomials.

In this section we also briefly develop just a few aspects of the idea of *automorphism group* of a larger field over a smaller field, in the context of finite fields. This is a forerunner of *Galois theory*, which is the systematic study of such automorphism groups.

Let $k = \mathbf{F}_q = GF(q)$ be a finite field with q elements, where $q = p^n$ is a power of a prime number p. Fix an integer $N > 1$, and suppose we have a larger finite field $K = \mathbf{F}_{q^N} = GF(q^N)$ containing k. The **Frobenius map** of K **over** k is simply

$$\Phi(\alpha) = \alpha^q$$

This is also sometimes called the **Frobenius automorphism** of K **over** k, for reasons that will be clarified somewhat in what follows. Since K is closed under multiplication, it is clear that Φ maps K to itself.

Remark: Yes, Φ is just the map that takes the qth power of things inside K, where q is the cardinality of the littler field k inside K. And, yes, the way we're writing it the notation does not forcefully tell us what the corresponding K and k are. This implicit reference to K and k is harmless, though, because we won't be doing anything devious with Φ.

Proposition.   The Frobenius map Φ of $K = \mathbf{F}_{q^N}$ over $k = \mathbf{F}_q$ is a bijection of K to K. In particular,

$$\Phi^N = \underbrace{\Phi \circ \Phi \circ \cdots \circ \Phi}_{N}$$

is the identity map on K (which maps every element of K to itself).

Proof: Again, since the Frobenius map Φ is just taking qth powers and K is closed under multiplication, Φ maps K to itself. What needs more attention is the injectivity and surjectivity. Some thought should make clear that proving Φ^N is the identity map on K is sufficient to prove that Φ is both injective and surjective.

The multiplicative group $\mathbf{K}^\times$ is of order $q^N - 1$, so by Lagrange's theorem and its corollaries the order of any $\beta \in K^\times$ is a divisor of $q^N - 1$, and

$$\beta^{q^N - 1} = 1$$

Therefore, for nonzero β in K,

$$\Phi(\beta) = \beta^{q^N} = \beta \cdot \beta^{q^N - 1} = \beta \cdot 1 = \beta$$

This proves the proposition.   ♣

Proposition.   The Frobenius map Φ restricted to k is the identity map. That is, for every α in $k = \mathbf{F}_q$, $\Phi(\alpha) = \alpha$. If $\alpha \in K$ has the property that $\Phi(\alpha) = \alpha$, then in fact $\alpha \in k$.

Proof: Half of the proposition is really just a corollary of Lagrange's theorem. The first point is that the multiplicative group $k^\times$ of nonzero elements in k has $q-1$ elements. So, by Lagrange's theorem and its corollaries, the *order* of any element α in k is a divisor d of $q-1$, and, further, $\alpha^{q-1} = 1$ for that reason. Then for nonzero $\alpha \in k$ we have

$$\Phi(\alpha) = \alpha^q = (\alpha)^{q-1} \cdot \alpha = 1 \cdot \alpha = \alpha$$

And certainly $0^q = 0$, so this proves half of the proposition.

Now suppose that $\alpha \in K$ and $\Phi(\alpha) = \alpha$. By the definition of Φ this means that α is a solution of the equation $x^q - x = 0$ lying inside the field K. By unique factorization of polynomials (with coefficients in a field), we know that a polynomial equation of degree q has at most q roots in a field. We already found q roots of this equation, namely the elements of the smaller field k sitting inside K. So there simply can't be any other roots of that equation other than the elements of k. This shows that $\Phi(\alpha) = \alpha$ implies $\alpha \in k$, which is the second half of the proposition.   ♣

Lemma.   Let 1_K be the multiplicative identity in K. Then

$$\underbrace{1_K + \cdots + 1_K}_{p} = 0$$

As a consequence, for any α in K,

$$\underbrace{\alpha + \cdots + \alpha}_{p} = 0$$

Remark: A more systematic development of general *field theory* would make the result of the last lemma much clearer, but would have taken more time altogether than the funny proof given below.

Proof: By Lagrange's theorem and its corollaries, in the group obtained by taking K with its addition (ignoring for the moment its multiplication), the order of any element α is a divisor of the order q^N of the group, and

$$q^N \cdot \alpha = \underbrace{\alpha + \cdots + \alpha}_{q^N} = 0$$

Since $q = p^n$, this is

$$p^{nN} \cdot \alpha = \underbrace{\alpha + \cdots + \alpha}_{p^{nN}} = 0$$

For the moment, use the abbreviation

$$t = \underbrace{1_K + \cdots + 1_K}_{p}$$

Taking $\alpha = 1_K$ in the formula above,

$$0 = \underbrace{1_K + \cdots + 1_K}_{q^N} = t^{nN}$$

Since K is a field, whenever the product of several elements is 0, one of the factors is itself 0. Thus, t is 0, as asserted in the lemma. And then

$$\underbrace{\alpha + \cdots + \alpha}_{p} = \underbrace{1_K \cdot \alpha + \cdots + 1_K \cdot \alpha}_{p} = \left(\underbrace{1_K + \cdots + 1_K}_{p}\right) \cdot \alpha = 0 \cdot \alpha = 0$$

This proves the lemma.   ♣

Proposition. The Frobenius map Φ of K over k has the property that for any α, β in K

$$\Phi(\alpha + \beta) = \Phi(\alpha) + \Phi(\beta)$$
$$\Phi(\alpha \cdot \beta) = \Phi(\alpha) \cdot \Phi(\beta)$$

That is, Φ preserves addition and multiplication. Since we already saw that Φ is bijective, Φ is said to be a **ring isomorphism**.

Proof: The second assertion, about preserving multiplication, is simply the assertion that the qth power of a product is the product of the qth powers. This is true in great generality as long as the multiplication is commutative, which it is here. This doesn't depend at all on what the particular exponent is.

The proof that Φ preserves addition makes quite sharp use of the fact that the exponent is q, which is a power of a prime number p. This wouldn't work for other exponents. To start with, we claim that for α, β in K

$$(\alpha + \beta)^p = \alpha^p + \beta^p$$

Expanding by the binomial theorem, the left-hand side is

$$\alpha^p + \binom{p}{1}\alpha^{p-1}b + \binom{p}{2}\alpha^{p-2}b^2 + \cdots + \binom{p}{p-1}\alpha^1 b^{p-1} + \beta^p$$

Here the multiplication of elements of K by positive integers means repeated addition. As observed in the proof of Fermat's Little Theorem, all those binomial coefficients in the middle of the expansion are integers divisible by p, so by the previous lemma all the middle terms of the expansion are 0 in K. Thus, we have proven that

$$(\alpha + \beta)^p = \alpha^p + \beta^p$$

Then, repeatedly invoking this result,

$$(\alpha + \beta)^{p^2} = (\alpha^p + \beta^p)^p = a^{p^2} + b^{p^2}$$

$$(\alpha + \beta)^{p^3} = (\alpha^p + \beta^p)^{p^2} = (a^{p^2} + b^{p^2})^p = \alpha^{p^3} + \beta^{p^3}$$

and so on, so by induction we could prove that

$$(\alpha + \beta)^{p^{nN}} = \alpha^{p^{nN}} + \beta^{p^{nN}}$$

as asserted. That is, the Frobenius map preserves addition.   ♣

Proposition. Let $P(x)$ be a polynomial with coefficients in $k = \mathbf{F}_q$. Let $\alpha \in K$ be a root of the equation $P(x) = 0$. Then $\Phi(\alpha) = \alpha^q$, $\Phi^2(\alpha) = \Phi(\Phi(\alpha)) = \alpha^{q^2}$, ... are also roots of the equation.

Proof: Let P have coefficients

$$P(x) = c_n x^n + c_{n-1}x^{n-1} + \cdots c_2 x^2 + c_1 x + c_0$$

with all the c_i's in k. Apply the Frobenius map to both sides of the equation

$$0 = c_n\alpha^n + c_{n-1}\alpha^{n-1} + \cdots c_2\alpha^2 + c_1\alpha + c_0$$

to obtain

$$\Phi(0) = \Phi(c_n)\Phi(\alpha)^n + \Phi(c_{n-1})\Phi(\alpha)^{n-1} + \cdots \Phi(c_2)\Phi(\alpha)^2 + \Phi(c_1)\Phi(\alpha) + \Phi(c_0)$$

since Φ preserves addition and multiplication in K, in the sense of the previous proposition. The coefficients c_i are in k, as is the 0 on the left-hand side, so Φ doesn't change them. Thus, in fact we have

$$0 = c_n\Phi(\alpha)^n + c_{n-1}\Phi(\alpha)^{n-1} + \cdots c_2\Phi(\alpha)^2 + c_1\Phi(\alpha) + c_0$$

That is, we have

$$0 = P(\Phi(\alpha))$$

That proves that $\Phi(\alpha)$ is a root of $P(x) = 0$ if α is. By repeating this, we obtain the assertion of the proposition.   ♣

Proposition. Let

$$A = \{\alpha_1, \ldots, \alpha_t\}$$

be a set of (t distinct) elements of K, with the property that for any α in A, $\Phi(\alpha)$ is again in A. Then the polynomial

$$(x - \alpha_1)(x - \alpha_2) \cdots (x - \alpha_t)$$

(when multiplied out) has coefficients in k.

Proof: For a polynomial

$$P(x) = c_n x^n + c_{n-1} x^{n-1} + \cdots c_2 x^2 + c_1 x + c_0$$

with coefficients in the larger field K, define a new polynomial $\Phi(P)$ by letting Φ just act on the coefficients:

$$\Phi(P)(x) = \Phi(c_n)x^n + \Phi(c_{n-1})x^{n-1} + \cdots \Phi(c_2)x^2 + \Phi(c_1)x + \Phi(c_0)$$

Since Φ preserves addition and multiplication in K, it is not hard to check that if also preserves addition and multiplication of polynomials with coefficients in K, in the sense that for two such polynomials P and Q

$$\begin{aligned} \Phi(P + Q) &= \Phi(P) + \Phi(Q) \\ \Phi(P \cdot Q) &= \Phi(P) \cdot \Phi(Q) \end{aligned}$$

Then applying Φ to the product

$$(x - \alpha_1)(x - \alpha_2) \cdots (x - \alpha_t)$$

will merely mix around the factors, by the hypothesis that Φ just permutes the elements of the set A. The order in which the factors are multiplied certainly doesn't matter here, so we have

$$\Phi((x - \alpha_1)(x - \alpha_2) \cdots (x - \alpha_t)) = (x - \alpha_1)(x - \alpha_2) \cdots (x - \alpha_t)$$

That means that the multiplied-out version

$$(x - \alpha_1)(x - \alpha_2) \cdots (x - \alpha_t) = c_n x^n + c_{n-1} x^{n-1} + \cdots c_2 x^2 + c_1 x + c_0$$

has the property that

$$c_n x^n + c_{n-1} x^{n-1} + \cdots c_2 x^2 + c_1 x + c_0$$

$$= \Phi(c_n) x^n + \Phi(c_{n-1}) x^{n-1} + \cdots \Phi(c_2) x^2 + \Phi(c_1) x + \Phi(c_0)$$

The meaning of 'equality' for polynomials is that the corresponding coefficients are equal, so the previous inequality implies that $\Phi(c_i) = c_i$ for all indices i. By now we know that this implies that $c_i \in k$, for all indices i.   ♣

Proposition. Let α be an element of $K = k[x]/Q$. There is exactly one monic irreducible polynomial P in $k[x]$ so that α is a root of $P(x) = 0$, namely

$$P(x) = (x - \alpha)(x - \Phi(\alpha))(x - \Phi^2(\alpha)) \cdots (x - \Phi^{d-1}(\alpha))$$

where d is the smallest positive integer so that $\Phi(\alpha) = \alpha$.

Proof: Consider the successive images $\Phi^i(\alpha)$ of α under the Frobenius map. Since the field is finite, at some point $\Phi^i(\alpha) = \Phi^j(\alpha)$ for some $0 \leq i < j$. Since Φ is a bijection of K to K, it has an inverse map Φ^{-1}. Applying this inverse i times to the equation $\Phi^i(\alpha) = \Phi^j(\alpha)$, we find

$$\alpha = \Phi^0(\alpha) = \Phi^{j-i}(\alpha)$$

That is, in fact $i = 0$. That means that in the list α, $\Phi(\alpha)$, $\Phi^2(\alpha)$, ..., for the smallest j so that $\Phi^j(\alpha)$ is already on the list, we have

$$\Phi^j(\alpha) = \alpha$$

rather than duplicating some *other* element further along on the list. Let

$$\alpha, \Phi(\alpha), \ldots, \Phi^{d-1}(\alpha)$$

be the distinct images of α under the Frobenius map. We just saw that $\Phi^d(\alpha) = \alpha$. Let

$$P(x) = (x - \alpha)(x - \Phi(\alpha))(x - \Phi^2(\alpha)) \cdots (x - \Phi^{d-1}(\alpha))$$

As just above, application of Φ to P only permutes the factors on the right-hand side, by shifting indices forward by one, and wrapping around at the end since

$\Phi^d(\alpha) = \alpha$. Thus, when multiplied out, the polynomial P is unchanged by application of Φ, so has coefficients in the smaller field k. We saw this phenomenon already in the discussion of the Frobenius map. And visibly α is a root of the equation $\mathbf{P}(x) = 0$.

From just above, if β is a root in K of a polynomial equation with coefficients in the smaller field k, then $\Phi(\beta)$ is also a root. So *any* polynomial with coefficients in k of which α is a zero must have factors $x - \Phi^i(\alpha)$ as well, for $1 \leq i < d$. By unique factorization of polynomials with coefficients in a field, this shows that this is the *unique* such polynomial.

In particular, P must be irreducible in $k[x]$, because if it properly factored in $k[x]$ as $P = P_1 P_2$ then (by unique factorization) α would be a root of either $P_1(x) = 0$ or $P_2(x) = 0$, and then all the d distinct elements $\Phi^i(\alpha)$ would be roots of the same equation as well. Since the number of roots is at most the degree, there cannot be any proper factorization, so P is irreducible in $k[x]$.   ♣

Corollary. Let β be the image of x in $K = \mathbf{F}_q[x]/Q$. Then

$$Q(x) = (x - \beta)(x - \Phi(\beta))(x - \Phi^2(\beta))\ldots(x - \Phi^{n-1}(\beta))$$

We have $\Phi^n(\beta) = \beta$, and n is the smallest positive integer so that this is so.

Proof: This is a special case of the proposition.   ♣

We need to develop one further abstraction. Let e denote the identity map of $K = \mathbf{F}_q[x]/Q$ to itself, and let

$$G = \{e, \Phi, \Phi^2, \ldots, \Phi^{n-1}\}$$

where Q is of degree n. This is a set of maps of K to itself. As noted above, each one of these maps when restricted to $\mathbf{F}_q$ is the identity map on $\mathbf{F}_q$. Since each Φ^i is the identity on $\mathbf{F}_q$ and maps K bijectively to itself, we say that G is a set of **automorphisms** of K over $\mathbf{F}_q$.

Proposition. This set G of automorphisms of K over $\mathbf{F}_q$ is a *group*, with identity e.

Proof: Let β be the image of x in K. We first check that $\Phi^n(\alpha) = \alpha$ for any α in K. We know that we can express α as a polynomial in β with coefficients in $\mathbf{F}_q$, say $\alpha = R(\beta)$. Then because Φ preserves addition and multiplication, and because $\Phi^n(\beta) = \beta$ by the previous corollary,

$$\Phi^n(\alpha) = \Phi^n(R(\beta)) = R(\Phi^n(\beta)) = R(\beta) = \alpha$$

Since $\Phi^n = e$, for any integer ℓ

$$\Phi^\ell = \Phi^{\ell \% n}$$

as a function from K to itself, where as usual $\% \ n$ means reduction modulo n. Therefore, the set G is closed under multiplication (meaning composition of functions):

$$\Phi^i \circ \Phi^j = \Phi^{(i+j) \% n}$$

Further, this shows that G is closed under inverses:

$$(\Phi^i)^{-1} = \Phi^{n-i}$$

The associativity follows as a consequence of the associativity of composition of functions from a set to itself. That the identity element of the group is the identity *map e* is clear. ♣

For α in K, the **stabilizer subgroup** G_α of α in G is defined to be

$$G_\alpha = \{g \in G : g(\alpha) = \alpha\}$$

Of course, we should verify that this really is a subgroup of G:

Proposition. For α in K the stabilizer subgroup G_α of α is a subgroup of G.

Proof: Certainly G_α contains the identity map e. Suppose that $g \in G$ so that $g(\alpha) = \alpha$. Applying the function g^{-1} to this equality gives

$$\alpha = g^{-1}(g(\alpha)) = g^{-1}(\alpha)$$

so G_α is closed under inverses. If g and h are both in G_α, then

$$g(h(\alpha)) = g(\alpha) = \alpha$$

which proves closure under multiplication. Thus, G_α really is a group. ♣

Proposition. Given α in $K = \mathbf{F}_q[x]/Q$, the number of distinct images $\Phi^i(\alpha)$ of α under repeated applications of the Frobenius map is a divisor of the degree n of Q.

Proof: What we should really claim here is that the collection of distinct images $\Phi^i(\alpha)$ is naturally in bijection with the collection of cosets G/G_α where G_α is the stabilizer subgroup of α in the automorphism G. Indeed, if $g \in G$ and $h \in G_\alpha$, then

$$(gh)(\alpha) = g(h(\alpha)) = g(\alpha)$$

This proves that $gG_\alpha \to g(\alpha)$ is well-defined. And if $g(\alpha) = g'(\alpha)$, then $\alpha = g^{-1}g'(\alpha)$, so $g^{-1}g'$ is in the stabilizer subgroup G_α. This proves that no two distinct cosets gG_α and $g'G_\alpha$ of G_α send α to the same thing. ♣

Corollary. For α in the field $K = k[x]/Q$, the degree of the unique monic irreducible polynomial P with coefficients in k so that $P(\alpha) = 0$ is a divisor of the degree n of Q.

Proof: From above,

$$P(x) = (x - \alpha)(x - \Phi(\alpha))(x - \Phi^2(\alpha)) \cdots (x - \Phi^{d-1}(\alpha))$$

where α, $\Phi(\alpha)$, $\Phi^2(\alpha)$, ..., $\Phi^{d-1}(\alpha)$ are the distinct images of α and d is then the degree of P. As was shown in the course of the proof of Lagrange's theorem and its corollaries, all cosets of G_α have the same cardinality. By this and by the previous proposition,

$$\text{card}\,(G) = d \cdot \text{card}\,(G_\alpha)$$

Likewise, in the special case of the image β of x in K, the stabilizer subgroup is just $\{e\}$, so

$$\text{card}\,(G) = n \cdot 1$$

so $\text{card}\,(G) = n$. This proves that d is a divisor of n.   ♣

Remark: In the discussion of this section we did *not* make any assumptions about the uniqueness of 'the' finite fields $\mathbf{F}_q$ and $\mathbf{F}_{q^N}$. Rather, we just used this notation as an occasional reminder of the number of elements in the finite fields k and K.

Exercises

29.6.01 Let S be a set, and $f : S \to S$ a function from S to itself. Suppose that $f \circ f$ is the identity map on S. Prove carefully that f is both injective and surjective.

29.6.02 Let S be a set, and $f : S \to S$ a function from S to itself. Suppose that

$$f^N = \underbrace{f \circ \cdots \circ f}_{N}$$

is the identity map on S. Prove carefully that f is both injective and surjective.

29.6.03 Let S be a finite set. Prove that if a function $f : S \to S$ is injective, then it is surjective. Prove that if f is surjective then it is injective.

29.7 Counting Irreducibles

Knowing that finite fields have primitive roots enables us to *count* the number of irreducible polynomials of a given degree. We make essential use of facts we've developed about Frobenius maps. Along the way, it is inevitable that we develop more structural properties of finite fields, and these are of interest in their own right.

An integer is usually said to be **square-free** if it is not divisible by the square of any prime number. Recall that the Möbius function μ is defined on positive integers by

$$\mu(n) = \begin{cases} (-1)^t & \text{if } n \text{ is square-free, divisible by exactly } t \text{ primes} \\ 1 & \text{if } n = 1 \\ 0 & \text{if } n \text{ is divisible by the square of some prime} \end{cases}$$

Theorem. The number of irreducible monic polynomials in $\mathbf{F}_q[x]$ of degree n is

$$\frac{1}{n} \sum_{1 \le d \le n,\; d | n} \mu(d)\, q^{n/d}$$

That is, this number is

$$\frac{1}{n} \cdot \left(q^n - \sum_{p_1 | n} q^{n/p_1} + \sum_{p_1, p_2 | n} q^{n/p_1 p_2} - \sum_{p_1, p_2, p_3 | n} q^{n/p_1 p_2 p_3} + \cdots \right)$$

where the sums are over collections of *distinct* prime divisors of n.

We can specialize this formula to some interesting and more memorable special cases:

Corollary. If $n = p_1$ is prime, then there are

$$\frac{q^n - q}{n}$$

irreducible monic polynomials of degree n in $\mathbf{F}_q[x]$.   ♣

Corollary. If $n = p_1 p_2$ is a product of two distinct primes p_1 and p_2, then there are

$$\frac{q^{p_1 p_2} - q^{p_1} - q^{p_2}}{p_1 p_2}$$

irreducible monic polynomials of degree $n = p_1 p_2$ in $\mathbf{F}_q[x]$.   ♣

Corollary. If $n = p_1^e$ is a power of a prime p_1, then there are

$$\frac{q^{p_1^e} - q^{p_1^{e-1}}}{n}$$

irreducible monic polynomials of degree $n = p_1^e$ in $\mathbf{F}_q[x]$.   ♣

Let Q be a fixed irreducible monic polynomial of degree n in $\mathbf{F}_q[x]$. We know that $K = \mathbf{F}_q[x]/Q$ is a field with q^n elements. Let

$$\Phi(\gamma) = \gamma^q$$

be the Frobenius automorphism of K over $k = \mathbf{F}_q$. From the discussion of the Frobenius automorphism above, we know that for any α in K there is a unique monic irreducible polynomial P with coefficients in $k = \mathbf{F}_q$ so that $P(\alpha) = 0$, and in fact

$$P(x) = (x - \alpha)(x - \Phi(\alpha))(x - \Phi^2(\alpha)) \cdots (x - \Phi^{d-1}(\alpha))$$

where d is the number of distinct images of α under repeated applications of the Frobenius automorphism Φ of K over $k = \mathbf{F}_q$. We have a converse:

Proposition. Let P be an irreducible monic polynomial of degree d with d dividing the degree n of irreducible Q. Then $P(x) = 0$ has d distinct roots in $K = k[x]/Q$, so $P(x)$ factors into distinct linear factors in K.

Proof: The quotient ring $L = k[x]/P$ is a field. Let α be the image of x there. We know that $P(\alpha) = 0$, and from discussion of the Frobenius map we know that

$$P(x) = (x - \alpha)(x - \Phi(\alpha))(x - \Phi^2(\alpha)) \cdots (x - \Phi^{d-1}(\alpha))$$

By Lagrange's theorem and its corollaries, we know that $\alpha^{q^d - 1} = 1$, since the order of $L^\times$ is $q^d - 1$. By unique factorization of polynomials with coefficients in a field, this implies that $P(x)$ divides $x^{q^d - 1} - 1$ as polynomials with coefficients in $k = \mathbf{F}_q$.

On the other hand, the existence of a primitive root g in K means exactly that $g^{q^n - 1} = 1$ but no smaller positive exponent makes this true. And, thus, the elements g^1, g^2, g^3, ..., $g^{q^n - 1}$ are all distinct (and nonzero). For any integer t

$$(g^t)^{q^n - 1} = (g^{q^n - 1})^t = 1^t = 1$$

so these $q^n - 1$ elements are all roots of $x^{q^n - 1} - 1 = 0$. On the other hand, this equation is of degree $q^n - 1$, so has at most $q^n - 1$ roots. We conclude that

$$x^{q^n - 1} - 1 = (x - g^1)(x - g^2)(x - g^3) \cdots (x - g^{q^n - 1})$$

in $K[x]$, that is, allowing coefficients in the larger field K.

For d dividing n, we have a basic algebra identity

$$q^n - 1 = (q^d - 1)(q^{(n-d)} + q^{(n-2d)} + q^{(n-3d)} + \cdots + q^d + 1)$$

Thus, $q^d - 1$ divides $q^n - 1$, and by the same basic identity $x^{q^d - 1} - 1$ divides $x^{q^n - 1} - 1$. As $P(x)$ divides $x^{q^d - 1} - 1$, $P(x)$ divides $x^{q^n - 1} - 1$. Thus, $P(x) = 0$ has d roots in K, since $x^{q^n - 1} - 1$ factors into *linear* factors in $K[x]$. ♣

Proof: At last we can count the elements of K by grouping them in d-tuples of roots of elements of irreducible monic polynomials with coefficients in $k = \mathbf{F}_q$, where d runs over positive divisors of n including 1 and n. Let N_d be the number of irreducible monic polynomials of degree d with coefficients in $k = \mathbf{F}_q$. Then this grouping and counting argument gives

$$q^n = \sum_{d|n} d \cdot N_d$$

By *Möbius inversion* we obtain the formula

$$d \cdot N_n = \sum_{d|n} \mu(d)\, q^{n/d}$$

which gives the assertion of the theorem. ♣

29.8 Counting Primitives

Our more refined discussion of finite fields just above also allows us to prove the counting formula for primitive polynomials, as a corollary of the characterization of primitive polynomials as irreducible factors of cyclotomic polynomials.

Fix a power q of a prime number, and let $k = \mathbf{F}_q$ be a finite field with q elements. Recall that a polynomial Q with coefficients in k of degree n is *primitive* if

$$x^{q^n - 1} = 1 \bmod Q(x)$$

and no smaller positive integer will do in place of this n. For brevity, let

$$N = q^n - 1$$

Theorem. A primitive polynomial Q of degree n in $\mathbf{F}_q[x]$ is an irreducible factor of the $(q^n - 1)$th cyclotomic polynomial. Conversely, every irreducible factor of the $(q^n - 1)$th cyclotomic polynomial is of degree n, and is primitive.

Let φ be Euler's phi-function. Recall that the degree of the Nth cyclotomic polynomial φ_N is $\varphi(N)$. Again, the counting corollary of the latter theorem is

Corollary. There are $\varphi(q^n - 1)/n$ primitive polynomials of degree n in the polynomial ring $\mathbf{F}_q[x]$.

Proof: By the theorem, every such primitive polynomial is an irreducible factor of the cyclotomic polynomial φ_N, where $N = q^n - 1$. And every irreducible factor of φ_N is primitive of degree n. Because $q^n - 1$ is relatively prime to the *characteristic* p of the fields in question, φ_N has no repeated factors, so no irreducible factor appears than once. Since the degree of a product is the sum of the degrees, we have   more

$$\text{degree } \varphi_N = (\text{number of primitives of degree } n) \cdot n$$

from which we obtain the formula of the corollary.   ♣

Proof: Without loss of generality, we only consider the case $n > 1$, since the linear case can be treated separately and easily. In particular, this excludes the case that an irreducible polynomial is divisible by x.

On one hand, suppose that Q divides the $(q^n - 1)$th cyclotomic polynomial φ_N and the degree of Q is n. Since φ_N divides $x^{q^n - 1} - 1$, certainly

$$x^{q^n - 1} = 1 \bmod Q(x)$$

If any smaller positive integer t were to have the property that

$$x^t = 1 \bmod Q(x)$$

then $Q(x)$ would divide $x^N - 1$. But from the discussion of cyclotomic polynomials, since p and $q^n - 1$ are relatively prime, φ_N and $x^t - 1$ have no common factor for $t < q^n - 1$. Thus, we see that the smallest power of x which is 1 modulo $Q(x)$ is $q^n - 1$, so Q is primitive of degree n.

On the other hand, suppose that Q is primitive of degree n. The condition

$$x^{q^n-1} = 1 \bmod Q(x)$$

is by definition equivalent to asserting that $Q(x)$ is a divisor of $x^{q^n-1} - 1$. Likewise, the condition that no smaller power of x is 1 modulo Q asserts that $Q(x)$ does *not* divide $x^N - 1$ for any smaller N. From the discussion of cyclotomic polynomials, using unique factorization, if we remove from $x^{q^n-1} - 1$ any factors that it has in common with $x^N - 1$ for $N < q^n - 1$, then what remains is the cyclotomic polynomial φ_N. Thus, primitive Q of degree n divides the $(q^n - 1)$th cyclotomic polynomial φ_N.

Now we will prove that all the irreducible factors of φ_N have degree n. Let Q be any irreducible factor of φ_N. Then $L = \mathbf{F}_q[x]/Q$ is a field, and the image α of x is of order $N = q^n - 1$ in the multiplicative group $L^\times$, by construction of the cyclotomic polynomial φ_N. Therefore, if d is the degree of Q, by Lagrange's theorem and its corollaries,

$$q^n - 1 \ \text{ divides } \ q^d - 1$$

In particular, $d \geq n$. That is, on one hand, any irreducible factor of φ_N has degree at least n. On the other hand, let Φ be the Frobenius map

$$\Phi(\beta) = \beta^q$$

of L over $\mathbf{F}_q$. The statement

$$x^{q^n-1} = 1 \bmod Q$$

is

$$\alpha^{q^n-1} = 1$$

which is equivalent to

$$\alpha^{q^n} = \alpha$$

which is

$$\Phi^n(\alpha) = \alpha$$

From the discussion of the Frobenius automorphism, this implies that the unique monic irreducible polynomial $f(x)$ in $\mathbf{F}_q[x]$ so that $f(\alpha) = 0$ is of degree at most n. At the same time, in the construction of finite fields we saw that $Q(\alpha) = 0$ as well. As a corollary of the discussion of the Frobenius automorphism, there is exactly *one* monic irreducible polynomial f so that $f(\alpha) = 0$, so $Q = f$. Since f has degree at most n, the degree of Q is at most n. Thus, all the irreducible factors of φ_N are of degree n, where $N = q^n - 1$.

Finally, we observe that primitive polynomials are necessarily irreducible. Indeed, a primitive polynomial Q of degree n in $\mathbf{F}_q[x]$ divides the cyclotomic polynomial φ_N with $N = q^n - 1$. Just above we proved that all the irreducible factors of φ_N are of degree n, so by unique factorization Q has no alternative but to be irreducible.   ♣

Appendices

Appendix 1: Sets and Functions

Here we review some relatively elementary but very important terminology and concepts about *sets* and *functions*, in a slightly abstract setting. We use the word **map** as a synonym for 'function', as is very often done.

Naively, a **set** is supposed to be a collection of 'things' described by 'listing' them or prescribing them by a 'rule'. Please note that this is *not* a terribly precise description, but it will be adequate for most of our purposes. We can also say that a **set** is an *unordered list* of *different* things.

There are standard symbols for some often-used sets:

$$
\begin{aligned}
\phi &= \{\} = \text{null set} = \text{set with no elements} \\
\mathbf{Z} &= \text{the integers} \\
\mathbf{Q} &= \text{the rational numbers} \\
\mathbf{R} &= \text{the real numbers} \\
\mathbf{C} &= \text{the complex numbers}
\end{aligned}
$$

484

A set described by a *list* is something like

$$S = \{1, 2, 3, 4, 5, 6, 7, 8\}$$

which is the set of integers bigger than 0 and less than 9. This set can also be described by a *rule* by

$$S = \{1, 2, 3, 4, 5, 6, 7, 8\} = \{x : x \text{ is an integer and } 1 \leq x \leq 8\}$$

This follows the general format and notation

$$\{x : \ x \text{ has some property}\}$$

If x is in a set S, then write $x \in S$ or $S \ni x$, and say that x is an *element* of S. Thus, a set is the collection of all its elements (although this remark only explains the *language*). It is worth noting that the *ordering* of a listing has no effect on a set, and if in the listing of elements of a set an element is *repeated*, this has no effect. For example,
$$\{1, 2, 3\} = \{1, 1, 2, 3\} = \{3, 2, 1\} = \{1, 3, 2, 1\}$$

A **subset** T of a set S is a set all of whose elements are elements of S. This is written $T \subset S$ or $S \supset T$. So always $S \subset S$ and $\phi \subset S$. If $T \subset S$ and $T \neq \phi$ and $T \neq S$, then T is a **proper** subset of S. Note that the empty set is a subset of *every* set. For a subset T of a set S, the **complement** of T (inside S) is

$$T^c = S - T = \{s \in S : s \notin T\}$$

Sets can also be elements of other sets. For example, $\{\mathbf{Q}, \mathbf{Z}, \mathbf{R}, \mathbf{C}\}$ is the set with 4 elements, each of which is a familiar set of numbers. Or, one can check that

$$\{\{1, 2\}, \{1, 3\}, \{2, 3\}\}$$

is the set of two-element subsets of $\{1, 2, 3\}$.

The **intersection** of two sets A, B is the collection of all elements which lie in *both* sets, and is denoted $A \cap B$. Two sets are **disjoint** if their intersection is ϕ. If the intersection is *not* empty, then we may say that the two sets **meet**. The **union** of two sets A, B is the collection of all elements which lie in *one or the other* of the two sets, and is denoted $A \cup B$.

Note that, for example, $1 \neq \{1\}$, and $\{\{1\}\} \neq \{1\}$. That is, the *set* $\{a\}$ with sole element a is *not* the same thing as the item a itself.

An **ordered pair** (x, y) is just that, a list of two things in which there is a *first* thing, here x, and a *second* thing, here y. Two ordered pairs (x, y) and (x', y') are **equal** if and only if $x = x'$ and $y = y'$.

The **(cartesian) product** of two sets A, B is the set of **ordered pairs** (a, b) where $a \in A$ and $b \in B$. It is denoted $A \times B$. Thus, the set $\{a, b\}$ might be thought of as an *unordered* pair, since, after all, order doesn't matter in the listing of elements of a set: by definition $\{a, b\} = \{b, a\}$. But for *ordered* pairs $(a, b) \neq (b, a)$ unless by chance $a = b$.

In case $A = B$, the cartesian power $A \times B$ is often denoted A^2. More generally, for a fixed positive integer n, the nth **cartesian power** A^n of a set is the set of ordered n-tuples $(a_1, a_2, \ldots, a_n)$ of elements a_i of A.

Some very important examples of cartesian powers are those of $\mathbf{R}$ or $\mathbf{Q}$ or $\mathbf{C}$, which arise in other contexts as well: for example, $\mathbf{R}^2$ is the collection of ordered pairs of real numbers, which we use to describe points in the plane. And $\mathbf{R}^3$ is the collection of ordered triples of real numbers, which we use to describe points in three-space.

The **power set** of a set S is the *set of subsets* of S. This is sometimes denoted by $\mathcal{P}S$. Thus,

$$\mathcal{P}\phi = \{\phi\}$$

$$\mathcal{P}\{1, 2\} = \{\phi, \{1\}, \{2\}, \{1, 2\}\}$$

Intuitively, a **function** f from one set A to another set B is supposed to be a 'rule' which assigns to each element $a \in A$ an element $b = f(a) \in B$. This is written as

$$f : A \to B$$

although the latter notation gives no information about the nature of f in any detail.

More rigorously, but less intuitively, we can define a 'function' by telling its *graph*: the formal definition is that a function $f : A \to B$ is a *subset* of the product $A \times B$ with the property that for every $a \in A$ there is a unique $b \in B$ so that $(a, b) \in f$. Then we would write $f(a) = b$.

This formal definition is worth noting, at least because it should make clear that there is absolutely no requirement that a function be described by any recognizable or simple 'formula'.

As a silly example of the formal definition of function, let $f : \{1, 2\} \to \{2, 4\}$ be the function 'multiply-by-two', so that $f(1) = 2$ and $f(2) = 4$. Then the 'official' definition would say that really f is the subset of the product set $\{1, 2\} \times \{2, 4\}$ consisting of the ordered pairs $(1, 2), (2, 4)$. That is, formally the function f is the *set*

$$f = \{(1, 2), (2, 4)\}$$

Of course, most often the description of a function is given in a manner more intuitive than bluntly giving its graph.

A function $f : A \to B$ is **surjective** (or **onto**) if for every $b \in B$ there is $a \in A$ so that $f(a) = b$. A function $f : A \to B$ is **injective** (or **one-to-one**) if $f(a) = f(a')$ implies $a = a'$. That is, f is *injective* if for every $b \in B$ there is *at most one* $a \in A$ so that $f(a) = b$. A map is a **bijection** if it is both injective and surjective.

The number of elements in a set is its **cardinality**. It is important to realize that two sets A and B have the same number of elements, so have the same cardinality, if and only if there is a *bijection* between them. That is, *if* they have the same number of elements, then those elements can be paired up in *some* manner. Conversely, if the elements can be paired up, then the two sets have the same number of elements.

Remark: The 'counting' definition of cardinality is completely acceptable for *finite* sets but is too naive in talking about *infinite* sets. In general, if we're trying to be very careful about 'counting' infinite sets, we will try to define cardinality first (in terms of 'number'), but rather define the property **have-the-same-cardinality** first: two sets have-the-same-cardinality if there is a *bijection* between them. This ploy of defining having-the-same-cardinality without defining 'cardinality' itself directly is a trick so that we don't have to actually *count* two sets to see whether they have the same number of elements. This sort of thing is interesting in itself, but is not essential for us here.

Since we *can* count the elements in a *finite* set in a traditional way, it is clear that *a finite set has no bijection to a proper subset of itself*. After all, a proper subset has *fewer elements*.

By contrast, for *infinite* sets it is easily possible that *proper* subsets have bijections to the whole set. For example, the set A of *all* natural numbers and the set E of *even* natural numbers have a bijection between them given by

$$n \to 2n$$

But certainly E is a *proper* subset of A! Even more striking examples can be arranged. In the end, we take as *definition* that a set is **infinite** if it has a bijection to a proper subset of itself.

Let $f : A \to B$ be a function from a set A to a set B, and let $g : B \to C$ be a function from the set B to a set C. The **composite function** $g \circ f$ is defined to be

$$(g \circ f)(a) = g(f(a))$$

for $a \in A$.

The **identity function** on a non-empty set S is the function $f : S \to S$ so that $f(a) = a$ for all $a \in A$. Often the identity function on a set S is denoted by id_S.

Let $f : A \to B$ be a function from a set A to a set B. An **inverse function** $g : B \to A$ for f (if such g exists at all) is a function so that $(f \circ g)(b) = b$ for all $b \in B$, and also $(g \circ f)(a) = a$ for all $a \in A$. That is, the inverse function (if it exists) has the two properties

$$f \circ g = \mathrm{id}_B, \qquad g \circ f = \mathrm{id}_A$$

An inverse function to f, if it exists at all, is usually denoted f^{-1}. (This is *not* at all the same as $1/f$!)

Proposition. A function $f : A \to B$ from a set A to a set B has an inverse if and only if f is a bijection. In that case, the inverse is unique (that is, there is only *one* inverse function).

Proof: We define a function $g : B \to A$ as follows. Given $b \in B$, let $a \in A$ be an element so that $f(a) = b$. Then define $g(b) = a$. Do this for each $b \in B$ to define g. Note that we use the *surjectivity* to know that there *exists* an a for each b, and the *injectivity* to be sure of its *uniqueness*.

To check that $g \circ f = \mathrm{id}_A$, compute: first, for any $a \in A$, $f(a) \in B$. Then $g(f(a))$ is, by definition, an element $a' \in A$ so that $f(a') = f(a)$. Since f is injective, it must be that $a' = a$. To check that $f \circ g = \mathbf{1}$, take $b \in B$ and compute: by definition of g, $g(b)$ is an element of A so that $f(g(b)) = b$. But that is (after all) just what we want.   ♣

Exercises

A.1.01 How many elements are in the set
$\{1, 2, 2, 3, 3, 4, 5\}$? How many in the set $\{1, 2, \{2\}, 3, \{3\}, 4, 5\}$? In $\{1, 2, \{2, 3\}, 3, 4, 5\}$?

A.1.02 Let $A = \{1, 2, 3, 4, 5\}$ and $B = \{3, 4, 5, 6, 7\}$. List (without repetition) the elements of the sets $A \cup B$, $A \cap B$, and of $\{x \in A : x \notin B\}$.

A.1.03 List all the elements of the *power set* (set of subsets) of $\{1, 2, 3\}$.

A.1.04 Let $A = \{1, 2, 3\}$ and $B = \{2, 3\}$. List (without repetition) all the elements of the *cartesian product* set $A \times B$.

A.1.05 How many functions are there from the set $\{1, 2, 3\}$ to the set $\{2, 3, 4, 5\}$?

A.1.06 How many injective functions are there from $\{1, 2, 3\}$ to $\{1, 2, 3, 4\}$?

A.1.07 How many surjective functions are there from $\{1, 2, 3, 4\}$ to $\{1, 2, 3\}$?

A.1.08 Show that if $f : A \to B$ and $g : B \to C$ are functions with inverses, then $g \circ f$ has an inverse, and this inverse is $f^{-1} \circ g^{-1}$.

A.1.09 Show that for a surjective function $f : A \to B$ there is a **right inverse** g, meaning a function $g : B \to A$ so that $f \circ g = \mathrm{id}_B$ (but not necessarily $g \circ f = \mathrm{id}_A$).

A.1.10 Show that for an injective function $f : A \to B$ there is a **left inverse** g, meaning a function $g : B \to A$ so that $g \circ f = \mathrm{id}_A$ (but not necessarily $f \circ g = \mathrm{id}_B$).

A.1.11 Give a *bijection* from the collection $2\mathbf{Z}$ of *even* integers to the collection $\mathbf{Z}$ of *all* integers.

A.1.12 (*) Give a *bijection* from the collection of *all* integers to the collection of *non-negative* integers.

A.1.13 (**) Give a *bijection* from the collection of all positive integers to the collection of all rational numbers.

A.1.14 (**) This illustrates a hazard in a too-naive notion of 'rule' for forming a set. Let S be the set of all sets which are not an element of themselves. That is, let

$$S = \{\text{sets } x : x \notin x\}$$

Is $S \in S$ or is $S \notin S$? (*Hint:* Assuming either that S is or isn't an element of itself leads to a contradiction. What's going on?)

Appendix 2: Searching, Sorting

Efficiency in basic sorting and searching algorithms is a fundamental building block in many other algorithms. We'll look at some generically slower sorting algorithms (*insertion sort*, *selection sort*, and *bubble sort*) and then faster algorithms that achieve better performance on generic data (*merge sort* and *quick sort*). This brief discussion certainly does not do justice to all the possibilities for sorting, but it should give some idea about possibilities for less naive algorithms.

In particular, to be sure that various computational algorithms run as fast as claimed, it is necessary to know

- A list of length n can be sorted using $O(n)$ comparisons.

- A specified element can be found in an an already-sorted list of length n (or certified not to appear in the list) using $O(\log n)$ comparisons.

Linear Search. Suppose that we have a list $L = (t_1, \ldots, t_n)$ of integers, for example. The problem we address is, *given another integer t, find $t_i \in L$ so that $t = t_i$, or ascertain that no such t_i exists.* The fairly obvious naive approach is to compare t to t_1, then to t_2, then to t_3, continuing until either a match is found or until we reach the end of the list. On average this would take $n/2$ comparisons. If we assume nothing whatsoever about the state of the list, in general we can do no better than this. This is **linear searching**.

Binary search. If the list $L = (s_1, \ldots, s_n)$ is *sorted* to begin with, say in ascending order, we can speed up enormously: given another element t, we can find $t_i \in L$ so that $t = t_i$, or ascertain that no such t_i exists, using at most

$$\text{ceiling}(\log_2 n)$$

comparisons of t with elements in the list. This is accomplished by a *divide-and-conquer* strategy that may be familiar from guessing games. For simplicity we assume that $n = 2^k$ for an integer k. (Or we can simply pad the list with some meaningless elements at the end to make its length a power of 2.) First compare t to $t_{n/2}$. If $t \leq t_{n/2}$, then we will continue our search in the length-$\frac{n}{2}$ list $(s_1, \ldots, s_{n/2})$, and if $t > t_{n/2}$, then we will continue our search in the length-$\frac{n}{2}$ list $(s_{\frac{n}{2}+1}, \ldots, s_n)$. This was one comparison. By induction on the length, either one of these half-sized searches will take at most

$$\log_2 \frac{n}{2} = (\log_2 n) - 1$$

(To get the induction started, note that the case that the list is length one does indeed require no comparisons at all.) Thus, by induction, recursively searching on lists of half the size, we need at most $\log_2 n$ comparisons. If n is not a power of two then there are minor inefficiencies, so it will take

$$\text{ceiling}(\log_2 n)$$

in general. This is **binary search**.

Remark: The speedup possible for binary search in a *sorted* list versus linear search in an unsorted list makes clear the importance of fast algorithms to sort lists.

Maxima and minima. To find the minimum (or maximum) integer in an unordered list $(t_1, \ldots, t_n)$ of integers t_i, $n - 1$ comparisons are necessary. One way to find the minimum in $n - 1$ comparions is as follows. Initially take $b = t_1$ as the candidate for the minimum. Compare $b = t_1$ to t_2. If $t_2 < t_1$, take $b = t_2$ as the new candidate for minimum, otherwise leave $b = t_1$ as candidate. Compare b to t_3. If $t_3 < b$, take $b = t_3$ as new candidate for minimum, otherwise leave b unchanged. Continue until a comparison has been made with all t_i. At that time the value of b will be the minimum.

Insertion sort is the type of sorting often done with hands of cards (although opponents can gain information from watching the sorting procedure). Insertion sort is slow with generic data. Given an unsorted list $L = (t_1, \ldots, t_n)$, a new list $M = (s_1, \ldots, s_n)$ is gradually built, as follows. Take s_1 to be the minimum of the list L. Take s_2 to be the minimum of the list L after s_1 is removed. Take s_3 to be the minimum of the list L after s_1 and s_2 are removed. Continue, so that s_{n-1} is the minimum of the list L after s_1, $\ldots$, s_{n-2} are removed. And then s_n is the last remaining element. This takes

$$(n - 1) + (n - 2) + \cdots + 3 + 2 + 1 = n(n-1)/2 = O(n^2)$$

comparisons.

Remark: Notice that in insertion sort we repeatedly discard the information acquired by the comparisons. It is not entirely clear how to make use of this information, but the repeated discard of it might lead one to suspect that there are inefficiencies that could be corrected. The same type of inefficiency occurs in selection sort. For example, *heapsort* is a smarter version of selection sort that does use the extra information by creating and maintaining a *heap* structure for the elements.

Selection sort is a little different from insertion sort, but takes about the same amount of runtime. To sort a list

$$L = (t_1, t_2, \ldots, t_n)$$

of positive integers by *size* in ascending order, *selection sort* proceeds as follows. First, find the smallest element t_{i_1} in the list, move it to the beginning of the list, moving other elements forward as necessary to make room. Second, find the second-smallest element t_{i_2}, move it to the second position, moving other elements forward as necessary to make room. Third, find the third-smallest element t_{i_3}, put it in the third position, and move other elements forward as necessary to make room. Continue. This requires $O(n^2)$ comparisons.

Bubble sort is a cleverer approach to sorting: repeatedly interchange adjacent elements that are out of order, until the whole list is ordered. This is slow for generic data, again requiring $O(n^2)$ operations in the worst-case scenario to sort a list of length n. On the other hand, if the data is 'almost' sorted to begin with, bubble sort can finish the sorting quickly. Thus, in more sophisticated sorting algorithms (*hybrid sorts*) a bubble sort is sometimes used as a component.

Merge sort is much faster with large generic data than the *sorts* above, running in $O(n \log n)$ time rather than $O(n^2)$. It uses a *divide and conquer* strategy. Suppose for simplicity that the list of things to be sorted has $n = 2^\ell$ elements. (If not, pad it with null elements until its number of elements is a power of 2.) The merge sort algorithm has a recursive definition: break the list into two parts, merge sort each half, and then merge them. The merge operation should take two *sorted* lists of size 2^{k-1} and combine them into a single sorted list of size $n = 2^k$. We can accomplish the merging of two sorted lists $L_1 = (s_1, \ldots s_a)$ and $L_2 = (t_1, \ldots, t_b)$ using at most

$$a + b - 1 = \text{length } L_1 \ + \text{length } L_1 \ - 1$$

comparisons, as follows. First, if $s_1 < t_1$, take s_1 as the first element of the merged list, removing it from L_1; otherwise, take t_1 as the first element of the merged list, removing it from L_2. In either case, the sum of the lengths of the *new* L_1 and L_2 is reduced by one, and one comparison has been made. By induction on the quantity

$$a + b = \text{length } L_1 \ + \text{length } L_1$$

this proves that the merging can be accomplished with *at most* $a+b-1$ comparisons.

After repeated subdivisions, merge sort is faced with the problem of ordering n separate rather degenerate lists consisting of single elements. Each of these requires no comparisons at all. Then merge sort merges $n/2$ pairs of single-element lists. Each such merge takes at most $1 + 1 - 1 = 1$ comparisons, so $(n/2) \cdot (1 + 1 - 1)$ comparisons are used. Then $n/4$ pairs of 2-element lists must be merged, requiring at most $(n/4) \cdot (2 + 2 - 1)$ comparisons. To simplify things let's ignore all those '-1's, since we can certainly say that to merge two sorted lists of lengths a and b at most $a + b$ comparisons are needed. Then, altogether, merge sort will make at most

$$\frac{n}{2} \cdot 2 + \frac{n}{4} \cdot 4 + \frac{n}{8} \cdot 8 + \frac{n}{8} \cdot 8 + \cdots + 8 \cdot \frac{n}{8} + 4 \cdot \frac{n}{4} + 2 \cdot \frac{n}{2}$$

$$\leq n \cdot \log_2 n$$

This is the desired estimate for merge sort. For large n this is much smaller than the roughly $n^2/2$ comparisons needed for the more naive sorting algorithms with generic data.

Remark: A bad feature of merge sort is that the simple implementation described roughly above requires extra memory, in an amount equal to the size of the original list.

Remark: Note that we're ignoring the cost of moving things around in all the previous algorithms. To a certain extent that's justified with the specific algorithms we've looked at, since the comparisons are a significant fraction of the total workload.

Quick sort is another divide-and-conquer sorting algorithm. We'll first describe its naive form, which has bad worst-case performance, and then we'll modify it to avoid disastrous worst-case behavior and take advantage of its excellent average-case behavior. It then runs as fast as merge sort, but does not use much memory if implemented a bit cleverly. These modified forms of quick sort are the 'sort' utilities in Unix/Linux, in Perl's *sort* built-in, and in C's *qsort*. Python's *sort* calls C's *qsort*. It is probabilistic in nature, unlike the other algorithms.

Given a list L to be sorted, quick sort first 'guesses' the midpoint of the whole list. The guessed value is called the *pivot*. It then partitions the list into two parts, the elements below the pivot, and the elements above the pivot. Each of these is then quick-sorted itself. Thus, this simplest version of the algorithm calls itself recursively, just as the simple merge sort does.

The simplest choice for pivot element is the last (or first) element in the list. A randomly chosen element is also a reasonable choice, although it costs something to generate a random number. The presumption is that the two parts into which the list is partitioned are roughly the same size. If so, then the runtime analysis is roughly the same as that of merge sort, $O(n \log n)$. However, if the pivots are repeatedly chosen badly, so that one half of the partition is much smaller than the other, the runtime deteriorates to $O(n^2)$.

A patch to the bad-pivot problem is the **median of three** trick in choosing a pivot. The median of three approach is to pick *three* 'random' elements in the list, and choose the middle value as the pivot. A probability calculation shows that this way of choosing pivots is more likely to product same-sized partitions, thus statistically ensuring the better runtime.

Remark: When programming quick sort and merge sort, it is possible to avoid having the operating system realize that the algorithm is calling itself recursively by explicitly managing the recursion, rather than having the operating system do it. This may speed things up a little, and avoids warnings often generated when recursions are very deep.

Appendix 3: Vectors

First, recall that in analytic geometry an ordered pair of real numbers (x, y) is often used to refer to a point in the plane, while an ordered triple (x, y, z) refers to a point in three-space. While we can just as easily write down ordered 7-tuples, we cannot as easily see how these might refer to any sort of 7-dimensional things. But this is not really an issue.

At the same time, the first version of **vector** one may see is that an n-dimensional vector is an ordered n-tuple (of real or complex numbers)

$$v = (v_1, \ldots, v_n)$$

How does one distinguish between 'vector' and 'point'? It's a nonissue, really: the use of a vector to refer to a point is an example of an *interpretation* of the notion of vector in a physical context.

Vectors x, y of the same dimension have a **vector addition**

$$\begin{aligned} x + y &= (x_1, \ldots, x_n) + (y_1, \ldots, y_n) \\ &= (x_1 + y_1, \ x_2 + y_2, \ \ldots, \ x_n + y_n) \end{aligned}$$

In this context, a **scalar** is simply a *number*. Note that the same $+$ sign is used for vector addition as for scalar addition, and that no overt reference is made to the dimension of the vectors. (There is no obligation to put arrows over variables that refer to vectors. You can if you want, though.) The n-dimensional **zero vector** is

$$0 = (0, 0, \ldots, 0)$$

(Yes, the same '0' is used for scalar as for vector, and for all dimensions. *Context* should make clear which is meant.)

There is **scalar multiplication** of vectors by scalars: for scalar c and vector $x = (x_1, \ldots, x_n)$,

$$c\,x = c\,(x_1, x_2, \ldots, x_n) = (cx_1, \ cx_2, \ \ldots, \ cx_n)$$

And we write

$$-x = (-x_1, -x_2, \ldots, -x_n)$$

and for $y = (y_1, \ldots, y_n)$

$$x - y = (x_1 - y_1, x_2 - y_2, \ldots, x_n - y_n)$$

From the Pythagorean theorem we get the distance formula in two dimensions:

$$\text{distance from } (x_1, x_2) \text{ to } (y_1, y_2) = \sqrt{(x_1 - y_1)^2 + (x_2 - y_2)^2}$$

Though we won't draw the picture here, this generalizes to a 3-dimensional formula as well:

$$\text{distance from } (x_1, x_2, x_3) \text{ to } (y_1, y_2, y_3) = \sqrt{(x_1 - y_1)^2 + (x_2 - y_2)^2 + (x_3 - y_3)^2}$$

In general, for an n-dimensional vector $x = (x_1, \ldots, x_n)$ the **norm** or **length** of x is

$$|x| = \sqrt{x_1^2 + x_2^2 + \cdots + x_n^2}$$

and the distance from (the point represented by) an n-vector $x = (x_1, \ldots, x_n)$ to an another (point represented by) n-vector $y = (y_1, \ldots, y_n)$ is

$$|x - y| = \sqrt{(x_1 - y_1)^2 + (x_2 - y_2)^2 + \cdots + (x_n - y_n)^2}$$

As a special case, $|x| = |x - 0|$, so the norm of x is the same as the distance from the point (designated by) x to 0.

The **inner product** or **scalar product** or **dot product** of two n-vectors $x = (x_1, \ldots, x_n)$ and $y = (y_1, \ldots, y_n)$ is

$$x_1 y_1 + x_2 y_2 + x_3 y_3 + \cdots + x_n y_n = x \cdot y = \langle x, y \rangle$$

Note that the values of the dot product are *scalars*, not *vectors*.

Proposition. Let x, y, and z be n-dimensional vectors, and c a scalar.

- $c(x + y) = cx + cy$
- $x + (y + z) = (x + y) + z$
- $x \cdot y = y \cdot x$
- $x \cdot (y + z) = x \cdot y + x \cdot z$ and $(y + z) \cdot x = y \cdot x + z \cdot x$
- $(cx) \cdot y = c(x \cdot y)$
- $|x| = \sqrt{x \cdot x}$

It may be a little surprising that the dot product can be expressed in terms of the norm (that is, in terms of *distance*):

Proposition. *(polarization identity)* For two n-vectors x and y,

$$\langle x, y \rangle = \frac{1}{4} \left(|x + y|^2 - |x - y|^2 \right)$$

Proof: If one resists the temptation to expand everything in terms of the components of the vectors, this is not hard. Use $|v|^2 = \langle v, v \rangle$ for vectors v, the distributive law for dot products, and the commutativity $x \cdot y = y \cdot x$:

$$|x + y|^2 - |x - y|^2 = \langle x + y, x + y \rangle - \langle x - y, x - y \rangle$$

$$= \langle x, x \rangle + \langle x, y \rangle + \langle y, x \rangle + \langle y, y \rangle - \langle x, x \rangle + \langle x, y \rangle + \langle y, x \rangle - \langle y, y \rangle$$

$$= 2\langle x, y \rangle + 2\langle y, x \rangle = 4\langle x, y \rangle$$

This is the result.   ♣

The least obvious and most useful property of the scalar/dot product is the following:

Theorem. Let x and y be two n-dimensional vectors, neither of which is 0. Let S_x be the line segment from the origin to (the point represented by) x, and let S_y be the line segment from the origin to (the point represented by) y. Let θ be the angle (at the origin) between S_x and S_y. Then

$$\cos \theta = \frac{\langle x, y \rangle}{|x| \, |y|}$$

Proof: We can reduce this to a 2-dimensional problem about triangles, as follows. Use the fact (similar to the polarization identity)

$$\langle x, y \rangle = \frac{1}{2} \left(|x|^2 + |y|^2 - |x - y|^2 \right)$$

Thus, the statement of the theorem is that

$$\cos \theta = \frac{|x|^2 + |y|^2 - |x - y|^2}{2 |x| |y|}$$

The right-hand side is an expression involving only the *distances* between x, y, and 0.

Certainly the three points 0, x, and y all lie in a common *plane*, no matter what the dimension of the larger space they're sitting in. And these three points are the vertices of a triangle T lying in that plane. The angle θ is the interior angle of T at the vertex 0. Thus, if the identity

$$\cos \theta = \frac{|x|^2 + |y|^2 - |x - y|^2}{2 |x| |y|}$$

holds for 2-dimensional vectors, then it holds for arbitrary dimensions. The 2-dimensional case is left as an exercise.   ♣

Theorem.   *(Cauchy–Schwarz–Bunyakowsky inequality)*   Let x and y be two N-dimensional vectors. Then

$$\langle x, y \rangle \le |x| |y|$$

with equality holding only if one of the vectors is a multiple of the other.

Proof: This is nearly a consequence of the formula for the cosine of the angle between two vectors, but we give a different proof that does not depend upon any presumptions about 'geometry'.

Let t be a scalar, and consider the function

$$f(t) = |x + ty|^2 = |x|^2 + 2t \langle x, y \rangle + t^2 |y|^2$$

(where the right-hand side is the expansion of $|x+ty|^2$ using properties from above). Certainly the norm of a vector is non-negative (being the sum of squares of real numbers) and is zero only if the vector is the zero vector. Thus, $f(t)$ is nonzero for all values of t, unless x is a multiple of y.

To continue, we may as well suppose that y is not the zero vector, or the assertion of the theorem is silly since both sides are 0. Then let's minimize $f(t)$: take its derivative with respect to t, set it equal to 0, and solve for t:

$$0 = 2\langle x, y \rangle + 2t|y|^2$$

Solving gives

$$t = \frac{-\langle x, y \rangle}{|y|^2}$$

(For all we know, this critical point might accidentally be giving a *maximum* instead of a minimum, but in fact we aren't presuming anything about that!) Certainly the value of f at this point is non-negative, so substitute this value into the expression and simplify a little to obtain

$$0 \leq f(\frac{-\langle x, y \rangle}{|y|^2}) = |x|^2 - \frac{\langle x, y \rangle^2}{|y|^2}$$

This rearranges to $\langle x, y \rangle^2 \leq |x|^2 |y|^2$, as desired. ♣

Exercises

A.3.01 Prove that for three vectors x, y, z of the same size, $x \cdot (y + z) = x \cdot y + x \cdot z$.

A.3.02 Prove that $|cx| = |c| |x|$ for scalar c and vector x.

A.3.03 Prove that

$$|x - y|^2 = |x|^2 - 2\langle x, y \rangle + |y|^2$$

A.3.04 Prove that

$$\langle x, y \rangle = \frac{1}{2} \left(|x|^2 + |y|^2 - |x - y|^2 \right)$$

A.3.05 Recall that a **rhombus** is a 'diamond-shaped' figure; that is, it is a polygon in the plane with four sides all of the same length, and so that opposite sides are parallel. Prove (by vector geometry!?) that the sum of the squares of the diagonals is equal to the circumference.

A.3.06 Prove that in two dimensions, for a triangle with vertices A, B, and C, the cosine of the angle θ at vertex C is

$$\cos \theta = \frac{|AC|^2 + |BC|^2 - |AB|^2}{2 |AC| |BC|}$$

where $|PQ|$ is the length of the line segment with endpoints P and Q. (This is a version of the so-called **law of cosines**.)

A.3.07 Prove that

$$(1 + 2 + 3 + \cdots + n)^2 \leq n \cdot (1^2 + 2^2 + \cdots + n^2)$$

Appendix 4: Matrices

An m-by-n **matrix** is just an m-by-n block of numbers

$$x = \begin{pmatrix} x_{11} & x_{12} & x_{13} & \cdots & x_{1n} \\ x_{21} & x_{22} & x_{23} & \cdots & x_{2n} \\ x_{31} & x_{32} & x_{33} & \cdots & x_{3n} \\ & & \cdots & & \\ x_{m1} & x_{m2} & x_{m3} & \cdots & x_{mn} \end{pmatrix}$$

The entry in the ith row and jth column is called the (i, j)th *entry*. If x is the whole matrix, often its (i, j)th entry is denoted by subscripts

$$x_{ij} = (i, j)\text{th entry of the matrix } x$$

Very often an n-by-1 matrix is called a **column vector** of size n, and a 1-by-n matrix is called a **row vector** of size n.

The **matrix addition** is the straightforward entry-by-entry addition *of two matrices of the same size*:

$$\begin{pmatrix} x_{11} & x_{12} & x_{13} & \cdots & x_{1n} \\ x_{21} & x_{22} & x_{23} & \cdots & x_{2n} \\ x_{31} & x_{32} & x_{33} & \cdots & x_{3n} \\ & & \cdots & & \\ x_{m1} & x_{m2} & x_{m3} & \cdots & x_{mn} \end{pmatrix} + \begin{pmatrix} y_{11} & y_{12} & y_{13} & \cdots & y_{1n} \\ y_{21} & y_{22} & y_{23} & \cdots & y_{2n} \\ y_{31} & y_{32} & y_{33} & \cdots & y_{3n} \\ & & \cdots & & \\ y_{m1} & y_{m2} & y_{m3} & \cdots & y_{mn} \end{pmatrix}$$

$$= \begin{pmatrix} x_{11} + y_{11} & x_{12} + y_{12} & x_{13} + y_{13} & \cdots & x_{1n} + y_{1n} \\ x_{21} + y_{21} & x_{22} + y_{22} & x_{23} + y_{23} & \cdots & x_{2n} + y_{2n} \\ x_{31} + y_{31} & x_{32} + y_{32} & x_{33} + y_{33} & \cdots & x_{3n} + y_{3n} \\ & & \cdots & & \\ x_{m1} + y_{m1} & x_{m2} + y_{m2} & x_{m3} + y_{m3} & \cdots & x_{mn} + y_{mn} \end{pmatrix}$$

The **additive identity** or **zero matrix** $0_{m,n}$ of size m-by-n is the m-by-n matrix with all entries 0. It has the obvious property that if it is added to any other matrix x of that same shape we just get

$$x + 0_{m,n} = x = 0_{m,n} + x$$

There is also **matrix multiplication**, whose meaning and computation is more complicated: for a k-by-m matrix x and an m-by-n matrix y the (i, j)th entry of the product xy depends only upon the ith row of x and the jth columns of y: it is

$$\begin{pmatrix} & \cdots & \\ \cdots & (xy)_{ij} & \cdots \\ & \cdots & \end{pmatrix} = \begin{pmatrix} & & \cdots & & \\ x_{i1} & x_{i2} & x_{i3} & \cdots & x_{im} \\ & & \cdots & & \end{pmatrix} \begin{pmatrix} \cdots & y_{1j} & \cdots \\ \cdots & y_{2j} & \cdots \\ \cdots & y_{3j} & \cdots \\ \cdots & \vdots & \cdots \\ \cdots & y_{mj} & \cdots \end{pmatrix}$$

$$= \begin{pmatrix} & & \ldots & & \\ \ldots & x_{i1}y_{1j} + x_{i2}y_{2j} + \cdots + x_{im}y_{mj} & \ldots \\ & & \ldots & & \end{pmatrix}$$

That is, the (i,j)th entry of the product is

$$\begin{aligned} (xy)_{ij} &= x_{i1}y_{1j} + x_{i2}y_{2j} + \cdots + x_{im}y_{mj} \\ &= \textstyle\sum_{1 \le \ell \le m} x_{i\ell}\, y_{\ell j} = \sum_{\ell=1}^{m} x_{i\ell}\, y_{\ell j} \end{aligned}$$

The (multiplicative) **identity matrix** 1_n of size n-by-n is the matrix

$$1_n = \begin{pmatrix} 1 & 0 & 0 & \ldots & & \\ 0 & 1 & 0 & \ldots & & \\ 0 & 0 & 1 & \ldots & & \\ & & & \ldots & & \\ & & & & 1 & 0 \\ & & \ldots & & 0 & 1 \end{pmatrix}$$

with all 1's on the **diagonal** (from upper left to lower right) and 0's everywhere else. This has the property that it's name suggests: for any m-by-n matrix x and/or n-by-m matrix y, we have

$$x \cdot 1_n = x, \qquad 1_n \cdot y = y$$

Since the product of a k-by-m matrix x and an m-by-n matrix is k-by-n, we note that for each positive integer n the collection of n-by-n *square matrices* has both addition and multiplication which give outcomes back in the same collection.

Some (but not all) n-by-n matrices x have a **multiplicative inverse** x^{-1}, meaning that

$$x \cdot x^{-1} = 1_n = x^{-1} \cdot x$$

Such square matrices are said to be **invertible**. In general, for large matrices, the process of finding an inverse (supposing there *is* one) can be computationally intensive.

Notice that all the above operations do not at all depend upon the details about what kind of 'numbers' we use in the vectors and matrices. In particular, everything makes sense if we use entries from $\mathbf{Z}_n$ (not to mention the *real, complex,* or *rational* entries). But what is it that we *expect* from matrices and matrix multiplication? For example:

Proposition. Matrix multiplication is *associative*. That is, for three matrices A, B, C of suitable sizes,

$$A\,(B\,C) = (A\,B)\,C$$

Proof: Let A_{ij}, B_{ij}, C_{ij} be the (i,j)th entries of A, B, C, respectively. Let $(AB)_{ij}$ be the (i,j)th entry of AB, and so on. To prove that the two matrix products are equal, we need to prove that the entries of the two products are the same: using the formula above for the entries of a product, we have

$$(A(BC))_{ij} = \sum_\ell A_{i\ell} (BC)_{\ell j}$$

$$= \sum_\ell A_{i\ell} \sum_k B_{\ell k} C_{kj}$$

$$= \sum_{\ell,k} A_{i\ell} B_{\ell k} C_{kj} = \sum_k \left(\sum_\ell A_{i\ell} B_{\ell k} \right) C_{kj}$$

$$= \sum_k (AB)_{ik} C_{kj} = ((AB)C)_{ij}$$

Thus, associativity follows by direct computation.   ♣

Let R be $\mathbf{Q}$, $\mathbf{R}$, $\mathbf{C}$, or $\mathbf{Z}_n$. The collection of all invertible n-by-n matrices with entries in R is denoted by $GL(n, R)$ or $GL_n(R)$ and is called the **general linear group** (of size n, with entries in R).

Exercises

A.4.01 Show that the matrix

$$\begin{pmatrix} 1 & 3 \\ 2 & 6 \end{pmatrix}$$

does not lie in $GL(2, \mathbf{R})$, that is, has no multiplicative inverse.

A.4.02 Find two 2-by-2 integer matrices A, B which do not *commute*, that is, so that $AB \neq BA$.

A.4.03 Find two 2-by-2 integer matrices A, B, neither one the 2-by-2 zero matrix, so that the product AB *is* the zero matrix.

A.4.04 Prove that for any positive integer N

$$\begin{pmatrix} 1 & 1 \\ 0 & 1 \end{pmatrix}^N = \begin{pmatrix} 1 & N \\ 0 & 1 \end{pmatrix}$$

A.4.05 Let

$$x = \begin{pmatrix} 1 & 1 & 0 \\ 0 & 1 & 1 \\ 0 & 0 & 1 \end{pmatrix}$$

Determine a formula for x^N for positive integers N, and prove that it is correct.

A.4.06 Let A, B be two n-by-n invertible matrices. Show that

$$(AB)^{-1} = B^{-1} A^{-1}$$

(rather than being $A^{-1}B^{-1}$).

A.4.07 How many elements are there in $GL(2, \mathbf{Z}/2)$ (out of the $2^4 = 16$ two-by-two matrices with entries in $\mathbf{Z}/2$)?

A.4.08 Define the **Fibonacci numbers** recursively by $F_0 = 0$, $F_1 = 1$, and

$$F_{n+1} = F_{n-1} + F_n$$

Let M be the two-by-two matrix

$$M = \begin{pmatrix} 0 & 1 \\ 1 & 1 \end{pmatrix}$$

Show that for every positive integer n

$$\begin{pmatrix} F_{n+1} \\ F_n \end{pmatrix} = M^n \begin{pmatrix} 1 \\ 0 \end{pmatrix}$$

A.4.09 Let F_n be the nth Fibonacci number, and let

$$M = \begin{pmatrix} 0 & 1 \\ 1 & 1 \end{pmatrix}$$

Show that

$$M^n = \begin{pmatrix} F_n & F_{n+1} \\ F_{n+1} & F_{n+2} \end{pmatrix}$$

A.4.10 Show that any matrix of the form

$$M = \begin{pmatrix} 0 & x & y \\ 0 & 0 & z \\ 0 & 0 & 0 \end{pmatrix}$$

has the property that $M^3 = 0_3$.

A.4.11 Let

$$M = \begin{pmatrix} 0 & x & y \\ 0 & 0 & z \\ 0 & 0 & 0 \end{pmatrix}$$

Show that $1_3 - M$ has a multiplicative inverse given by

$$(1_3 - M)^{-1} = 1_3 + M + M^2$$

A.4.12 A matrix M with entries M_{ij} is called **strictly upper-triangular** if $M_{ij} = 0$ for $i \geq j$. Show that an n-by-n upper-triangular matrix M has the property that $M^n = 0_n$.

A.4.13 Let M be a strictly upper-triangular n-by-n matrix. Show that $1_n - M$ has a multiplicative inverse given by

$$(1_n - M)^{-1} = 1_n + M + M^2 + M^3 + \cdots + M^{n-1}$$

Appendix 5: Stirling's Formula

The properties of the **factorial** function

$$n! = 1 \cdot 2 \cdot 3 \cdot 4 \cdot 5 \cdot \ldots \cdot (n-2) \cdot (n-1) \cdot n$$

are important to understand, considering that many counting problems have answers involving factorials, or in terms of binomial coefficients (which are made from factorials).

The most obvious feature of the factorial function $n!$ is that it grows very rapidly as a function of n. Therefore, in many situations the question is not to compute factorials *exactly*, but rather only to express them in terms of simpler functions whose size (large though it may be) we can discuss more easily. The approximation we obtain here is nearly the simplest case of **Stirling's approximation**, but it suffices for our purposes. The proof itself is fairly memorable.

(This estimate also plays a role in elementary approaches to the Prime Number Theorem.)

Proposition. The limit

$$\lim_{n \to \infty} \frac{n!}{n^{n+\frac{1}{2}} e^{-n}}$$

exists. Its value is $\sqrt{2\pi}$. Further, in fact, for $n \geq 2$

$$\sqrt{2\pi}\, n^{n+\frac{1}{2}} e^{-n} \cdot e^{\frac{1}{12(n+1)}} < n! < \sqrt{2\pi}\, n^{n+\frac{1}{2}} e^{-n} \cdot e^{\frac{1}{12n}}$$

Proof: The proof starts by comparing

$$\ln(n!) = \ln 1 + \ln 2 + \ln 3 + \cdots + \ln n$$

to the integrals

$$\int_1^{n+1} \ln x \, dx = [x \ln x - x]_1^{n+1} = (n+1) \ln(n+1) - (n+1)$$

and

$$\int_0^n \ln x \, dx = [x \ln x - x]_0^n = n \ln n - n$$

(The latter integral is 'improper' at 0, but converges.) First, for each $n = 2, 3, 4, \ldots$, since ln is an increasing function,

$$\int_{t-1}^t \ln x \, dx \leq \ln t \leq \int_t^{t+1} \ln x \, dx$$

From this we get

$$n \ln n - n \leq \ln n! \leq (n+1) \ln(n+1) - (n+1)$$

Already this is interesting: if we exponentiate we get

$$n^n e^{-n} \leq n! \leq (n+1)^{n+1} e^{-(n+1)}$$

The key quantity to consider is $(n + \frac{1}{2}) \ln n - n$, which is a moderately clever choice of an average between the lower and upper bounds we just obtained. Then let

$$E_n = \ln n! - [(n + \frac{1}{2}) \ln n - n]$$

be the error in estimating $\ln n!$ by this average. We have

$$
\begin{aligned}
E_n - E_{n+1} &= \ln n! - [(n + \tfrac{1}{2}) \ln n - n] - [\ln (n+1)! \\
&\qquad -[(n + 1 + \tfrac{1}{2}) \ln(n+1) - (n+1)]] \\
&= (n + \tfrac{1}{2}) \ln(1 + \tfrac{1}{n}) - 1
\end{aligned}
$$

after simplifying and rearranging. Next use the Taylor expansion

$$\ln(1 + x) = x - \frac{x^2}{2} + \frac{x^3}{3} - \frac{x^4}{4} + \cdots$$

to obtain

$$
\begin{aligned}
E_n - E_{n+1} &= (n + \tfrac{1}{2})(\tfrac{1}{n} - \tfrac{1}{2n^2} + \tfrac{1}{3n^3} - \cdots) - 1 \\
&= (\tfrac{1}{1} - \tfrac{1}{2n} + \tfrac{1}{3n^2} - \cdots) + \tfrac{1}{2}(\tfrac{1}{n} - \tfrac{1}{2n^2} + \tfrac{1}{3n^3} - \cdots) - 1 \\
&= (\tfrac{1}{3} - \tfrac{1}{4})\tfrac{1}{n^2} + (-\tfrac{1}{4} + \tfrac{1}{6})\tfrac{1}{n^3} + (\tfrac{1}{5} - \tfrac{1}{8})\tfrac{1}{n^4} + (-\tfrac{1}{6} + \tfrac{1}{10})\tfrac{1}{n^5} + \cdots
\end{aligned}
$$

by cancelling the '1' and the $\frac{1}{2n}$. For any $n \geq 1$ this is an alternating decreasing sequence.

Recall that, generally, for an alternating decreasing sequence

$$a_1 - a_2 + a_3 - a_4 + \cdots$$

(that is, with each $a_i > 0$ and $a_i > a_{i+1}$ for all i), we have inequalities such as

$$a_1 - a_2 < a_1 - a_2 + a_3 - a_4 + \cdots < a_1 - a_2 + a_3$$

Therefore,

$$\frac{1}{12}\left(\frac{1}{n^2} - \frac{1}{n^3}\right) < E_n - E_{n+1} < \frac{1}{12n^2} - \frac{1}{12n^3} + \frac{1}{40n^4}$$

In particular, since the left-hand side is always positive, each of the values $E_n - E_{n+1}$ is *positive*, so the sequence E_n itself is *decreasing*.

Subtracting $\frac{1}{12n}$ and adding $\frac{1}{12(n+1)}$ to the right-hand inequality here, we get

$$(E_n - \frac{1}{12n}) - (E_{n+1} - \frac{1}{12(n+1)}) < \frac{1}{12n^2} - \frac{1}{12n^3} + \frac{1}{40n^4} - \frac{1}{12n} + \frac{1}{12(n+1)}$$

The right-hand side (miraculously) simplifies to

$$\frac{12 - 28n}{12 \cdot 40 \cdot n^3(n+1)}$$

which is *negative* for all $n \geq 1$. Therefore, the sequence $E_n - \frac{1}{12n}$ is *increasing*.

Since E_n is decreasing and $E_n - \frac{1}{12n}$ is increasing, and since $\frac{1}{12n}$ goes to 0, we conclude that E_n is a *bounded* decreasing sequence, so has a limit C. This limit is actually $\sqrt{2\pi}$, but we'll not prove that just now.

Similarly, subtracting $\frac{1}{12(n+1)}$ and adding $\frac{1}{12((n+1)+1)}$ to the left-hand inequality, we have

$$\frac{1}{12}(\frac{1}{n^2} - \frac{1}{n^3}) - \frac{1}{12(n+1)} + \frac{1}{12((n+1)+1)}$$

$$< (E_n - \frac{1}{12(n+1)}) - (E_{n+1} - \frac{1}{12((n+1)+1)})$$

The left-hand side simplifies (not as miraculously as the previous episode) to

$$\frac{2n^2 - n - 2}{n^3 \cdot 12(n+1) \cdot 12((n+1)+1)}$$

The numerator satisfies

$$2n^2 - n - 2 = 2 \cdot [(n - \frac{1}{4})^2 - \frac{1}{16} - 1] \geq 2 \cdot [(2 - \frac{1}{4})^2 - \frac{17}{16}] = 4 > 0$$

for $n \geq 2$. Therefore, at least starting with $n \geq 2$, the sequence

$$E_n - \frac{1}{12(n+1)}$$

is *decreasing*.

In summary,

$$\lim_n E_n = C$$

and since the sequences $\frac{1}{12n}$ and $\frac{1}{12(n+1)}$ go to 0,

$$E_n - \frac{1}{12n} \quad \text{increases to} \quad C$$

$$E_n - \frac{1}{12(n+1)} \quad \text{decreases to} \quad C$$

Therefore, for $n \geq 2$,

$$C + \frac{1}{12(n+1)} < E_n < C + \frac{1}{12n}$$

That is,

$$C + \frac{1}{12(n+1)} + (n+\frac{1}{2})\ln n - n < \ln n! < C + \frac{1}{12n} + (n+\frac{1}{2})\ln n - n$$

This is the statement of the proposition.   ♣

Exercises

A.5.01 Using Stirling's formula, show that there is a constant C so that we can estimate the "middle" binomial coefficient by

$$\binom{2n}{n} \cdot \leq C \cdot 2^{2n} \cdot \frac{1}{\sqrt{n}}$$

A.5.02 Show that the probability that *exactly* n heads come up in $2n$ flips of a fair coin is less than $C/\sqrt{n}$ for some constant C.

A.5.03 Let $a_1 > a_2 > a_3 > \ldots$ be a sequence of positive real numbers with $\lim_n a_n = 0$. Let

$$S_n = a_1 - a_2 + a_3 - \cdots + (-1)^{n-1}a_n$$

be the nth partial sum of this **alternating decreasing sum**. Show that for all indices n

$$S_{2n} < S_{2n+2}, \qquad S_{2n-1} > S_{2n+1}$$

(That is, the even partial sums are increasing and the odd partial sums are decreasing.)

A.5.04 Let $a_1 > a_2 > a_3 > \ldots$ be a sequence of positive real numbers with $\lim_n a_n = 0$. Grant that the limit

$$L = a_1 - a_2 + a_3 - a_4 + \cdots$$

exists. Prove that for all indices k

$$a_1 - a_2 + a_3 - a_4 + \cdots + a_{2k-1} - a_{2k} < L < a_1 - a_2 + a_3 - a_4 + \cdots + a_{2k-1}$$

A.5.05 (*) Prove that an alternating decreasing infinite sum converges. That is, let S_n be the nth partial sum, as in the previous problem. Prove that for every $\varepsilon > 0$ there is an index N so that $|S_i - S_j| < \varepsilon$ for all $i, j \geq N$.

Tables

It may seem silly to include such modest tables when relatively high-powered computing is so widely available. However, in more mundane practical terms it seems to have proven useful to have a few tables available for times when machine computation is infeasible.

Table 1: Factorizations under 600

2 = 2	3 = 3	4 = 2.2	5 = 5
6 = 2.3	7 = 7	8 = 2.2.2	9 = 3.3
10 = 2.5	11 = 11	12 = 2.2.3	13 = 13
14 = 2.7	15 = 3.5	16 = 2.2.2.2	17 = 17
18 = 2.3.3	19 = 19	20 = 2.2.5	21 = 3.7
22 = 2.11	23 = 23	24 = 2.2.2.3	25 = 5.5
26 = 2.13	27 = 3.3.3	28 = 2.2.7	29 = 29
30 = 2.3.5	31 = 31	32 = 2.2.2.2.2	33 = 3.11
34 = 2.17	35 = 5.7	36 = 2.2.3.3	37 = 37
38 = 2.19	39 = 3.13	40 = 2.2.2.5	41 = 41
42 = 2.3.7	43 = 43	44 = 2.2.11	45 = 3.3.5
46 = 2.23	47 = 47	48 = 2.2.2.2.3	49 = 7.7

$50 = 2.5.5$	$51 = 3.17$	$52 = 2.2.13$	$53 = 53$
$54 = 2.3.3.3$	$55 = 5.11$	$56 = 2.2.2.7$	$57 = 3.19$
$58 = 2.29$	$59 = 59$	$60 = 2.2.3.5$	$61 = 61$
$62 = 2.31$	$63 = 3.3.7$	$64 = 2.2.2.2.2.2$	$65 = 5.13$
$66 = 2.3.11$	$67 = 67$	$68 = 2.2.17$	$69 = 3.23$
$70 = 2.5.7$	$71 = 71$	$72 = 2.2.2.3.3$	$73 = 73$
$74 = 2.37$	$75 = 3.5.5$	$76 = 2.2.19$	$77 = 7.11$
$78 = 2.3.13$	$79 = 79$	$80 = 2.2.2.2.5$	$81 = 3.3.3.3$
$82 = 2.41$	$83 = 83$	$84 = 2.2.3.7$	$85 = 5.17$
$86 = 2.43$	$87 = 3.29$	$88 = 2.2.2.11$	$89 = 89$
$90 = 2.3.3.5$	$91 = 7.13$	$92 = 2.2.23$	$93 = 3.31$
$94 = 2.47$	$95 = 5.19$	$96 = 2.2.2.2.2.3$	$97 = 97$
$98 = 2.7.7$	$99 = 3.3.11$	$100 = 2.2.5.5$	$101 = 101$
$102 = 2.3.17$	$103 = 103$	$104 = 2.2.2.13$	$105 = 3.5.7$
$106 = 2.53$	$107 = 107$	$108 = 2.2.3.3.3$	$109 = 109$
$110 = 2.5.11$	$111 = 3.37$	$112 = 2.2.2.2.7$	$113 = 113$
$114 = 2.3.19$	$115 = 5.23$	$116 = 2.2.29$	$117 = 3.3.13$
$118 = 2.59$	$119 = 7.17$	$120 = 2.2.2.3.5$	$121 = 11.11$
$122 = 2.61$	$123 = 3.41$	$124 = 2.2.31$	$125 = 5.5.5$
$126 = 2.3.3.7$	$127 = 127$	$128 = 2.2.2.2.2.2.2$	$129 = 3.43$
$130 = 2.5.13$	$131 = 131$	$132 = 2.2.3.11$	$133 = 7.19$
$134 = 2.67$	$135 = 3.3.3.5$	$136 = 2.2.2.17$	$137 = 137$
$138 = 2.3.23$	$139 = 139$	$140 = 2.2.5.7$	$141 = 3.47$
$142 = 2.71$	$143 = 11.13$	$144 = 2.2.2.2.3.3$	$145 = 5.29$
$146 = 2.73$	$147 = 3.7.7$	$148 = 2.2.37$	$149 = 149$
$150 = 2.3.5.5$	$151 = 151$	$152 = 2.2.2.19$	$153 = 3.3.17$
$154 = 2.7.11$	$155 = 5.31$	$156 = 2.2.3.13$	$157 = 157$
$158 = 2.79$	$159 = 3.53$	$160 = 2.2.2.2.2.5$	$161 = 7.23$
$162 = 2.3.3.3.3$	$163 = 163$	$164 = 2.2.41$	$165 = 3.5.11$
$166 = 2.83$	$167 = 167$	$168 = 2.2.2.3.7$	$169 = 13.13$
$170 = 2.5.17$	$171 = 3.3.19$	$172 = 2.2.43$	$173 = 173$
$174 = 2.3.29$	$175 = 5.5.7$	$176 = 2.2.2.2.11$	$177 = 3.59$
$178 = 2.89$	$179 = 179$	$180 = 2.2.3.3.5$	$181 = 181$
$182 = 2.7.13$	$183 = 3.61$	$184 = 2.2.2.23$	$185 = 5.37$
$186 = 2.3.31$	$187 = 11.17$	$188 = 2.2.47$	$189 = 3.3.3.7$
$190 = 2.5.19$	$191 = 191$	$192 = 2.2.2.2.2.2.3$	$193 = 193$
$194 = 2.97$	$195 = 3.5.13$	$196 = 2.2.7.7$	$197 = 197$
$198 = 2.3.3.11$	$199 = 199$	$200 = 2.2.2.5.5$	$201 = 3.67$
$202 = 2.101$	$203 = 7.29$	$204 = 2.2.3.17$	$205 = 5.41$
$206 = 2.103$	$207 = 3.3.23$	$208 = 2.2.2.2.13$	$209 = 11.19$
$210 = 2.3.5.7$	$211 = 211$	$212 = 2.2.53$	$213 = 3.71$
$214 = 2.107$	$215 = 5.43$	$216 = 2.2.2.3.3.3$	$217 = 7.31$
$218 = 2.109$	$219 = 3.73$	$220 = 2.2.5.11$	$221 = 13.17$
$222 = 2.3.37$	$223 = 223$	$224 = 2.2.2.2.2.7$	$225 = 3.3.5.5$
$226 = 2.113$	$227 = 227$	$228 = 2.2.3.19$	$229 = 229$
$230 = 2.5.23$	$231 = 3.7.11$	$232 = 2.2.2.29$	$233 = 233$

$234 = 2.3.3.13$	$235 = 5.47$	$236 = 2.2.59$	$237 = 3.79$
$238 = 2.7.17$	$239 = 239$	$240 = 2.2.2.2.3.5$	$241 = 241$
$242 = 2.11.11$	$243 = 3.3.3.3.3$	$244 = 2.2.61$	$245 = 5.7.7$
$246 = 2.3.41$	$247 = 13.19$	$248 = 2.2.2.31$	$249 = 3.83$
$250 = 2.5.5.5$	$251 = 251$	$252 = 2.2.3.3.7$	$253 = 11.23$
$254 = 2.127$	$255 = 3.5.17$	$256 = 2^8$	$257 = 257$
$258 = 2.3.43$	$259 = 7.37$	$260 = 2.2.5.13$	$261 = 3.3.29$
$262 = 2.131$	$263 = 263$	$264 = 2.2.2.3.11$	$265 = 5.53$
$266 = 2.7.19$	$267 = 3.89$	$268 = 2.2.67$	$269 = 269$
$270 = 2.3.3.3.5$	$271 = 271$	$272 = 2.2.2.2.17$	$273 = 3.7.13$
$274 = 2.137$	$275 = 5.5.11$	$276 = 2.2.3.23$	$277 = 277$
$278 = 2.139$	$279 = 3.3.31$	$280 = 2.2.2.5.7$	$281 = 281$
$282 = 2.3.47$	$283 = 283$	$284 = 2.2.71$	$285 = 3.5.19$
$286 = 2.11.13$	$287 = 7.41$	$288 = 2.2.2.2.2.3.3$	$289 = 17.17$
$290 = 2.5.29$	$291 = 3.97$	$292 = 2.2.73$	$293 = 293$
$294 = 2.3.7.7$	$295 = 5.59$	$296 = 2.2.2.37$	$297 = 3.3.3.11$
$298 = 2.149$	$299 = 13.23$	$300 = 2.2.3.5.5$	$301 = 7.43$
$302 = 2.151$	$303 = 3.101$	$304 = 2.2.2.2.19$	$305 = 5.61$
$306 = 2.3.3.17$	$307 = 307$	$308 = 2.2.7.11$	$309 = 3.103$
$310 = 2.5.31$	$311 = 311$	$312 = 2.2.2.3.13$	$313 = 313$
$314 = 2.157$	$315 = 3.3.5.7$	$316 = 2.2.79$	$317 = 317$
$318 = 2.3.53$	$319 = 11.29$	$320 = 2.2.2.2.2.2.5$	$321 = 3.107$
$322 = 2.7.23$	$323 = 17.19$	$324 = 2.2.3.3.3.3$	$325 = 5.5.13$
$326 = 2.163$	$327 = 3.109$	$328 = 2.2.2.41$	$329 = 7.47$
$330 = 2.3.5.11$	$331 = 331$	$332 = 2.2.83$	$333 = 3.3.37$
$334 = 2.167$	$335 = 5.67$	$336 = 2.2.2.2.3.7$	$337 = 337$
$338 = 2.13.13$	$339 = 3.113$	$340 = 2.2.5.17$	$341 = 11.31$
$342 = 2.3.3.19$	$343 = 7.7.7$	$344 = 2.2.2.43$	$345 = 3.5.23$
$346 = 2.173$	$347 = 347$	$348 = 2.2.3.29$	$349 = 349$
$350 = 2.5.5.7$	$351 = 3.3.3.13$	$352 = 2.2.2.2.2.11$	$353 = 353$
$354 = 2.3.59$	$355 = 5.71$	$356 = 2.2.89$	$357 = 3.7.17$
$358 = 2.179$	$359 = 359$	$360 = 2.2.2.3.3.5$	$361 = 19.19$
$362 = 2.181$	$363 = 3.11.11$	$364 = 2.2.7.13$	$365 = 5.73$
$366 = 2.3.61$	$367 = 367$	$368 = 2.2.2.2.23$	$369 = 3.3.41$
$370 = 2.5.37$	$371 = 7.53$	$372 = 2.2.3.31$	$373 = 373$
$374 = 2.11.17$	$375 = 3.5.5.5$	$376 = 2.2.2.47$	$377 = 13.29$
$378 = 2.3.3.3.7$	$379 = 379$	$380 = 2.2.5.19$	$381 = 3.127$
$382 = 2.191$	$383 = 383$	$384 = 2^7.3$	$385 = 5.7.11$
$386 = 2.193$	$387 = 3.3.43$	$388 = 2.2.97$	$389 = 389$
$390 = 2.3.5.13$	$391 = 17.23$	$392 = 2.2.2.7.7$	$393 = 3.131$
$394 = 2.197$	$395 = 5.79$	$396 = 2.2.3.3.11$	$397 = 397$
$398 = 2.199$	$399 = 3.7.19$	$400 = 2.2.2.2.5.5$	$401 = 401$
$402 = 2.3.67$	$403 = 13.31$	$404 = 2.2.101$	$405 = 3.3.3.3.5$
$406 = 2.7.29$	$407 = 11.37$	$408 = 2.2.2.3.17$	$409 = 409$
$410 = 2.5.41$	$411 = 3.137$	$412 = 2.2.103$	$413 = 7.59$
$414 = 2.3.3.23$	$415 = 5.83$	$416 = 2.2.2.2.2.13$	$417 = 3.139$

$418 = 2.11.19$	$419 = 419$	$420 = 2.2.3.5.7$	$421 = 421$
$422 = 2.211$	$423 = 3.3.47$	$424 = 2.2.2.53$	$425 = 5.5.17$
$426 = 2.3.71$	$427 = 7.61$	$428 = 2.2.107$	$429 = 3.11.13$
$430 = 2.5.43$	$431 = 431$	$432 = 2.2.2.2.3.3.3$	$433 = 433$
$434 = 2.7.31$	$435 = 3.5.29$	$436 = 2.2.109$	$437 = 19.23$
$438 = 2.3.73$	$439 = 439$	$440 = 2.2.2.5.11$	$441 = 3.3.7.7$
$442 = 2.13.17$	$443 = 443$	$444 = 2.2.3.37$	$445 = 5.89$
$446 = 2.223$	$447 = 3.149$	$448 = 2.2.2.2.2.2.7$	$449 = 449$
$450 = 2.3.3.5.5$	$451 = 11.41$	$452 = 2.2.113$	$453 = 3.151$
$454 = 2.227$	$455 = 5.7.13$	$456 = 2.2.2.3.19$	$457 = 457$
$458 = 2.229$	$459 = 3.3.3.17$	$460 = 2.2.5.23$	$461 = 461$
$462 = 2.3.7.11$	$463 = 463$	$464 = 2.2.2.2.29$	$465 = 3.5.31$
$466 = 2.233$	$467 = 467$	$468 = 2.2.3.3.13$	$469 = 7.67$
$470 = 2.5.47$	$471 = 3.157$	$472 = 2.2.2.59$	$473 = 11.43$
$474 = 2.3.79$	$475 = 5.5.19$	$476 = 2.2.7.17$	$477 = 3.3.53$
$478 = 2.239$	$479 = 479$	$480 = 2.2.2.2.2.3.5$	$481 = 13.37$
$482 = 2.241$	$483 = 3.7.23$	$484 = 2.2.11.11$	$485 = 5.97$
$486 = 2.3.3.3.3.3$	$487 = 487$	$488 = 2.2.2.61$	$489 = 3.163$
$490 = 2.5.7.7$	$491 = 491$	$492 = 2.2.3.41$	$493 = 17.29$
$494 = 2.13.19$	$495 = 3.3.5.11$	$496 = 2.2.2.2.31$	$497 = 7.71$
$498 = 2.3.83$	$499 = 499$	$500 = 2.2.5.5.5$	$501 = 3.167$
$502 = 2.251$	$503 = 503$	$504 = 2.2.2.3.3.7$	$505 = 5.101$
$506 = 2.11.23$	$507 = 3.13.13$	$508 = 2.2.127$	$509 = 509$
$510 = 2.3.5.17$	$511 = 7.73$	$512 = 2^9$	$513 = 3.3.3.19$
$514 = 2.257$	$515 = 5.103$	$516 = 2.2.3.43$	$517 = 11.47$
$518 = 2.7.37$	$519 = 3.173$	$520 = 2.2.2.5.13$	$521 = 521$
$522 = 2.3.3.29$	$523 = 523$	$524 = 2.2.131$	$525 = 3.5.5.7$
$526 = 2.263$	$527 = 17.31$	$528 = 2.2.2.2.3.11$	$529 = 23.23$
$530 = 2.5.53$	$531 = 3.3.59$	$532 = 2.2.7.19$	$533 = 13.41$
$534 = 2.3.89$	$535 = 5.107$	$536 = 2.2.2.67$	$537 = 3.179$
$538 = 2.269$	$539 = 7.7.11$	$540 = 2.2.3.3.3.5$	$541 = 541$
$542 = 2.271$	$543 = 3.181$	$544 = 2.2.2.2.2.17$	$545 = 5.109$
$546 = 2.3.7.13$	$547 = 547$	$548 = 2.2.137$	$549 = 3.3.61$
$550 = 2.5.5.11$	$551 = 19.29$	$552 = 2.2.2.3.23$	$553 = 7.79$
$554 = 2.277$	$555 = 3.5.37$	$556 = 2.2.139$	$557 = 557$
$558 = 2.3.3.31$	$559 = 13.43$	$560 = 2.2.2.2.5.7$	$561 = 3.11.17$
$562 = 2.281$	$563 = 563$	$564 = 2.2.3.47$	$565 = 5.113$
$566 = 2.283$	$567 = 3.3.3.3.7$	$568 = 2.2.2.71$	$569 = 569$
$570 = 2.3.5.19$	$571 = 571$	$572 = 2.2.11.13$	$573 = 3.191$
$574 = 2.7.41$	$575 = 5.5.23$	$576 = 2^6 \cdot 3^2$	$577 = 577$
$578 = 2.17.17$	$579 = 3.193$	$580 = 2.2.5.29$	$581 = 7.83$
$582 = 2.3.97$	$583 = 11.53$	$584 = 2.2.2.73$	$585 = 3.3.5.13$
$586 = 2.293$	$587 = 587$	$588 = 2.2.3.7.7$	$589 = 19.31$
$590 = 2.5.59$	$591 = 3.197$	$592 = 2.2.2.2.37$	$593 = 593$
$594 = 2.3.3.3.11$	$595 = 5.7.17$	$596 = 2.2.149$	$597 = 3.199$
$598 = 2.13.23$	$599 = 599$	$600 = 2.2.2.3.5.5$	$601 = 601$

Table 2: Primes Below 10,000

3, 5, 7, 11, 13, 17, 19, 23, 29, 31, 37, 41, 43, 47, 53, 59, 61, 67, 71, 73, 79, 83, 89, 97, 101, 103, 107, 109, 113, 127, 131, 137, 139, 149, 151, 157, 163, 167, 173, 179, 181, 191, 193, 197, 199, 211, 223, 227, 229, 233, 239, 241, 251, 257, 263, 269, 271, 277, 281, 283, 293, 307, 311, 313, 317, 331, 337, 347, 349, 353, 359, 367, 373, 379, 383, 389, 397, 401, 409, 419, 421, 431, 433, 439, 443, 449, 457, 461, 463, 467, 479, 487, 491, 499, 503, 509, 521, 523, 541, 547, 557, 563, 569, 571, 577, 587, 593, 599, 601, 607, 613, 617, 619, 631, 641, 643, 647, 653, 659, 661, 673, 677, 683, 691, 701, 709, 719, 727, 733, 739, 743, 751, 757, 761, 769, 773, 787, 797, 809, 811, 821, 823, 827, 829, 839, 853, 857, 859, 863, 877, 881, 883, 887, 907, 911, 919, 929, 937, 941, 947, 953, 967, 971, 977, 983, 991, 997, 1009, 1013, 1019, 1021, 1031, 1033, 1039, 1049, 1051, 1061, 1063, 1069, 1087, 1091, 1093, 1097, 1103, 1109, 1117, 1123, 1129, 1151, 1153, 1163, 1171, 1181, 1187, 1193, 1201, 1213, 1217, 1223, 1229, 1231, 1237, 1249, 1259, 1277, 1279, 1283, 1289, 1291, 1297, 1301, 1303, 1307, 1319, 1321, 1327, 1361, 1367, 1373, 1381, 1399, 1409, 1423, 1427, 1429, 1433, 1439, 1447, 1451, 1453, 1459, 1471, 1481, 1483, 1487, 1489, 1493, 1499, 1511, 1523, 1531, 1543, 1549, 1553, 1559, 1567, 1571, 1579, 1583, 1597, 1601, 1607, 1609, 1613, 1619, 1621, 1627, 1637, 1657, 1663, 1667, 1669, 1693, 1697, 1699, 1709, 1721, 1723, 1733, 1741, 1747, 1753, 1759, 1777, 1783, 1787, 1789, 1801, 1811, 1823, 1831, 1847, 1861, 1867, 1871, 1873, 1877, 1879, 1889, 1901, 1907, 1913, 1931, 1933, 1949, 1951, 1973, 1979, 1987, 1993, 1997, 1999, 2003, 2011, 2017, 2027, 2029, 2039, 2053, 2063, 2069, 2081, 2083, 2087, 2089, 2099, 2111, 2113, 2129, 2131, 2137, 2141, 2143, 2153, 2161, 2179, 2203, 2207, 2213, 2221, 2237, 2239, 2243, 2251, 2267, 2269, 2273, 2281, 2287, 2293, 2297, 2309, 2311, 2333, 2339, 2341, 2347, 2351, 2357, 2371, 2377, 2381, 2383, 2389, 2393, 2399, 2411, 2417, 2423, 2437, 2441, 2447, 2459, 2467, 2473, 2477, 2503, 2521, 2531, 2539, 2543, 2549, 2551, 2557, 2579, 2591, 2593, 2609, 2617, 2621, 2633, 2647, 2657, 2659, 2663, 2671, 2677, 2683, 2687, 2689, 2693, 2699, 2707, 2711, 2713, 2719, 2729, 2731, 2741, 2749, 2753, 2767, 2777, 2789, 2791, 2797, 2801, 2803, 2819, 2833, 2837, 2843, 2851, 2857, 2861, 2879, 2887, 2897, 2903, 2909, 2917, 2927, 2939, 2953, 2957, 2963, 2969, 2971, 2999, 3001, 3011, 3019, 3023, 3037, 3041, 3049, 3061, 3067, 3079, 3083, 3089, 3109, 3119, 3121, 3137, 3163, 3167, 3169, 3181, 3187, 3191, 3203, 3209, 3217, 3221, 3229, 3251, 3253, 3257, 3259, 3271, 3299, 3301, 3307, 3313, 3319, 3323, 3329, 3331, 3343, 3347, 3359, 3361, 3371, 3373, 3389, 3391, 3407, 3413, 3433, 3449, 3457, 3461, 3463, 3467, 3469, 3491, 3499, 3511, 3517, 3527, 3529, 3533, 3539, 3541, 3547, 3557, 3559, 3571, 3581, 3583, 3593, 3607, 3613, 3617, 3623, 3631, 3637, 3643, 3659, 3671, 3673, 3677, 3691, 3697, 3701, 3709, 3719, 3727, 3733, 3739, 3761, 3767, 3769, 3779, 3793, 3797, 3803, 3821, 3823, 3833, 3847, 3851, 3853, 3863, 3877, 3881, 3889, 3907, 3911, 3917, 3919, 3923, 3929, 3931, 3943, 3947, 3967, 3989, 4001, 4003, 4007, 4013, 4019, 4021, 4027, 4049, 4051, 4057, 4073, 4079, 4091, 4093, 4099, 4111, 4127, 4129, 4133, 4139, 4153, 4157, 4159, 4177, 4201, 4211, 4217, 4219, 4229, 4231, 4241, 4243, 4253, 4259, 4261, 4271, 4273, 4283, 4289, 4297, 4327, 4337, 4339, 4349, 4357, 4363, 4373, 4391, 4397, 4409, 4421, 4423, 4441, 4447, 4451, 4457, 4463, 4481, 4483,

4493, 4507, 4513, 4517, 4519, 4523, 4547, 4549, 4561, 4567, 4583, 4591, 4597, 4603,
4621, 4637, 4639, 4643, 4649, 4651, 4657, 4663, 4673, 4679, 4691, 4703, 4721, 4723,
4729, 4733, 4751, 4759, 4783, 4787, 4789, 4793, 4799, 4801, 4813, 4817, 4831, 4861,
4871, 4877, 4889, 4903, 4909, 4919, 4931, 4933, 4937, 4943, 4951, 4957, 4967, 4969,
4973, 4987, 4993, 4999, 5003, 5009, 5011, 5021, 5023, 5039, 5051, 5059, 5077, 5081,
5087, 5099, 5101, 5107, 5113, 5119, 5147, 5153, 5167, 5171, 5179, 5189, 5197, 5209,
5227, 5231, 5233, 5237, 5261, 5273, 5279, 5281, 5297, 5303, 5309, 5323, 5333, 5347,
5351, 5381, 5387, 5393, 5399, 5407, 5413, 5417, 5419, 5431, 5437, 5441, 5443, 5449,
5471, 5477, 5479, 5483, 5501, 5503, 5507, 5519, 5521, 5527, 5531, 5557, 5563, 5569,
5573, 5581, 5591, 5623, 5639, 5641, 5647, 5651, 5653, 5657, 5659, 5669, 5683, 5689,
5693, 5701, 5711, 5717, 5737, 5741, 5743, 5749, 5779, 5783, 5791, 5801, 5807, 5813,
5821, 5827, 5839, 5843, 5849, 5851, 5857, 5861, 5867, 5869, 5879, 5881, 5897, 5903,
5923, 5927, 5939, 5953, 5981, 5987, 6007, 6011, 6029, 6037, 6043, 6047, 6053, 6067,
6073, 6079, 6089, 6091, 6101, 6113, 6121, 6131, 6133, 6143, 6151, 6163, 6173, 6197,
6199, 6203, 6211, 6217, 6221, 6229, 6247, 6257, 6263, 6269, 6271, 6277, 6287, 6299,
6301, 6311, 6317, 6323, 6329, 6337, 6343, 6353, 6359, 6361, 6367, 6373, 6379, 6389,
6397, 6421, 6427, 6449, 6451, 6469, 6473, 6481, 6491, 6521, 6529, 6547, 6551, 6553,
6563, 6569, 6571, 6577, 6581, 6599, 6607, 6619, 6637, 6653, 6659, 6661, 6673, 6679,
6689, 6691, 6701, 6703, 6709, 6719, 6733, 6737, 6761, 6763, 6779, 6781, 6791, 6793,
6803, 6823, 6827, 6829, 6833, 6841, 6857, 6863, 6869, 6871, 6883, 6899, 6907, 6911,
6917, 6947, 6949, 6959, 6961, 6967, 6971, 6977, 6983, 6991, 6997, 7001, 7013, 7019,
7027, 7039, 7043, 7057, 7069, 7079, 7103, 7109, 7121, 7127, 7129, 7151, 7159, 7177,
7187, 7193, 7207, 7211, 7213, 7219, 7229, 7237, 7243, 7247, 7253, 7283, 7297, 7307,
7309, 7321, 7331, 7333, 7349, 7351, 7369, 7393, 7411, 7417, 7433, 7451, 7457, 7459,
7477, 7481, 7487, 7489, 7499, 7507, 7517, 7523, 7529, 7537, 7541, 7547, 7549, 7559,
7561, 7573, 7577, 7583, 7589, 7591, 7603, 7607, 7621, 7639, 7643, 7649, 7669, 7673,
7681, 7687, 7691, 7699, 7703, 7717, 7723, 7727, 7741, 7753, 7757, 7759, 7789, 7793,
7817, 7823, 7829, 7841, 7853, 7867, 7873, 7877, 7879, 7883, 7901, 7907, 7919, 7927,
7933, 7937, 7949, 7951, 7963, 7993, 8009, 8011, 8017, 8039, 8053, 8059, 8069, 8081,
8087, 8089, 8093, 8101, 8111, 8117, 8123, 8147, 8161, 8167, 8171, 8179, 8191, 8209,
8219, 8221, 8231, 8233, 8237, 8243, 8263, 8269, 8273, 8287, 8291, 8293, 8297, 8311,
8317, 8329, 8353, 8363, 8369, 8377, 8387, 8389, 8419, 8423, 8429, 8431, 8443, 8447,
8461, 8467, 8501, 8513, 8521, 8527, 8537, 8539, 8543, 8563, 8573, 8581, 8597, 8599,
8609, 8623, 8627, 8629, 8641, 8647, 8663, 8669, 8677, 8681, 8689, 8693, 8699, 8707,
8713, 8719, 8731, 8737, 8741, 8747, 8753, 8761, 8779, 8783, 8803, 8807, 8819, 8821,
8831, 8837, 8839, 8849, 8861, 8863, 8867, 8887, 8893, 8923, 8929, 8933, 8941, 8951,
8963, 8969, 8971, 8999, 9001, 9007, 9011, 9013, 9029, 9041, 9043, 9049, 9059, 9067,
9091, 9103, 9109, 9127, 9133, 9137, 9151, 9157, 9161, 9173, 9181, 9187, 9199, 9203,
9209, 9221, 9227, 9239, 9241, 9257, 9277, 9281, 9283, 9293, 9311, 9319, 9323, 9337,
9341, 9343, 9349, 9371, 9377, 9391, 9397, 9403, 9413, 9419, 9421, 9431, 9433, 9437,
9439, 9461, 9463, 9467, 9473, 9479, 9491, 9497, 9511, 9521, 9533, 9539, 9547, 9551,
9587, 9601, 9613, 9619, 9623, 9629, 9631, 9643, 9649, 9661, 9677, 9679, 9689, 9697,
9719, 9721, 9733, 9739, 9743, 9749, 9767, 9769, 9781, 9787, 9791, 9803, 9811, 9817,
9829, 9833, 9839, 9851, 9857, 9859, 9871, 9883, 9887, 9901, 9907, 9923, 9929, 9931,
9941, 9949, 9967, 9973.

Table 3: Primitive Roots under 100

3 has primitive root 2.

5 has primitive roots 2, 3.

7 has primitive roots 3, 5.

11 has primitive roots 2, 6, 7, 8.

13 has primitive roots 2, 6, 7, 11.

17 has primitive roots 3, 5, 6, 7, 10, 11, 12, 14.

19 has primitive roots 2, 3, 10, 13, 14, 15.

23 has primitive roots 5, 7, 10, 11, 14, 15, 17, 19, 20, 21.

29 has primitive roots 2, 3, 8, 10, 11, 14, 15, 18, 19, 21, 26, 27.

31 has primitive roots 3, 11, 12, 13, 17, 21, 22, 24.

37 has primitive roots 2, 5, 13, 15, 17, 18, 19, 20, 22, 24, 32, 35.

41 has primitive roots 6, 7, 11, 12, 13, 15, 17, 19, 22, 24, 26, 28, 29, 30, 34, 35.

43 has primitive roots 3, 5, 12, 18, 19, 20, 26, 28, 29, 30, 33, 34.

47 has primitive roots 5, 10, 11, 13, 15, 19, 20, 22, 23, 26, 29, 30, 31, 33, 35, 38, 39, 40, 41, 43, 44, 45.

53 has primitive roots 2, 3, 5, 8, 12, 14, 18, 19, 20, 21, 22, 26, 27, 31, 32, 33, 34, 35, 39, 41, 45, 48, 50, 51.

59 has primitive roots 2, 6, 8, 10, 11, 13, 14, 18, 23, 24, 30, 31, 32, 33, 34, 37, 38, 39, 40, 42, 43, 44, 47, 50, 52, 54, 55, 56.

61 has primitive roots 2, 6, 7, 10, 17, 18, 26, 30, 31, 35, 43, 44, 51, 54, 55, 59.

67 has primitive roots 2, 7, 11, 12, 13, 18, 20, 28, 31, 32, 34, 41, 44, 46, 48, 50, 51, 57, 61, 63.

71 has primitive roots 7, 11, 13, 21, 22, 28, 31, 33, 35, 42, 44, 47, 52, 53, 55, 56, 59, 61, 62, 63, 65, 67, 68, 69.

73 has primitive roots 5, 11, 13, 14, 15, 20, 26, 28, 29, 31, 33, 34, 39, 40, 42, 44, 45, 47, 53, 58, 59, 60, 62, 68.

79 has primitive roots 3, 6, 7, 28, 29, 30, 34, 35, 37, 39, 43, 47, 48, 53, 54, 59, 60, 63, 66, 68, 70, 74, 75, 77.

83 has primitive roots 2, 5, 6, 8, 13, 14, 15, 18, 19, 20, 22, 24, 32, 34, 35, 39, 42, 43, 45, 46, 47, 50, 52, 53, 54, 55, 56, 57, 58, 60, 62, 66, 67, 71, 72, 73, 74, 76, 79, 80.

89 has primitive roots 3, 6, 7, 13, 14, 15, 19, 23, 24, 26, 27, 28, 29, 30, 31, 33, 35, 38, 41, 43, 46, 48, 51, 54, 56, 58, 59, 60, 61, 62, 63, 65, 66, 70, 74, 75, 76, 82, 83, 86.

97 has primitive roots 5, 7, 10, 13, 14, 15, 17, 21, 23, 26, 29, 37, 38, 39, 40, 41, 56, 57, 58, 59, 60, 68, 71, 74, 76, 80, 82, 83, 84, 87, 90, 92.

Bibliography

[Adleman 1994] L. Adleman, "The function field sieve," in *Algorithmic Number Theory,* Lecture Notes in Computer Science, vol. 877, pp. 108–121, 1994.

[Alford, Granville, Pomerance 1994] W. Alford, A. Granville, and C. Pomerance, "There are infinitely many Carmichael numbers," *Ann. of Math.*, vol. 140 (1994), pp. 703–722.

[Anschel, Anschel, Goldfeld 1999] I. Anschel, M. Anschel, and D. Goldfeld, "An algebraic method for public-key cryptography," *Math. Research Letters*, vol. 6 (1999), pp. 1–5.

[Bach 1991] E. Bach, "Toward a theory of Pollard's rho method," *Information and Computation*, vol. 90 (1991), pp. 139–155.

[Bach, Shallit 1996] E. Bach and J. Shallit, *Algorithmic Number Theory*, vol. 1: *Efficient Algorithms*, MIT Press, 1996. ISBN 0-262-02405-5.

[Bell 1993] J. Bell, *Speakable and Unspeakable in Quantum Mechanics*, Cambridge Univ. Press, London and New York, 1993.

[Birman, Ko, Lee 1998] J. Birman, K. Ko, and S. Lee, "A new approach to the word and conjugacy problems in the braid groups," *Adv. in Math.*, vol. 139 (1998), pp. 322–353.

[Blake, Seroussi, Smart 2000] I. Blake, G. Seroussi, and N. Smart, *Elliptic Curves in Cryptography*, London Mathematics Society Lecture Notes no. 265, Cambridge University Press, 2000.

[Blum, Blum, Shub 1986] L. Blum, M. Blum, and M. Shub, "A simple unpredictable random number generator," SIAM J. on Computing, vol. 15 (1986), pp. 364–383.

[Boneh, 1999], D. Boneh, "20 years of attacks on RSA," *Notices of A.M.S.*, vol. 46, no. 2 (1999), pp. 203–213.

[Boneh, Durfee, Frankel 1998], D. Boneh, G. Durfee, and Y. Frankel, "An attack on RSA given a fraction of the private key bits," in *AsiaCrypt98*, Lecture Notes in Computer Science, Springer-Verlag, 1998.

[Calderbank, Shor 1996] A.R. Calderbank, and P. Shor, "Good quantum error-correcting codes exist," *Phys. Rev. A*, vol. 54 (1996), pp. 1098–1105.

[Cohen 1993] Henri Cohen, *A Course in Computational Algebraic Number Theory*, Springer-Verlag, 1993. ISBN 3-540-55640-0.

[Coppersmith 1993] D. Coppersmith, "Modifications to the number field sieve," *J. Crypto*, vol. 6 (1993), pp. 169–180.

[Coppersmith 1998] D. Coppersmith, "Small solutions to polynomial equations, and low exponent RSA vulnerabilities," *J. Crypto*, vol. 10 (1998), pp. 233–260.

[Coppersmith, Shamir 1997] D. Coppersmith, and A. Shamir, "Lattice attacks on NTRU," *Eurocrypto 1997*.

[Diffie, Hellman 1976] W. Diffie and W. Hellman, "New directions in cryptography," *IEEE Transactions on Information Theory*, vol. IT-22 (1976), pp. 644–654.

[Einstein, Podolsky, Rosen 1935] A. Einstein, B. Podolsky, and N. Rosen, "Can quantum-mechanical description of physical reality be considered complete?," *Phys. Rev.*, vol. 47, no. 777 (1935).

[ElGamal 1985] T. ElGamal, "A public key cryptosystem and signature scheme based on discrete logarithms," *IEEE Transactions on Information Theory*, vol. IT-31 (1985), pp. 469–473.

[Fellows, Koblitz 1992] M. Fellows and N. Koblitz, "Self-witnessing polynomial time complexity and prime factorization," *Designs, Codes and Cryptography*, vol. 2 (1992), pp. 231–235.

[Garrett 1997] P. Garrett, *Buildings and Classical Groups*, CRC Press, 1997.

[Golomb 1982] S. Golomb, *Shift Register Sequences*, 2d ed., 1982, Aegean Park Press, Laguna Hills, CA. ISBN 0-89412-048-4.

[Hoffstein, Pipher, Silverman 1996] J. Hoffstein, J. Pipher, and J. Silverman, "NTRU: A new high speed public-key cryptosystem,' presented at *Crypto 96* rump session.

[Hughes, Tannenbaum 2000] J. Hughes, and A. Tannenbaum, "Length-based attacks for certain group-based encryption rewriting systems,' preprint, 2000.

[Kahn 1996] D. Kahn, *The Codebreakers*, 2d ed., Scribner, 1967, 1996. ISBN 0-684-83130-9.

[Karatsuba 1990] A. A. Karatsuba, "The distribution of prime numbers," *Russian Math. Surveys*, vol. 45 (1990), pp. 99–171.

[Knill, Laflamme, Martinez, Tseng 2000], E. Knill, R. Laflamme, R. Martinez, and C.-H. Tseng, "An algorithmic benchmark for quantum information processing," *Nature*, vol. 404 (2000), pp. 368–370.

[Knuth 1997] Donald Knuth, *The Art of Computer Programming. Vol. 1: Fundamental Algorithms*, 2d ed., Addison-Wesley, 1973. ISBN 0-201-03809-9. *Vol. 2: Semi-Numerical Algorithms*, 2d ed., 1989. ISBN 0-201-03822-6. *Vol. 3: Sorting and Searching*, 1979. ISBN 0-201-03803-X. (*Third* editions are available.)

[Koblitz 1994] Neal Koblitz, *A Course in Number Theory and Cryptography*, 2d ed., Springer-Verlag, 1994. ISBN 3-540-94293-9.

[Kocher 1996] P. Kocher, "Timing attacks on implementations of Diffie-Hellman, RSA, DSS, and other systems," *Crypto96*, Lecture Notes in Computer Science, Springer-Verlag, pp. 104–113.

[Kumanduri, Romero 1997] R. Kumanduri and C. Romero, *Number Theory with Computer Applications*, Prentice Hall, Upper Saddle River, NJ, 1997. ISBN 0-13-801812-X.

[Lenstra, Lenstra, Lovasz 1982] A. Lenstra, H. Lenstra, L. Lovasz, "Factoring polynomials with polynomial coefficients," *Math. Ann.*, vol. 261 (1982), pp. 515–534.

[Menezes, van Oorschot, Vanstone 1997] A. Menezes, P. van Oorschot, and S. Vanstone, *Handbook of Applied Cryptography*, CRC Press, 1997, ISBN 0-8493-8523-7.

[Merkle, Hellman 1978] R. Merkle and M. Hellman, "Hiding information and signatures in trapdoor knapsacks," *IEEE Transactions on Information Theory*, vol. IT-24 (1978), pp. 525–530.

[Naor, Reingold 1995] M. Naor, and O. Reingold, "Synthesizers and their application to the parallel construction of pseudo-random functions," *Proc. 36th IEEE Symp. on Foundations of Computer Science* (1995), pp. 170–181.

[Pati, Braunstein 2000] A. Pati, and S. Braunstein, "Impossibility of deleting an unknown quantum state," *Nature*, vol. 404 (2000), pp. 164–165.

[Pinch 1993] R. Pinch, "The Carmichael numbers up to 10^{15}," *Math. Comp.*, vol. 61 (1993), pp. 381–391.

[Pollard 1975] J. Pollard, "A Monte Carlo method for factorization', *BIT*, vol. 15 (1975), pp. 331–334.

[Proth 1878] F. Proth, "Théorèmes sur les nombres premiers', *C. R. Acad. Sci. Paris*, vol. 87 (1878), p. 926.

[Rivest, Shamir, Adleman 1978] R. Rivest, A. Shamir, and L. Adleman: "A method for obtaining digital signatures and public-key cryptosystems," *Comm. ACM*, vol. 21 (1978), pp. 120–126.

[Salomaa 1996] Arto Salomaa, *Public-Key Cryptography*, 2d ed., Springer, 1996. ISBN 3-540-61356-0.

[Shamir 1982] A. Shamir, "A polynomial-time algorithm for breaking the Merkle-Hellman cryptosystem," *Proc. 23d FOCS Symp.* (1982), pp. 145–152.

[Shor 1996a] P. Shor, "Polynomial-time algorithms for prime factorization and discrete logarithms on a quantum computer," *SIAM J. Computation*, vol. 26, no. 5 (1997), pp. 1484–1509.

[Shor 1996b] P. Shor, "Fault-tolerant computation," in *Proc. 37th Symposium on Foundations of Computing* (1996), IEEE Computer Society Press, pp. 56–65.

[Schneier 1996] Bruce Schneier, *Applied Cryptography*, 2d ed., John Wiley, 1996. ISBN (cloth) 0-471-12845-7 (paper) 0-471-11709-9.

[Schnorr, Euchner 1994] C. Schnorr, and M. Euchner, "Lattice basis reduction: improved practical algorithms and solving subset sum problems," *Mathematical Programming*, vol. 66 (1994), pp. 181–194.

[Silverman 1986] J. Silverman, *The Arithmetic of Elliptic Curves*, Springer-Verlag, New York, 1986.

[Stinson 1997] Douglas Stinson, *Cryptography: Theory and Practice*, 4th ed., CRC Press, 1997. ISBN 0-8493-8521-0.

[Wagner, Magyarik 1985] N. Wagner, and M. Magyarik, "A public key cryptosystem based on the word problem," *Adv. in Crypto: Proc. Crypto 84*, Lecture Notes in Computer Science, vol. 196 (1985), Springer, New York, pp. 19–36.

[Walfisz 1963] A. Walfisz, *Weylsche Exponentialsummen in der neueren Zahlentheorie*, VEB Deutscher Verlag der Wissenschaften, Berlin, 1963.

[Wiener 1990] M. Wiener, "Cryptanalysis of short RSA secret exponents," *IEEE Transactions on Information Theory*, vol. 36 (1990), pp. 553–558.

Selected Answers

1.01.01 'GUVF VF GUR ZRFFNTR'

1.01.02 'AOPZ PZ AOL TLZZHNL'

1.01.07 'Take me out to the ball game'

1.01.08 'These are times that make us tired'

1.01.09 'Oh, what a beautiful morning'

1.01.11 'Shark has pretty teeth'

1.02.01 10

1.02.02 29

1.02.03 10

1.02.06 78

1.02.07 44

1.02.08 122

1.02.09 56

1.02.18 77

1.02.20 69

1.03.01 'RBXICEWFV'

1.03.02 'VHDSJKBTV'

1.03.05 'DBZ LDW QFZIS'

1.04.01 'RTTM RT HM RFQUFZCM'

1.04.02 'DTTC DT BC DLIOLPAC'

1.04.06 $(9, 15)$

1.04.08 $(15, 7)$

1.04.12 $(a, b) = (2, 25)$

1.04.13 $(a, b) = (9, 18)$

1.04.15 $(a, b) = (7, 9)$

1.04.16 $(a, b) = (17, 10)$

2.01.01 $3! = 6$

2.01.03 $5! = 120$

2.01.06 $\binom{9}{3} = 84$

2.01.08 $\binom{10}{5} = 252$

2.02.02 $\binom{10}{5}/2^{10} \approx 0.24609$

2.02.04 $\left(\binom{8}{5} + \binom{8}{6} + \binom{8}{7} + 1\right)/2^8$

2.02.07 $\frac{5}{5+6} \cdot \frac{5}{5+6} = \frac{25}{121} \approx 0.2066$

2.04.01 'Better late than never'

3.01.02 'Unicode is a relatively new idea for encoding larger alphabets and ideographic systems by using two bytes per character'

3.01.03 'From the theorem just proven the ratio of primitive roots to all elements is most often above one quarter'

3.02.02 'theme'

3.02.04 'grimy'

3.02.08 'finally' and 'bicycle'

3.03.02 (1 2 5) (3 4 7 6), order 12

3.03.04 (1 6) (2 5 7 3 4), order 10

3.03.05 $\begin{pmatrix} 1 & 2 & 3 & 4 & 5 & 6 & 7 \\ 5 & 1 & 7 & 2 & 7 & 6 & 3 \end{pmatrix}$

3.03.07 $\begin{pmatrix} 1 & 2 & 3 & 4 & 5 & 6 & 7 \\ 5 & 1 & 7 & 2 & 6 & 4 & 3 \end{pmatrix}$

3.03.09 $6 \cdot 5 \cdot 4 \cdot 3/4 = 90$

3.04.04 $(1\ 2\ 4\ 8\ 3\ 6\ 12\ 11\ 9\ 5\ 10\ 7)$

3.04.06   8-cycles $(1\ 2\ 4\ 8\ 16\ 15\ 13\ 9)$, $(3\ 6\ 12\ 7\ 14\ 11\ 5\ 10)$

3.05.03   Using $0, 1, 2, \ldots, 11$:
$(0)\ (11)\ (1\ 3\ 9\ 5\ 4)\ (2\ 6\ 7\ 10\ 8)$

4.01.02   'BERW AV IC TUH OCLTY NIHVR BIQQWXHI'

4.01.04   'TSVK UJ QP AVV RTQMA HTKVZ RQFUWXYB'

4.02.02   3, 90

4.02.06   1, 1457

4.02.09   79

4.04.02   50/14

4.04.03   60/15

4.04.05   1/2

4.04.06   3

5.01.01 $n \cdot 2^{n-1}$

5.01.05 $x(1 + x)/(1 - x)^3$

5.02.02   35/6

5.03.02   By Chebycheff's inequality, probability is less than or equal to 1/40.

5.04.02   8 rolls

7.01.02 $1, 2, 4, 5, 8, 10, 16, 20, 40, 80$

7.01.04   1, 2, 3, 4, 6, 8, 12, 16, 24, 32, 48, 96

7.01.09 $10510100501 =$
$1 \cdot 100^5 + 5 \cdot 100^4 + 10 \cdot 100^3 + 10 \cdot 100^2 + 5 \cdot 100 + 1 = (100 + 1)^5$

7.02.03   110111101111011
$= 11011 \cdot 100000^2 + 11011 \cdot 100000 + 11011$
$= 11011 \cdot (100000^2 + 100000 + 1)$, so 11011 is a proper factor. Also 3, 7, 11, 13, 31, 37 by trial division, if you insist.

7.03.02   347

7.03.05 $1 = 117 \cdot (-34) + 173 \cdot (23)$

7.03.07 $3 = 12345 \cdot (3617) + 54321 \cdot (-822)$

7.04.03   8

7.04.05   5

7.04.08 $(n - 3)$

7.05.02   19

7.05.05   19

7.05.07   3239

7.07.05   Eight: 1, 5, 7, 11, 13, 17, 19, 23 mod 24

7.07.08   8

7.07.10   1

7.07.15 $1, 12, 131, 142$

7.08.02 $2^2 = 4$, $2^3 = 8$, $2^4\ \%\ 11 = 5$, $2^5\ \%\ 11 = 10$, $2^6\ \%\ 11 = 9$, $2^7\ \%\ 11 = 7$, $2^9\ \%\ 11 = 3$, $2^{10}\ \%\ 11 = 1$

7.08.06   2

7.08.08   7

7.08.10   29

10.02.02   187183

10.02.05   9611

12.01.02   16

12.01.04   8

12.01.06   3

12.04.03 $1, 7, 37, 5 \cdot 5 \cdot 7, 11 \cdot 71, 7 \cdot 13 \cdot 37$, $14197, 5 \cdot 5 \cdot 7 \cdot 337, 37 \cdot 6553, 7 \cdot 11 \cdot 71 \cdot 181$, $23 \cdot 174659, 5 \cdot 5 \cdot 7 \cdot 13 \cdot 37 \cdot 193, 131 \cdot 500, 111$, $7 \cdot 7 \cdot 379 \cdot 14, 197, 11 \cdot 37 \cdot 61 \cdot 71 \cdot 601$

12.05.02   334

12.05.04   559

12.05.06   17

12.05.08   18

12.06.02   5

12.06.04   60

12.06.07   928

12.07.02   59

12.07.03   31

12.07.05   19 (Also 34, 50.)

13.02.02   1

13.02.04   89

13.02.06   385

13.03.05   1, 103, 118, 220

13.04.02   315520, 1456041

13.04.04   1068, 14557

13.06.02   12, 6, 12

13.07.05   12

13.07.08   6

13.07.11   102

13.08.02   Yes.

13.08.03   No.

13.08.06   No.

13.08.08   Yes.

14.01.02 $(3+1) \cdot (1+1) = 8$

14.01.04 $(1+3+9+27) \cdot (1+37) = 1520$

14.03.02   0

14.03.04 -1

15.05.02 $+1$, yes.

15.05.04 $+1$, yes.

15.05.09 $+1$, no.

15.05.10 $+1$, no.

16.02.03   25, 325, 561, 703, 817, 1105

17.02.06   For $d = 0, 1, 2, 3, 4, 6, 8, 12$, the collection of multiples of d mod 24 is a subgroup, and these are all the subgroups.

19.01.06 $1, 5, 7, 11$ mod 12.

19.01.17 $3 \cdot 7 = 0$ mod 21, $6 \cdot 7 = 0$ mod 21, $9 \cdot 7 = 0$ mod 21, $3 \cdot 14 = 0$ mod 21, etc.

19.02.02 $7 \cdot 1 = 7 \cdot 12$ mod 77 but $1 \neq 12$ mod 77.

19.03.02   5 mod 7 and 6 mod 7

19.03.04   5 mod 13 and 8 mod 13

19.04.02 $x^8 + x^7 + x^6 + x^2 + x + 1$

19.04.05 $x^2 + x + 1$

19.04.07 $x^8 + x^6 + x^3 + 1$

20.02.02 $x^3 + x^2 + x + 1$

20.02.04 $x^3 + x + 1$

20.05.02   3, 5, 6, 7, 10, 11, 12, 14

22.02.02   5, 8

27.01.02   22

27.01.04   11

27.01.06   47

27.01.08   6

27.01.10   11

27.01.12   28

27.02.02   9

27.02.04   10

27.02.06   19

27.02.08   8

27.02.10   740

27.02.13   17

27.02.15 16

27.02.17 14

27.02.19 109

Index